To Wyeth

a huge fan.

Best Wishes

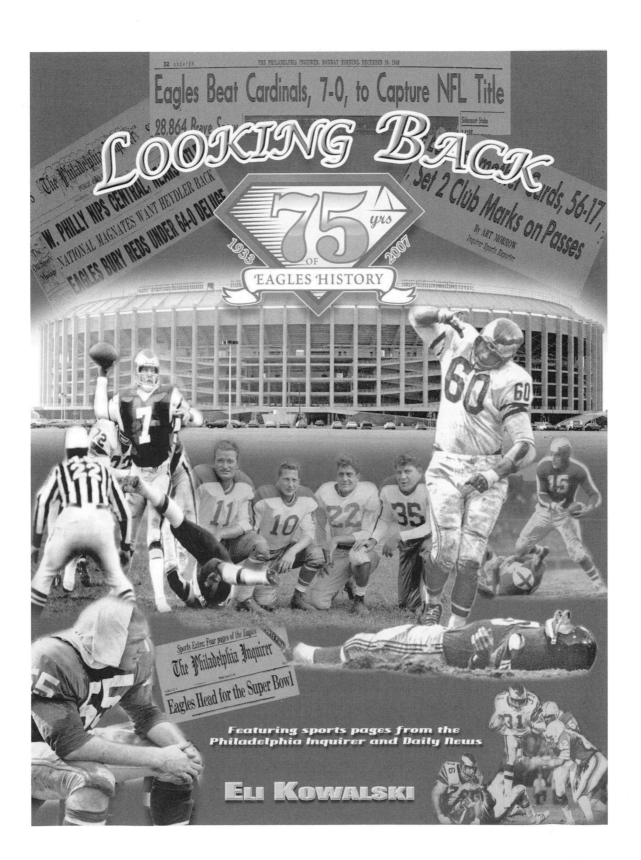

LOOKING BACK

75 yrs
1933 OF 2007
EAGLES HISTORY

Eagles Beat Cardinals, 7-0, to Capture NFL Title

Set 2 Club Marks on Passes

Featuring sports pages from the
Philadelphia Inquirer and Daily News

ELI KOWALSKI

Looking Back…75yrs of Eagles History
Copyright © 2007 Eli Kowalski
All Rights Reserved
First Published 2007
Printed in the United States of America

ISBN: 978-0-615-15195-3

Cover Designed by Bright Imaging
Typesetting by: A-C Reproduction

The following individuals and organizations generously gave permission to reproduce photographs in this book:

The Philadelphia Inquirer and Philadelphia Daily News pages were reprinted with permission by Philadelphia Newspapers, LLC.
Urban Archives, Temple University Libraries, page 189
Maple Leaf Productions for their History of the Eagles Uniform, pages 190-195
Hall of Fame Illustrations by Bob Carroll, pages 213-218

The photo collage on the front cover courtesy of Urban Archives, Temple University Libraries (from left to right), #55 Maxie Baughan, #7 Ron Jaworski, #11 Tommy Thompson, #10 Al Sherman, #22 Bill Mackrides, #35 Pete Pihos, #60 Chuck Bednarik, #15 Lou Tomasetti, #31 Wilbert Montgomery and Veterans Memorial Stadium.

The photo on the back cover courtesy of Urban Archives, Temple University Libraries, Head Coach Dick Vermeil sitting on the shoulders of #65 Charlie Johnson and #87 Claude Humphrey.

The NFL or its teams do not sanction this book.

Publisher
Sports Challenge Network
Philadelphia, PA 19102

www.sportschallengenetwork.com
email: elik@sportschallengenetwork.com

Dedication

This book is dedicated to my father, Peter Kowalski, who passed away in July 2007 while I was completing this book. My dad was a man who enjoyed sports and who was loved deeply by his family and the countless friends who had the privilege to know him.

Acknowledgements

Without the assistance of so many individuals, this project didn't have a chance. I would like to express my sincere gratitude to the following for their enormous contributions to this book.

First, I have to thank the staff at the Philadelphia Inquirer and Philadelphia Daily News for their incredible patience and hard work pulling the various sports pages. I am especially grateful for the countless of hours it took looking up all these sports pages and never, never giving up on this project.

To Jim Gallagher, retired Eagles Public Relations Director and member of the Eagles Honor Roll, for his wisdom and for exposing me to some of the former Eagles players. His memories of the Eagles are priceless. Thanks Jimmy!

Over the years, I have spent many days researching in a small room located in the basement of the Temple University Library, flipping through boxes of old photographs, looking through miles and miles of micro-film. John Pettit and the staff at Urban Archives, Temple University Libraries were always so helpful and cooperative.

I would like to thank the many local sportscasters and writers who shared with me some of their fondest Eagles memories. Thanks to Ray Didinger, Michael Barkann, Lou Tilley, Jody McDonald, Sam Carchidi, Don Tollefson, Bill Campbell, Vinnie "the crumb", Glen Macnow and Steve Sabol.

Many thanks go out to the both the current and former Eagles players who shared with me their fondest memories as players. They include, Chuck Bednarik, Tom Brookshier, Pete Retzlaff, Tommy McDonald, Garry Cobb, Randall Cunningham, Brian Dawkins, Billy Ray Barnes, Jon Runyan, Bill Mackrides, David Akers, William Thomas, Sheldon Brown, Harold Carmichael, Fred Barnett, Mike Quick, Hugh Douglas, Ed Khayat, Vaughn Hebron, Bill Bergey, Vince Papale, Ike Reese, Ron Jaworski, Via Sikahema, Jeremiah Trotter, Brian Westbrook, and Donovan McNabb.

To the various die-hard Eagles fans whom I spoke with that shared their memories, Shaun Young, Gary Discount, Jason Bloom, Ben (Socratese), Mark Zeserman, John Spitzkopf, Adam Poppel, Ray (the Midas Man), Mitch Rosenberg, Stanley Higbee, Kim Sinclair, Larry Kagel, Steve Odabashian, Carl Henderson, Saul Braverman, Jerry D'Addesi, Paul Parone, Neil Poppel, Jim Murray, Brian "Shifty" Schiff, and Neil Tobin, Birdheadz Darulah and Jimmy Gallagher.

To Garry Cobb of GCobb.com who was instrumental assisting me with player interviews. I thank you for all your hard work and your commitment!

To Sean Miller and A-C Reproduction for putting together all my loose pieces of paper with scratch notes, going through all the revisions and finally creating this great looking book. Thank You!

Some of my research resources were, The Eagles Encyclopedia, by Ray Didinger and Bob Lyons; Philadelphia Eagles Media Guides; Eagles by the Numbers, John Maxymuk; The Professional Football Researchers Association; The Philadelphia Inquirer and Daily News newspapers.

To my family members, for their patience and understanding during some troubling times.

Preface

My goal in writing this book was very simple. I wanted to look back at the Eagles 75 years of professional football. I hoped to provide you, the reader, an entertaining and informative compilation of Eagles information along with a statistical chronicle of the franchise. There has never been a book with such a comprehensive collection of actual sports pages used from both the Philadelphia Inquirer and Philadelphia Daily News newspapers, which covered the Eagles games for the past 75 years. I wanted people to relive game memories by looking back at these sports pages.

I have incorporated chapters that you should enjoy looking back on. You will be able to look at the stats for every game played during the past 75 years, see where all the training camps were, and view a pictorial history of the evolution of the various Eagles uniforms. Also included are all retired jerseys numbers and, in chronological order, every jersey number worn and the corresponding players who wore them over the past 75 years. You will be able to look back on all the Head coaches, owners, Eagles in the Hall of Fame, the Eagles Honor Roll, a section on all the Monday Night Football games the Eagles played in, first draft selections per year, and finally a section with the all-time players roster.

What really made this an interesting project was the ability to contact former and current Eagles players to get their views and hear some of their fondest memories as an Eagles player. I also contacted many of the local sportscasters and writers who covered the Eagles over the past 75 years, and of course the fans, for their memories as well.

Enjoy looking back at the past 75 years of Eagles history.

Contents

Preface	vii
30s Decade in Review	10
40s Decade in Review	26
50s Decade in Review	48
60s Decade in Review	70
70s Decade in Review	82
80s Decade in Review	114
90s Decade in Review	136
2000s Decade in Review	158
Fondest Eagles Memories	176
Training Camp Locations	189
Eagles Uniform History	190
Retired Eagles Jerseys	196
Players by the Numbers	197
Eagles Home Records	209
Eagles Head Coaches	210
Eagles Owners	211
Eagles in the Hall of Fame	213
Eagles Honor Roll	219
Monday Night Football Games	220
First Draft Selections by Year	233
All-Time Eagles Records	234
All-Time Eagles Roster	237

30's Decade in Review

Decade Win-Loss Record:
18-55-3
Home Field:
Baker Bowl 1933-35; Temple Stadium 1934-35;
Municipal Stadium 1936-39
Playoff Appearances:
None
Championships:
None
Head Coaches:
Lud Wray 1933-35 (9-21-1), Bert Bell 1936-1939 (9-34-2)
Hall of Fame Inductees:
Bert Bell, Bill Hewitt
Award Winners:
None
All Pro:
Swede Hanson 1933-34, Joe Carter 1935-36 and 1938, Ed Manske 1935,
Bill Hewitt 1937-38, Davey O'Brien 1939
All-Star Game Selections:
Joe Carter 1938-39, Davey O'Brien 1939
First Game of the Decade:
October 15, 1933 crushing loss to New York Giants 56-0
Last Game of the Decade:
December 3, 1939 loss to Cleveland Rams 35-13
Largest Margin of Victory:
November 6, 1934 vs. Cincinnati Reds 64-0
Largest Margin of Defeat:
October 16, 1933 vs. New York Giants 56-0

Eagle Firsts of the Decade:
First Touchdown
35-yard touchdown pass from Roger Kirkman to Swede Hanson
on October 29, 1933 vs. Green Bay
First Safety
by George Kenneally on October 29, 1933 vs. Green Bay
First Field Goal
Guy Turnbow kicked a 20-yard field goal on
November 12, 1933 vs. Chicago Bears
First Win
November 15, 1933 vs. Cincinnati Reds, 6-0
First Shutout
17-0 over the Pirates in Pittsburgh on September 26, 1934
First Draft Pick
Jay Berwanger in 1936

30's Decade in Review

In 1931, Philadelphia's representative in the National Football League, the Frankford Yellow Jackets, went bankrupt and ceased operations midway through the season. After more than a year searching for a suitable replacement, the NFL awarded its dormant Philadelphia franchise to a syndicate headed by former University of Pennsylvania teammates Lud Wray and Bert Bell, in exchange for an entry fee of $2,500. Drawing inspiration from the insignia of the centerpiece of President Franklin D. Roosevelt's New Deal, the National Recovery Act, Bell and Wray named the new franchise the Philadelphia Eagles. Neither the Eagles nor the NFL officially regard the two franchises as the same, citing the aforementioned period of dormancy. The Eagles simply inherited the right to take over from the Yellow Jackets.

The new team played its first game on October 15, 1933, against the New York Giants in New York in which the Giants destoryed the Eagles 56-0. The Eagles struggled over the course of their first decade, enduring repeated losing seasons. For the most part, the Eagles' rosters were comprised of former Penn, Temple and Villanova players who put in a few years before going on to other things. In 1935, Bert Bell, the team's General Manager, proposed an annual college draft to equalize talent across the league. The draft was a revolutionary concept in professional sports. Having teams select players in inverse order of their finish in the standings, a practice still followed today, strove to increase fan interest by guaranteeing that even the worst teams would have the opportunity for annual infusions of the best college talent. Previously, the Chicago Bears and New York Giants and Green Bay Packers had won all but one title since 1927.

Having finished last in the standings, the Eagles were "honored" with the first pick, an opportunity they squandered by selecting the University of Chicago's Heisman Trophy-winning back, Jay Berwanger. Berwanger, who had no interest in playing professional football, elected to go to medical school instead. Fortunately for the Eagles, they had managed by then to trade his rights to the Chicago Bears.

The Eagles' first major recruiting success would come in 1939, with the signing of Texas Christian's All-America quarterback, Davey O'Brien; O'Brien proceeded to shatter numerous existing single-season NFL passing records in his rookie season. That year, the Eagles participated in the first televised football game, against the Brooklyn Dodgers, at Ebbets Field in Brooklyn (as was to be expected of the 1930's Eagles, they lost the game, 23-14).

TRIVIA QUESTION

Q1 DURING WHICH SEASON DID THE EAGLES ONLY SCORE 51 POINTS FOR THE ENTIRE SEASON?

(a) 1933 (b) 1934 (c) 1936 (d) 1939

answer on page 254

TRIVIA QUESTION

Q2 HOW MANY GAMES DID THE EAGLES WIN IN THEIR FIRST DECADE?

(a) 15 (b) 18 (c) 21 (d) 27

answer on page 254

1933

RECORD: 3-5-1, 4TH IN NFL EAST
HEAD COACH: LUD WRAY

Schedule
Regular Season

Wk. 5	Oct 15	L	56-0	at New York Giants
Wk. 6	Oct 18	L	25-0	vs Portsmouth Spartans
Wk. 7	Oct 29	L	35-9	at Green Bay Packers
Wk. 8	Nov 5	W	6-0	at Cincinnati Reds
Wk. 9	Nov 12	T	3-3	vs Chicago Bears
Wk. 10	Nov 19	W	25-6	vs Pittsburgh Pirates
Wk. 11	Nov 26	W	20-3	vs Cincinnati Reds
Wk. 12	Dec 3	L	10-0	vs Green Bay Packers
Wk. 13	Dec 10	L	20-14	vs New York Giants

After the Frankford Yellow Jackets folded, a syndicate headed by Bert Bell and Lud Wray paid $25,000 for the franchise for the purpose of placing a NFL team in Philadelphia. The club was christened "Eagles" in honor of the symbol of the New Deal's National Recovery Act. On October 15, the Eagles made their debut, with Lud Wray holding the coaching reigns, in New York by getting slaughtered by the Giants 56-0. A week later they did not do much better in their debut before the home fans of Philly, being shut out by the Portsmouth Spartans 25-0. After losing to the Packers in Green Bay the Eagles finally won their first game on November 5 by beating the Cincinnati Reds 6-0 at the Baker Bowl. The Eagles would go on to finish their inaugural season with a 3-5-1 record.

1933 Philadelphia Eagles Stats

Passing	Comp	Att	Comp %	Yds	Y/Att	TD	Int	Rating
Red Davis	2	6	33.3	62	10.33	1	3	72.9
Jack Roberts	4	10	40.0	97	9.70	1	3	69.6
Nick Prisco	0	2	0.0	0	0.00	0	0	39.6
Red Kirkman	22	73	30.1	354	4.85	2	13	17.0
Reb Russell	8	32	25.0	0	0.00	0	2	13.5
Dick Thornton	2	13	15.4	52	4.00	0	4	4.2
Swede Hanson	7	28	25.0	50	1.79	0	4	0.0
Jodie Whire	1	5	20.0	10	2.00	0	2	0.0
Harry O'Boyle	0	2	0.0	0	0.00	0	1	0.0
Les Woodruff	0	1	0.0	0	0.00	0	1	0.0
Rick Lackman	0	1	0.0	0	0.00	0	1	0.0

Rushing	Rush	Yds	Avg	TD
Swede Hanson	133	475	3.6	3
Jack Roberts	91	261	2.9	1
Reb Russell	32	96	3.0	0
Les Woodruff	22	74	3.4	1
Rick Lackman	17	59	3.5	0
Red Davis	15	57	3.8	1
Red Kirkman	22	43	2.0	0
Jodie Whire	8	14	1.8	0
Dick Thornton	5	14	2.8	0
Nick Prisco	7	6	0.9	0
Harry O'Boyle	2	4	2.0	0

Receiving	Rec	Yds	Avg	TD
Swede Hanson	10	186	18.6	1
Joe Carter	5	109	21.8	2
Red Kirkman	4	84	21.0	1
Red Davis	4	50	12.5	0
Les Woodruff	3	57	19.0	0
George Kenneally	2	37	18.5	0
Dick Thornton	2	14	7.0	0
Nick Prisco	2	7	3.5	0
Dick Fencl	1	20	20.0	0
Porter Lainhart	1	20	20.0	0
Jodie Whire	1	15	15.0	0
Ev Rowan	1	12	12.0	0
Nip Felber	1	8	8.0	0
Jack Roberts	1	6	6.0	0
Larry Steinbach	1	5	5.0	0

Interceptions	Int	Yds	Avg	TD
Swede Hanson	3	0	0.0	0
Jack Roberts	2	0	0.0	0
Ray Smith	2	0	0.0	0
Rick Lackman	1	0	0.0	0
Lipski	1	0	0.0	0
Reb Russell	1	0	0.0	0
Les Woodruff	1	0	0.0	1

Punting	Punts	Yds	Avg	Blocked
Davey O'Brien	6	246	41.0	0
Elmer Kolberg	10	401	40.1	0
Joe Bukant	15	568	37.9	0
Franny Murray	30	1098	36.6	0
John Cole	10	336	33.6	0
Foster Watkins	2	45	22.5	0

Kicking	PAT Made	PAT Att	PAT %	FG Made	FG Att	FG %	Pts
Joe Carter	1	1	100	0	0	0.0	13
Reb Russell	0	1	0	0	0	0.0	12
Red Davis	3	5	60	0	0	0.0	9
Red Kirkman	2	3	67	0	0	0.0	8

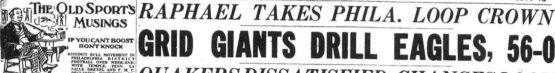

SPORTS **The Philadelphia Inquirer** **SPORTS**

PHILADELPHIA, MONDAY MORNING, OCTOBER 16, 1933

abce 13

RAPHAEL TAKES PHILA. LOOP CROWN

GRID GIANTS DRILL EAGLES, 56-0

QUAKERS DISSATISFIED; CHANGES LOOM

THE OLD SPORT'S MUSINGS

IF YOU CAN'T BOOST DON'T KNOCK

NEWMAN HERO FOR N. Y. TEAM AS BIRDS FALL

Former Michigan Star Flips Pass After Pass to Crush Lud Wray's Gridmen in League Debut

Eagle Moleskinners No Match for Coogan's Bluff Clan as Steady Stream of Touchdowns Makes Tilt One-sided

TABBUTT HURLS 7-HIT GAME TO CAPTURE TITLE

Holds South Phillies Runless After Opening Inning and Raphael Takes Game and Crown

Error by Black Foozles Double Play, Then Logan Follows With Fumble to Settle Tilt in Fourth Frame

Yep, Still Playing Ball — and He's Safe at Third

After a long, vigorous and strenuous campaign of six months ball playing the curtain finally fell on the Philadelphia League yesterday when Raphael defeated South Phillies in the final game for the title. Here is Maitland, sliding into third in the sixth frame of the series. He beat Logan's throw to Brakefield, the former handling Holstein's slow infield grounder on which Maitland reached third by a sweet dash from second.

Where Is That Scoring Punch?

When a Smart Team Blunders

Drexel-LaSalle in Notable Wins

ST. CHARLES ELEVEN BEATS SUN VILLAGE ON 1ST PERIOD PASS

Joe Regan Tosses to Tony Dekovitch for Lone Score of Battle

PENN STARTS DRIVE FOR INDIANS TODAY

Mentors to Meet and Hear Miller's Report on Next Foe; "Engle Brilliant, But Isn't He Always?" Fox; Stofko, Soph Tackle, Pleases Coach

HAGEN'S BRILLIANCY EARNS PRO GOLFERS "ALL-EVEN" VERDICT

Detroit Ace and Smith Rally to Draw With Brinke and Gunn

By GEORGE KINGSTON

Cycling Knights of Old Revive Yesteryear's Stunts

Bywood Hornets Push Over Tally to Sting Tinicum

Clearview Eleven Wins 27th Straight

Coach Defends Tactics of Cats Against Bisons

1934

**RECORD: 4-7-1, 3RD IN NFL EAST
HEAD COACH: LUD WRAY**

Schedule
Regular Season

Wk. 2	Sep 16	L	19-6	at Green Bay Packers
Wk. 4	Sep 26	W	17-0	at Pittsburgh Pirates
Wk. 5	Oct 7	L	9-7	vs Pittsburgh Pirates
Wk. 6	Oct 14	L	10-0	vs Detroit Lions
Wk. 7	Oct 21	L	6-0	at Boston Redskins
Wk. 8	Oct 28	L	17-0	at New York Giants
Wk. 9	Nov 6	W	64-0	vs Cincinnati Reds
Wk. 10	Nov 11	L	10-7	vs Brooklyn Dodgers
Wk. 11	Nov 18	L	14-7	vs Boston Redskins
Wk. 12	Nov 25	W	13-0	at Brooklyn Dodgers
Wk. 14	Dec 2	W	6-0	vs New York Giants

The Eagles continued to struggle in their second season, losing five of their first six games and going on to finish with a 4-7 record. Amazingly the Eagles four wins of the season were all shutouts. They defeated, in order, Pittsburgh 17-0, Cincinnati 64-0 (this was their only win at Temple Stadium), Brooklyn 13-0, and the NY Giants 6-0 in the final game of the season.

1934 Philadelphia Eagles Stats

Passing	Comp	Att	Comp %	Yds	Y/Att	TD	Int	Rating
Dan Barnhart	1	1	100.0	4	4.00	1	0	122.9
Reds Weiner	3	6	50.0	40	6.67	2	0	111.1
Jim Leonard	2	10	20.0	29	2.90	0	0	39.6
Ed Matesic	20	60	33.3	278	4.63	2	5	25.6
Swede Ellstrom	3	14	21.4	40	2.86	1	5	23.8
Red Kirkman	7	23	30.4	38	1.65	1	2	18.2
Swede Hanson	4	12	33.3	28	2.33	0	2	2.8
Ed Storm	8	30	26.7	97	3.23	0	6	1.0
Jack Knapper	0	7	0.0	0	0.00	0	3	0.0

Rushing	Rush	Yds	Avg	TD
Swede Hanson	146	805	5.5	7
Swede Ellstrom	72	287	4.0	1
Ed Storm	81	281	3.5	2
Jim Leonard	55	207	3.8	1
Ed Matesic	63	181	2.9	0
Reds Weiner	9	37	4.1	0
Jack Roberts	10	28	2.8	0
Jack Knapper	10	19	1.9	0
Red Kirkman	6	12	2.0	0
Rick Lackman	4	9	2.3	0
George Kavel	2	5	2.5	0
Joe Pilconis	1	5	5.0	0
Lorne Johnson	1	0	0.0	0

Receiving	Rec	Yds	Avg	TD
Joe Carter	16	238	14.9	4
Red Kirkman	8	114	14.3	1
Ed Storm	5	34	6.8	0
Swede Hanson	5	22	4.4	0
Rick Lackman	4	83	20.8	0
Ed Matesic	3	38	12.7	1
Jim Leonard	3	7	2.3	0
Swede Ellstrom	1	18	18.0	0
George Kenneally	1	12	12.0	0
Bob Gonya	1	4	4.0	1
Joe Pilconis	1	3	3.0	0

Interceptions	Int	Yds	Avg	TD
Swede Hanson	4	0	0.0	1
John Lipski	2	0	0.0	0
Diddie Willson	2	0	0.0	0
Chuck Hajek	1	0	0.0	0
Jack Knapper	1	0	0.0	0
Ed Matesic	1	0	0.0	0
Joe Pilconis	1	0	0.0	0
Reds Weiner	1	0	0.0	0

Kicking	PAT Made	PAT Att	PAT %	FG Made	FG Att	FG %	Pts
Swede Hanson	2	2	100	0	0	0.0	50
Jim Leonard	5	7	71	0	0	0.0	11
Red Kirkman	5	7	71	0	0	0.0	11
Reds Weiner	3	4	75	1	2	50.0	6

1934

November 7, 1934
Largest Shutout Win; 64-0 against Cincinnati Reds

1935

RECORD: 2-9, 5TH IN NFL EAST
HEAD COACH: LUD WRAY

Schedule

Regular Season

Wk. 1	Sep 13	L	17-7	vs Pittsburgh Pirates
Wk. 2	Sep 20	L	35-0	at Detroit Lions
Wk. 5	Oct 9	W	17-6	at Pittsburgh Pirates
Wk. 5	Oct 13	L	39-0	vs Chicago Bears
Wk. 7	Oct 27	L	17-6	at Brooklyn Dodgers
Wk. 8	Nov 3	W	7-6	at Boston Redskins
Wk. 8	Nov 5	L	3-0	vs Brooklyn Dodgers
Wk. 9	Nov 10	L	12-3	at Chicago Cardinals
Wk. 11	Nov 24	L	10-0	at New York Giants
Wk. 12	Dec 1	L	21-14	vs New York Giants
Wk. 13	Dec 8	L	13-6	vs Green Bay Packers

The Eagles kept on struggling, finishing with a horrid 2-9 record. Their two wins came on the road, defeating Pittsburgh 17-6 and Boston 7-6. General Manager Bert Bell proposed an annual college draft to balance the talent in the league. The proposal was adopted on May 19, 1935, for the upcoming 1936 season. An unusual signing occurred when the Eagles signed Alabama Pitts upon his release from Sing Sing Prison. Following the '35 season Bert Bell bought out Lud Wray and became the team's sole owner.

1935 Philadelphia Eagles Stats

Passing	Comp	Att	Comp %	Yds	Y/Att	TD	Int	Rating
Swede Hanson	1	1	100.0	23	23.00	0	0	118.8
Red Kirkman	1	1	100.0	1	1.00	1	0	118.8
Ed Storm	15	44	34.1	372	8.45	3	10	48.9
Irv Kupcinet	1	5	20.0	6	1.20	0	0	39.6
Steve Banas	0	2	0.0	0	0.00	0	0	39.6
Ed Matesic	15	64	23.4	284	4.44	2	13	16.4
Jim Leonard	11	32	34.4	119	3.72	0	3	7.2
Bob Rowe	1	11	9.1	6	0.55	0	2	0.0
Mike Sebastian	0	4	0.0	0	0.00	0	1	0.0

Receiving	Rec	Yds	Avg	TD
Joe Carter	11	260	23.6	2
Eggs Manske	9	205	22.8	4
Izzy Weinstock	8	107	13.4	0
Rick Lackman	5	49	9.8	0
Swede Hanson	4	82	20.5	0
Ed Storm	3	44	14.7	0
Alabama Pitts	2	21	10.5	0
Mike Sebastian	1	19	19.0	0
Burle Robison	1	18	18.0	0
Glenn Campbell	1	2	2.0	0

Rushing	Rush	Yds	Avg	TD
Swede Hanson	77	209	2.7	0
Izzy Weinstock	58	176	3.0	0
Jim Leonard	74	171	2.3	1
Ed Storm	84	164	2.0	0
Ed Matesic	50	138	2.8	1
Mike Sebastian	17	76	4.5	0
Rick Lackman	22	56	2.5	0
Bob Rowe	7	21	3.0	0
Joe Carter	7	19	2.7	0
Stumpy Thomason	3	14	4.7	0
Eggs Manske	3	9	3.0	0
Steve Banas	5	3	0.6	0
Bill Brian	1	2	2.0	0
George Kenneally	3	-4	-1.3	0

Kicking	PAT Made	PAT Att	PAT %	FG Made	FG Att	FG %	Pts
Hank Reese	4	6	67	1	0	0.0	7
Bud Jorgensen	1	1	100	0	0	0.0	4
Red Kirkman	1	1	100	0	0	0.0	1

German Soccermen Defeat Scots-Americans to Grab Sixth Straight Win

SPORTS — **The Philadelphia Inquirer** — **SPORTS**

PUBLIC LEDGER

PHILADELPHIA, MONDAY MORNING, OCTOBER 14, 1935

abcde 13

CHI BEARS CRUSH EAGLES, 39-0

PETILLO WINS, SETS WORLD RECORD

THE OLD SPORT'S MUSINGS

IF YOU CAN'T BOOST DON'T KNOCK

PENN OWES HUMILIATING DEFEAT TO WEAKNESS IN FUNDAMENTALS; QUAKER TACKLING AND BLOCKING ATROCIOUS; TEMPLE AND VILLANOVA IMPRESSIVE IN WEEK-END TRIUMPHS; ALBRIGHT HAS WHAT IT TAKES

TIME may soften but can never erase the chagrin of those who follow the football fortunes of Penn as they slowly and sadly melted away from Franklin Field after seeing the Quakers blotted out by Yale, 31 to 20.

It is idle to say that here was a game that Penn should have won because the Red and Blue once held a lead of 20 to 6. Had the Quakers led 200 to 6, with unlimited time to play, the Bulldogs would have overtaken them, as Harmon's pupils were performing in that second half.

Football teams can be pounded into submission by superior opponents; when they are overpowered and beautifully executed play may decide the issue—but when a team that musters the individual strength of Penn yields a total of 229 yards in four plays FOR FOUR TOUCHDOWNS, something is radically wrong.

Something is radically wrong with Penn and that something was evident to everyone who witnessed the downfall of the Quakers against Yale. They are not wanting in the fundamentals; there was no finality about their tackling; their blocking was atrocious and their defense was without elasticity.

Three of Yale's five touchdowns were scored on long runs developed from the same type of play—a reverse which feinted at the long side of Penn's line and then struck at the short side. In each case the ball carrier got loose to score without a Penn tackler having a fair shot at the runner.

Quaker Blocking Without Finality

NO TEAM can get anywhere without blocking—the type of blocking that puts a potential tackler definitely out of the play. Simply hitting a defensive player does not suffice; he must be definitely cut down, rendered temporarily impotent.

POLLOCK STAR AS CHI ELEVEN BATTERS BIRDS

22,000 See Second-Period Onslaught Roll Up 27 Points in Phils' Park Combat

Ex-Northeast and P. M. C. Hero Scores Three Touchdowns; Pitts' Ramble Gives Philly Rooters Only Thrill

By STAN BAUMGARTNER

Gangway for Petillo · · · Orendorf Cracks Up

Kelly Petillo, winner of the most recent Indianapolis Speed classic, won the feature event at Langhorne yesterday and set a world mark for the 100-mile grind on a one-mile track. Top picture shows Petillo, left, coming on his way at the 60-mile mark. Lower pictures the wreckage of Vern Orendorf's racing car. Directly in front of the pits, he blew a tire during the "century" test, skidded and crashed into the rail. Fortunately, neither Orendorf nor his mechanic was injured.

CLIFTON GRIDMEN UPSET PASSYUNK IN AERIAL BATTLE

All Touchdowns Result of Passes as Delaware Countians Triumph

By FRED BYROD

HOOSIER HERO HANDY WINNER AT LANGHORNE

Indianapolis Victor Lowers Mark for "Century" on One-mile Track Before 18,000

Winn Finishes Second and Roberts Third; Winnai and Paulowski Injured Slightly in Mishap; Fowler Also Crashes

By PERRY LEWIS

TALLY BY ALTEMOSE GIVES GERMANS GAME

Inside Left Ace Scores in Opening Half to Give Philadelphians Victory Over Scots-Americans and Sixth Straight Conquest of Season

By GEORGE BUTZ

WENTZ OLNEY TRIPS DIGGERS RIVAL, 2-0, IN SEASON'S OPENER

Tigers Tally Safety in Second Quarter to Win Initial Tussle

The Lineup

RUNYAN CAPTURES LOUISVILLE OPEN

AUDUBON COUNTRY CLUB, Louisville, Ky., Oct. 13

KEN STRONG GLEAMS AS GIANTS TRIUMPH

NEW YORK, Oct. 13

Cards Seek Third Baseman, Martin Back to Outfield

ST. LOUIS, Oct. 13

KUNES BLASTS PAR IN PRACTICE ROUND

OKLAHOMA CITY, Oct. 13

October 14, 1935
Second shutout loss of over 35 points in the season, 39-0 to Chicago Bears;
Eagles had four shutout losses in 1935

1936

RECORD: 1-11, 5TH IN NFL EAST
HEAD COACH: BERT BELL

Schedule
Regular Season

Wk. 1	Sep 13	W	10-7	vs New York Giants
Wk. 2	Sep 20	L	26-3	vs Boston Redskins
Wk. 3	Sep 27	L	17-0	vs Chicago Bears
Wk. 4	Oct 4	L	18-0	at Brooklyn Dodgers
Wk. 5	Oct 11	L	23-0	vs Detroit Lions
Wk. 6	Oct 14	L	17-0	at Pittsburgh Pirates
Wk. 7	Oct 18	L	17-7	at Boston Redskins
Wk. 8	Oct 25	L	21-17	at New York Giants
Wk. 9	Nov 5	L	6-0	vs Pittsburgh Pirates (at Johnstown, PA)
Wk. 10	Nov 8	L	13-0	at Chicago Cardinals
Wk. 11	Nov 22	L	28-7	vs Chicago Bears
Wk. 12	Nov 29	L	13-7	vs Brooklyn Dodgers

Bert Bell was now the sole owner of the Eagles and also took over as head coach, though he did not have any more success than Lud Wray on the field, losing six games by shutouts. His only win occurred in the second game of the season against the NY Giants, winning 10-7 at home. Then the Eagles hit an all-time low, losing the next 10 games. The 1936 season was their worst season on record, as the Eagles scored only 51 points and finished with an awful record of 1-11. Also, in the very first draft the Eagles had the first pick and they selected QB Jay Berwanger, who recently had won the first Heisman Trophy. However, Berwanger had no intention of ever playing pro-football so he never signed.

1936 Philadelphia Eagles Stats

Passing	Comp	Att	Comp %	Yds	Y/Att	TD	Int	Rating
Dave Smukler	21	68	30.9	345	5.07	3	6	26.9
Jim Leonard	2	6	33.3	45	7.50	0	2	21.5
John Kusko	6	27	22.2	108	4.00	0	8	4.2
Reds Bassman	1	3	33.3	3	1.00	0	1	2.8
Don Jackson	7	35	20.0	80	2.29	0	11	0.0
Stumpy Thomason	1	10	10.0	11	1.10	0	3	0.0
Walt Masters	1	6	16.7	11	1.83	0	1	0.0
Swede Hanson	0	15	0.0	0	0.00	0	4	0.0

Rushing	Rush	Yds	Avg	TD
Swede Hanson	119	359	3.0	1
Stumpy Thomason	109	333	3.1	0
Dave Smukler	99	321	3.2	0
John Kusko	49	209	4.3	1
Don Jackson	46	76	1.7	0
Jim Leonard	33	72	2.2	0
Reds Bassman	4	19	4.8	0
Walt Masters	7	18	2.6	0
Glenn Frey	7	8	1.1	0

Receiving	Rec	Yds	Avg	TD
Eggs Manske	17	325	19.1	0
Jim Leonard	5	46	9.2	1
Joe Pilconis	4	51	12.8	1
Joe Carter	4	42	10.5	1
Glenn Frey	3	65	21.7	0
Swede Hanson	3	33	11.0	0
Reds Bassman	2	38	19.0	0
George Mulligan	1	3	3.0	0

Kicking	PAT Made	PAT Att	PAT %	FG Made	FG Att	FG %	Pts
Hank Reese	3	3	100	2	0	0.0	9
Stumpy Thomason	1	1	100	0	0	0.0	7
Dave Smukler	2	2	100	1	0	0.0	5

September 14, 1936
Only win of the '36 season happened in the first game; 10-7 vs. NY Giants
Hank Reese kicks the game winning field goal

1937

RECORD: 2-8-1, 5TH IN NFL EAST
HEAD COACH: BERT BELL

Schedule
Regular Season

Wk. 1	Sep 5	L	27-14	at Pittsburgh Pirates
Wk. 2	Sep 10	L	13-7	vs Brooklyn Dodgers
Wk. 3	Sep 21	L	21-3	vs Cleveland Rams
Wk. 4	Sep 26	T	6-6	vs Chicago Cardinals
Wk. 5	Oct 3	L	16-7	vs New York Giants
Wk. 6	Oct 10	W	14-0	at Washington Redskins
Wk. 7	Oct 17	L	21-0	at New York Giants
Wk. 8	Oct 24	L	10-7	vs Washington Redskins
Wk. 9	Oct 31	L	16-7	at Pittsburgh Pirates
Wk. 10	Nov 7	W	14-10	at Brooklyn Dodgers
Wk. 11	Nov 14	L	37-7	at Green Bay Packers
				(at Milwaukee, WI)

The Eagles signed the last NFL player not to wear a helmet, Bill Hewitt. After losing their first three games, the Eagles snap a 14-game losing streak spread over two seasons by tying the Chicago Cardinals 6-6 at Municipal Stadium. In week five, they lost to the NY Giants 16-7, then they finally got a win by stunning the eventual NFL Champion Redskins 14-0 in Washington. The Eagles would go on to finish with a 2-8-1 record.

1937 Philadelphia Eagles Stats

Passing	Comp	Att	Comp %	Yds	Y/Att	TD	Int	Rating
Dave Smukler	42	118	35.6	432	3.66	5	14	21.5
Rabbit Keen	1	5	20.0	86	17.20	1	0	118.8
Swede Hanson	0	2	0.0	0	0.00	0	0	39.6
Glenn Frey	0	1	0.0	0	0.00	0	0	39.6
Winnie Baze	0	3	0.0	0	0.00	0	0	39.6
Emmett Mortell	18	71	25.4	320	4.51	2	8	15.7
John Kusko	2	7	28.6	11	1.57	0	2	0.0

Rushing	Rush	Yds	Avg	TD
Emmett Mortell	100	312	3.1	0
Dave Smukler	92	247	2.7	1
Rabbit Keen	34	154	4.5	0
Swede Hanson	18	59	3.3	1
Bob Masters	9	32	3.6	0
John Kusko	17	27	1.6	0
Joe Pilconis	2	21	10.5	0
Winnie Baze	3	14	4.7	0
Glenn Frey	5	11	2.2	0
Jay Arnold	5	7	1.4	0

Receiving	Rec	Yds	Avg	TD
Bill Hewitt	16	197	12.3	5
Joe Carter	15	282	18.8	3
Jay Arnold	8	142	17.8	0
Joe Pilconis	6	59	9.8	0
Rabbit Keen	5	45	9.0	0
Bob Masters	4	60	15.0	0
Glenn Frey	4	19	4.8	0
John Kusko	2	47	23.5	0
Winnie Baze	1	2	2.0	0
Emmett Mortell	1	0	0.0	0
Dave Smukler	1	-4	-4.0	0

Kicking	PAT Made	PAT Att	PAT %	FG Made	FG Att	FG %	Pts
Dave Smukler	8	9	89	1	0	0.0	17
Hank Reese	3	3	100	0	0	0.0	3

1937

November 15, 1937
*Last game of a horrible season (winning only two games)
losing 37-7 to Green Bay*

1938
RECORD: 5-6, 4TH IN NFL EAST
HEAD COACH: BERT BELL

Schedule
Regular Season

Wk. 2	Sep 11	L	26-23	vs Washington Redskins
Wk. 3	Sep 16	W	27-7	at Pittsburgh Pirates (at Buffalo, NY)
Wk. 4	Sep 25	W	14-10	vs New York Giants
Wk. 5	Oct 2	L	28-6	vs Chicago Bears
Wk. 7	Oct 16	L	17-7	at New York Giants
Wk. 8	Oct 23	L	20-14	at Washington Redskins
Wk. 9	Oct 26	W	7-0	at Chicago Cardinals (at Erie, PA)
Wk. 10	Nov 6	L	10-7	vs Brooklyn Dodgers
Wk. 11	Nov 13	L	32-14	at Brooklyn Dodgers
Wk. 12	Nov 20	W	14-7	at Pittsburgh Pirates (at Charleston, WV)
Wk. 14	Dec 4	W	21-7	at Detroit Lions

The Eagles showed signs of improvement, playing solid football at times on the way to a 5-6 record, which was bolstered by two straight wins to close the season. They defeated Pittsburgh 14-7 and Detroit 21-7. The Eagle training camp was moved to West Chester State Teachers College.

1938 Philadelphia Eagles Stats

Passing	Comp	Att	Comp %	Yds	Y/Att	TD	Int	Rating
Dave Smukler	42	102	41.2	524	5.14	7	8	48.0
Joe Bukant	1	1	100.0	14	14.00	0	0	118.8
Emmett Mortell	12	57	21.1	201	3.53	6	7	37.3
Dick Riffle	9	31	29.0	178	5.74	2	4	32.9

Rushing	Rush	Yds	Avg	TD
Dave Smukler	96	313	3.3	1
Emmett Mortell	110	296	2.7	0
Dick Riffle	65	227	3.5	1
Joe Bukant	48	119	2.5	0
Jay Arnold	19	22	1.2	0
Woody Dow	4	20	5.0	0
Rabbit Keen	3	10	3.3	0
John Cole	1	4	4.0	0

Receiving	Rec	Yds	Avg	TD
Joe Carter	27	386	14.3	7
Bill Hewitt	18	237	13.2	4
Jay Arnold	6	74	12.3	2
Red Ramsey	5	122	24.4	1
Woody Dow	5	88	17.6	1
John Cole	2	9	4.5	0
Bob Pylman	1	1	1.0	0

Kicking	PAT Made	PAT Att	PAT %	FG Made	FG Att	FG %	Pts
Joe Carter	1	1	100	0	0	0.0	13
Jay Arnold	3	3	100	0	1	0.0	27
Dave Smukler	6	6	100	0	2	0.0	18
Hank Reese	10	13	77	1	6	16.7	13

Punting	Punts	Yds	Avg	Blocked
Dick Riffle	17	683	40.2	0

1938

September 17, 1938
First win of five for the season defeating Pittsburgh 27-7;
game played in Buffalo, NY

1939
RECORD: 1-9-1, T-4TH IN NFL EAST
HEAD COACH: BERT BELL

Schedule
Regular Season

Wk. 2	Sep 17	L	7-0	vs Washington Redskins
Wk. 3	Sep 24	L	13-3	vs New York Giants
Wk. 4	Oct 1	T	0-0	vs Brooklyn Dodgers
Wk. 6	Oct 15	L	27-10	at New York Giants
Wk. 7	Oct 22	L	23-14	at Brooklyn Dodgers
Wk. 9	Nov 5	L	7-6	at Washington Redskins
Wk. 10	Nov 12	L	23-16	vs Green Bay Packers
Wk. 11	Nov 19	L	27-14	at Chicago Bears
Wk. 12	Nov 23	W	17-14	vs Pittsburgh Pirates
Wk. 12	Nov 26	L	24-12	at Pittsburgh Pirates
Wk. 13	Dec 3	L	35-13	at Cleveland Rams
				(at Colorado Springs, CO)

Davey O'Brien, an All-American QB, signed with the Eagles for a reported $12,000 per year salary and a percentage of the gate. O'Brien played in every game and set an NFL passing yardage record with 1,324 yards. Despite the success of O'Brien, the Eagles could only muster a 1-9-1 record; their only win was on Thanksgiving Day against Pittsburgh, 17-14. However the Eagles would make history that year. On October 22nd, the Eagles played in the first televised NFL game and fell to the host Brooklyn Dodgers, 23-14. Allan "Skip" Walz broadcast the game for WNBC from Ebbetts field to the approximately 1,000 TV sets then in Brooklyn.

1939 Philadelphia Eagles Stats

Passing	Comp	Att	Comp %	Yds	Y/Att	TD	Int	Rating
Davey O'Brien	99	201	49.3	1324	6.59	6	17	45.3
Joe Bukant	10	1	1000.0	0	0.00	0	0	79.2
Emmett Mortell	12	41	29.3	134	3.27	1	0	48.8
Dave Smukler	7	20	35.0	56	2.80	0	4	4.2
Dick Riffle	1	4	25.0	2	0.50	0	1	0.0

Rushing	Rush	Yds	Avg	TD
Dave Smukler	45	218	4.8	0
Franny Murray	49	137	2.8	1
Joe Bukant	59	136	2.3	3
Emmett Mortell	37	88	2.4	0
Dick Riffle	18	61	3.4	0
Drew Ellis	1	6	6.0	0
Joe Carter	1	4	4.0	0
Jay Arnold	8	1	0.1	0
Bill Hewitt	1	1	1.0	0
Chuck Newton	1	0	0.0	0
Woody Dow	1	-7	-7.0	0
Davey O'Brien	108	-14	-0.1	1

Receiving	Rec	Yds	Avg	TD
Red Ramsey	31	359	11.6	1
Joe Carter	24	292	12.2	2
Bill Hewitt	15	243	16.2	1
Jay Arnold	13	207	15.9	1
Franny Murray	13	144	11.1	1
Chuck Newton	9	123	13.7	1
Dick Riffle	6	57	9.5	0
Woody Dow	5	58	11.6	0
Elmer Kolberg	3	33	11.0	0

Kicking	PAT Made	PAT Att	PAT %	FG Made	FG Att	FG %	Pts
Joe Carter	1	1	100	0	0	0.0	13
Franny Murray	8	12	67	2	4	50.0	26
Hank Reese	1	1	100	2	4	50.0	7

Punting	Punts	Yds	Avg	Blocked
Joe Bukant	1	54	54.0	0
Dave Smukler	10	483	48.3	0
Jay Arnold	1	42	42.0	0
Davey O'Brien	3	120	40.0	0
Emmett Mortell	23	907	39.4	0
Franny Murray	33	1220	37.0	0
Dick Riffle	14	479	34.2	0

EAGLES WIN ON O'BRIEN'S PASS, 17 TO 14

The Philadelphia Inquirer

PHILADELPHIA, FRIDAY MORNING, NOVEMBER 24, 1939

TOMASETTI — BOYD — O'BRIEN

O'BRIEN DISCOURAGES COMPETITION FOR HIS PASSING LAURELS

Not only did Davey O'Brien pass his Eagles to a sensational 17-14 triumph over the Pittsburgh Pirates yesterday, but he saw to it that no one else stole his aerial thunder. Here he is about to rush in and spear a pass that is bouncing off the finger tips of Sam Boyd, Pirate end. Lou Tomasetti, 1939 Inquirer A. A. All-Star player, threw the pass. Davey returned it to the Eagles 25-yard line. Two other Eagles—Murray (11) and Dow (14)—also are seeking to intercept the heave.

1939

Strictly Sports
Penna.-New York Pact Ideal, But Will It Work?
Empire State Boxing Commission's Previous Nullification Recalled

Burrs Beaten By W. Phila.
Sigholtz Kicks Goal To Beat W. Catholic Before 12,000 Fans

12th in Row For San Jose
'Pop' Warner's Team Beats Fresno State

La Salle Jars P. M. C., 20-0
Explorers Score In Three Periods; 5000 Watch Game

Late Aerial Beats Pirates
Bill Hewitt Catches Forward in Last Minute, Laterals to Arnold for Deciding Score as 20,000 Look On

South Catholic Ties Southern

Catholic University Gains 8th Victory

California Gridder Dies of Injuries

Frankford Beats N. Catholic, 18-6

Report Maryland Coach to Resign

Spiegal Rally Overcomes Tony Saraullo

Bowl Test Won By Sourdoughs

First Setback For Richmond

Holiday Football Scores

Girard Estate Loses

Collingdale Turns Back Darby,

40's Decade in Review

Decade Win-Loss Record:
58-47-5, (3-1 postseason record)

Home Field:
1940-49 Shibe Park, 1941 and 1947 Municipal Stadium

Playoff Appearances:
1947, 1948 and 1949

Championships:
Divisional Championship 1947 (NFL East), 1948 (NFL East) and 1949 (NFL East)
NFL Championship Games 1947, 1948, 1949
NFL Champions 1948, 1949

Head Coaches:
1940 Bert Bell (1-10); 1941-49 Greasy Neale (67-45-7) (3-1 postseason record);
1943 Walt Kiesling as the Steagles (5-4-1)

Hall of Fame Inductees:
Chuck Bednarik, Bert Bell, Bill Hewitt, Greasy Neale, Pete Pihos,
Steve Van Buren, Alex Wojciechowicz

Award Winners:
Greasy Neale, Coach of the Year 1948

All Pro:
Dick Bassi 1940, Don Looney 1940, Davey O'Brien 1940, Dick Humbert 1941,
Phil Ragazzo 1941, Bob Suffridge 1941, Tommy Thompson 1942 and 1948-49,
Jack Hinkle 1943, Eberle Schultz 1943, Vic Sears 1943 and 1945, Ernie Steele 1943,
Leroy Zimmerman 1943-44, Steve Van Buren 1944-49, Al Wistert 1944-49,
Bruno Banducci 1945, Jack Ferrante 1945 and 1949, Augie Lio 1946,
Pete Pihos 1947-49, Bucko Kilroy 1948-49, Joe Muha 1948, Cliff Patton 1949

All-Star Game Selections:
Dick Bassi 1940, Don Looney 1940, Dick Humbert 1941, Enio Conti 1942,
Tommy Thompson 1942, Bosh Pritchard 1942

First Game of the Decade:
September 15, 1940 lost to Green Bay 27-20

Last Game of the Decade:
December11, 1949 defcated NY Giants 17-3

Largest Margin of Victory:
October 10, 1948 vs. NY Giants 45-0, October 17, 1948 vs. Washington Redskins 45-0,
November 14, 1948 vs. Boston Yanks 45-0

Largest Margin of Defeat:
November 30, 1941 vs. Chicago Bears 49-14

Eagle Firsts of the Decade:
First Game at Shibe Park, September 28, 1940, loss to NY Giants
First Winning Season – 1943, 5-4-1 as Steagles
First 300-Yard Passing Game – Davey O'Brien completed 33 of 60 passes totaling 316 yards in a
losing effort against the Washington Redskins, December 1, 1940
First 200-Yard Rushing Game – Steve Van Buren rushed 27 times gaining 205 yards in a win over the
Pittsburgh Steelers, November 27, 1949
First 100 points scored – Steve Van Buren scored 110 points during the 1945 season
First 20 Touchdown Passes – Tommy Thompson threw 25 touchdown passes in the 1948 season
First Postseason Game – Shut out Pittsburgh Steelers 21-0 in their first playoff game on December 21, 1947

40's Decade in Review

The 1940's would prove a tumultuous and ultimately triumphant decade for the young club. In 1940, the team moved from Philadelphia Municipal Stadium to Shibe Park. Lud Wray's half-interest in the team was purchased by Art Rooney, who had just sold the Pittsburgh Steelers to Alexis Thompson. Soon thereafter, Bell/Rooney and Thompson swapped franchises, but not teams. Bell/Rooney's entire Eagles' corporate organization, including most of the players, moved to Pittsburgh (The Steelers' corporate name remained "Philadelphia Football Club, Inc." until 1945) and Thompson's Steelers moved to Philadelphia, leaving only the team nicknames in their original cities. Since NFL franchises are territorial rights distinct from individual corporate entities, the NFL does not consider this a franchise move and considers the current Philadelphia Eagles as a single unbroken entity from 1933.

After assuming ownership, Thompson promptly hired Greasy Neale as the team's head coach. In its first years under Neale, the team continued to struggle. In 1943, when manpower shortages stemming from World War II made it impossible to fill the roster, the team temporarily merged with the Steelers to form a team popularly known as the "Steagles." The merger, never intended as a permanent arrangement, was dissolved at the end of the 1943 season. This season saw the team's first winning season in its 11-year history, with a finish of 5-4-1. In 1944, however, the Eagles finally experienced good fortune, as they made their finest draft pick to date: running back Steve Van Buren. At last, the team's fortunes were about to change.

Led by future Hall of Famers Van Buren and Neale, the Eagles became a serious competitor for the first time. They had their first winning season as a separate team in 1944. After two more second-place finishes (1945 and 1946), the Eagles reached the NFL title game for the first time in 1947. Van Buren, end Pete Pihos and Bosh Pritchard fought valiantly, but the young team fell to the Chicago Cardinals, 28-21, at Chicago's Comiskey Park. Undeterred, the young squad rebounded and returned to face the Cardinals once more in the 1948 championship. With home-field advantage (and a blinding snowstorm) on their side, the Eagles won their first NFL Championship, 7-0. Due to the severity of the weather, few fans were on hand to witness the joyous occasion. That would not be the case the following season, however, when the Eagles returned to the NFL championship game for the third consecutive year and won in dominating fashion in front of a large crowd in Los Angeles, beating the Los Angeles Rams, 14-0.

1949 also saw the sale of the team by Thompson to a syndicate of 100 buyers, each of whom paid a fee of $3,000 for their share of the team. While the leader of the "Happy Hundred" was noted Philadelphia businessman James P. Clark, one unsung investor was Leonard Tose, a name that would eventually become very familiar to Eagles fans. The new regime's first draft pick was Chuck Bednarik, an All-American lineman/linebacker from the University of Pennsylvania. Bednarik would go on to become one of the greatest and most beloved players in Eagles history. An eventual Hall of Famer and the last of the great two-way players, Bednarik may have been the toughest man in football history.

TRIVIA QUESTION
Q3 DURING THE '30S, WHICH EAGLES PLAYER KICKED THE MOST SUCCESSFUL FIELD GOALS?

(a) Guy Turnbow (b) Dave Smukler
(c) Hank Reese (d) Joe Carter

answer on page 254

TRIVIA QUESTION
Q4 IN WHAT YEAR DID THE EAGLES FINALLY HAVE THEIR FIRST WINNING SEASON?

(a) 1941 (b) 1943 (c) 1945 (d) 1949

answer on page 254

1940

RECORD: 1-10, 5TH IN NFL EAST
HEAD COACH: BERT BELL

Schedule

Regular Season

Wk. 2	Sep 15	L	27-20	at Green Bay Packers
Wk. 3	Sep 22	L	21-13	at Cleveland Rams
Wk. 4	Sep 28	L	20-14	vs New York Giants
Wk. 5	Oct 4	L	30-17	at Brooklyn Dodgers
Wk. 6	Oct 13	L	17-7	at New York Giants
Wk. 7	Oct 20	L	34-17	vs Washington Redskins
Wk. 8	Oct 26	L	21-7	vs Brooklyn Dodgers
Wk. 10	Nov 10	L	7-3	at Pittsburgh Pirates
Wk. 11	Nov 17	L	21-0	vs Detroit Lions
Wk. 13	Nov 28	W	7-0	vs Pittsburgh Pirates
Wk. 13	Dec 1	L	13-6	at Washington Redskins

After selling the Pittsburgh Steelers to Alexis Thompson, Art Rooney bought a half interest in the Eagles, who move their games to Shibe Park (later known as Connie Mack Stadium). However, the Eagles would limp along again, finishing with an awful 1-10 record. Following the season Rooney, along with Eagles co-founder Bert Bell, swapped franchises with Thompson. Bell, who also departed his post as Eagles coach, would one day go on to be commissioner of the NFL. The struggling Eagles won only one game that season, against Pittsburgh 7-0, thus ending a nine-game losing streak. One positive note was that Don Looney's 58 receptions set a new club record that stood for many years.

1940 Philadelphia Eagles Stats

Passing	Comp	Att	Comp %	Yds	Y/Att	TD	Int	Rating
Davey O'Brien	124	277	44.8	1290	4.66	5	17	39.2
Foster Watkins	28	85	32.9	565	6.65	1	3	46.4

Rushing	Rush	Yds	Avg	TD
Dick Riffle	81	238	2.9	4
Elmer Hackney	32	101	3.2	1
Frank Emmons	29	77	2.7	1
John Cole	26	75	2.9	0
Joe Bukant	18	50	2.8	1
Franny Murray	8	7	0.9	0
Theodore Schmitt	1	6	6.0	0
Jay Arnold	39	0	0.0	7
Les McDonald	2	-2	-1.0	0
Joe Carter	1	-3	-3.0	0
Don Looney	2	-4	-2.0	0
Foster Watkins	14	-76	-5.4	0
Davey O'Brien	100	-180	-1.8	1

Receiving	Rec	Yds	Avg	TD
Jay Arnold	145	0	0.0	0
Don Looney	58	707	12.2	4
Red Ramsey	17	143	8.4	0
Les McDonald	14	289	20.6	0
Joe Carter	12	201	16.8	0
Franny Murray	12	125	10.4	0
Joe Wendlick	8	67	8.4	0
Dick Riffle	8	58	7.3	1
Elmer Kolberg	6	43	7.2	0
Frank Emmons	3	19	6.3	1
John Cole	2	11	5.5	0
Elmer Hackney	2	4	2.0	0
Chuck Newton	1	22	22.0	0
Joe Bukant	1	13	13.0	0
Theodore Schmitt	1	8	8.0	0

Punting	Punts	Yds	Avg	Blocked
Davey O'Brien	6	246	41.0	0
Elmer Kolberg	10	401	40.1	0
Joe Bukant	15	568	37.9	0
Franny Murray	30	1098	36.6	0
John Cole	10	336	33.6	0
Foster Watkins	2	45	22.5	0

Interceptions	Int	Yds	Avg	TD
Davey O'Brien	4	92	23.0	0
Franny Murray	2	10	5.0	0
Elmer Kolberg	1	15	15.0	0
Chuck Newton	1	12	12.0	0
Joe Bukant	1	10	10.0	0
Red Ramsey	1	5	5.0	0
Jay Arnold	1	4	4.0	0
Chuck Cherundolo	1	0	0.0	0

Kicking	PAT Made	PAT Att	PAT %	FG Made	FG Att	FG %	Pts
Joe Carter	1	1	100	0	0	0.0	13
George Somers	1	1	100	2	9	22.2	7
Franny Murray	6	8	75	0	1	0.0	6
John Cole	3	4	75	1	1	100.0	6
Foster Watkins	2	2	100	0	0	0.0	2

THE PHILADELPHIA INQUIRER, FRIDAY MORNING, NOVEMBER 29, 1940

FOOTBALL FAREWELL: DAVEY O'BRIEN'S LAST STAND WITH EAGLES HERE; F. B. I. NEXT STOP

November 29, 1940
Eagles only win for the season
was a 7-0 shutout versus Pittsburgh

1941

RECORD: 2-8-1, 4TH IN NFL EAST
HEAD COACH: GREASY NEALE

Schedule
Regular Season

Wk. 2	Sep 13	L	24-0	vs New York Giants
Wk. 3	Sep 21	W	10-7	at Pittsburgh Steelers
Wk. 4	Sep 27	L	24-13	vs Brooklyn Dodgers
Wk. 6	Oct 12	L	16-0	at New York Giants
Wk. 7	Oct 19	L	21-17	vs Washington Redskins
Wk. 8	Oct 26	W	21-14	vs Chicago Cardinals
Wk. 9	Nov 2	L	15-6	at Brooklyn Dodgers
Wk. 10	Nov 9	T	7-7	vs Pittsburgh Steelers
Wk. 11	Nov 16	L	21-17	at Detroit Lions
Wk. 13	Nov 30	L	49-14	vs Chicago Bears
Wk. 14	Dec 7	L	20-14	at Washington Redskins

Bell and Rooney swapped franchises with Thompson. The new owner hired Earl (Greasy) Neale as the new head coach of the Eagles. With Neale as head coach the Eagles continued to struggle, posting a 2-8-1 record (with wins over Pittsburgh 10-7 and Chicago 21-14), while returning to play in Municipal Stadium for one season.

1941 Philadelphia Eagles Stats

Passing	Comp	Att	Comp %	Yds	Y/Att	TD	Int	Rating
Tommy Thompson	86	162	53.1	959	5.92	8	14	51.4
Foster Watkins	6	10	60.0	62	6.20	1	0	111.3
Dan DeSantis	3	7	42.9	78	11.14	1	1	84.2
Wes McAfee	1	4	25.0	4	1.00	0	0	39.6
Len Barnum	19	55	34.5	260	4.73	0	10	11.0
Jim Castiglia	0	7	0.0	0	0.00	0	1	0.0
Nick Basca	0	4	0.0	0	0.00	0	1	0.0

Rushing	Rush	Yds	Avg	TD
Jim Castiglia	60	183	3.1	4
Dan DeSantis	45	125	2.8	0
Terry Fox	21	97	4.6	0
Jack Banta	27	92	3.4	1
Mort Landsberg	23	69	3.0	0
Sam Bartholomew	21	69	3.3	0
Len Barnum	35	64	1.8	0
Fred Gloden	22	55	2.5	0
Nick Basca	15	44	2.9	1
Lou Tomasetti	10	37	3.7	0
Foster Watkins	15	11	0.7	0
Wes McAfee	9	6	0.7	0
Lou Ghecas	2	0	0.0	0
Enio Conti	1	-1	-1.0	0
Tommy Thompson	54	-2	-0.0	0

Receiving	Rec	Yds	Avg	TD
Dick Humbert	29	332	11.4	2
Bob Krieger	19	240	12.6	2
Hank Piro	10	141	14.1	1
Terry Fox	6	71	11.8	0
Lou Tomasetti	5	54	10.8	1
John Shonk	5	52	10.4	0
Mort Landsberg	5	51	10.2	0
Larry Cabrelli	4	90	22.5	1
Dan DeSantis	4	53	13.3	0
Foster Watkins	4	36	9.0	0
Tommy Thompson	4	30	7.5	1
Jim Castiglia	4	24	6.0	0
Wes McAfee	3	30	10.0	1
Sam Bartholomew	3	15	5.0	0
Nick Basca	2	45	22.5	0
Jack Banta	2	42	21.0	0
Jack Ferrante	2	22	11.0	0
Fred Gloden	2	13	6.5	0
Len Barnum	1	11	11.0	0
Kirk Hershey	1	11	11.0	0

Punting	Punts	Yds	Avg	Blocked
Jack Banta	9	412	45.8	0
Len Barnum	41	1788	43.6	0
Tommy Thompson	1	43	43.0	0
Nick Basca	10	348	34.8	0
Wes McAfee	1	32	32.0	0
Dan DeSantis	7	206	29.4	0

Kicking	PAT Made	PAT Att	PAT %	FG Made	FG Att	FG %	Pts
Nick Basca	9	9	100	1	2	50.0	18
Len Barnum	2	2	100	2	6	33.3	8
Wes McAfee	2	2	100	0	0	0.0	8
Dan DeSantis	1	1	100	0	0	0.0	1

Eagles Check Cardinals' Rally to Win, 21-14

Strictly Sports

Penn's Fresh Grid Power Suggests a Victory Cycle

Championship Class Instilled Spirit Spreads to Spark Lowest Subs

By CY PETERMAN

The Philadelphia Inquirer

PHILADELPHIA, MONDAY MORNING, OCTOBER 27, 1941

La Salle Conquers Canisius, 7-0

Byron Scores For Explorers In 3d Period

Forwards Pave Way for La Salle Victory in Buffalo

Rookie Tallies Twice

Castiglia Star In Eagles' 2d Triumph

By PERRY LEWIS

EAGLES BREAK UP CHICAGO CARDINALS' PASS IN END ZONE
Nick Basca (No. 47) deflects heave intended for Chicago's John Hall

Passes Win For St. Mary's Over Loyola

Penn Bankers 2d In Pistol Shoot

Canadian Draft May Take Hockey Players

W. Catholic Beats South

Temple, Penn Among 5 Unbeaten, Untied

By FRED BYROD

Catholic Tops St. John's, 6-0

Parker Stars, Giants Lose To Brooklyn

St. Carthage Retains Grid League Lead

Kaplan 7-5 Choice to Beat Padlo in Arena Ring Tonight

By JOHN WEBSTER

Flop Last Week, Kimbrough Stars as Yanks Win, 31-14

Unbeaten, Untied

	G.	Pts.	Opp. Pts.
Temple	5	112	42
Duquesne	5	111	20
Penn	4	125	19
Fordham	4	98	20
Army	4	79	33

1941

October 27, 1941
One of only two wins for the entire '41 season,
21-14 against the Chicago Cardinals

1942

RECORD: 2-9, 5TH IN NFL EAST
HEAD COACH: GREASY NEALE

Schedule
Regular Season

Wk. 1	Sep 13	W	24-14	at Pittsburgh Steelers
Wk. 2	Sep 20	L	24-14	at Cleveland Rams (at Akron, OH)
Wk. 3	Sep 27	L	35-14	vs Brooklyn Dodgers (at Buffalo, NY)
Wk. 4	Oct 4	L	14-10	vs Washington Redskins
Wk. 5	Oct 11	L	35-17	at New York Giants
Wk. 6	Oct 18	L	14-0	vs Pittsburgh Steelers
Wk. 7	Oct 25	L	45-14	at Chicago Bears
Wk. 8	Nov 1	L	30-27	at Washington Redskins
Wk. 9	Nov 8	L	14-0	vs New York Giants
Wk. 10	Nov 15	W	14-7	at Brooklyn Dodgers
Wk. 12	Nov 29	L	7-0	vs Green Bay Packers

After moving back to Shibe Park full time, the Eagles continued to be one of the worst teams in the NFL, posting a wretched 2-9 record. They won their first game against Pittsburgh 24-14, but then flew to an eight game losing streak until finally they defeated Brooklyn 14-7. In the final game of the season they lost to Green Bay 7-0, which landed them in last place, again.

1948 Philadelphia Eagles Stats

Passing	Comp	Att	Comp %	Yds	Y/Att	TD	Int	Rating
Tommy Thompson	95	203	46.8	1410	6.95	8	16	50.3
Billy Jefferson	0	1	0.0	0	0.00	0	0	39.6
Len Barnum	1	9	11.1	6	0.67	0	1	0.0

Rushing	Rush	Yds	Avg	TD
Bob Davis	43	207	4.8	2
Bosh Pritchard	35	193	5.5	0
Ted Williams	50	183	3.7	2
Ernie Steele	24	124	5.2	0
Lou Tomasetti	45	102	2.3	0
Dick Erdlitz	21	69	3.3	1
Len Barnum	30	64	2.1	0
Billy Jefferson	11	57	5.2	0
Bert Johnson	27	54	2.0	0
Jack Stackpool	15	47	3.1	0
Irv Hall	8	14	1.8	0
Fred Meyer	2	13	6.5	0
Bob Masters	1	3	3.0	0
Len Supulski	1	1	1.0	0
John Binotto	1	-10	-10.0	0
Tommy Thompson	92	-32	-0.3	1

Receiving	Rec	Yds	Avg	TD
Fred Meyer	16	324	20.3	1
Larry Cabrelli	15	229	15.3	1
Bert Johnson	9	123	13.7	2
Ted Williams	9	58	6.4	0
Len Supulski	8	149	18.6	1
Ernie Steele	7	114	16.3	1
Bob Davis	6	93	15.5	1
Dick Erdlitz	5	78	15.6	0
Bob Priestly	4	47	11.8	0
Bill Combs	4	44	11.0	1
Lou Tomasetti	4	22	5.5	0
Len Barnum	3	54	18.0	0
Jack Stackpool	2	59	29.5	0
Irv Hall	2	18	9.0	0
Bosh Pritchard	2	4	2.0	0

Punting	Punts	Yds	Avg	Blocked
Billy Jefferson	1	50	50.0	0
Len Barnum	50	2106	42.1	0
Irv Hall	1	36	36.0	0
Bosh Pritchard	17	595	35.0	0
Ernie Steele	2	61	30.5	0

Interceptions	Int	Yds	Avg	TD
Tommy Thompson	4	28	7.0	0
Bosh Pritchard	3	23	7.7	0
Ernie Steele	2	49	24.5	0
Bob Davis	2	35	17.5	0
Lou Tomasetti	1	23	23.0	0
Len Barnum	1	11	11.0	0
Ken Hayden	1	5	5.0	0
Len Supulski	1	5	5.0	0
Dick Erdlitz	1	0	0.0	0
Woody Gerber	1	0	0.0	0
Ray Graves	1	0	0.0	0

Kicking	PAT Made	PAT Att	PAT %	FG Made	FG Att	FG %	Pts
Len Barnum	7	8	88	3	7	42.9	16
Dick Erdlitz	8	8	100	0	0	0.0	14
Ernie Steele	1	1	100	0	0	0.0	13
Ed Kasky	0	0	0.	0	1	0.0	0

St. Joseph's Wins, 7-0; Villanova Loses, 9-0

Strictly Sports

State, Not Penn, Beat Penn in So-Called Upset

Lion Defenders, Notably Cenci, Made Rival Quarterbacks Look Bad

By LEO RIORDAN

JOE COLONE

The Philadelphia Inquirer

PHILADELPHIA, MONDAY MORNING, NOVEMBER 16, 1942   abdefgh 23

LA SALLE HIGH MISSES THIS EARLY CHANCE TO SCORE AGAINST ST. JOSEPH'S
Bob Fitzmyer, St. Joseph's centre (No. 21) thrust aside this pass as LaSalle's Pete Villari stood with waiting arms on the threshold of a touchdown.

Early Drive Decides

Titans Score, Trap Postus For Safety

By PERRY LEWIS
Inquirer Sports Reporter

DETROIT, Mich., Nov. 15.

Americans Prevail, Top Soccer League

By GEORGE BUTZ

St. Joseph's Jolts La Salle

By KEN HAY

Eagles Stop Losing; Beat Dodgers, 14-7

By FRANK O'GARA
Inquirer Sports Reporter

BROOKLYN, N. Y., Nov. 15.

West Catholic Jars St. John's

Magnolia Rally Tops Zuni A. A.

Don't Look Now, But—

Jack O'Brien and the Long Count

By CHARLEY McCROSSEN

U. S. G. A. Slates New Treasurer

Fairman Seeks Strong Team For Batesville in Tourney

By JOHN WEBSTER

St. James Beats Malvern Prep

COLLEGIANS—Penn Charter

42,787 See Bears Sink Packers, 38-7

CHICAGO, Nov. 15 (A. P.)

Continued on Page 24, Column 6
Continued on Page 25, Column 6
Continued on Page 25, Column 6
Continued on Page 25, Column 6
Continued on Page 25, Column 2
Continued on Page 25, Column 2
Continued on Page 24, Column 7
Continued on Page 24, Column 1
Continued on Page 35, Column 2

November 16, 1942
In what was the lowest attended game,
3,858 watched the Eagles defeat the Brooklyn Dodgers 14-7

1943

RECORD: 5-4-1, 3RD IN NFL EAST
HEAD COACH: GREASY NEALE &
WALT KIESLING

Schedule
Regular Season

Wk. 3	Oct 2	W	17-0	vs Brooklyn Dodgers (at Philadelphia, PA)
Wk. 4	Oct 9	W	28-14	vs New York Giants (at Philadelphia, PA)
Wk. 5	Oct 17	L	48-21	at Chicago Bears
Wk. 6	Oct 24	L	42-14	at New York Giants
Wk. 7	Oct 31	W	34-13	vs Chicago Cardinals (at Pittsburgh, PA)
Wk. 8	Nov 7	T	14-14	vs Washington Redskins (at Philadelphia, PA)
Wk. 9	Nov 14	L	13-7	at Brooklyn Dodgers
Wk. 10	Nov 21	W	35-34	vs Detroit Lions (at Pittsburgh, PA)
Wk. 11	Nov 28	W	27-14	at Washington Redskins
Wk. 12	Dec 5	L	38-28	vs Green Bay Packers (at Philadelphia, PA)

With a shortage of players due to World War II, the Eagles merged with the Pittsburgh Steelers, and become the Phil-Pitt Steagles, with both teams' coaches (Walt Kiesling and Greasy Neale) splitting duties. The Steagles would actually play competitive football, posting a solid 5-4-1 record and their first winning season for the franchise. Another Eagles record occurred while defeating the Giants 28-14; the Eagles fumbled a record ten times. Following the season Eagles owner Alex Thompson dissolved the merger.

1943 Philadelphia Eagles Stats

Passing	Comp	Att	Comp %	Yds	Y/Att	TD	Int	Rating
Roy Zimmerman	43	124	34.7	846	6.82	9	17	44.0
Allie Sherman	16	37	43.2	208	5.62	2	1	68.3
Johnny Butler	6	13	46.2	84	6.46	0	1	35.4
Ernie Steele	0	1	0.0	0	0.00	0	1	0.0

Rushing	Rush	Yds	Avg	TD
Jack Hinkle	116	571	4.9	3
Ernie Steele	85	409	4.8	4
Johnny Butler	87	362	4.2	3
Bob Thurbon	71	291	4.1	5
Charlie Gauer	12	69	5.8	0
Ben Kish	22	50	2.3	0
Ted Laux	9	23	2.6	0
Tony Bova	1	11	11.0	0
Bob Masters	2	6	3.0	0
Steve Sader	3	5	1.7	0
Dean Steward	1	-6	-6.0	0
Allie Sherman	17	-20	-1.2	0
Roy Zimmerman	33	-41	-1.2	1

Receiving	Rec	Yds	Avg	TD
Tony Bova	17	419	24.6	5
Larry Cabrelli	12	199	16.6	1
Ernie Steele	9	168	18.7	2
Ben Kish	8	67	8.4	1
Bob Thurbon	6	100	16.7	1
Johnny Butler	3	63	21.0	0
Tom Miller	3	60	20.0	1
Bill Hewitt	2	22	11.0	0
Ted Laux	2	19	9.5	0
Charlie Gauer	2	18	9.0	0
Jack Hinkle	1	3	3.0	0

Punting	Punts	Yds	Avg	Blocked
Dean Steward	2	84	42.0	0
Ben Kish	1	42	42.0	0
Johnny Butler	11	407	37.0	0
Roy Zimmerman	44	1521	34.6	0
Jack Hinkle	4	78	19.5	0

Kicking	PAT Made	PAT Att	PAT %	FG Made	FG Att	FG %	Pts
Roy Zimmerman	26	28	93	1	6	16.7	35
Ted Laux	2	2	100	0	0	0.0	2
Gordon Paschka	2	2	100	0	0	0.0	2

Interceptions	Int	Yds	Avg	TD
Ben Kish	5	114	22.8	1
Roy Zimmerman	5	19	3.8	0
Jack Hinkle	4	98	24.5	0
Larry Cabrelli	1	24	24.0	1
Ted Laux	1	24	24.0	0
Ray Graves	1	15	15.0	0
Al Wukits	1	7	7.0	0
Bob Thurbon	1	3	3.0	0
Enio Conti	1	0	0.0	0
Charlie Gauer	1	0	0.0	0
Tom Miller	1	0	0.0	0

THE PHILADELPHIA INQUIRER, SUNDAY MORNING, OCTOBER 3, 1943

N.C. Navy Jarred by Duke, 42-0

Blue Devils Score Early on Pass, Luper to Blount

DURHAM, N.C., Oct. 2 (A.P.)—Duke University's Blue Devils celebrated Navy Day today by beating the North Carolina Navy Preflight School football team, 42-0.

The Blue Devils, scoring almost at will, scored in the first quarter when Lloyd Blount snagged a 42-yard pass from Buddy Luper and stepped across the goal line, less than two minutes after the start of the game.

Caught 1914 Series

BOSTON (A.P.)—Major Hank Gowdy, the first major leaguer to enlist in World War I, caught all four games as the Miracle Braves swept the 1914 Series against the Athletics.

Army-Navy Play At West Point

EAGLES' BEN KISH STOPPED AFTER 12-YARD GAIN
Ray Wehba (center figure) and Dean McAdams, Brooklyn Dodgers, are the tacklers

N. Dame Jars Georgia Tech

Holy Cross Defeats Brown, 20-0

WORCESTER, Oct. 2 (A.P.)—Stan Koslowski, who managed to regain his passing form during the week, figured in all of the scoring plays while the durable Holy Cross football team was overwhelming Brown, 20-0, today before 4000 at Fitton Field.

Kansas State Beats Washburn, 13-7

MANHATTAN, Kan., Oct. 2 (A.P.)—Kansas State College resumed intercollegiate football competition on a winning note.

Southwestern Beats Texas, 14-7

By DAVE CHEAVENS

AUSTIN, Tex., Oct. 2 (A.P.)—Southwestern University trounced a young but stubborn University of Texas football team, 14-7, today.

North Texas Wins, 20-6, Over S.M.U.

DALLAS, Tex., Oct. 2 (A.P.)—Pete Stout, North Texas Aggies quarterback, who does 100 yards in less than 10 seconds, blasted Southern Methodist into a 20-6 defeat today.

Navy Sailing Team Defeats Stevens

ANNAPOLIS, Md., Oct. 2 (A.P.)—Navy's sailing team opened its fall racing season today with a 170-133 victory over Stevens Institute of Technology, of Hoboken, N.J.

Eagles Jar Dodgers; Butler Ace

Pitt Loses, 40-0, To Great Lakes

Ex-Navy Back

College of Pacific Beats U.C.L.A.

Iowa Pre-Flight Triumphs, 33-13

S. California T-Formation Baffles California, Wins, 7-0

"BOMBING A PATH TO BERLIN"

Brigadier General Sorenson says strategic bombing will destroy the enemy's industries and save Allied soldiers' lives.

Headline in N. Y. TIMES, September 19th

Far from the fighting lines but nevertheless important, Mrs. Elinor Greene is welding an airplane part in the Budd plant. It takes millions of workers on the home front to supply our fighting Armies and Navy.

Here in Philadelphia is produced materiel which makes bombing possible. Here are made bombs and shells, and cargo ships and planes to carry them to the battle lines. Here were built warships which stood off the Salerno beaches and rained shells on the Germans in the hills.

War workers can now see PRODUCTION fighting—and saving the lives of American boys. Your production is helping blast the Japs out of South Pacific islands and destroying Nazi submarine yards. It will bring victory quicker.

Isn't this good reason to take a war job now, if you are not in an essential industry? Philadelphia's war plants need thousands more, men and women. It is a patriotic service—taking the places of scores of thousands of young men who have gone to fight for their country—and for you. From the Budd plant alone, 2915 men have joined the armed forces. Edward G. Budd Manufacturing Company, 2450 Hunting Park Avenue.

★ By buying an extra Bond, YOU can put a gun in a soldier's hand.

1943

October 3, 1943
First game of the Steagles season
defeating the Brooklyn Dodgers 17-0

1944

RECORD: 7-1-2, 2ND IN NFL EAST
HEAD COACH: GREASY NEALE

Schedule

Regular Season

Wk. 2	Sep 26	W	28-7	at Boston Yanks
Wk. 4	Oct 8	T	31-31	vs Washington Redskins
Wk. 6	Oct 22	W	38-0	vs Boston Yanks
Wk. 7	Oct 29	W	24-17	at New York Giants
Wk. 8	Nov 5	W	21-7	at Brooklyn Tigers
Wk. 9	Nov 12	T	21-21	vs New York Giants
Wk. 10	Nov 19	W	37-7	at Washington Redskins
Wk. 11	Nov 26	L	28-7	vs Chicago Bears
Wk. 12	Dec 3	W	34-0	vs Brooklyn Tigers
Wk. 13	Dec 10	W	26-13	vs Cleveland Rams

Steve Van Buren, the Eagles' top pick in the 1944 draft, debuted as halfback, providing the spark that the Eagles needed as they went unbeaten through their first seven games, on the way to posting a winning season at 7-1-2. Their only loss was to the Chicago Bears, 28-7. However, they would miss winning the division championship by a half game.

1944 Philadelphia Eagles Stats

Passing	Comp	Att	Comp %	Yds	Y/Att	TD	Int	Rating
Roy Zimmerman	39	105	37.1	785	7.48	8	10	50.0
Allie Sherman	16	31	51.6	156	5.03	1	2	49.9

Rushing	Rush	Yds	Avg	TD
Steve Van Buren	80	444	5.6	5
Jack Hinkle	92	421	4.6	2
Mel Bleeker	60	315	5.3	4
Ernie Steele	59	247	4.2	5
Jack Banta	38	198	5.2	3
Ben Kish	22	96	4.4	0
Art Macioszczyk	16	55	3.4	0
Toimi Jarvi	5	16	3.2	0
Ted Laux	2	-1	-0.5	0
Tom Miller	1	-2	-2.0	0
Larry Cabrelli	1	-2	-2.0	0
Allie Sherman	22	-42	-1.9	1
Roy Zimmerman	26	-84	-3.2	2

Punting	Punts	Yds	Avg	Blocked
Ben Kish	4	182	45.5	0
Jack Banta	9	398	44.2	0
Roy Zimmerman	39	1531	39.3	0
Steve Van Buren	1	35	35.0	0
Allie Sherman	1	27	27.0	0
Ted Laux	1	18	18.0	0

Kicking	PAT Made	PAT Att	PAT %	FG Made	FG Att	FG %	Pts
Roy Zimmerman 32	34	94	4	8	50.0		56
Ben Kish	1	1	100	0	0	0.0	7

Receiving	Rec	Yds	Avg	TD
Larry Cabrelli	14	169	12.1	1
Mel Bleeker	8	299	37.4	4
Tom Miller	8	135	16.9	0
Ben Kish	5	73	14.6	1
Flip McDonald	4	26	6.5	1
Jack Ferrante	3	66	22.0	1
Art Macioszczyk	3	28	9.3	0
Charlie Gauer	2	35	17.5	0
Jack Hinkle	2	34	17.0	0
John Durko	2	31	15.5	1
Ernie Steele	1	22	22.0	0
Jack Banta	1	18	18.0	0
Toimi Jarvi	1	9	9.0	0
Ted Laux	1	6	6.0	0

Interceptions	Int	Yds	Avg	TD
Ernie Steele	6	113	18.8	0
Steve Van Buren	5	47	9.4	0
Ben Kish	4	52	13.0	0
Roy Zimmerman	4	36	9.0	0
Jack Hinkle	2	62	31.0	1
Allie Sherman	2	34	17.0	0
Vic Lindskog	1	65	65.0	1
Tom Miller	1	35	35.0	1
Jack Banta	1	34	34.0	0
Duke Maronic	1	32	32.0	0
Bap Manzini	1	16	16.0	0
Flip McDonald	1	14	14.0	0
Bob Friedlund	1	2	2.0	0
Charlie Gauer	1	2	2.0	0
Mel Bleeker	1	0	0.0	0
Toimi Jarvi	1	0	0.0	0

October 23, 1944
The first of two 30-plus points shutout games in the season,
this one was against the Boston Yanks 38-0

1945

RECORD: 7-3, 2ND IN NFL EAST
HEAD COACH: GREASY NEALE

Schedule

Regular Season

Wk. 3	Oct 7	W	21-6	vs Chicago Cardinals
Wk. 4	Oct 14	L	28-24	at Detroit Lions
Wk. 5	Oct 21	L	24-14	at Washington Redskins
Wk. 6	Oct 28	W	28-14	vs Cleveland Rams
Wk. 7	Nov 4	W	45-3	at Pittsburgh Steelers
Wk. 8	Nov 11	W	38-17	vs New York Giants
Wk. 9	Nov 18	W	30-6	vs Pittsburgh Steelers
Wk. 10	Nov 25	W	16-0	vs Washington Redskins
Wk. 11	Dec 2	L	28-21	at New York Giants
Wk. 12	Dec 9	W	35-7	vs Boston Yanks

Steve Van Buren led the NFL with 838 rushing yards and 110 points. He also set the NFL record for the most touchdowns in a single season, with 18. The Eagles finished in second place again with a 7-3 record.

1945 Philadelphia Eagles Stats

Passing	Comp	Att	Comp %	Yds	Y/Att	TD	Int	Rating
Roy Zimmerman	67	127	52.8	991	7.80	9	8	75.9
Allie Sherman	15	29	51.7	172	5.93	2	3	53.3
Steve Van Buren	0	1	0.0	0	0.00	0	0	39.6
Tommy Thompson	15	28	53.6	146	5.21	0	2	38.7
Ernie Steele	1	2	50.0	12	6.00	0	1	29.2

Rushing	Rush	Yds	Avg	TD
Steve Van Buren	143	832	5.8	15
Ernie Steele	20	212	10.6	2
Mel Bleeker	50	167	3.3	2
Abe Karnofsky	41	134	3.3	2
Ben Kish	9	82	9.1	0
Johnny Butler	21	61	2.9	1
Jack Banta	15	49	3.3	1
Gil Steinke	7	46	6.6	1
Jack Hinkle	11	40	3.6	0
Jim Castiglia	13	29	2.2	0
Dick Erdlitz	6	24	4.0	0
John Rogalla	2	2	1.0	0
Allie Sherman	16	-7	-0.4	1
Busit Warren	1	-7	-7.0	0
Roy Zimmerman	29	-11	-0.4	1
Tommy Thompson	8	-13	-1.6	0

Receiving	Rec	Yds	Avg	TD
Jack Ferrante	21	464	22.1	7
Larry Cabrelli	15	140	9.3	0
Steve Van Buren	10	123	12.3	2
Ben Kish	8	78	9.8	0
Flip McDonald	8	75	9.4	1
Dick Humbert	6	53	8.8	0
Abe Karnofsky	5	113	22.6	0
Ernie Steele	3	42	14.0	0
Mel Bleeker	3	32	10.7	0
Johnny Butler	2	14	7.0	0
Gil Steinke	2	12	6.0	0
John Rogalla	2	2	1.0	0
Jack Banta	1	10	10.0	0
Jack Hinkle	1	8	8.0	0

Interceptions	Int	Yds	Avg	TD
Roy Zimmerman	7	90	12.9	0
Tommy Thompson	2	33	16.5	0
Johnny Butler	1	32	32.0	0
Abe Karnofsky	1	27	27.0	0
Vic Lindskog	1	22	22.0	0
Jack Hinkle	1	17	17.0	0
Jack Ferrante	1	15	15.0	0
Ernie Steele	1	15	15.0	0
Dick Erdlitz	1	3	3.0	0
Steve Van Buren	1	2	2.0	0
Larry Cabrelli	1	1	1.0	0
Ben Kish	1	0	0.0	0

Punting	Punts	Yds	Avg	Blocked
Roy Zimmerman	47	1778	37.8	0

Kicking	PAT Made	PAT Att	PAT %	FG Made	FG Att	FG %	Pts
Roy Zimmerman	29	33	88	4	8	50.0	47

20 adelph   THE PHILADELPHIA INQUIRER, MONDAY MORNING, NOVEMBER 5, 1945

Football Afterthoughts

Navy's Football Pains The Pains of Peace?

Jarmoluk Bolsters Unbeaten Temple, But Penn State, Holy Cross Threats

By ART MORROW

28,000 Watch Roman Jar West, 13-0

Eagles Rout Pittsburgh, Tie for 2d

Ferrante Scores Twice on Passes In 45-3 Victory

By HANK LITTLEHALES

Inquirer Sports Reporter

FINAL PASS PLAY IN HECTIC NOTRE DAME-NAVY GAME

Defeat 1st in League For Burrs Since 1940

Defending Titlists Get Initial 1st Down In 4th Quarter; Tucker, Ladner Score

By KEN HAY

289 at Richmond Wins for Hogan

Metz' 293 Second; Ghezzi, Bulla Tie For 3d, Hines 5th

Bears Upset Packers, 28-24; Redskins, Lions, Rams Win

By LOWELL REIDENBAUGH

Devore Certain Colella Scored

CLEVELAND, Nov. 4

Holy Cross Beats Sub Base for 6th

St. Matthew's Jars Malvern

Nelson May Play In British Open

Donosa Golf Victor

St. Joseph's Routs St. Thomas, 30-0

Nicetown Blues Lose

Billy Arnold Rated Favorite Over Zannelli Here Tonight

Russian Soccer Team Arrives in England

Jacksonville Wins Sixth

Camp Peary Wins

Clubs in Inquirer Tourney Welcome Novices to Ring

By JOHN WEBSTER

Marine Wins Title, Diller 7th in Run

Abrams, Fritchie in Final

W. Nottingham Wins

Air Transport Team Shatters Bainbridge Streak at 21

Special to The Inquirer

Sports Results

Professional

1945

November 5, 1945
Eagles largest win of the season defeating Pittsburgh 45-3
Roy Zimmerman threw two TD passes while Jack Ferrante scored two TDs

1946

RECORD: 6-5, 2ND IN NFL EAST
HEAD COACH: GREASY NEALE

Schedule

Regular Season

Wk. 2	Sep 29	W	25-14	at Los Angeles Rams
Wk. 3	Oct 6	W	49-25	vs Boston Yanks
Wk. 4	Oct 13	L	19-7	vs Green Bay Packers
Wk. 5	Oct 13	L	21-14	at Chicago Bears
Wk. 6	Oct 27	W	28-24	at Washington Redskins
Wk. 7	Nov 3	W	24-14	vs New York Giants
Wk. 8	Nov 10	L	45-17	at New York Giants
Wk. 9	Nov 17	L	10-7	at Pittsburgh Steelers
Wk. 10	Nov 24	L	27-10	vs Washington Redskins
Wk. 11	Dec 1	W	10-7	vs Pittsburgh Steelers
Wk. 12	Dec 8	W	40-14	at Boston Yanks

The Eagles played mediocre football all season and wound up settling for second place for the past three years after posting a disappointing 6-5 record. There was one high note; after trailing Washington 24-0 at half-time the Eagles came back to win their October 27 game, 28-24 and set a new team record for the biggest comeback.

1946 Philadelphia Eagles Stats

Passing	Comp	Att	Comp %	Yds	Y/Att	TD	Int	Rating
Tommy Thompson	57	103	55.3	745	7.23	6	9	61.3
Steve Van Buren	1	1	100.0	35	35.00	0	0	118.8
Allie Sherman	17	33	51.5	264	8.00	4	3	80.1
Roy Zimmerman	41	79	51.9	597	7.56	4	8	54.1
Bosh Pritchard	0	1	0.0	0	0.00	0	0	39.6

Rushing	Rush	Yds	Avg	TD
Steve Van Buren	116	529	4.6	5
Bosh Pritchard	42	218	5.2	3
Gil Steinke	38	154	4.1	1
Ernie Steele	31	108	3.5	1
Russ Craft	27	108	4.0	0
Jim Castiglia	39	87	2.2	1
Roy Zimmerman	23	43	1.9	1
Joe Muha	12	41	3.4	0
Jack Hinkle	18	33	1.8	0
Pete Kmetovic	5	30	6.0	0
Ben Kish	6	13	2.2	0
Elliott Ormsbee	4	12	3.0	0
Allie Sherman	21	8	0.4	0
Dick Humbert	1	2	2.0	0
Mel Bleeker	6	-7	-1.2	0
Tommy Thompson	34	-116	-3.4	0

Receiving	Rec	Yds	Avg	TD
Jack Ferrante	28	451	16.1	4
Dick Humbert	18	191	10.6	3
Bosh Pritchard	14	309	22.1	3
Jim Castiglia	11	51	4.6	0
Larry Cabrelli	8	98	12.3	1
Steve Van Buren	6	75	12.5	0
Gil Steinke	5	107	21.4	2
Ernie Steele	5	69	13.8	0
Pete Kmetovic	4	68	17.0	0
Russ Craft	4	48	12.0	0
Rudy Smeja	3	45	15.0	0
Mel Bleeker	3	29	9.7	0
Ben Kish	3	16	5.3	0
Bob Krieger	2	47	23.5	0
Jay MacDowell	1	28	28.0	0
Bert Kuczynski	1	9	9.0	1

Punting	Punts	Yds	Avg	Blocked
Steve Van Buren	1	41	41.0	0
Ben Kish	4	163	40.8	0
Roy Zimmerman	23	890	38.7	0
Joe Muha	22	843	38.3	0
Bosh Pritchard	7	242	34.6	0

Interceptions	Int	Yds	Avg	TD
Gil Steinke	6	72	12.0	1
Ernie Steele	3	69	23.0	0
Roy Zimmerman	3	58	19.3	0
Bosh Pritchard	3	7	2.3	0
Jack Hinkle	2	37	18.5	0
Al Wistert	1	27	27.0	0
Ben Kish	1	13	13.0	0
Vic Lindskog	1	10	10.0	0
Joe Muha	1	8	8.0	0
Duke Maronic	1	7	7.0	0
Bucko Kilroy	1	0	0.0	0

Kicking	PAT Made	PAT Att	PAT %	FG Made	FG Att	FG %	Pts
Augie Lio	27	27	100	6	11	54.5	45
Roy Zimmerman	2	2	100	2	4	50.0	14

October 7, 1946
11 combined touchdowns scored as Eagles defeat Boston 49- 25
Van Buren, Pritchard each score twice

1947

RECORD: 8-4, 1ST IN NFL EAST
HEAD COACH: GREASY NEALE

Schedule

Regular Season

Wk. 2	Sep 28	W	45-28	vs Washington Redskins
Wk. 3	Oct 5	W	23-0	at New York Giants
Wk. 4	Oct 12	L	40-7	at Chicago Bears
Wk. 5	Oct 19	L	35-24	at Pittsburgh Steelers
Wk. 6	Oct 26	W	14-7	vs Los Angeles Rams
Wk. 7	Nov 2	W	38-14	at Washington Redskins
Wk. 8	Nov 9	W	41-24	at New York Giants
Wk. 9	Nov 16	W	32-0	vs Boston Yanks
Wk. 10	Nov 23	L	21-14	at Boston Yanks
Wk. 11	Nov 30	W	21-0	vs Pittsburgh Steelers
Wk. 12	Dec 7	L	45-21	vs Chicago Cardinals
Wk. 13	Dec 14	W	28-14	vs Green Bay Packers

Post Season

Divisional Playoffs				
	Dec 21	W	21-0	at Pittsburgh Steelers
League Championship				
	Dec 28	L	28-21	at Chicago Cardinals

The addition of rookie end Pete Pihos turned out to be the final piece of the puzzle, as the Eagles finished in a tie for first place with a franchise record of eight wins and four losses. In the Divisional Playoff the Eagles overpowering defense shut down the Steelers all day in a convincing 21-0 win in Pittsburgh. However, the Eagles would fall 28-21 in a heart stopping (their first) NFL Championship game with the Cardinals in Chicago .

1947 Philadelphia Eagles Stats

Passing	Comp	Att	Comp %	Yds	Y/Att	TD	Int	Rating
Tommy Thompson	106	201	52.7	1680	8.36	16	15	76.3
Bill Mackrides	8	17	47.1	58	3.41	2	3	55.1
Allie Sherman	2	5	40.0	23	4.60	0	1	15.0

Rushing	Rush	Yds	Avg	TD
Steve Van Buren	217	1008	4.6	13
Bosh Pritchard	69	294	4.3	1
Pat McHugh	22	171	7.8	1
Ernie Steele	26	138	5.3	1
Joe Muha	27	107	4.0	1
Art Macioszczyk	30	104	3.5	0
Tommy Thompson	23	52	2.3	2
Gil Steinke	16	50	3.1	0
Noble Doss	11	45	4.1	0
Allie Sherman	17	17	1.0	1
Jack Hinkle	1	2	2.0	0
Russ Craft	5	-1	-0.2	0
Ben Kish	3	-1	-0.3	0
Bill Mackrides	7	-15	-2.1	1

Receiving	Rec	Yds	Avg	TD
Pete Pihos	23	382	16.6	7
Jack Ferrante	18	341	18.9	4
Neill Armstrong	17	197	11.6	2
Bosh Pritchard	16	315	19.7	3
Dick Humbert	13	139	10.7	0
Steve Van Buren	9	79	8.8	0
Gil Steinke	4	90	22.5	1
Ernie Steele	4	62	15.5	0
Art Macioszczyk	3	20	6.7	0
Russ Craft	2	66	33.0	1
Noble Doss	2	17	8.5	0
Pat McHugh	2	16	8.0	0
Hal Prescott	1	15	15.0	0
Ben Kish	1	12	12.0	0
Joe Muha	1	10	10.0	0

Punting	Punts	Yds	Avg	Blocked
Joe Muha	53	2303	43.5	0
Ben Kish	8	301	37.6	0
Bosh Pritchard	2	64	32.0	0

Interceptions	Int	Yds	Avg	TD
Ernie Steele	6	103	17.2	0
Pat McHugh	3	52	17.3	0
Hal Prescott	3	5	1.7	0
Noble Doss	2	31	15.5	0
Dick Humbert	2	12	6.0	0
Ben Kish	1	37	37.0	3
Gil Steinke	1	17	17.0	0
Vic Lindskog	1	15	15.0	0
Bosh Pritchard	1	12	12.0	0
Alex Wojciechowicz	1	3	3.0	0
Russ Craft	1	0	0.0	0
Steve Van Buren	1	0	0.0	0

Kicking	PAT Made	PAT Att	PAT %	FG Made	FG Att	FG %	Pts
Cliff Patton	36	40	90	3	14	21.4	45
Joe Muha	0	0	0	1	5	20.0	15
Jim Kekeris	2	3	67	0	1	0.0	2

20 abcdefgh THE PHILADELPHIA INQUIRER, MONDAY MORNING, DECEMBER 29, 1947

Eagles Bow to Cardinals, 28-21, in NFL Title Playoff

Sidecourt Stabs
6 West Fives To Play Here This Week

Santa Clara, Utah, Kansas State Head Visiting Quintets

By HANK LITTLEHALES

THERE GOES ELMER ANGSMAN ON 70-YARD SCORING SPRINT FOR CARDINALS
Halfback outdistances his interferer, Tackle Joe Coomer, and eludes Eagles' Ernie Steele (37) on way to second-period touchdown in playoff game yesterday in Chicago. The Cards won.

Angsman, Trippi Score 2 Each; Thompson Completes 27 Passes

Chicago Tallies Come on Jaunts of 75, 70, 70 and 44 Yards; McHugh, Van Buren, Craft Register Phila. Touchdowns

By FRANK O'GARA
Inquirer Sports Reporter

CHICAGO, Dec. 28.—The Philadelphia Eagles made the disconcerting discovery today in refrigerated Comiskey Park that a superlative game of fighting football was not enough to counteract their deficiency in the art of ice skating.

Eagles Did Everything But Beat Cards—Neale

By JERRY LISKA

Playoff Facts

Tourney Battles Carded Tonight

By JOHN WEBSTER
Tournament Director

Rockets Tie Ramblers, 3-3, On Wochy's Penalty Shot

Reading Central Beats Roman

Jardine Dies In Ski Mishap

Bombers Triumph; Doll Stars With 23

USGA Handicap System Offers Uniform Ratings

By FRED BYRD

Hulse, Thompson Set Track Marks

By HAROLD V. RATLIFF

Munn and Ben Rose Take Pin Doubles

Profits Decline for Players

CHICAGO, Dec. 28.

Higgins, Bell See Trouble Ahead

Phila. CC Defeats Merion in Shoot

Lesnevich Selected 'Fighter of '47'

By GAYLE TALBOT

1947

December 29, 1947
Eagles play their first NFL Championship Game, losing to Chicago Cardinals 28-21

1948

RECORD: 9-2-1, 1ST IN NFL EAST
HEAD COACH: GREASY NEALE

Schedule

Regular Season

Wk. 2	Sep 24	L	21-14	at Chicago Cardinals
Wk. 3	Oct 3	T	28-28	at Los Angeles Rams
Wk. 4	Oct 10	W	45-0	vs New York Giants
Wk. 5	Oct 17	W	45-0	at Washington Redskins
Wk. 6	Oct 24	W	12-7	vs Chicago Bears
Wk. 7	Oct 31	W	34-7	at Pittsburgh Steelers
Wk. 8	Nov 7	W	35-14	at New York Giants
Wk. 9	Nov 14	W	45-0	vs Boston Yanks
Wk. 10	Nov 21	W	42-21	vs Washington Redskins
Wk. 11	Nov 28	W	17-0	vs Pittsburgh Steelers
Wk. 12	Dec 5	L	37-14	at Boston Yanks
Wk. 13	Dec 12	W	45-21	vs Detroit Lions

Post Season

League Championship

| | Dec 19 | W | 7-0 | vs Chicago Cardinals |

After losing and tying their first two games, the Eagles take off, winning the next eight games including two back-to-back 45-0 shutouts over the NY Giants and Washington. The Eagles soared to a 9-2-1 record, which helped them easily capture the Eastern Division Championship. Making the Eagles fiercer was a defense that allows just 156 points on the season. In the NFL Championship Game, the Eagles found themselves in a rematch with the Chicago Cardinals. The game would be played in a blinding blizzard at Shibe Park. In the game known as the "Blizzard Bowl," the Eagles defense smothered the Cardinals on the way to a 7-0 victory that earned the Eagles its first NFL Championship.

1948 Philadelphia Eagles Stats

Passing	Comp	Att	Comp %	Yds	Y/Att	TD	Int	Rating
Tommy Thompson	141	246	57.3	1965	7.99	25	11	98.4
Bill Mackrides	53	276	19.2	2	0.01	4	0	44.4
Steve Van Buren	0	1	0.0	0	0.00	0	0	39.6

Rushing	Rush	Yds	Avg	TD
Steve Van Buren	201	945	4.7	10
Bosh Pritchard	117	517	4.4	4
Noble Doss	62	193	3.1	0
Jim Parmer	30	167	5.6	3
Jack Myers	21	118	5.6	1
Ben Kish	10	106	10.6	1
Ernie Steele	13	99	7.6	1
Joe Muha	5	90	3.6	0
Russ Craft	13	67	5.2	0
Tommy Thompson	12	46	3.8	1
Gil Steinke	5	17	3.4	0
Pat McHugh	4	12	3.0	0
Bill Mackrides	7	4	0.6	0
Pete Pihos	8	-3	-0.4	0

Receiving	Rec	Yds	Avg	TD
Pete Pihos	46	766	16.7	11
Jack Ferrante	28	444	15.9	7
Bosh Pritchard	27	252	9.3	2
Neill Armstrong	24	325	13.5	3
Steve Van Buren	10	96	9.6	0
Noble Doss	8	96	12.0	0
Jack Myers	7	57	8.1	0
Russ Craft	4	138	34.5	2
Ernie Steele	2	43	21.5	1
Joe Muha	2	22	11.0	1
Dick Humbert	1	2	2.0	0

Punting	Punts	Yds	Avg	Blocked
Joe Muha	57	2694	47.3	0
Les Palmer	4	148	37.0	0
Tom Johnson	1	5	5.0	0

Interceptions	Int	Yds	Avg	TD
Ernie Steele	6	55	9.2	0
Dick Humbert	4	35	8.8	0
Ben Kish	3	32	10.7	0
Steve Van Buren	2	32	16.0	0
Neill Armstrong	2	30	15.0	0
Pat McHugh	2	27	13.5	0
Jack Myers	2	9	4.5	0
Jim Parmer	1	6	6.0	0
Alex Wojciechowicz	1	2	2.0	0

Kicking	PAT Made	PAT Att	PAT %	FG Made	FG Att	FG %	Pts
Joe Carter	1	1	100	0	0	0.0	13
Cliff Patton	50	50	100	8	12	66.7	74
Joe Muha	0	0	0	0	5	0.0	6

1948

December 20, 1948
*Eagles win first NFL Championship Game
against Chicago Cardinals 7-0*

1949

RECORD: 11-1, 1ST IN NFL EAST
HEAD COACH: GREASY NEALE

Schedule

Regular Season

Wk. 1	Sep 22	W	7-0	at New York Bulldogs
Wk. 2	Oct 3	W	22-14	at Detroit Lions
Wk. 3	Oct 8	W	28-3	vs Chicago Cardinals
Wk. 4	Oct 16	L	38-21	at Chicago Bears
Wk. 5	Oct 23	W	49-14	vs Washington Redskins
Wk. 6	Oct 30	W	38-7	at Pittsburgh Steelers
Wk. 7	Nov 6	W	38-14	vs Los Angeles Rams
Wk. 8	Nov 13	W	44-21	at Washington Redskins
Wk. 9	Nov 20	W	42-0	vs New York Bulldogs
Wk. 10	Nov 27	W	34-17	vs Pittsburgh Steelers
Wk. 11	Dec 4	W	24-3	at New York Giants
Wk. 12	Dec 11	W	17-3	vs New York Giants

Post Season

League Championship				
	Dec 18	W	14-0	at Los Angeles Rams

The Eagles were sold to one hundred buyers, each of whom paid $3,000 for one of the 100 shares. They were called the "Happy Hundred" or the "Hundred Brothers." Their leader was James P. Clark, a Philadelphia sportsman and business executive, and the hundred investors included some of the leading names in Philadelphia business, government and politics, including Leonard Tose. University of Pennsylvania All-American center and linebacker Chuck Bednarik was the team's first round draft choice. The addition of Bednarik made the Eagles defense even stronger as they allow just 134 points while posting a franchise best 11-1 record to win their third straight Eastern Division. Their only loss was to Chicago in week four, by the score 38-21. In the NFL Championship Game the Eagles continued to soar, smothering the Rams all day on the way to a 14-0 win in Los Angeles. This was the first time a team won back-to-back championship with shutouts (and the only time to date), for a second straight NFL Championship. The team ended the decade with 14 consecutive home wins, dating from December 14, 1947, through December 11, 1949.

1949 Philadelphia Eagles Stats

Passing	Comp	Att	Comp %	Yds	Y/Att	TD	Int	Rating
Tommy Thompson	116	214	54.2	1727	8.07	16	11	84.4
Bill Mackrides	14	36	38.9	182	5.06	2	2	50.9
Bosh Pritchard	0	1	0.0	0	0.00	0	1	0.0

Rushing	Rush	Yds	Avg	TD
Steve Van Buren	263	1146	4.4	11
Bosh Pritchard	84	506	6.0	3
Frank Ziegler	84	283	3.4	1
Jim Parmer	66	234	3.5	5
Clyde Scott	40	195	4.9	1
Jack Myers	48	182	3.8	1
Joe Muha	3	19	6.3	0
Tommy Thompson	15	17	1.1	2
Bill Mackrides	14	17	1.2	1
Russ Craft	11	5	0.5	0
Pat McHugh	2	5	2.5	0
Ben Kish	2	-2	-1.0	0

Receiving	Rec	Yds	Avg	TD
Jack Ferrante	34	508	14.9	5
Pete Pihos	34	484	14.2	4
Neill Armstrong	24	271	11.3	5
Bosh Pritchard	8	185	23.1	2
Clyde Scott	8	148	18.5	1
Jack Myers	7	98	14.0	0
Jim Parmer	5	33	6.6	0
Steve Van Buren	4	88	22.0	1
Frank Ziegler	3	33	11.0	0
Russ Craft	1	37	37.0	0
Dick Humbert	1	14	14.0	0
Joe Muha	1	10	10.0	0

Punting	Punts	Yds	Avg	Blocked
Frank Reagan	8	362	45.3	0
Joe Muha	45	1800	40.0	0

Interceptions	Int	Yds	Avg	TD
Frank Reagan	7	146	20.9	0
Russ Craft	7	70	10.0	0
Dick Humbert	7	69	9.9	0
Pat McHugh	6	89	14.8	1
Joe Muha	2	31	15.5	1
Alex Wojciechowicz	2	26	13.0	0
Jim Parmer	2	12	6.0	0
Frank Ziegler	1	16	16.0	0
Mike Jarmoluk	1	3	3.0	0

Kicking	PAT Made	PAT Att	PAT %	FG Made	FG Att	FG %	Pts
Cliff Patton	42	43	98	9	18	50.0	69
Joe Muha	5	5	100	0	1	0.0	11

THE PHILADELPHIA INQUIRER, MONDAY MORNING, DECEMBER 19, 1949

Eagles Beat Rams, 14-0, in Rain, Retain NFL Title

LOUISIANA LIGHTNING STRIKES, VITAMIN PROVES EFFICIENCY AND SMACKOVER GETS SMACKED IN PRO FOOTBALL'S MUDDY TITLE TILT AT LOS ANGELES

Philadelphia's Steve Van Buren, who gained record 196 yards yesterday as Eagles kept National Football League crown with 14-0 victory over Rams, is shown at left being tackled by Jerry Williams after a 25-yard gain. In photo at right, Vitamin Smith, speedy Ram halfback, has broken into clear and awaits pass tossed by Bob Waterfield. Los Angeles reached Eagles' 28 with eight-yard gain. (Another picture on Page 33.) (AP Wirephotos)

Year-End Reflections

Chandler, Tops in Pop-Off, Made Comeback in 1949

By LEO RIORDAN
Inquirer Executive Sports Editor

Pihos, Skladany Get Touchdowns; Van Buren Stars, Sets 2 Records

By FRANK O'GARA

Lineups, Facts Of Title Game

Owners Agree But—

Bell Refuses To Defer Game

Special to The Inquirer
LOS ANGELES, Dec. 18.

Clyde (Smackover) Scott is about to be tackled for no gain by Rams' Dick Huffman.

Lakers, Pistons Win NBA Games

Mrs. duPont Ranked No. 1 In Tennis; Louise Brough 2d

Bad Weather Routine to Eagles

Brooklyn Polo Victor

N. Catholic Wins In Final 26 Secs.

Villemain in Paris

First Belt Elimination Bouts At Cambria Next Monday

By MORT BERRY

Kramer Boosts Lead Over Gonzales to 32-5

'They Were All Great,' But That Van Buren . . .

'Best I Ever Saw a Man Run,' Neale Says

By PETE ARTHUR

Inquirer Track Meet

Mail Your Order For Tickets Now

December 19, 1949
Eagles win back-to-back NFL Championship games
defeating LA Rams 14-0

50's Decade in Review

Decade Win-Loss Record:
51-64-5
Home Field:
Shibe Park 1950-57, Franklin Field 1958-59
Playoff Appearances:
None
Championships:
None
Head Coaches:
Greasy Neale 1950 (6-6); Bo McMillian 1951 (2-0); Wayne Milner 1951 (2-8);
Jim Trimble 1952-55 (25-20-3); Hugh Devore 1956-67 (7-16-1); Buck Shaw 1958-59 (9-14-1)
Hall of Fame Inductees:
Chuck Bednarik, Sony Jurgensen, Tommy McDonald, Pete Pihos,
Norm Van Brocklin, Steve Van Buren, Alex Wojciechowicz
Award Winners:
Bobby Walston, Rookie of the Year 1951
All Pro:
Chuck Bednarik 1950-57; Bucko Kilroy 1950-54; Joe Muha 1950; Pete Pihos 1950 and 1952-55;
Vic Sears 1950 and 1952; Steve Van Buren 1950; Al Wistert 1950-51; Vic Lindskog 1951;
Bobby Walston 1951; Lum Snyder 1952-55; Bobby Thomason 1953; Norm Willey 1953-55;
Frank Wydo 1953; Wayne Robinson 1955; Tom Scott 1955-56; Pete Retzlaff 1958; Tom Brookshier 1959;
Tommy McDonald 1959
Pro Bowl Selections:
Walter Barnes 1951; Chuck Bednarik 1951-55 and 1957-58; John Green 1951; Pete Pihos 1951-56;
Al Wistert 1951; Russ Craft 1952-53; Mike Jarmoluk 1952; Bucko Kilroy 1953-55; Ken Farragut 1954;
Lum Snyder 1954-55; Bobby Thomason 1954 and 1956-57; Adrian Burk 1955-56; Wayne Robinson 1955-56;
Norm Willey 1955-56;Jim Weatherall 1956-57; Buck Lansford 1957; Billy Ray Barnes 1958-59;
Jerry Norton 1958-59; Tommy McDonald 1959; Pete Retzlaff 1959; Norm Van Brocklin 1959
First Game of the Decade:
September 16, 1950 in a loss to the Cleveland Browns 35-10
Last Game of the Decade:
December 13, 1959 losing to the Cleveland Browns 28-21
Largest Margin of Victory:
October 25, 1953 vs. Chicago Cardinals 56-17
Largest Margin of Defeat:
October 19, 1952 vs. Cleveland Browns 49-7

Eagle Firsts of the Decade:
First African-American Eagles – In 1952, Ralph Goldston and Don Stevens were draft selections.
First Pro Bowlers – In 1950, Piggy Barnes, Chuck Bednarik, John Green, Pete Pihos, and
Al Wistert took part in the first Prow Bowl game.
First 400 Yards Passing – On November 8, 1953, Bobby Thomason completed two of
44 passes for437 yards in a win over the New York Giants 30-7.
First 200 Yards Passing – On December 7, 1952, Bud Grant caught 11 passes for 203
yards in a win over the Dallas Texans 38-21.
First 1,000-Yard Receiving – in 1953, Pete Pihos gained 1,049 yards.
First 90-Yard Pass Play – On November 14, 1954, Tommy McDonald caught Norm
Van Brocklin's pass for a 91-yard touchdown in a win over the New York Giants 27-24.
First Game at Franklin Field – On September 28, 1958 in a loss to the Washington Redskins 24-14.

50's Decade in Review

With the turn of the decade came another turn in team fortunes. After a whipping by the AAFC champion Cleveland Browns, who had just (with the other AAFC franchises) joined the NFL, the Eagles stumbled in the standings. 1950 proved Greasy Neale's last as head coach, and in 1951, Neale was replaced by Alvin "Bo" McMillan. McMillan, in turn, would get seriously ill the night before the season opener, and was replaced by Wayne Millner, who would last for all of one year before being replaced by Jim Trimble. While the remnants of the great 1940's teams managed to stay competitive for the first few years of the decade, and while younger players like Bobby Walston and Sonny Jurgensen occasionally provided infusions of talent, the team lacked the stuff of true greatness for most of the 1950s. In 1958, however, the franchise took key steps to improve, hiring Buck Shaw as Head Coach and acquiring future Hall of Famer Norm Van Brocklin in a trade with the Los Angeles Rams. That year also saw the team move from Connie Mack Stadium (formerly Shibe Park) to Franklin Field, and attendance doubled. The 1959 squad showed real flashes of talent, and finished in second place in the Eastern Division.

TRIVIA QUESTION

Q5 IN WHAT YEAR WAS JOHN MADDEN DRAFTED IN THE 21ST ROUND BY THE EAGLES?

(a) 1955 (b) 1958
(c) 1961 (d) Eagles Never Drafted Him

answer on page 254

TRIVIA QUESTION

Q6 WHO WAS THE EAGLES' MVP IN 1955 AND THE LAST LINEMAN IN THE LEAGUE TO PLAY WITHOUT A FACEMASK?

(a) Jess Richardson (b) Bucko Kilroy
(c) Mike Jarmoluk (d) Lum Snyder

answer on page 254

TRIVIA QUESTION

Q7 WHICH EAGLE SET A CLUB RE-CORD BY SCORING 25 POINTS IN A SINGLE GAME?

(a) Don Johnson   (b) Jerry Williams
(c) Pete Pihos   (d) Bobby Walston

answer on page 254

TRIVIA QUESTION

Q8 IN 1953, AGAINST WHICH TEAM DID CHUCK BEDNARIK SCORE HIS ONLY REGULAR SEASON TOUCHDOWN FOR THE EAGLES?
(a) San Francisco 49ers (b) Baltimore Colts
(c) Cleveland Browns   (d) Pittsburgh Steelers

answer on page 254

1950

RECORD: 6-6, T-3RD IN AFC
HEAD COACH: GREASY NEALE

Schedule
Regular Season

Wk. 1	Sep 16	L	35-10	vs Cleveland Browns
Wk. 2	Sep 24	W	45-7	at Chicago Cardinals
Wk. 4	Oct 7	W	56-20	vs Los Angeles Rams
Wk. 5	Oct 15	W	24-14	at Baltimore Colts
Wk. 6	Oct 22	W	17-10	at Pittsburgh Steelers
Wk. 7	Oct 29	W	35-3	vs Washington Redskins
Wk. 8	Nov 5	L	9-7	vs Pittsburgh Steelers
Wk. 9	Nov 12	W	33-0	at Washington Redskins
Wk. 10	Nov 19	L	14-10	vs Chicago Cardinals
Wk. 11	Nov 26	L	7-3	at New York Giants
Wk. 12	Dec 3	L	13-7	at Cleveland Browns
Wk. 13	Dec 10	L	9-7	vs New York Giants

The two-time NFL champs lost their home opener 35-10 to Cleveland. After playing solid football for most of the season the Eagles went into a sudden tailspin, falling out of competition with a season ending four-game losing streak that ended their season with a disappointing 6-6 record. Following the season Coach Greasy Neale was fired. Bo McMillan replaced him.

1950 Philadelphia Eagles Stats

Passing	Comp	Att	Comp %	Yds	Y/Att	TD	Int	Rating
Tommy Thompson	107	239	44.8	1608	6.73	11	22	44.4
Bill Mackrides	14	46	30.4	228	4.96	4	6	37.5

Rushing	Rush	Yds	Avg	TD
Frank Ziegler	172	733	4.3	1
Steve Van Buren	188	629	3.3	4
Toy Ledbetter	67	320	4.8	1
Jim Parmer	60	203	3.4	7
Jack Myers	29	159	5.5	0
Bill Mackrides	21	82	3.9	0
Frank Reagan	3	55	18.3	0
Russ Craft	8	52	6.5	0
Clyde Scott	13	46	3.5	0
Tommy Thompson	15	34	2.3	0
Pat McHugh	4	14	3.5	0
Joe Sutton	1	1	1.0	0

Receiving	Rec	Yds	Avg	TD
Pete Pihos	38	447	11.8	6
Jack Ferrante	35	588	16.8	3
Frank Ziegler	13	216	16.6	2
Jack Myers	12	204	17.0	0
Neill Armstrong	8	124	15.5	1
Jim Parmer	6	103	17.2	2
Toy Ledbetter	4	81	20.3	2
Steve Van Buren	2	34	17.0	0
Billy Hix	2	25	12.5	0
Russ Craft	1	14	14.0	0

Punting	Punts	Yds	Avg	Blocked
Frank Reagan	54	2270	42.0	0
Joe Muha	2	48	24.0	0

Interceptions	Int	Yds	Avg	TD
Joe Sutton	8	67	8.4	0
Frank Reagan	4	132	33.0	1
Pat McHugh	4	34	8.5	0
Neill Armstrong	3	4	1.3	0
Russ Craft	2	61	30.5	0
Joe Muha	2	40	20.0	1
Norm Willey	1	41	41.0	1
Chuck Bednarik	1	9	9.0	0
Alex Wojciechowicz	1	4	4.0	0

Kicking	PAT Made	PAT Att	PAT %	FG Made	FG Att	FG %	Pts
Cliff Patton	32	33	97	8	17	47.1	56
Joe Muha	0	0	0	0	5	0.0	6

| California 14 | Purdue 28 | Princeton 34 | Army 41 | Cornell 26 | Michigan 27 | Oklahoma 34 | Nebraska 32 | Maryland 34 |
| Penn 7 | Notre Dame 14 | Rutgers 28 | Penn St. 7 | Syracuse 7 | Dartmouth 7 | Texas Ag 28 | Minnesota 26 | Mich. St. 7 |

68,098 See Yanks Beat Phillies, 5-2, to Sweep Series

SPORTS BASEBALL

The Philadelphia Inquirer

PUBLIC LEDGER
An Independent Newspaper for All the People

RACING MAIL ORDER

SUNDAY MORNING, OCTOBER 8, 1950

Kids Get Two in 9th After 2 Outs As Woodling Drops Seminick's Fly

Reynolds Relieves Ford, Fans Lopata With Two on Base
For Final Out; N. Y. Chases Miller, Tallies 3 Off Konstanty

By STAN BAUMGARTNER
Inquirer Sports Reporter

NEW YORK, Oct. 7.—The Fightin' Phillies, who won the acclaim of the sports world when they captured Philadelphia's first National League pennant in 35 years, today became the 13th team since 1921 to bow before the New York Yankees in the World Series.

Purdue Snaps Notre Dame Streak

Sports Results

College
FOOTBALL
PHILADELPHIA DISTRICT

Irish Beaten First Time In 40 Games

Soph Samuels Stars in Upset

Illustrated on Page 5

By CHARLES CHAMBERLAIN

SOUTH BEND, Ind.-Oct. 7 (AP)—Purdue today ended Notre Dame's reign of terror on the gridiron which had gone unchecked through 39 games without defeat, the greatest record in modern college football.

GENE WOODLING SCORES YANKS' INITIAL RUN IN 1ST INNING
New York outfielder tallies easily from second base on Yogi Berra's single at Yankee Stadium in fourth game of World Series. Phils' catcher, Andy Seminick, after taking throw, makes sure Yogi doesn't try to go to second on peg. The umpire is Charley Berry. Yanks won, 5-2, to win Series in four straight games. (Other pictures on Page 5.)

Official Series Box Score

FOURTH GAME
PHILLIES (N. L.)

Army Routs Penn State

WEST POINT, Oct. 7 (AP). — Sparked by Bobby Blaik's flashy passing, Army's football team today humbled Penn State a 41-7 trimming before 26,252 in Michie Stadium.

California Victor As Penn Rally Fails

Illustrated on Page 7
By MORT BERRY
Inquirer Sports Reporter

BERKELEY, Calif., Oct. 7.—If defeat can be glorious, Pennsylvania lost in that manner today when it extended a shockingly powerful California football team to a 14-7 score in the presence of 64,000 surprised onlookers.

Oklahoma Beats Texas Aggies

NORMAN, Okla., Oct. 7 (AP)—A desperate passing attack covering 65 yards and capped by a four-yard touchdown pass to Leon Heath with 37 seconds remaining pulled Oklahoma past the Texas Aggies, 34-28, here today.

Eagles Vanquish Rams, 56-20

By FRANK O'GARA

The Los Angeles Rams, the "natural rival" of the Philadelphia Eagles, once again proved a 14-karat "natural" for our champions last night.

Series Runs Set Record Low Despite Yanks' Final Splurge

By ART MORROW
Inquirer Sports Reporter

NEW YORK, Oct. 7.—The National Leaguers' worst fears were realized today when the pent-up power of the Yankees exploded in the face of the Phillies for the final and most decisive victory of the brief 1950 World Series.

Facts, Figures On World Series

Title for Yanks Is 13th Out of 17

YANKEE STADIUM, New York, Oct. 7 (AP)—Today's World Series victory by the New York Yankees saw the Phillies was...

Eagle River, I Will Finish In Dead Heat at Camden

Illustrated on Page 9
By TEDDY COX

Colgate Wins, 47-6, After Nine Losses

Hill Prince Beats Noor for Gold Cup

NEW YORK, Oct. 7 (UP)—C. T. Chenery's Hill Prince, the "running-est" horse in the land, sent Irish-bred Noor down to his third straight defeat today in the $50,000 Jockey Club gold cup.

Jim Konstanty Says:
Trouble With Control Costly As Yankees Scored 3 in 6th

By Jim Konstanty
Phillies Pitcher

NEW YORK, Oct. 7.

Blew Chances For Runs-Sawyer

By HANK LITTLEHALES
Inquirer Sports Reporter

Justice Won't Play Any Pro Football

CHAPEL HILL, N. C., Oct. 7 (AP)—All-America football player Charlie Justice said today he won't play pro ball with the Washington Redskins or anybody else.

LaBeach Runs 100 Meters In 0:10.1; Betters Mark

GUAYAQUIL, Ecuador, Oct. 7 (AP)—Lloyd LaBeach, Panama, bettered the accepted world record for the 100-meter dash today when he ran the distance in 0:10.1 in the Bolivarian Games.

1951

**RECORD: 4-8, 5TH IN AFC
HEAD COACH: BO McMILLIAN &
WAYNE MILLNER**

Schedule
Regular Season

Wk. 1	Sep 30	W	17-14	at Chicago Cardinals
Wk. 2	Oct 6	W	21-14	vs San Francisco 49ers
Wk. 3	Oct 14	L	37-24	at Green Bay Packers
Wk. 4	Oct 21	L	26-24	at New York Giants
Wk. 5	Oct 28	L	27-23	vs Washington Redskins
Wk. 6	Nov 4	W	34-13	at Pittsburgh Steelers
Wk. 7	Nov 11	L	20-17	at Cleveland Browns
Wk. 8	Nov 18	L	28-10	vs Detroit Lions
Wk. 9	Nov 25	L	17-13	vs Pittsburgh Steelers
Wk. 10	Dec 2	W	35-21	at Washington Redskins
Wk. 11	Dec 9	L	23-7	vs New York Giants
Wk. 12	Dec 16	L	24-9	vs Cleveland Browns

The Eagles won their first two games under Coach Bo McMillan. However, the new coach was forced to resign after becoming ill. Under his replacement Wayne Millner the Eagles would struggle, winning just two of their remaining ten games on the way to a 4-8 record.

1951 Philadelphia Eagles Stats

Passing	Comp	Att	Comp %	Yds	Y/Att	TD	Int	Rating
Adrian Burk	92	218	42.2	1329	6.10	14	23	44.5
Bill Mackrides	23	54	42.6	333	6.17	3	5	43.2
Johnny Rauch	5	12	41.7	51	4.25	0	1	19.8

Rushing	Rush	Yds	Avg	TD
Frank Ziegler	113	418	3.7	2
Steve Van Buren	112	327	2.9	6
Jim Parmer	92	316	3.4	2
Clyde Scott	45	161	3.6	1
Al Pollard	24	119	5.0	0
Dan Sandifer	35	113	3.2	1
Ebert Van Buren	16	60	3.8	0
Johnny Rauch	6	21	3.5	0
Adrian Burk	28	12	0.4	1
Bill Mackrides	7	9	1.3	0
Bosh Pritchard	31	6	0.2	0

Receiving	Rec	Yds	Avg	TD
Pete Pihos	35	536	15.3	5
Bobby Walston	31	512	16.5	8
Jim Parmer	13	80	6.2	0
Clyde Scott	10	212	21.2	3
Bosh Pritchard	8	103	12.9	0
Frank Ziegler	8	59	7.4	0
Steve Van Buren	4	28	7.0	0
Red O'Quinn	3	58	19.3	0
Neill Armstrong	3	44	14.7	0
Al Pollard	3	17	5.7	0
Dan Sandifer	2	36	18.0	1
Vic Lindskog	0	21	0.0	0
John Magee	0	7	0.0	0

Interceptions	Int	Yds	Avg	TD
Frank Reagan	4	60	15.0	0
Neill Armstrong	4	18	4.5	0
Pete Pihos	2	30	15.0	0
Joe Sutton	2	8	4.0	0
Russ Craft	1	32	32.0	1
Dan Sandifer	1	28	28.0	0
Ebert Van Buren	1	23	23.0	0
Pat McHugh	1	19	19.0	0
Mike Jarmoluk	1	9	9.0	0

Punting	Punts	Yds	Avg	Blocked
Adrian Burk	67	2646	39.5	0
Frank Reagan	10	367	36.7	0

Kicking	PAT Made	PAT Att	PAT %	FG Made	FG Att	FG %	Pts
Bobby Walston	28	31	90	6	1	600.0	94

THE PHILADELPHIA INQUIRER, MONDAY MORNING, OCTOBER 15, 1951   abdefgh★ 25

Football Reflections

Princeton's Ace Trumps Penn; Villanova Soaring

By Leo Riordan
Inquirer Executive Sports Editor

APPROPRIATELY enough, a new type of rubber football was used experimentally in the LSU-Georgia Tech game Saturday. The way the sport is acting up this year, you need a rubber ball to absorb the extra quota of crazy bounces. Repeat crazy bounces.

Bounce No. 1: For example, in pre-season estimates, observers have recently tended to rate the Columbia-at-Pennsylvania date a "Boy Scout game." This it meant as no reflection on the Scouts. It merely meant an automatic victory for Penn, with a chance to try out soph and enjoy the tang of the October air. And with fan interest tepid, the university would be inclined to invite Scouts and other well-behaved groups as a civic gesture and as a means of steaming up some enthusiasm in the stands.

Well, folks, Lou Little's visit to his alma mater next Saturday will find Columbia a genuine menace. For while Penn looked better losing, 13-7, to Princeton Saturday than it had the previous week beating Dartmouth, 38-14, its thin ranks are further reduced. Glenn Adams, triple-threat back who suffered an injured knee, cannot face Columbia.

Bounce No. 2: Suppose that one week after Villanova beat Army, 21-7, Dartmouth had taken the Cadets, 28-14—as it did Saturday. Everybody would have said. Ho hum or something equally explosive to indicate the magnitude of Villanova's triumph.

But, in fact, Villanova extended its West Point success by upending a good Penn State team, 20-14, and then in a nationally resounding victory, clawed up cubs a phrase: Alabama, 41-18, Friday night.

ED BELL

(remaining article text continues)

Rate Princeton, Villanova, Cornell Best in the East

NEW YORK, Oct 14 (AP)—In a turbulent football season so far, with spike-s plentiful, but it less rampage through the debris you can find 13 teams still strongly in the running for national honors.

Princeton Star Out for Season

PRINCETON, N.J., Oct. 14 (AP)—Unbeaten Princeton today lost Jack Newell, place-kick artist and defensive halfback, for the rest of the season.

18,792 See NL Stars Beat AL Aces in Denver

DENVER, Oct. 14 (AP)—Denver's largest baseball crowd on history, 18,792 paid, turned out today to watch a team of National League players whip an American League team, 10-1.

Missouri Halfback Suffers Concussion

BOULDER, Colo., Oct. 14 (AP)—Missouri halfback Bob Harris, 20, remained in a hospital here today with a severe brain concussion suffered on Saturday's Big Seven football game between Missouri and Colorado.

Red Smith's next "Views of Sport" column will appear in The Inquirer tomorrow.

Eagan Wins Langhorne Title Race

Marriott Second In Stock Event

Dick Eagan, Springfield, Mass., driving in relief of Holly Bunn, also of Springfield, won the curtailed 100-mile National sportsman stock car championship before 10,000 yesterday at Langhorne Speedway.

Pete Fleming Wins Ozark Golf Title

SPRINGFIELD, Mo., Oct. 14 (AP)—Pete Fleming, Hot Springs, Ark., today won the Ozark Open golf tournament with a 54-hole score of 203, winning $1000.

Americans Top New York, 3-0

Philadelphia Americans ushered in the American soccer League season by handing New York Americans a 3-0 defeat at Lighthouse Field yesterday before 1500.

Donahue Wins Title

Frank Donahue won the men's singles tennis championship of the Philadelphia Country Club yesterday, defeating the defending titleholder, E. W. Overton, 7-5, 6-4.

(AP Wirephoto)
EAGLES' CLYDE SCOTT RUNS INTO TRAFFIC JAM OF PACKERS
Eagles' speedboy is hemmed in by Green Bay players after gaining six yards in first quarter yesterday at Green Bay. Identifiable Packers include (left to right) Abner Wimberly, Rebel Steiner and Dick Wildung. Packers won, 37-24.

Unbeaten Giants Rally in 4th to Top Cards; Rams Upset Lions; Bears, Browns Triumph

By HANK LITTLEHALES

A 14-point rally in the fourth quarter gave the New York Giants a 28-17 triumph over the Chicago Cardinals yesterday at the Polo Grounds and left Steve Owen's well-balanced machine the only unbeaten entry in the 12-club National Football League.

10 Autos Pile Up In Flames in Race

Continued From First Page

N.J., a mechanic, on the face and right hand.

Packers Hand Eagles 1st NFL Loss, 37-24

Green Bay Rolls After 10-10 Tie In Third Period; Fumbles Ruin Birds

By FRANK O'GARA
Inquirer Sports Reporter

GREEN BAY, Wis., Oct. 14—The Philadelphia Eagles were knocked out of their league lead and almost out of their sox by the bone-crushing power of the Green Bay Packers today in a 37-24 battle that delighted 18,680 partisans at City Stadium.

TIED IN 3D QUARTER

South Tops North; West, Roman, St. Joseph's Win

By JOHN DELL

North Catholic's high hopes of a third straight football championship in the Catholic League were ground down beneath the feet of John McDonnell yesterday. The South half-back made a fine, deciding run after taking a short pass from Lou Solari to complete a 38-yard touchdown maneuver which sent North to its second defeat in three league games. The score was 7-0.

Babe Zaharias Wins Fourth Texas Open

FORT WORTH, Tex., Oct. 14 (AP)—Babe Zaharias of Tampa won the fourth women's Texas Open golf title at River Crest Country Club today with a 6 and 7 victory over defending champion Betty Hanson, Inola, Calif.

Stranahan Triumphs in Willard Golf

FORT SMITH, Ark., Oct. 14 (AP)—Frank Stranahan, Toledo, won the Willard Memorial amateur golf tournament today, defeating George Bigelow, Oklahoma A. & M., 3 and 2.

Santa Clara Winner Over Loyola, 20-16

SAN FRANCISCO, Oct. 14 (AP)—Santa Clara survived a mild fourth-quarter rally by Loyola, 20-16, today in Kezar Stadium.

Campanella's All-Stars Beat Hodges' Team, 4-1

NORFOLK, Va., Oct. 14 (AP)—Roy Campanella's All-Stars today slugged out a three-game winning streak of a team of major league standouts piloted by Gil Hodges, 4-1, before 4000.

Caps Win 2d in Row

PROVIDENCE, R.I., Oct. 14 (AP)—The Indianapolis Capitols scored a second straight victory in the American Hockey League campaign by defeating the Rhode Island Reds, 5-4, tonight at the Auditorium.

(AP Wirephoto)
WHOOPS, DEAR, WATCH THAT HOLDING
The Pi Beta Phis ran "perfect" interference for halfback Lou Laidlaw (right) in annual Powder Bowl game between Ohio University sorority teams yesterday at Athens, O., and beat Alpha Xi Deltas, 12-0. Pi Phi at left (holding opponent's arm) is taking slight liberty with rules.

1951

October 15, 1951
Eagles lose to Green Bay giving up
the largest number of points for the season, 37-24

53

1952

RECORD: 7-5, T-2ND AFC
HEAD COACH: JIM TRIMBLE

Schedule
Regular Season

Wk. 1	Sep 28	W	31-25	at Pittsburgh Steelers
Wk. 2	Oct 4	L	31-7	vs New York Giants
Wk. 3	Oct 12	W	26-21	vs Pittsburgh Steelers
Wk. 4	Oct 19	L	49-7	vs Cleveland Browns
Wk. 5	Oct 26	W	14-10	at New York Giants
Wk. 6	Nov 2	L	12-10	at Green Bay Packers (at Milwaukee, WI)
Wk. 7	Nov 9	W	38-20	vs Washington Redskins
Wk. 8	Nov 16	W	10-7	vs Chicago Cardinals
Wk. 9	Nov 23	W	28-20	at Cleveland Browns
Wk. 10	Nov 30	L	28-22	at Chicago Cardinals
Wk. 11	Dec 7	W	38-21	vs Dallas Texans
Wk. 12	Dec 14	L	27-21	at Washington Redskins

When Jim Trimble took over the coaching reigns the Eagles went back to playing solid football, landing in second place with a 7-5 record. The Eagles signed their first African-American players, halfbacks Ralph Goldston and Don Stevens.

1952 Philadelphia Eagles Stats

Passing	Comp	Att	Comp %	Yds	Y/Att	TD	Int	Rating
Bobby Thomason	95	212	44.8	1334	6.29	8	9	60.5
Adrian Burk	37	82	45.1	561	6.84	4	5	59.0
Fred Enke	22	67	32.8	377	5.63	1	5	26.8

Rushing	Rush	Yds	Avg	TD
John Huzvar	105	349	3.3	2
Ralph Goldston	65	210	3.2	3
John Brewer	50	188	3.8	2
Al Pollard	55	186	3.4	1
Frank Ziegler	67	172	2.6	2
Don Stevens	33	95	2.9	0
Bobby Thomason	17	88	5.2	0
Adrian Burk	7	28	4.0	0
Fred Enke	14	25	1.8	0
Jim Parmer	12	23	1.9	0
Bob Stringer	2	5	2.5	0
Ebert Van Buren	7	1	0.1	0

Receiving	Rec	Yds	Avg	TD
Bud Grant	56	997	17.8	7
Bobby Walston	26	469	18.0	3
Don Stevens	13	174	13.4	0
John Huzvar	13	37	2.8	0
Pete Pihos	12	219	18.3	1
Frank Ziegler	8	120	15.0	2
Al Pollard	8	59	7.4	0
John Brewer	5	19	3.8	0
Ebert Van Buren	4	73	18.3	0
Bibbles Bawel	2	60	30.0	0
Fred Enke	2	19	9.5	0
Ralph Goldston	2	12	6.0	0
Jim Parmer	2	10	5.0	0
Bob Stringer	1	4	4.0	0

Interceptions	Int	Yds	Avg	TD
Bibbles Bawel	8	121	15.1	0
Joe Sutton	3	54	18.0	0
Mike Jarmoluk	2	48	24.0	1
Chuck Bednarik	2	14	7.0	0
Russ Craft	1	32	32.0	1
Vic Sears	1	9	9.0	1
Bob Stringer	1	9	9.0	0
Clyde Scott	1	0	0.0	0
Norm Willey	1	0	0.0	0
Neil Ferris	0	3	0.0	0

Punting	Punts	Yds	Avg	Blocked
Adrian Burk	83	3335	40.2	0

Kicking	PAT Made	PAT Att	PAT %	FG Made	FG Att	FG %	Pts
Bobby Walston	31	31	100	11	20	55.0	82

THE PHILADELPHIA INQUIRER, MONDAY MORNING, DECEMBER 8, 1952

Football on Television
Unlimited TV Called Aid to Learning Sports

Do you favor a one-game-a-week plan for televising college football games or an uncontrolled system? Readers of The Inquirer are expressing their opinions in these columns.

Majors Approve 2-Loop Waivers, Adopt Bonus Rule

Big Leagues Put Ban On 24-Hour Recall Of Optioned Players

PHOENIX, Ariz., Dec. 7 (AP).—The major leagues adopted a rule requiring two-league waivers after the June 15 trading deadline today and backed up the hard-pressed minors by adopting the bonus rule and closing the 24-hour recall of optioned players.

Eagles Beat Texans, 38-21, Take Undisputed 2d Place; Browns Win, 10-0, Retain One-Game Lead Over Birds

Cleveland Tops Cards, Clinches Tie for Conf. Title

CHICAGO, Dec. 7 (UP)—The Cleveland Browns clinched at least a tie for the American Conference title in the National Football League today by beating the Chicago Cardinals, 10-0, before 24,941.

Grant Catches 11 Passes, Sets 2 Club Marks

By FRANK O'GARA

Harry 'Bud' Grant, the Eagles' extraordinary end, enjoyed the most successful pass-catching afternoon a member of that organization has experienced in its 20-year history and also erased the club's seasonal record for aerial yardage yesterday before 18,516 at Shibe Park to aid a filip to the Philadelphians' 38-21 conquest of the homeless, hapless Dallas Texans.

A Texan from Dallas "bulldozed" a rampaging "steer" in the Eagles' backfield when Jim Lansford tackled the Birds' Al Pollard after a seven-yard gain in the first quarter yesterday at Shibe Park. John Petitbon (23), Dallas, and Frank Ziegler (31), Eagles, are others in foreground. Eagles won the National Football League game, 38-21.

Warriors Shaded, 94-92, By Royals' Strong Surge

ROCHESTER, N. Y., Dec. 7.—Dominating the play almost all the way, the Philadelphia Warriors ran out of gas in the closing minutes and dropped a 94-92 decision to the Rochester Royals before the largest crowd of the season in the National Basketball Association.

Redskins Blast Giants' Title Bid

NEW YORK, Dec. 7 (AP).—Eddie Le Baron threw four touchdown passes, three to Hugh Taylor, as the jolly Washington Redskins whipped the New York Giants, 27-17, and wrecked any chance the Giants had for championship honors in the National Football League's American Conference race.

Lions Rout Bears, 45-21, To Near Title Tie; Box Ace

DETROIT, Dec. 7 (AP).—End Cloyce Box triggered the Detroit Lions to within shooting distance of a pro football championship by grabbing two over-the-shoulder touchdown passes within a 96-second span of the first period today, and from there the Lions went on to trounce the Chicago Bears, 45-21, before 38,618.

Americans Win, Lead League

The Philadelphia Americans defeated the Philadelphia Nationals, 5-1, in their American Soccer League game at Holmes Stadium.

College Basketball Roundup
Indiana Victim of Upset; La Salle, Kansas State Win

By RIP WATSON

NEW YORK, Dec. 7 (AP).—With the college football season completed only a few hours before, college basketball's season broke out like a mustard oil over the country last night.

Rams Roll, 45-27, Over Green Bay

LOS ANGELES, Dec. 7 (UP)—The Los Angeles Rams capitalized on pass interceptions to take the Green Bay Packers, 45-27, and maintain a first-place tie in the National Conference of the National Football League before 49,922.

Meyer Is 'Serious' After Heart Attack

PHOENIX, Ariz., Dec. 7 (AP).—Billy Meyer, 59, recently returned as manager of the Pittsburgh Pirates, suffered a heart attack in his Arizona winter home tonight and was rushed to Memorial Hospital.

Wings, Bruins Tie, 1-1

DETROIT, Dec. 7 (AP).—The Boston Bruins and Detroit Red Wings battled to a 1-1 tie in their National Hockey League game.

Americans Win, Lead League

Nats' Rally in 4th, Top Hawks, 71-67

SYRACUSE, N. Y., Dec. 7 (AP).—The Syracuse Nationals came from behind in the fourth period to rout the Milwaukee Hawks, 71-67.

Flukes Score TD

Pistons Down Knicks As Meineke Scores 27

FORT WAYNE, Ind., Dec. 7 (AP).—The New York Knickerbockers came up within two points in the fourth quarter but couldn't knock off Fort Wayne off in winning streak tonight, and the Pistons won, 102-91.

Rangers, Canadiens Tie

NEW YORK, Dec. 7 (AP).—Defenseman Hy Buller fired home a tying score at 7:33 of the third period to earn the New York Rangers a 2-2 tie with the Montreal Canadiens tonight in a bruising National Hockey League game.

15 Finished Unbeaten, Untied

NEW YORK, Dec. 7 (AP).—The 1952 college football season finished with 15 teams on unbeaten lists.

Notre Dame Plans Commercial Television Station

CHICAGO, Dec. 7 (UPR)—Revelations that legal action to fight it... University of Notre Dame may be taken against the National Collegiate Athletic Association concerning NCAA TV football plans, that Notre Dame would carry commercial television in South Bend and that the Notre Dame football team...

Sports Results
Professional
FOOTBALL
BASKETBALL
HOCKEY
SOCCER

College
FOOTBALL
BASKETBALL

School
BASKETBALL

December 8, 1952
Eagles rout the Dallas Texans, 38-21
Bud Grant catches 11 passes for 203 yards and scores two touchdowns

55

1953
RECORD: 7-4-1, 2ND IN NFL EAST
HEAD COACH: JIM TRIMBLE

Schedule
Regular Season

Wk. 1	Sep 27	L	31-21	at San Francisco 49ers
Wk. 2	Oct 2	T	21-21	vs Washington Redskins
Wk. 3	Oct 10	L	37-13	at Cleveland Browns
Wk. 4	Oct 17	W	23-7	vs Pittsburgh Steelers
Wk. 5	Oct 25	W	56-17	at Chicago Bears
Wk. 6	Nov 1	W	35-7	at Pittsburgh Steelers
Wk. 7	Nov 8	W	30-7	vs New York Giants
Wk. 8	Nov 15	W	45-14	vs Baltimore Colts
Wk. 9	Nov 21	W	38-0	vs Chicago Cardinals
Wk. 10	Nov 29	L	37-28	at New York Giants
Wk. 11	Dec 6	L	10-0	at Washington Redskins
Wk. 12	Dec 13	W	42-27	vs Cleveland Browns

Bobby Thomason and Adrian Burk combined to pass for a league-high 3,089 yards, while Pete Pihos caught 63 passes for 1,049 yards and 10 touchdowns to lead the league. Rookie defenseman Tom Brookshier led the team with eight interceptions while Chuck Bednarik returned an interception for a touchdown against Baltimore. The Eagles finish in second place again with a 7-4-1 record, while snapping the Cleveland Browns 11-game winning streak with 42-27 win in the season finale.

1953 Philadelphia Eagles Stats

Passing	Comp	Att	Comp %	Yds	Y/Att	TD	Int	Rating
Bobby Thomason	162	304	53.3	2462	8.10	21	20	75.8
Adrian Burk	56	119	47.1	788	6.62	4	9	48.6
Frank Ziegler	0	1	0.0	0	0.00	0	0	39.6
Bob Gambold	6	14	42.9	107	7.64	0	2	30.1

Rushing	Rush	Yds	Avg	TD
Don Johnson	83	439	5.3	5
Jerry Williams	61	345	5.7	3
Frank Ziegler	83	320	3.9	5
Jim Parmer	38	158	4.2	2
Hal Giancanelli	44	131	3.0	1
Toy Ledbetter	41	120	2.9	1
John Brewer	17	85	5.0	1
Adrian Burk	8	54	6.8	3
Al Pollard	23	44	1.9	0
Bobby Thomason	9	23	2.6	1
Bob Stringer	1	5	5.0	0
Bob Gambold	2	-2	-1.0	0

Receiving	Rec	Yds	Avg	TD
Pete Pihos	63	1049	16.7	10
Bobby Walston	41	750	18.3	5
Jerry Williams	31	438	14.1	1
Hal Giancanelli	20	346	17.3	5
Frank Ziegler	15	211	14.1	0
Jim Parmer	14	89	6.4	0
Toy Ledbetter	13	137	10.5	2
Don Johnson	12	227	18.9	2
Al Pollard	7	33	4.7	0
John Brewer	4	43	10.8	0
Bob Schnelker	4	34	8.5	0

Punting	Punts	Yds	Avg	Blocked
Adrian Burk	41	1765	43.0	0
Chuck Bednarik	12	483	40.3	0

Interceptions	Int	Yds	Avg	TD
Tom Brookshier	8	41	5.1	0
Chuck Bednarik	6	116	19.3	1
Russ Craft	4	46	11.5	0
Bob Hudson	3	74	24.7	0
Ebert Van Buren	1	13	13.0	0
Bob Stringer	1	7	7.0	0
Mike Jarmoluk	1	2	2.0	0

Kicking	PAT Made	PAT Att	PAT %	FG Made	FG Att	FG %	Pts
Bobby Walston	45	48	94	4	13	30.8	87
Al Pollard	1	1	100	0	2	0.0	1

24 abdefgh★   THE PHILADELPHIA INQUIRER, MONDAY MORNING, OCTOBER 26, 1953

Browns Capture 5th NFL Victory, Trip Giants, 7-0

Eagles Smother Cards, 56-17, Set 2 Club Marks on Passes

By Art Morrow
Inquirer Sports Reporter

CHICAGO, Oct. 25—Chicago's downtrodden Cardinals had the impudence to score first at Comiskey Park today, and the Eagles wreaked a horrible vengeance. Jim Trimble's inspired Philadelphians, growing more ferocious with every period, rolled to a 56-17 victory as 22,060 looked on in amazement.

It was the worst defeat in history for the Cardinals, a charter member of the National Football League, and a new modern victory margin for the Eagles.

Jim Christy still is on his back in mid-air after carrying North Catholic's John Latsis over goal line on four-yard touchdown jaunt with seven-yard pass from his brother Dick in first period yesterday at Connie Mack Stadium. In foreground is North's Ray Ranes. St. James won No. 6, over North, snapped city champion Falcons' unbeaten string at 17 games and gave undefeated St. James the Catholic League lead.

St. James Turns Back North, 9-0

17-Game Streak Of Falcons Ends; D. Christy Star

By Hal Freeman

Reflections

Penn Spirit, Gambles, Tradition Upset Navy

By Leo Riordan
Inquirer Executive Sports Editor

Kelly Wins Pair In Mexico City; Miller Is Victor

49,546 See Rams Jar Bears, 38-24

54,862 Watch Lions Trip 49ers on Layne's Passing

Hogan Cards 72 'Against' Britons

46 Grid Teams Still Unbeaten

Piedmont League To Stay in Business

Boston College Wallops Xavier

Leahy Reported In Good Condition

Giants Boom to Victory On Rhodes' Grand Slam

Sports Results
Professional

Football Roundup: Purdue's Upset of MSC Boosts Notre Dame Status

October 26, 1953
Eagles handed the Chicago Cardinals their worst
defeat in team history by the score 56-17

1954

RECORD: 7-4-1, 2ND IN NFL EAST
HEAD COACH: JIM TRIMBLE

Schedule

Regular Season

Wk. 1	Sep 26	W	28-10	vs Cleveland Browns
Wk. 2	Oct 3	W	35-16	at Chicago Cardinals
Wk. 3	Oct 9	W	24-22	vs Pittsburgh Steelers
Wk. 4	Oct 17	W	49-21	at Washington Redskins
Wk. 5	Oct 23	L	17-7	at Pittsburgh Steelers
Wk. 6	Oct 30	L	37-14	vs Green Bay Packers
Wk. 7	Nov 7	W	30-14	vs Chicago Cardinals
Wk. 8	Nov 14	L	27-14	at New York Giants
Wk. 9	Nov 21	L	6-0	at Cleveland Browns
Wk. 10	Nov 28	W	41-33	vs Washington Redskins
Wk. 11	Dec 5	T	13-13	at Detroit Lions
Wk. 12	Dec 12	W	29-14	vs New York Giants

After winning their first four games, the Eagles continued to be one of the NFL's strongest teams, finishing with a 7-4-1 record, to finish in second place for the third season in a row. Leading the Eagles success was punter Bobby Watson who led the NFL with 114 points and seta club record by scoring 25 points in a single game (3 touchdowns and 7 extra points) against Washington 49-21.

1954 Philadelphia Eagles Stats

Passing	Comp	Att	Comp %	Yds	Y/Att	TD	Int	Rating
Adrian Burk	123	231	53.2	1740	7.53	23	17	80.4
Bobby Thomason	83	170	48.8	1242	7.31	10	13	61.0

Rushing	Rush	Yds	Avg	TD
Jim Parmer	119	408	3.4	0
Toy Ledbetter	81	241	3.0	1
Jerry Williams	47	183	3.9	1
Neil Worden	58	128	2.2	1
Dom Moselle	29	114	3.9	1
Hal Giancanelli	33	47	1.4	0
Bobby Thomason	10	45	4.5	0
Adrian Burk	15	18	1.2	0
Don Johnson	7	16	2.3	0
Pete Pihos	1	-1	-1.0	0
Jerry Norton	1	-3	-3.0	0

Receiving	Rec	Yds	Avg	TD
Pete Pihos	60	872	14.5	10
Jerry Williams	44	668	15.2	3
Bobby Walston	31	581	18.7	11
Dom Moselle	17	242	14.2	2
Toy Ledbetter	15	192	12.8	3
Hal Giancanelli	14	195	13.9	4
Jim Parmer	12	40	3.3	0
Neil Worden	7	63	9.0	0
Don Luft	3	59	19.7	0
Norm Willey	2	50	25.0	0
Don Johnson	1	20	20.0	0

Punting	Punts	Yds	Avg	Blocked
Adrian Burk	73	2918	40.0	0

Kicking	PAT Made	PAT Att	PAT %	FG Made	FG Att	FG %	Pts
Bobby Walston	36	39	92	4	10	40.0	114

Interceptions	Int	Yds	Avg	TD
Bob Hudson	8	89	11.1	0
Jerry Norton	5	110	22.0	1
Wayne Robinson	4	41	10.3	0
Bucko Kilroy	4	29	7.3	0
Harry Dowda	2	34	17.0	0
Roy Barni	2	0	0.0	0
Jess Richardson	1	10	10.0	0
Chuck Bednarik	1	9	9.0	0
Ed Sharkey	1	4	4.0	0

THE PHILADELPHIA INQUIRER, MONDAY MORNING, OCTOBER 18, 1954

26 abcdefgh★

Eight Buy Stock of Connie, Earle; Keep A's Here

Group to Invest Four Million, Hire Top Gen. Manager, Pilot

By ART MORROW

The new order is congratulated by the old as A's change hands in deal consummated yesterday. Arthur A. Gallagher, one of the eight new stockholders who is expected to become president of the club, is congratulated by 91-year-old Connie Mack, retiring president, while Roy Mack looks on. Connie will be honorary president, while Roy, who retained one-ninth of the team's stock, is expected to serve the club in an executive capacity. He had been executive vice president and served as general manager.

Sketches of 8 New Stockholders in A's

Burk's 7 TD Passes Tie Mark; Eagles Win

Rout Redskins; Birds Take 4th In Row, 49-21

Sports Results
Professional
School

Steelers Romp; Worst Loss for Browns, 55-27

Reflections

Penn Improves, Needs Drills on Fundamentals
By LEO RIORDAN
Inquirer Executive Sports Editor

Rookie Ace in Victory

Corbitt Takes First In AAU Marathon

Rodenberger Duo Wins Hatfield Race

Bryan Triumphs in 100-Mile Race

Eagles' end Bobby Walston takes a first-quarter pass from Adrian Burk as Harry Gilmer, Washington Redskins' halfback, makes a futile try at a block. Walston raced for a touchdown after grabbing ball at Washington. (AP Wirephoto)

1954

October 18, 1954
Eagles QB Adrian Burk throws league-tying record of seven touchdown passes as the Eagles smothered Washington 49-21

1955

RECORD: 4-7-1, T-4TH IN NFL EAST
HEAD COACH: JIM TRIMBLE

Schedule
Regular Season

Wk. 1	Sep 24	W	27-17	vs New York Giants
Wk. 2	Oct 1	L	31-30	vs Washington Redskins
Wk. 3	Oct 8	L	21-17	at Cleveland Browns
Wk. 4	Oct 15	L	13-7	at Pittsburgh Steelers
Wk. 5	Oct 23	T	24-24	at Chicago Cardinals
Wk. 6	Oct 30	W	24-0	vs Pittsburgh Steelers
Wk. 7	Nov 6	L	34-21	at Washington Redskins
Wk. 8	Nov 13	W	33-17	vs Cleveland Browns
Wk. 9	Nov 20	L	31-7	at New York Giants
Wk. 10	Nov 27	L	23-21	vs Los Angeles Rams
Wk. 11	Dec 4	W	27-3	vs Chicago Cardinals
Wk. 12	Dec 11	L	17-10	at Chicago Bears

Pete Pihos again led all NFL pass receivers with 62 catches for 864 yards. However, the Eagles struggled to a meager 4-7-1 record. Eagles All-Pro tackle Bucko Kilroy started in 101st consecutive game against the Giants, then suffered a career-ending knee injury. Pete Pihos retired at the end of the season. In his nine-year career he managed to catch 373 receptions for 5,619 yards and 63 touchdowns. Hugh Devore replaced Jim Trimble as head coach following the season.

1955 Philadelphia Eagles Stats

Passing	Comp	Att	Comp %	Yds	Y/Att	TD	Int	Rating
Bobby Thomason	88	171	51.5	1337	7.82	10	7	80.0
Adrian Burk	110	228	48.2	1359	5.96	9	17	49.2
Jerry Norton	0	1	0.0	0	0.00	0	0	39.6

Rushing	Rush	Yds	Avg	TD
Hal Giancanelli	97	385	4.0	2
Rob Goode	76	274	3.6	0
Jerry Norton	36	144	4.0	1
Adrian Burk	36	132	3.7	2
Jim Parmer	34	129	3.8	1
Ted Wegert	26	120	4.6	2
Dick Bielski	28	67	2.4	1
Toy Ledbetter	21	48	2.3	0
Bobby Thomason	17	29	1.7	0
Don Johnson	3	1	0.3	0
Bobby Walston	1	-3	-3.0	0
Ralph Goldston	14	-7	-0.5	0

Receiving	Rec	Yds	Avg	TD
Pete Pihos	62	864	13.9	7
Bill Stribling	38	568	14.9	6
Bobby Walston	27	443	16.4	3
Hal Giancanelli	25	379	15.2	1
Jerry Norton	11	125	11.4	1
Rob Goode	10	137	13.7	0
Dick Bielski	8	48	6.0	0
Toy Ledbetter	7	88	12.6	1
Ted Wegert	3	17	5.7	0
Ralph Goldston	2	8	4.0	0
Bibbles Bawel	1	6	6.0	0
Jim Parmer	1	-4	-4.0	0

Punting	Punts	Yds	Avg	Blocked
Adrian Burk	61	2615	42.9	0

Interceptions	Int	Yds	Avg	TD
Bibbles Bawel	9	168	18.7	2
Bob Hudson	3	48	16.0	0
Chuck Bednarik	1	36	36.0	0
Eddie Bell	1	30	30.0	0
Wayne Robinson	1	20	20.0	0
Jerry Norton	1	0	0.0	0

Kicking	PAT Made	PAT Att	PAT %	FG Made	FG Att	FG %	Pts
Dick Bielski	23	24	96	9	23	39.1	56
Bobby Walston	6	7	86	2	3	66.7	30

30 abdefgh★   THE PHILADELPHIA INQUIRER, MONDAY MORNING, NOVEMBER 14, 1955

Trailing by 17, Eagles Rally to Trounce Browns, 33-17, Before Record 39,303

Burk Passes To Stribling Bring 2 TDs

By HERB GOOD

Cleveland's Otto Graham scores from the one in the first quarter as the Eagles' Norm Willey (right) tries to pry the ball out of his hands. The Birds' player with a headlock on Graham is unidentified.

The Eagles also provided their share of thrills in the game yesterday at Connie Mack Stadium. Here's Pete Pihos being tackled in air by Browns' Ray Renfro after catching a pass from Adrian Burk.

Skins Stall 49ers, 7-0, Trail Browns by Game

WASHINGTON, Nov. 13 (AP)—It was thievery in broad daylight today as the Washington Redskins beat the San Francisco 49ers, 7-0.

Sports Results

Professional

33,982 Watch Giants Turn Back Colts, 17-7

NEW YORK, Nov. 13 (UP)—The New York Giants put a tight rein on Alan (The Horse) the Baltimore Colts today and rolled to a 17-7 victory that ruined the Colts' chance to move into a tie for the National Football League's Western Division lead.

Rote, Packers Rout Cardinals

GREEN BAY, Wis., Nov 13 (UP)—Tobin Rote, returning to an old football axiom that the best defense is a good offense, passed, ran and quarterbacked the Green Bay Packers to a 31-14 victory over the Chicago Cardinals today.

UCLA Loses Knox Until Rose Bowl

LOS ANGELES, Nov. 13 (AP)—The UCLA Bruins have lost their air arm via a broken leg.

Tom Hopkins (52), LaSalle fullback, crowds past off-balance Bob Mastripolito, St. Thomas More fullback, on four-yard rush leading up to Catholic League champions' first touchdown in 22-0 victory. Defenders Jim DiSantis (25) and Gaspare Pallegrini (27) are moving in to stop play. Story on Page 32.

Bears Deadlock Rams for Lead, Win 5th Straight

Chicago Scores 24 In First 19 Minutes; 50,187 Watch Rout

CHICAGO, Nov. 13 (UP)—The Chicago Bears riddled the Los Angeles Rams with merciless efficiency today to rack up their fifth straight victory, 24-2, before 50,187 fans and move into a first place tie in the National Football League's Western Division.

HOFFMAN RUNS 47

Yanks Rout Stars; End Tour Unbeaten

TOKYO, Nov. 13 (AP)—The New York Yankees whipped the Japan All-Stars, 9-3, before 45,000 today to wind up their 16-game Japan tour without a defeat.

November 14, 1955
Eagles explode for two touchdowns and a field goal within three minutes and 54 seconds to defeat Cleveland 33-17

1956

RECORD: 3-8-1, 6TH IN NFL EAST
HEAD COACH: HUGH DEVORE

Schedule

Regular Season

Wk. 1	Sep 30	L	27-7	at Los Angeles Rams
Wk. 2	Oct 6	W	13-9	vs Washington Redskins
Wk. 3	Oct 14	W	35-21	at Pittsburgh Steelers
Wk. 4	Oct 21	L	20-6	vs Chicago Cardinals
Wk. 5	Oct 28	L	20-3	at New York Giants
Wk. 6	Nov 4	L	28-17	at Chicago Cardinals
Wk. 7	Nov 11	W	14-7	vs Pittsburgh Steelers
Wk. 8	Nov 18	L	16-0	vs Cleveland Browns
Wk. 9	Nov 25	T	10-10	vs San Francisco 49ers
Wk. 10	Dec 2	L	17-14	at Cleveland Browns
Wk. 11	Dec 9	L	19-17	at Washington Redskins
Wk. 12	Dec 15	L	21-7	vs New York Giants

The fans witnessed 17 players getting injured during the season, while losing another seven starters to retirement. The Eagles offense never took flight, as they struggled to score 143 points on the season while landing in last place with a terrible 3-8-1 record. Despite the struggles during the frustrating season, the Eagles defense continued to be one of the strongest in the league, allowing just 215 points.

1956 Philadelphia Eagles Stats

Passing	Comp	Att	Comp %	Yds	Y/Att	TD	Int	Rating
Bobby Thomason	82	164	50.0	1119	6.82	4	21	40.7
Don Schaefer	1	3	33.3	11	3.67	1	0	84.7
Adrian Burk	39	82	47.6	426	5.20	1	6	36.9

Rushing	Rush	Yds	Avg	TD
Ken Keller	112	433	3.9	4
Don Schaefer	102	320	3.1	2
Dick Bielski	52	162	3.1	1
Hal Giancanelli	42	148	3.5	1
Ted Wegert	47	127	2.7	1
Will Berzinski	15	72	4.8	0
Adrian Burk	17	61	3.6	0
Bobby Thomason	21	48	2.3	2
Bob Smith	9	8	0.9	0
Jim Parmer	1	-2	-2.0	0

Receiving	Rec	Yds	Avg	TD
Bobby Walston	39	590	15.1	3
Don Schaefer	13	117	9.0	0
Pete Retzlaff	12	159	13.3	0
Hank Burnine	10	208	20.8	2
John Bredice	10	146	14.6	1
Hal Giancanelli	10	104	10.4	0
Dick Bielski	8	63	7.9	0
Ken Keller	7	36	5.1	0
Ted Wegert	6	46	7.7	0
Will Berzinski	3	35	11.7	0
Bill Stribling	2	11	5.5	0
Rocky Ryan	1	31	31.0	0
Lee Riley	1	10	10.0	0

Interceptions	Int	Yds	Avg	TD
Eddie Bell	4	61	15.3	1
Lee Riley	3	57	19.0	0
Jerry Norton	2	34	17.0	0
Chuck Bednarik	2	0	0.0	0
Bibbles Bawel	1	33	33.0	0
Tom Brookshier	1	31	31.0	0
Rocky Ryan	1	17	17.0	0
Tom Scott	1	12	12.0	0
Marion Campbell	1	1	1.0	0

Punting	Punts	Yds	Avg	Blocked
Adrian Burk	68	2843	41.8	0

Kicking	PAT Made	PAT Att	PAT %	FG Made	FG Att	FG %	Pts
Bobby Walston	17	18	94	6	13	46.2	53
Dick Bielski	0	0	0	0	1	0.0	6

October 7, 1956
Eagles rallied to defeat the Redskins 13-9

1956

1957

RECORD: 4-8, 5TH IN NFL EAST
HEAD COACH: HUGH DEVORE

Schedule

Regular Season

Wk. 1	Sep 29	L	17-13	at Los Angeles Rams
Wk. 2	Oct 5	L	24-20	vs New York Giants
Wk. 3	Oct 13	L	24-7	at Cleveland Browns
Wk. 4	Oct 20	W	17-7	vs Cleveland Browns
Wk. 5	Oct 27	L	6-0	at Pittsburgh Steelers
Wk. 6	Nov 3	W	38-21	at Chicago Cardinals
Wk. 7	Nov 10	L	27-16	vs Detroit Lions
Wk. 8	Nov 17	L	13-0	at New York Giants
Wk. 9	Nov 24	W	21-12	vs Washington Redskins
Wk. 10	Dec 1	W	7-6	vs Pittsburgh Steelers
Wk. 11	Dec 8	L	42-7	at Washington Redskins
Wk. 12	Dec 14	L	31-27	vs Chicago Cardinals

The Eagles continued to struggle, finishing with a 4-8 record. However, rookie quarterback Sonny Jurgensen played solid football all season, showing signs of brilliance at times. In their best college draft to date, the Eagles selected Billy Ray Barnes, Tommy Mc-Donald, Clarence Peaks, and Sonny Jurgensen. Following the season Coach Hugh Devore was fired and replaced by Buck Shaw.

1957 Philadelphia Eagles Stats

Passing	Comp	Att	Comp %	Yds	Y/Att	TD	Int	Rating
Tommy McDonald	1	1	100.0	11	11.00	0	0	112.5
Clarence Peaks	2	3	66.7	56	18.67	0	1	70.1
Sonny Jurgensen	33	70	47.1	470	6.71	5	8	53.6
Bobby Thomason	46	92	50.0	630	6.85	4	10	47.2
Billy Barnes	0	1	0.0	0	0.00	0	0	39.6
Jerry Norton	0	1	0.0	0	0.00	0	0	39.6
Al Dorow	17	36	47.2	212	5.89	1	4	35.6

Rushing	Rush	Yds	Avg	TD
Billy Barnes	143	529	3.7	1
Clarence Peaks	125	495	4.0	1
Ken Keller	57	195	3.4	0
Neil Worden	42	133	3.2	0
Jerry Norton	2	73	36.5	0
Bobby Thomason	15	62	4.1	3
Al Dorow	17	52	3.1	2
Tommy McDonald	12	36	3.0	0
Bobby Walston	1	7	7.0	0
Sid Youngelman	0	3	0.0	0
Sonny Jurgensen	10	-3	-0.3	2

Receiving	Rec	Yds	Avg	TD
Billy Barnes	19	212	11.2	1
Bill Stribling	14	194	13.9	1
Bobby Walston	11	266	24.2	1
Clarence Peaks	11	99	9.0	0
Pete Retzlaff	10	120	12.0	0
Tommy McDonald	9	228	25.3	3
Dick Bielski	8	81	10.1	2
Hank Burnine	7	63	9.0	0
Rocky Ryan	4	91	22.8	2
Ken Keller	4	31	7.8	0
Neil Worden	1	3	3.0	0
Bob Gaona	1	-9	-9.0	0

Punting	Punts	Yds	Avg	Blocked
Jerry Norton	68	2798	41.1	0

Interceptions	Int	Yds	Avg	TD
Jerry Norton	4	155	38.8	1
Tom Brookshier	4	74	18.5	0
Jimmy Harris	3	99	33.0	1
Chuck Bednarik	3	51	17.0	0
Eddie Bell	2	38	19.0	0
Frank Wydo	1	25	25.0	0

Kicking	PAT Made	PAT Att	PAT %	FG Made	FG Att	FG %	Pts
Bobby Walston	20	21	95	9	12	75.0	53
Dick Bielski	0	0	0	0	2	0.0	12

1957

November 4, 1957
QB Bobby Thomason scores twice on quarterback sneaks and passes
for two more touchdowns to defeat the Chicago Cardinals 38-21

1958

RECORD: 2-9-1, T-5TH IN NFL EAST
HEAD COACH: BUCK SHAW

Schedule

Regular Season

Wk. 1	Sep 28	L	24-14	vs Washington Redskins
Wk. 2	Oct 5	W	27-24	vs New York Giants
Wk. 3	Oct 12	L	24-3	at Pittsburgh Steelers
Wk. 4	Oct 19	L	30-24	vs San Francisco 49ers
Wk. 5	Oct 26	L	38-35	at Green Bay Packers
Wk. 6	Nov 2	T	21-21	at Chicago Cardinals
Wk. 7	Nov 9	L	31-24	vs Pittsburgh Steelers
Wk. 8	Nov 16	W	49-21	vs Chicago Cardinals
Wk. 9	Nov 23	L	28-14	at Cleveland Browns
Wk. 10	Nov 30	L	24-10	at New York Giants
Wk. 11	Dec 7	L	21-14	vs Cleveland Browns
Wk. 12	Dec 14	L	20-0	at Washington Redskins

To give the team a veteran quarterback, the Eagles acquired Norm Van Brocklin from the Los Angels Rams. In week two Van Brocklin threw a club record 91-yard touchdown pass to Tommy McDonald to defeat the Giants 27-24. After that game, the Eagles lost the next four games, then tied Chicago 21-21, lost to Pittsburgh, defeated Chicago, and lost their last four games. They struggled throughout the season and ended in last place with a 2-9-1 record. However, despite the struggles the Eagles would double attendance, moving to historic Franklin Field on the campus of Pennsylvania University.

1958 Philadelphia Eagles Stats

Passing	Comp	Att	Comp %	Yds	Y/Att	TD	Int	Rating
Norm Van Brocklin	198	374	52.9	2409	6.44	15	20	64.1
Billy Barnes	4	6	66.7	104	17.33	3	0	149.3
Sonny Jurgensen	12	22	54.5	259	11.77	0	1	77.7

Rushing	Rush	Yds	Avg	TD
Billy Barnes	156	551	3.5	7
Clarence Peaks	115	386	3.4	3
Billy Wells	24	92	3.8	1
Walt Kowalczyk	17	43	2.5	1
Brad Myers	9	23	2.6	0
Norm Van Brocklin	8	5	0.6	1
Sonny Jurgensen	1	1	1.0	0
Tommy McDonald	3	-4	-1.3	0
Pete Retzlaff	1	-4	-4.0	0

Receiving	Rec	Yds	Avg	TD
Pete Retzlaff	56	766	13.7	2
Billy Barnes	35	423	12.1	0
Tommy McDonald	29	603	20.8	9
Clarence Peaks	29	248	8.6	2
Dick Bielski	23	234	10.2	1
Bobby Walston	21	298	14.2	3
Walt Kowalczyk	8	72	9.0	0
Billy Wells	4	49	12.3	0
Brad Myers	4	25	6.3	0
Gene Mitcham	3	39	13.0	1
Andy Nacrelli	2	15	7.5	0

Interceptions	Int	Yds	Avg	TD
Bob Pellegrini	4	90	22.5	0
Eddie Bell	2	33	16.5	0
Tom Scott	2	15	7.5	0
Rocky Ryan	1	38	38.0	0
Bob Hudson	1	15	15.0	0
Lee Riley	1	8	8.0	0
Bill Koman	1	5	5.0	0
Walt Kowalczyk	1	2	2.0	0
Tom Brookshier	1	0	0.0	0
Jerry Norton	1	0	0.0	0

Punting	Punts	Yds	Avg	Blocked
Norm Van Brocklin	54	2225	41.2	0

Kicking	PAT Made	PAT Att	PAT %	FG Made	FG Att	FG %	Pts
Bobby Walston	31	31	100	6	14	42.9	67

26 sbdh★   THE PHILADELPHIA INQUIRER, MONDAY MORNING, NOVEMBER 17, 1958

Peaks Gets 4 TDs as Eagles Romp, 49-21

Cards Battered In Birds' Best Attack Since '54

By HERB GOOD

Snapping violently out of a five-week slump, the Eagles crushed the Chicago Cardinals, 49-21, with their most devastating all-around play of the season to the delight of 18,325 at Franklin Field yesterday.

Clarence Peaks scored four touchdowns and Walt Kowalczyk, Tommy McDonald, and Bobby Walston chipped in with one each as the Philadelphia pros exploded for their greatest offensive effort since scoring the same number of points against Washington in 1954.

RECEIVERS HELP

Sharing the spotlight with this quartet were Norm Van Brocklin and Billy Barnes. The former riddled the Cards' defense with 18 completions in 29 attempts for 318 yards and two of the touchdowns. Barnes contributed 204 yards with his running, pass catching and two pass completions.

The strikes thrown by Van Brocklin, who came within two yards of equalling the best NFL individual passing performance of the season, were made all the more effective by the unusual spirited, hard-running of his receivers.

BREAK 1-7 TIE

Three touchdowns within a five and a half-minute stretch of the second period broke a 7-7 deadlock and gave the Eagles complete control of a lively battle, filled with long pass plays and thrilling runs.

The offense clicked so well that the Eagles outgained the visitors, 515 net yards to 321, surely the best possible answer for their troublesome pass defense.

Peaks scored all three of the rapid-fired TDs that rent the Cards reeling in the second period. He started the deluge by romping into the end zone on a 37-yard pass play that concluded an 86-yard drive.

Then he ploughed over from the one and the two on drives of 37 and 44, respectively. His second tally stemmed from a pass interception by Bill Koman and the third from a sparkling 35-yard punt return by McDonald, a brilliant performer throughout the cloudy, misty afternoon.

CAPS 86-YARD DRIVE

Peaks made his other TD from the one to conclude another 86-yard drive in the final minute of the third quarter. Kowalczyk also scored from the one at the end of a 60-yard drive that gave the Eagles a 7-0 first-quarter lead.

McDonald tallied on a 47-yard pass from Van Brocklin in the third quarter and Walston put the finishing touches to the rout by scoring on a 71-yard, pass-and-run dazzler, engineered by Barnes in the final period.

Barnes' pass, made on the run after taking a pitchout from Van Jurgenson, was one of four attempted after Van Brocklin was given a much deserved rest in the fourth quarter.

The only opportunity the Eagles muffed was in the early moments of the final period when they gave up the ball on downs on the 16 after Tom Scott intercepted a pass and ran 16 to the nine on the last play of the previous period.

MATSON HELD TO 22

The Eagles' defensive unit, spearheaded by Marion Campbell, Ed Meadows and Tom Brookshier, did such a good job that the ever-dangerous Ollie Matson was limited to a mere 22 yards rushing as the Cards were held to 105 yards on the ground.

Rushing tactics by the Eagles also made the passing of rookie M. C. Reynolds and Lamar Mc-Han considerably less effective than in the 21-21 stalemate at Chicago two weeks ago.

However, McHan managed to fire a 35-yard pass to Joe Childress...

Continued on Page 27, Column 4

A view from the point of Chicago Cardinals' linebacker shows how Clarence Peaks mounted the line to move half a yard for one of his four touchdowns.

Quarterback Norm Van Brocklin (11) watches after having made the handoff. Cardinal defenders include Jack Patera (61), Ed Culpepper (73), Ed Husmann (66).

Steelers Upset Giants, 31-10, on Layne's Passes

PITTSBURGH, Nov. 16 (AP)—Quarterback Bobby Layne's pinpoint passing and some of the most aggressive line play ever turned in by a Pittsburgh team gave the Steelers a 31-10 victory over the New York Giants today in a National Football League game.

The upset, in which the Steelers captured their third consecutive victory by overcoming a 10-point deficit, was a severe blow to the Giants' hopes for the Eastern Conference title. The Giants had won three in a row until today, starting the three three weeks ago by beating the Steelers, 17-6, at New York. They now trail Cleveland by one game.

30,830 SEE GAME

A crowd of 30,830 in balmy weather at Pitt Stadium saw victory by overcoming a passing attack which finally carried the Eastern Conference title. The Giants had won three in a row until today, starting the three three weeks ago by beating the Steelers, 17-6, at New York. They...

GIFFORD SCORES

The Giants' lone touchdown came in the first period. Gifford plunged over for the score from three yards out, climaxing a 61-yard drive.

The Giants got their other three points on a 43-yard field goal by Pat Summerall in the second period. He missed two other field goal attempts.

Tom Miner accounted for seven Steeler points, kicking a 43-yard field goal and four conversions.

LaSalle Hits Top On 40-14 Victory

LaSalle High School, defending league and City champion, trampled St. James, 40-14, to stand alone in the lead. After Monsignor Bonner lowered St. James to a second-place tie.

The Chester team's 21-12 upset by Bonner gave St. James and Bishop Neumann identical 6-2 records. LaSalle has a 7-1 mark. Each team plays nine league games.

Neumann stayed in the race by beating Father Judge, 28-6, while in other games, West Catholic defeated North, 28-13, and Roman downed St. Thomas More, 28-0.

QUARDS STARS

Howard Guarini had a field day in leading LaSalle. He scored the first touchdown from the one, passed for three others. His scoring throws all came in the 32-point second quarter, during which LaSalle iced the game.

First he hit Fred Shaughnessy from the 30, then he tossed from the 20 to Gerry Weltemate, who made a diving catch. Finally he threw 40 yards to Tom Morey, who ran another 25 to complete a 65-yard play.

Joey Maxwell's 17-yard run and Tom Koss' four-yard and swept ground for other LaSalle TDs. Dougherty (3-5-1) tallied as John Grispon blocked a punt, recovered the ball and carried it five yards, with Dave Peak running the last 10.

Bob G.io's 46-yard run gave Neumann its upset of St. James. It was followed by Bill Grubb's two-point pass to Fran Welsh to give Bonner the lead for keeps, 14-8.

GRUBB'S SNEAK 7TES

A run of similar distance by Vince Czyzewski had given St. James a 6-0 start, but Bonner tied on Grubb's one-yard sneak at the end of a 77-yard drive.

After Giffin scored, St. James closed the gap on Charley O'Hara's 45-yard run. But Bonner's lead (14-12) was preserved when Tony Dolcemore blocked Al Filorsio's pass try for two points.

Later, Charley Ricevuto ran...

Continued on Page 28, Column 3

Colts Win, 17-0, Over Bears to Near West Title

CHICAGO, Nov. 16 (AP)—The running of Alan Ameche and the passing of George Shaw with a great defense to hand the Chicago Bears a 17-0 shutout—their first in 149 National Football League games.

The last time the Bears were blanked was in 1946 by the New York Giants, 14-0.

The Colts, who crushed the Bears earlier this season, 51-38, took a stranglehold on the Western Conference lead with a 17-0 record, while the Bears' bid collapsed with their third defeat.

49,664 SEE GAME

At one stage of the game, which attracted Wrigley Field's largest crowd of the season—49,664—quarterback Shaw hit on nine passes in a row, including 15 straight in a 49-yard scoring surge at the start of the second quarter.

During this drive, Shaw's serial accounted for 79 yards and was capped by his seven-yard toss to Ray Berry, who made a diving catch in the end zone.

Later in the second period, the Colts secured their only other touchdown on Ameche's 4-yard smash that ended a 95-yard thrust in four plays. Shaw's 23-yard pass to Lenny Moore touched it off and a 39-yard pass interference infraction set up Ameche's TD from the one.

AMECHE GAINS 142

In all, Ameche hammered 142 yards in 26 carries and Shaw made good on 10 of 23 passes for 191. Steve Myhra booted his 13-yard field goal in the last quarter.

In losing to the Colts for the fourth straight time, the Bears come closest to threatening a touchdown in the first quarter when they reached the 17 behind Willie Galimore's 17-yard dash. But a field goal attempt by George Blanda failed.

Galimore again broke loose in the second half in returning a punt 68 yards to the Colt 24. After moving to the 22 they fumbled away the ball.

Penn, Army Win With Haymakers

By JOHN DELL

In boxing parlance, it went something like this: Penn and Army were near-knockouts against opponents...

landed several roundhouse clouts; Temple, although overmatched again, gave a good account of itself, but Gettysburg caught it twice with its guard down.

Penn's 42-0 victory, the highest scorer in the five seasons under Steve Sebo, came on touchdown plays of 90, 87, 54, 41, 33 and 29 yards.

DAWKINS BRILLIANT

Villanova, despite Army's high statistical advantage to maintaining its unbeaten mark with a 26-6 victory, had the stopper for almost every Army maneuver, except the long ones made by particularly brilliant Pete Dawkins. He scored three times, on an 86-yard punt return, a 46-yard pass play from Joe Caldwell and a six-yard run. Army drove from its own territory to Villanova's end zone only once, late in the game.

Similarly, Gettysburg marched from beyond the midfield stripe once against Temple. The Bullets' other two touchdowns in a 33-6 victory stemmed from recoveries of Temple fumbles 30 and 12 yards from the goal.

Penn, now winner of four straight Ivy League games, has a chance to finish tied for second place on a combination of results, including a Penn victory over Cornell, also 4-2 in the league, on Thanksgiving.

TITLE TILT SATURDAY

Princeton, a 50-14 victor over Yale, and Dartmouth, which beat Cornell, 32-15, meet Saturday at Princeton to decide the title. Princeton coach Dick Colman thinks his Tigers have an excellent chance of retaining their championship, because they have momentum up. Colman also denied charges by Yale's Jordan Olivar that Princeton deliberately ran up the score to where it matched the previous high made against Yale by Penn in 1942. Colman declared, "We had everybody and his brother in there, includ...

Continued on Page 28, Column 3

Brown Clips Record, Browns Jolt 'Skins

WASHINGTON, Nov. 16 (UPI)—Jim Brown broke Steve Van Buren's 10-year National Football League rushing record today and led the Cleveland Browns to a 20-10 victory over the Washington Redskins. The big Cleveland fullback, needing 135 yards to tie Van Buren's mark of 1146 yards in a single season, made it with room to spare—152 yards in 27 carries. He also scored twice to come within one touchdown of matching another record—18 TD's in a season—and would have done it except for 62-yard scoring run that was called back for clipping.

But Brown was not the only hero of Cleveland's hard-fought victory, which bounced the Browns back into sole possession of first place in the NFL's Eastern Conference before 32,382.

It was veteran Lou Groza who contributed what proved to be the winning points with a 25-yard field goal in the closing minutes, a boot that broke a 10-10 tie. Brown's final touchdown—a five-yard cruise around end—came after Cleveland intercepted a desperation Washington pass on the Tribe's 11 with seconds to play.

BROWNS' EARLY LEAD

Until the last five minutes, the underdog Redskins played the Browns to a standstill. They spotted Cleveland an early lead when Milt Plum caught them napping on the third play of the game with a 74-yard pass play to Preston Carpenter. That put the ball on the Washington six and four plays later Brown scored from off tackle.

Ralph Guglielmi got the 'Skins back in the game a few minutes later when he threw a 64-yard scoring strike to halfback Jim Podoley, and the Redskins went in front briefly on Sam Baker's 35-yard field goal in the second period. But the boot was only necessary because two plays earlier, Podoley dropped Guglielmi's easiest pass in the open, in the clear zone for what would have been a certain TD.

Groza evened the count on a 10-yard field goal midway through the second quarter and the game stayed deadlocked in a bruising defensive battle until the Browns finally got a sustained drive going with nine minutes left to play.

What happened? Well, it seems as if Ram halfback Jack Morris (right) has deflected a pass and Packer Max McGee (85) is about to catch the ball for a score. That's what happened. Story on page 27.

Gedman Stars As Lions Win

DETROIT, Nov. 16 (UPI)—Gene Gedman, who hadn't thrown a pass all season, today fired one touchdown pass, set up another with a 30-yard toss and scored twice to lead the Detroit Lions to a 35-21 victory over the San Francisco 49ers before 54,523.

Gedman and quarterback Tobin Rote methodically picked apart the 49er pass defense, with Rote clicking for three touchdown passes for the second straight week.

The 49ers led briefly, 7-0, after recovering a fumble on the Detroit 28. But San Francisco didn't threaten again until the final period, when the Lions held a 28-7 margin.

Actually, the play that broke the 49ers' spirit came on Detroit's first play from scrimmage after San Francisco had scored. Rote handed off to Gedman, who fired a 26-yard pass to Cassady. The first Detroit halfback raced the remaining 46 yards.

The second touchdown capped a 91-yard drive. Gedman broke away 28 yards to the San Francisco 22 then rifled a pass to Steve Junker for the touchdown.

Rocky Delayed, Ramblers Fret

By FRANK DOLSON

Sickness in Rocky Bukavina's family has delayed the little winger's return to the Ramblers and may, in fact, force him to remain at his Kapuskasing, Ont., home, the Inquirer learned last night.

The Ramblers had announced Monday that Bukavina, a holdout, had agreed to terms over the phone and would report soon. Bukavina had been suspended by the Ramblers for failure to report to camp.

"It's up to Rocky now," Rambler president-manager George...

Chirp Signs

Edgar (Chirp) Brenchley, who resigned as coach and manager of the Ramblers last season, has signed as manager-coach of the Niagara Falls (Ont.) Rockets.

One of Brenchley's players is Alex Zabrluk, a Rambler in 1957-58.

Davis admitted, "I talked to him Friday night and thought he'd be on his way by now."

The 5-4½ winger was still in Kapuskasing last night, although unavailable for comment. His father didn't think Rocky would report.

"It's not a matter of salary terms, but family details that are holding him back," Davis emphasized. "I'll have to try to get hold of him tomorrow to see what I can do to help . . . It sure is a mess, but maybe something can still be worked out. We'll know better in a day or two."

Rambler player-coach Doug Adam refused comment except to say: "There'll be an official statement when we get to the bottom of this."

Davis indicated that word of Bukavina's resumption had not been sent to Kapuskasing through a mix-up in the Eastern Hockey League office. Because of that, Rocky has been playing for his home-town team, the Huskies. His injury factor slight but last Saturday night, according to his father.

Born Jan. 3, 1907, in Marquam, Oregon, Mr. Ridings was a high school and basketball star at the University of Oregon.

He served at Lt. Commander in the Navy during the Second World War and was with the Fourth Fleet in Brazil.

Blades Turn Back Clippers by 4-2

NEW HAVEN, Conn., Nov. 16 (AP)—The New Haven Blades defeated the Charlotte Clippers, 4-2, in an Eastern Hockey League game tonight before 3200 at the New Haven Arena.

Ivan Chadic, Don Davidson, Nick Donaldson and Hugh Riopelle scored for the winners who tied an early goal by Charlotte in the first period, added two more in the second and then split goals with the Clippers in the third.

Herve Lalonde and Ken Murphy scored for Charlotte.

Presidents Win In Overtime, 6-5

JOHNSTOWN, Pa., Nov. 16 (AP)—Winger Wally Kullman boosted in a goal at 1:11 of a sudden-death overtime period to give the Washington Presidents a 6-5 victory over the Johnstown Jets in an Eastern Hockey League game.

Steve Kuzma led the Presidents' attack with two goals. Frank Kuzma, Bernie Bernaqueur and Moose Lallo each contributed a tally for the winners.

Sports Results

Professional

FOOTBALL

NATIONAL LEAGUE

EAGLES 49 .... Chicago Cards 21
Cleveland 20 ...... Washington 10
Baltimore 17 ...... Chicago Bears 0
Detroit 35 .... San Francisco 21
Green Bay 20 ...... Los Angeles 7
PITTSBURGH 31 .... N. Y. Giants 10

Standings

Eastern Conference
	W	L	T	Pct.
Cleveland	7	2	0	.778
New York	6	3	0	.667
Pittsburgh	5	4	0	.556
EAGLES	2	6	1	.250
Washington	3	6	0	.333
Chi. Cards	2	7	0	.222

Western Conference
	W	L	T	Pct.
Baltimore	8	1	0	.889
Chi. Bears	6	3	0	.667
Los Angeles	6	4	0	.600
San Fran.	4	5	0	.444
Detroit	3	5	1	.375
Green Bay	1	8	1	.111

BASKETBALL

NATIONAL ASSOCIATION

Eastern Division				

HOCKEY

NATIONAL LEAGUE

AMERICAN LEAGUE

SOCCER

School

FOOTBALL

CATHOLIC LEAGUE

LaSalle 40 .... St. James 14
Neumann 28 .... Father Judge 6
Bonner 21 .... Chester 12

Cards Win Two In Japan Finale

TOKYO, Nov. 16 (AP)—The St. Louis Cardinals (14-2) wound up their 16-game Japan tour today by handing the Japan All Stars a double drubbing, 8-2, 4-1.

More than 40,000 American and Japanese, including U. S. Ambassador Douglas MacArthur, 2d, saw the American team overtake the Japanese with a three-run seventh-inning rally to win the second game.

The Cards hammered out 22 hits in the first game, including two home runs by catcher Gene Green. They scored five runs in the third inning to put the game on ice. Sad Sam Jones and Phil Paine limited the Japanese to five hits.

Ridings Dies at 51; Columbia Coach

NEW YORK, Nov. 16 (UPI)—Gordon Ridings, who guided Columbia's basketball team to three Eastern Intercollegiate League championships in five years, died early today of a heart attack. He was 51.

Ridings was head coach at Columbia from 1946 to 1952. His teams won a total of 94 games and lost 12 for an .810 percentage. He won the Eastern title in 1949-47 with a 11-5 mark, repeated and won a third title in 1951-52 with a 22-1 mark.

Born Jan. 3, 1907, in Marquam, Oregon, Mr. Ridings was a high school and basketball star at the University of Oregon.

Amerks Beat Bears

ROCHESTER, N. Y., Nov. 16 (AP)—The Rochester Americans snapped a five-game losing streak by defeating the Hershey Bears, 5-1, in an American Hockey League game tonight.

As lines clash in a T-formation play, St. James High quarterback Al Filoreta prepares to hand off ball to Ronald Rogers in second quarter of yesterday's game with Monsignor Bonner at Villanova Stadium. Bonner won, 21-12.

Musical Foes Run the Scale

A trumpet player ran a scale ranging from 35 to 58 yards to make three touchdowns and lead the Philadelphia Music Academy to a 26-12 victory over Curtis Institute in the "Melody Bowl" football game yesterday at Merchantville, N. J.

The winners also scored on a 45-yard pass from a clarinetist to another trumpeter. The losers' heavy work was done by a tuba player, who raced on an interception, and a trombonist, on a pass reception, for a touchdown. The players on the seven-man team (four linemen, three backs) played without music. Neither school had a band at the game.

November 17, 1958
Clarence Peaks scores four touchdowns as the Eagles crush the Chicago Cardinals 49-21

1959

RECORD: 7-5, T-2ND IN NFL EAST
HEAD COACH: BUCK SHAW

Schedule
Regular Season

Wk. 1	Sep 27	L	24-14	at San Francisco 49ers
Wk. 2	Oct 4	W	49-21	vs New York Giants
Wk. 3	Oct 11	W	28-24	vs Pittsburgh Steelers
Wk. 4	Oct 18	L	24-7	at New York Giants
Wk. 5	Oct 25	W	28-24	at Chicago Cardinals (at Minneapolis, MN)
Wk. 6	Nov 1	W	30-23	vs Washington Redskins
Wk. 7	Nov 8	L	28-7	at Cleveland Browns
Wk. 8	Nov 15	W	27-17	vs Chicago Cardinals
Wk. 9	Nov 22	W	23-20	vs Los Angeles Rams
Wk. 10	Nov 29	L	31-0	at Pittsburgh Steelers
Wk. 11	Dec 6	W	34-14	at Washington Redskins
Wk. 12	Dec 13	L	28-21	vs Cleveland Browns

Quarterback Norm Van Brocklin became one of the league's top passers, hitting targets like Tommy McDonald (47 receptions for 846 yards and 10 touchdowns) and Pete Retzlaff (34 catches for 595 yards and one touchdown). Tragedy struck as NFL commissioner (and once Eagles owner) Bert Bell collapsed and died while watching the Eagles defeat Pittsburgh 28-24 at Franklin Field. The Eagles would finish the season with a 7-5 record and tied for second place with the Cleveland Browns.

1959 Philadelphia Eagles Stats

Passing	Comp	Att	Comp %	Yds	Y/Att	TD	Int	Rating
Norm Van Brocklin	191	340	56.2	2617	7.70	16	14	79.5
Sonny Jurgensen	3	5	60.0	27	5.40	1	0	114.2
Billy Barnes	0	7	0.0	0	0.00	0	2	0.0

Rushing	Rush	Yds	Avg	TD
Billy Barnes	181	687	3.8	7
Clarence Peaks	124	451	3.6	3
Theron Sapp	41	145	3.5	1
Walt Kowalczyk	26	37	1.4	0
Norm Van Brocklin	11	13	1.2	2
Bobby Walston	2	8	4.0	0
Joe Pagliei	2	-5	-2.5	0
Tommy McDonald	2	-10	-5.0	0
Pete Retzlaff	2	-11	-5.5	0

Receiving	Rec	Yds	Avg	TD
Tommy McDonald	47	846	18.0	10
Pete Retzlaff	34	595	17.5	1
Billy Barnes	32	314	9.8	2
Clarence Peaks	28	209	7.5	0
Bobby Walston	16	279	17.4	3
Dick Bielski	15	264	17.6	1
Walt Kowalczyk	9	33	3.7	0
Theron Sapp	6	47	7.8	0
Ken MacAfee	5	48	9.6	0
Joe Pagliei	2	9	4.5	0

Punting	Punts	Yds	Avg	Blocked
Joe Pagliei	1	45	45.0	0
Norm Van Brocklin	53	2263	42.7	0

Interceptions	Int	Yds	Avg	TD
Jimmy Carr	5	65	13.0	0
Bob Pellegrini	3	42	14.0	0
Art Powell	3	17	5.7	0
Tom Brookshier	3	13	4.3	0
Chuck Weber	2	8	4.0	0
Gene Johnson	1	22	22.0	0
Marion Campbell	1	0	0.0	0
Ed Khayat	1	0	0.0	0
Lee Riley	1	0	0.0	0

Kicking	PAT Made	PAT Att	PAT %	FG Made	FG Att	FG %	Pts
Bobby Walston	33	34	97	0	1	0.0	51
Paige Cothren	1	1	100	8	18	44.4	25
Dick Bielski	0	0	0	0	5	0.0	6

24 abdh★ THE PHILADELPHIA INQUIRER, MONDAY MORNING, OCTOBER 5, 1959

Record Crowd Plays Part in Dodger Win

Key Single Is Blamed On White Background

By ALLEN LEWIS
Inquirer Reporter

LOS ANGELES, Oct. 4.—For the first time in World Series history, the crowd may have been the deciding factor in victory or defeat Sunday. The greatest collection of baseball fans—92,294—in major league annals gathered in the huge, odd-sized Coliseum and their very presence influenced the Los Angeles Dodgers 3-1 win over the Chicago White Sox.

In the infield and outfield and even behind the plate, players of both teams agreed it was extremely hard to follow the ball against the multitude of white shirts that formed the background in the third game of the Series.

Carl Furillo's ground single to center that scored the first two runs might well have been handled in a normal ball park with a normal background.

HIT LOOKED LIKE OUT

Furillo's key seventh-inning hit looked as if it could have been fielded when it left the bat—particularly since Sox shortstop Luis Aparicio is an accredited fielding magician.

"I can't see the ball come off the bat," the pleasant Venezuelan said in his locker cubicle after the game. "I got a pretty good jump on the ball but not like I would normally.

"If I had I would have been more in front of the ball. As it was I had to reach for it. I thought I was going to get it, but the ball hopped over my glove." he added with a shrug of his thin shoulders.

BOTHERED CARL, TOO

Furillo himself, a veteran of two seasons here, admitted that the tough background was the only thing he was worried about when he went up to the plate to bat for Don Demeter in the climax of a rather dull game.

"You know how it is here for most day games," the former Reading Ride said. "We never have anyone sitting out in center field, and before I left the dugout I knew it was going to be tough to follow the ball from what our fellows had told me.

"One reason I took that first pitch—a curve ball—was because I wanted to find out how hard it was see. Then he threw me a sinker and I hit it and that was that.

BIG HIT IN PLAYOFF

"But the big hit for me was the one the other day against the Braves (that helped win the game in the 12th inning). I'd have to say this was sort of an anti-climax," said Furillo, who added he hoped to play two more years and then retire — as a Dodger, if possible.

Dodger Manager Walter Alston, who it seems has smiled more in the past week than in the past three seasons combined, thought the background was a factor.

"I not only think it influenced this game," Alston said, "but I think it's going to continue to be a big factor with 92,000 at every game.

"I don't say it will always help us too much, though, because we hardly ever play any day games here. We only played about 12 here this season and then never had that many people. But I think the pitching to capitalize on it."

LOPEZ CAUTIOUS

Sox Manager Al Lopez, cautious because he doesn't want to make excuses for his club's defeat, said, "It's a park, a beautiful stadium," implying it wasn't his doing. "But if the Sox had rallied to pull out the victory in the eighth when they trailed, 2-0, the "goat"

Series Lineups

White Sox	Dodgers
11 Aparicio, ss	19 Gilliam, 3b
3 Fox, 2b	42 Neal, 2b
1 Landis, cf	9 Moon, rf
8 Kluszewski, 1b	1 Larker, lf
10 Lollar, c	14 Hodges, 1b
4 Goodman, 3b	24 Demeter, cf
16 Smith, lf	41 Roseboro, c
5 Phillips, 3b	30 Wills, ss
34 Wynn, p	36 Craig, p

WHITE SOX—3 McAnany; 6 Goodman; 31 Esposito; 15 Mc-Bride; 17 Torgeson; 16 Latman; 19 Pierce; 28 Romano; 21 Shaw; 32 Donovan; 26 Battey; 27 Lown; 29 Moore; 23 Cicotello, coach; 34 Cooney, coach; 25 Shaw; 37 Berres, coach; 36 Cash; 20 Gutteridge, coach; 42 Lopez, manager; 49 Arias.

DODGERS—Reese, coach; 4 Snider; 6 Furillo; 7 Dressen, coach; 8 Fairly; 16 McDevitt; 38 Repulski; 22 Fowler; 33 Zimmer; 24 Alston, manager; 25 Essegian; 31 Mulleavy, coach; 32 Koufas; 35 Labine; 45 Klippstein; 40 Williams; 41 Labine; 45 Churn; 51 Sherry; 53 Drysdale; 58 Pignatano.

TELEVISION—WRCV, Channel 3, 4:45 P. M.; RADIO—WRCV, 1000, 1:45 P. M.

Jim Rivera rides an invisible sled and the White Sox outfielder coasts toward second on an attempted steal in the second inning. Maury Wills covers.

Wills jumps clear of Rivera after tagging him out. Dodgers won to lead World Series, 2-1.
AP Photos

Eagles Romp as McDonald Scores 4

By HERB GOOD

Lifted to startling heights by the tornado-like performance of speedy Tommy McDonald, the Eagles walloped the New York Giants in the soundling tune of 49-21 before 27,035 delighted sunbaked onlookers at Franklin Field Sunday.

McDonald, a jet-propelled 182-pounder who always has that vital extra boost in reserve, scored four big touchdowns as the Eagles rebounded with stunning violence from their opening-game loss at San Francisco to even their NFL ledger in their home debut.

Enjoying his greatest hours since coming here from the University of Oklahoma campus three years ago, McDonald scored on pass plays of 32, 55 and 19 yards and returned a punt 81 thrilling yards for the final tally.

Quarterback Norm Van Brocklin, who threw perfect strikes for McDonald's first two scores, rookie Theron Sapp and line-backer Chuck Weber, who fell on a fumble in the end zone, also made touchdowns as the Eagles handed the Giants their worst setback since the Cleveland Browns beat them, 62-14, in 1953.

It was the most one-sided Philadelphia conquest of the New Yorkers since a 45-0 romp in 1948. It was the second straight year that Buck Shaw's

Picture on Page 29

charges upset the Giants here after losing their opening game.

The Giants, who overcame last year's loss in the Eastern title, were never in this one although you'd never believe it by the statistics, which gave the invaders a 333-259 net yardage edge rushing and passing.

The Eagles grabbed an early 14-0 lead, led at halftime, 21-7, and skyrocketed their edge to 42-7 in the second half before the Giants were able to rally for two fourth-period TDs.

Rookie Art Powell, who contributed one of the key blocks on McDonald's punt-return TD in the closing minutes of the first half, provided one of the sunny day's big thrills when he returned the second-half kickoff 95 yards, probably the longest non-scoring such return in the league's history.

Powell had a clear path to the goal, but inside the five he tried to take an extra long stride and

Other National League Football Games Page 29

stumbled and fell on the two. Assistant Coach Charley Gauer said later he thought Powell slipped in a hole in the name time the rookie lengthened his stride.

Powell had no regrets since Van Brocklin scored on a one-yard sneak three plays later.

But this was a McDonald story from start to finish, another superlative chapter in a career that seems destined to be one of the most glorious in Eagle history.

Although a marked man, Mc-Donald caught six passes for 133 yards all told, and in addition to his spectacular punt return he

Continued on Page 28, Column 3

'Leetle' Bad Bounce Becomes Nightmare For Aparicio, Chisox

LOS ANGELES, Oct. 4 (AP)—A "leetle" bad bounce and a heroic pitcher who tried changing into the glum White Sox dressing room. "If the ball stays down I have a chance to get it," said Sox shortstop Luis Aparicio of Carl Furillo's pinch single that broke up Sunday's third World Series game.

Furillo's shot bounded just out of Aparicio's reach into center field, scoring the first two Dodger runs in the seventh inning.

Venezuelan Aparicio, tabbed as one of the greatest shortstops ever to play in the American League, said:

"I got a good enough start on Furillo's ball, but it took a leetle bad bounce over my glove. The background is rough on fielders on."

"You can't see the ball coming off the bat."

World Series At a Glance

STANDINGS

	W.	L.	Pct.
Los Angeles	2	1	.667
Chicago	1	2	.333

FIRST GAME

At Chicago, Oct. 1
Los Angeles 0 0 0 0 0 0 0 0 0—0 8 0
Chicago 2 0 7 0 0 0 2 0 x—11 11 0

CRAIG, Churn (3), Labine (4), Koufax (5), Klippstein (7) and Roseboro; WYNN, Staley (8) and Lollar.
Home runs—Chicago, Kluszewski 2.

SECOND GAME

At Chicago, Oct. 2
Los Angeles 0 0 0 1 2 0 0 0 0—4 9 1
Chicago 0 0 0 0 1 0 2 0 0—3 8 1

PODRES, Sherry (7) and Roseboro; SHAW, Lown (8) and Lollar.
Home runs—Los Angeles, Neal 2, Essegian.

THIRD GAME

At Los Angeles, Oct. 4
Chicago 0 0 0 0 0 0 0 1 0—1 8 1
Los Angeles 0 0 0 0 0 0 3 0 x—3 5 0

DONOVAN, Staley (7) and Lollar, Chicago; DRYSDALE, Sherry (8) and Roseboro, Los Angeles.

REMAINING GAMES

Fourth game, at Los Angeles, Monday, Oct. 5.
Fifth game, at Los Angeles, Tuesday, Oct. 6.
Sixth game, if necessary, at Chicago, Thursday, Oct. 8.
Seventh game, if necessary, at Chicago, Friday, Oct. 9.

THIRD GAME FINANCIAL FIGURES

Attendance 92,294
receipts $594,971.24
Players' share $260,026.66
Commissioner's share $82,260.70
Clubs and Leagues' share $49,622.19

THREE-GAME TOTALS

Attendance 187,625
Total receipts $917,452.63
Players' share $811,606.86
Commissioner's share $179,726.33
Clubs and Leagues' share $267,164.61

Rangers Win, 4-2

ST. PAUL, Minn., Oct. 4 (AP)—The New York Rangers wound up their week-end exhibition series with the Winnipeg Warriors Sunday with a 4-2 victory.

'Lucky to Win,' Alston Concedes

LOS ANGELES, Oct. 4 (UPI)—Walt Alston frankly conceded the White Sox out-played his Dodgers Sunday and made no secret that he felt "we were lucky to win."

"What else can you say when they get 12 hits and so many walks, and we get only five" commented the soft-spoken Los Angeles skipper.

"Nope, I'm not going to make any predictions on how many games it will take us to win. (I) added. "A lot of things can happen yet."

For the most part, the Dodgers' dressing room was uncommonly quiet and one might have gotten the idea they had lost instead of won. Even Carl Furillo, whose two-run single in the seventh proved the key blow, wasn't shouting or carrying on.

'LITTLE SURPRISED'

"I thought that ball I hit was going through the infield," he said, "although I didn't spend too much time looking. I was a little surprised when they called on me to hit for (Don) Demeter. I figured they were going to use (Duke (Snider)."

Alston made it plain he needed someone up there who doesn't strike out," Alston explained. "Furillo was the perfect choice because he generally meets the ball. If I wanted the long ball, I would've gone for either (Chuck) Essegian or Snider."

DON'S NOT UPSET

Don Drysdale, who started for the Dodgers, pitched his way in and out of trouble, and gave way to Larry Sherry in the eighth, said he wasn't particularly upset over being pulled.

"Naturally, I would have liked to stay in the ball game," he said, "but he (Alston) came out and told me I had thrown a lot of balls and Sherry was warm. As long as we win, I don't care who wins it."

Rudy Larussa, former Dartmouth star and the St. Louis Browns, former minor leaguer, got into the game in the seventh.

Haney Refuses New Pact, Quits As Braves' Pilot

LOS ANGELES, Oct. 4 (AP)—Fred Haney resigned Sunday night as manager of the Milwaukee Braves, of the National League.

Haney, who led the Braves to two pennants and one world championship in the 2¾ years he handled the team, met with owner Lou Perini, president Joseph Cairns, vice president Birdie Tebbetts and general manager John McHale to discuss his future.

He was offered a one-year contract to return as Braves' manager but turned it down.

FAMILY COMES FIRST

Haney said he was perfectly happy with the Braves, but that he wanted to spend more time with his family.

"It is not fair to myself or to my family with whom I have not spent much time while managing," he said.

"Nothing whatsoever that happened during the past season influenced my decision," said Haney.

He obviously was referring to the fact that the Braves lost the National League pennant to the Los Angeles Dodgers in a playoff.

WANTS VACATION

"All the officials of the club have given me 100 percent cooperation," he added. "Right now I have nothing on my mind except to take a vacation with Mrs. Haney."

The 62-year-old Haney replaced Charley Grimm as manager of the Braves on June 15, 1956. He previously had managed the Pittsburgh Pirates and the St. Louis Browns. He spent most of his playing career with the Detroit Tigers.

Haney won the pennant in '57 and beat the New York Yankees in seven games in the World series. He won the pennant in '58, but lost to the Yanks in seven games after winning three of the first four.

Dodgers Win, 3-1, On Hit by Furillo

By OSCAR FRALEY
Continued From First Page

Up to this point, Donovan had appeared invincible, not even giving up a walk.

Neal went to second as Wally Moon grounded out to Nellie Fox, but then Donovan wearied. He walked Norm Larker on four straight pitches and walked Gil Hodges on three pitches to fill the bases.

That was all for the big Irishman, Staley, the White Sox relief ace, came on—and so did Furillo.

Furillo, batting for Don Demeter, lashed the single which sent Neal and Larker barrelling across the plate with two big runs as Hodges held up at second. Staley got out of it when he slid into third and Roseboro lined to Fox to end the rally.

The White Sox roared back in a vain attempt to pull it out. Big Ted Kluszewski laced a single to left and went to second as Sherry Lollar followed with a single to right field which Wally Moon lost in the sun.

That was when Drysdale left. Sherry caused a faint uproar among the few White Sox fans when he hit Billy Goodman on the right knee to fill the bases. But then he fed a double play ball to Al Smith which let Big Klu score with one run, but ended the threat by getting Jim Rivera on a pop to Roseboro.

The Dodgers got that one right back when Maury Wills led off the eighth with a single to right and Sherry sacrificed him to second. He went to third as Gilliam was grounded out and scored on Neal's double off Sam Esposito's glove.

Staley kept Neal there as he got Moon to ground out—and then it was up to Sherry.

That was when Drysdale left. Young Larry didn't let the Dodgers down. He struck out pinch-hitter Norm Cash, sent a third strike whistling past Aparicio, allowed Fox a single—and then finished striking out the side by getting Fox.

Wynn, Craig Duel Again

Early Wynn and Roger Craig, the starting pitchers in last Thursday's World Series opener, again will face each other Monday in another battle of righthanders at the Coliseum.

Wynn, 22-10 during the regular season for the White Sox, beat Craig in the first game, 11-0, although forced to leave in the eighth inning when his elbow stiffened. Craig (11-5) was routed by the Sox in a three-run third inning.

But He Has Faith

Furillo's Son Shuns Prayer

From Our Wire Services

LOS ANGELES, Oct. 4.—CARL FURILLO'S 10-year-old son, Butch, sat next to sports writer Dick Young in the Coliseum press box Sunday. When his dad came up to pinch hit, Young whispered to the youngster: "Say a prayer for your old man."

"I don't have to say a prayer," was the answer. "I know my pop. He'll get a hit!" (He did).

Nellie Fox broke out in fever blisters around the mouth and White Sox trainer Ed Froehlich applied medicine to soothe his lips. Looked like lipstick and he took a ribbing.

"I don't have to make any explanations," he laughed.

Continued on Page 28, Column 6

Dodgers 17-10 Series Pick

NEW YORK, Oct. 4 (UPI)—The Los Angeles Dodgers became a 17-10 pick to win the World Series after taking a 2-1 lead in games over the White Sox in Sunday's third game. Monday's fourth game was rated an 11-10 pick 'em affair by New York odds-makers.

Celtics Defeat Lakers, 107-84

BOSTON, Oct. 4 (AP)—Boston outmaneuvered Minneapolis on a slippery floor Sunday night in a 107-84 National Basketball Association exhibition victory.

The Celtics, defending world champions, made it four straight over the Lakers in their first game exhibition tour minus Bob Cousy and Tommy Heinsohn. Cousy was out with the flu and Heinsohn was sidelined by water on the knee.

Continued on Page 28, Column 1

DICK ACTS BITTER

Donovan, who pitched magnificently through the first six innings, was crestfallen, perhaps a little bitter.

"No. I wasn't tired." he snapped. "All didn't ask me. After all, he won the pennant and I guess he knew what he was doing."

The Go-Go Sox expressed admiration for Dodger catcher

Continued on Page 28, Column 3

Here's that catch. Jim Landis, White Sox center-fielder, makes a belly-flop dive for ball hit by Junior

Gilliam in the first inning. Jim Rivera, Sox left-fielder, has closest view of play of the day.
UPI Telephoto

The hit that won it bounds into the outfield, beyond White Sox shortstop Luis Aparicio. Nelson Fox (2) watches the ball, which Carl Furillo hit for a two-run single in the seventh inning.
AP Wirephoto

October 5, 1959
Tommy McDonald scores four touchdowns as the Eagles soar pass the NY Giants 49-21

60's Decade in Review

Decade Win-Loss Record:
57-76-5; (1-0 postseason record)

Home Field:
Franklin Field 1960-69

Playoff Appearances:
None

Championships:
NFL Champion Game 1960
NFL Champions 1960

Head Coaches:
Buck Shaw 1960 (10-2), (1-0 postseason record); Nick Skorich 1961-63 (15-24-3);
Joe Kuharich 1964-68 (28-41-1); Jerry Williams 1969 (4-9-1)

Hall of Fame Inductees:
Chuck Bednarik, Bill Bradley, Tom Brookshier, Timmy Brown, Jim Gallagher (executive),
Sonny Jurgensen, Tommy McDonald, Pete Retzlaff, Norm Van Brocklin

Award Winners:
Norm Van Brocklin, MVP 1960; Buck Shaw, Coach of the Year 1960; Pete Retzlaff, MVP 1965

All Pro:
Chuck Bednarik 1960-61; Tom Brookshier 1960; Don Burroughs 1960-62;
Tommy McDonald 1960-62; Jess Richardson 1960; Norm Van Brocklin 1960;
Maxie Baughan 1961 and 1964-65; Sonny Jurgensen 1961; Leo Sugar 1961;
Tim Brown 1963 and 1965-66; Bob Brown 1964-68; Pete Retzlaff 1964-66;
Jim Ringo 1964 and 1966; Tom Woodeschick 1968-69

Pro Bowl Selections:
Billy Ray Barnes 1960, Jess Richardson 1960, Maxie Baughan 1961-62 and 1964-66;
Chuck Bednarik 1961; Tom Brookshier 1960-61; Marion Campbell 1960-61;
Tommy McDonald 1960-63; Pete Retzlaff 1961 and 1964-65; Norm Van Brocklin 1960-61;
Ted Dean 1962; Bobby Walston 1962; Sonny Jurgensen 1962; J.D. Smith 1962;
Tim Brown 1963-64 and 1966; Sam Baker 1965 and 1969; Irv Cross 1965-66; Floyd Peters 1965-68;
Jim Ringo 1965-66 and 1968; Bob Brown 1966-67; Norm Snead 1966; Tom Woodeschick 1969

First Game of the Decade:
September 25, 1960, loss to the Cleveland Browns 41-24

Last Game of the Decade:
December 21, 1969, loss to San Francisco 49ers 14-13

Largest Margin of Victory:
October 22, 1961, huge win over the Dallas Cowboys 43-7

Largest Margin of Defeat:
October 9, 1966, losing to the Dallas Cowboys 56-7

Eagle Firsts of the Decade:
First Hall of Fame Inductee Bert Bell became a charter member of the
Pro Football Hall of Fame in 1963
First 3,000-Yard Passer – Sonny Jurgensen threw 3,723 total yards in 1961
First 30 TD Passes – Sonny Jurgensen threw 32 touchdowns during the 1961 season
First 2 Kickoff Returns for touchdowns in one game – November 6, 1966, Tim Brown returned
two kickoffs for touchdowns of 93 and 90 yards respectively

60's Decade in Review

1960 remains the most celebrated year in Eagle history. Shaw, Van Brocklin and Bednarik (each in his last season before retirement) led a team more notable for its grit than its talent (one observer later quipped that the team had "nothing but a championship") to its first division title since 1949. On December 26, 1960, one of the coldest days in recorded Philadelphia history, the Eagles faced Vince Lombardi's Green Bay Packers in the NFL title game and dealt the mighty Lombardi the sole championship game loss of his storied career. Bednarik was the last NFL player to play an entire game without leaving the field in that game, lining up at center on offense and at linebacker on defense. Fittingly, the game ended as Bednarik tackled a struggling Jim Taylor and refused to allow him to stand until the last seconds had ticked away.

Flush with excitement from the 17-13 victory, with the talented Jurgensen poised to take the reigns of the offense, the future looked promising indeed. That promise, however, proved illusory.

In 1961, the Eagles finished just a half-game behind the New York Giants for first place in the Eastern Conference standings with a 10-4 record. Despite the on-the-field success, however, the franchise was in turmoil. Van Brocklin had come to Philadelphia and agreed to play through 1960 with the tacit understanding that, upon his retirement as a player, he would assume the mantle of Head Coach. Ownership, however, opted to hire Nick Skorich upon Buck Shaw's retirement, and Van Brocklin quit the organization in a fit of pique. In 1962, the bottom dropped out as the team was decimated by injury and managed only three wins. The off-field chaos would continue through 1963, as the remaining 65 shareholders out of the original Happy Hundred sold the team to Jerry Wolman, a 36-year-old Washington developer who outbid local bidders for the team, paying an unprecedented $5,505,000 for control of the club. In 1964, Wolman hired former Cardinals and Washington Redskins coach Joe Kuharich to a lifetime contract.

Kuharich would prove utterly unworthy of the honor, wasting top-tier talent such as Timmy Brown, Ollie Matson, Ben Hawkins and Jurgensen and effectively running the franchise into the ground. At Kuharich's insistence, Jurgensen was traded to the Redskins for Norm Snead in 1964: Jurgensen would go on to a Hall of Fame career while Snead, although serviceable, lacked the talent to lift the team out of mediocrity. By 1968, fans were in full revolt. Chants of "Joe must go" echoed through the increasingly empty bleachers of Franklin Field. Adding insult to injury, the Eagles managed to eke out meaningless wins in two of the last three games of the season, costing the franchise the first pick in the draft, and with it the opportunity to add O.J. Simpson to the roster. (With the second pick, the Eagles chose Leroy Keyes, who played only four years in an Eagles uniform.) The last game of 1968 helped cement the rowdy reputation of Philadelphia fans when they booed and threw snowballs at depiction of Santa Claus. By 1969, Wolman, a former millionaire, was bankrupt and the franchise under the administration of a federal bankruptcy court. At the end of the bankruptcy proceedings, the Eagles were sold to Leonard Tose, the self-made trucking millionaire and original member of the Happy Hundred. Tose's first official act was to fire Kuharich.

1960

RECORD: 10-2, 1ST IN NFL EAST
HEAD COACH: BUCK SHAW

Schedule

Regular Season

Wk. 3	Sep 25	L	41-24	vs Cleveland Browns
Wk. 4	Sep 30	W	27-25	at Dallas Cowboys
Wk. 5	Oct 9	W	31-27	vs St. Louis Cardinals
Wk. 6	Oct 16	W	28-10	vs Detroit Lions
Wk. 7	Oct 23	W	31-29	at Cleveland Browns
Wk. 9	Nov 6	W	34-7	vs Pittsburgh Steelers
Wk. 10	Nov 13	W	19-13	vs Washington Redskins
Wk. 11	Nov 20	W	17-10	at New York Giants
Wk. 12	Nov 27	W	31-23	vs New York Giants
Wk. 13	Dec 4	W	20-6	at St. Louis Cardinals
Wk. 14	Dec 11	L	27-21	at Pittsburgh Steelers
Wk. 15	Dec 18	W	38-28	at Washington Redskins

Post Season

League Championship

Dec 26	W	17-13	vs Green Bay Packers

The Eagles started the season out on the wrong foot by losing their season opener at home to the Cleveland Browns 41-24. A week later the Eagles would barely beat the expansion Cowboys by a score of 27-25 in Dallas. However, from there the Eagles would soar, winning nine straight to capture the Eastern Division with a 10-2 record. Spurring on the Eagles was quarterback Norm Van Brocklin, who had a spectacular season by passing for 2,471 yards, and Chuck Bednarik, who played sixty minutes a game at center and linebacker. Bednarik made his presence felt in a big way in a 17-10 win over the Giants in New York on November 20, when he laid a ferocious hit on Frank Gifford that nearly ended the star wide receiver's career. In the NFL Championship Game at Franklin Field, the Eagles faced the Green Bay Packers. After holding a 10-6 lead throughout the third quarter, the Eagles suddenly found themselves trailing 13-10 when the Packers scored early in the fourth. However, Ted Dean would return the ensuing kickoff deep into Packers territory as the Eagles retook the lead 17-13 with 5:21 left in the game. The Packers would not go down quietly, driving deep into Eagles territory. However, Bednarik would save the game with a crushing tackle of Jim Taylor on the eight-yard line as time expired, clinching the Eagles third NFL Championship. Following the season both Coach Buck Shaw and quarterback Norm Van Brocklin retired.

1960 Philadelphia Eagles Stats

Passing	Comp	Att	Comp %	Yds	Y/Att	TD	Int	Rating
Norm Van Brocklin	153	284	53.9	2471	8.70	24	17	86.5
Sonny Jurgensen	24	44	54.5	486	11.05	5	1	122.0
Billy Barnes	0	3	0.0	0	0.00	0	2	0.0

Rushing	Rush	Yds	Avg	TD
Clarence Peaks	86	465	5.4	3
Billy Barnes	117	315	2.7	4
Ted Dean	113	304	2.7	0
Timmy Brown	9	35	3.9	2
Theron Sapp	9	20	2.2	0
Sonny Jurgensen	4	5	1.3	0
Pete Retzlaff	2	3	1.5	0
Norm Van Brocklin	11	-13	-1.2	0

Receiving	Rec	Yds	Avg	TD
Pete Retzlaff	46	826	18.0	5
Tommy McDonald	39	801	20.5	13
Bobby Walston	30	563	18.8	4
Billy Barnes	19	132	6.9	2
Ted Dean	15	218	14.5	3
Clarence Peaks	14	116	8.3	0
Timmy Brown	9	247	27.4	2
Dick Lucas	3	34	11.3	0
Theron Sapp	2	20	10.0	0

Punting	Punts	Yds	Avg	Blocked
Norm Van Brocklin	60	2585	43.1	0

Interceptions	Int	Yds	Avg	TD
Don Burroughs	9	124	13.8	0
Chuck Weber	6	48	8.0	0
Bobby Freeman	4	67	16.8	0
Maxie Baughan	3	50	16.7	0
Gene Johnson	3	34	11.3	0
Jimmy Carr	2	4	2.0	0
Chuck Bednarik	2	0	0.0	0
Tom Brookshier	1	14	14.0	0

Kicking	PAT Made	PAT Att	PAT %	FG Made	FG Att	FG %	Pts
Bobby Walston	39	40	98	14	20	70.0	105

December 27, 1960
Eagles come from behind victory over the Green Bay Packers,
17-13 to win the NFL Championship. Coach Buck Shaw
and Norm Van Brocklin retire after season

73

1961

RECORD: 10-4, 2ND IN NFL EAST
HEAD COACH: NICK SKORICH

Schedule
Regular Season

Wk. 2	Sep 17	W	27-20	vs Cleveland Browns
Wk. 3	Sep 24	W	14-7	vs Washington Redskins
Wk. 4	Oct 1	L	30-27	vs St. Louis Cardinals
Wk. 5	Oct 8	W	21-16	vs Pittsburgh Steelers
Wk. 6	Oct 15	W	20-7	at St. Louis Cardinals
Wk. 7	Oct 22	W	43-7	at Dallas Cowboys
Wk. 8	Oct 29	W	27-24	at Washington Redskins
Wk. 9	Nov 5	W	16-14	vs Chicago Bears
Wk. 10	Nov 12	L	38-21	at New York Giants
Wk. 11	Nov 19	L	45-24	at Cleveland Browns
Wk. 12	Nov 26	W	35-13	vs Dallas Cowboys
Wk. 13	Dec 3	W	35-24	at Pittsburgh Steelers
Wk. 14	Dec 10	L	28-24	vs New York Giants
Wk. 15	Dec 17	W	27-24	at Detroit Lions

Nick Skorich was named the new head coach as Sonny Jurgensen took over as the starting quarterback. Jurgensen won seven of the first eight games and ended up with a record season, passing for 3,723 yards and connecting on 32 touchdown passes. However, the Eagles who finished with a 10-4 record and had to settle for second place after two costly losses to the New York Giants.

1961 Philadelphia Eagles Stats

Passing	Comp	Att	Comp %	Yds	Y/Att	TD	Int	Rating
Sonny Jurgensen	235	416	56.5	3723	8.95	32	24	88.1
King Hill	6	12	50.0	101	8.42	2	2	78.8
Clarence Peaks	0	1	0.0	0	0.00	0	0	39.6

Rushing	Rush	Yds	Avg	TD
Clarence Peaks	135	471	3.5	5
Timmy Brown	50	338	6.8	1
Ted Dean	66	321	4.9	2
Billy Barnes	92	309	3.4	1
Sonny Jurgensen	20	27	1.4	0
Theron Sapp	7	24	3.4	1
King Hill	2	9	4.5	0
Pete Retzlaff	1	8	8.0	0

Receiving	Rec	Yds	Avg	TD
Tommy McDonald	64	1144	17.9	13
Pete Retzlaff	50	769	15.4	8
Bobby Walston	34	569	16.7	2
Clarence Peaks	32	472	14.8	0
Ted Dean	21	335	16.0	1
Billy Barnes	15	194	12.9	3
Timmy Brown	14	264	18.9	2
Dick Lucas	8	67	8.4	5
Theron Sapp	3	10	3.3	0

Punting	Punts	Yds	Avg	Blocked
King Hill	55	2403	43.7	0

Interceptions	Int	Yds	Avg	TD
Don Burroughs	7	90	12.9	0
Irv Cross	2	36	18.0	0
Chuck Bednarik	2	33	16.5	0
Tom Brookshier	2	20	10.0	0
Jimmy Carr	2	20	10.0	0
Maxie Baughan	1	22	22.0	0
Chuck Weber	1	15	15.0	0
John Nocera	0	3	0.0	0

Kicking	PAT Made	PAT Att	PAT %	FG Made	FG Att	FG %	Pts
Bobby Walston	43	46	93	14	25	56.0	97

SPORTS **The Philadelphia Inquirer** MAIL ORDER

An Independent Newspaper for All the People

SPORTS SECTION SUNDAY, MORNING, JANUARY 7, 1962 PAGE ONE

Jurgensen Hurt as Lions Shock Eagles

This is the play on which Sonny Jurgensen suffered a shoulder separation. Lions' Wayne Walker is hitting Sonny (No. 9) with jarring block while Yale Lary makes 66-yard run with intercepted pass. UPI Telephoto

By HERB GOOD
Inquirer Reporter

MIAMI, Jan. 6.—If Eastern pro coaches were embarrassed by what happened to the Giants at Green Bay, they'll be going into hiding after what happened to the Eagles in the National Football League's second Playoff Bowl Saturday afternoon.

The Detroit Lions, apparently stimulated by the memory of four successive losses to the Flock in the last two years, handed the Philadelphians a 38-10 shellacking before a shirt-sleeved crowd of 25,612 in the Orange Bowl and a National television audience.

In winning third-place honors for the second straight year, the Western Conference runnersup made the most of three interceptions and a recovered fumble as they jumped off to a quick 10-0 lead and increased it to 24-0 before the Eagles got their only points in the third quarter.

It wasn't much of a show for the crowd, which enjoyed only the 81-degree temperature, and especially was a bitter disappointment for some 500 Eagle fans who made the trip by chartered plane, train and automobile.

The Eagles, who had squeezed out a 27-24 last-second win over the Lions in the final regular-season game at Detroit to finish just a half-game behind Eastern champ New York, not only came out of the rather dull game with bruised pride, but with six cripples to boot.

All-league quarterback Sonny Jurgensen and offensive tackle J. D. Smith were so badly hurt that they'll miss the Pro Bowl game at Los Angeles next Sunday.

Jurgensen received a badly separated right shoulder early in the second period when he was blocked on an interception run by Yale Lary that led to Detroit's second TD. He watched the rest of the game from the sidelines with his arm in a cast. Dr. Mike Mandarino said an operation would be necessary Tuesday in Philadelphia.

Smith received a fracture of the right tibia, similar to the injury that put Tom Brookshier on the sidelines half the season. He was treated at Jackson Hospital.

Others hurt were linebacker John Nocera, who received a bad spike wound on his left hand, requiring six stitches, in the early minutes; defensive end Leo Sugar, sprained knee, and fullback Clarence Peaks, a pulled leg muscle.

It was just one of those bad days when nothing went right. The Eagles, who started the season the first week of July and who were completing the longest season ever for an NFL team, were flat to start with and, when the injuries started piling up, what little enthusiasm they might have had for the game soon evaporated.

Even so, the Eagles managed to outgain the Lions, 177 net yards to 151 in the air, but were outgained 180 net yards to 58 on the ground.

Jim Ninowski and Earl Morrall directed the rout for the Lions, each tossing two TD passes, two of which were caught

Continued on Page 5, Column 2

Fun in the Sun?

Jurgensen Expected To Be OK Next Year, Smith Career in Doubt

Special to The Inquirer

MIAMI, Jan. 6.—Although Sonny Jurgensen came out of the debacle with the Lions with the "worst shoulder separation" Dr. Mike Mandarino has ever seen, the Eagles' team physician insisted that the injury wouldn't harm the all-NFL quarterback's passing next season.

Dr. Mandarino said Sonny would be throwing the ball as sharp as ever next season. He predicted Sonny would be playing with the Eagles' basketball team within eight weeks after an operation Tuesday at the Hahnemann Hospital in Philadelphia.

The leg fracture received by tackle J. D. Smith looms more serious as far as his pro future is concerned. He may be in a cast as long as six months and he might not be ready to join the Eagles by the time they report to camp next July.

BREAK WORSE THAN BROOKSHIER'S

Smith has a compound fracture of the right tibia, lower on the leg than that received by Tom Brookshier in the Bears game, and this means it will take longer to heal, according to Dr. Mandarino. Smith had his leg set at Jackson Memorial Hospital and will remain there until Tuesday.

Jurgensen was hit hard by a shoulder block thrown by Detroit linebacker Wayne Walker as the Eagles' star was rushing to tackle Yale Lary on a runback of an interception. The collision tore two sets of ligaments in Jurgensen's shoulder and forced the clavicle several inches out of the shoulder.

Dr. Mandarino said future trouble with the shoulder would be avoided with the repairing of the ligaments Tuesday. Jurgensen, who completed eight of 17 passes for 62 yards, had his arm put in a cast immediately at the Orange Bowl and watched the second half from the sidelines.

Back at his hotel, Jurgensen was in obvious pain, although under sedation. He said it was the first serious injury he had ever had in football. Early in the season he had been bothered with an injured toe.

HE'LL MISS PRO BOWL GAME

Jurgensen, who threw 32 touchdown passes and gained more yardage in the air this season than any other NFL quarterback in history, was bitterly disappointed that the injury would keep him out of the Pro Bowl game. He would have been the starting East quarterback next Sunday. It was a similar blow to Smith who, like Jurgensen, had been selected for the Los Angeles classic for the first time.

The injuries will cost the two players $800 or $600, the winning and losing players' shares in the Pro Bowl.

Bobby Walston, Tommy McDonald, Ted Dean and Maxie Baughan, the other Eagles in the Pro Bowl, left for the West Coast by air immediately after the game.

—*HERB GOOD*

Temple Whips Scranton, 90-70, For 4th Straight

SCRANTON, Pa., Jan. 6.—Temple led all the way Saturday night to rout the University of Scranton Royals, 90-70, before 1200 fans at the Scranton CYC.

The once-beaten Owls ran up an 8-0 lead in the early minutes as they streaked to their fourth straight victory and ninth of the year. Scranton's loss was the fifth in 10 games.

The Temple starters were in action only about 20 of the 40 minutes as Coach Harry Litwack cleared his bench and gave 13 players an opportunity to play.

GORDON GETS 19

All managed to score, with Russ Gordon leading the parade with 19. Bruce Drysdale hit for 18, three points under his average.

Drysdale, Earl Proctor, Gordon and Ed Devery got the Owls off to the 8-0 lead before Joe Barbuti finally hit for Scranton after 2:30 had elapsed.

The Owls went from there to a 19-4 lead after five minutes and prevailed 30-10 after 10 minutes. Litwack began substituting and the Royals managed to hold the Temple advantage to 20 points at halftime, 46-25, thanks to an eight-point spree near the end of the half.

BECOMES ROUT

At the start of the second half, the Temple regulars turned the game into a complete rout before Litwack waved in his scrubs. The count went to 70-38 before the shock troops took over.

The Owls hit on 44.7 percent of their shots from the field, making 38 of 85. Scranton was 33.3, with 21 of 63. Gordon hit on seven of 10 shots and led in rebounds with 13. Temple outrebounded Scranton, 59-53.

Scranton	G	F	P	Temple	G	F	P
Barbuti	[illegible]	[illegible]	[illegible]	Devery	[illegible]	[illegible]	[illegible]
Wilkerson	[illegible]	[illegible]	[illegible]	Krohimes	[illegible]	[illegible]	[illegible]
Jordan	[illegible]	[illegible]	[illegible]	Spooner	[illegible]	[illegible]	[illegible]
Cruin	[illegible]	[illegible]	[illegible]	Gordon	[illegible]	[illegible]	[illegible]
Ryan	[illegible]	[illegible]	[illegible]	Drysdale	[illegible]	[illegible]	[illegible]
Roche	[illegible]	[illegible]	[illegible]	Gold	[illegible]	[illegible]	[illegible]
Glynn	[illegible]	[illegible]	[illegible]	Kramer	[illegible]	[illegible]	[illegible]
Shaffer	[illegible]	[illegible]	[illegible]	Bishop	[illegible]	[illegible]	[illegible]
Stark	0	0	0	Ladar	[illegible]	[illegible]	[illegible]
				Kristiunas	[illegible]	[illegible]	[illegible]
				Siethen	[illegible]	[illegible]	[illegible]
				Harrington	[illegible]	[illegible]	[illegible]
				Proctor	[illegible]	[illegible]	[illegible]
Totals	21	28-39	70	Totals	38	14-26	90

Halftime—Temple, 46-25

W. Virginia Snaps Villanova's Streak; Penn, St. Joseph's Victors at Palestra

Referees Criticized By NYU

By FRANK DOLSON

It was a rough Saturday night for visiting coaches at the Palestra, but an enjoyable one for 4038 fans.

Princeton's Jack McCandless watched his defending Ivy League champions lose to Penn, 64-56, then had to rush to the hospital to check on the condition of his injured Capt. Al Kaemmerlen.

Then New York University's Lou Rossini saw his high-jumping sophomores lose a 59-55 thriller to St. Joseph's—and spent the next 15 minutes pacing up and down in front of his dressing room, battling successfully not to say anything he might regret later.

McCandless, the first-year coach who replaced the late Cappy Cappon, went home with a high regard for Penn high scorers Dave Robinson and John Wideman, and god news about Kaemmerlen, who survived a jolting collision with a mild concussion. Rossini went home full of admiration for St. Joseph's Jimmy Lynam and Tom Wynne—and bad thoughts about local officiating.

Penn-Princeton

Princeton, surprising Penn with a 1-2-2 zone, stayed in contention until the last two minutes despite scoring ace Pete Campbell's 2-for-17 shooting night and a freak accident that knocked out Capt. Al Kaemmerlen.

Kaemmerlen was carried off the court on a stretcher with 14:48 left and taken to University Hospital for observation. He was KO'd in a collision with Campbell after Penn's Sid Amira had heaved the ball high in the air over his head in an attempt to stop it from sailing out of bounds.

Kaemmerlen, Princeton's best rebounder, Campbell, and Penn's Robinson leaped for it as they converged from three directions. Campbell was knocked down but uninjured. Robinson was untouched and Kaemmerlen wound up flat on his back, unconscious.

THE LITTLE TAILOR

"I went up for the ball," said Robinson, "and the next thing I saw was the two of them on the ground, moaning. I thought Kaemmerlen was faking for a second, then I looked at his eyes and I knew he wasn't. I felt like

Continued on Pag. 6, Column 2

Anxious Al Kaemmerlen elbows Princeton mate Jim Day (30) out of way to grab rebound. Kaemmerlen was later KO'd in scramble for another rebound. Quakers are John Wideman (10) and J. D. Graham.

Fouls Hurt Wildcats in 88-82 Loss

By JOHN DELL
Inquirer Reporter

MORGANTOWN, W. Va., Jan. 6—The clock struck 12 for Philadelphia's Cinderella team Saturday night.

Coach Jack Kraft's Villanovans lost their first game after 12 straight victories, 88-82, in the valley between the human palisades at Mountaineer Field House, home of the University of West Virginia.

A sellout crowd of 6800 drowned out the cries of protest that Villanova's handful made against certain calls by officials.

"For a game this good, we should have had two top-flight officials. We didn't have them tonight," was Kraft's only comment.

FOULS HURT WILDCATS

Villanova was in the game nearly all the way against a team that has lost only twice in six seasons on its home court, even though the Wildcats were forced to sacrifice some of their aggressiveness after Wally Jones, Jim McMonagle and Jim O'Brien ran into early foul trouble.

All had three personals well before halftime and Jones was forced to the bench for six minutes to preserve his eligibility against the tallest team Villanova has met so far.

But with White scoring 28 points, Jones 19 and George Leftwich 18, Villanova, after holding the lead through most of the first half, trailed by only a point at intermission. The Wildcats were only four points behind with 1:26 left in a game in which the lead changed seven times and the score was tied five times.

FINALLY CATCH UP

Villanova took the lead on a White jump shot which severed the last tie, 59-59, with 12:31 left. White also added a foul but West Virginia came back on an overhead set shot by 6-6 Paul Miller and tap-in by Rod Thorn, 6-4 Mountaineer star who was game-high scorer with 29 points.

West Virginia stayed ahead after that, but Villanova never slipped entirely out of contention. With less than two minutes left, McMonagle was fouled and his right knee injured as White was sinking a short jump from the side. Kraft substituted Joe McGill, who made the most of the one-and-one award to McMonagle to reduce the Mountaineer lead to 82-78 with 1:47 left.

STOLEN PASS HURTS

McMonagle shortly afterward threw a cross-court pass that West Virginia's Jim McCormick intercepted in the backcourt. McCormick dribbled in for a field goal. Then Thorn drew two shots

Continued on Page 6, Column 4

Dietzel Signs Pact At Army for 5 Years

WEST POINT, N. Y., Jan. 6 (UPI).—Paul Dietzel, after an exhausting, day-long trip from Louisiana, signed a five-year contract late Saturday night as the new head coach of the Army football team.

The 37-year-old Dietzel, who gained his release as head coach at Louisiana State Friday although he had four years remaining on a five-year contract, arrived at the U. S. Military Academy about 10:30 P. M.

He signed to succeed Dale Hall as the Cadets' head coach at 11 P. M. in the quarters of Col. Emory S. Adams, Jr., the Academy's director of athletics.

Terms of the contract were not announced but it was learned Dietzel will be paid approximately $20,000 a year.

Originally, Dietzel was supposed to have signed at 4 P. M., but bad weather caused delay in his arrival.

FLIES TO WASHINGTON

Upon landing in Atlanta this morning from Baton Rouge, La., Dietzel learned that rain and fog had closed in the airport at New York. He then boarded a plane to Washington and made the remainder of the trip to New York by train.

The former LSU coach was met at the New York train terminal by Col. Red Reeder, Capt. Don Holleder and publicity director Joe Cahill, all of whom accompanied him on the 65-mile automobile trip to the Military Academy.

Dietzel said his first official order of business will be meeting his staff Sunday morning after which he will leave for Greenville, S. C., to serve as guest speaker at an Atlantic Coast Conference meeting on Monday.

Sports Results

Professional

FOOTBALL

RUNNERUP BOWL

Detroit 38 EAGLES 10

ICE HOCKEY

NATIONAL LEAGUE

[illegible]

AMERICAN LEAGUE

[illegible]

EASTERN LEAGUE

[illegible]

BASKETBALL

NATIONAL LEAGUE

[illegible]

AMERICAN LEAGUE

[illegible]

Continued on Page 6, Column 6

Ellen Gery Wins Harder Hall Golf

SEBRING, Fla., Jan. 6 (AP).—Ellen Gery, of Miami, won the sixth annual Harder Hall Women's Golf Tournament Saturday by two strokes in a nine-hole playoff with champion Marge Burns after both completed 54 holes in 236.

The rubber round was played in rain so intense it caused a delay after eight holes. Rain was still falling when they shot par 3s on the ninth. The winner used 38 strokes.

Miss Burns, Greensboro, N. C., missed a chance to win her fourth consecutive Harder Hall title in 54 holes when she got a bogey on No. 18 for 38-41—79. Miss Gery carded 41-38—79.

Jinny Dyson, Sugar Loaf, Pa., finished seventh with a 246 total.

Mississippi State Stays Unbeaten

STATE COLLEGE, Miss., Jan. 6 (AP).—Undefeated Mississippi State had a close call but remained one of the Nation's two basketball teams with perfect records by defeating Auburn, 51-48, Saturday night.

It was the 10th straight victory for the ninth-ranked defending Southeastern Conference champions, who stand with Ohio State in the unbeaten class. The game was the SEC opener for both schools.

Sophomore Doug Hutton sank a fall-away shot with six seconds to play to put State ahead, 50-48. The Maroons had stalled for three minutes following the fourth of four straight free throws by W. D. Stroud that tied the score.

State Comeback Tops Pitt, 74-62

PITTSBURGH, Jan. 6 (AP).—Penn State's basketball team scored 48 points in the second half Saturday night for a come-from-behind 74-62 victory over Pittsburgh.

The game was tied four times and the lead changed hands five times.

Pitt led 30-26 at the half, but the Nittany Lions closed the gap and with 12:36 remaining, John Mitchell hit on a jump shot that gave Penn State a 39-38 lead. State was never headed after that.

Gene Harris led the State with 19. Pitt's high scorer was Cal Sheffield with 13.

Penn State	G	F	P	Pittsburgh	G	F	P
Hutchinson	[illegible]	[illegible]	[illegible]	Sheffield	[illegible]	[illegible]	[illegible]
Phillips	[illegible]	[illegible]	[illegible]	Generals	[illegible]	[illegible]	[illegible]
Harris	[illegible]	[illegible]	19	Krieger	[illegible]	[illegible]	[illegible]
Mitchell	[illegible]	[illegible]	[illegible]	Sauer	[illegible]	[illegible]	[illegible]
Marin	[illegible]	[illegible]	[illegible]	Jinks	[illegible]	[illegible]	[illegible]
Kart	[illegible]	[illegible]	[illegible]	Maloney	[illegible]	[illegible]	[illegible]
Hoffman	[illegible]	[illegible]	[illegible]	Maczuzak	[illegible]	[illegible]	[illegible]
				Sankey	[illegible]	[illegible]	[illegible]
				Greurich	[illegible]	[illegible]	[illegible]
Totals	25	24-28	74	Totals	22	18-27	62

Halftime—Pitt, 30-26

Palestra Lineups

G. field goals; ST, shots tried; F, fouls made; FT, fouls tried; R, rebounds; A, assists; Per., personal fouls; Pts., points scored.

FIRST GAME

Penn	G-ST	F-FT	R	A	Per	Pts
Wideman	[illegible]	[illegible]	[illegible]	[illegible]	[illegible]	[illegible]
Robinson	[illegible]	[illegible]	[illegible]	[illegible]	[illegible]	[illegible]
Graham	[illegible]	[illegible]	[illegible]	[illegible]	[illegible]	[illegible]
Amira	[illegible]	[illegible]	[illegible]	[illegible]	[illegible]	[illegible]
Casale	[illegible]	[illegible]	[illegible]	[illegible]	[illegible]	[illegible]
Sturgis	[illegible]	[illegible]	[illegible]	[illegible]	[illegible]	[illegible]
Purdy	[illegible]	[illegible]	[illegible]	[illegible]	[illegible]	[illegible]
Babcock	[illegible]	[illegible]	[illegible]	[illegible]	[illegible]	[illegible]
Totals	[illegible]	[illegible]	[illegible]	[illegible]	[illegible]	64
Princeton	G-ST	F-FT	R	A	Per	Pts
Whitehouse	[illegible]	[illegible]	[illegible]	[illegible]	[illegible]	[illegible]
Day	[illegible]	[illegible]	[illegible]	[illegible]	[illegible]	[illegible]
Kaemmerlen	[illegible]	[illegible]	[illegible]	[illegible]	[illegible]	[illegible]
Campbell	[illegible]	[illegible]	[illegible]	[illegible]	[illegible]	[illegible]
Hyland	[illegible]	[illegible]	[illegible]	[illegible]	[illegible]	[illegible]
Harlow	[illegible]	[illegible]	[illegible]	[illegible]	[illegible]	[illegible]
Butler	[illegible]	[illegible]	[illegible]	[illegible]	[illegible]	[illegible]
Totals	[illegible]	[illegible]	[illegible]	[illegible]	[illegible]	56

Halftime—Penn, 28-22. Officials—Jim Lennon and Phil Fox.

SECOND GAME

NYU	G-ST	F-FT	R	A	Per	Pts
Filardi	[illegible]	[illegible]	[illegible]	[illegible]	[illegible]	[illegible]
Bonn	[illegible]	[illegible]	[illegible]	[illegible]	[illegible]	[illegible]
Hairston	[illegible]	[illegible]	[illegible]	[illegible]	[illegible]	[illegible]
Kramer	[illegible]	[illegible]	[illegible]	[illegible]	[illegible]	[illegible]
Reiner	[illegible]	[illegible]	[illegible]	[illegible]	[illegible]	[illegible]
Williams	[illegible]	[illegible]	[illegible]	[illegible]	[illegible]	[illegible]
Blaha	[illegible]	[illegible]	[illegible]	[illegible]	[illegible]	[illegible]
Totals	[illegible]	[illegible]	[illegible]	[illegible]	[illegible]	55
St. Joseph's	G-ST	F-FT	R	A	Per	Pts
Dickey	[illegible]	[illegible]	[illegible]	[illegible]	[illegible]	[illegible]
Bosle	[illegible]	[illegible]	[illegible]	[illegible]	[illegible]	[illegible]
Tiller	[illegible]	[illegible]	[illegible]	[illegible]	[illegible]	[illegible]
Lynam	[illegible]	[illegible]	[illegible]	[illegible]	[illegible]	[illegible]
Gormley	[illegible]	[illegible]	[illegible]	[illegible]	[illegible]	[illegible]
Wynne	[illegible]	[illegible]	[illegible]	[illegible]	[illegible]	[illegible]
Hoy	[illegible]	[illegible]	[illegible]	[illegible]	[illegible]	[illegible]
Kelley	[illegible]	[illegible]	[illegible]	[illegible]	[illegible]	[illegible]
Courtin	[illegible]	[illegible]	[illegible]	[illegible]	[illegible]	[illegible]
Totals	[illegible]	[illegible]	[illegible]	[illegible]	[illegible]	59

Halftime—NYU, 28-22. Officials—Jerry Rollo and Lou Soodler.

Art Tokle Repeats At Bear Mountain

BEAR MOUNTAIN, N. Y., Jan. 6 (AP).—Art Tokle, veteran Brooklyn skier, won the Torger Tokle Memorial Ski Jump at Bear Mountain for the sixth straight year Saturday. He had leaps of 139 and 140 feet that netted 204 points.

It was the seventh time in the 17 years of the competition that Art Tokle won the award in the meeting named for his brother, who was killed in action while with the U. S. Forces in northern Italy during the Second World War.

Charley Scott Upsets Ortega in TV Match

By JACK CUDDY

NEW YORK, Jan. 6 (UPI).—Charley Scott of Philadelphia, a substitute in a substitute national TV fight, scored a mild upset Saturday night by left-hooking his way to a unanimous 10-round decision over welterweight contender Gaspar Ortega of Mexico at Madison Square Garden.

Ortega, the ninth-ranking welterweight contender, was favored at 6-5 for the 10-rounder.

Unrated Scott, who accepted the bout last Sunday, weighed 148½ pounds to Ortega's 148, and forced the action in most of the rounds.

NO KNOCKDOWNS

Because of his harder punching, he won the decisions on a rounds basis as follows: referee Harry Kessler, 6-3-1; judge Tony Castelano, 5-4-1 and judge Bill Recht, 6-1-3.

There were no knockdowns. Ortega's nose began bleeding in the fourth round and he suffered a nick at the outside corner of his left brow in the eighth.

Ortega, probably the world's busiest fighter, was competing for the 16th time in 12 months. He had 15 fights in the last 11 months of 1961. He went into the ring Saturday night with a string of three straight knockouts.

It seemed in some of the rounds that Ortega would be knocked out because of the bombing he took from the 25-year-old Scott's left hooks. Lanky Ortega's knees were buckled five times in the second round.

He was sent swaying into the ropes by a right and left hook to the head in the third, and was hanging on in the fifth. His knees were buckled by left hooks in the ninth and he was groggy at the bell.

The Detroit Tigers' personnel and problems are reviewed by Allen Lewis in the first of a mid-winter series on the major league baseball teams . . . . Page 4

West Chester Loses 1st Game

EAST ORANGE, N. J., Jan. 6 (AP).—Upsala converted four free throws down the stretch to nip West Chester (Pa.) State College, 77-75, in basketball Saturday night.

The setback was the first of the season for West Chester, which entered the game with a 6-0 record. Upsala is 3-7.

With the score tied at 73, Upsala's Bob Brandes was awarded two free throws and converted both. West Chester missed a field goal attempt and Upsala recovered the rebound. West Chester battled to get the ball back and in the process fouled Chuck Engler. He converted both shots.

Brandes finished with 21 points and Engler had 20 to pace Upsala. Dale Waters was high for the losers with 23.

Paul Walker Held For Grand Jury

RALEIGH, N. C., Jan. 6 (UPI).—New Yorker Paul Walker, accused of conspiring to bribe two North Carolina State basketball plays in 1960, waived preliminary hearing Saturday before Justice of the Peace H. A. Bland.

The 30-year-old Walker was bound over to Wake County Superior Court and returned to county jail in lieu of $25,000 bond.

District Solicitor Lester V. Chalmers said a bill of indictment naming Walker, a New York trucking official, will be presented Monday to the Wake County grand jury. The grand jury opens a regular term at that time.

2

1961

January 7, 1961
Eagles lose to the Detroit Lions, 38-10, in the Playoff Bowl.

1962

RECORD: 3-10-1, 7TH IN NFL EAST
HEAD COACH: NICK SKORICH

Schedule
Regular Season

Wk. 2	Sep 16	L	27-21	vs St. Louis Cardinals
Wk. 3	Sep 23	L	29-13	vs New York Giants
Wk. 4	Sep 30	W	35-7	vs Cleveland Browns
Wk. 5	Oct 6	L	13-7	at Pittsburgh Steelers
Wk. 6	Oct 14	L	41-19	at Dallas Cowboys
Wk. 7	Oct 21	L	27-21	vs Washington Redskins
Wk. 8	Oct 28	L	31-21	at Minnesota Vikings
Wk. 9	Nov 4	T	14-14	at Cleveland Browns
Wk. 10	Nov 11	L	49-0	vs Green Bay Packers
Wk. 11	Nov 18	L	19-14	at New York Giants
Wk. 12	Nov 25	W	28-14	vs Dallas Cowboys
Wk. 13	Dec 2	W	37-14	at Washington Redskins
Wk. 14	Dec 9	L	26-17	vs Pittsburgh Steelers
Wk. 15	Dec 16	L	45-35	at St. Louis Cardinals

An unpredicted number of injuries hampered the Eagles all season as they crashed into last place with a disappointing 3-10-1 record. Tommy McDonald passed for a touchdown to Tim Brown on a busted play as the Eagles defeated Washington 37-14. Following the season Chuck Bednarik, the last true two-way player, would retire at age 37, after 14 ferocious seasons.

1962 Philadelphia Eagles Stats

Passing	Comp	Att	Comp %	Yds	Y/Att	TD	Int	Rating
Sonny Jurgensen	196	366	53.6	3261	8.91	22	26	74.3
Tommy McDonald	1	1	100.0	10	10.00	1	0	147.9
King Hill	31	61	50.8	361	5.92	0	5	34.9

Rushing	Rush	Yds	Avg	TD
Timmy Brown	137	545	4.0	5
Clarence Peaks	137	447	3.3	3
Theron Sapp	23	53	2.3	2
Sonny Jurgensen	17	44	2.6	2
King Hill	4	40	10.0	1
Ralph Smith	1	13	13.0	0
Merrill Douglas	4	7	1.8	0
Hopalong Cassady	1	6	6.0	0

Receiving	Rec	Yds	Avg	TD
Tommy McDonald	58	1146	19.8	10
Timmy Brown	52	849	16.3	6
Clarence Peaks	39	347	8.9	0
Pete Retzlaff	30	584	19.5	3
Dick Lucas	19	236	12.4	1
Hopalong Cassady	14	188	13.4	2
Theron Sapp	6	80	13.3	0
Frank Budd	5	130	26.0	1
Bobby Walston	4	43	10.8	0
Ralph Smith	1	29	29.0	0

Punting	Punts	Yds	Avg	Blocked
King Hill	64	2747	42.9	0

Kicking	PAT Made	PAT Att	PAT %	FG Made	FG Att	FG %	Pts
Bobby Walston	36	38	95	4	15	26.7	48
John Wittenborn	0	0	0	2	4	50.0	6

Interceptions	Int	Yds	Avg	TD
Don Burroughs	7	96	13.7	0
Irv Cross	5	46	9.2	0
Ben Scotti	4	72	18.0	0
Jimmy Carr	3	59	19.7	0
Mike McClellan	3	2	0.7	0
Bob Harrison	2	14	7.0	0
Maxie Baughan	1	0	0.0	0
John Nocera	1	0	0.0	0

1962

The Philadelphia Inquirer
33 MONDAY DECEMBER 3, 1962 h★

TODAY'S SPORTS

Also in this section . . .
Classified
Death Notices

Brown Runs 99, Eagles Rout 'Skins, 37-14

Timmy Brown is off on 99-yard kickoff return for Eagles' first touchdown. With J. D. Smith and Merrill Douglas leading the way, Tim starts to cut at his 12 as John Nocera forces Ron Hatcher wide and John Wittenborn starts to block Allen Miller.

Timmy's 3-TD Burst Triggers Comeback

By HERB GOOD
Inquirer Reporter

WASHINGTON, D. C., Dec 2.—It was a grand day of firsts for the Eagles as they exploded for their highest score this season while drubbing the Washington Redskins, 37-14, before 32,229 in sunny D. C. Stadium Sunday afternoon.

Tommy McDonald thew a touchdown pass, Frank Budd, former Villanova Olympian, scored a TD and John Wittenborn kicked a field goal, each an individual first as pros, as the Eagles gained their third victory.

Timmy Brown scored three touchdowns, one a 99-yard kickoff return.

EAGLES MOVE UP

In avenging an early-season 27-21 setback, the Eagles moved into undisputed possession of sixth place by handing the Redskins their fifth loss, third in a row and fifth in their last six games.

The reverse dropped the Redskins from third to fourth place in the National Football League's Eastern Division.

While McDonald, Budd and Wittenborn provided the unusual, Brown, Pete Retzlaff and Sonny Jurgensen made tremendous contributions as the Eagles overcame a 14-0 deficit in a wide-open game marked by long runs and big aerial bombs.

The slippery Brown, voted the outstanding Eagle by the Sports Writers Football Club last week, had one of his best days; Retzlaff scored one TD while catching eight passes for 135 yards in one of his finest efforts, and Jurgensen made another big climb on the comeback road by stealing the show from Washington's Norm Snead with 14 completions in just 19 attempts.

STAR ON DEFENSE

Also prominent in the victory were Maxie Baughan, who recovered two fumbles that led to touchdowns; rookie Mike McClellan, who also recovered a fumble and intercepted a pass; Jimmy Carr, who intercepted a pass and was the "glue man" in the secondary that was efficient when it counted, and tackle Riley Gunnels, who was his usual aggressive self.

After Snead got the Redskins off to a flying start by tossing short TD passes to Steve Junker and Dick James, it was the nimble-footed Brown who put the Eagles back in the game and fired their comeback with a 99-yard kickoff return for the first Philadelphia score.

It was his second scoring dash of that impressive distance this season, the first coming on the return of a missed field goal against the Cardinals in the opening game at Philadelphia.

This time he went all the way on the kickoff that followed Washington's second score, which came on the first play of the second quarter.

KEYS' BLOCK HELPS

Brown used his speed and shiftiness to break into the clear near the left sideline. Upon crossing midfield, he cut inside a screening block by Howard Keys on James to leave the last enemy at his heels.

Brown's second TD came on a spinning three-yard run on which he fell backward into the end zone on the ninth play of a 77-yard drive after the second-half

Continued on Page 34, Column 4

Wittenborn knocked Miller to his knees and Brown, now at Eagles' 19-yard line, cuts back to the right, still following teammate J. D. Smith.

J. D. Smith tried to block Washington's Ben Davidson at Eagles' 30. He couldn't knock him down but he knocked him off stride and Brown races by.

At midfield, Dick James is lone Redskin defender between Brown and the goal. Howard Keys takes care of James by almost running over him.

Magic Eye Photos by Robert L. Mooney, Inquirer Staff Photographer
Brown is in the clear at the Redskins' 36 and the chase given by Davidson and Doug Elmore is futile. This fine run started Eagles' comeback.

Eagles' passer Sonny Jurgensen, thrown for 19-yard loss in second quarter, complained that Redskin John Paluck illegally grabbed his face mask, as shown here. Officials brushed off complaint.

Unable to Catch Ball, McDonald Tosses for TD on 'Broken' Play

Special to The Inquirer

WASHINGTON, Dec. 2.—Irrepressible Tommy McDonald, frustrated in his favorite ploy of catching the football, turned the tables and left a lot of Redskins red-faced in embarrassment Sunday by throwing a touchdown pass on a "busted" play.

"I don't catch 'em any more," cracked McDonald, "so they're starting to let me throw 'em now. I'm like Jim Brown—my first completion for a touchdown."

Employed mostly as a decoy, McDonald caught only one pass, but his 16-yard scoring pitch to Tim Brown eased some of the sting and helped the Eagles pile up their 37-14 margin.

NEARLY INTERCEPTED

"I've thrown passes in college," related McDonald, "but this was the first for the Eagles."

"Funny thing," mused Tommy, "I nearly didn't get it off. Somebody (end Andy Stynchula) on the Redskins blitzed and I thought for a minute he was going to intercept the pitchout and run for a touchdown."

The play began as an end around and McDonald circled deep, under heavy pressure, and ran for his life. When he did get off the toss, it was deflected off Dale Hackbart, whose interception at Philadelphia killed a late Eagle rally and saved the Redskins' victory in the first meeting.

HAD TO LOB IT

"I knew I never had a chance to run it in," McDonald said. "Then I saw Hackbart coming across, I knew I had to lob it. If I threw it hard, it would have sailed right out of the end zone."

Less than seven minutes later, the Eagles had another first when Frank Budd settled under Sonny Jurgensen's long toss for a 49-yard touchdown.

"I've been waiting a long time

Continued on Page 36, Column 2

Eagles Statistics

TEAM

	Redskins	Eagles
First downs	26	21
Net yds. rushing	75	120
Net yds. passing	272	252
Passing	22-39	15-22
Passes int'cep'd by	1	2
Punts, average	2-30	3-49
Yards penalized	15	90
Fumbles lost	3	1

INDIVIDUAL LEADERS

RUSHING

EAGLES—Peaks, 7 carries for 18 net yards; Brown, 16 for 41 and 2 TD's; Jurgensen, 2 for 13.
REDSKINS—Jackson, 13 for 44; Bossler, 5, for 20; Snead, 1 for 9.

PASSING

EAGLES—Jurgensen, 14 completions in 19 attempts for 261 yards and 2 TD's; McDonald, 1 for 1 for 16 yds. and 1 TD.
REDSKINS—Snead, 16 of 29 for 211 and 2 TDs; Hall, 6 of 10 for 61.

PASS RECEIVING

EAGLES—Retzlaff, 8 catches for 135 yds.; Budd 2 for 63 and 1 TD; Brown 2 for 24 and 1 TD; McDonald 1 for 16.
REDSKINS—Mitchell, 8 for 114; Junker, 4 for 36 and 1 TD; James, 2 for 30 and 1 TD; Jackson 3 for 60.

Giants Conquer Bears, 26-24, to Win Title in East

CHICAGO, Dec. 2 (AP).—The New York Giants clinched their second straight Eastern Conference title of the National Football League on Sunday by defeating the Chicago Bears, 26-24, on two touchdown passes by Y. A. Tittle and four field goals by Don Chandler.

The first meeting between the clubs since New York pasted the Bears, 47-7, in the 1956 championship game was a rough, hardplayed contest that kept an overflow Wrigley Field crowd of 49,043 alternating boos with cheers.

Several fist-swinging incidents charged up the battle. The only player ejected was the Bears' Ed O'Bradovich, who started punching Phil King in the third period. King was forced to the Giant bench to rest with an ice pack against his face.

O'Bradovich's flare-up cost the Bears a 15-yard penalty and set up Chandler's 27-yard field goal that pushed the Giants ahead, 23-17. Chandler, who booted a 26-yard field goal in the first quarter and a 47-yarder early in the third, added his fourth from 16 yards midway in the final period.

He also booted extra points after the two touchdowns to total 14 points.

5TH IN 7 YEARS

The triumph, assuring the Giants their fifth divisional crown in the last seven years, was their seventh straight. It gave them a 10-2 record with two games to play.

After Chandler's field goal put New York in front, 26-17, in the fourth, the Bears scored on a 59-yard drive capped by Bill Wade's 25-yard pass to Angelo Coia. Roger Leclerc converted for the third time. He also kicked a 31-yard field goal in the third.

It was Wade's second touchdown pass. He hit Johnny Morris in the corner for a 30-yard tally in the first period to end a 66-yard push in four plays.

The veteran Tittle hurled

Continued on Page 46, Column 3

Records

GIANTS LOG

[illegible]

BEARS LOG

[illegible]

Hornung Back, Packers Romp Over LA, 41-10

MILWAUKEE, Dec. 2 (UPI).—Green Bay's Paul Hornung made his long-awaited comeback Sunday and teamed with quarterback Bart Starr and fullback Jim Taylor to lead the Packers to a 41-10 victory over the Los Angeles Rams before 46,833.

Hornung, who hadn't seen extended action since an injury seven weeks ago, scored the Packers' first touchdown on a 30-yard pass from Starr and later took a 35-yard pass from Starr to set up Green Bay's second score.

Taylor scored twice to run his National Football League-leading total to 102 points. Starr also passed to Ron Kramer for four yards and a touchdown, and Jerry Kramer kicked 35 and 37 yard field goals as well as adding five extra points.

The Packers now need win only one of two games on the West Coast against the Rams and San Francisco to wrap up at least a tie for a third successive Western Division crown.

Hornung, who has played only briefly since Oct. 14, gained 27 yards in nine carries, caught two passes and threw one, which was intercepted.

He left the game limping in the third quarter.

Records

PACKERS LOG

[illegible]

RAMS LOG

[illegible]

[illegible]

Valley Forge Loses in Polo

Harley Williams scored six goals and Fred Fortungo five to lead the Oxford Royals, of Kelton, Pa., to a 14-7 indoor polo victory over Valley Forge Military Academy on Sunday at Wayne. The loss ended a 12-game winning streak by the Cadets.

[illegible]

Celtics Defeat Royals, 128-127

CINCINNATI, Dec. 2 (UPI).—The Boston Celtics cooled off the hot Cincinnati Royals Sunday night, coming from behind for a 128-127 overtime victory on the clutch shooting of Tom Heinsohn before 8719, the largest crowd of the local season.

[illegible]

Sports Results

Professional FOOTBALL

NFL

EAGLES 37	Washington 14
Pittsburgh 19	St. Louis 7
New York 26	Chicago 24
Dallas 45	Cleveland 21
Green Bay 41	Los Angeles 10
Detroit 21	Baltimore 14
San Francisco 35	Minnesota 12

STANDINGS

EASTERN DIVISION

	W	L	T	Pct.	Pts.	OP
x-New York	10	2	0	.833	340	239
Pittsburgh	7	5	0	.583	259	322
Cleveland	6	5	1	.545	265	230
Washington	5	5	2	.500	260	315
Dallas	5	6	1	.455	347	309
EAGLES	3	8	1	.273	220	285
St. Louis	2	9	1	.182	190	306

x-New York wins Eastern title.

WESTERN DIVISION

	W	L	T	Pct.	Pts.	OP
Green Bay	11	1	0	.917	384	110
Detroit	10	2	0	.833	278	151
Chicago	7	5	0	.583	288	273
San Francisco	6	6	0	.500	251	287
Baltimore	5	7	0	.417	217	238
Minnesota	2	9	1	.182	214	331
Los Angeles	1	10	1	.091	189	284

AFL

[illegible]

Continued on Page 46, Column 2

West Beats Judge for Title

By BILL SIMMONS

Father Judge had the All-Stars but West Catholic had the team Sunday at Franklin Field

Picture on Page 46

as it spotted the Crusaders eight early points and then came roaring back to score a surprisingly easy 38-16 victory before 25,000.

The triumph, 10th in 11 games this year for Vince McAneny's Burrs, gave them their first Catholic League championship since 1951 and the right to meet Public League titlist Southern High for the City Title Saturday on the same field.

Tommy DeFelice, seeing his first action since suffering a thigh injury a month ago, looked as sound as ever passing with deadly accuracy and faking beautifully on running plays while his All-Catholic backfield mate Bobby Mahan scored four touchdowns and passed for another to lead West's attack.

The Crusaders, who placed six on the all-Catholic squad, scored with 2:10 gone in the

Continued on Page 46, Column 3

Broken Ribs For Don?

Don Burroughs, Eagles' defensive back, will be x-rayed Monday for a possible fracture of two ribs on the right side. He suffered the injury when he was caught in a pile-up on the last play of the first half against the Redskins Sunday. Burroughs was in such pain he played only three minutes of the second half.

Tackle Jim McCusker required two stitches for a cut on his forehead. Clarence Peaks has a sprained right ankle and Timmy Brown a sprained right knee. It is expected that all three will be able to play against the Steelers next Sunday, however.

Ailing Ramblers Lose to Ducks

COMMACK, L. I., Dec. 2.—Rambler center Chuck Stuart boosted his league-leading point total with two goals Sunday night—but the second one proved to be costly.

Stuart crashed into the boards after scoring on a game-tying, first-period breakaway and was carried off on a stretcher. Without him, the Ramblers lost to the Long Island Ducks, 8-5, before 3239 fans.

Stuart was hurt moments after netting his 20th goal and his eighth in three games. He left with an injured left knee, which will be X-rayed Monday.

The Ramblers played without winger Don Graham, who hurt his knee Saturday night and was placed on the 30-day disabled list. His replacement, 20-year-old Art Chiupka, made his Rambler debut and had two assists.

Buzz Deschamps' second goal broke a 4-4 tie at 2:03 of the third period and the Ducks never

Continued on Page 36, Column 5

December 3, 1962
Eagles romp over the Washington Redskins, 37-14
Tommy McDonald throws his first career touchdown pass to Tim Brown.
Also Tim Brown scores on a 99-yard kick-off return

1963

**RECORD: 2-10-2, 7TH IN NFL EAST
HEAD COACH: NICK SKORICH**

Schedule
Regular Season

Wk. 2	Sep 15	T	21-21	vs Pittsburgh Steelers
Wk. 3	Sep 22	L	28-24	vs St. Louis Cardinals
Wk. 4	Sep 29	L	37-14	vs New York Giants
Wk. 5	Oct 6	W	24-21	vs Dallas Cowboys
Wk. 6	Oct 13	W	37-24	at Washington Redskins
Wk. 7	Oct 20	L	37-7	at Cleveland Browns
Wk. 8	Oct 27	L	16-7	at Chicago Bears
Wk. 9	Nov 3	L	23-17	vs Cleveland Browns
Wk. 10	Nov 10	L	42-14	at New York Giants
Wk. 11	Nov 17	L	27-20	at Dallas Cowboys
Wk. 12	Nov 24	L	13-10	vs Washington Redskins
Wk. 13	Dec 1	T	20-20	at Pittsburgh Steelers
Wk. 14	Dec 7	L	38-14	at St. Louis Cardinals
Wk. 15	Dec 15	L	34-13	vs Minnesota Vikings

Timmy Brown set a new NFL record for total offense (2,436 yards; 841 rushing, 487 receiving, 11 passing, 945 kickoff returns, and 152 punt returns) in a season. With the club's outstanding shares now held by 65 stockholders, club president Frank L. McNamee said it would be put up for sale with an asking price of 4.5 million dollars. Jerry Wolman, a 36-year old builder and self-made millionaire from Washington, outbid Philadelphia businessman Jack Wolgin and became the new owner. The sale price was 5.5 million dollars. However, the Eagles flapped their wings right into last place, finishing with a dreadful 2-10-2 record. Following the season Nick Skorich was fired and replaced by Joe Kuharich.

1963 Philadelphia Eagles Stats

Passing	Comp	Att	Comp %	Yds	Y/Att	TD	Int	Rating
Sonny Jurgensen	99	184	53.8	1413	7.68	11	13	69.4
King Hill	91	186	48.9	1213	6.52	10	17	49.9
Timmy Brown	1	3	33.3	11	3.67	1	1	45.1
Ralph Guglielmi	2	7	28.6	29	4.14	0	0	44.3

Rushing	Rush	Yds	Avg	TD
Timmy Brown	192	841	4.4	6
Ted Dean	79	268	3.4	0
Clarence Peaks	64	212	3.3	1
Sonny Jurgensen	13	38	2.9	1
Paul Dudley	11	21	1.9	0
Theron Sapp	8	21	2.6	0
Ralph Guglielmi	1	20	20.0	0
Tom Woodeshick	5	18	3.6	0
King Hill	3	-1	-0.3	0

Receiving	Rec	Yds	Avg	TD
Pete Retzlaff	57	895	15.7	4
Tommy McDonald	41	731	17.8	8
Timmy Brown	36	487	13.5	4
Clarence Peaks	22	167	7.6	1
Ron Goodwin	15	215	14.3	4
Ted Dean	14	108	7.7	0
Ralph Smith	5	63	12.6	1
Paul Dudley	1	8	8.0	0
Tom Woodeshick	1	-3	-3.0	0
Theron Sapp	1	-5	-5.0	0

Punting	Punts	Yds	Avg	Blocked
King Hill	69	2972	43.1	0

Interceptions	Int	Yds	Avg	TD
Don Burroughs	4	36	9.0	0
Dave Lloyd	3	30	10.0	0
Irv Cross	2	6	3.0	0
Lee Roy Caffey	1	87	87.0	1
Jimmy Carr	1	25	25.0	0
Ben Scotti	1	17	17.0	0
Maxie Baughan	1	9	9.0	0
Mike McClellan	1	0	0.0	0
Nate Ramsey	1	0	0.0	0

Kicking	PAT Made	PAT Att	PAT %	FG Made	FG Att	FG %	Pts
Mike Clark	29	32	91	7	15	46.7	50

Choking Steeler, Saved From Death

DEATH was cheated Sunday on Franklin Field before 58,205 onlookers, unaware of the drama developing before them.

Only quick, skilled work by team doctors and trainers saved John Reger, Pittsburgh Steelers' linebacker, from choking to death. Reger was knocked unconscious and went into convulsions after tackling Theron Sapp of the Eagles on the last play of the first quarter.

Reger's face was blue-black from his inability to breathe after swallowing his tongue, those who rushed to his aid said.

Dr. James Nixon, the Eagles' physician, took one look at Reger writhing on the ground and rushed off for a knife with which he planned to make an on-the-spot, emergency tracheotomy if no other way could be found to give Reger life-saving air.

Meanwhile, Pittsburgh trainer Roger McGill attempted artificial respiration and then Dr. John Best, the team's physician, forced scissors between the player's teeth. When the scissors became caught in Reger's mouth, several teeth were dislodged as the instrument was withdrawn. Through the hole left by the missing teeth, it was possible to pry open Reger's mouth so that the obstruction could be removed.

IT was obvious from the moment that Reger went down that he was in serious trouble, but only a few of those present realized its nature.

As soon as the doctors saw him, they summoned a cabulance, which was driven right to his side on the playing field.

When the desperate first aid efforts partially restored Reger's breathing, treatment was continued on the field for several minutes before he was lifted on a stretcher to the cabulance and driven to nearby University Hospital.

There it was later announced that his condition was satisfactory. He was detained overnight for observation to guard against possibility of a brain injury.

— HERB GOOD

STEELERS' JOHN REGER RECEIVES OXYGEN AFTER FIRST-PERIOD INJURY.

The Philadelphia Inquirer

TODAY'S SPORTS

31 | MONDAY, SEPTEMBER 16, 1963 | h★

Also in this section...

Classified Advertising

Comics, Puzzles

Trailing by a point in the fourth period, the Eagles shift into a shotgun formation—and Sonny Jurgensen fires as Steelers' Lou Michaels and Ernie Stautner apply pressure. Sonny's on his 11 as he throws the ball.

Inquirer Magic Eye Photos by Robert L. Mooney, Staff Photographer
The pass sails 50 yards through the air and falls into the waiting arms of Tommy McDonald, who grabs it in full stride and heads for the goal line. Here, he's crossing the Steelers' 35 with Glenn Glass in pursuit.

Phils Win, 6-1, Shave Dodger Lead to 1 Game

By ALLEN LEWIS

Cards Sweep Braves, Extend Win Streak to 10

ST. LOUIS, Sept. 15 (AP) —

WHITE BELTS 27TH

Remaining Games

BURDETTE WALKS NONE

Steelers' Late PAT Fails, Eagles Tie in Opener, 21-21

By HERB GOOD
Continued from First Page

Tittle's Passes Carry Giants to Win Over Colts

BALTIMORE, Sept. 15 (UPI) — Y. A. Tittle, the 36-year-old pass master, threw three scoring passes and ran nine yards for a go-ahead touchdown Sunday before leaving with an injury as the New York Giants scored a 37-28 victory over the Baltimore Colts.

It's a race between McDonald and Glass, who dives in an effort to catch Tommy on the 23.

McDonald's home free on a 75-yard TD play as he leaves Glass sprawled behind him on the 20.

Baseball Facts
Standings, Statistics

(September 16, 1963)

NATIONAL LEAGUE
Sunday's Results

PHILLIES, 6; Los Angeles, 1.
San Francisco, 13; Pittsburgh, 5.
Cincinnati, 3; Chicago, 1.
St. Louis, 3; Milwaukee, 1, 1st. St. Louis, 5; Milwaukee, 0, 2d.
Houston, 5; New York, 4, 1st. Houston, 0, New York, 0, 2d.

Eagles' Statistics

TEAM
	Eagles	Steelers
First downs	14	21
Net Yards rushing	58	300
Net Yards passing	295	200
Passes completed	16 of 26	18 of 34
Passes intercepted by	0	2
Punts	6-45.3	4.20.3
Yards penalized	40	15
Fumbles lost	1	1

September 16, 1963
Eagles tie the Steelers, 21-21
Tommy McDonald has seven catches for 179 yards and two touchdowns

1964

RECORD: 6-8, T-3RD IN NFL EAST
HEAD COACH: JOE KUHARICH

Schedule
Regular Season

Wk. 1	Sep 13	W	38-7	vs New York Giants
Wk. 2	Sep 20	L	28-24	vs San Francisco 49ers
Wk. 3	Sep 27	L	28-20	vs Cleveland Browns
Wk. 4	Oct 4	W	21-7	vs Pittsburgh Steelers
Wk. 5	Oct 11	L	35-20	at Washington Redskins
Wk. 6	Oct 18	W	23-17	at New York Giants
Wk. 7	Oct 25	W	34-10	at Pittsburgh Steelers
Wk. 8	Nov 1	L	21-10	vs Washington Redskins
Wk. 9	Nov 8	L	20-10	at Los Angeles Rams
Wk. 10	Nov 15	W	17-14	at Dallas Cowboys
Wk. 11	Nov 22	L	38-13	vs St. Louis Cardinals
Wk. 12	Nov 29	L	38-24	at Cleveland Browns
Wk. 13	Dec 6	W	24-14	vs Dallas Cowboys
Wk. 14	Dec 13	L	36-34	at St. Louis Cardinals

In the first of a series of major trades, Kuharich traded safety Jim Carr and quarterback Sonny Jurgensen to the Washington Redskins for Norm Snead in a swap of signal callers. He then traded Tommy McDonald to Dallas, Clarence Peaks to Pittsburgh, Ted Dean to Minnesota, and Lee Roy Caffey and a draft pick to Green Bay. The team that was clearly in a rebuilding mode slowly showed improvement by eventually finishing the season with a 6-8 record.

1964 Philadelphia Eagles Stats

Passing	Comp	Att	Comp %	Yds	Y/Att	TD	Int	Rating
Norm Snead	138	283	48.8	1906	6.73	14	12	69.6
Jack Concannon	12	23	52.2	199	8.65	2	1	92.5
King Hill	49	88	55.7	641	7.28	3	4	71.3
Earl Gros	0	1	0.0	0	0.00	0	0	39.6
Timmy Brown	0	2	0.0	0	0.00	0	1	0.0

Rushing	Rush	Yds	Avg	TD
Earl Gros	154	748	4.9	2
Ollie Matson	96	404	4.2	4
Timmy Brown	90	356	4.0	5
Tom Woodeshick	37	180	4.9	2
Jack Concannon	16	134	8.4	1
Norm Snead	16	59	3.7	2
Izzy Lang	12	37	3.1	0
King Hill	8	27	3.4	0
Ron Goodwin	1	-23	-23.0	0

Receiving	Rec	Yds	Avg	TD
Pete Retzlaff	51	855	16.8	8
Ray Poage	37	479	12.9	1
Earl Gros	29	234	8.1	0
Ron Goodwin	23	335	14.6	3
Ollie Matson	17	242	14.2	1
Timmy Brown	15	244	16.3	5
Red Mack	8	169	21.1	1
Izzy Lang	6	69	11.5	0
Roger Gill	4	58	14.5	0
Ralph Smith	4	35	8.8	0
Tom Woodeshick	4	12	3.0	0
Claude Crabb	1	14	14.0	0

Punting	Punts	Yds	Avg	Blocked
Sam Baker	49	2073	42.3	0
King Hill	24	968	40.3	0

Interceptions	Int	Yds	Avg	TD
Nate Ramsey	5	31	6.2	0
Irv Cross	3	109	36.3	1
Dave Lloyd	3	68	22.7	0
Joe Scarpati	3	41	13.7	1
Don Burroughs	2	5	2.5	0
Glenn Glass	1	18	18.0	0

Kicking	PAT Made	PAT Att	PAT %	FG Made	FG Att	FG %	Pts
Sam Baker	36	37	97	16	26	61.5	84

THE PHILADELPHIA INQUIRER. MONDAY MORNING, SEPTEMBER 14, 1964   a h   31

Too Many Eagles in Backfield
Make It Trying Day for Tittle

Inquirer Photos by Alexander Deans, Staff Photographer

Eagles' blitzing defense kept catching up with Giants' signal-caller, as linebacker Baughan applies "collar" tackle and Morgan zeroes on Yat's underpinnings.

Giants' Y. A. Tittle (left) found that his "pocket" Sunday consisted all too often of Eagles instead of Giants. Floyd Peters (72), Mike Morgan (89) and Max Baughan (55) apply first-quarter rush.

Even the news on the sidelines wasn't good. Tittle relaxes glumly while Giants' coach Allie Sherman talks with aides upstairs as disaster unfolds.

To make day "complete," Tittle had to run 248-pound Eagle linebacker Dave Lloyd (left) out of bounds after latter had stolen Yat's pass in fourth period and returned it to Giants' nine-yard line.

September 14, 1964
Eagles snap a six-game losing streak against the Giants by winning 38-7. QB Norm Snead makes his Eagles debut.

1964

1965

RECORD: 5-9, T-5TH IN NFL EAST
HEAD COACH: JOE KUHARICH

Schedule
Regular Season

Wk. 2	Sep 19	W	34-27	vs St. Louis Cardinals
Wk. 3	Sep 26	L	16-14	vs New York Giants
Wk. 4	Oct 3	L	35-17	vs Cleveland Browns
Wk. 5	Oct 10	W	35-24	at Dallas Cowboys
Wk. 6	Oct 17	L	35-27	at New York Giants
Wk. 7	Oct 24	L	20-14	vs Pittsburgh Steelers
Wk. 8	Oct 31	L	23-21	at Washington Redskins
Wk. 9	Nov 7	L	38-34	at Cleveland Browns
Wk. 10	Nov 14	W	21-14	vs Washington Redskins
Wk. 11	Nov 21	L	34-24	at Baltimore Colts
Wk. 12	Nov 28	W	28-24	at St. Louis Cardinals
Wk. 13	Dec 5	L	21-19	vs Dallas Cowboys
Wk. 14	Dec 12	W	47-13	at Pittsburgh Steelers
Wk. 15	Dec 19	L	35-28	vs Detroit Lions

Despite solid seasons from quarterback Norm Snead and his favorite target, tight end Pete Retzlaff (66 receptions for 1,190 and 10 touchdowns), the Eagles still had a disappointing season. The Eagles did manage to tie an NFL record with nine interceptions against Pittsburgh in 47-13 win. Unfortunately the team continued to sputter, finishing with a 5-9 record. However, the Eagles did end the season on a strong note by winning three of their last four games.

1965 Philadelphia Eagles Stats

Passing	Comp	Att	Comp %	Yds	Y/Att	TD	Int	Rating
Norm Snead	150	288	52.1	2346	8.15	15	13	78.0
King Hill	60	113	53.1	857	7.58	5	10	55.8
Earl Gros	1	2	50.0	63	31.50	1	0	135.4
Ray Poage	0	1	0.0	0	0.00	0	0	39.6
Timmy Brown	0	1	0.0	0	0.00	0	0	39.6
Jack Concannon	12	29	41.4	176	6.07	1	3	33.8

Rushing	Rush	Yds	Avg	TD
Timmy Brown	158	861	5.4	6
Earl Gros	145	479	3.3	7
Tom Woodeshick	28	145	5.2	0
Jack Concannon	9	104	11.6	0
Ollie Matson	22	103	4.7	2
Norm Snead	24	81	3.4	3
Izzy Lang	10	25	2.5	1
King Hill	7	20	2.9	2
Joe Scarpati	1	6	6.0	0

Receiving	Rec	Yds	Avg	TD
Pete Retzlaff	66	1190	18.0	10
Timmy Brown	50	682	13.6	3
Ray Poage	31	612	19.7	5
Earl Gros	29	271	9.3	2
Ron Goodwin	18	252	14.0	1
Glenn Glass	15	201	13.4	0
Tom Woodeshick	6	86	14.3	0
Claude Crabb	2	41	20.5	0
Izzy Lang	2	30	15.0	0
Ollie Matson	2	29	14.5	1
Roger Gill	1	27	27.0	0
Fred Hill	1	21	21.0	0

Interceptions	Int	Yds	Avg	TD
Nate Ramsey	6	74	12.3	0
Jim Nettles	3	84	28.0	1
Joe Scarpati	3	4	1.3	0
Irv Cross	3	1	0.3	0
Dave Lloyd	2	35	17.5	0
Al Nelson	2	23	11.5	0
John Meyers	2	12	6.0	0
George Tarasovic	1	40	40.0	1
Maxie Baughan	1	33	33.0	1
Don Hultz	1	6	6.0	0
Mike Morgan	1	1	1.0	0

Punting	Punts	Yds	Avg	Blocked
King Hill	19	813	42.8	0
Sam Baker	37	1551	41.9	0

Kicking	PAT Made	PAT Att	PAT %	FG Made	FG Att	FG %	Pts
Sam Baker	38	40	95	9	23	39.1	65
Dave Lloyd	7	7	100	1	2	50.0	10

The Philadelphia Inquirer — *Today's* SPORTS

32   MONDAY, DECEMBER 13, 1965   h★

Also in this section
Financial News
Classified
Advertising
Comics, Puzzles

Eagles Steal 9 Passes, Rip Steelers, 47-13

6 Interceptions Turned Into TDs; Nettles Grabs 3

Astros Fire Richards, Harris in Shakeup

Pittsburgh Suffers 11th Loss as Thefts Equal NFL Record

By HERB GOOD
Of The Inquirer Staff

PITTSBURGH, Dec. 12. — Using enemy passes as their most potent weapon, the Eagles rolled over the Pittsburgh Steelers on Sunday with ridiculous ease, 47-13, for their fifth victory before 22,002 in Pitt Stadium.

With rookie Jim Nettles stealing three, the Eagles intercepted nine passes to tie the National Football League record as they handed the Steelers their sixth straight loss and 11th reverse of the season.

Three of the interceptions were returned for touchdowns and three other scores stemmed from the thefts as the Eagles avenged a 20-14 setback received in a Franklin Field upset.

NETTLES SCORES

Nettles, diminutive former Wisconsin star who was pressed into service at strong-side safety when Nate Ramsey was injured early in the game, returned his second interception 50 yards for his first pro TD Maxie Baughan, seeing most of his action at middle linebacker, raced 33 yards and George Tarasovic, a former Steeler, dashed 46 yards for scores on their interceptions.

Marv Woodson also raced 61 yards with an interception for Pittsburgh's second TD on the last play of the first half. Thus, four scoring interceptions by the two teams set a new NFL record, and the three by the Eagles tied the league mark for one team.

It was a weird, sloppy game, almost a travesty on the sport, and was played in unseasonable 64-degree weather on a somewhat soggy field outlined by sawdust at the wettest spots. Brief flurries of fisticuffs broke out three times as frustrations ignited tempers.

RETZLAFF SETS MARKS

Veteran tight end Pete Retzlaff wiped out two of Tommy McDonald's Eagle season records with five catches for 52 yards and one TD, all in the first half. He now has 66 catches, one more than McDonald made in 1961, and 1171 yards, compared with the 1146 yards McDonald contributed in 1962.

Except for that bright point, the Eagles did little to brag about offensively although running up a 34-0 lead in the first 16 minutes and scoring the most points ever made against the Steelers in this long rivalry.

Believe it or not, the Steelers had a 19-17 edge in first downs and had a total net yardage advantage of 356 to 302.

Norm Snead directed the Eagles to first-period scores on

Continued on Page 34, Column 6

'Guilty Conscience'
Lucky to Intercept 3, Rookie Nettles Claims

Special to The Inquirer

PITTSBURGH, Dec. 12 — Nobody bothered to draft Jim Nettles when his football eligibility expired at the University of Wisconsin two years ago, so he stayed in school to pick up his degree in landscape architecture and worked at a variety of jobs.

He helped plan a John F. Kennedy Memorial Library in his home town—Muncie, Ind.—and as a member of the General Motors labor relations staff helped negotiate a contract with a Muncie local.

Sunday, the pint-sized defensive halfback negotiated a place for himself in the Eagles future history as he intercepted three Pittsburgh Steeler passes—a total that fell one short of a prediction he'd made before the game.

Continued on Page 34, Column 2

Hornung Gets 5 TDs As Packers Top Colts To Take Division Lead

BALTIMORE, Dec. 12 (AP)—Paul Hornung scored five touchdowns in leading the Green Bay Packers to a 42-27 victory over the crippled Baltimore Colts Sunday and moved the Packers into first place in the National Football League's Western Conference.

The Packers, winning their 10th game against three losses, took a one-half game lead over the Colts and can clinch a championship playoff berth Jan. 2 against Cleveland by beating San Francisco in the final game next Sunday.

The scoring outburst by the Packers was their highest of the season and Hornung's five touchdowns were the most ever by a Packer. The Golden Boy had scored only three in the 12 previous games this season.

42-YARD PASS PLAY

As the Colts were staging their second attempt at a comeback in the last quarter, Hornung and quarterback Bart Starr pulled off a 42-yard pass and scoring play.

In the first quarter, the same pair worked a 50-yard touchdown and Hornung ran for three more.

The Colts, with quarterback John Unitas on crutches on the sideline, and his substitute Gary Cuozzo playing the last half with an injured shoulder, had trouble with their offense until the last quarter.

They scored twice then to chop the Packer lead to 35-27. Cuozzo set up the first score with a 40-yard pass and Raymond Berry and hit him for the second on a five-yard toss.

The Colts were blanked in the third quarter when Cuozzo was hurt and the Packers ran up a 35-13 lead with Hornung scoring twice.

47-YARD RETURN

They muffed an opportunity to take the lead at halftime instead of trailing, 21-13.

They were on the Packer two and scored down when Cuozzo lofted a soft pass to the flat on his right.

Linebacker Dave Robinson intercepted the ball and rambled 47 yards to the Colt 10 before being dragged down from behind. On the first play, Starr rifled a touchdown pass to end Boyd Dowler.

The sudden turn of events extinguished what had been a rally by the Colts to overcome a 14-3 Packer lead in the first quarter.

Although the Colts drew first blood on Lou Michaels' 14-yard field goal after Lenny Lyles returned an intercepted pass to the Green Bay 11, the Packers stormed for touchdowns the next two times with the ball.

They ran and passed through the Colts for 64 yards on six plays, with Hornung ramming over the last two. Hornung worked his way out in the clear the next time the Packers were in possession and Starr hit him with a pass for a 50-yard scoring play.

Michaels kicked another field goal of 43 yards and Lyles provided the offense with another chance to score by recovering a

Continued on Page 34, Column 1

See Red Smith's Column on Page 36

Sports Results

Professional
FOOTBALL
NATIONAL LEAGUE

EAGLES 47	Pittsburgh 13
Green Bay 42	Baltimore 27
Chicago 61	San Francisco 20
New York 27	Cleveland 2
Minnesota 29	Washington 21
Dallas 27	Detroit 7

Saturday's Result
St. Louis 13

Eastern Conference

	W	L	T	Pct.	Pts.	Op.
*Cleveland	10	3	0	.769	349	301
New York	6	7	0	.538	258	398
Dallas	6	7	0	.462	287	268
EAGLES	5	8	0	.385	344	361
St. Louis	5	8	0	.385	345	372
Pittsburgh	2	11	0	.154	188	352

*Clinched conference title.

Western Conference

	W	L	T	Pct.	Pts.	Op.
Green Bay	10	3	0	.769	292	200
Baltimore	9	3	1	.750	369	267
Chicago	8	4	0	.692	382	234
S.Francisco	6	6	0	.538	397	378
Minnesota	7	6	0	.462	350	386
Detroit	5	7	1	.417	227	267
Los Angeles	4	9	0	.308	252	269

AMERICAN LEAGUE

San Diego 37	Houston 26
Oakland 24	New York 14
Boston 26	Denver 28

Eastern Division

	W	L	T	Pct.	Pts.	Opp.
Buffalo	10	2	1	.833	301	212
New York	4	8	1	.333	271	291
Houston	3	9	0	.308	281	387
Boston	3	8	2	.273	202	288

Western Division

	W	L	T	Pct.	Pts.	Opp.
*San Diego	8	2	1	.800	314	213
Oakland	7	6	0	.538	301	281
Kansas City	6	5	2	.545	275	248
Denver	4	9	0	.308	288	347

*Clinched divisional title.

Waiting eagerly for this pre-Christmas gift, Eagles' Maxie Baughan prepares to make shoestring catch of pass thrown by Steelers' sub quarterback, Tommy Wade, on Steeler 33 late in the first quarter.

In full stride after making the interception, Baughan veers to his right as he nears the Steelers' 15. Ray Mansfield and Dan James race cross-field in an effort to cut him off.

Inquirer Magic Eye Photos by Robert L. Mooney, Staff Photographer

Running more like a young halfback than a veteran linebacker, Maxie keeps his feet and manages to stay in bounds as he eludes Mansfield at the eight and heads for the Steeler goal line.

Crossing the five, Maxie runs into Steelers' Charlie Bradshaw, who appears to have a clean shot at the ball-carrier. But Baughan, cutting back to the inside, escapes Bradshaw's grasp.

Running hard and low, Maxie is home free at the end of his fancy-stepping dash, crossing the goal line an instant before Steelers' Mike Lind hits him. Baughan's TD gave Eagles a 27-0 lead.

Grady Hatton Promoted to Manager's Job

Tal Smith Is Named Head of Personnel; Robinson Bounced

HOUSTON, Tex., Dec. 12 (UPI).—The Houston Astros, ninth in the National League for the past three years, Sunday fired general manager Paul Richards and field manager Luman Harris in a major top-level shakeup.

The Astros' owner, Judge Roy Hofheinz, announced that former Cincinnati third baseman Grady Hatton will replace Harris as manager.

The 43-year-old Hatton moves up to the post from the managership of the Astros' Class Triple-A minor league club at Oklahoma City, which he guided to two pennants and a third-place finish in three years.

ROBINSON OUT ALSO

Also losing his job in the shakeup was Astros' farm director Eddie Robinson.

Hofheinz said Tal Smith, a key figure in laying out the fabulous Harris County domed stadium for baseball, will become a vice-president of the Astros and director of player personnel.

"Hatton and Smith will handle all decisions regarding player personnel and development throughout the Houston organization," Hofheinz said.

Hofheinz said he wished "Richards the very best in any endeavor he may undertake."

CONTRACT THROUGH 1970

Richards, who had a 65-97 record with the Astros last season, had another year to go on his contract. Hofheinz said he will be offered another position with the club.

Richards had a contract that ran through 1970.

Hatton only last Friday announced that he had an offer from the Chicago White Sox to succeed Al Lopez as manager, an offer that the White Sox denied making. The unusual nature of the Hatton announcement led to widespread speculation that he was on his way up in the Houston organization.

SOME COACHES OUT

Hatton said that he will choose his own coaches under his new job, and indicated that "some" of his present staff would not stay on. He did not say who would be fired.

Hatton joined the Houston organization less than a month

Continued on Page 35, Column 2

Sayers' 6 TDs Equal Mark as Bears Win, 61-20

CHICAGO, Dec. 12 (AP).— Fabulous Gale Sayers scored six touchdowns Sunday, pushing his season total to 21 to set a National Football League season record, and the Chicago Bears routed the San Francisco 49ers, 61-20.

Sayers' touchdown spree established a Bear single game scoring record and also matched the one-game NFL mark.

His total of 21 bettered the league record of 20 registered last season by Baltimore's Lenny Moore and duplicated this season by Cleveland's Jimmy Brown.

BEARS AVENGE LOSS

The triumph, avenging an opening 52-24 defeat at San Francisco, kept alive the Bears' mathematical chance of sharing the Western Conference title. They now have a 8-4 mark.

The remarkable rookie from Kansas tallied this way on a rain-slick field as 46,278 fans gave him standing ovations:

First quarter — Rudy Bukich hit Sayers on a screen pass and he streaked 80 yards.

SAYERS BOLTS OVER

Second quarter—After John Arnett ran back a punt 77 yards to the 49ers' 21, Sayers bolted across on the first play. Bukich's 51-yard pass to Jimmy Jones set up Sayers' next scoring smash from the seven on a pitchout.

Third quarter — Sayers cut through tackle and raced 30

Continued on Page 35, Column 3

1966

RECORD: 9-5, T-2ND IN NFL EAST
HEAD COACH: JOE KUHARICH

Schedule

Regular Season

Wk. 2	Sep 11	L	16-13	at St. Louis Cardinals
Wk. 3	Sep 18	W	23-10	vs Atlanta Falcons
Wk. 4	Sep 25	W	35-17	vs New York Giants
Wk. 5	Oct 2	L	41-10	vs St. Louis Cardinals
Wk. 6	Oct 9	L	56-7	at Dallas Cowboys
Wk. 7	Oct 16	W	31-14	at Pittsburgh Steelers
Wk. 8	Oct 23	W	31-3	at New York Giants
Wk. 9	Oct 30	L	27-13	vs Washington Redskins
Wk. 10	Nov 6	W	24-23	vs Dallas Cowboys
Wk. 11	Nov 13	L	27-7	at Cleveland Browns
Wk. 12	Nov 20	W	35-34	at San Francisco 49ers
Wk. 14	Dec 4	W	27-23	vs Pittsburgh Steelers
Wk. 15	Dec 11	W	33-21	vs Cleveland Browns
Wk. 16	Dec 18	W	37-28	at Washington Redskins

Despite more trades and switching between three different quarterbacks (Norm Snead, Jack Concannon and King Hill) the Eagles actually played solid football all year, finishing with a 9-5 record for their first winning season in five years. However, the Eagles record was only good enough to land them in second place.

1966 Philadelphia Eagles Stats

Passing	Comp	Att	Comp %	Yds	Y/Att	TD	Int	Rating
Norm Snead	103	226	45.6	1275	5.64	8	11	55.1
Izzy Lang	2	3	66.7	51	17.00	0	0	109.7
King Hill	53	97	54.6	571	5.89	5	7	59.3
Earl Gros	0	1	0.0	0	0.00	0	0	39.6
Jack Concannon	21	51	41.2	262	5.14	1	4	31.7

Rushing	Rush	Yds	Avg	TD
Timmy Brown	161	548	3.4	3
Earl Gros	102	396	3.9	7
Tom Woodeshick	85	330	3.9	4
Izzy Lang	52	239	4.6	1
Jack Concannon	25	195	7.8	2
Ollie Matson	29	101	3.5	1
Norm Snead	15	32	2.1	1
Sam Baker	1	15	15.0	0
Fred Hill	1	5	5.0	0
King Hill	7	-2	-0.3	0

Receiving	Rec	Yds	Avg	TD
Pete Retzlaff	40	653	16.3	6
Timmy Brown	33	371	11.2	3
Fred Hill	29	304	10.5	0
Earl Gros	18	214	11.9	2
Ron Goodwin	16	212	13.3	1
Ben Hawkins	14	143	10.2	0
Izzy Lang	12	107	8.9	0
Tom Woodeshick	10	118	11.8	1
Ollie Matson	6	30	5.0	1
Jack Concannon	1	7	7.0	0

Punting	Punts	Yds	Avg	Blocked
Sam Baker	42	1726	41.1	0
King Hill	23	862	37.5	0

Interceptions	Int	Yds	Avg	TD
Joe Scarpati	8	182	22.8	0
Jim Nettles3	57	19.0	1	
Dave Lloyd	3	46	15.3	0
Aaron Martin	1	47	47.0	0
Harold Wells	1	8	8.0	0
Mike Morgan	1	5	5.0	0
Al Nelson	1	0	0.0	0
Nate Ramsey	1	0	0.0	0
Fred Whittington	1	0	0.0	0

Kicking	PAT Made	PAT Att	PAT %	FG Made	FG Att	FG %	Pts
Sam Baker	38	39	97	18	25	72.0	92

1966

The Philadelphia Inquirer
43 MONDAY, JANUARY 9, 1967

Today's SPORTS

Also in this section
Classified
Advertising
Comics, Puzzles

Colts Down Eagles in Final 14 Seconds

With only 14 seconds left in game, Colts' Tom Matte (41) crosses goal with winning touchdown after taking handoff from Johnny Unitas (19). Matte's score defeated Eagles, 20-14, in Playoff Bowl.

Intercepted Pass Sets Up 20-14 Playoff Bowl Win

By GORDON FORBES
Of the Inquirer Staff

MIAMI, Fla., Jan. 8.—None of the plungers at Miami's gambling dens blew as much over the weekend as Jack Concannon did on one tragic play Sunday in the Orange Bowl. The Baltimore Colts latched on to an unexpected Concannon pass which they converted into a last-second touchdown and a 20-14 Playoff Bowl victory before 58,088 shirt-sleeved fans and a Nation-wide television audience.

The interception cost the Eagles a cool $28,000, the difference between $48,000, and $1200 per player for the winning team, and $20,000, and $500 per man, for the losing team.

DULL SECOND HALF

Actually, there was such a dull flavor to the second half that many of the fans were streaming for the exits when Concannon made his ill-fated pitch.

It came when the Eagles had second down at their 25 and needed only three yards for a first down with a little more than three minutes left to play.

Instead of hammering out a first down, Concannon shoved the entire stakes on his ability to hit tight end Pete Retzlaff on a sprint-out play to his right.

LOGAN INTERCEPTS

Jerry Logan, however, ranged up to grab the ball at the Eagles' 40 and joyfully dashed with it to the 35.

That left it up to Johnny Unitas, who proceeded to guide the Colts into the end zone, with Tom Matte, hero of last season's Playoff Bowl win over the Dallas Cowboys, slamming the final foot with just 14 seconds left.

It was an ironic windup for the Eagles, who had laughed at odds all season while compiling a 9-5 record.

And it was especially bitter for Concannon, who had wrested the quarterback job away from King Hill and Norm Snead with his daring, sometimes nondescript style of moving the offense.

'JUST HUNG IT UP THERE'

"I just got jammed up when I rolled out and thought I saw Retzlaff open," said a dejected Concannon in the Eagles' locker room. "I just hung it up there."

After the theft, the Eagles could have braced at the 17 when the Colts went to third-and-nine. But even so, Baltimore had Lou Michaels available for a field goal that would have erased the Eagles' 14-13 lead.

Michaels wasn't called on then because Matte ripped past Don Hultz, Gary Pettigew and Dave Lloyd for a 10-yard gain and a first down at the seven with 1:25 to play.

INTERFERENCE PENALTY

A motion penalty pushed the Colts momentarily back to the 12 but Jim Nettles, defensing Ray Berry, was guilty of interference and Baltimore got a first down at the six.

In the final minute, it took the Colts three plays to score. Fullback Jerry Hill smashed for three; Matte went over right tackle for almost three more and then slid off linebacker Har-

Continued on Page 44, Column 3

Frank Dolson

Miami Fans Missed TV Fun

Look, there on the screen,
Is it a soap opera?
Is it a variety show?
Well, it's certainly not Super Bowl.

OKAY, so the temperature in Miami was in the 80s, the sun was shining and the voice kept saying, "It's a beautiful day for football."

And . . . let's be honest. It was a miserable day in Philadelphia, damp and dismal. Good for nothing much but sitting in front of a television screen and watching the Eagles play the Colts in the sixth annual Lesser Bowl.

FRANK DOLSON

Still, that's no reason to be jealous of those 58,088 live ones, basking in the Orange Bowl. Oh sure, they got a tan and saw a football game. But think of what they missed.

Studio audiences never see as much of a TV show as the home viewers. And, let's face it. The NFL's Lesser Bowl, pitting the team that didn't quite win the Eastern title against the team that didn't quite win the Western title, is basically a TV show. So it shouldn't be surprising that those poor, sun-bathing ticket-buyers in Miami missed practically all the fun.

* * *

COUNTING pre-game and post-game shows, they missed 25 commercials, all in living color. While the folks in the Orange Bowl yawned through all those dull, minute-long time-outs, those of us lucky enough to be home thrilled to the sight of people hawking four brands of cigarets, two makes of TV sets, two deodorants, cars, trucks, gasoline, razor blades, sun glasses, cigars, after-shave lotion, shaving cream, tires, an airline and a beer.

Best of all, was an inspired commercial for Ford pickup trucks, starring Harry Gilmer, "coach of the Detroit Lions." Gilmer played his role with striking realism, considering he was fired a couple of days ago by the owner of the Lions, William Clay Ford.

Apparently, there was a breakdown in communications between the auto branch and the football branch of the Ford family. Now that the auto branch has used Gilmer to plug cars, the football branch may get even by using the Lions to plug Edsels.

The studio audience also missed a lot of other goodies. There were isolated videotape reruns in color and slow-motion reruns in black and white. There were close-up shots of the Orange Bowl queen and her court. And there was a pre-game interview with Eagles' coach Joe Kuharich, who told home viewers: "We're hopeful that with variations of defensive maneuvers we can stymie them, at least periodically."

The Lesser Bowl, though, was much more than a TV show. In reality, it was a gigantic, three-hour-

Continued on Page 44, Column 4

Subs' 12-5 Spurt Propels 76ers By Bulls, 117-108

Full-Court Press Decisive: Celtics Fall 9 Games Back

By JACK CHEVALIER
Of The Inquirer Staff

CHICAGO, Jan. 8. — A scrambling, pressing defense — executed by the 76ers' reserves while the strong men were catching their breath for the fourth quarter — carried Philadelphia to a stormy, 117-108 victory over the Chicago Bulls on Sunday night.

The unexpected surge came in the last 3:42 of the third period with Wilt Chamberlain resting his injured ankle and four other regulars out of the lineup. It changed the game, which Chicago had dominated, and sent the 76ers limping into the All-Star break with a 39-4 record.

By breaking the Bulls' spirit and silencing an International Amphitheater crowd of 7353, the 76ers opened a fat, nine-game bulge on the second-place Boston Celtics in the National Basketball Association's Eastern Division.

SUBS GET 12-5 SPURT

While the subs tied up Chicago with a sticky, full-court press, the 76ers went on a 12-5 spurt to take a 92-88 lead after three quarters. Then Chamberlain, Luke Jackson and Hal Greer returned to turn on the usual power and make the 76ers' record 7-0 against this expansion club.

With Larry Costello out for three weeks with torn knee ligaments, coach Alex Hannum started the game with a thin backcourt crew. Things got worse after only 7:33 when Villanova grad Wally Jones was ejected for fighting with Temple grad Guy Rodgers.

Rodgers also got the thumb and was sorely missed by Bulls' coach Johnny Kerr. "Nevertheless, it was the press that killed us," Kerr admitted after the game. "I'm surprised Philly didn't try it earlier."

WILT GETS REST

The proper time came with Chicago on top, 81-80, and Chamberlain—whose right achilles tendon was kicked in Friday's game against Baltimore — due for a rest. The personal foul situation strongly favored the 76ers and Hannum decided to gamble.

Dave Gambee and Chet Walker took care of the rebounds, rookies Bill Melchionni and Matt Guokas fired the points, and the Bulls made repeated mistakes in the next 3:42.

Melchionni's first hoop of the game put the 76ers on top, 84-83. He and Walker sank free throws, then Walker stole the ball at midcourt and drove for a 15-foot jumper.

Guokas, tighter than a drum during the first half, caught the

Continued on Page 44, Column 1

No 'Star' Tilt For Wilt?

CHICAGO, Jan. 8. — Wilt Chamberlain, hobbled by a swollen achilles tendon in his right ankle, said Sunday night he may not play in the NBA All-Star game on Tuesday in San Francisco.

"If this ankle doesn't feel any better tomorrow, I'll tell them I can't play," Wilt said. "I won't request it. I'll tell them."

Chamberlain, Hal Greer and Chet Walker are scheduled to represent the 76ers in the East-West game. The Knicks' Walt Bellamy, the logical replacement if Chamberlain can't play, will be in San Francisco because New York is making a West Coast swing.

Subperb

G—Goals; ST—Shots tried; F—Fouls; FT—Fouls tried; R—Rebounds; A—Assists; P—Personal fouls; PTS—Total points.

[illegible]

Guokas Plays Well

Jones, Rodgers Banished for 1st-Period Fight

Special to The Inquirer

CHICAGO, Jan. 8. — Wally Jones and Guy Rodgers, old head-to-head playground and professional basketball rivals, were ejected from Sunday night's 76ers-Chicago game after a fist fight in the first quarter.

The scuffle, in which both participants landed a couple of solid punches, occurred at 7:33 of the period after Jones tripped Rodgers, who was trying to drive toward the basket.

Chicago's Rodgers came up swinging and it took 76ers' coach Alex Hannum and the Bulls' Jim Washington, a former teammate of Jones at Villanova, to prevent Wally from making it a 10-round bout. Jones and Hannum later said that an incident earlier in the game led to the fight.

JONES CLOUTED

"Guy did something to me, physically," Jones said. "He knows what it is—I don't want to say."

Hannum revealed that Rodgers had clouted Jones in the mouth with an elbow during a rebound battle.

"It was a dirty, malicious play," the coach said. "Wally

Continued on Page 44, Column 7

Concannon Wanted to Run On Pivotal Interception Play

By JOHN DELL
Of the Inquirer Staff

MIAMI, Fla., Jan. 8.—"Did you get paid yet," Timmy Brown asked, holding his $300 loser's share from Sunday's Playoff Bowl game. "They're not going to give me any," Jack Concannon answered. This was in the Eagles' locker room at the Orange Bowl stadium, after the Eagles blew a whole locker-room load of $1200 winning shares.

Concannon was feeling lowest of the low, after an interception of his pass gave the Baltimore Colts a chance to get fat piggy banks, 20-14, on a touchdown 14 seconds before the end.

"I was surprised that he threw the ball," said Jerry Logan, Colts' right safetyman, who was playing his zone, on the left side, and hoping more than expecting that the ball would be propelled within his reach on a second-and-three situation on the Eagles' 25. Logan intercepted and returned 14 to the Eagles' 35.

LOGAN CONFIDENT

"I was just happy," was the reaction of Logan, who also made an interception in the Colts' 34-24 victory over the Eagles last season, a win made possible by Bobby Boyd's interception.

"I thought John (Unitas) would take us in or we'd get

Continued on Page 41, Column 6

Inquirer Games

Tickets Now At 3 Outlets

BUY your tickets now for the 23d annual Inquirer Track Games, Saturday, Feb. 4, at Civic Center Convention Hall.

Prices are:

$5.50	$3.50
$4.50	$2.50

Tickets are now on sale at these Central City Ticket Offices:

1422 Chestnut st.
10 A. M.-5:30 P. M.
69th Street Terminal Concourse
41 Roosevelt plaza, Camden

For mail orders make check payable to Philadelphia Inquirer Charities, Inc., and mail to Central City Ticket Office, 1422 Chestnut st., Philadelphia, Pa. 19102. Include 25 cents for postage and handling.

Sports Results

Professional

FOOTBALL
NFL PLAYOFF BOWL
Baltimore 20 EAGLES 14

BASKETBALL
NATIONAL BASKETBALL ASSN.
76ERS 117 Chicago 108
Cincinnati 126 Baltimore 94
St. Louis 117 Detroit 115
New York 121 Los Angeles 118
(Only games scheduled)

[illegible]

HOCKEY
NATIONAL LEAGUE

[illegible]

AMERICAN LEAGUE

[illegible]

EASTERN LEAGUE

[illegible]

School

BASKETBALL
CATHOLIC LEAGUE

[illegible]

SUBURBAN CATHOLIC LEAGUE

[illegible]

NON LEAGUE

[illegible]

Independent

BASKETBALL
SCHUYLKILL NAVY LEAGUE

[illegible]

JEWISH LEAGUE

[illegible]

Campbell's Body Still Not Found

CONISTON, England, Jan. 8 (AP).—While prayers were said for him in village churches Sunday, divers continued searching for the body of speed king Donald Campbell who died when his jet boat Bluebird crashed on Coniston Lake last Wednesday.

Bluebird's steering wheel was dredged up, but the boat's hull still lay stuck in a bed of silt 142 feet down.

The violence of pro football is well demonstrated on this play as Colts' linebacker Mike Curtis takes the legs out from under Eagles' Ron Goodwin, who has just caught a Jack Concannon pass for nine-yard gain.

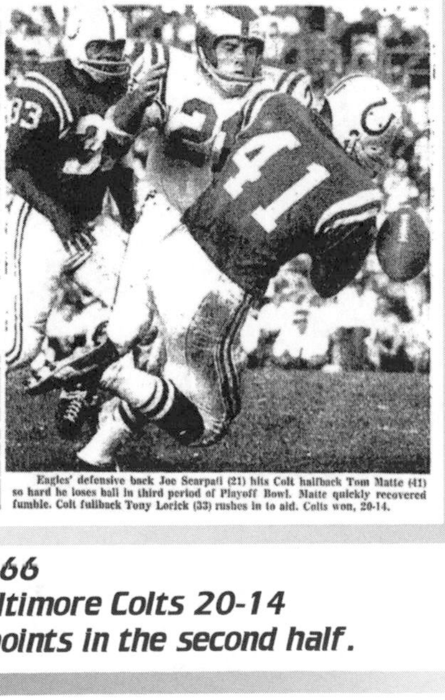

Eagles' defensive back Joe Scarpati (21) hits Colt halfback Tom Matte (41) so hard he loses ball in third period of Playoff Bowl. Matte quickly recovered fumble. Colt fullback Tony Lorick (33) rushes in to aid. Colts won, 20-14.

January 9, 1967 for 1966
Eagles lose in the Playoff Bowl to the Baltimore Colts 20-14 as the Colts come back with 10 unanswered points in the second half.

1967

RECORD: 6-7-1, 2ND IN NFL CAPITOL
HEAD COACH: JOE KUHARICH

Schedule

Regular Season

Wk. 3	Sep 17	W	35-24	vs Washington Redskins
Wk. 4	Sep 24	L	38-6	vs Baltimore Colts
Wk. 5	Oct 1	W	34-24	vs Pittsburgh Steelers
Wk. 6	Oct 8	W	38-7	at Atlanta Falcons
Wk. 7	Oct 15	L	28-27	vs San Francisco 49ers
Wk. 8	Oct 22	L	48-14	at St. Louis Cardinals
Wk. 9	Oct 29	W	21-14	vs Dallas Cowboys
Wk. 10	Nov 5	L	31-24	at New Orleans Saints
Wk. 11	Nov 12	L	33-17	at Los Angeles Rams
Wk. 12	Nov 19	W	48-21	vs New Orleans Saints
Wk. 13	Nov 26	L	44-7	at New York Giants
Wk. 14	Dec 3	T	35-35	at Washington Redskins
Wk. 15	Dec 10	L	38-17	at Dallas Cowboys
Wk. 16	Dec 17	W	28-24	vs Cleveland Browns

Quarterback Norm Snead and flanker Ben Hawkins set team passing (3,399 yards for 29 touchdowns) and receiving records (59 completions gaining 1,265 yards and 10 touchdowns), respectively. However, injuries to key players and a poor showing by the defense allowing 409 points led the team to a disappointing 6-7-1 record.

1967 Philadelphia Eagles Stats

Passing	Comp	Att	Comp %	Yds	Y/Att	TD	Int	Rating
Norm Snead	240	434	55.3	3399	7.83	29	24	80.0
Izzy Lang	1	1	100.0	26	26.00	0	0	118.8
King Hill	2	7	28.6	33	4.71	1	0	86.3
Benjy Dial	1	3	33.3	5	1.67	0	0	42.4

Rushing	Rush	Yds	Avg	TD
Tom Woodeshick	155	670	4.3	6
Izzy Lang	101	336	3.3	2
Timmy Brown	53	179	3.4	1
Norm Snead	9	30	3.3	2
Harry Jones	8	17	2.1	0
Gary Ballman	1	17	17.0	1
Ron Goodwin	1	1	1.0	0

Receiving	Rec	Yds	Avg	TD
Ben Hawkins	59	1265	21.4	10
Gary Ballman	36	524	14.6	6
Tom Woodeshick	34	391	11.5	4
Mike Ditka	26	274	10.5	2
Izzy Lang	26	201	7.7	3
Timmy Brown	22	202	9.2	1
Jim Kelly	21	345	16.4	4
Fred Hill	9	144	16.0	0
Ron Goodwin	6	65	10.8	0
Harry Jones	3	32	10.7	0
Harry Wilson	2	20	10.0	0

Interceptions	Int	Yds	Avg	TD
Joe Scarpati	4	99	24.8	1
Jim Nettles	4	52	13.0	0
Fred Brown	2	29	14.5	0
Ron Medved	2	23	11.5	0
Aaron Martin	2	8	4.0	0
Ike Kelley	1	18	18.0	0
Harold Wells	1	17	17.0	0
Don Hultz	1	16	16.0	1
Bob Shann	1	8	8.0	0
Floyd Peters	1	3	3.0	0
Dave Lloyd	1	1	1.0	0
Mike Morgan	1	0	0.0	0

Punting	Punts	Yds	Avg	Blocked
Sam Baker	61	2335	38.3	0

Kicking	PAT Made	PAT Att	PAT %	FG Made	FG Att	FG %	Pts
Sam Baker	45	45	100	12	19	63.2	81

1967

The Philadelphia Inquirer

25 MONDAY, NOVEMBER 20, 1967 h

Today's SPORTS

Also in this section
Classified
Advertising
Comics, Puzzles

Snead Stars as Eagles Rout Saints, 48-21

Sandy Padwe

Tom's Policy: Get Rid of Joe

IT WAS not a good day for Tom Woodruff. It was cold in Franklin Field, the wind was blowing and it took a long while to gain the attention of the hot chocolate vendors.

SANDY PADWE

Besides that, the Eagles won, 48-21, over New Orleans. Normally that would make Tom Woodruff happy. But these are not normal times. And they won't be until Joe Kuharich is coaching some place else. Like about 12 years from now.

Tom Woodruff is the president of a rather informal society known as the "Let's Get Rid of Joe Kuharich Club."

Woodruff is the manager of an insurance agency in Abington. He's in his 30s and looks very much like Ed Snider, the former vice president of the Eagles.

"I wish I had his money," Tom Woodruff said. If he did, you know the first thing he would do. He would head straight for the Eagles office and buy up Joe Kuharich's contract.

"Listen," Woodruff said. "I like Jerry Wolman. He's a courteous man and I want to see him get out of those financial problems he's in. But if someone bought the Eagles from him, I wouldn't mind. The new owners would get rid of Kuharich.

"What did Kuharich ever do to earn a contract (15 years) like that?"

* * *

EXACTLY what is Woodruff's gripe about Kuharich? "We know it doesn't mean a thing to him to hear what the fans think," Woodruff said. "He's demonstrated that on television and through his statements in the papers.

"It's frustrating. The fans made this league what it is. I know the fans can't run the teams, but the sentiment around our section of Franklin Field and the sentiment of lots of people I've spoken to is the same as mine.

"What has he done here? He asked for four years to build a championship team. Well? What has he done to improve the defensive line? And his trades? He never gets anything in return for any of his trades.

"The man never admits individual weaknesses among his players and he has no imagination. None. If he did, he might have compensated for some of those injuries last week."

Tom Woodruff is no wild-eyed radical. He dresses conservatively. Lives in the quiet, Chestnut Hill area.

"I just love the Eagles," he said. "We have about 25 people in this club. Some work with me. I know there are a lot of people who feel this way. You hear it all over town."

Last week, the club acted officially for the first time. It sent a telegram to Maxie Baughan and Irv Cross, two players Kuharich traded to the Los Angeles Rams.

* * *

IT READ: "We're true Eagle fans, but when Mister Double Talk traded you two guys it was the biggest steal since the Louisiana Purchase. We're asking you and the rest of the Rams not just to win, but play like you've never played before and humiliate him (Kuharich) so bad that he'll want to walk home to Philadelphia just to clear his head. Our sincere wishes for the Rams to win the Western Conference."

—Tom Woodruff, president, *Get Rid of Joe Kuharich Fan Club.*

The Rams complied. But Joe took the team plane back to Philadelphia.

The club's next official act is a secret. A march around City Hall? The Eagles office? Perhaps Franklin Field at halftime of the Browns game Dec. 17?

"I'm not afraid of being called a crank," Tom Woodruff said. "There are a lot of people out there every Sunday who pay good money to see that team play. I just get mad and when I get mad I work my frustrations off by writing letters."

The man he corresponds with is Jerry Wolman. "I've never met Mr. Woodruff," Wolman said, "but I do consider him my pen pal."

It has been a long association. "Ever since the third game of the 1964 season, I've sat down after every Eagles game and written Wolman a letter," Woodruff said. "I just tell him what I think. He answers most of them, too. That's why I consider him a gentleman. How many other men in his position would take the time? On Fridays, the guys at my office have a ritual. They all come up to me and ask me if I've gotten my weekly reply from Jerry."

Wolman laughed. "If he's working his frustration off," Jerry said, "he does a good job of it."

He's got 12 more years to go, too. The post office department should be happy about that.

Inquirer Color Photo by Alexander L. Deans, Staff Photographer

Eagles' Timmy Brown runs for daylight and four-yard gain at Franklin Field before Saints' Mike Tilleman (74) moves in for tackle. Other Eagles are Jim Skaggs (70), Tom Woodeshick (37) and Lynn Hoyem (63). Saints' 81 is Doug Atkins.

60,751 See Norm Complete Four Scoring Passes

Birds Roll Up 28 In Second Period To Avenge Upset

By GORDON FORBES
Of The Inquirer Staff

For one period at least, the Eagles played like a club worth $15 million Sunday while the New Orleans Saints played like a club looking for the first decent road to the airport.

Favored by such environment quarterback Norm Snead hurled four touchdown passes in less than 20 minutes as the Eagles made off with a 48-21 romp before 60,751 chilled onlookers at Franklin Field.

REVENGE VICTORY

The lopsided victory avenged an upset dealt the Eagles in New Orleans two weeks ago. It halted an Eagles' slump which had resulted in four defeats in their last five games and gave them a 5-5 record for the season.

Snead was brilliant during the almost three periods he played. But throughout the second quarter, when the Eagles broke the game open with 24 points, and part of the third, he was close to perfect.

COMPLETES 8 IN ROW

In the second period alone, he completed eight successive passes for 145 yards and three touchdowns. And in the early minutes of the third quarter, Snead struck for a fourth score before retreating to the bench in favor of backup King Hill.

Over-all, Snead completed 19 of 27 attempts for 309 yards, including a pair of touchdown strikes to flanker Ben Hawkins and one each to running backs Tom Woodeshick and Izzy Lang.

"The game plan was to send our backs out to work on their linebackers," Snead said in the winners' dressing room. "And we noticed their backs had been playing deep in recent games.

SHORT GAME WORKS

"So we relied on our short game most of the time—and it worked."

The Eagles seized undisputed control of the game after a whacky first period dominated by cold-weather fumbles.

On the first play of that quarter, Snead completed his fourth pass and his third to tight end Jim Kelly on a drive that swept to the Saints' 31. Two plays later, Snead missed Gary Ballman in the end zone — but he didn't miss again until after halftime.

HAWKINS' GREAT CATCH

His 18-yard bullet was grabbed by a lunging Hawkins in the left corner for a touchdown, leaving defender Dave Whitsell sprawling alongside, and the Saints behind, 10-0. That completion touched off Sneads eight-in-a-row string.

A blend of Don McCall's 68-yard kickoff return, a foolish piling on penalty by bomb squad leader Ike Kelley, which cost 15 more yards, and Gary Cuozzo's 22-yard pitch to rookie split end Dan Abramowicz got the Saints back in contention at 10-7.

After that, the Saints disappeared from view.

SCARPATI INTERCEPTS

An interference call against John Douglas, defending Hawkins on a fly pattern, cost the Saints 44 yards on the next series. It put the ball on the five and Woodeshick barreled over on the next play. Sam Baker, who kicked field goals of 21 and 37 yards, converted for a 17-7 margin.

The Eagles couldn't cash in on Ernie Wheelwright's second fumble near midfield but turned

Continued on Page 26, Column 4

Flyers Nip Blues, 3-2, Then 2 Brawls Erupt As Teams Leave Ice

By JACK CHEVALIER
Of The Inquirer Staff

If they had played a fourth period Sunday night at the Spectrum, it might have been the most exciting 20 minutes in hockey history. That's because tempers were boiling, the score was close and 7102 fans were roaring after the final buzzer in the Flyers' 3-2 victory over the St. Louis Blues.

The game, actually decided by the Flyers' three-goal flurry in the first period, ended in a wild melee, with both teams conducting shoving matches on the ice around two heated fights.

Blues' defenseman Noel Picard jarred the Flyers Larry

Picture, Related Article On Page 28

Zeidel with a sucker punch and it took two linesmen and three Flyers to restrain Zeidel and push him off the ice.

POUNCES ON VAN IMPE

It was a lifeless contest until St. Louis scored twice in the third period, then pulled goalie Glenn Hall for most of the final minute.

The Blues' six-forward attack failed to produce the tying goal, so the visitors decided to have some postgame fireworks. Defenseman Gordie Kannegiessen started the brawl by pouncing on Ed Van Impe, who had scored the Flyers' winning goal.

"We were tangled up in the corner and as he pulled free, my stick hit his face," Van Impe said. "I guess he thought I hit him on purpose, so he jumped me. Pat Hannigan came over to help out and I was glad to see him."

GETS CLOUT UNDER EYE

The game had ended and some of the players were headed toward the locker rooms when they noticed Hannigan and Kannegiessen starting their main bout. They received five-minute fighting penalties, officially timed at 20:00 of the period, but they'll never be served.

Then Zeidel, who hadn't played since the first period, skated out as a peacemaker and was clouted under the left eye by Picard. Zeidel will have a shiner Monday, but he never got a solid return punch at the Blues' defenseman.

IT'LL COST 'EM $50 EACH

"They say Picard knocked out Harry Sinden (the Boston coach) with a sucker punch like that," Zeidel said later. "I must be pretty tough. I didn't go down."

Both of these combatants were

Continued on Page 28, Column 5

Answer Today?

Penn State May Go to Gator Bowl

A MEMBER of the selection committee admitted Sunday that the Gator Bowl is "very much interested" in Penn State as a participant in the Dec. 30 postseason contest in Jacksonville, Fla.

"We like to have an Eastern team because we get good press coverage and a good viewing

Related Articles, Page 29

area for television," Van Fletcher said by telephone from Jacksonville. "But we won't know anything for sure until tomorrow."

The earliest any bowl bid may be offered and accepted under NCAA regulations is 10:30 A. M. Monday.

Fletcher spiked a report that Penn State might be left at home in favor of a team it had beaten. "It's untrue that Penn State is being excluded in favor of Syracuse," Fletcher said in response to one report that had Syracuse playing the Florida-Florida State victor in the Gator Bowl.

Sports Results

Professional
FOOTBALL
NATIONAL LEAGUE
Sundays Results

EAGLES 48	New Orleans 21
Baltimore 41	Detroit 7
L. Angeles 31	Atlanta 3
Cleveland 14	Minnesota 10
New York 28	Pittsburgh 20
Chicago 30	St. Louis 3
Green Bay 13	S. Francisco 0
Washington 27	Dallas 20

Standings
Eastern Conference
Capitol Division

	W.	L.	T.	Pct.	Pts.	Opp.
Dallas	7	3	0	.700	225	183
EAGLES	5	5	0	.500	264	268
Washg'tn	4	4	2	.500	246	236
N. Orl'ns	1	9	0	.100	146	280

Century Division

	W.	L.	T.	Pct.	Pts.	Opp.
Cl'v'land	6	4	0	.600	224	202
St. Louis	5	4	1	.556	251	233
N. York	5	5	0	.500	267	304
Pitt'sb'gh	2	7	1	.222	196	233

Western Conference
Central Division

	W.	L.	T.	Pct.	Pts.	Opp.
Gr. Bay	7	2	1	.778	244	118
Chicago	5	5	0	.500	165	183
Detroit	3	5	2	.375	195	194
Minn's'ta	2	6	2	.250	152	213

Coastal Division

	W.	L.	T.	Pct.	Pts.	Opp.
Baltimore	8	0	2	1.000	305	128
L. Ang'l's	7	1	2	.875	286	152
San Fran.	5	5	0	.500	192	239
Atlanta	1	8	1	.111	106	318

AMERICAN LEAGUE

New York 29	Boston 24
Oakland 31	Miami 17
Denver 21	Buffalo 20
San Diego 17	Kansas City 16

Standings
Eastern Division

	W.	L.	T.	Pct.	Pts.	Opp.
New York	7	2	1	.778	269	204
Houston	5	3	1	.625	142	133
Boston	3	7	1	.300	226	277
Buffalo	3	7	1	.300	145	201
Miami	1	8	0	.111	96	279

Continued on Page 28, Column 2

Locker Room Report

Eagles' Ferocity Surprises Saint

By JOHN DELL
Of The Inquirer Staff

"I knew you fellows were mad, but I didn't think you were that mad," said Ray Rissmiller, the one-time Eagle who plays tackle for the New Orleans Saints, after the Eagles' 48-21, get-even victory Sunday at Franklin Field.

"It was a good day all around," said Jim Ringo, the durable center who was glad some of the sting of a 31-24 upset two weeks ago at New Orleans was eased on his day.

"I thought we had played our bad game against Cleveland," said Ed Khayat, a defensive tackle from the Eagles' 1960 championship team who now coaches the Saints' defensive line. Cleveland beat the Saints, 42-7, in the third game of the season and the fledgings haven't been as thoroughly humbled since. The Saints did a bit of early grave digging but their mistakes only served to make things easier for an Eagles' offense that was functioning so well that the score would have gone into the 50's if Joe Kuharich had not pulled a number of first-liners in the last quarter.

"We didn't do much different on offense than we did against them in the first game," Kuharich said of the plays that gave the Eagles a tidy 421 yards in total offense. They had made 339 yards at New Orleans.

"We added a few man-in-motion plays but 90 to 95 percent of the plays were the same as we used against them before and against Los Angeles," Kuharich said.

The man-in-motion maneuver accounted for the Eagles' easiest touchdown. On it, Norm Snead passed to Jim Kelly for the 35-yard second-quarter touchdown that made the game a runaway. It upped the lead to 24-7 and the momentum carried on until the Eagles built up a 48-7 lead.

"Timmy (Brown) was in mo-

Continued on Page 28, Column 5

Ballman Injured

Gary Ballman, Eagles split end, pulled a hamstring muscle in his right leg Sunday and will be out for possibly two weeks.

Ballman was hurt while running out for a pass in the second quarter of the Eagles 48-21 victory over the New Orleans Saints at Franklin Field. Ballman missed one game because of a similar injury earlier in the season.

Mike Ditka, tight end who tore a medial collateral ligament in his left knee in the 31-24 loss at New Orleans two weeks ago, had his cast removed after the game by Dr. James E. Nixon.

"Mike will start swimming and exercising this week and will miss at least one or two more games," Dr. Nixon said.

Concannon Tosses for 3 TDs

Bears Wallop Cards, 30-3

CHICAGO, Nov. 19 (AP). — Quarterback Jack Concannon threw three touchdown bombs, including a 93-yard strike to Dick Gordon, spiralling the Chicago Bears to a 30-3 victory Sunday over the St. Louis Cardinals in a National Football League game.

The 93-yard pass play, longest in the NFL this year, touched off a 20-point second period in which Concannon hit Bob Jones on a 51-yard scoring pass and then found Gordon again with a 67-yard touchdown pass.

The Cardinals, yielding the ball seven times on pass interceptions and twice on fumbles, scored the first time they got the ball on a 37-yard field goal by Jim Bakken but couldn't get going again.

Following Bakken's field goal, the Bears marched 70 yards with Concannon capping the drive on a six-yard run to go ahead to stay.

Early in the second quarter, St. Louis gained field position on a punt by Chuck Latourette deep into Bear territory. But Concannon, who had thrown only one touchdown pass all season, let go with a long pitch which bounced off the hands of Pat Fischer and Larry Wilson and into the hands of Gordon, who rambled the 48 yards untouched.

Midway in the period, Curt Gentry made the first of his three interceptions. After the Cardinals were hit with two penalties, Concannon threw his 51-yard touchdown pass to rookie Bob Jones, a 22-year-old hurdle champion from San Diego State.

The next time the Bears got the ball, Concannon hit Gordon with a 67-yard touchdown pass.

The victory was the third straight for the Bears who boosted their record to 5-5 while

Continued on Page 28, Column 1

4 TD Aerials Beat Cowboys

Jurgensen Passes Win for Redskins

DALLAS, Nov. 19 (UPI). — Sonny Jurgensen, working from an almost air-tight pocket, picked the Dallas Cowboys' defense apart for four touchdown passes Sunday and the Washington Redskins kept their Capitol Division hopes alive with a 27-20 victory before 75,538.

Jurgensen ran his season touchdown total to 21 with 29 and 4-yard scoring tosses to Jerry Smith, a 14-yarder to A. D. Whitfield and a 5-yard pitch to Bobby Mitchell to even the Redskins' record to 4-4-2.

The Cowboys, snake-bitten with dropped touchdown passes and fumbles for most of three quarters, staged another of their patented fourth-quarter finishes that have marked this series when Craig Morton came on for limping Don Meredith and sparked the Cowboys to two touchdowns.

Morton hit Frank Clarke with a 15-yarder for one touchdown. Then, after Cowboys linebacker, Dave Edwards recovered an onside kickoff at the Washington 45, he guided them to another touchdown, which came on a 6-yard pass to Pettis Norman with Redskins hanging all over him.

The Cowboys got the ball on their own 10-yard line with 2:33 left and the crowd kept anticipating another of the final minute surges that has seen these clubs divide their last four games with each one won in the final two minutes.

But Redskins defensive back, Paul Krause abruptly blotted out that hope with a sparkling interception, the Redskins' fourth of the day, at the Dallas 49-yard line with 1:40 remaining.

The Cowboys got one more chance from their own 17-yard line with 58 seconds left, but could work their way out only to the Washington 37 by game's end in the face of a terrific rush put on Morton by the Redskins' front line of Ron Snidow, Walt Barnes, Joe Rutgens and Earl Kammerer.

It was this same group that got to Meredith time and time again in the first three quarters, forced him to throw hastily or smother him for losses. He took a heavy beating and finally had to retire.

Jurgensen hit 23 of 33 passes for 265 yards and suffered only one interception, while he was not thrown for a loss a single time by the once-feared Cowboys' front line.

In contrast, Meredith hit 14 of 27 for 189 yards, Morton hit 10 of 16 for 131 yards and half-

Continued on Page 26, Column 1

November 20, 1967
Eagles enjoy their highest single-game offensive output in eight years, defeating New Orleans 48-21

1968

RECORD: 2-12, 4TH IN NFL CAPITOL
HEAD COACH: JOE KUHARICH

Schedule
Regular Season

Wk. 2	Sep 15	L	30-13	at Green Bay Packers
Wk. 3	Sep 22	L	34-25	vs New York Giants
Wk. 4	Sep 29	L	45-13	vs Dallas Cowboys
Wk. 5	Oct 6	L	17-14	at Washington Redskins
Wk. 6	Oct 13	L	34-14	at Dallas Cowboys
Wk. 7	Oct 20	L	29-16	vs Chicago Bears
Wk. 8	Oct 27	L	6-3	at Pittsburgh Steelers
Wk. 9	Nov 3	L	45-17	vs St. Louis Cardinals
Wk. 10	Nov 10	L	16-10	vs Washington Redskins
Wk. 11	Nov 17	L	7-6	at New York Giants
Wk. 12	Nov 24	L	47-13	at Cleveland Browns
Wk. 13	Nov 28	W	12-0	at Detroit Lions
Wk. 14	Dec 8	W	29-17	vs New Orleans Saints
Wk. 15	Dec 15	L	24-17	vs Minnesota Vikings

The Eagles struggled, losing their first 11 games (a team record), and then winning their last two games. By winning those two games, they ruined the probability of selecting O.J. Simpson in the draft. In the last game of the season, a 24-17 loss to Minnesota, Eagles fans where so unhappy with Coach Joe Kuharich that they turned on Santa Claus by pelting him with snowballs.

1968 Philadelphia Eagles Stats

Passing	Comp	Att	Comp %	Yds	Y/Att	TD	Int	Rating
Norm Snead	152	291	52.2	1655	5.69	11	21	51.8
Sam Baker	1	1	100.0	58	58.00	1	0	158.3
Joe Scarpati	1	2	50.0	3	1.50	0	0	56.3
John Huarte	7	15	46.7	110	7.33	1	2	54.2
King Hill	33	71	46.5	531	7.48	3	6	50.9

Receiving	Rec	Yds	Avg	TD
Ben Hawkins	42	707	16.8	5
Tom Woodeshick	36	328	9.1	0
Fred Hill	30	370	12.3	3
Gary Ballman	30	341	11.4	4
Izzy Lang	17	147	8.6	1
Cyril Pinder	16	166	10.4	0
Mike Ditka	13	111	8.5	2
Harry Jones	5	87	17.4	1
Chuck Hughes	3	39	13.0	0
John Mallory	1	58	58.0	1
Sam Baker	1	3	3.0	0

Rushing	Rush	Yds	Avg	TD
Tom Woodeshick	217	947	4.4	3
Izzy Lang	69	235	3.4	0
Cyril Pinder	40	117	2.9	0
Gary Ballman	1	30	30.0	0
Norm Snead	9	27	3.0	0
Harry Jones	22	24	1.1	0
Larry Conjar	8	21	2.6	0
John Huarte	2	9	4.5	0
King Hill	1	1	1.0	0

Punting	Punts	Yds	Avg	Blocked
Rick Duncan	5	228	45.6	0
Sam Baker	55	2248	40.9	0

Interceptions	Int	Yds	Avg	TD
Al Nelson	3	7	2.3	0
Joe Scarpati	2	22	11.0	0
Nate Ramsey	2	0	0.0	0
Harold Wells	2	0	0.0	0
Randy Beisler	1	12	12.0	0
Alvin Haymond	1	10	10.0	0
Ron Medved	1	0	0.0	0
Floyd Peters	1	0	0.0	0

Kicking	PAT Made	PAT Att	PAT %	FG Made	FG Att	FG %	Pts
Sam Baker	17	21	81	19	30	63.3	74

The Philadelphia Inquirer
33 FRIDAY, NOVEMBER 29, 1968 h ★★ — *Today's* **SPORTS** — Comics, Puzzles, Classified, Advertising

76ers' Romp Ruins Lakers' 'Super' Image

Eagles' Sam Baker was set to try for field goal near the end of first half when high pass from center caused holder Joe Scarpati to start running.

Scarpati is running to the left looking for someone to throw the ball to while Baker watches and Lions' defensive back Mike Weger starts to chase the Eagle, who is now at the 48.

Realizing he is trapped by several Lions, and unable to find an eligible receiver free downfield, Scarpati turns and starts to pass the ball to Baker, who was a fullback at Oregon State.

Inquirer Magic Eye Sequence Photos by Alexander Deans, Staff Photographer

Baker makes the catch at about the Lions' 42, turns and starts to run as tacklers converge.

Hit at the 41, Baker manages to keep going in the sloppy footing until he reaches the 37.

Locker Room Report
Baker Gets New Experience After 14 Years in Pro Ball
By ROGER KEIM
Of The Inquirer Staff

DETROIT, Nov. 28.—Sam Baker has been kicking in the National Football League for 14 years. Thursday he received a new experience. "I never played on a field like that in the pros," said Baker after booming a field goal in each quarter at Tiger Stadium to keep the Eagles from achieving the longest one-season losing streak in NFL history.

Sandy Padwe
In the Long Run, Effort Pays Off

IT WAS cold and dark and the terrain was a bit unfamiliar. There were no police around, however, and that made things a little easier.

Eagles Defeat Lions, 12-0, for 1st Win of '68
Continued from First Page

L.A. Troubles Aired by Coach After Setback
By ERNIE ACCORSI
Of The Inquirer Staff

Cowboys Win, Redskins' Coach Cries 'Robbery'
From Our Wire Services

AFL Roundup
Chiefs Topple Oilers, Clinch Crown for Jets
From Our Wire Services

Sugar Goes To Arkansas

Tickets Available

Sports Results

College
FOOTBALL
EAST

Professional
FOOTBALL
NATIONAL LEAGUE

Continued on Page 28, Column 6
Continued on Page 36, Column 7
Continued on Page 28, Column 4
Continued on Page 38, Column 1
Continued on Page 36, Column 4
Continued on Page 34, Column 4

November 29, 1968
After eleven straight losses, Sam Baker kicks four field goals as the Eagles defeat Detroit 12-0 for their first win of the season

1969

RECORD: 4-9-1, 4TH IN NFL CAPITOL
HEAD COACH: JERRY WILLIAMS

Schedule
Regular Season

Wk. 2	Sep 21	L	27-20	vs Cleveland Browns
Wk. 3	Sep 28	W	41-27	vs Pittsburgh Steelers
Wk. 4	Oct 5	L	38-7	vs Dallas Cowboys
Wk. 5	Oct 13	L	24-20	at Baltimore Colts
Wk. 6	Oct 19	L	49-14	at Dallas Cowboys
Wk. 7	Oct 26	W	13-10	vs New Orleans Saints
Wk. 8	Nov 2	W	23-20	at New York Giants
Wk. 9	Nov 9	T	28-28	at Washington Redskins
Wk. 10	Nov 16	L	23-17	vs Los Angeles Rams
Wk. 11	Nov 23	W	34-30	at St. Louis Cardinals
Wk. 12	Nov 30	L	26-17	at New Orleans Saints
Wk. 13	Dec 7	L	34-29	vs Washington Redskins
Wk. 14	Dec 14	L	27-3	vs Atlanta Falcons
Wk. 15	Dec 21	L	14-13	at San Francisco 49ers

Financial ruin forced owner Jerry Wolman to sell the Eagles to Leonard Tose, a millionaire trucking executive, who purchased the Eagles for a record price of 16.1 million dollars. Tose fired Kuharich immediately and replaced him with GM Pete Retzlaff, who in turn promoted assistant coach Jerry Williams to head coach. Despite the change at the top the Eagles continued to struggle, finishing in last place again with a terrible 4-9-1 record.

1969 Philadelphia Eagles Stats

Passing	Comp	Att	Comp %	Yds	Y/Att	TD	Int	Rating
Norm Snead	190	379	50.1	2768	7.30	19	23	65.7
Leroy Keyes	1	2	50.0	14	7.00	0	0	72.9
Bill Bradley	0	1	0.0	0	0.00	0	0	39.6
George Mira	25	76	32.9	240	3.16	1	5	19.6

Rushing	Rush	Yds	Avg	TD
Tom Woodeshick	186	831	4.5	4
Leroy Keyes	121	361	3.0	3
Cyril Pinder	60	309	5.2	1
Ronnie Blye	8	25	3.1	0
George Mira	3	16	5.3	0
Harold Jackson	2	10	5.0	0
Harry Wilson	4	7	1.8	0
Bill Bradley	1	5	5.0	0
Norm Snead	8	2	0.3	2
Harry Jones	1	0	0.0	0
Ben Hawkins	1	-3	-3.0	0

Receiving	Rec	Yds	Avg	TD
Harold Jackson	65	1116	17.2	9
Ben Hawkins	43	761	17.7	8
Gary Ballman	31	492	15.9	2
Leroy Keyes	29	276	9.5	0
Tom Woodeshick	22	177	8.0	0
Cyril Pinder	12	77	6.4	0
Fred Hill	6	64	10.7	1
Chuck Hughes	3	29	9.7	0
Ronnie Blye	2	-6	-3.0	0
Fred Brown	1	20	20.0	0
Kent Lawrence	1	10	10.0	0
Harry Wilson	1	6	6.0	0

Punting	Punts	Yds	Avg	Blocked
Bill Bradley	74	2942	39.8	0

Interceptions	Int	Yds	Avg	TD
Joe Scarpati	4	54	13.5	1
Al Nelson	3	10	3.3	0
Nate Ramsey	2	26	13.0	1
Dave Lloyd	2	22	11.0	0
Bill Bradley	1	56	56.0	1
Wayne Colman	1	11	11.0	0
Adrian Young	1	0	0.0	0

Kicking	PAT Made	PAT Att	PAT %	FG Made	FG Att	FG %	Pts
Sam Baker	31	31	100	16	30	53.3	79

26   a d h   THE PHILADELPHIA INQUIRER, MONDAY MORNING, SEPTEMBER 29, 1969

The Norman Conquest—Snead Style

Inquirer Magic-Eye Pictures by Alexander L. Deans and William M. Brown, Staff Photographers

Gentle Ben a Better Show Than Oliver

With Eagles trailing 13-0 in second period, quarterback Norm Snead fired pass from pocket formed by three linemen. Steelers' Joe Greene fails in his leap to block first of 5 TD passes.

Wide receiver Ben Hawkins turns toward scrimmage line and leaps over defender Clarence Oliver for catch.

As ball settles in Hawkins' chest, his speed and momentum carry him toward goal line.

Hawkins falls into end zone to complete 26-yard touchdown play and ignite the rally which carried Eagles' to 41-27 victory. Eagles declined pass interference call against Steelers.

Rookie Flips Over Hawk's Move

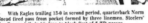

It looks like Ben Hawkins is going nowhere after catching this sideline pass in front of Steelers' Coach Chuck Noll near midfield.

But Hawkins, without touching the ground, flips Clarence Oliver over his shoulder and keeps going.

Hawkins leaves Oliver, a rookie from San Diego State, on the turf and crosses the midfield stripe.

Headed off by linebacker Andy Russell, Hawkins changes direction and gets hemmed in by three defenders.

Hawkins' pivot fools the Steelers, however, and Gary Ballman rushes over to help Ben gain more yardage on third-quarter play.

Defensive end Lloyd Voss finally wrestles down Hawkins at Pittsburgh's 46. Play gained 15 yards.

Good Way to Get a Shiner

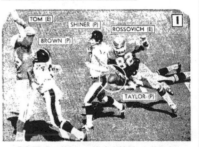

Eagles' Tim Rossovich bats arm of Steelers' Dick Shiner on third-period passing attempt and forces fumble. Tackle John Brown blocks Eagles' Mel Tom.

As Rossovich forces Shiner to the turf, ball bounces loose near the Steelers' 33-yard line. Tackle Mike Taylor, on all fours, spots the pigskin.

Taylor grabbed ball on Steelers' 29, but advanced only to the 36 before Floyd Peters nailed him. Loss of 12 yards forced Pittsburgh to punt.

September 29, 1969
Hawkins ties a club record with four touchdowns as the Eagles defeated Pittsburgh 41-27

70's Decade in Review

Decade Win-Loss Record:
56-84-4; (1-2 postseason record)
Home Field:
Franklin Field 1970; Veterans Stadium 1971-79
Playoff Appearances:
1978 and 1979
Championships:
None
Head Coaches:
Jerry Williams 1970-71 (3-13-1); Ed Khayat 1971-1972 (8-15-2);
Mike McCormack 1973-75 (16-25-1); Dick Vermeil 1976-1979 (29-31) (1-2 postseason record)
Hall of Fame Inductees:
None
Award Winners:
Roman Gabriel, Comeback Player of the Year 1973; Charlie Young, Rookie of the Year 1973;
Dick Vermeil, Coach of the Year 1979
All Pro:
Bill Bradley 1971-1973, Harold Jackson 1972; Harold Carmichael 1973 and 1979;
Charlie Young 1973-1974; Bill Bergey 1974-78; Wilbert Montgomery 1978-79;
Charlie Johnson 1979; Stan Walters 1979
Pro Bowl Selections:
Dave Lloyd 1970; Tim Rossovich 1970; Bill Bradley 1972-74; Harold Jackson 1970 and 1973;
Harold Carmichael 1974; Roman Gabriel 1974; Charlie Young 1974-76;
Bill Bergey 1975 and 1977-79; Mike Boryla 1976; Wilbert Montgomery 1979; Stan Walters 1979
First Game of the Decade:
September 20, 1970, lost to Dallas Cowboys 17-7
Last Game of the Decade:
December 16, 1979, defeated by the Houston Oilers 26-20
Largest Margin of Victory:
December 2, 1979 vs. Detroit Lions 44-7
Largest Margin of Defeat:
November 26, 1972 vs. New York Giants 62-10

Eagle Firsts of the Decade:
First Game at Veterans Stadium
September 19, 1971, loss to the Cincinnati Bengals 37-14
First Playoff game at the Vet
December 23, 1979, defeated the Chicago Bears in their first postseason home game 27-17
First Overtime Game
September 27, 1976, lost to Washington Redskins 20-17
First Monday Night Football
November 23, 1970, win over the New York Giants 23-20 at Franklin Field
First Exhibition Game Outside the US
August 5, 1978, the New Orleans Saints defeat the Eagles 14-7 in a preseason game held in Mexico City
First Soccer-Style Kicker
In 1975, Horst Muhlmann became the Eagles first Soccer-Style Kicker.

70's Decade in Review

In 1971, the Eagles moved from Franklin Field to brand-new Veterans Stadium. In its first season, the "Vet" was widely acclaimed as a triumph of ultra-modern sports engineering, a consensus that would be short-lived. Equally short-lived was Williams's tenure as head coach: after a 3-10-1 record in 1970 and three consecutive blowout losses to open the 1971 season, Williams was fired and replaced by assistant coach Ed Khayat. Khayat proved little better, and was released after another dismal season in 1972. Khayat was replaced by offensive guru Mike McCormick, who, aided by the skills of Roman Gabriel and towering young receiver Harold Carmichael, managed to infuse a bit of vitality into a previously moribund offense. New general manager Jim Murray also began to add talent on the defensive side of the line, most notably through the addition of future Pro Bowl linebacker Bill Bergey. Overall, however, the team was still mired in mediocrity. McCormick was fired after a 4-10 1975 season, and replaced by a college coach unknown to most Philadelphians. That coach would become one of the most beloved names in Philadelphia sports history: Dick Vermeil.

Vermeil faced numerous obstacles as he attempted to rejuvenate a franchise that had not seriously contended in well over a decade. Despite the team's young talent and Gabriel's occasional flashes of brilliance, the Eagles finished 1976 with the same result – a 4-10 record – as in 1975. 1977, however, saw the first seeds of hope begin to sprout. Rifle-armed quarterback Ron Jaworski was obtained by trade with the Los Angeles Rams in exchange for popular tight end Charlie Young. The defense, led by Bergey and defensive coordinator Marion Campbell, began earning a reputation as one of the hardest hitting in the league. By the next year, the Eagles had fully taken Vermeil's enthusiastic attitude, and made the playoffs for the first time since 1960. Young running back Wilbert Montgomery became the first Eagle since Steve Van Buren to exceed 1,000 yards in a single season. (1978 also bore witness to one of the greatest, and unquestionably most surreal moment in Eagles history: "The Miracle at the Meadowlands," when Herman Edwards returned a late-game fumble by Giants' quarterback Joe Pisarcik for a touchdown with 20 seconds left, resulting in a 19-17 Eagles victory) By 1979, in which the Eagles tied for first place with an 11-5 record and Wilbert Montgomery shattered club rushing records with a total of 1,512 yards, the Eagles were poised to join the NFL elite.

TRIVIA QUESTION

Q9 IN THEIR 1960 CHAMPIONSHIP SEASON, WHO LED THE EAGLES IN BOTH RECEPTIONS AND RECEIVING YARDS?

(a) Tommy Mcdonald   (b) Billy Barnes
(c) Bobby Walston   (d) Pete Retzlaff

answer on page 254

TRIVIA QUESTION

Q10 WHICH ONE OF THE FOLLOWING EAGLES WAS INDUCTED INTO THE PRO FOOTBALL HALL OF FAME IN 1970?

(a) Tommy Mcdonald (b) Steve Van Buren
(c) Pete Retzlaff   (d) Pete Pihos

answer on page 254

1970

RECORD: 3-10-1, 5TH IN NFC EAST
HEAD COACH: JERRY WILLIAMS

Schedule

Regular Season

Wk. 1	Sep 20	L	17-7	vs Dallas Cowboys
Wk. 2	Sep 27	L	20-16	at Chicago Bears
Wk. 3	Oct 4	L	33-21	vs Washington Redskins
Wk. 4	Oct 11	L	30-23	at New York Giants
Wk. 5	Oct 18	L	35-20	vs St. Louis Cardinals
Wk. 6	Oct 25	L	30-17	at Green Bay Packers (at Milwaukee, WI)
Wk. 7	Nov 1	L	21-17	at Dallas Cowboys
Wk. 8	Nov 8	W	24-17	vs Miami Dolphins
Wk. 9	Nov 15	T	13-13	vs Atlanta Falcons
Wk. 10	Nov 23	W	23-20	vs New York Giants
Wk. 11	Nov 29	L	23-14	at St. Louis Cardinals
Wk. 12	Dec 6	L	29-10	at Baltimore Colts
Wk. 13	Dec 13	L	24-6	at Washington Redskins
Wk. 14	Dec 20	W	30-20	vs Pittsburgh Steelers

The Eagles began the new decade on a sour note, losing their first seven games on the way to another wretched last place 3-10-1 season; it was their last season at Franklin Field. The Eagles would actually win their final game at Franklin Field 30-20 over the Pittsburgh Steelers on December 20, 1970. Also, the Eagles played in their first Monday Night Football game on November 23, 1970, when they defeated the NY Giants 23-20.

1970 Philadelphia Eagles Stats

Passing	Comp	Att	Comp %	Yds	Y/Att	TD	Int	Rating
Norm Snead	181	335	54.0	2323	6.93	15	20	66.1
Rick Arrington	37	73	50.7	328	4.49	1	3	50.5
Lee Bouggess	0	1	0.0	0	0.00	0	0	39.6
Gary Ballman	0	1	0.0	0	0.00	0	0	39.6

Rushing	Rush	Yds	Avg	TD
Cyril Pinder	166	657	4.0	2
Lee Bouggess	159	401	2.5	2
Tom Woodeshick	52	254	4.9	2
Larry Watkins	32	96	3.0	1
Harry Jones	13	44	3.4	0
Norm Snead	18	35	1.9	3
Rick Arrington	4	33	8.3	1
Bill Bradley	1	14	14.0	0
Leroy Keyes	2	7	3.5	0
Ben Hawkins	2	3	1.5	0
Harold Jackson	1	-5	-5.0	0

Receiving	Rec	Yds	Avg	TD
Lee Bouggess	50	401	8.0	2
Gary Ballman	47	601	12.8	3
Harold Jackson	41	613	15.0	5
Ben Hawkins	30	612	20.4	4
Cyril Pinder	28	249	8.9	0
Steve Zabel	8	119	14.9	1
Tom Woodeshick	6	28	4.7	0
Fred Hill	3	10	3.3	1
Larry Watkins	3	6	2.0	0
Harry Jones	1	12	12.0	0
Billy Walik	1	0	0.0	0

Punting	Punts	Yds	Avg	Blocked
Bill Bradley	61	2246	36.8	0
Mark Moseley	10	350	35.0	0

Interceptions	Int	Yds	Avg	TD
Al Nelson	2	45	22.5	0
Steve Preece	2	19	9.5	0
Adrian Young	2	19	9.5	0
Ray Jones	2	17	8.5	0
Ed Hayes	1	2	2.0	0
Nate Ramsey	1	0	0.0	0

Kicking	PAT Made	PAT Att	PAT %	FG Made	FG Att	FG %	Pts
Mark Moseley	25	28	89	14	25	56.0	67

Page 19 Monday
September 21, 1970

The Philadelphia Inquirer / SPORTS

h ★

Financial

Eagles Fall to Cowboys, 17-7, in Opener

FRANK DOLSON

Sacrificial Lambs Played Like Tigers

THEY CAME OUT BREATHING FIRE, riding a tide of emotion that helped them keep the Dallas Cowboys off the scoreboard for nearly the entire first half. Two rookies. Two second-year pros. Only one starter, middle linebacker Dave Lloyd, with more than five years' experience. But this green defensive unit came ready to play football.

The sacrificial lambs played like tigers Sunday, slamming down the big names in the white jerseys, play after play, until a strange sound filled Franklin Field. Cheers.

"Boy, were they fired up!" Roger Staubach said. "Our first two series we didn't do anything. Either they were fired up or we were fired down."

They were up. Up so high you could sense it in the top row of the upper deck.

The first time Calvin Hill carried the ball he was slammed down for a one-yard loss. The first time Walt Garrison carried the ball, it was belted out of his hands. The first time Staubach scrambled, the Eagles scrambled him, jolting the ball loose five yards behind the line of scrimmage.

For 28 minutes, the team that is rated odds-on to win the National East title couldn't score a point against the 1000-to-one longshots. All that preparation—the unusually long practices, the written tests, the six and seven-hour work days that made up what Lloyd called "the hardest week I've ever spent for a league game"—paid off. The Eagles lost another football game, but at least it was a respectable loss. And then the game was 57 minutes old before the first loud boos floated across the field. At least the people who paid $5 to get in got something in return.

Cowboys Have to Work

AT LEAST THE DALLAS COWBOYS had to work and sweat and strain for this victory.

"I feel exhausted," Calvin Hill said in that soft, pleasant voice die after absorbing the brutal pounding the Eagles were dishing out. "I'm just drained emotionally ... They've got a good team. Golly. They're so much better than last year ..."

Had Hill made that statement 24 hours earlier, there would have been laughter. Not now. The Eagles' defensive team made Calvin earn every one of the 117 yards he gained on this opening day. Time after time, it prevented him from breaking loose for the long gainer he wanted so badly.

Perhaps the best measure of the Eagles' tenacity was Hill's frustration, which bubbled over early in the third quarter when Mel Tom reached out from behind and hauled him down near the Dallas bench, turning a potential big play into a modest six-yarder. Calvin fired the ball at the artificial turf in disgust.

Four plays later he nearly broke another one, but the hotly pursuing Eagles held him to 11 yards. Again Hill slammed the football—and drew a 15-yard penalty for unsportsmanlike conduct.

"I was ticked off at myself," the Yale man said. "I was pretty psyched up. I was upset. Throwing the ball down is like banging your fist against the turf ... I wish they'd define the rules. Sometimes you can jump (hurdle for extra yardage, sometimes you can't. Sometimes you can slam the ball down, sometimes you can't ..."

"You mean you didn't say anything when you slammed down the ball?" a newspaperman asked.

Hill grinned. "I might have said, 'Damnit Calvin, c'mon,'" he replied. "Or maybe 'Dammit Calvin ...'" The grin spread. "Or maybe something worse than that."

Anger, Frustration Subside

THE ANGER AND FRUSTRATION he felt on the football field had subsided. It had been a good day for Calvin Hill, despite all the Eagles did to stop him. Sure that one reporter suggested that he bore a startling resemblance to Jimmy Brown.

"There's only one Jim Brown," Hill said softly. "The only resemblance is we're both black, and we both have numbers in the 30s ..."

And then he talked about how well the Cowboys had blocked for him, and how much he had to learn about using his blockers. "If O. J. (Simpson) had the blocking I had, he'd gain 3000 yards," Calvin said.

Not against a defensive team that hit as hard and pursued as well as the Eagles did Sunday, he wouldn't. Not against the charged-up unit that might have held Dallas scoreless for the first half, if Tom Woodeshick hadn't fumbled on his own 34 with 5½ minutes to go.

"I'm real proud of the defense," Dave Lloyd said. "If they hadn't scored that first touchdown, if they'd gone in the locker room seven points down instead of even, I don't think they'd have scored the second one ..."

But the Cowboys had scored the first one and the second one, and they had won the football game. The 1000-to-one longshots, the pre-season laughing stocks were 0-1, as advertised.

"It's better than losing the game like we lost before," Lloyd argued. "We were determined if they beat us, it was going to be a marginal score. Not like before. Not 56-7."

So it was only 17-7. A tough 17-7. A come-from-behind 17-7. Don't sneer. This is a year when moral victories may have to do.

Cowboys' Calvin Hill Sheds Eagles' Adrian Young
Hill gained four yards on this second-quarter carry, finished the game with 117 yards rushing in 25 attempts

Lions Win in Rout, Hand Packers 1st Shutout Since '58

GREEN BAY, Wis., Sept. 20 (AP)—Mel Farr scored two touchdowns and Erroll Mann kicked four field goals as the Detroit Lions crushed the Green Bay Packers, 40-0, in a National Football League opener Sunday.

It was the first time the Packers were blanked in Green Bay since 1958, when the Baltimore Colts stomped them, 56-0.

Gretel Spurts On 5th Leg to Beat Intrepid

From Our Wire Services
NEWPORT, R. I., Sept. 20.—Skipper Jim Hardy found the right spinnaker to complement Gretel II's speed as the Australian challenger rallied on the fifth leg to push Detroit's lead to 10-0, then added another tally on a 13-yard burst in the fourth period.

Staubach Hits Rentzel For Key TD

Birds Lead, 7-0, Before Lapsing Into Exhibition Form

By GORDON FORBES
Of The Inquirer Staff

Unsaddled in the first half, the Dallas Cowboys were remounted by Roger Staubach and Calvin Hill and proceeded on to a 17-7 victory over the Eagles before 59,728 fans Sunday at Franklin Field.

The Eagles, rated by some as the worst team in pro football, and the Cowboys, ranked by many as the best, played far out of character.

It took a pretty 31-yard touchdown strike from Staubach to Lance Rentzel in the third period to crack an even-up grudge match between the Eastern Division rivals. Before that, the Eagle defensive line had laughed in the faces of Tom Landry's multiple offense.

Pictures, Related Article On Pages 24 and 25

'PRESEASON FORM'

Say, Jerry ...?

Snead Still No. 1 For a Starter

Eagles' Coach Jerry Williams answers questions from the fans telephoned to The Inquirer during the game and relayed to sports writer Chuck Newman at the scene of action. While watching or listening to next week's game at Chicago, if you have a question, dial Say Jerry at LO 3-3288 before the end of the game.

Q. Why did you start Snead over Arrington?

A. Because Norm Snead is our No. 1 quarterback and he has not been displaced by Rick Arrington.
— Chuck Armstrong, Swarthmore

Q. Why didn't the Eagles play more ball control when they got the lead in the first half?

A. Snead went to the air on the first down after we had the lead. I corrected him and we did try to control the ball after that.
— Tillman Hann, Philadelphia

Q. What did you say to Tom Woodeshick after he fumbled in the second period?

A. Nothing. Physical errors that are not the result of lack of effort are not the object of my wrath.
— Chip Barrett, Wayne

Q. Why did you punt on fourth down and inches to go in the third period?

A. The idea of going for it crossed my mind, but only briefly. A good punt would have given us ideal field position. If we had gone for the first down and missed, it would
— Cathy Kinsay, Philadelphia

Pirates Split With Mets, Lead by 2

From Our Wire Services
NEW YORK, Sept. 20.—Willie Stargell's first homer touched off a four-run spree in the 10th inning that gave the Pittsburgh Pirates a 6-5 victory over the New York Mets.

Mets' Donn Clendenon Slides In With Run
Pirates' Manny Sanguillen awaits throw in fourth inning of first game

---

September 21, 1970
Eagles lose home opener to the Dallas Cowboys 17-7

1971

RECORD: 6-7-1, 3RD IN NFC EAST
HEAD COACH: JERRY WILLIAMS & ED KHAYAT

Schedule
Regular Season

Wk. 1	Sep 19	L	37-14	at Cincinnati Bengals
Wk. 2	Sep 26	L	42-7	vs Dallas Cowboys
Wk. 3	Oct 3	L	31-3	vs San Francisco 49ers
Wk. 4	Oct 10	L	13-0	vs Minnesota Vikings
Wk. 5	Oct 17	L	34-10	at Oakland Raiders
Wk. 6	Oct 24	W	23-7	vs New York Giants
Wk. 7	Oct 31	W	17-16	vs Denver Broncos
Wk. 8	Nov 7	T	7-7	at Washington Redskins
Wk. 9	Nov 14	L	20-7	at Dallas Cowboys
Wk. 10	Nov 21	W	37-20	at St. Louis Cardinals
Wk. 11	Nov 28	L	20-13	vs Washington Redskins
Wk. 12	Dec 5	W	23-20	at Detroit Lions
Wk. 13	Dec 12	W	19-7	vs St. Louis Cardinals
Wk. 14	Dec 19	W	41-28	at New York Giants

In their first season at Veterans Stadium, the Eagles did not start out any better than before, losing their first three games, including the first at the Vet 42-7 to the Dallas Cowboys on September 26th, when coach Jerry Williams wasfired and replaced by Ed Khayat. Under Khayat the Eagles would continue to struggle, losing their next two games. Now 0-5, the Eagles were looking for there first win both for the season and at the Vet. It finally happened on October 24, 1971,when the Eagles defeated the New York Giants 23-7. The Eagles played solid football the rest of the season, posting a 6-7-1 record, as they finished the season on a strong note by winning their last three games. Tom Dempsey made his Eagles kicking debut and earned his first win by kicking three field goals against St. Louis, with a final score of 37-20. Then, just three weeks later, the Eagles played St. Louis again and Dempsey tied a club record with four field goals, one of which was a 54-yarder---the longest in the NFL that season.

1971 Philadelphia Eagles Stats

Passing	Comp	Att	Comp %	Yds	Y/Att	TD	Int	Rating
Pete Liske	143	269	53.2	1957	7.28	11	15	67.1
Rick Arrington	55	118	46.6	576	4.88	2	5	49.3
Ronnie Bull	1	1	100.0	15	15.00	0	0	118.8
Jim Ward	1	1	100.0	4	4.00	0	0	83.3
Sonny Davis	0	1	0.0	0	0.00	0	0	39.6

Rushing	Rush	Yds	Avg	TD
Ronnie Bull	94	351	3.7	0
Lee Bouggess	97	262	2.7	2
Tom Woodeshick	66	188	2.8	0
Sonny Davis	17	163	9.6	1
Larry Watkins	35	98	2.8	1
Tony Baker	17	49	2.9	0
Tom Bailey	23	41	1.8	1
Harold Jackson	5	41	8.2	0
Pete Liske	13	29	2.2	1
Rick Arrington	5	23	4.6	0
Ben Hawkins	4	8	2.0	0
Steve Zabel	1	-5	-5.0	0

Receiving	Rec	Yds	Avg	TD
Harold Jackson	47	716	15.2	3
Ben Hawkins	37	650	17.6	4
Lee Bouggess	24	170	7.1	1
Harold Carmichael	20	288	14.4	0
Gary Ballman	13	238	18.3	0
Sonny Davis	11	46	4.2	0
Ronnie Bull	9	75	8.3	1
Fred Hill	7	92	13.1	0
Tom Bailey	7	55	7.9	0
Kent Kramer	6	65	10.8	1
Larry Watkins	6	40	6.7	0
Tom Woodeshick	6	36	6.0	1
Tony Baker	4	36	9.0	0
Steve Zabel	2	4	2.0	2
Jim Whalen	1	41	41.0	0

Punting	Punts	Yds	Avg	Blocked
Tom McNeill	73	3063	42.0	0
Bill Bradley	2	76	38.0	0

Interceptions	Int	Yds	Avg	TD
Bill Bradley	11	248	22.5	0
Leroy Keyes	6	31	5.2	0
Al Nelson	2	63	31.5	1
Tim Rossovich	1	24	24.0	0
Steve Zabel	1	14	14.0	0
Don Hultz	1	4	4.0	0

Kicking	PAT Made	PAT Att	PAT %	FG Made	FG Att	FG %	Pts
Tom Dempsey	13	14	93	12	17	70.6	49
Happy Feller	10	10	100	6	20	30.0	28

NFL Playoff Picture
(Stories on Page 36)

| Cowboys vs. Vikings (Sat., Ch. 10, 1 P.M.) | Dolphins vs. Chiefs (Sat., Ch. 3, 4 P.M.) | Browns vs. Colts (Sun., Ch. 3, 1 P.M.) | Redskins vs. 49ers (Sun., Ch. 10, 4 P.M.) |

Monday, Dec. 20, 1971
b★ 35

The Philadelphia Inquirer / SPORTS

Television—Radio

Act Surprised, Pete

This Was the Day Scrooge Became Santa Claus

FRANK DOLSON

NEW YORK.
LEONARD TOSE ARRIVED at Yankee Stadium on Sunday wearing a red plaid sports jacket. If he had only known what was going to happen, he might have worn more fitting attire. Say, a red suit with white trim on it. Ho-ho-ho.

For the owner of the Philadelphia Eagles it was a strange, new role, but Leonard Tose played it convincingly. Maybe he was Scrooge to Jerry Williams, but on this long, cold afternoon in the Bronx he looked like Santa Claus to Pete Retzlaff and Eddie Khayat.

As the day dragged on, as the score mounted, the jolly old elf in Leonard Tose took charge. By the third quarter he was smiling, even laughing. By the fourth quarter his mind was made up. It was time to end all those nasty rumors. Time to rehire his general manager and his head coach.

"It was an easy decision to make," Tose said. "I saw no point in having these guys hang over Christmas."

Not after turning a 0-5 start into a 6-7-1 finish. Not after outclassing the New York Giants on the final day of the season.

"I thought we completely dominated the game," the Eagles' owner gushed. "I said, 'Why not (make the announcement)?'"

Complete domination. That was the key, the magic phrase that turned Scrooge into Santa. Anything short of that would have prolonged the agony.

"I would say that's a fair assessment, yes," Tose said. "I would say if this game was up for grabs I would've given it

more thought. But I don't say my decision would have been different . . ."

NOR DID HE SAY HIS DECISION would have been the same.

In fact, there's some question as to exactly what Leonard Tose did say at the moment he decided to keep Retzlaff and Khayat for another two years.

"I was told about it before the announcement was made," the general manager said.

When?

"Prior to coming down here (to the locker room). Let me put it that way. He told me what he was going to say . . ."

Continued on Page 38, Column 1

★ ★ ★

"I said to myself, 'If you make a decision there's no sense vacillating.' I didn't want to be accused of killing Santa Claus." — LEN TOSE

★ ★ ★

A Gathering of Clean-Shaven, Victorious and Happy-for-the-Boss Eagles
Leroy Keyes (left) and Al Davis lead cheers after 'dunked' head coach Ed Khayat (right) was given two-year contract

(Inquirer photos by GERVASE ROZANSKI)

Liske Hurls For 3 TDs in Eagle Romp

By GORDON FORBES
Of The Inquirer Staff

NEW YORK. — The Eagles ended their turn-around season Sunday by humiliating the pathetic New York Giants and thrilling their demanding owner.

Minutes after the 41-28 rout was completed, Len Tose swaggered into the Eagle dressing room and announced that his interim coach, Ed Khayat, and his general manager, Pete Retzlaff, had been rehired.

Khayat and Retzlaff earned two-year contracts that reflect Tose's belief in the future of his once-shaky football team.

"Eddie's going to be our coach," Tose told a cluster of reporters after posing for pictures. "And Retzlaff is coming back, too. That's official."

Given three touchdown passes by Pete Liske and vicious gang-tackling by the defense, the Eagles wrapped up the

victory as early as the third period.

Liske, who earlier hit Steve Zabel and Ben Hawkins for second-period scoring passes, hooked up with speedy Harold Jackson on a 63-yarder. That gave the Eagles a 38-14 lead and by then Tose was overjoyed.

Randy Johnson, who went all the way in place of Fran Tarkenton as the Giant quarterback, threw two meaningless touchdown passes in the final period. Johnson wound up with impressive statistics, 30 of 47 attempts for 372 yards and three TDs.

Earlier in the game when the Giants needed the big play, however, Johnson was ineffective in the face of constant pressure from the Eagle pass rush and blitzing linebackers.

Liske, on the other hand, contributed another strong

Continued on Page 38, Column 1

Flyers Fall To Plante, Leafs, 4-0

By CHUCK NEWMAN
Of The Inquirer Staff

Bernie Parent enjoyed another "homecoming" Sunday night. Smiled all the way through the Toronto Maple Leafs' 4-0 blanking of the Flyers. Never once lifted a stick, never stopped a puck.

"I always like coming back," the ex-Flyer goaltender said after watching ageless Jacques Plante sheepwalk his way through a 25-shot (you should excuse the expression) shutout.

DATE VIVIDLY RECALLED

The date of Jan. 31, 1971, came back vividly to the Flyers' again last night. That was the date they sent Parent to the Leafs and failed to hold on to winger Mike Walton, who might help with a couple of goals here. If they forget the people involved, Walton's name went up on the scoreboard after he scored a goal for the Bruins against Pittsburgh.

The Flyers also got goalie Bruce Gamble and a first-round draft choice in the deal. The draft pick turn out to be Pierre Plante, now with Richmond. Gamble got into the act last night, rescuing Doug Favell after the score was 4-0.

FANS REMEMBER

Parent, whom Plante says will be the best in the NHL very soon, likes to know he's remembered here. The sign in black letters that read, "This is 'Your' Home, Bernie," made him happy as did the one in red which said, "Hi, Bernie."

Parent has yet to play a game for Toronto here, and he has only met them once in

Continued on Page 40, Column 4

Everyone Was All Smiles After the Game, But...
GM Pete Retzlaff, left, coach Ed Khayat, right, receive Leonard Tose's congratulations

Lakers Beat 76ers for 25th; Wilt Nets 32, 33 Rebounds

Special to The Inquirer

INGLEWOOD, Calif. — The Los Angeles Lakers won a record 25th consecutive game Sunday night, repelling a determined bid by the 76ers, 154-132.

The 76ers trailed only 121-119 with 6:48 to play but then made it close with the Lakers outscored the Philadelphians, 18-1, late in the fourth quarter. Wilt Chamberlain led the way with 32 points, 33 rebounds and blocked 12 shots. It was Los Angeles'

highest point total of its record-smashing season.

Bob Rule led the 76ers with 33 points while Billy Cunningham contributed 28. Gail Goodrich had 31 for the Lakers.

The 76ers started fast in hopes of accomplishing what the Lakers' last 24 opponents couldn't.

Kevin Loughery made a three-point play off the opening tipoff, and Dave Kohl followed with a short jumper for a 5-0 lead.

But the Lakers quickly caught up, and went ahead, 8-7, on a pair of free throws by Jim McMillian.

Then, the Lakers went of a

Continued on Page 40, Column 1

COLLEGE FOOTBALL

Sports on TV
9 P.M.—Liberty Bowl: Tennessee vs. Arkansas, Ch. 6.

Sports Results

Professional
FOOTBALL
Sunday's Results

EAGLES...41	N.Y. Giants 28
N.Y. Jets 35	Cincinnati 21
Cleveland 21	Washington 17
Miami 27	Green Bay 6
Los Angeles 20	Pittsburgh 14
Houston 9	Cleveland 27
Atlanta 24	New Orleans 20
Minnesota 27	Chicago 10
Kansas City 22	Buffalo 9
San Diego 30	Denver 17
Dallas 31	St. Louis 12

BASKETBALL
NATIONAL BASKETBALL
Sunday's Results

Atlanta 101	Cincinnati 97
Chicago 119	Cleveland 97

...Retzlaff's Fate Was a Questionable Pre-Game Matter
Tose confers with rumored-on-the-way-out Pete as the Eagles warmed up

December 20, 1971
Eagles close out the season with third consecutive win over the NY Giants 41-28

1972

RECORD: 2-11-1, 5TH IN NFC EAST
HEAD COACH: ED KHAYAT

Schedule

Regular Season

Wk. 1	Sep 17	L	28-6	at Dallas Cowboys
Wk. 2	Sep 24	L	27-17	vs Cleveland Browns
Wk. 3	Oct 2	L	27-12	vs New York Giants
Wk. 4	Oct 8	L	14-0	at Washington Redskins
Wk. 5	Oct 15	L	34-3	vs Los Angeles Rams
Wk. 6	Oct 22	W	21-20	at Kansas City Chiefs
Wk. 7	Oct 29	L	21-3	at New Orleans Saints
Wk. 8	Nov 5	T	6-6	vs St. Louis Cardinals
Wk. 9	Nov 12	W	18-17	at Houston Oilers
Wk. 10	Nov 19	L	28-7	vs Dallas Cowboys
Wk. 11	Nov 26	L	62-10	at New York Giants
Wk. 12	Dec 3	L	23-7	vs Washington Redskins
Wk. 13	Dec 10	L	21-12	vs Chicago Bears
Wk. 14	Dec 17	L	24-23	at St. Louis Cardinals

Wide receiver Harold Jackson hada spectacular year, leading the NFL in both catches (62) and yards (1,048). Dempsey set another club record by scoring all the points in an 18-17 win against Houston (the Eagles second win for the season) when he kicked six field goals. However, the Eagles played terrible football all season long and finish with a wretched 2-10-1 season. Following the disastrous season, Tose accepts general manager Retzlaff's resignation and releases the entire coaching staff as part of a shake-up from the front office to the field.

1972 Philadelphia Eagles Stats

Passing	Comp	Att	Comp %	Yds	Y/Att	TD	Int	Rating
Pete Liske	71	138	51.4	973	7.05	3	7	60.4
John Reaves	108	224	48.2	1508	6.73	7	12	58.4
Rick Arrington	5	13	38.5	46	3.54	0	1	16.8

Rushing	Rush	Yds	Avg	TD
Po James	182	565	3.1	0
Tony Baker	90	322	3.6	0
Larry Watkins	67	262	3.9	1
John Reaves	18	109	6.1	1
Harold Jackson	9	76	8.4	0
Tom Bailey	7	22	3.1	0
Pete Liske	7	20	2.9	0
Tom Sullivan	13	13	1.0	0
Rick Arrington	1	2	2.0	0
Larry Crowe	1	2	2.0	0
Ben Hawkins	3	0	0.0	0

Receiving	Rec	Yds	Avg	TD
Harold Jackson	62	1048	16.9	4
Ben Hawkins	30	512	17.1	1
Harold Carmichael	20	276	13.8	2
Po James	20	156	7.8	1
Tony Baker	16	114	7.1	0
Kent Kramer	11	176	16.0	1
Gary Ballman	9	183	20.3	0
Larry Watkins	6	-2	-0.3	0
Tom Bailey	5	32	6.4	0
Tom Sullivan	4	17	4.3	0
Billy Walik	1	15	15.0	1

Punting	Punts	Yds	Avg	Blocked
Tom McNeill	7	290	41.4	0
Bill Bradley	56	2250	40.2	0

Interceptions	Int	Yds	Avg	TD
Bill Bradley	9	73	8.1	0
Nate Ramsey	3	14	4.7	0
Ron Porter	2	10	5.0	0
Leroy Keyes	2	0	0.0	0
John Bunting	1	45	45.0	0
Chuck Allen	1	15	15.0	0
Dick Absher	1	7	7.0	0

Kicking	PAT Made	PAT Att	PAT %	FG Made	FG Att	FG %	Pts
Tom Dempsey	11	12	92	20	35	57.1	71

Houston a Panacea to Ailing Philadelphians

HOUSTON.

AH, FINALLY A CITY with pro teams we can handle.

Saturday night the Houston Rockets.

Sunday afternoon the Houston Oilers.

Tomorrow the world . . .

Derek Sanderson was right. Think positive. Any time your pro football team can get outscored, two touchdowns to none, and win — well, things can't be THAT bad.

Although, in all honesty, they almost were.

The Eagles came within a few inches — a foot perhaps? — of losing to a team that seemed capable of clobbering. And yet with 16 seconds to go, there was Skip Butler flexing his right leg, getting ready to kick the 43-yard field goal that would win it for the Oilers.

Skip Butler, of all people.

For Tom Dempsey, who had booted six field goals in seven tries, it would have been an awful way to lose. After all, Butler was the guy who took Dempsey's job in New Orleans last year.

"He took it with a 13-yard field goal and three kickoffs out of bounds," Tom said in a voice that still contained a hint of bitterness.

And now Butler was on the verge of stealing the glory on Dempsey's most productive day.

FRANK DOLSON

heller themselves hoarse.

Dempsey stood in front of the Eagles' bench, hoping the ball would curve to the left of the yellow upright, thinking not about the six field goals he had kicked, but the one he hadn't kicked.

"I was watching the official," Tom said.

And he was listening to the people in the end zone seats, waiting for their reaction . . .

"The fans started yelling, I thought, 'Oh . . . '"

But the ball curved. The yell died. The Eagles won. Now Tom Dempsey could think about the six field goals he had kicked, and forget about the 22-yarder he had pulled to the left of the same yellow upright.

Wipe Away the Tears

And Skip Butler could do nothing but stand in front of his locker, press a towel to his face and wipe away the tears.

Like Dempsey, he lived for the moment when a place-kick could make the difference.

And, like Dempsey and Jim Bakken last week in Philadelphia, he failed.

"It missed by a foot," Butler said in a voice choked by emotion. "A foot . . . . "

But it missed. That's all that mattered. "It should have been down the gut," he kept saying. "That's what a kicker gets paid for. When you miss one, especially one like that . . . ."

The voice trailed away. He was sobbing again. Finally, with a visible effort, he controlled himself.

"You want to help the team so damn much. Seems like when you need it most you can't come through. . . . That's what the game's all about. It's a game of inches. A game of pressure. . . ." He seemed startled by his own words. "No," he said, "I don't think it was the pressure. I just hit the ball bad. I got a good snap, a good hold and I just came across it a little bit."

So little that for a few, excruciating moments nobody on the sidelines could possibly tell.

A Save for Pastorini

So little that Dan Pastorini, the young, hard-throwing Oiler quarterback, thought Skip Butler had blown him off the hook.

"I thought he made it," Pastorini said, and he tore a strip of tape off his ankle, crushed it into a ball and threw it past his locker.

He wasn't angry at Butler's miss. He was angry at his own stupidity. If Dan Pastorini had known what down it was in the final minute of the first half, when he drove the Oilers deep into Eagles' territory, it would have been a different ball game.

It was third-and-seven on the Eagles' 17 when Pastorini dumped a screen pass to Fred Willis, who could have settled for a first down, but tried to go for six points instead. Retreating a yard or so as he looked for running room, Willis was thrown just inside the 11. Now it was fourth-and-one. Pastorini thought it was first-and-10.

Had he known it was fourth down, he would have called Houston's last time out of the first half and given Butler a chance to kick an 18-yard field goal. Instead he threw a pass that Bill Bradley intercepted in the end zone.

"We had sent in word from the bench," Oiler coach Bill Peterson said. "If it's fourth down, take a time out. . . . But Dan thought he made first down. Hell, anybody can make mistakes. Fred had run around. It was one of those things . . . ."

"It was a screw-up on my part," Pastorini said, holding a hand to the side of his head, the anger still flashing in his eyes.

"Mental mistakes . . . ." He was talking to himself. "How do you expect to make a quarterback with mistakes like that?" He looked up, seemingly aware of his audience for the first time. "That game was my fault," the kid said. "Nobody else's."

Okay, they were both willing to accept full blame for the defeat — the quarterback who didn't know what down it was in the last minute of the first half, the place-kicker who missed by a foot in the last minute of the game.

And the Eagles were just as willing to accept Sunday afternoon's one-point victory over the Oilers as the 76ers were to take Saturday night's two-pointer over the Rockets.

Helluva town, Houston.

A kicker lives for the moment when it's just him and one second (to go)," Tom said. "If he doesn't live for that he shouldn't be out there . . . . That's when it's fun to kick, unless you miss."

The snap was good. The snap was perfect. The kick was in the air . . ."

For the better part of three hours the fans in the half-filled Astrodome had done more booing than rooting. Now they were on their feet, ready to

The Philadelphia Inquirer / SPORTS

Monday, Nov. 13, 1972 ♦ 13

Dial a Score LO 3-2842
For Late Results

Dempsey's Boots Beat Oilers, 18-17

Eagles Win on 6 Field Goals

By GORDON FORBES
Of The Inquirer Staff

HOUSTON—The Eagle offense fainted seven times at the sight of the end zone Sunday.

Fortunately, Tom Dempsey took the notoriously in-and-out unit of a giant book with a flurry of six field goals. The Eagles needed every one to pull out an 18-17 victory over the incredibly inept Houston Oilers inside the glittering Astrodome.

As sometimes happens in one of these pro football capers, the ending was packed with drama. Skip Butler, the newest in a succession of Oiler placekickers, barely missed a 43-yard try with 16 seconds left to play.

"It didn't miss by a helmet," said Super Bill Bradley. "It missed by (the width of) a football. I thought it was going to hit the bar."

When Butler's kick curled to the left of the upright, the Eagles were assured of their second one-point victory of the season against its losses and a tie.

The Oilers, roundly jeered by a half-filled Astrodome including many millionaire Texans trying to stay awake in their super-suites, dropped to 1-8, the worst record of any team in pro football.

"I was plain nervous when Butler lined up," admitted Bob Creech, the young Eagle linebacker. "I thought it missed by about three feet. I was just happy to see it go by."

With any kind of offensive thrust in the scoring zones, the Eagles should have been coasting in the final period.

As it was, Dempsey's sixth field goal, a 22-yarder in the first minute of the final period, provided an uneasy cushion of 18-10.

Quarterback Dan Pastorini, the adopted scapegoat of Oiler fans, somehow brought his team back to within a point with an unorthodox 44-yard thrust midway through the fourth quarter. It was unusual because the drive included only one tough pass, a 14-yard play-action toss to right end Alvin Reed. It was called on, of all downs, fourth-and-one.

A fail-safe flat pass to Paul Robinson gained five more yards and Pastorini scrambled for six to the Eagle 30.

Robinson then got two vicious blocks from guards Tom Regner and Ron Saul, located a power alley up the right side, and exploded for a 30-yard touchdown. Butler's kick with 5:39 left cut the Eagle lead to a single point, 18-17.

The offense then put the Eagles in a big hole. Pete Liske ran Ben Hawkins on a deep reverse that lost 15 yards back to the 15. That series ended with Bradley getting off a towering punt that fluttered away from returner Ken Houston and was finally downed at the Oiler 11 with 3:27 to go.

"It was left up to us, just like at Kansas City," grinned Richard Harris, the big end. "We decided we couldn't give it (a field goal) up.

"I was thinking all we had to do was try to contain Pastorini from running. Put on a big rush. Hope the backs could cover the receivers.

"OUR PURPOSE then was to keep them out of field goal range. They got inside but we just kept up the pressure. It was a lucky shot for us."

Fullback Fred Willis, who rushed for 119 yards, rammed for two tough yards and a first down at the 22 to get the drive started. Pastorini

Continued on Page 18, Column 1

Longest of Tom Dempsey's six field goals was this 52-yarder for Eagles in first period. UPI Telephoto

Now he has it (left), now he doesn't (right) as Eagles' Harold Carmichael catches pass and fumbles to Oilers' Gar Boyette UPI Telephoto

★★★
Tom's Feat One Short

Tom Dempsey of the Eagles was one short of the National Football League record when he kicked six field goals in the Eagles' 18-17 victory over the Oilers Sunday at Houston.

Jim Bakken of the 1967 St. Louis Cardinals kicked seven against the Pittsburgh Steelers.

Here's rundown of Dempsey's connections:

Distance	Score
First Quarter	
33 yards	3-0
52 yards	6-0
Second Quarter	
22 yards	9-3
12 yards	12-3
38 yards	15-3
Fourth Quarter	
20 yards	18-10

Giant Coach Accuses 'Skins Of Trying to Run Up Score

WASHINGTON (AP). With 24 seconds remaining and Washington leading New York, 20-13, Redskin Coach George Allen called it timeout to stop the clock, much to the dismay of Giant Coach Alex Webster.

On the next play, running back Larry Brown plowed four yards for a touchdown.

Webster said afterward. "Why did he call the time out? You guys know what he's like, don't you."

IN REPLY Allen said, "Somebody said Larry needed only one yard to go over 1,000 yards for the season." said Allen. "My only thought was to give Larry an opportunity to crack the mark.

"And you have to remember, the score was only 20-13 at the time, so another touchdown wouldn't have hurt. You know, anything can happen at

the end of a game"

Brown, the NFL's leading ground-gainer, carried the ball 30 times for 106 yards, the sixth time this season he has rushed for 100 or more

Related Story, Photo on Page 18

yards. He was shy of the 1,000-yard mark by five.

Allen also denied giving Webster the cold shoulder.

"Before a game, I'm too tight that I don't say anything to anyone," he said. "And

afterward, I would have liked to shake hands with Red Webster's nicknames) but I was concerned with more fights breaking out. I didn't want Sam to break his hand."

ALLEN SAID he thought there were two points in the game where the Redskins assured themselves of victory.

The Giants ran the second-half kickoff back to the Redskins 13, but six plays later had to settle for a field goal.

The second turning point was in the Redskins series of downs after the field goal.

On a second-and-19 on Washington's 13-yard line, quarterback Bill Kilmer's pass hit Giant linebacker Jim Files on the hands and bounced out but Redskins receiver Roy Jefferson made a one-hand catch for a 14-yard gain. The Skins went on to score.

NFL RESULTS

Sunday's Results

EAGLES 18, Houston 17

Washington 20, St. Louis 24
Pittsburgh 33, Kansas City 7
Minnesota 37, L.A. Rams 6
N.Y. Jets 41, Buffalo 3
Dallas 28, Detroit 24
Miami 30, New England 14
Atlanta 36, New Orleans 20
Green Bay 33, Chicago 17
Minnesota 27, Detroit 13
San Francisco 24, Baltimore 21
Denver 16, San Diego 13

NATIONAL CONFERENCE
East Division

	W	L	T	Pct.	PF	PA
Washington	7	2	0	.778	227	154
Dallas	6	3	0	.667	222	155
St. Louis	3	5	1	.389	155	175
EAGLES	1	6	2	.222	110	197
N.Y. Giants	4	5	0	.444	236	210

Central Division

Green Bay	6	3	0	.667	187	131
Detroit	5	3	1	.611	231	173
Minnesota	5	4	0	.556	210	167
Chicago	3	6	0	.333	149	207

West Division

Los Angeles	5	3	1	.611	172	146
Atlanta	5	4	0	.556	196	172
S. Francisco	5	4	0	.556	237	166
New Orleans	1	7	1	.167	137	223

AMERICAN CONFERENCE
East Division

Miami	9	0	0	1.000	235	104
N.Y. Jets	6	3	0	.667	257	193
Baltimore	4	5	0	.444	155	150
Buffalo	3	6	0	.333	162	229
New England	2	7	0	.222	136	231

Central Division

Pittsburgh	7	2	0	.778	210	133
Cleveland	6	3	0	.667	180	166
Cincinnati	5	4	0	.556	213	176
Houston	1	8	0	.111	103	223

West Division

Oakland	5	2	1	.667	216	157
Kansas City	5	4	0	.556	186	153
Denver	3	5	1	.389	207	213
San Diego	3	5	1	.389	203	198

Flyers Score 8 Goals in Last 2 Periods To Wallop Seals, 8-3, Take Lead in West

By CHUCK NEWMAN
Of The Inquirer Staff

Former City Representative Abe Rosen would have taped it. It wasn't even in style in his days in office. "We're No. 1. We're No. 1."

The chant, that has been heard in Pittsburgh, Dallas, Baltimore, Boston and points east, west, north and south of the city, came to Philadelphia at 9:42 P.M. "We're No. 1, We're No. 1."

It rang out from 15,074 assembled at the Spectrum at 9:02 P.M. Sunday night. "We're No. 1, We're No. 1." The Flyers had made it possible by burying the California Golden Seals, 8-3, on eight goals in the last two periods as the scoreboard showed the New York Rangers on their way to a win over Los Angeles. And an uproar at the happen-

ing summed it up the best. "Even if it's only for one day," he said, "the fans have waited a long while."

IT HASN'T been since the 1967-68 hockey and basketball seasons here that a city sports team has been in first place this deep into the season. The Flyers are there. In first place in the West Division of

the National Hockey League.

They made it in convincing fashion. Unlike their predecessors they went out and ate up a 1-0 deficit after one period played here in a 4-1 loss to the last-place Seals on Oct. 21 came back.

But, according to Coach Fred Shero and the players, this is no longer a defensive hockey team. Defenseman Brent Hughes tied the game and the Flyers were off to four straight goals and first

place.

Shero has heard the chant before. In Buffalo when his teams were 20 points ahead of the pack in the American Hockey League. "It feels good even then. It gives you a lift," Shero said, almost showing some elation.

"I'd like to be there at the end," he rationalized. "But

THE FLYERS got even 1-1 on Bobby Clarke's goal at 2:15. At 4:23 of the second period they were down again, 2-1. Visions of the stinker they played here in a 4-1 loss to the

Continued on Page 14, Column 3

Inside Our Pages

BLAZERS lose to Ottawa, 3-1 .... Page 14
BENNIE BRISCOE and Carlos Monzon are offered title rematch in Philadelphia .... Page 14
ST. JAMES defeats Bonner in battle of Catholic League unbeatens .... Page 17
BUDDY BAKER wins Texas 500 stock car race .... Page 19
TAIWAN captures golf's World Cup .... Page 19

November 13, 1972
Tom Dempsey sets club record by kicking
six field goals to defeat the Houston Oilers 18-17.

1973

RECORD: 5-8-1, 3RD IN NFC EAST
HEAD COACH: MIKE McCORMACK

Schedule
Regular Season

Wk. 1	Sep 16	L	34-23	vs St. Louis Cardinals
Wk. 2	Sep 23	T	23-23	at New York Giants
Wk. 3	Sep 30	L	28-7	vs Washington Redskins
Wk. 4	Oct 7	L	27-26	at Buffalo Bills
Wk. 5	Oct 14	W	27-24	at St. Louis Cardinals
Wk. 6	Oct 21	L	28-21	at Minnesota Vikings
Wk. 7	Oct 28	W	30-16	vs Dallas Cowboys
Wk. 8	Nov 4	W	24-23	vs New England Patriots
Wk. 9	Nov 11	L	44-27	vs Atlanta Falcons
Wk. 10	Nov 18	L	31-10	at Dallas Cowboys
Wk. 11	Nov 25	W	20-16	vs New York Giants
Wk. 12	Dec 2	L	38-28	at San Francisco 49ers
Wk. 13	Dec 9	W	24-23	vs New York Jets
Wk. 14	Dec 16	L	38-20	at Washington Redskins

Under new head coach Mike McCormick and new quarterback Roman Gabriel, the Eagles had an exciting offensive season but could only muster a 5-8-1 record. In his first year as a full-time receiver, Harold Carmichael became the second consecutive Eagle to lead the NFL in receptions with 67. Meanwhile quarterback Roman Gabriel became the NFL Comeback Player of the Year, after passing for 3,219 yards and 23 touchdowns.

1973 Philadelphia Eagles Stats

Passing	Comp	Att	Comp %	Yds	Y/Att	TD	Int	Rating
Roman Gabriel	270	460	58.7	3219	7.00	23	12	86.0
John Reaves	5	19	26.3	17	0.89	0	1	17.7

Rushing	Rush	Yds	Avg	TD
Tom Sullivan	217	968	4.5	4
Norm Bulaich	106	436	4.1	1
Po James	36	178	4.9	1
Tom Bailey	20	91	4.6	0
Harold Carmichael	3	42	14.0	0
Lee Bouggess	15	34	2.3	1
Charlie Young	4	24	6.0	1
Roman Gabriel	12	10	0.8	1
Greg Oliver	1	6	6.0	0
John Reaves	2	2	1.0	0
Bill Bradley	1	0	0.0	0\

Receiving	Rec	Yds	Avg	TD
Harold Carmichael	67	1116	16.7	9
Charlie Young	55	854	15.5	6
Tom Sullivan	50	322	6.4	1
Norm Bulaich	42	403	9.6	3
Don Zimmerman	22	220	10.0	3
Po James	17	94	5.5	0
Tom Bailey	10	80	8.0	1
Ben Hawkins	6	114	19.0	0
Lee Bouggess	4	18	4.5	0
Greg Oliver	1	9	9.0	0
Stan Davis	1	6	6.0	0

Punting	Punts	Yds	Avg	Blocked
Tom McNeill	46	1881	40.9	0
Bill Bradley	18	735	40.8	0

Interceptions	Int	Yds	Avg	TD
Randy Logan	5	38	7.6	0
Bill Bradley	4	21	5.3	0
John Outlaw	2	48	24.0	1
Steve Zabel	2	13	6.5	0
John Sodaski	1	0	0.0	0
Dennis Wirgowski	1	0	0.0	0

Kicking	PAT Made	PAT Att	PAT %	FG Made	FG Att	FG %	Pts
Tom Dempsey	34	34	100	24	40	60.0	106

Monday, Dec. 17, 1973 — The Philadelphia Inquirer / SPORTS — Dial **a** Score LO 3-2842 For Late Results — Section C

Associated Press
O. J. Simpson gets hero's ride from mates after breaking NFL rushing mark

2,003

O. J. Runs to Records as Bills Bury Jets

By SKIP MYSLENSKI
Inquirer Staff Writer

NEW YORK. — He had endured a hectic week, so now, as the Buffalo Bills chartered jet flew toward New York, O. J. Simpson was able to more appreciate the moments alone.

But as he relaxed, Johnny Ray, the team's irrepressible linebacker coach, moved down the aisle, noted his fashionable three-piece gray suit and chortled. "Hey, Juice," Ray kidded, "you look so good someone would think you're on your way to close some business deal."

Simpson looked up and smiled wanly. "That," he answered, "all depends."

At 1:25 Sunday afternoon in a snowy Shea Stadium, all doubts were removed. Joe Ferguson, Buffalo's rookie quarterback, knelt in the huddle and called "I-5 right," once again for O. J. Simpson to run the ball. At the snap, he turned and handed it to Simpson, then watched as this splendid runner followed fullback Jim Braxton over left tackle for six yards.

As they lay on the ground together, Braxton looked over. "That a big enough hole for ya?" he asked.

"Yea, man," Simpson said back. "Not bad. Not bad at all."

With that simple run the momentous countdown ended. O.J. Simpson upped his season total to 1,869 yards and eclipsed Jim Brown's old mark by six.

Before the game ended in a Bills' 34-14 victory, others too would fall. Simpson himself would go on to carry 34 times for a season-total of 332, breaking the old mark by 27; he would run for 200 yards, his season total then ending at a prodigious 2,003; and the Bills as a team gained 314 yards rushing, surpassing the
(See O.J. on 2-C)

JIM BROWN, 1963				O. J. SIMPSON, 1973			
Opponent	Atts.	Yds.	Avg.	Opponent	Atts.	Yds.	Avg.
Washington	15	162	10.8	New England	29	250	8.6
Dallas	20	232	11.6	San Diego	22	103	4.7
Los Angeles	22	95	4.3	New York Jets	24	123	5.1
Pittsburgh	21	175	8.3	Philadelphia	27	171	6.3
Philadelphia	23	123	5.3	Baltimore	22	166	7.5
New York Giants	23	144	5.8	Miami	14	55	3.9
New York Giants	9	40	4.4	Kansas City	39	157	4.0
Philadelphia	28	223	8.0	New Orleans	20	79	3.9
Pittsburgh	19	99	5.2	Cincinnati	29	99	4.9
St. Louis	22	154	7.0	Miami	20	120	6.0
Dallas	17	51	3.0	Baltimore	24	137	8.3
St. Louis	29	179	6.2	Atlanta	24	137	5.7
Detroit	13	61	4.7	New England	22	219	10.0
Washington	28	125	4.5	New York Jets	34	200	5.9
TOTALS	291	1,863	6.4	TOTALS	332	2,003	6.9

Redskins Defeat Eagles, Gain Playoffs

FRANK DOLSON

Eagles Still Believe After Final Defeat

WASHINGTON.—Sure, it would have been nice to end the season with a victory. Especially a victory over a team fighting to make the playoffs. And most especially a victory over a team coached by George Allen.

But Mike McCormack's first season as Eagles' head coach had ended with a defeat, and now, as the writers entered the locker room, he was walking from locker to locker, player to player. He patted Kermit Alexander on the back, shook hands with Bill Bradley, embraced Jerry Sisemore, playfully mussed Mark Nordquist's hair, thanked them all for what they had done. And what they had tried to do.

MIKE McCORMACK
...looks to next year

Maybe to his old boss—the guy down the hall in the winners' locker room on this dismal day—losing was like death. But not this defeat. Not to this man.

Mike McCormack's Eagles had started something this season—something that didn't end in the snow and mud and disappointment of Sunday's game.

"I think we have an outstanding young football team," the losing coach said after he had patted the last back, grasped the last hand, mussed the last lock of hair.

Sure, this was a painful defeat. But it wasn't the end of the world, merely the end of the first season—even if the winning coach was named George Allen.

"We had a lot of guys on this team who wanted to win the game so bad it hurt," said super rookie Charley Young, and he began ticking off names. McCormack ... Alexander ... Boyd Dowler ... Roman Gabriel ... Marlin McKeever, all the Eagles who had been with Allen in past years. "You could see it in their faces."

"Maybe so. But now that it was over, you could see something else in most of those faces. And it wasn't despair. Nor humiliation.

George Allen had won the game he simply had to win against a team crippled on defense. Nothing extraordinary about that.

"He's a great coach," Gabriel said. "No doubt about it. His record proves that. We had a lot of emotion going today because we had the opportunity of knocking them out of the
(See DOLSON on 4-C)

Charley Young is hot as his touchdown catch, against Redskins' Ken Houston, gives Eagles 10-0 lead ...

... but Young is cold and forlorn on snow-kissed bench late in game
Philadelphia Inquirer / RICHARD H. TITLEY

Playoff Picture

The lineup for National Football League playoff games (all times Eastern Standard):

NATIONAL CONFERENCE
FIRST ROUND
Dec. 22—Washington (10-4) at Minnesota (12-2), 1 P.M., CBS-TV (Ch. 10).
Dec. 23—Los Angeles (12-2) at Dallas (10-4), 4 P.M., CBS-TV (Ch. 10).

CHAMPIONSHIP GAME
Dec. 30—At Dallas or Los Angeles, time to be announced, CBS-TV (Ch. 10).

AMERICAN CONFERENCE
FIRST ROUND
Dec. 22—Pittsburgh (10-4) at Oakland (9-4-1), 4 P.M., NBC-TV (Ch. 3).
Dec. 23—Cincinnati (10-4) at Miami (12-2), 1 P.M., NBC-TV (Ch. 3).

CHAMPIONSHIP GAME
Dec. 30—Site priority: Miami, Oakland, Cincinnati, time to be announced; NBC-TV (Ch. 3).

SUPER BOWL
Jan. 13—National champion vs. American champion at Rice Stadium, Houston, 1:30 P.M., CBS-TV (Ch. 10).

Brown Stars in 38-20 Win

By GORDON FORBES
Inquirer Staff Writer

WASHINGTON — Confronted by natural and manmade obstacles, Larry Brown cut loose for four touchdowns Sunday to propel the desperate Washington Redskins into the playoffs for the third straight season.

Neither a swirling snowstorm that made footing treacherous at RFK Stadium nor an off-beat 4-4 defense could halt Brown throughout the Redskins' 38-20 triumph over the outmanned Eagles.

Brown scored twice as the Redskins erupted for 24 points in an intimidating show of offensive firepower in the second period.

"We couldn't stop them," said Coach Mike McCormack, conceding the obvious. "Larry came alive today. I think he scored four times without being touched."

George Allen, a fanatic for perfection on the Redskin specialty teams, had the pleasure of seeing McCormack's units break down repeatedly. In the second period alone, a roughing-the-punter penalty and a high snap generously helped the Redskins to their second and third touchdowns.

The Eagles managed to offset the Redskins flurry, getting a 15-yard field goal from Tom Dempsey just before halftime to trail, 24-13.

Then Brown fled 64 yards with a screen pass from Billy Kilmer to finish the Eagles late in the third period.

"He was my coverage on the screen," said linebacker Dean Halverson. "I got cut down by Charley Taylor. Hell, I was down all the time. The ice and mud would just cake up on your cleats."

Halverson slipped and fell trying to defend Brown while the Eagles were trying to protect a 10-0 lead. The result was an easy 14-yard touchdown pass to Brown that triggered the Redskin surge.

After the Redskins had gone ahead, 31-13, on the screen pass to Brown, the Eagle options narrowed to Roman Gabriel throwing deep.

Harold Carmichael outleaped 5-9 cornerback Pat Fischer for one of Gabe's tosses, shook off Brig Owens with a vicious stiff-arm and legged it to the one-yard line for a 73-yard play.

Tom Sullivan, who fell 32 yards short in his quest for 1,000 yards rushing, scored from the one for the final Eagle touchdown.

Gabriel wound up unloading 39 passes into the tough Redskin defense, completing 22 for 302 yards. He managed to reach Carmichael twice more
(See EAGLES on 5-C)

Flyers Whip Islanders, 4-0

By CHUCK NEWMAN
Inquirer Staff Writer

Denis Potvin, the New York Islander's $300,000-plus draft choice, missed the bus. That's not only the laughing stock of the National Hockey League is so bad. It's really because their general manager, Bill Torrey, missed the boat when it came to choosing a profession.

"Torrey's Turkeys" lost another one last night, 4-0, to the Flyers at the Spectrum. And they bored the 13,181 paying customers who had braved the snowstorm.

The Islanders were saved from falling to the position they are so accustomed to, last in the East Division, by another Vancouver nosedive.

Potvin, who lives a five-minute drive in his $17,000 Mercedes from the Nassau County Coliseum where the Islanders allegedly play, couldn't make the distance. The Islanders' bus left for Philadelphia at 10:06. But Coach Al Arbour, who deserves a better fate, waited. The bus was scheduled to leave at 10 o'clock.

"I know I wouldn't make it and would be suspended and fined anyway so I just forgot about it," Potvin told a New York reporter.

But stay tuned; they're only one point away and charging.

"He'll face something," Arbour, who probably can't do much about Potvin, said after the game. "We'll sit down and talk to the boy."

The worse they can do to Potvin is make him rejoin this crew, which Torrey is molding into the same type of failure he fashioned at California.

The victory kept the Flyers one point ahead of Chicago in the West Division of the NHL.
(See FLYERS on 6-C)

Sports on the Air

TELEVISION
College Football
1 P.M.—Liberty Bowl, North Carolina, Kansas, Ch. 3.

RADIO
Thoroughbred Racing
6:15 P.M.—Races of the Day from J.P.M. By Bell Park, WCAU-1210, WTMR-800.

1974

RECORD: 7-7, 4TH IN NFC EAST
HEAD COACH: MIKE McCORMACK

Schedule
Regular Season

Wk. 1	Sep 15	L	7-3	at St. Louis Cardinals
Wk. 2	Sep 23	W	13-10	vs Dallas Cowboys
Wk. 3	Sep 29	W	30-10	vs Baltimore Colts
Wk. 4	Oct 6	W	13-7	at San Diego Chargers
Wk. 5	Oct 13	W	35-7	vs New York Giants
Wk. 6	Oct 20	L	31-24	at Dallas Cowboys
Wk. 7	Oct 27	L	14-10	at New Orleans Saints
Wk. 8	Nov 3	L	27-0	at Pittsburgh Steelers
Wk. 9	Nov 10	L	27-20	vs Washington Redskins
Wk. 10	Nov 17	L	13-3	vs St. Louis Cardinals
Wk. 11	Nov 24	L	26-7	at Washington Redskins
Wk. 12	Dec 1	W	36-14	vs Green Bay Packers
Wk. 13	Dec 8	W	20-7	at New York Giants
Wk. 14	Dec 15	W	28-17	vs Detroit Lions

The Eagles made a trade with Cincinnati to acquire linebacker Bill Bergey. Bergey bolstered the defense and wons Pro Bowl honors along with Charlie Young, who becomes the third consecutive Eagle to lead the league in pass receptions with 63. Newly acquired linebacker Bill Bergey led an improved defense as the Eagles get off to a solid start, winning four of their first five games. However, a six-game losing streak would doom the Eagles playoff hopes, as they needed to win their final three games just to finish with a 7-7 record.

1974 Philadelphia Eagles Stats

Passing	Comp	Att	Comp %	Yds	Y/Att	TD	Int	Rating
Mike Boryla	60	102	58.8	580	5.69	5	3	78.9
Roman Gabriel	193	338	57.1	1867	5.52	9	12	66.8
Harold Carmichael	0	1	0.0	0	0.00	0	0	39.6
John Reaves	5	20	25.0	84	4.20	0	2	5.0

Rushing	Rush	Yds	Avg	TD
Tom Sullivan	244	760	3.1	11
Po James	67	276	4.1	2
Norm Bulaich	50	152	3.0	0
Roman Gabriel	14	76	5.4	0
Charlie Young	6	38	6.3	0
Tom Bailey	10	32	3.2	0
Mike Boryla	6	25	4.2	0
Greg Oliver	7	19	2.7	0
John Reaves	1	8	8.0	0
Randy Jackson	7	3	0.4	2
Merritt Kersey	1	2	2.0	0
Harold Carmichael	2	-6	-3.0	0

Receiving	Rec	Yds	Avg	TD
Charlie Young	63	696	11.0	3
Harold Carmichael	56	649	11.6	8
Tom Sullivan	39	312	8.0	1
Po James	33	230	7.0	0
Don Zimmerman	30	368	12.3	2
Norm Bulaich	28	204	7.3	0
Randy Jackson	17	0	0.0	0
Tom Bailey	6	27	4.5	0
Charlie Smith	1	28	28.0	0

Punting	Punts	Yds	Avg	Blocked
Merritt Kersey	82	2959	36.1	0
Bill Bradley	2	67	33.5	0

Interceptions	Int	Yds	Avg	TD
Bill Bergey	5	57	11.4	0
John Bunting	2	23	11.5	0
John Outlaw	2	22	11.0	0
Bill Bradley	2	19	9.5	0
Steve Zabel	2	12	6.0	0
Randy Logan	2	2	1.0	0
Joe Lavender	1	37	37.0	1
Jerry Patton	1	4	4.0	0
Dean Halverson	1	0	0.0	0

Kicking	PAT Made	PAT Att	PAT %	FG Made	FG Att	FG %	Pts
Tom Dempsey	26	30	87	10	16	62.5	56

Sportscene 3
Scoreboard 6
Calendar 6
Horse Racing 7
High Schools 8

The Philadelphia Inquirer
sports

section **C**

♦♦ Monday, Dec. 2, 1974

In Packer Weather, Boryla Makes Impressive Debut

BILL LYON

For four nights Mike Boryla had a squirrel scurrying around inside his stomach.

For four nights Mike Boryla counted blitzing linebackers in his sleep and listened to the wild pounding of his own heart, dreaming of the ecstasy of a touchdown pass, the agony of an interception.

Because last Wednesday Mike McCormack decided to rest Roman Gabriel's battered body and start Mike Boryla, whose regular-season experience his rookie season had consisted of 59 seconds of one game.

"Mike just told me I'd start and he was going to keep it quiet so the Packers wouldn't be able to prepare for me, set up blitzes and stunts to pressure me," Mike Boryla said.

"So that gave Mike Boryla four nights to wait. And worry. And stew in his own bubbling juices. And feel that damned squirrel running around loose in his gut.

"Sure, I got the shakes and the nerves," Mike Boryla admitted. "But I think I would rather know in advance that I was starting instead of the last minute.

"A lot of people on the team talked to me. They all had advice for me," he smiled.

"I just told myself this is what you were waiting for. Now it's your chance. I've always felt I could play up here. If I didn't feel that way, I wouldn't belong in the pros. I've always had confidence. But you don't always have to be talking about it just to prove it."

So Mike Boryla, low key, quiet, a rookie in experience only, went out and completed 16 of 32 passes, two of them for scores, engineered two impressive touchdown drives of 89 and 41 yards, and the Eagles took out six weeks worth of frustration on fumbling, butter-fingered Green Bay, 36-14.

It was an impressive debut for the QB from Stanford, because the game was played in the kind of weather the Packers invented.

The sky was black and glowering. The Vet echoed with thunderclaps. Sheets of rain splattered down. And the wind was whirlpool treacherous, blowing in cold, buffeting currents with downdrafts that grabbed spirals and drove them into the artificial turf.

Yet Mike Boryla threw with accuracy and variety. Lobs to skyscraping Harold Carmichael. Darts to Charles Young. Flares to Norm Bulaich. Sideline zingers to Don Zimmerman.

(See LYON on 4-C)

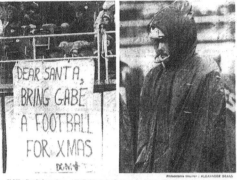

If Mike Boryla keeps it up, will Christmas be the next time Roman Gabriel (right) gets the ball?

Eagles' Will Wynn pounces on one of five fumbles Packers lost, this by MacArthur Lane (36) ...

... picks it up and takes off 87 yards for a touchdown with a phalanx of blockers to protect him ...

Eagles End Slump, Rack Pack, 36-14

By GORDON FORBES
Inquirer Staff Writer

Mike Boryla made his quarterback debut in the pro football bigs Sunday and it would be nice to say that he corrected everything that was wrong with the Eagle offense when it belonged to Roman Gabriel.

It would also be untrue.

Sure, Boryla played with poise against natural and human obstacles, but what accelerated the Eagles in their totally enjoyable 36-14 win over the bungling Green Bay Packers was an awesome defense.

"That was the best defensive effort we've had all around," said middle linebacker Bill Bergey. "The guys in front of me were just knocking people over. And the defensive secondary played well.

"After six straight losses," Bergey added, fingering a long, thin cigar, "maybe we had to go back to basic things. We gave the game ball to Mike McCormack, but I thought 30 or 40 people could have gotten game balls."

McCormack handled the ball flawlessly. The Packers should have been so fortunate. They fumbled eight times against the aroused Eagle defense, losing the ball five times. Out of those five turnovers, the Eagles gleefully produced 29 points to the delight of the 42,030 fans in attendance. The miserable weather accounted for 24,022 no-shows.

Boryla, who got the call from McCormack over an unhappy John Reaves, had to battle swirling winds and a tough Packer defense that had limited its last three opponents to 10 points. Bergey's hitters removed much of the pressure by turning the ball over to the offense three times in Packer territory and supplying a touchdown outright on Will Wynn's spectacular 87-yard run with MacArthur Lane's fumble.

The rookie took the Eagles 89 yards late in the second period for their fourth straight touchdown and a 29-0 lead over the dazed Packers.

Green Bay got it together offensively in the second half, closing to within 29-14 on quarterback John Had's three-yard rollout pass to MacArthur Lane. And on the

(See EAGLES on 4-C)

Now find the other 24,558 who watched the Browns-49ers game

A No-Show Sunday

From Inquirer Wire Services

Things were rough all over Sunday.

An ice storm forced cancellation of the 10-race program at Penn National Race Course in Grantville, Pa.

The World Hockey Association game between the Cleveland Crusaders and the Michigan Stags at Richfield, O., was snowed out.

So was the National Hockey League game between the Toronto Maple Leafs and the Detroit Red Wings. It seems the Maple Leafs made it to Olympic Stadium in Detroit just fine, but all except one Red Wing were stranded at their homes.

And although no National Football League games were called off, maybe a few should've been.

An NFL record for no-shows was set in Chicago where 36,951 decided not to attend a Bears-New York Giants game played in freezing rain and snow. Some 18,602 did show up.

But the record didn't last out the day. Two hours later in Atlanta, where it was 33 degrees with 15-MPH winds, 18,448 ticket holders stayed and 40,392 didn't.

In other sellouts, there were 29,368 no-shows in Cleveland (24,559 showed); 24,022 at Veterans Stadium, where 42,030 watched the Eagles; 9,155 no-shows in Pittsburgh (43,195 braved freezing rain); approximately 4,000 in Buffalo (79,543 showed) and 3,900 in Oakland, where 51,620 attended in good weather.

Elsewhere, attendance was 44,402 at Minnesota, 41,863 in snowy St. Louis and 44,688 at Shea Stadium where the New York Jets beat San Diego, 27-14, in showers and blustery winds.

K.C.'s Not-So-Good Scouts Lambasted by Flyers, 10-0

By CHUCK NEWMAN
Inquirer Staff Writer

Tom Capaccio and Mike Fore were the starting linesmen in Sunday night's so-called hockey game between the Flyers and the Kansas City Scouts.

Don't look for them in the National Hockey League roster of officials. They usually wash Junior A games in South Jersey and toil as stickboys at the Flyers' games at the Spectrum. Ironically, Capaccio and Fore were not out of place when fouled-up weather forced the use of stand-ins until relief could manage the three-hour car drive from Washington.

In a game that should erase all thoughts of further expansion, the Flyers scored five times in the first period and four more times in the second en route to a 10-0 annihilation of the Scouts.

The win pushed the Flyers back atop Division One of the NHL, two points ahead of idle Atlanta.

"It was a tough game to coach," Flyers' Coach Fred Shero explained. "You have to stop the players from giving goals."

Shero used four lines in an effort to hold the score down and held a seminar with his team after the first and second periods, concentrating on the mistakes his team was making.

"I told them after the second period that we could go out there and score five more goals and give two more goals and give up two more (See FLYERS on 6-C)

Jabbar Scores 35, Bucks Zap 76ers

Special to The Inquirer

RACINE, Wis.—Kareem Abdul-Jabbar scored 20 of his 35 points in the third period and the revived Milwaukee Hawks beat the 76ers, 117-112, before 5,032 Sunday night.

The loss was the 76ers' fourth in succession and the victory was the Bucks' sixth in seven games. They lost 13 of their first 14 while Jabbar was sidelined with a broken hand.

Jabbar spent the last 15 minutes of the first half on the bench after picking up his third personal foul but the Bucks led at intermission, 58-36, on a field goal by Gary Brokaw, the only basket in the half by the rookie from Notre Dame.

In the third period, Jabbar dominated the boards and began scoring regularly. He was a one-man show for the Bucks, although the 76ers twice forged four-point leads, 79-75 and 83-79.

But Jabbar paced a Buck rally and Brokaw scored his second field goal on a fast break to put the Bucks ahead to stay, 89-87, as the third period ended.

The Bucks gradually increased their lead in the final period as the losers ran into foul trouble. With 4½ minutes to play, Jabbar made a perfect pass to Mickey Davis underneath for a goal and a 107-96 Milwaukee advantage.

The 76ers then rallied as Doug Collins and Allan Bristow led the way. Bristow's second three-point play at the spurt cut the Milwaukee edge to 109-108 before Jim Price, fouled by Steve Mix with 2:01 (See 76ERS on 6-C)

NFL Playoff Picture

Standings and remaining games for teams in contention for National Football League playoff berths (six division champions and the second-place team with the best record in each conference qualify):

NATIONAL CONFERENCE
Eastern Division

	W	L	T	Dec. 8	Dec. 15
y-St. Louis	9	3	0	at N. Orleans	N. Y. Giants
Washington	8	4	0	at L. Ang. (M)	Chicago
Dallas	7	5	0	Cleveland (S)	at Oakland (S)

Central Division

	W	L	T		
x-Minnesota	8	4	0	Atlanta (S)	at Ken. City (S)
Detroit	6	6	0	at Cincinnati	at Eagles

Western Division

	W	L	T		
x-L. Angeles	9	3	0	Washing. (M)	Buffalo

AMERICAN CONFERENCE
Eastern Division

	W	L	T		
Buffalo	9	3	0	at N. Y. Jets	at Los Angeles
Miami	8	3	0	at Baltimore	New England
N. England	7	5	0	Pittsburgh	at Miami

Central Division

	W	L	T		
Pittsburgh	8	3	1	at N. England	Cincinnati (S)
Cincinnati	7	4	1	Detroit	at Pitts. (S)

Western Division

	W	L	T		
x-Oakland	10	2	0	at Ken. City	Dallas (S)
Denver	6	5	1	Houston	at San Diego

x-clinched division title   y-clinched playoff berth
S-scheduled preceding Saturday; M-following Monday

... so it's no wonder he has a Wynning smile

December 2, 1974
In his Eagles debut QB Mike Boryla defeats the Green Bay Packers 36-14

1975

RECORD: 4-10, 5TH IN NFC EAST
HEAD COACH: MIKE McCORMACK

Schedule
Regular Season

Wk. 1	Sep 21	L	23-14	vs New York Giants
Wk. 2	Sep 28	L	15-13	at Chicago Bears
Wk. 3	Oct 5	W	26-10	vs Washington Redskins
Wk. 4	Oct 12	L	24-16	at Miami Dolphins
Wk. 5	Oct 19	L	31-20	at St. Louis Cardinals
Wk. 6	Oct 26	L	20-17	vs Dallas Cowboys
Wk. 7	Nov 3	L	42-3	vs Los Angeles Rams
Wk. 8	Nov 9	L	24-23	vs St. Louis Cardinals
Wk. 9	Nov 16	W	13-10	at New York Giants
Wk. 10	Nov 23	L	27-17	at Dallas Cowboys
Wk. 11	Nov 30	W	27-17	vs San Francisco 49ers
Wk. 12	Dec 7	L	31-0	vs Cincinnati Bengals
Wk. 13	Dec 14	L	25-10	at Denver Broncos
Wk. 14	Dec 21	W	26-3	at Washington Redskins

The Eagles suffered a season of setbacks, finishing in last place with a terrible 4-10 record. Following the season coach Mike McCormick was fired and replaced by fiery UCLA coach Dick Vermeil.

1975 Philadelphia Eagles Stats

Passing	Comp	Att	Comp %	Yds	Y/Att	TD	Int	Rating
Roman Gabriel	151	292	51.7	1644	5.63	13	11	67.8
Mike Boryla	87	166	52.4	996	6.00	6	12	52.7

Rushing	Rush	Yds	Avg	TD
Tom Sullivan	173	632	3.7	0
James McAlister	103	335	3.3	1
Art Malone	101	325	3.2	0
Po James	43	196	4.6	1
Charlie Smith	9	85	9.4	0
Roman Gabriel	13	70	5.4	1
Mike Boryla	8	33	4.1	0
John Tarver	7	20	2.9	0
Charlie Young	2	1	0.5	0
Spike Jones	1	-1	-1.0	0

Receiving	Rec	Yds	Avg	TD
Charlie Young	49	659	13.4	3
Harold Carmichael	49	639	13.0	7
Charlie Smith	37	515	13.9	6
Po James	32	267	8.3	1
Tom Sullivan	28	276	9.9	0
Art Malone	20	120	6.0	0
James McAlister	17	134	7.9	2
John Tarver	5	14	2.8	0
Keith Krepfle	1	16	16.0	0

Punting	Punts	Yds	Avg	Blocked
Spike Jones	68	2742	40.3	0
Merritt Kersey	15	489	32.6	0

Interceptions	Int	Yds	Avg	TD
John Outlaw	5	23	4.6	0
Frank LeMaster	4	133	33.3	1
Artimus Parker	4	15	3.8	0
Joe Lavender	3	59	19.7	1
Bill Bergey	3	48	16.0	0
John Bunting	1	6	6.0	0
Randy Logan	1	4	4.0	0

Kicking	PAT Made	PAT Att	PAT %	FG Made	FG Att	FG %	Pts
Horst Muhlmann	21	24	88	20	29	69.0	81

The Scene 3
High Schools 5
Classified Ads 7
Comics 16
Feature Page 17

The Philadelphia Inquirer
sports

section
D

✦✦✦ Tuesday, Nov. 4, 1975

A Helpless McCormack

By FRANK DOLSON

It was quite a switch for Howard. Two nights before he had been in New York City doing Saturday Night Live. Last night he was in Philadelphia doing Monday Night Dead . . .

Game-time approached and you could feel the excitement mounting. So what if the Eagles were 1-and-5? The nation was watching, the stadium was packed.

Half a minute before the opening kickoff and a roar thundered across Veterans Stadium, imploring the home team to win one for Mike McCormack or Roone Arledge or Leonard Tose's friend, Gene Mauch, who was sitting in the owner's box . . . or somebody. Anybody . . .

The people were ready. The Eagles weren't. What a shame for the 64,601 in the Vet and the 40 million non-paying spectators who missed Archie Bunker to see this.

And especially what a shame for Mike McCormack . . .

"I like Mike McCormack," Bill Bergey had said 24 hours before the dreadful mismatch. "I think he's a good coach. I think he prepares us well. He's got a knack of keeping things going when things are dark and dismal."

But last night, with all these people watching, with Howard Cosell talking, with all those friends of the owner sitting in the executive box, things got so dark, so dismal that the fired-up crowd started leaving in the third quarter. One disgruntled group in the end zone went so far as to hold up a sign they had brought along in the event of just such a shellacking. "Bring Back Joe," it said, apparently referring to former Eagles Coach Joe Kuharich.

Poor Mike McCormack. He stood there near midfield, his arms folded across his huge chest, watching the game get out of control, listening to the cheers turn to jeers.

Bill Bergey isn't the only person who likes Mike McCormack. To know the man is to like him . . . and, at a time like this, to feel sorry for him. When a game disintegrates there is nothing a coach can do — except maybe wish it hadn't disintegrated with the nation watching.

"I couldn't think of anything to stem the tide," McCormack said. "I'd have taken messages from Heaven, from the pressbox, from anyplace if anybody knew how to stop it."

Outwardly, he was still calm, still in control of his emotions. But there was one clue to the agony he must have felt inside. In his left hand, he held a red-colored lead pencil, and as he stood there, leaning against the wooden platform in his office, he gripped the pencil tighter and tighter until, finally, it snapped in two.

Before the ordeal was over, the pencil was in tiny fragments, the lead was jammed through the rubber eraser. Here was a man going through hell—and yet, no matter how unpleasant the question, never once acting anything but a man.

"I don't know any other profession that affects you so much personally," he had said before the game. "You

Mike McCormack: "I'd have taken messages from Heaven"

get in a losing streak, you don't want to go out of the house, to see anyone . . .

It happened to Nick Skorich. It happened to Jerry Williams, and to Eddie Khayat, and now it was happening to Mike McCormack.

"In professional sports," he knew, "people pay to see a winner."

(See DOLSON on 2-D)

> 'In seven years, we haven't made any progress at all.'
> —Leonard Tose

Rams Humiliate Eagles

Sixth Defeat (42-3)
Worst Since 1972

By GORDON FORBES
Inquirer Staff Writer

The Eagles suffered another of those humiliating defeats last night that have so often marked their pathetic past. This time it was a 42-3 drubbing at the hands of the awesome Los Angeles Rams before a jeering sellout crowd of 64,601 fans and a national television audience of 40 million.

The last time the Eagles were wiped out that badly was three years ago in a 62-10 wipeout by the New York Giants. That was the season that owner Len Tose chose to fire Eddie Khayat and replace him with Mike McCormack. And out of the Monday Night Massacre came the obvious question: Is Tose in the mood to replace McCormack?

The owner wasn't saying. But McCormack, wearing his customary grim face after watching his team taken apart, admitted this was the worst defeat in his three-year head coaching career.

"It's going to be short and sweet this time gentlemen," he told reporters afterwards. "We had our butts kicked by a very good football team. They did everything they wanted to and we couldn't seem to do anything against them."

The Eagles, now 1-6 and badly slipping, fell behind, 21-3 at halftime as quarterback James Harris whipped both cornerbacks on deep touchdown passes to fleet Harold Jackson, the former Eagle gamebreaker. On the first of Harris' throws, a 54-yard

bomb, Jackson ran past defender John Outlaw. On the second, he beat Cliff Brooks for a 30-yard score.

The Rams turned it into a rout in the third quarter, scoring twice more. Harris hurled a 42-yard touchdown strike to backup receiver Jack Snow and later Fred Dryer, the flanky defensive end, rubbed it in by grabbing a fumble by Roman Gabriel and racing 20 yards for another score.

"They weren't as good as we made them out to be," Outlaw said in the silent Eagle dressing room. "We knew they were going to put the ball in the air. We just didn't do the job.

"He (Jackson) just ran a short out and then a fly. I just didn't come out of my turn quick enough. He just outran me. With Snow, we were in zone coverage and he just split the seam on us," Outlaw said as he stared off into space. "You just want to go somewhere and bury yourself. There's not a whole lot you can say."

Dryer's touchdown opened a 35-3 lead for the Rams (6-1) and McCormack gave Gabriel a 10th series before turning the sputtering offensive over to Mike Boryla with 6:36 left in the third period.

Boryla produced a touchdown all right—for the Rams. On the second play of the final period, the young quarterback tried to go short but linebacker Isiah Robertson intercepted and sprinted 76 yards down the left sideline to wrap up the scoring.

"It wasn't any fun," Dryer said

(See EAGLES on 2-D)

On the bench, Tom Sullivan (right) rages against a hopeless situation . . .

Leonard Tose: A Bitter Man

By BILL LYON

Leonard Tose went on the Mutual Radio Network at halftime last night and did what Howard Cosell is always braying about. He told it like it is.

"In seven years," said the Eagles' owner, "We haven't made any progress at all in my opinion."

"We're 1-and-5 and we're headed for 1-and-6 and that doesn't make me happy. We've slipped a lot."

Tose did not amplify on that. Not during the game. But afterwards.

Two weeks ago he was asked if he thought his coach, Mike McCormack, was doing a good job. He refused comment, and that of course triggered all sorts of speculation that McCormack, in his third year of a three-year contract, faced the ultimatum that confronts all coaches—win or else.

The Eagles, facing a grim schedule, would have to sweep the second half of their season to emerge with a winning record. In the wake of last night's humiliation, you can make your own odds on that possibility.

"Well, I'll tell ya," said Fred Dryer. "I empathesize with these guys (the Eagles).

"I've been through that before, Man, I could stand here and talk to you 'til next week about my days with the Giants."

Dryer, a defensive end traded from New York to the Rams, rumbled 20 yards with a Roman Gabriel fumble to score one of six LA TDs against the Eagles. And the Eagles, he said, reacted predictably.

"Some of 'em quit and some of 'em didn't," he said. "I'm not gonna name names. I imagine the films will show that. It happens when you get behind. Believe me, I know. They got

half a season left. They can either say, screw it, or they can try to correct whatever is wrong. I'll tell you, they got some damn good players."

So does the fault lie with the coaches?

"Who the hell knows?" replied Dryer. "From what I can tell McCormack is a good coach. Look at Atlanta. They fire a coach and the next day they beat New Orleans. Now figure that.

"I think the Eagles can turn themselves around. I hope they do. Really. Otherwise, it's a long damn season.

"I think if they get some points on us early they'd have really stuck it to us."

But the sticking was done instead by the Roadrunner, Harold Jackson, Ex-Eagle. Two TD catches.

"The first one is called 68 X-go. If you really care," Jackson said with a grin. "John Outlaw was setting on me, hanging for the short stuff. So on the sideline I said, hey, let me run a fly right by him.

"The second one, (Clifford) Brooks was expecting me to go inside. So I

(See LYON on 2-D)

. . . while on the field, the hopelessness is the reality of a Roman Gabriel fumble, following Larry Brooks' sack

November 4, 1975
Eagles get clobbered by the LA Rams 42-3,
worst loss since 1972.

1976

RECORD: 4-10, 4TH IN NFC EAST
HEAD COACH: DICK VERMEIL

Schedule
Regular Season

Wk. 1	Sep 12	L	27-7	at Dallas Cowboys
Wk. 2	Sep 19	W	20-7	vs New York Giants
Wk. 3	Sep 27	L	20-17	vs Washington Redskins (OT)
Wk. 4	Oct 3	W	14-13	at Atlanta Falcons
Wk. 5	Oct 10	L	33-14	at St. Louis Cardinals
Wk. 6	Oct 17	L	28-13	at Green Bay Packers
Wk. 7	Oct 24	L	31-12	vs Minnesota Vikings
Wk. 8	Oct 31	W	10-0	at New York Giants
Wk. 9	Nov 7	L	17-14	vs St. Louis Cardinals
Wk. 10	Nov 14	L	24-3	at Cleveland Browns
Wk. 11	Nov 21	L	26-7	vs Oakland Raiders
Wk. 12	Nov 28	L	24-0	at Washington Redskins
Wk. 13	Dec 5	L	26-7	vs Dallas Cowboys
Wk. 14	Dec 12	W	27-10	vs Seattle Seahawks

After 10 straight non-winning seasons, the Eagles new coach Dick Vermeil was a change of direction. Vermeil, a workaholic perfectionist, came into camp and worked the Eagles hard. Many players rejected the hard-driving Vermeil, as the Eagles did not play any better posting another 4-10 record. However, they did win their home opener 20-7 against the NY Giants.

1976 Philadelphia Eagles Stats

Passing	Comp	Att	Comp %	Yds	Y/Att	TD	Int	Rating
Mike Boryla	123	246	50.0	1247	5.07	9	14	53.4
Spike Jones	1	1	100.0	-4	-4.00	0	0	79.2
Roman Gabriel	46	92	50.0	476	5.17	2	2	63.5
Harold Carmichael	0	2	0.0	0	0.00	0	0	39.6
John Walton	12	28	42.9	125	4.46	0	2	26.6

Rushing	Rush	Yds	Avg	TD
Mike Hogan	123	561	4.6	0
Tom Sullivan	99	399	4.0	2
Dave Hampton	71	267	3.8	1
James McAlister	68	265	3.9	0
Herb Lusk	61	254	4.2	0
Mike Boryla	29	166	5.7	2
Bill Olds	36	120	3.3	1
Charlie Smith	9	25	2.8	1
Art Malone	2	14	7.0	1
Charlie Young	1	6	6.0	0
Roman Gabriel	4	2	0.5	0
John Walton	2	1	0.5	0

Receiving	Rec	Yds	Avg	TD
Harold Carmichael	42	503	12.0	5
Charlie Young	30	374	12.5	0
Charlie Smith	27	412	15.3	4
Mike Hogan	15	89	5.9	0
Tom Sullivan	14	116	8.3	1
Herb Lusk	13	119	9.2	0
James McAlister	12	72	6.0	0
Dave Hampton	12	57	4.8	0
Bill Olds	9	29	3.2	0
Keith Krepfle	6	80	13.3	1
Art Malone	1	-3	-3.0	0
Frank LeMaster	1	-4	-4.0	0

Punting	Punts	Yds	Avg	Blocked
Spike Jones	94	3445	36.6	0

Kicking	PAT Made	PAT Att	PAT %	FG Made	FG Att	FG %	Pts
Horst Muhlmann	18	19	95	11	16	68.8	51

Interceptions	Int	Yds	Avg	TD
Bill Bradley	2	63	31.5	0
Bill Bergey	2	48	24.0	0
John Outlaw	2	19	9.5	0
Randy Logan	1	38	38.0	0
Tom Ehlers	1	27	27.0	0
Al Clark	1	0	0.0	0

1976

Scoreboard 2
The Scene 3
Horse racing 6
High schools 7

The Philadelphia Inquirer
sports

section C

Monday, Nov. 1, 1976

Eagles win with basics

By FRANK DOLSON

Sports Editor

Tale of Jolly Lean Giants

EAST RUTHERFORD, N.J. — Come to think of it, this has been a heckuva sports year for New York. The Yankees made it to the World Series. The Knicks won three games before losing. The Islanders got off to a flying start in the National Hockey League. And, perhaps best of all from the standpoint of rebuilding the city's sports image, the Giants left town.

Their record might be the worst this side of Tampa Bay. Their execution might be abysmal. Their personnel might be questionable. Their offense might be invisible. But nobody can criticize their timing.

What better season to escape to the other side of the river. What more perfect year to flee across state lines. The move was sheer genius. As the New York Giants, descendants of a proud heritage, this club would be a disgrace. But as the East Rutherford Giants (Midgets?) they're — well, they're the best damned football team East Rutherfordians have ever had.

A great sports town, East Rutherford. Maybe the greatest of all time. Imagine selling 76,000 tickets — at $9 and $11.50 a crack — to see a 0-and-7 team that hasn't scored a point in five quarters extend their winless streak to eight and their scoreless streak to nine.

Listing flagship

Across the way, on the other side of the Hudson, the natives must be laughing themselves silly. Not only is it now possible for them to totally disown this team, but yesterday — thanks to the foresight of the local CBS television station — it was impossible to watch the Giants play in New York. Given a choice between carrying the sold-out East Rutherford-Philadelphia game or Dallas-Washington, the station chose the latter. It may have been CBS' sharpest move since the cancellation of "Ball Four."

"When you're talking about the Giants you're talking about the flagship of the NFL," East Rutherford's new head coach, John McVay told a New York writer the other day. Either McVay has a good sense of humor or the NFL has a bad flagship.

The Giants were so impotent yesterday that even the most loyal East Rutherfordians were tempted to act like hardened New Yorkers. Their boos floated across these reclaimed marshlands; their frustrations over the inability of Craig Morton to put points on those fancy, electronic scoreboards drove them to chant: "We want Snead ... We want Snead." (In fairness to the East Rutherford sports fans, however, those may have been Eagles' rooters screaming for McVay to use Snead.)

Poor McVay. A short, chunky, personable man who inherited this mess from Bill Arnsparger days before, he handled the postgame inquisition with patience and grace.

"We moved the ball a little bit," he said in the tone of voice of a coach grateful for small favors, "but we dropped a touchdown pass in the end zone and we missed a field goal. You're not supposed to do things like that in a professional football game."

First and no goal

Nor are you supposed to get a first down on the other team's 3, try three running plays and wind up with a fourth down on the 6. But the Giants did in the fourth quarter — with a major assist from the Eagles' defensive unit, and no small help from themselves. On the first play Marsh White slipped and lost 3. Second-and-goal on the 6. In came another play from the sidelines, designed for a goal-line defense. But the Eagles weren't in a goal-line defense, and Morton called time.

A conference, then a handoff to — surprise! — Larry Csonka, only his seventh carry of the day. He struggled to the 5. Then a quick pitch to Doug Kotar, and a loss as Manny Sistrunk hauled him down from behind. And finally, a pass that bounced harmlessly in the end zone, far over the head of wide-receiver Ray Rhodes, who obviously didn't run the pattern Morton expected him to run. BOO-O-O.

"We were down in there (close)," McVay said. "It was my decision, let's go in for a score. Then an on-side kick, then ..."

That was quite a finish John McVay had worked out in his mind, but it bore no resemblance to what the Giants came up with on the field.

"Holding hurt us," the coach was saying. "And our inability to get outside. And we dropped some balls."

They did what losing football teams have been doing for years in much more exotic places than East Rutherford, N.J. And McVay said what his predecessor had been saying for weeks: "We've got good personnel ... football players."

"Well," Csonka would say later in that big, plush locker room, "we'd

(See DOLSON on 5-C)

Associated Press

His footing unsecure, tight end Bob Tucker of the Giants goes down at the hands of the Eagles' John Bunting in the last period

Defeat Giants by 10-0

By Gordon Forbes
Inquirer Staff Writer

After seven weeks of frustration in the defensive trenches, the Eagles finally discovered an offensive line they could handle and a quarterback they could knock down.

They needed both edges to achieve a 10-0 victory over the winless, struggling New York Giants yesterday at the Meadowlands Complex on a day when the Eagle offense didn't dazzle anybody either.

"We just went back to basics," said Bill Dunstan, who went all the way inside at both tackle spots as the Eagles put together their first shutout in 105 games, or since late in 1968. "We stressed coming off the football and it finally is coming around now. We just began rolling off the ball ... starting with step one and reading our keys second."

"We knew beginning on Wednesday that we weren't going to be doing that much blitzing," said Blenda Gay, the strongside end. "That's because they flared their backs a lot. Most teams give solid protection and the backs can help defense the ends."

Gay grinned. "You know," he said, "it's much easier to hit a still target than a moving target."

The still target was poor Craig Morton, the beleaguered Giant quarterback, who was sacked six times by the furious Eagle rush and booed continually by angry fans who pleaded for a relief appearance by Norm Snead.

The boos began as early as the second period when Morton was on the field for three running plays and then off. On the next two series, quarterback Mike Boryla guided the Eagles to a 10-point lead that stood up only because they were playing the Giants.

It would have stood up in their first game when the Giants scored a single touchdown. And it was enough yesterday because the Giants, playing their first game under new coach John McVay, never developed any offensive rhythm or consistency.

"I've seen three Giant games on film," said linebacker John Bunting, "and our defensive front four has just played unbelievable against the Giants. It makes it so much easier on the linebackers. They play that way and you know Bill Bergy will make all-pro. Hell, even Frank LeMaster and me might be all-pro, too."

Boryla gave the Eagles a 7-0 lead

(See EAGLES on 5-C)

Wind-helped kick levels Vikings

Associated Press

CHICAGO — Bob Parsons plays for the Chicago Bears who play in the Windy City and knows something about shifting winds.

Parsons outdueled Neil Clabo in a kicking game that went a long way in providing the Chicago Bears with a 14-13 victory yesterday as they handed the Minnesota Vikings their first loss of the season.

A pair of squibbed punts by Clabo into a 17-m.p.h. wind quickly were turned into touchdowns by the Bears and Parsons recalled that he had shanked three punts at Minnesota earlier in the season when the Vikings edged the Bears, 20-19.

"I felt sorry for Clabo," said Parsons. "I know how he feels. I work on kicking into the wind every day. I was able to get my punts high into the wind which enabled our guys to cover well."

Clabo admitted the wind was a factor but said, "All kickers have bad days," and Minnesota Coach Bud Grant added, "Kicking definitely was a factor. Our's was as bad as it has been since I can remember."

Bear Coach Jack Pardee said the wind was against the Vikings on their last possession and was a factor in keeping them from getting into range for a game-winning field goal.

Walter Payton's 29-yard touchdown run in the first quarter and a couple of breaks which led to another touchdown in the fourth period helped the Bears even their record at 4-4.

Minnesota is now 6-1-1.

With the Bears leading, 7-6, after Fred Cox had booted a pair of 24-yard field goals for the Vikings, Nate Wright was called for pass interference which gave the Bears the ball on the Viking 3-yard line. Johnny Musso then fumbled and recovered the ball in the end zone for what proved to be the winning touchdown

Minnesota came right back with a touchdown on an 80 yard drive which was helped by a pass interference call before Fran Tarkenton, who earlier broke the last of Johnny Unitas' passing records, rolled out 2 yards to score.

Tarkenton completed 24 of 46 passes for 272 yards and a career total of 40,421, surpassing Unitas' total of 40,239.

It marked the Bears' first victory over the Vikings since 1972 after eight regular-season losses.

Tarkenton, who a year ago sur-

(See BEARS on 4-C)

Bakken's OT kick wins for Cards

Associated Press

ST. LOUIS — "We just blew them out," guard Bob Young said. "They stunted some in the first half, but they never beat us one on one."

The 270-pound Young was describing the 39-yard St. Louis Cardinals march in overtime, overcoming the vaunted defense of the San Francisco 49ers in a 23-20 National Football League game yesterday.

The Cards, after recovering a fumble at the 49er 43-yard line, called on Jim Otis for five straight carries in their parade to within the shadow of the San Francisco goalpost.

Then, after Otis was halted at the 4 on third down, veteran Jim Bakken coolly kicked a 21-yard field goal for the triumph with 6 minutes 42 seconds gone in the extra period.

"We have nothing to be ashamed about in losing," said San Francisco Coach Monte Clark, who watched his team begin with a costly mistake and lose in the same fashion.

"Aside from a couple mistakes, I thought we outplayed them, but they (Cardinals) are a championship-type team," Clark added.

"Our effort was great," Clark said. "It's just too bad that as great as

(See CARDINALS on 4-C)

Flyers blast LoPresti to wallop Stars, 9-1

Gary Ronberg
Inquirer Staff Writer

Down there on the frosty Spectrum ice, his head encased in white plastic and the rest of him wrapped in pads that would never be more vital to his survival, Pete LoPresti was all alone last night. Into his pads, against his stick, clanging off the glass and the bright red posts on either side of him, and feeling like hot coals when it wound up in his glove, more rubber was poured at LoPresti than into tire factory molds.

And many times — too many times — it billowed in the net behind him as the Flyers thrashed the Minnesota North Stars, 9-1, and pulled into a first-place tie with the New York Islanders, pending the outcome of tonight's Islanders-Canucks match in Vancouver.

"It's hard to explain," said LoPresti, son of Sam LoPresti, a former National Hockey League goaltender who after he gets word of last night may wish his son had chosen other endeavors.

"You just try to keep going. You give it your best, so that at least you can walk out of the building with your head up. Everybody has bad games now and then. But with a goaltender, it goes up there on the board where everybody can see it."

The thing is, LoPresti was probably the best North Star on the ice. Indeed, if he gave up a bad goal, it was only one — Reggie Leach's short-side strike on a first-period power play.

"If you saw a bad goal against him tonight, I didn't," said Minnesota Coach Ted Harris. "None of what happened tonight was his fault. I wouldn't have been him (LoPresti) tonight for a million bucks."

Perhaps it was the game at Long Island Saturday night that aroused these Flyers. Or maybe it was that they decided to cease playing down to

(See FLYERS on 2-C)

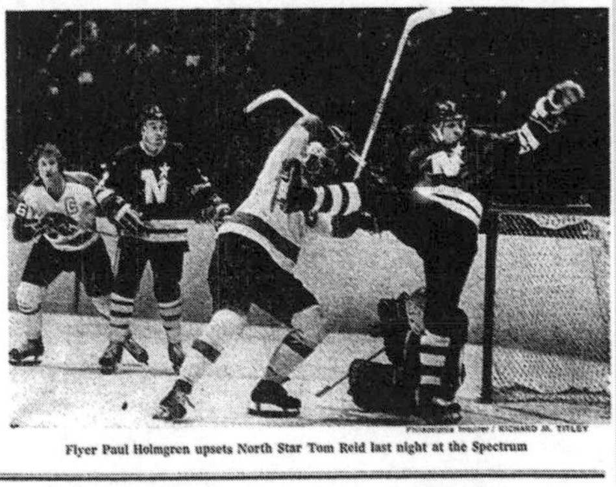

Philadelphia Inquirer / RICHARD M. TITLEY

Flyer Paul Holmgren upsets North Star Tom Reid last night at the Spectrum

Syracuse coach: No honest day's work by officials

By Chuck Newman
Inquirer Staff Writer

College roundup

Syracuse Coach Frank Maloney will violate football decorum at his weekly football press conference today. Not only will he question the judgment of the officials who worked his game at Pittsburgh Saturday, but he will question their INTEGRITY.

"I'm going to ask for an investigation of the whole thing," he said after viewing films of two downs on which Syracuse short yardage specialist Jim Sessler failed — according to head linesman Cliff Fair — to make inches for a first down at the Panther 10-yard line, with second-ranked Pitt nursing a 7-point lead. Pitt won, 23-13.

Maloney drew a 15-yard penalty after Syracuse was stopped with 3 minutes 23 seconds left to play for questioning the placement of the ball. "It was obvious in the films that his (Sessler's) shoulders were inside the 10-yard line," he said yesterday. "He made it even if he was carrying the ball between his legs."

There are extenuating circumstances to the controversy. The official who made the call on the placement of the ball is a member of the Tri-State officials, who mainly handle Pitt, Penn State and West Virginia games. He was one of four Tri-State officials in the crew Two others were assigned from the ECAC, of which Syracuse is a member.

Maloney left the field thinking he had been bilked. He vent his ire on two officials, neither of whom had anything to do with the marking of the ball. "I couldn't find Fair," he said.

"They are a great football team," he said of the Panthers. "Maybe, if we had scored, they would have come back to win. But we had a chance at one of the major college upsets of the year if not many years."

You could understand his thinking had his team been given the first down. Quarterback Bill Hurley was doing a surgical number (365 yards in offense) on Pitt's vaunted defense and there seemed no way they could have stopped him from getting 10 yards in four more downs.

"People say you're supposed to keep quiet," Maloney steamed. "I get attacked when I make bad calls, so why can't I attack them. I have no control over the officials who work the game. We coaches don't have as much power as you think. It's ridiculous. Everybody knows those Tri-State officials better not offend anybody if they want to keep working the games of those three schools.

"I'm not going to milquetoast this thing. Question not only the judg-

(See COLLEGES on 7-C)

November 1, 1976
Eagles first shutout since 1968, when they defeated the NY Giants 10-0.

1977

RECORD: 5-9, 4TH IN NFC EAST
HEAD COACH: DICK VERMEIL

Schedule
Regular Season

Wk. 1	Sep 18	W	13-3	vs Tampa Bay Buccaneers
Wk. 2	Sep 25	L	20-0	at Los Angeles Rams
Wk. 3	Oct 2	L	17-13	at Detroit Lions
Wk. 4	Oct 9	W	28-10	at New York Giants
Wk. 5	Oct 16	L	21-17	vs St. Louis Cardinals
Wk. 6	Oct 23	L	16-10	vs Dallas Cowboys
Wk. 7	Oct 30	L	23-17	at Washington Redskins
Wk. 8	Nov 6	W	28-7	vs New Orleans Saints
Wk. 9	Nov 13	L	17-14	vs Washington Redskins
Wk. 10	Nov 20	L	21-16	at St. Louis Cardinals
Wk. 11	Nov 27	L	14-6	at New England Patriots
Wk. 12	Dec 4	L	24-14	at Dallas Cowboys
Wk. 13	Dec 11	W	17-14	vs New York Giants
Wk. 14	Dec 18	W	27-0	vs New York Jets

QB Ron Jaworski was obtained from the Los Angeles Rams in exchange for the rights to tight end Charlie Young. Bill Bergey, keying the newly installed 3-4 defense of coordinator Marion Campbell, won All-Pro and All-Conference honors and was selected to play in his third Pro Bowl. , The Eagles would end the lackluster season on a strong note by taking their last two games in convincing fashion to finish with a 5-9 record. The Birds did show improvement on the field, but earned only one more victory than the previous season.

1977 Philadelphia Eagles Stats

Passing	Comp	Att	Comp %	Yds	Y/Att	TD	Int	Rating
Ron Jaworski	166	346	48.0	2183	6.31	18	21	60.4
Roman Gabriel	1	3	33.3	15	5.00	0	0	50.7

Rushing	Rush	Yds	Avg	TD
Mike Hogan	155	546	3.5	0
Keith Krepfle	27	530	19.6	3
Tom Sullivan	125	363	2.9	0
James Betterson	62	233	3.8	1
Herb Lusk	52	229	4.4	2
Wilbert Montgomery	45	183	4.1	2
Ron Jaworski	40	127	3.2	5
Frank LeMaster	1	30	30.0	0
Charlie Smith	2	13	6.5	0
Cleveland Franklin	1	0	0.0	0
Wally Henry	1	-2	-2.0	0

Receiving	Rec	Yds	Avg	TD
Harold Carmichael	46	665	14.5	7
Charlie Smith	33	464	14.1	4
Tom Sullivan	26	223	8.6	2
Mike Hogan	19	118	6.2	1
Herb Lusk	5	102	20.4	1
James Betterson	4	41	10.3	0
Wilbert Montgomery	3	18	6.0	0
Wally Henry	2	16	8.0	0
Vince Papale	1	15	15.0	0
Richard Osborne	1	6	6.0	0

Punting	Punts	Yds	Avg	Blocked
Spike Jones	93	3463	37.2	0

Kicking	PAT Made	PAT Att	PAT %	FG Made	FG Att	FG %	Pts
Horst Muhlmann	17	19	89	3	8	37.5	26
Nick Mike-Maye	7	7	100	3	3	100.0	16
Ove Johannson	1	3	33	1	4	25.0	4

Interceptions	Int	Yds	Avg	TD
Deac Sanders	6	122	20.3	0
Herman Edwards	6	9	1.5	0
Randy Logan	5	124	24.8	0
John Outlaw	2	41	20.5	0
Bill Bergey	2	4	2.0	0

1977

Sports/People 2
NFL roundup 4
Horse racing 6
Colleges 7
Schools 7

The Philadelphia Inquirer
sports

section
C

Monday, December 19, 1977

Another titanic battle, another big Flyers loss

By Gary Ronberg
Inquirer Staff Writer

After a buildup of 10 weeks, it was equal to what the most rabid Montreal or Flyers fan might have expected. One of grand emotion, of gut-wrenching skating, an absolute blur of red and white shirts up and down the frosty ice of the Spectrum. And when it was over, after a final, desperate chance by the Flyers had been destroyed by a referee's whistle with only 2 minutes 6 seconds to play, the Montreal Canadiens again had defeated the Flyers, this time by 2-0 last night.

Obviously it was not an explosive struggle, replete with heart-stopping opportunities and sprawling saves; but to observe the effort put forth by these rivals was worth double the admission price of the Spectrum's most expensive ticket. All one had to do was drop by the dressing cubicle of Joe Watson, that veteran defenseman who has been through so many games he has stopped counting, and the entire evening was put into perspective.

"Wasn't that," Watson sighed, "a titanic struggle? It seemed like one out there, but you watched it."

Yes, Joe, it was.

For the Flyers, riding the crest of an 11-game undefeated streak, leading the National Hockey League with 46 points, and already flirting with the same Stanley Cup spirit that had infused them several years ago, this was the night to put an end to the Canadiens' jinx once and for all. It was a night, THE NIGHT, to puncture that 0-11-1 Flyers' record against Montreal dating to Feb. 15, 1976.

For these Canadiens were not only hurting, they were sick. The finest player in the world today, Guy Lafleur, was back in Montreal with tonsillitis and the flu. So was an all-star defenseman, Guy LaPointe, with a bad knee and the flu. So were Yvan Cournoyer and Pierre LaRouche, both with knee injuries.

And coming into the Spectrum,
(See FLYERS on 3-C)

Philadelphia Inquirer / RICHARD M. TITLEY
Mel Bridgman attacks, but only to find the Canadiens' Dan Dryden waiting — again

By FRANK DOLSON

Sports Editor

Nothing game? Not for Eagles

There was so much water on the artificial turf yesterday they should have renamed the place Veterans Lake.

There were so many empty seats in the upper deck you'd have thought Temple was playing.

It was raining so hard you kept expecting to see the Phillies take the field for a playoff game against the Dodgers.

The weather was so downright miserable Club Feeney should have been forced to spend the entire two and a half hours sitting in an uncovered box seat without an umbrella.

"The halftime show," quipped a member of the Eagles' official family, "is being produced by Aquarama. For the highlight, Johnny Weissmuller is going to dive off the 30-second clock."

Yes, friends, it was THAT bad yesterday at the Vet, where the Eagles and the Jets played one of those nothing games that dot the NFL schedule this time of the year. It was a day when you might expect a 3-10 team and a 4-9 team to go through the motions ... but only the 3-10 team did.

They played for keeps

The Eagles played this nothing game with the Jets as if it really mattered to them that they finish Dick Vermeil's second season 5-9 instead of 4-10. Neither the weather nor the strange-looking collection of starters the Jets threw out into the rain nor those 43,000-plus empty seats could kill their lust for battle.

If you didn't know better you'd have sworn a playoff berth was on the line in those closing minutes. Why else would Vince Papale come leaping off the bench in ecstasy as Bill Bergey intercepted a soggy, misdirected Richard Toss pass? Why else would Bergey display all that emotion as the clock ran down on yet another losing season, balling his battered hands into fists and thrusting them high over his head as the faithful chanted his name?

The Eagles, with all their losing tradition, have won meaningless, season-ending games before; in fact, they've now closed out four straight seasons with victories. But the way they acted yesterday you'd have thought they were challenging the Cowboys for first place, not the Giants for last. Grown men don't embrace at the end of nothing games, so obviously to the Eagles — to Bergey and Keith Krepfle and Randy Logan and all the others wrapped in last-minute bear hugs — this game, this 27-0 victory, meant something.

Praise from Vermeil

"I get a kick out of playoff teams saying they can't get up for nothing games," Vermeil said. "I wonder how some of those teams would play in the Eagles' situation, when half of the season is nothing games."

Would they go through the motions on a day like this? Or would they play the way this team played, would they care the way Bill Bergey and John Bunting cared?

"With about four minutes to go John Bunting threw a little fit out there," Bergey said. "He wanted that shutout."

The members of the defensive unit had been talking shutout all week — big talk when you consider that Eagles teams had won only two shutouts in two decades, and hadn't blanked anybody before the home fans since 1955, when home was Connie Mack Stadium.

"We kept saying and yelling and screaming for a shutout all week in practice," Bergey said. And so, with 4 minutes left and the Jets on their first drive of the day, Bunting ex-
(See DOLSON on 5-C)

Eagles swamp Jets, 27-0

Philadelphia Inquirer / EDWARD J. FREEMAN
The Eagles' Wilbert Montgomery (31), with Mike Hogan (35) and Wade Key (72) leading the way, makes a third-quarter gain

End year with five victories

By Gordon Forbes
Inquirer Staff Writer

It was the kind of miserable weather in which the winners invariably pull away to an early lead, grind out the yards with a running attack and try to destroy the senses of the other team's quarterback.

In gusting winds and swirling rain yesterday at the Vet, the Eagles did all three to humiliate the New York Jets, 27-0 and set quarterback Richard Todd's education back at least another season. It was all over after the first 12 minutes for the Jets, who fell behind, 17-0, and then fell victim to a solid if not spectacular Eagle ground game and a wild pass rush off Merion Campbell's 3-4 defense.

"I think under those conditions, we had it put away when it was 17-0," said Eagle quarterback Ron Jaworski. "It's really difficult to throw the ball when you get behind as they did. We kept the pressure on Todd and that ball, it must have weighed four pounds."

The lopsided win enabled the Eagles to finish 5-9, an improvement over last year's 4-10 record that was much more significant than the statistics if you believe Coach Dick Vermeil. The Jets, who lost nine of their last 10 games, fell to 3-11, but managed to escape the AFC East cellar by a single point in head-to-head competition with the lowly Buffalo Bills.

"There isn't any comparison between the two squads," Vermeil said. "This squad is totally committed to working together and getting better. Nobody is grumbling to go anywhere else and nobody is mad at this coach and that coach. We have the foundation. It'll just take time."

It was an afternoon in which the Eagles kept approaching and passing old records and the Jets put on display their team of the '80s by starting eight backup players. The Eagle pass rush, led by third-down specialist Lem Burnham, got to Todd seven times, bringing the season sack total to 47 to match a club record. Split end Harold Carmichael routinely caught two passes, the first extending his consecutive-game streak to 50 games, tieing another club mark, and the second giving him 300 catches in his accelerating seven-year career.

Only 19,241 Eagle fanatics turned out (prompting record 43,013 no-
(See EAGLES on 5-C)

The playoffs: Who's in, who's not

Associated Press

In a dramatic final day of the regular-season that included one critical game that went into overtime and another in which the winner came back from an 18-point deficit, the National Football League yesterday filled its lineup for next weekend's playoffs.

With the dust — and snow — now cleared, the first round of the playoffs shapes up like this:

In the NFC, the Eastern Division champion Dallas Cowboys (12-2) will face the wild-card entry Chicago Bears (9-5) at Dallas and the Western Division champion Los Angeles Rams (10-4) will play the Central Division champion Minnesota Vikings (9-5) at Los Angeles, both next Monday.

In the AFC, the Eastern Division champion Baltimore Colts (10-4) will meet the wild-card Oakland Raiders (11-3) at Baltimore and the Western Division champion Denver Broncos (12-2) will play the Central Division champion Pittsburgh Steelers (9-5) at Denver, both on Saturday.

The Bears, Colts, and Steelers wrapped up the last four playoff berths yesterday, with the Bears and Colts doing it in particularly dramatic fashion.

Chicago, which had to defeat the New York Giants to wrest the NFC wild-card spot from the Washington Redskins, succeeded by a 12-9 margin in overtime on a snow-covered field at East Rutherford, N.J., winning on Bob Thomas' 28-yard field goal with 9 seconds left in the sudden-death overtime.

The Colts got their playoff spot — and bumped out the Miami Dolphins — by coming back to a 30-24 victory over the New England Patriots after New England had taken a 21-3 lead early in the third quarter. Quarterback Bert Jones threw three touchdown passes in the Baltimore rally.

Pittsburgh, which needed a Cincinnati Bengals defeat to have a shot at the AFC Central title, got that when the Houston Oilers upset the Bengals, 21-16, and then took advantage of the break by edging the San Diego Chargers, 10-9, to clinch its berth.

More joy in Tampa Bay

By Skip Myslenski
Inquirer Staff Writer

TAMPA, Fla. — When, eight days ago, it was about to happen for the very first time, Lee Roy Selmon looked long and lovingly at the scoreboard in the New Orleans Superdome. The clock was stopped for the 2-minute warning, and the numbers showed that his team, the Tampa Bay Buccaneers, was leading the Saints, 33-14, and at last he was certain. "They shouldn't be able to score that many points," he thought. Then he smiled softly and a single word popped into his mind: "Wow!"

At the same time linebacker Richard Wood looked at the people suddenly surrounding the Buc bench and said to no one in particular, "I can't wait to get into the dressing room so I can cry. A grown man ought not to cry out here in front of these people."

"It was a totally different feeling," Lee Roy Selmon recalled. "It was great. It's one of the best I've ever had. It's hard to describe. To see a little success after so long, well" — and here his voice trailed off before he continued — "right
(See BUCS on 8-C)

Associated Press
Walter Payton managed only 47 yards

Bears make it; Payton doesn't

"Oh, my life is worth more than 6 seconds. It couldn't pass in front of me in 6 seconds. But, if I'd missed, I saw an exit sign over to the left. I figure the Giants would've been happy, they'd have let me run through 'em, and I could've got away.

"I'd probably have forwarded my mail to Asia."

—Chicago placekicker Bob Thomas

By Bill Livingston
Inquirer Staff Writer

EAST RUTHERFORD, N.J. — Actually, it all happened with 9 seconds left in overtime, but let us not accuse Bob Thomas of being overly dramatic.

The 28-yard field goal he nailed through flying sleet and snow, after skittering up to the football over treacherous patches of ice with 9 seconds to play, gave the Chicago Bears a 12-9 victory over the New York Giants and their *first* NFL playoff berth in 14 years.

So, although Bear running back Walter Payton was able to slalom his way to only 47 yards in 15 carries, a full 151 short of O.J. Simpson's surreal one-season record, the game need no hype.

It needed little more than the actual, numbing sequences of opportunity and futility that sent the Bears pratfalling around the field for 74 minutes and 51 seconds in their frantic pursuit of the National Conference wild-card playoff spot.

It needed little more than Thomas' final frantic kick, which redeemed the third-year kicker from Notre Dame for two earlier missed field goals of 23 and 35 yards (the second
(See BEARS on 4-C)

December 19, 1977
Wilbert Montgomery makes his first NFL start and the Eagles achieve their only shutout for the season by defeating the NY Jets 27-0

1978

RECORD: 9-7, 2ND IN NFC EAST
HEAD COACH: DICK VERMEIL

Schedule

Regular Season

Wk. 1	Sep 3	L	16-14	vs Los Angeles Rams
Wk. 2	Sep 10	L	35-30	at Washington Redskins
Wk. 3	Sep 17	W	24-17	at New Orleans Saints
Wk. 4	Sep 24	W	17-3	vs Miami Dolphins
Wk. 5	Oct 1	W	17-14	at Baltimore Colts
Wk. 6	Oct 8	L	24-14	at New England Patriots
Wk. 7	Oct 15	W	17-10	vs Washington Redskins
Wk. 8	Oct 22	L	14-7	at Dallas Cowboys
Wk. 9	Oct 29	L	16-10	vs St. Louis Cardinals
Wk. 10	Nov 5	W	10-3	vs Green Bay Packers
Wk. 11	Nov 12	W	17-9	vs New York Jets
Wk. 12	Nov 19	W	19-17	at New York Giants
Wk. 13	Nov 26	W	14-10	at St. Louis Cardinals
Wk. 14	Dec 3	L	28-27	at Minnesota Vikings
Wk. 15	Dec 10	L	31-13	vs Dallas Cowboys
Wk. 16	Dec 17	W	20-3	vs New York Giants

Post Season

Wild Card Playoffs

	Dec 24	L	14-13	at Atlanta Falcons

The Eagles continued to show improved as they post a 9-7 record, their first winning season since 1966, and making the playoffs for the first time since 1960. Wilbert Montgomery, in his first starting season, rushes for 1,220 yards to become the first Eagle since Steve Van Buren to surpass 1,000 in a season. In a game against the Giants dubbed the "Miracle of the Meadowlands," the Giants were trying to run out the clock and with the Eagles were seemingly headed towards defeat. Somehow Eagle Herman Edwards started the "Miracle" when he scooped up a fumbled handoff from Joe Pisarcik to Larry Csonka and races 26 years for a TD in the final 20 seconds of play before a stunned Giants Stadium. The win propels the Eagles into the playoffs for the first time since 1960. In the NFC Wild Card playoff game in Atlanta, the Eagles lost on what was to be 34-yard game winning field goal when Eagles Kicker Mike Michel missed the attempt with only 1:34 left to play.

1978 Philadelphia Eagles Stats

Passing	Comp	Att	Comp %	Yds	Y/Att	TD	Int	Rating
Ron Jaworski	206	398	51.8	2487	6.25	16	16	67.9
Rick Engles	1	1	100.0	-2	-2.00	0	0	79.2
John Walton	0	1	0.0	0	0.00	0	0	39.6
John Sciarra	0	1	0.0	0	0.00	0	0	39.6

Rushing	Rush	Yds	Avg	TD
Wilbert Montgomery	259	1220	4.7	9
Mike Hogan	145	607	4.2	4
Billy Campfield	61	247	4.0	0
Cleveland Franklin	60	167	2.8	0
Ron Jaworski	30	79	2.6	0
James Betterson	11	32	2.9	0
Frank LeMaster	2	29	14.5	0
Harold Carmichael	1	21	21.0	0
Ken Payne	1	17	17.0	0
Rick Engles	1	16	16.0	0
John Sciarra	8	11	1.4	2
Louie Giammona	4	6	1.5	0
Larry Barnes	1	4	4.0	1
John Walton	2	0	0.0	0
Mike Michel	1	0	0.0	0

Receiving	Rec	Yds	Avg	TD
Harold Carmichael	55	1072	19.5	8
Wilbert Montgomery	34	195	5.7	1
Mike Hogan	31	164	5.3	1
Keith Krepfle	26	374	14.4	3
Billy Campfield	15	101	6.7	0
Ken Payne	13	238	18.3	1
Richard Osborne	13	145	11.2	0
Charlie Smith	11	142	12.9	2
Cleveland Franklin	7	46	6.6	0
James Betterson	2	8	4.0	0

Punting	Punts	Yds	Avg	Blocked
Rick Engles	33	1307	39.6	0
Mike Michel	58	2078	35.8	0

Interceptions	Int	Yds	Avg	TD
Herman Edwards	7	59	8.4	0
Deac Sanders	5	43	8.6	1
Bill Bergey	4	70	17.5	0
Frank LeMaster	3	22	7.3	1
Bob Howard	3	15	5.0	0
Randy Logan	2	15	7.5	0
John Sciarra	1	21	21.0	0
Dennis Harrison	1	12	12.0	0
John Bunting	1	9	9.0	0
Drew Mahalic	1	5	5.0	0

Kicking	PAT Made	PAT Att	PAT %	FG Made	FG Att	FG %	Pts
Nick Mike-Mayer	21	22	95	8	17	47.1	45
Mike Michel	9	12	75	0	0	0.0	9

The Philadelphia Inquirer
Sports Extra

section **D**

◆ Monday, Dec. 25, 1978

Eagles fail to follow through and the Falcons win by 14-13

Amidst the jubilation of Atlanta players and fans sits dejected Eagles kicker Mike Michel as teammate John Sciarra (21) walks off after a missed field goal

Philadelphia Inquirer / AKIRA SUWA

Missed FG ends season

By Gordon Forbes
Inquirer Staff Writer

ATLANTA — The Eagles lost their first NFL playoff in 18 years yesterday — in a cold drizzle, to the amazing Atlanta Falcons, and by a 14-13 score. They will be forced to remember it as a game they tried to win without a field-goal kicker.

With 13 seconds left and the crowd at Atlanta-Fulton County Stadium in an uproar after the Falcons had scored twice in 3 minutes 17 seconds to take a 14-13 lead, Mike Michel lined up to try a 34-yard, game-winning field goal. He missed.

But don't blame Michel. He is the Eagle punter who was pressed into double-duty as a placekicker six weeks ago when Nick Mike-Mayer broke two ribs.

"Mike is a punter who was sort of transposed to kicker," said linebacker Frank LeMaster in the silent Eagle dressing room. "He did all he could. I think he did an adequate job. I'd be more upset if it was his job and it came down to that. I know Mike feels terrible. It came down to (the point where) he could have been the villain or the hero and he missed being the hero by three or four inches."

Michel also missed a conversion after the first Eagle touchdown. So when the Falcons, who have won four games in the final 18 seconds and six in the final two minutes, exploded for two touchdowns in the last five minutes yesterday, they had the winning margin.

There were some glaring breakdowns in the coverage by the Eagle secondary which allowed Falcon quarterback Steve Bartkowski to hurl a 20-yard scoring pass to tight end Jim Mitchell with 4:56 left and a 37-yarder to split end Wallace Francis with 1:39 to play. Rookie Tim Mazzetti, the former Penn kicker

(See EAGLES on 5-D)

Michel took his darkest moment like a man

ATLANTA — Sports can be so cruel. So damnably, relentlessly cruel. So often the big game — the entire season — comes down to a matter of seconds, or a matter of inches. After more than 160 baseball games, after 17 football games, one player becomes all or nothing, one man becomes hero or goat.

Two months ago, Garry Maddox, who can practically catch fly balls in his sleep, failed to catch one in Dodger Stadium and wound up facing the toughest inquisition of his life. To his credit, he handled it like the man he is.

Yesterday it was Mike Michel's

By FRANK DOLSON

Sports editor

turn ... and he, too, handled it like a man.

With the final seconds ticking off on the Atlanta Stadium clock, Michel went through with the giddiest high and the most shattering low of his career. Bang-bang, just like that.

One moment he was leaving his

feet, his arm raised, his hopes soaring to the cloudy skies. This punter-turned-emergency-place-kicker had never kicked a field goal in a regular season or postseason National Football League game, but for a giddy instant he thought, his teammates thought, we all thought that he had kicked the Atlanta Falcons into oblivion and the Eagles into the next round of the playoffs.

"I hit it good," the slender, dark-haired, bearded young man would say later.

The ball seemed headed for three-point territory just inside the right post. For a right-footed kicker, that should have meant success. Usually,

Michel's kicks hook to the left. But his first point-after-touchdown try didn't. And neither did this field-goal attempt. Instead of a hook, Michel got the tiniest slice. Not much. Just enough to send those fans who hadn't quit on the Falcons when they were down, 13-0, into a wild celebration.

Just enough to turn what had started out as a jump for joy by Mike Michel into a backward somersault of despair. The football sailed to the right of the upright ... and in that moment Mike Michel's ecstasy turned into agony.

"I thought it would come back," he said, "They usually do. They usually

have a slight hook on them. This one didn't come back at all."

And so this finest Eagle season in more than a decade was suddenly, shatteringly over. Thousands of Atlanta fans poured onto the field, delaying the final 13 seconds of the game for fully five minutes. While the fans cavorted, Michel remained on the wet ground for what seemed like a very long time, then got up slowly edged through the mob.

God, how a moment like this can tear a man apart. He had come so close to being the storybook hero, so close to making his first official NFL field goal one of the most memorable in the history of the franchise. If

only that kick had hooked when it was supposed to hook; if only Mike Michel had followed all the way through with that right leg.

"I just didn't come back enough. I didn't swing through it well enough."

A crowd gathered in front of his locker, as luck would have it, Michel's stall was the one nearest the main entrance to the visiting locker room. Then another crowd. And another. Michel made no effort to hide, or to run or to plead for privacy. Handling those waves of questioners at a time like this had to be as difficult as ... well, as kicking a 34-

(See DOLSON on 4-D)

'Dual' catch saves Falcons, leaves bitter taste for Birds

By Allen Lewis
Inquirer Staff Writer

ATLANTA — To Atlanta Falcons quarterback Steve Bartkowski, it was the key play of the game. To Falcons flanker Wallace Francis, it was the play that set up Atlanta's first touchdown. To Eagles defensive back John Sanders, it was an official's decision that will live in infamy.

THE play occurred when the Eagles seemingly had the National Football League playoff game sewed up. They were riding the crest of a 13-0 lead and stopping the Falcons' offense with consistency.

There was less than 8 minutes left, and it was second down and 10 yards to go for the Falcons with the ball on their 26 when Bartkowski faded back and fired a bomb down the middle.

Free safety Sanders leaped at the Eagles' 26-yard line and was joined by Wallace a split second after the Philadelphia player seemingly had the ball. They went down in a heap. An official ran over and signaled Atlanta first down — a 49-yard gain.

Sanders couldn't believe it. "He never had the ball," Sanders said emphatically after Atlanta's thrill-

ing 14-13 victory. "I caught the ball before he ever got to me. I rolled over with the ball and I had it until I saw the official signal first down. Then is the first time I gave it up. And besides, he pushed me before the ball got there.

"He said he caught it?" Sanders asked incredulously. "He knew he didn't."

As for the official, Sanders said, "He must have been intimidated by the crowd."

Francis, of course, had a different view of the controversial play.

"He may have caught it first, I don't know," the six-year veteran said. "But I know I came down with it. I'd have to look at the films to see who caught it first. I know I didn't push him."

As controversial as that catch was, there was no problem involved with either Atlanta scoring pass. Four plays after the dual-possession pass, Atlanta got on the scoreboard as Bartkowski threw a 20-yard strike to tight end Jim Mitchell, who caught the ball a step from the goal line and went in untouched.

When the Falcons gained possession again, they drove 49 yards in six

plays, and the scoring toss was a 37-yarder to a wide-open Francis, who made a fall-down grab and landed on his back just over the goal line.

"We used three wide receivers on that play," Francis said. "I took the place of the tight end in the slot. I ran a post pattern. If it was zone, I was supposed to hook up in the middle. If it was man, I was supposed to keep going, and that's what I did. Steve (Bartkowski) read the coverage real well and I was open.

"I didn't know how open I was and I didn't know I was at the goal. I just concentrated on catching the ball. It was the same play as the other one (dual catch play).

"My greatest day? I don't know. My greatest day hasn't happened yet. It was my best since I caught seven against the Giants."

"On the touchdown, I caught him playing me square, and I gave him a step to the inside and he went for it.

"I had told Steve I was open on the pattern a few plays before the touchdown."

He was so open, Eagles Coach Dick Vermeil said, "Someone was responsible, that's definite."

Celebrating his TD reception is Atlanta's Wallace Francis

United Press International

Pastorini leads Oilers over Miami

By Dan Sewell
Associated Press

MIAMI — Dan Pastorini, wearing a specially designed flak jacket able to withstand the pounding of onrushing defensive linemen, had his best passing game in three seasons, leading the Houston Oilers to a 17-9 victory over the Miami Dolphins in an NFL wild-card playoff game yesterday.

Pastorini completed 20 of 29 passes for 306 yards, including a 13-yard touchdown pass to Tim Wilson, despite knee and rib injuries.

The Oilers quarterback took a pain-killing shot and wore a brace to ward off the effects of a wrenched knee, and wore the flak jacket given to him by a man in Houston.

The jacket's effectiveness was demonstrated to him by the man, who wore the jacket while a friend pounded him — without effect — with a baseball bat.

"I said, 'I want one of those,'" Pastorini recalled.

"The flak jacket spreads the shock

(See OILERS on 6-D)

December 25, 1978
Eagles lose their first NFL playoff game in 18 years to the Atlanta Falcons 14-13, when Mike Michel with 13 seconds left in the game missed a 34-yard game winning field goal.

1979

RECORD: 11-5, 2ND IN NFC EAST
HEAD COACH: DICK VERMEIL

Schedule

Regular Season

Wk. 1	Sep 2	W	23-17	vs New York Giants
Wk. 2	Sep 10	L	14-10	vs Atlanta Falcons
Wk. 3	Sep 16	W	26-14	at New Orleans Saints
Wk. 4	Sep 23	W	17-13	at New York Giants
Wk. 5	Sep 30	W	17-14	vs Pittsburgh Steelers
Wk. 6	Oct 7	W	28-17	vs Washington Redskins
Wk. 7	Oct 14	W	24-20	at St. Louis Cardinals
Wk. 8	Oct 21	L	17-7	at Washington Redskins
Wk. 9	Oct 28	L	37-13	at Cincinnati Bengals
Wk. 10	Nov 4	L	24-19	vs Cleveland Browns
Wk. 11	Nov 12	W	31-21	at Dallas Cowboys
Wk. 12	Nov 18	W	16-13	vs St. Louis Cardinals
Wk. 13	Nov 25	W	21-10	at Green Bay Packers
Wk. 14	Dec 2	W	44-7	vs Detroit Lions
Wk. 15	Dec 8	L	24-17	vs Dallas Cowboys
Wk. 16	Dec 16	W	26-20	at Houston Oilers

Post Season

Wild Card Playoffs				
	Dec 23	W	27-17	vs Chicago Bears
Divisional Playoffs				
	Dec 29	L	24-17	at Tampa Bay Buccaneers

The Eagles came soaring out of the gate, winning six of their first seven games. Then a midseason three-game slide threatened their season. The Eagles would end their slide with a 31-21 win over the Cowboys in Dallas that got them right in thick of the race for first place. Unfortunately the Eagles could never shake off the Cowboys, and with a record of 10-4 entered a showdown in the Vet with the NFC East on the line. The Eagles would fall 24-17 as the Cowboys held on to win the division via tiebreaker, as the Eagles settled for a Wild Card with an 11-5 record. In the playoffs the Eagles beat the Chicago Bears 27-17 in the first playoff game in Philadelphia in 19 years. However, a week later their season ended with a disappointing 24-17 loss to the Buccaneers in Tampa. Wilbert Montgomery set a club record with 1,512 rushing yards, and Harold Carmichael set an NFL record on November 4, 1979, by catching a pass in his 106th consecutive game. Rookie barefoot kicker Tony Franklin booted the second longest field goal in NFL history---59 yards---in a 31-21 win at Dallas. Dick Vermeil was voted NFL Coach of the Year.

1979 Philadelphia Eagles Stats

Passing	Comp	Att	Comp %	Yds	Y/Att	TD	Int	Rating
Ron Jaworski	190	374	50.8	2669	7.14	18	12	76.8
John Walton	19	36	52.8	213	5.92	3	1	86.9

Rushing	Rush	Yds	Avg	TD
Wilbert Montgomery	338	1512	4.5	9
Leroy Harris	107	504	4.7	2
Billy Campfield	30	165	5.5	3
Ron Jaworski	43	119	2.8	2
Larry Barnes	25	74	3.0	1
Louie Giammona	5	38	2.5	0
Frank LeMaster	1	15	15.0	0
Harold Carmichael	1	0	0.0	0
Earl Carr	1	-1	-1.0	0
John Walton	6	-5	-0.8	0

Receiving	Rec	Yds	Avg	TD
Harold Carmichael	52	872	16.8	11
Keith Krepfle	41	760	18.5	3
Wilbert Montgomery	41	494	12.0	5
Charlie Smith	24	399	16.6	1
Leroy Harris	22	107	4.9	0
Billy Campfield	16	115	7.2	0
Scott Fitzkee	8	105	13.1	1
John Spagnola	2	24	12.0	0
Larry Barnes	1	6	6.0	0
Earl Carr	1	2	2.0	0
Jerrold McRae	1	-2	-2.0	0

Punting	Punts	Yds	Avg	Blocked
Max Runager	74	2927	39.6	0
Tony Franklin	1	32	32.0	0

Interceptions	Int	Yds	Avg	TD
Brenard Wilson	4	70	17.5	0
Randy Logan	3	57	19.0	0
Bob Howard	3	34	11.3	0
Herman Edwards	3	6	2.0	0
John Sciarra	2	47	23.5	0
Al Chesley	2	39	19.5	0
John Bunting	2	13	6.5	0
Reggie Wilkes	2	0	0.0	0
Bill Bergey	1	0	0.0	0

Kicking	PAT Made	PAT Att	PAT %	FG Made	FG Att	FG %	Pts
Tony Franklin	36	39	92	23	31	74.2	105

The NBA 2
Scoreboard 4
Colleges 9
Horse racing 10
High schools 12

The Philadelphia Inquirer

sports

section D

Sunday, December 30, 1979

Bucs end Eagles' season, 24-17

Philadelphia Inquirer / VICKI VALERIO

Ricky Bell, whom the Eagles had a difficult time figuring out yesterday, appears to be casting a spell on linebacker Reggie Wilkes

Bell, Williams engineer upset

By Gordon Forbes
Inquirer Staff Writer

TAMPA, Fla. — Doug Williams and the young, ambitious Tampa Bay Buccaneers came out running yesterday, and the Eagles came out retreating, all the way out of the National Football Conference playoffs.

The Bucs lined up in a double-tight-end formation, pulled both guards, led into the power alley with their fullback and pitched the ball back to magnificent Ricky Bell. They ran all the way to a 24-17 victory over the helpless Eagles before 71,402, mostly fanatical Bucs' lovers.

The Eagles were overpowered in the trenches, especially the left side of their wilting defense — end Claude Humphrey, outside linebacker John Bunting and cornerback Bobby Howard. Bell, who set an NFL playoff record with 38 carries and rushed for 142 yards, kept beating the Eagles defenders to the corner, at least those who were still standing.

"If you're asking me where to put the blame," Humphrey said afterward in the subdued losers' dressing room, "I don't know where to put it. I do know this. They've got a better football team. That's where to put some of the blame."

As lopsided as the game statistics were in favor of the tough-hitting Bucs, 318 total yards to 227, 186 rushing yards to 48, 70 offensive plays to 58, the Eagles miraculously still had a chance to pull it out in the final, dramatic 2 minutes.

For maybe the first time in the game, Humphrey got penetration and slammed Bell down for a seven-yard loss on third-and-one, forcing the Bucs to punt. With 2 minutes, 11 seconds left, quarterback Ron Jaworski led his battered offense back onto the field for one last shot.

"I was confident," said Jaworski, who hooked up with Harold Carmichael on a late 37-yard touchdown pass that brought the Eagles within 24-17 with 3:36 left. "But I was also realistic, too. I realized you're limited in what you can do. You get down to no timeouts and you can't be going for five or six yards. And it's a risky thing when you throw downfield."

While cornerback Jeris White was dropping two game-ending interceptions, Jaworski kept firing. The Polish Rifle completed a low, 16-yarder to Carmichael, an 18-yard crossover on fourth down (which was nullified by a penalty) and a 25-yarder to Charlie Smith at the Bucs 45 with a little more than a minute left.

It was the kind of drive of which miracles are made. But it ended 17 tense seconds later after three incompletions and a dropped third-down pass by Billy Campfield.

On fourth-and-10 from the 45, Jaworski backpedaled, searched for Carmichael along the right sideline and threw. The ball flew out of bounds as Carmichael broke inside.

"It was good coverage," said Jaworski, who was pressured into a dreadful 15-for-38 afternoon in bright, balmy Florida weather. "I just tried to lead him away from the defense. They had him covered, and by the time he came off the ball, I had already let it go."

The Eagles already had let go of their chance for another eagerly awaited rematch with Dallas, assuming that the Cowboys get past the Los Angeles Rams in today's other NFC divisional playoff. The Eagles' greatest contribution to the Bucs' highly emotional upset was an inability to handle Tampa Bay's running game.

"They were like cutting it back," said Howard, who may have played his final game as an Eagle. "They started out and they executed real well. Their execution really helped them. They had us (the Eagles defense) down real well. They played super today. You could tell from the start. It was like they were caged and they were letting them out."

Incredibly, the no-offense Bucs (11-

(See EAGLES on 6-D)

Eagles' title hopes were drowned in a sea of orange

By FRANK DOLSON

Sports editor

TAMPA, Fla. — The stadium was a sea of orange, and from the very start of yesterday's playoff game the Philadelphia Eagles were battling desperately to stay afloat. At the end, the wonder of it wasn't that the Tampa Bay Bucs, a 4-year-old professional football team, won the game, 24-17, but that the Eagles were that close.

Seldom has an underdog football team so thoroughly dominated a game of this importance ... and yet each time the visitors were on the verge of sinking out of sight, somebody threw them a life raft and the Eagles clutched it, prolonging the agony. Had they somehow pulled out yesterday's game — and Stan Walters, among others, thought "we were going to get overtime; I really did" — it would have been a terrible miscarriage of justice. Even the most partisan of Eagles fans would have been forced to admit that.

In retrospect, it might be fair to say the Eagles really lost this game — and with it the chance to go to the NFC championship game — three weeks ago at Veterans Stadium, when the Dallas Cowboys beat them out of the Eastern Division championship and the home-field playoff advantage that went with it. Had that sea of orange been an ocean of green, perhaps the Eagles would have been inspired to play the kind of game that the Bucs played yesterday.

"I realize now," Walters said after the Eagles had finally gone down for the last time, "the importance of playing at home. If I had to make one objective statement, it would be that if we ever get another shot to win a game for the division (title), we've got to take full advantage of it and get the home field and the week's rest and everything else that goes with it."

Don't underestimate the importance of that home field, the impact of a roaring crowd. Above all, don't underestimate the importance of getting a week off before plunging into the playoffs.

"Their execution showed two weeks of practice," Dick Vermeil said. "We've been practicing since Wednesday."

It was not an excuse, merely a simple statement of the facts. But not even those facts should have added up to so great a superiority on the playing field as the Bucs displayed. "It's just impossible to gain a mental edge in a playoff game," Vermeil had said, "because there's no such thing as a team not being ready to play." Maybe not, but the Bucs were more ready to play than the Eagles. That much was clear.

The team that wasn't supposed to have much of an offense, the team that had scored a not-so-grand total of 10 points in its last three games, merely took the opening kickoff and rammed the ball down the Eagles' throats. For 18 plays the Bucs controlled the football. For close to 9½ minutes they ran Ricky Bell again and again and again. Sweep right. Sweep right. A draw, then another sweep, this time to the left.

And it was "draft choices right" and "draft choices left." The Eagles, no great shakes against the run all year as Vermeil was quick to point out, simply were incapable on this day of stopping Tampa Bay's basic plays.

"The Eagles are not good enough to win unless we play super," Vermeil

(See DOLSON on 6-D)

Flyers edge the rallying Rockies, 3-2

By Al Morganti
Inquirer Staff Writer

DENVER — Just another night on the road with the usual stuff: a record-breaking crowd jacked up beyond belief; an opposing team jacked up even higher, and the usual uneven officiating.

Despite it all, just as they seemingly have done for an eternity, the Flyers rumbled out of McNichols Arena with a gasping, 3-2 win over the Colorado Rockies, thus extending their unbeaten streak to 33 games and raising their lead over Buffalo, which lost to Montreal, to seven points with two games in hand.

The Flyers looked as if they finally were going to win one with a little room to spare when they went into the final period leading, 3-0, but two frantic Colorado goals within less than two minutes of the final period — one very controversial — made the Flyers sweat their usual bullets through the closing seconds.

With 9 minutes, 22 seconds remaining, Rene Robert scored the first Rockies goal, ending Phil Myre's shutout bid and throwing the record-crowd of 16,452 into ecstacy.

Like the night before in Winnipeg, where a record-breaking crowd went out to see the Flyers, the Colorado crowd was primed to see the Flyers' streak come to a halt.

"This whole team, this whole place was ready for us," Bob Dailey said. "We knew this was going to be a tough place to play when we got here."

It got very tough in that last period when, with 7:57 left, Mike McEwen scored a disputed goal that ignited a final Colorado charge.

The goal began as a simple icing call when linesman Bob Luther put

(See FLYERS on 3-D)

Philadelphia Inquirer / VICKI VALERIO

Jimmy Giles rejoices after scoring the touchdown that put Tampa Bay ahead, 24-10, on a nine-yard pass from Doug Williams

Up from the dump: How sweet it is for Bucs

By BILL LYON

TAMPA, Fla. — You say you don't believe in miracles?

Try this one: In its four-year history, a football team tha has played 61 games and managed to lose 43 of them is one step from the Super Bowl.

"Yeah, it kinda blows your mind, doesn't it?" said Steve Wilson, standing there with a grin cutting a wide swath through his bush of a beard.

Wilson is an original Buccaneer, which, until now, was a dubious distinction at best. Kind of like being the driver of the getaway car for The Gang That Couldn't Shoot Straight. Or the navigator aboard the Titanic.

Wilson is the center for Tampa Bay, the only one they've ever had, so he stood there amid the locker room frenzy yesterday and sucked in deep gulps of air, almost as if he were trying to cleanse the purgatory of the last four seasons.

One of the attendants came by to take his helmet so the dents could be hammered out, and on the back of the attendant's shirt was the Tampa Bay slogan:

"Five Year Plan — From Worst To First."

The Bucs certainly fulfilled the first part of that plan. For a long time they were the worst team in pro football. Second worst was far behind.

"What was it like?" Wilson repeated the question. "Well, it was depressing. Like living in a garbage dump, I uess. You know how a bad smell won't go away no matter what you do? That's what it was like. We'd work and work and work, but nothing good would ever seem to happen.

"Then you'd start doubting yourself, wondering if you were good enough to play up here. That's a terrible thing, doubting yourself. It's slow death."

Well, the Bucs moved out of the low-rent district yesterday. They vacated the garbage dump and moved uptown to a fancy address. And now, despite a record of 18 wins and 43 defeats, the Bucs are close to taking up residence in the penthouse of the NFL.

They achieved that by blowing out

(See LYON on 7-D)

Oilers stifle Chargers in 17-14 upset

Associated Press

SAN DIEGO — Safety Vernon Perry, leading an aroused Houston defense that took up the slack for missing offensive stars, intercepted four passes by Dan Fouts and blocked a field-goal attempt, and the Oilers, riding Gifford Nielsen's clutch touchdown pass to Mike Renfro, beat San Diego, 17-14, yesterday in the American Football Conference playoffs.

Nielsen, making only his second career start in the NFL, teamed with Renfro on a 47-yard scoring play with 2 minutes, 5 seconds left to play in the third quarter for the touchdown that vaulted Houston into the AFC championship game Jan. 6, against the winner of today's contest between Miami and the defending Super Bowl champion Pittsburgh Steelers.

"Ain't no such thing as a one- or two-man team," said Perry, whose play helped compensate for the absence of NFL rushing champion Earl Campbell and quarterback Dan Pastorini.

"We knew when we signed him as a free agent out of Canada that the kid was a player," Houston coach Bum Phillips said of Perry, who came out of Jackson State, failed to make it as a Chicago Bears draft choice and wound up with the Canadian Football League's Montreal Alouettes.

"If the Canadian League never does anything else for the NFL," Phillips said, "they did something for us."

In fact, the last big game Perry had was in the Canadian Grey Cup. In that game he had two interceptions and a blocked punt.

"He was a college teammate of (Houston linebacker) Robert Bra-

(See OILERS on 5-D)

1979

December 30, 1979
Tampa Bay rolls over the Eagles 24-17
in the NFC Divisional Playoff game.

80's Decade in Review

Decade Win-Loss Record:
76-74-2; (2-4 postseason record)

Home Field:
Veterans Stadium 1980-89

Playoff Appearances:
1980, 1981, 1988, and 1989

Championships:
Division Champions 1980 (NFC East)
NFL/NFC Champion Game 1980
Super Bowl Appearance XV (1980)

Head Coaches:
Dick Vermeil 1980-83 (25-16) (2-2 postseason record);
Marion Campbell 1983-85 (17-29-1); Fred Bruney 1985 (1-0);
Buddy Ryan 1986-89 (33-29-1) (0-2 postseason record)

Hall of Fame Inductees:
None

Award Winners:
Ron Jaworski MVP 1980; Randall Cunningham MVP 1988;
Reggie White Defensive MVP 1987; Keith Jackson Rookie of the Year 1988;
Paul McFadden NFC Rookie of the Year 1984

All Pro:
Harold Carmichael 1980; Charlie Johnson 1980-81; Randy Logan 1980;
Jerry Robinson 1980-81 and 1983; Mike Quick 1983, 1985 and 1987;
Wes Hopkins 1984-85; Reggie White 1986-89; Randall Cunningham 1988:
Keith Jackson 1988-89; Jerome Brown 1989

Pro Bowl Selections:
Wilbert Montgomery 1980; Stan Walters 1980; Wally Henry 1980;
Harold Carmichael 1980-81; Ron Jaworski 1981; Charlie Johnson 1980-81;
Randy Logan 1980-81; Frank LeMaster 1982; Jerry Robinson 1982; Jerry Sisemore 1980 and 82;
Roynell Young 1982; Dennis Harrison 1983; Mike Quick 1984-88; Wes Hopkins 1986;
Reggie White 1987-89; Randall Cunningham 1989-89; Keith Jackson 1989

First Game of the Decade:
September 7, 1980 defeated the Denver Broncos 27-6

Last Game of the Decade:
December 24, 1989 defeated the Phoenix Cardinals 31-14

Largest Margin of Victory:
November 18, 1981 vs. the St. Louis Cardinals 52-10

Largest Margin of Defeat:
October 16, 1983 vs. the Dallas Cowboys 37-7

Eagle Firsts of the Decade:
First Quarterback to lead team in Rushing,
Randall Cunningham did it from 1987-1990

80's Decade in Review

In 1980, the team, led by coach Dick Vermeil, quarterback Ron Jaworski, running back Wilbert Montgomery, wide receiver Harold Carmichael, and linebacker Bill Bergey, dominated the NFC, facing its chief nemesis, the Dallas Cowboys, in the NFC Championship. The game was played in cold conditions in front of the Birds' faithful fans at Veterans Stadium. Led by an incredible rushing performance from Wilbert Montgomery, whose long cutback TD run in the first half is surely one of the most memorable plays in Eagles history, and a gutsy performance from fullback Leroy Harris, who scored the Eagles' only other TD that day, the Birds earned a berth in Super Bowl XV with a 20-7 victory.

The Eagles traveled to New Orleans for Super Bowl XV and were heavy favorites to knock off the upstart Oakland Raiders. Things did not go the Eagles' way, beginning with the disastrous decision by Tose to bring comedian Don Rickles into the pregame locker room to lighten the mood. Jaworski's first pass of the game was intercepted by Rod Martin, setting up an Oakland touchdown. Later in the first quarter, a potential game-tying 40-yard touchdown pass to Rodney Parker was nullified by an illegal motion penalty. Veteran journeyman quarterback Jim Plunkett was named the game's MVP. In a bizarre coincidence, Joe Kuharich died on the same day.

The Eagles got off to a great start in the 1981 season, winning their first six games. They eventually ended up 10-6 and earned a wild card berth. However, they were unable to repeat as NFC champs when they got knocked out in the wild card round by the New York Giants, 27-21. Exhausted, Vermeil quit the team, citing "burnout." he was replaced by defensive coordinator Marion Campbell, aka "the Swamp Fox." Campbell had helped to popularize the "bend-don't-break" defensive strategy in the 1970's. Under Campbell, however, the team struggled, although his stweardship was notable in that it saw the arrival of all-time football greats Reggie White and Randall Cunningham.

Campbell's reign of error ended in 1986, when Buddy Ryan was named head coach. Immediately infusing the team with his tough, hard-as-nails attitude, the Eagles quickly became known for their tough defense and tougher personalities. Under Ryan, the Eagles made the first of three straight playoff appearances in 1988, although the team did not win a postseason game in any of those years. This failure was greatly frustrating to many Eagles fans, as the team was commonly acknowledged as among the most talented in the NFL. On offense, the Eagles were led by quarterback Cunningham, one of the most exciting players of his generation; tight end Keith Jackson; and running back Keith Byars. The defense is commonly acknowledged as among the greatest in league history, and as the best never to win a championship. In 1991, the Eagles became the first NFL team since 1975 to rank first in the league in both rushing and passing yardage allowed, but were unable to reach the playoffs despite a 10-6 record. along with White, notable defensive stars included Jerome Brown, Clyde Simmons, Seth Joyner, Eric Allen, Wes Hopkins, and Andre Waters.

Perhaps most reflective of this era was a playoff loss to the Chicago Bears on December 31, 1988, in the infamous "Fog Bowl" at Soldier Field in Chicago. The Eagles were poised that season to make a run toward the Super Bowl, but in a turn of bad luck, a thick fog clouded Soldier Field that day, keeping the Eagles from playing their usual style and leading to a devastating loss, 20-12.

On November 12, 1990, during a Monday Night Football game at the Vet, the Eagles crushed the Washington Redskins by a score of 28-14, with the defense scoring three of the team's four touchdowns. More lopsided than its score would indicate, the game quickly acquired the sobriquet "the Body Bag Game," attesting to the physical damage inflicted by the tougher Eagles squad. The Eagles knocked out the starting Washington quarterback, and then seriously injured his replacement as well. Running back Brian Mitchell, who would later be signed by the Eagles, was forced to play quarterback for the Redskins.

1980

RECORD: 12-4, 1ST IN NFC EAST
HEAD COACH: DICK VERMEIL

Schedule

Regular Season

Wk. 1	Sep 7	W	27-6	vs Denver Broncos
Wk. 2	Sep 14	W	42-7	at Minnesota Vikings
Wk. 3	Sep 22	W	35-3	vs New York Giants
Wk. 4	Sep 28	L	24-14	at St. Louis Cardinals
Wk. 5	Oct 5	W	24-14	vs Washington Redskins
Wk. 6	Oct 12	W	31-16	at New York Giants
Wk. 7	Oct 19	W	17-10	vs Dallas Cowboys
Wk. 8	Oct 26	W	17-14	vs Chicago Bears
Wk. 9	Nov 2	W	27-20	at Seattle Seahawks
Wk. 10	Nov 9	W	34-21	at New Orleans Saints
Wk. 11	Nov 16	W	24-0	at Washington Redskins
Wk. 12	Nov 23	W	10-7	vs Oakland Raiders
Wk. 13	Nov 30	L	22-21	at San Diego Chargers
Wk. 14	Dec 7	L	20-17	vs Atlanta Falcons
Wk. 15	Dec 14	W	17-3	vs St. Louis Cardinals
Wk. 16	Dec 21	L	35-27	at Dallas Cowboys

Post Season

Divisional Playoffs				
	Jan 3	W	31-16	vs Minnesota Vikings
Conference Championship				
	Jan 11	W	20-7	vs Dallas Cowboys
Superbowl				
	Jan 25	L	27-10	vs Oakland Raiders (at New Orleans, LA)

The Eagles led by QB Ron Jaworski threw for 3,527 yards and 27 touchdowns. He was named NFL player of the year by the Maxwell Football Club and NFC player of the year by UPI. As the Eagles won 11 of their first 12 games and went on to a 12-4 capturing the NFC East Championship. Harold Carmichael's then-record NFL receiving streak is snapped at 127 games when he fails to catch a pass in the regular season finale at Dallas after sustaining a back injury in the first half. In the divisional playoffs, the Eagles trounced on the Vikings 31-16, then in the NFC Championship game against the Cowboys. The Eagles defeated them 20-7, as the Cowboys wore their blue uniforms on a frigid day in Philadelphia before a loud sellout crowd at the Vet and a berth in Super Bowl XV. In their first Super Bowl, the Eagles were matched up against the Oakland Raiders in New Orleans. The Eagles would go into the game, as the heavy favorite because the Raiders were just a wild card team. The Oakland Raiders prevailed in the game 27-10.

1980 Philadelphia Eagles Stats

Passing	Comp	Att	Comp %	Yds	Y/Att	TD	Int	Rating
Ron Jaworski	257	451	57.0	3529	7.82	27	12	91.0
Louie Giammona	3	3	100.0	55	18.33	1	0	158.3
Joe Pisarcik	15	22	68.2	187	8.50	0	0	94.3
Wilbert Montgomery	0	1	0.0	0	0.00	0	0	39.6

Rushing	Rush	Yds	Avg	TD
Wilbert Montgomery	193	778	4.0	8
Louie Giammona	97	361	3.7	4
Leroy Harris	104	341	3.3	3
Perry Harrington	32	166	5.2	1
Billy Campfield	44	120	2.7	1
Ron Jaworski	27	95	3.5	1
Mike Hogan	12	44	3.7	1
Charlie Smith	5	33	6.6	0
Frank LeMaster	2	21	10.5	0
Scott Fitzkee	1	15	15.0	0
John Sciarra	3	11	3.7	0
Zachary Dixon	2	8	4.0	0
Jim Culbreath	1	3	3.0	0
Keith Krepfle	1	2	2.0	0
Joe Pisarcik	3	-3	-1.0	0

Receiving	Rec	Yds	Avg	TD
Wilbert Montgomery	50	407	8.1	2
Harold Carmichael	48	815	17.0	9
Charlie Smith	47	825	17.6	3
Keith Krepfle	30	450	15.0	4
Billy Campfield	26	275	10.6	2
John Spagnola	18	193	10.7	3
Louie Giammona	17	178	10.5	1
Leroy Harris	15	207	13.8	1
Rodney Parker	9	148	16.4	1
Scott Fitzkee	6	169	28.2	2
Wally Henry	4	68	17.0	0
Perry Harrington	3	24	8.0	0
Lewis Gilbert	1	7	7.0	0
Zachary Dixon	1	5	5.0	0

Punting	Punts	Yds	Avg	Blocked
Max Runager	75	2947	39.3	0

Interceptions	Int	Yds	Avg	TD
Brenard Wilson	6	79	13.2	0
Roynell Young	4	27	6.8	0
Herman Edwards	3	12	4.0	0
Charles Johnson	3	9	3.0	0
Jerry Robinson	2	13	6.5	0
Richard Blackmore	2	0	0.0	0
Randy Logan	1	16	16.0	0
Bill Bergey	1	7	7.0	0
Frank LeMaster	1	7	7.0	0
Carl Hairston	1	0	0.0	0
Reggie Wilkes	1	0	0.0	0

Kicking	PAT Made	PAT Att	PAT %	FG Made	FG Att	FG %	Pts
Tony Franklin	48	48	100	16	31	51.6	96

Sports Extra: Four pages of the Eagles

SPORTS FINAL

The Philadelphia Inquirer

Vol. 304, No. 12 · © 1981, The Philadelphia Inquirer · Monday, January 12, 1981 · 20 CENTS

Eagles Head for the Super Bowl

Softer line from Iran on money

Bill could be a compromise

From Inquirer Wire Services

The Iranian Parliament went into closed session today to discuss what was believed to be a bill concerning compromises with the United States on financial terms of negotiations for the release of the 52 American hostages.

Iran has dropped its demand that the U.S. deposit $24 billion in Algerian banks before the release of the hostages, a top Iranian negotiator was quoted as saying yesterday.

In the first indication from Iran that it would waive the deposit demand, negotiator Ahmad Azizi told the Iranian newspaper Enghelab Islami: "The Iranian government has accepted Algerian proposals asking the United States for international guarantees instead of placing a deposit with the Algerian bank."

U.S. officials in Washington said they had not been notified by Iran that their demand had been dropped and could not independently confirm Azizi's statement.

However, sources close to the Algerian delegation in Tehran, which is serving as intermediary in the hostage talks, said yesterday that the Algerians believe a breakthrough is near.

And Iranian government spokesman and Executive Affairs Minister Benzad Nabavi, a key figure in the negotiations Azizi, presented a bill in the parliament early today "concerning the financial and legal problems" between the two countries.

There was no immediate indication of the bill's contents, but it was believed to be a compromise resulting from intensive negotiating over the last few days.

Negotiator Azizi would not specify the kind of guarantees his government would accept, but they presumably would be connected with Iranian claims on assets frozen in the United States and claims on the wealth of the late shah, Mohammed Reza Pahlavi.

He was quoted as saying that Iran would formally respond to the Algerian suggestion today or tomorrow.

On Saturday, Azizi told another Tehran newspaper, Kayhan, that Iran "in all likelihood" would accept the Algerian draft and that he thought the initiative would also be acceptable to the United States.

Last week, an American official who asked not to be identified said that Iran was prepared to revise its demand for the Algerian bank deposit, but Azizi's comments yesterday were the first indication from Iran that the deposit condition was negotiable.

American negotiators extended their stay in the Algerian capital yesterday to reply to additional Iranian questions about the latest American proposal. American officials said Deputy Secretary of State Warren M.

(See IRAN on 2-A)

The Big Act

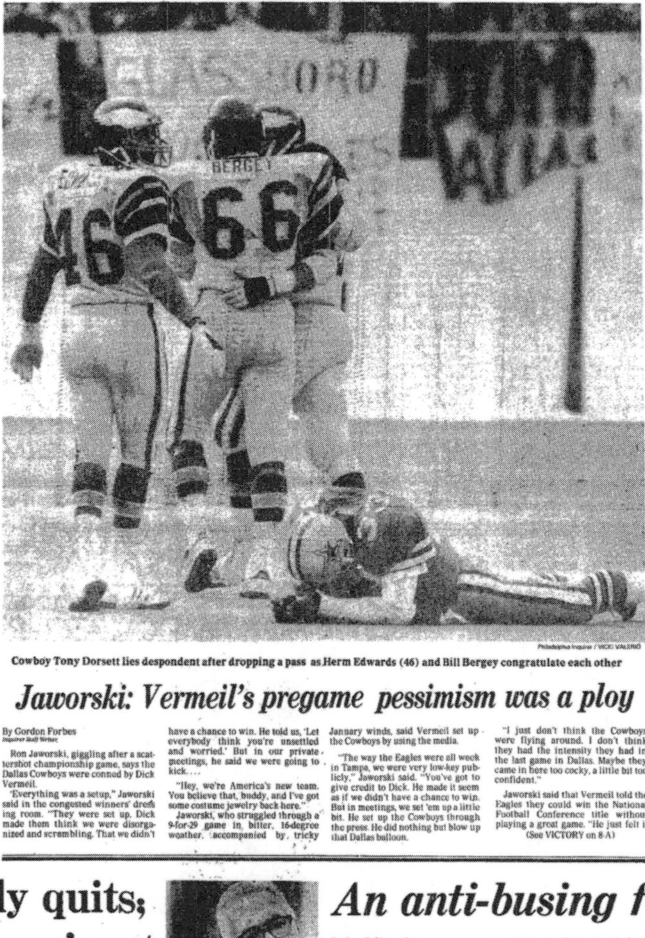

Philadelphia Inquirer / VICKI VALERIO

Cowboy Tony Dorsett lies despondent after dropping a pass as Herm Edwards (46) and Bill Bergey congratulate each other

Jaworski: Vermeil's pregame pessimism was a ploy

By Gordon Forbes
Inquirer Staff Writer

Ron Jaworski, giggling after a scattershot championship game, says the Dallas Cowboys were conned by Dick Vermeil.

"Everything was a setup," Jaworski said in the congested winners' dressing room. "They were set up. Dick made them think we were disorganized and scrambling. That we didn't have a chance to win. He told us, 'Let everybody think you're unsettled and worried.' But in our private meetings, he said we were going to kick. . . .

"Hey, we're America's new team. You believe that, buddy, and I've got some costume jewelry back here."

Jaworski, who struggled through a 9-for-29 game in bitter, 16-degree weather, accompanied by tricky January winds, said Vermeil set up the Cowboys by using the media.

"The way the Eagles were all week in Tampa, we were very low-key publicly," Jaworski said. "You've got to give credit to Dick. He made it seem as if we didn't have a chance to win. But in meetings, we set 'em up a little bit. He set up the Cowboys through the press. He did nothing but blow up that Dallas balloon.

"I just don't think the Cowboys were flying around. I don't think they had the intensity they had in the last game in Dallas. Maybe they came in here too cocky, a little bit too confident."

Jaworski said that Vermeil told the Eagles they could win the National Football Conference title without playing a great game. "He just felt if

(See VICTORY on 8-A)

Cowboys fall; on to Raiders

The Philadelphia Eagles yesterday won their first trip to the Super Bowl with a 20-7 thrashing of their nemesis, the Dallas Cowboys, at Veterans Stadium.

A sellout crowd of 70,696 endured a combination of cold and brisk winds that made the temperature feel as though it was 15 degrees below zero. Most sat bundled like Eskimos, but several inspired fans paraded through the stands bare-chested.

The victory gave the Eagles the National Football Conference championship and a berth in Super Bowl XV against the American Football Conference champion Oakland Raiders, who beat the San Diego Chargers 34-27. The Jan. 25 game in the New Orleans Superdome will be the first time the Eagles have played for the National Football League championship since 1960, when they defeated the Green Bay Packers 17-13.

The victory touched off the second jubilant celebration at the South Philadelphia stadium in three months — since that day in October when the Philadelphia Phillies won the World series, setting off a mad celebration that gripped the city for days.

There was much cause for reminiscence yesterday. Just as in October, the Philadelphia police encircled the field with mounted officers and police dogs to contain the crowd as the final moments ticked away.

Like the Phillies

Just as in October, a cordon of helmeted officers escorted the coach — this time Dick Vermeil, the architect of the Eagles' rise from mediocrity — to the jubilant locker room.

And as the victorious Eagles filed off the field, CBS television announcer Brent Musburger proclaimed Philadelphia, just as in October, the "city of champions."

Indeed, the Eagles' ticket to the Super Bowl completes a remarkable sports year for the city. In 1980, all four of the city's major sport teams — the Sixers, the Phillies, the Flyers and the Eagles — have made it to the final round of championship play. The Flyers and Sixers were unsuccessful in their bids for the top, but then on came the Phillies.

There was little dancing in the streets after the latest triumph, but that was more a reflection on the frigid temperatures than the mood of the fans in the city.

Many of those who attended the game refused to leave, prancing through the stands chanting and cheering long after the players had left the field. Then they piled into cars and headed home through congested streets with horns honking wildly.

Those who headed north toward Center City were greeted at Broad Street and Snyder Avenue by several hundred celebrants.

Additional police were also summoned to Frankford and Cottman Avenues in the Northeast to control a crowd estimated at more than 150.

Game coverage, Page 1-B.

Begin ally quits; collapse imminent

By William Claiborne
Washington Post Service

JERUSALEM — Israeli Finance Minister Yigael Hurvitz made good on his threat to resign yesterday, thereby virtually assuring the collapse of the government of Prime Minister Menachem Begin.

Yigael Hurvitz
Israeli finance minister

After nearly eight hours of uninterrupted debate in which Begin fruitlessly sought to reach a compromise in a ministerial impasse over Israel's deteriorating economy, Begin announced through a spokesman that the cabinet would meet again today to discuss the "political implications" of Hurvitz's resignation.

But because Hurvitz will take with him the three votes of the parliamentary Rafi faction, thus further diminishing Begin's already paper-thin Likud coalition majority, the only practical option that appeared available to the prime minister was to submit a motion to dissolve the Knesset (parliament) and schedule national elections.

The cabinet ministers appeared unanimous on the inevitability of the collapse of the government, with Justice Minister Moshe Nissim saying, "I think this can be assumed," and Health Minister Eliezer Shostak declaring, "Of course the government will (fall). One has to go to early elections, and I think this will be the opinion of the prime minister."

The opposition Labor Party said yesterday that it would give the government until Wednesday to dissolve

(See BEGIN on 2-A)

AS MAYOR of Philadelphia, James H.J. Tate was not known for long talks with the press. But now years out of office, Tate talks freely. People, Page 1-C.

Weather & Index

MOSTLY SUNNY today. High 15 to 20. Partly cloudy and not so cold tonight. Low 10 to 15. Mostly cloudy tomorrow with a chance of snow flurries. Full weather report, Page 17-D.

Action Line	2-C	Horoscope	16-D
The Arts	6-C	Obituaries	18-D
Business	4-D	People	1-C
Classified	5-D	Puzzles	17-D
Comics	16-D	Sports	1-B
Editorials	6-A	TV/Radio	14-D

An anti-busing folk hero

By Jane P. Shoemaker
Inquirer Staff Writer

ALEXANDRIA, La. — The judge's office is overflowing with mementos of past conquests — photographs of the fallen deer, of the record fishing catch, of the ducks hunted with a passion.

Richard E. Lee takes his competition seriously, against fish or game — or any man who interferes with the way he runs his court.

It was in a Rapides Parish courtroom here that Lee gave his blessing to a hastily arranged custody agreement that, in effect, allowed three white teenage girls to avoid being bused away from all-white Buckeye High School under a federal desegregation plan.

And it was a block away in the granite and marble federal courthouse that U.S. District Judge Nauman Scott, who wrote the desegregation plan, ruled that Lee was out of line to interfere with desegregation. Scott ordered the three girls out of Buckeye High and into a school with a racially mixed enrollment.

Lee ordered them back to Buckeye. Scott ordered them out. Lee ordered them back. Scott ordered them out.

Lee took them back. Scott ordered them out, filed contempt citations against parents, guardians, school officials and Lee, and threatened everyone with fines of $500 to $1,000 a day if the girls returned to Buckeye High. They did not, and will not be going to any school pending a courtroom confrontation between Scott and Lee Thursday.

Is this the end of the battle, with the federal government proving it

(See JUDGE on 4-A)

A bitter federal prison strike wears on

By David Zucchino
Inquirer Staff Writer

MARION, Ill. — The first day of refusal, Sept. 15, began with a passive retreat. The men of Marion Prison declined, silently and almost to a man, to answer the morning work call.

For Marion, a secluded warehouse for the nation's most resourceful and independent felons, a work stoppage was hardly a remarkable event. Two other strikes had come and gone earlier in 1980, each aborted with a whimper as the prison ladled out minor concessions.

But now, as the strike enters its 18th week, the men who run Marion find themselves struggling to keep the lid on what has become the longest strike in federal prison history. It is now no ordinary strike — and fittingly, for Marion is no ordinary prison.

For years, career convicts have come to know and fear Marion. From the day it opened in 1962 as the federal government's maximum-security prison, it was "the lab," "behavior mod," the new Alcatraz, the toughest turn of the screw in the federal prison system.

Marion is a catch basin for the men who, in the judgment of prison officials, cannot be "controlled" in any

(See PRISON on 4-A)

1980

January 12, 1981
After 20 years the Eagles make it to the Super Bowl, however lose to Oakland Raiders 27-10

1981

RECORD: 10-6, 2ND IN NFC EAST
HEAD COACH: DICK VERMEIL

Schedule

Regular Season

Wk. 1	Sep 6	W	24-10	at New York Giants
Wk. 2	Sep 13	W	13-3	vs New England Patriots
Wk. 3	Sep 17	W	20-14	at Buffalo Bills
Wk. 4	Sep 27	W	36-13	vs Washington Redskins
Wk. 5	Oct 5	W	16-13	vs Atlanta Falcons
Wk. 6	Oct 11	W	31-14	at New Orleans Saints
Wk. 7	Oct 18	L	35-23	at Minnesota Vikings
Wk. 8	Oct 25	W	20-10	vs Tampa Bay Buccaneers
Wk. 9	Nov 1	L	17-14	vs Dallas Cowboys
Wk. 10	Nov 8	W	52-10	at St. Louis Cardinals
Wk. 11	Nov 15	W	38-13	vs Baltimore Colts
Wk. 12	Nov 22	L	20-10	vs New York Giants
Wk. 13	Nov 30	L	13-10	at Miami Dolphins
Wk. 14	Dec 6	L	15-13	at Washington Redskins
Wk. 15	Dec 13	L	21-10	at Dallas Cowboys
Wk. 16	Dec 20	W	38-0	vs St. Louis Cardinals

Post Season

Wild Card Playoffs				
	Dec 27	L	27-21	vs New York Giants

With running back Wilbert Montgomery's return from injury to rush for 1,402 yards, the Eagles got off to a high flying start by winning their first 6 games. The Eagles would continue to play solid football and sat atop the NFC East at 9-2. However, a four-game losing streak would drop them out of first. The Eagles won their final game to finish with a 10-6 record, and appear in the playoffs for the fourth consecutive year, but were upset at home in the NFC Wild Card Game by the NY Giants, 27-21 at the Vet. The Birds' defense ranked first in the NFL in fewest yards allowed (4,447) and fewest points allowed (221). On offense, Harold Carmichael enjoyed the third 1,000-yard receiving year of his career and Wilbert Montgomery rushed for 1,402 yards.

1981 Philadelphia Eagles Stats

Passing	Comp	Att	Comp %	Yds	Y/Att	TD	Int	Rating
Ron Jaworski	250	461	54.2	3095	6.71	23	20	73.8
Joe Pisarcik	8	15	53.3	154	10.27	2	2	89.3

Rushing	Rush	Yds	Avg	TD
Wilbert Montgomery	286	1402	4.9	8
Hubie Oliver	75	329	4.4	1
Perry Harrington	34	140	4.1	2
Calvin Murray	23	134	5.8	0
Ron Jaworski	22	128	5.8	0
Booker Russell	38	123	3.2	4
Billy Campfield	31	115	3.7	1
Louie Giammona	35	98	2.8	1
Steve Atkins	1	21	21.0	0
Frank LeMaster	1	7	7.0	0
Ron Smith	1	7	7.0	0
Charlie Smith	2	5	2.5	0
Joe Pisarcik	7	1	0.1	0
Harold Carmichael	1	1	1.0	0
John Sciarra	1	0	0.0	0
Wally Henry	1	-2	-2.0	0

Receiving	Rec	Yds	Avg	TD
Harold Carmichael	61	1028	16.9	6
Wilbert Montgomery	49	521	10.6	2
Charlie Smith	38	564	14.8	4
Billy Campfield	36	326	9.1	3
Keith Krepfle	20	210	10.5	5
Hubie Oliver	10	37	3.7	0
Wally Henry	9	145	16.1	2
Perry Harrington	9	27	3.0	0
Rodney Parker	8	168	21.0	2
John Spagnola	6	83	13.8	0
Louie Giammona	6	54	9.0	1
Ron Smith	4	84	21.0	0
Calvin Murray	1	7	7.0	0
Booker Russell	1	-5	-5.0	0

Interceptions	Int	Yds	Avg	TD
Brenard Wilson	5	73	14.6	0
Roynell Young	4	35	8.8	0
Herman Edwards	3	1	0.3	0
Al Chesley	2	66	33.0	0
Richard Blackmore	2	43	21.5	0
Frank LeMaster	2	28	14.0	0
Reggie Wilkes	2	18	9.0	0
Randy Logan	2	-1	-0.5	0
Jerry Robinson	1	3	3.0	0
Charles Johnson	1	0	0.0	0
Ray Phillips	1	0	0.0	0
John Sciarra	1	0	0.0	0

Punting	Punts	Yds	Avg	Blocked
Max Runager	63	2567	40.7	0
Tony Franklin	1	13	13.0	0

Kicking	PAT Made	PAT Att	PAT %	FG Made	FG Att	FG %	Pts
Tony Franklin	41	43	95	20	31	64.5	101

The Philadelphia Inquirer
Sports Extra

section **C**

* ♦ ♦ Monday, December 28, 1981

Eagles dig hole, Giants bury 'em

Carpenter heroic in 27-21 win

By Gordon Forbes
Inquirer Staff Writer

The strategy that was supposed to send the Eagles winging toward Super Bowl XVI was simple enough.

On defense, to gang-tackle the Giants' Rob Carpenter and force young Scott Brunner to throw before his receivers made their break. On offense, to control the ball with a unique, three-back I-formation and just enough passes to keep the tough New York defense honest.

It all sounded nice enough, but on a dreary afternoon at Veterans Stadium yesterday, the Giants kicked the aging Eagles and Dick Vermeil's game plans around in a stunning 27-21 upset before 71,611 gloomy fans. The unexpected victory sends the wild-card Giants to San Francisco for a divisional playoff against the 49ers on Sunday.

How bad were the Eagles?

The Giants (10-7), jumping on two disastrous kick fumbles by Wally Henry, rushed out to a 20-0 first-period lead before Ron Jaworski got to throw a pass. The Eagles (10-7) never recovered from that nightmarish start, although they finally found their poise to close within a touchdown of victory with 2 minutes, 51 seconds left.

Carpenter gains 161

That left it up to the defense to gang up on Carpenter, who carried 33 times for 161 yards — more than any other runner had gained against the Eagles this season. He did it with classic inside cutbacks from a one-back set. Philadelphia's 3-4 defense, with its reputation for jamming up the run, suddenly seemed old and never got the ball back for Jaworski's offense.

"It was a shock that they did that much in so short a time," said defensive end Carl Hairston in a crushing room where the mood was a perfect match for the weather. "I'm hurting. I was looking forward to winning this game. This one was tougher to take than the Super Bowl because we didn't play well. This was almost like a championship game for us."

Linebacker Frank LeMaster stood in disbelief in front of his locker stall. "This loss is the most disappointing and frustrating I've ever had," he said, "mainly because my expectations were higher. We've got too much talent here. The higher your expectations are, the more frustration there is. I wish I had the answers."

Reece recovers

The Eagles began their fumbling and bumbling exit from the NFC playoffs on the first Giants series. Continuing a streak of dreadful special-teams play, Henry fumbled Jennings' punt with the Giants' Pro Bowl linebacker, rookie Lawrence Taylor, in his face. Beasley Reece recovered for the Giants at the 25-yard line.

Brunner, who completed only nine passes but burned the Eagles for three touchdowns, took the Giants into the end zone in six plays. After Carpenter moved it to the four on five power runs, tackle Gordon King was called for a false start, leaving the Giants with third-and-goal at the nine.

Brunner overcame. The Giants flowed their receivers inside and sent Leon Bright, a speed runner,

(See EAGLES on 5-C)

Dick Vermeil makes sure that Eagles assistant coach John Becker (left) wigwags correct signal to Ron Jaworski; sub QB Joe Pisarcik (center) also flashes sign

Philadelphia Inquirer / VICKI VALERIO

Their 'science' left in rubble, erring Eagles reveal courage

By FRANK DOLSON
Sports editor

They talk about the "science" of pro football. The Dick Vermeils of the world work deep into the night studying films, looking for a clue here, an edge there before coming up with that precious thing known as a "game plan."

And then the game begins and almost quicker than you can say "Wait 'til next year," the plan is shot to pieces.

That's the crazy thing about football. All those hours running a projector, all that precise, scientific planning, all those brilliant X's and O's aren't worth a hoot when a team keeps giving away the football, when a fumbled punt and a fumbled kickoff add up to two gift touchdowns in the very first period.

As the Eagles discovered yesterday, a game plan is reduced to rubble when your offensive unit has been on the field for a total of four plays (for a net gain of one yard) in the first quarter and the score is 20-0 against you.

Suddenly, shockingly, sickeningly, the game they found themselves in bore absolutely no resemblance to the tight, tough, defensive game they had made such elaborate plans to play.

In this season of devastating mistakes, that was the final irony. Not even the hardest-working, best-prepared coaching staff in all of football could have foreseen the rash of blunders that shot down the '81 Philadelphia Eagles.

There were those holding penalties by the kickoff-return team that kept the Eagles stuck in terrible field position the first time they played Dallas. There was the fumbled snap on what was supposed to be the game-winning field-goal try at Washington. And the fumbled punt that cost the Eagles

(See DOLSON on 4-C)

Wally Henry tries to get ball after fumbling kickoff

Philadelphia Inquirer / JOHN PAUL FILO

Bills roll up early lead, then hold off Jets, 31-27

By Chuck Newman
Inquirer Staff Writer

NEW YORK — Jim Haslett, who has, on occasion, publicly pronounced his hatred for the New York Jets and the horse they play in, was praying at the end.

"Lord, please give us one more break," thought Haslett, a linebacker for the Buffalo Bills, who were staggering at the end of yesterday's AFC wild-card game at Shea Stadium.

While Haslett was praying, teammate Joe Cribbs had his eyes closed. "I couldn't bear to watch the last 2 minutes," the Bills' 1,000-yard runner said. "I kept thinking about last year."

Last year, the Bills lost a playoff game to the Chargers in the final minutes, when Ron Smith (now an Eagle) scored on a pass play that will live in infamy in Haslett's mind.

The victim of Smith's reception was safety Bill Simpson, who yesterday answered Haslett's prayers, intercepting a Richard Todd pass at the Buffalo one-yard line with 2 seconds left to play to secure a 31-27 victory. The win sent the Bills (11-6) to Cincinnati, for a second-round NFL playoff game on Sunday, and the frustrated Jets (10-6-1) went to an early vacation, to ponder what might have been.

Simpson's second interception of the game killed a frantic Jets drive that began at the New York 20-yard line with 2:36 to play. The Jets devoured 69 yards before the Bills were able to cut short what would have been one of the great comebacks in NFL history.

That the game would have come down to the final seconds had seemed highly unlikely.

Buffalo built a 24-0 lead in just over 24 minutes of play, fueled by the fastest touchdown in an NFL playoff since 1974. Cornerback Charles Romes picked up a fumble on the

(See BILLS on 6-C)

Buffalo wide receiver Frank Lewis wins the race to the end zone for a first-quarter touchdown

Associated Press

NFL playoffs

CONFERENCE SEMIFINALS

Saturday
Tampa Bay Buccaneers (9-7) at Dallas Cowboys (12-4), 1 p.m.
San Diego Chargers (10-6) at Miami Dolphins (11-4-1), 5 p.m.

Sunday
Buffalo Bills (11-6) at Cincinnati Bengals (12-4), 1 p.m.
New York Giants (10-7) at San Francisco 49ers (13-3), 5 p.m.

CONFERENCE CHAMPIONSHIPS
Jan. 10
Sites and times to be determined.

SUPER BOWL XVI
Jan. 24
Pontiac, Mich., 4 p.m.

Sixers, unable to overcome their Phoenix jinx, tumble to 99-96 loss

By George Shirk
Inquirer Staff Writer

PHOENIX, Ariz. — The 76ers always save their worst for Phoenix. It's a tradition.

Last night, after four days of rest, the Sixers gave their worst shooting performance of the season and lost to the Suns, 99-96.

On paper, the loss appeared unlikely. The Suns were playing their third game in three days and, by all rights, should have been two steps slower and three times more ragged. But it didn't turn out that way at all. So, in front of a capacity crowd of 14,666 — the Suns' first sellout of the season — with Truck Robinson collecting 25 points and 15 rebounds, Phoenix beat the Sixers again.

The loss was Philadelphia's fifth straight here since March 1978. To make matters worse, it dropped the Sixers, now 20-6, a half-game behind Boston in the NBA's Atlantic Division.

Phoenix, which jumped its record to 16-12, had lost to Golden State on Saturday evening in Oakland and had lost to Los Angeles at home on Friday. Yet it was the Sixers, who were playing without injured Bobby Jones, who were a step slow and off balance.

"It was hard to tell which team was the one that had played three games in three nights," coach Billy Cunningham said with a wry laugh after the game. "We just didn't get anything generated on a consistent basis, either defensively or offensively. I thought we had several opportunities to win the game, but we either committed a foul, didn't get a rebound, missed foul shots, etc. I can name about 20 [opportunities]."

The Sixers shot a pitiful 40.2 percent from the field. It was not only their poorest effort this season but worse than any last season.

Julius Erving, who led the club with 20 points, was 7 for 17. Darryl Dawkins, who fouled out of the game in the fourth quarter and who scored nine points, all in the first half, shot 2 for 7. Mo Cheeks, who had nine points and six assists, was three for 11, Lionel Hollins 6 for 15 and Caldwell Jones 3 for 8.

In addition, the Sixers were pounded on the boards, losing the rebounding battle, 58-40.

Given those circumstances, it was remarkable that they were even in the game when time began running out on them in the fourth quarter. But they were indeed in it, thanks to 22 Phoenix turnovers, right up until the last seconds.

They were down by 99-96 and had the ball and a timeout with 14 seconds to go. They also had Andrew Toney, who, with 41 seconds left, had hit a three-point field goal to bring them that close.

All eyes, therefore, were on Toney, who is the best three-point man on the club, as the Sixers put the ball in bounds.

Cunningham had designed a play that would have gotten the ball first to C. Jones, who would have the option of passing to Erving, Cheeks, Toney or Steve Mix for a three-point try. The play went awry.

"We were looking for a three-point shot, obviously," Cunningham said. "We were going to have five people *(See SIXERS on 7-C)*

December 28, 1981
*Eagles lose in the NFC Wild Card game
27-21 to the NY Giants*

1982

RECORD: 3-6, 13TH IN NFC
HEAD COACH: DICK VERMEIL

Schedule
Regular Season

Wk. 1	Sep 12	L	37-34	vs Washington Redskins (OT)
Wk. 2	Sep 19	W	24-21	at Cleveland Browns
Wk. 10	Nov 21	L	18-14	vs Cincinnati Bengals
Wk. 11	Nov 28	L	13-9	at Washington Redskins
Wk. 12	Dec 5	L	23-20	vs St. Louis Cardinals
Wk. 13	Dec 11	L	23-7	at New York Giants
Wk. 14	Dec 19	W	35-14	vs Houston Oilers
Wk. 15	Dec 26	W	24-20	at Dallas Cowboys
Wk. 16	Jan 2	L	26-24	vs New York Giants

An NFL players' strike took place after two games and stopped play for eight weeks. When play resumed on November 21, 1982, the long layoff hurt the Eagles. After splitting the first two games of the season, the Birds came back from the strike to lose four in a row and miss the playoff for the first time since 1977. A 24-20 Eagles victory at Dallas on December 26, 1982, is the last victory in the Philadelphia career of head coach Dick Vermeil, who resigned sighting burnout shortly following the season after compiling a 56-51-0 overall record.

1982 Philadelphia Eagles Stats

Passing	Comp	Att	Comp %	Yds	Y/Att	TD	Int	Rating
Ron Jaworski	167	286	58.4	2076	7.26	12	12	77.5
Joe Pisarcik	1	1	100.0	24	24.00	0	0	118.8
Louie Giammona	0	1	0.0	0	0.00	0	1	0.0

Rushing	Rush	Yds	Avg	TD
Wilbert Montgomery	114	515	4.5	7
Perry Harrington	56	231	4.1	1
Leroy Harris	17	39	2.3	2
Louie Giammona	11	29	2.6	1
Ron Jaworski	10	9	0.9	0
Melvin Hoover	1	5	5.0	0
Billy Campfield	1	2	2.0	0
Frank LeMaster	1	-1	-1.0	0

Receiving	Rec	Yds	Avg	TD
Harold Carmichael	35	540	15.4	4
Ron Smith	34	475	14.0	1
John Spagnola	26	313	12.0	2
Wilbert Montgomery	20	258	12.9	2
Billy Campfield	14	141	10.1	1
Perry Harrington	13	74	5.7	0
Mike Quick	10	156	15.6	1
Louie Giammona	8	67	8.4	0
Vyto Kab	4	35	8.8	1
Leroy Harris	3	17	5.7	0
Lawrence Sampleton	1	24	24.0	0

Punting	Punts	Yds	Avg	Blocked
Max Runager	44	1784	40.5	0

Interceptions	Int	Yds	Avg	TD
Herman Edwards	5	3	0.6	0
Roynell Young	4	0	0.0	0
Jerry Robinson	3	19	6.3	0
Richard Blackmore	1	20	20.0	1
John Bunting	1	0	0.0	0
Brenard Wilson	1	0	0.0	0

Kicking	PAT Made	PAT Att	PAT %	FG Made	FG Att	FG %	Pts
Tony Franklin	23	25	92	6	9	66.7	41

The Philadelphia Inquirer
Sports Extra

section C

♦ ♦ Monday, September 20, 1982

Carmichael, Eagles seem to have 'picks' down pat

Gordon Forbes:
Inside report

CLEVELAND — It is one of the slickest tricks in pro football, one that defensive coaches scream about and offensive coaches swear they never use.

Coach Dick Vermeil said that the Eagles put together those two superb touchdown drives yesterday to stun the Cleveland Browns without benefit of a single "pick" play. But Harold Carmichael, his dead-honest receiver, who set up the winning score by beating a loo-w safety named Judson Flint, wasn't so sure.

"Well, yeah, you could say that I

was using the pick," Carmichael said, with a sheepish grin, following the 24-21 thriller at Cleveland Stadium. "I could pick on it or get open on it. I'm trying to get open, but if the guy holds me up and if I can see him in 'man' (man-to-man coverage), I can set a pick. I pick the other guy."

Pick plays usually work inside the 20-yard line. With the defense almost always in man-to-man coverage, one

(See FORBES on 6-C)

Harold Carmichael beats Judson Flint, sets up winning score

Eagles' offense strikes in time

By Jere Longman
Inquirer Staff Writer

CLEVELAND — These were the Cardiac Kids all right, but they were in different jerseys now, wearing Eagles green instead of Cleveland brown.

(See EAGLES on 5-C)

Pro football

Dallas 24, St. Louis 7
Detroit 19, L. A. Rams 14
Pittsburgh 26, Cincinnati 20, ovt.
L. A. Raiders 38, Atlanta 14
New York Jets 31, New England 7
New Orleans 10, Chicago 0
Kansas City 19, San Diego 12
Denver 24, San Francisco 21
Houston 23, Seattle 21
Washington 21, Tampa Bay 13
Miami 24, Baltimore 20
Detailed coverage Pages 4-C and 5-C

If this was the end, it sure was a beauty

By BILL LYON

CLEVELAND — The first three quarters here in Baghdad-by-the-Sewer had been as inconclusive as mud-wrestling.

(See LYON on 6-C)

Leroy Harris barrels over Eddie Johnson for the Eagles' game-winning TD with 22 seconds left

Phils fall to Bucs, 8-1, find backs against wall

By Jayson Stark
Inquirer Staff Writer

In the context of great Philadelphia disasters, this one isn't even in the top 10.

A day for Stargell
Phils honor a star-studded career

By Gary Ronberg
Inquirer Staff Writer

Willie Stargell: 'My final season has been like a gourmet meal'

Kenyan breezes to world half-marathon record in Phila. Distance Run

By Ron Reid
Inquirer Staff Writer

In a performance as stunning as it appeared effortless, Michael Musyoki of Kenya won the Philadelphia Distance Run yesterday, covering the 13.1-mile course in the world-record time of 1 hour, 1 minute, 35 seconds.

(See RUN on 6-C)

September 20, 1982
Jaworski is successful with his second consecutive 300-yard game as the Eagles defeat the Cleveland Browns 24-21

1983

RECORD: 5-11, 4TH IN NFC EAST
HEAD COACH: MARION CAMPBELL

Schedule
Regular Season

Wk. 1	Sep 3	W	22-17	at San Francisco 49ers
Wk. 2	Sep 11	L	23-13	vs Washington Redskins
Wk. 3	Sep 18	W	13-10	at Denver Broncos
Wk. 4	Sep 25	L	14-11	vs St. Louis Cardinals
Wk. 5	Oct 2	W	28-24	at Atlanta Falcons
Wk. 6	Oct 9	W	17-13	at New York Giants
Wk. 7	Oct 16	L	37-7	at Dallas Cowboys
Wk. 8	Oct 23	L	7-6	vs Chicago Bears
Wk. 9	Oct 30	L	22-21	vs Baltimore Colts
Wk. 10	Nov 6	L	27-20	vs Dallas Cowboys
Wk. 11	Nov 13	L	17-14	at Chicago Bears
Wk. 12	Nov 20	L	23-0	vs New York Giants
Wk. 13	Nov 27	L	28-24	at Washington Redskins
Wk. 14	Dec 4	W	13-9	vs Los Angeles Rams
Wk. 15	Dec 11	L	20-17	vs New Orleans Saints (OT)
Wk. 16	Dec 18	L	31-7	at St. Louis Cardinals

Marion Campbell replaced Dick Vermeil as head coach after six seasons as the defensive coordinator. Owner and president Leonard Tose announced in January that his daughter, Susan Fletcher, the Eagles vice president and legal counsel, would eventually succeed him as primary owner of the Eagles. The Eagles got off to a solid start, winning four of their first six games. However, they came crashing down to earth quickly during a crippling seven game losing streak. The Eagles went on to finish in last place with a 5-11 record. The Birds' offense was highlighted by first-team all-pro and AFC-NFC Pro Bowl selection Mike Quick, who led the league and set club records with 1,409 yards receiving on 69 catches.

1983 Philadelphia Eagles Stats

Passing	Comp	Att	Comp %	Yds	Y/Att	TD	Int	Rating
Ron Jaworski	235	446	52.7	3315	7.43	20	18	75.1
Harold Carmichael	1	1	100.0	45	45.00	1	0	158.3
Joe Pisarcik	16	34	47.1	172	5.06	1	0	72.2
Dan Pastorini	0	5	0.0	0	0.00	0	0	39.6

Rushing	Rush	Yds	Avg	TD
Hubie Oliver	121	434	3.6	1
Michael Williams	103	385	3.7	0
Michael Haddix	91	220	2.4	2
Wilbert Montgomery	29	139	4.8	0
Ron Jaworski	25	129	5.2	1
Perry Harrington	23	98	4.3	1
Major Everettt	5	7	1.4	0
Max Runager	1	6	6.0	0
Dan Pastorini	1	0	0.0	0
Joe Pisarcik	3	-1	-0.3	0

Receiving	Rec	Yds	Avg	TD
Mike Quick	69	1409	20.4	13
Hubie Oliver	49	421	8.6	2
Harold Carmichael	38	515	13.6	3
Michael Haddix	23	254	11.0	0
Vyto Kab	18	195	10.8	1
Michael Williams	17	142	8.4	0
Melvin Hoover	10	221	22.1	0
Wilbert Montgomery	9	53	5.9	0
Tony Woodruff	6	70	11.7	2
Al Dixon	4	54	13.5	0
Glen Young	3	125	41.7	1
Lawrence Sampleton	2	28	14.0	0
Major Everettt	2	18	9.0	0
Perry Harrington	1	19	19.0	0
Ron Smith	1	8	8.0	0

Punting	Punts	Yds	Avg	Blocked
Max Runager	59	2459	41.7	0
Tom Skledany	27	1062	39.3	0

Interceptions	Int	Yds	Avg	TD
Anthony Griggs	3	61	20.3	0
Ray Ellis	1	18	18.0	0
Herman Edwards	1	0	0.0	0
Elbert Foules	1	0	0.0	0
Randy Logan	1	0	0.0	0
Roynell Young	1	0	0.0	0

Kicking	PAT Made	PAT Att	PAT %	FG Made	FG Att	FG %	Pts
Tony Franklin	24	27	89	15	26	57.7	69

The Philadelphia Inquirer
Sports Extra
section D
Monday, December 19, 1983

Eagles fall on their faces one last time

By FRANK DOLSON

Sports editor

The Eagles go slip-slidin' away

ST. LOUIS — Somewhere, that old, ex-Eagle, Tom Brookshier, was probably sitting in an easy chair in front of a warm fire yesterday, his feet propped up, looking at a television screen and laughing.

Red-jerseyed Cardinals were romping up and down the snow-slicked field while red-faced Eagles were slipping and sliding on a day when the wind-chill factor was minus-10 degrees. And to think, the big shots at CBS-TV thought they were *punishing* Brookshier by taking him off the game, a suspension for comments made on the air during last week's Eagles-Saints game.

It was a day unfit for man, beast or television announcer, and the game was perfectly suited to the day — a virtually meaningless exercise in which grown men took pratfalls in the snow and 21,902 spectators thumbed their frozen noses at double pneumonia.

It was so miserable out there that Cardinals' veteran Dan Dierdorf, retiring at the end of this, his 13th pro season, accepted a plaque before the game, stepped to the microphone and said, "I don't want anybody to think I'm going to talk long enough to delay the start of this football game. I'm as cold as you are."

Unfortunately for the Eagles, Dierdorf quit talking at that point and let the game begin.

It was horrendous, a game only a Cardinals fanatic could love. The playing surface looked more like a hockey rink than a football field, and the Eagles, getting into the spirit of things, looked like the New Jersey Devils.

The only thing the visitors were to win on this frostbitten afternoon was the opening toss. They elected to receive. Had they known then what they know now, they would have elected to leave.

While the Eagles' running backs spun their wheels and went nowhere, collectively gaining a net 14 yards, the Cardinals' Ottis Anderson personally ran for 156.

"They had good traction ... a lot better traction than we had," Eagles coach Marion Campbell said when it was over, indicating that the Cardinals wore shoes better suited to the playing suface.

Maybe so. But watching this game between a Cardinals team that had won six of its last nine and an Eagles team that had lost eight of its last nine, you got the feeling they could have been playing in Miami Beach and it wouldn't have made much difference in the final result.

The Eagles were so helpless that they didn't gain anything until their eighth play from scrimmage — a Ron Jaworski-to-Hubie Oliver pass that picked up three yards on a second-and-12 play. Their first seven offensive plays netted minus-14 yards.

Their running game was so bad that they went 12½ minutes before

(See DOLSON on 6-D)

Associated Press

Ottis Anderson (32) darts past Eagles linebackers Reggie Wilkes (51) and Jerry Robinson for a 12-yard, first-period touchdown

Cardinals cruise, 31-7, in the snow

By Jere Longman
Inquirer Staff Writer

ST. LOUIS — The other shoe dropped on the Eagles yesterday.

Make that the wrong shoe.

In a season in which everything imaginable has gone askew, the Eagles reached a new low in yesterday's finale, a 31-7 loss to St. Louis — they wore the wrong shoes.

That's right.

The Cardinals appeared relatively immune to the blowing snow and 10-degree temperature at Busch Stadium, but the Eagles went skating across the frozen turf like Eric Heiden.

St. Louis, it seems, wore a brand of shoe called Acton, which was originally designed for rainy weather and is often used in the Canadian Football League. Its most attractive feature is longer rubber cleats than the standard turf shoe.

The Eagles, meanwhile, went slip-sliding around in their normal turf shoes, missing tackles, falling on pass patterns and generally being unable to generate any traction.

"I almost fell down just coming out of the huddle," center Guy Morriss said.

Partly because the Eagles couldn't stay on their feet, they slipped to their 11th loss in 16 games. Yesterday's inglorious conclusion marked their worst season since Dick Vermeil was hired as coach in 1976 and posted a 4-10 record. The last time the Eagles lost 11 games was 1972, when they finished 2-11-1.

"It was just a poor performance on our part," said coach Marion Campbell, that master of understatement. "We didn't get anything going offensively or defensively."

Some examples:

- The Eagles managed a grand total of 14 yards rushing on 12 carries. If Max Runager hadn't skated for 6 yards on a fake punt, that total would have been 8 yards on 11 carries. It was the most pitiful rushing performance by the Eagles since they plowed up 10 yards against the Giants on Nov. 20.

- Ron Jaworski completed 21 of 45 passes for 298 yards, but he also threw four interceptions, matching his career high. The pickoffs were costly, setting up three St. Louis touchdowns and a field goal.
- Jaworski, hounded all day by a fierce pass rush, also was sacked 11 times; 4½ sacks went to defensive end Curtis Greer and three more went to defensive end Bubba Baker.

The only reason the Eagles scored was St. Louis' insistence on passing even with a 31-0 lead in the fourth quarter. With 28 seconds remaining, quarterback Neil Lomax lost the ball while trying to scramble, and Jaworski salvaged the day with a 20-yard touchdown pass to Mike Quick at the final gun.

With his four catches, Quick set an Eagles season record of 69 receptions. His touchdown also tied Tommy McDonald's club mark of 13 in a season. There was another record of sorts. Harold Carmichael, with five catches, tied Fred Biletnikoff for fifth place on the all-time NFL list, with 589 career receptions.

But yesterday's frosty denouement will not be remembered for records.

(See EAGLES on 6-D)

Wild finishes complete playoff field

From Inquirer Wire Services

The battle for the last playoff berths in the National Football Conference went down to the final seconds yesterday when field goals eliminated two of the five teams vying for the three spots available on the final Sunday of the National Football League regular season.

Mike Lansford's 42-yard field goal with 2 seconds left gave the visiting Los Angeles Rams a 26-24 victory, earned them a postseason date and dashed the playoff hopes of the New Orleans Saints, who were bidding also for the first winning season in the franchise's 17-year history.

Minutes later in Chicago, Bob Thomas kicked a 22-yard field goal with 10 seconds remaining to give the Bears a 23-21 victory over Green Bay and eliminate the Packers from playoff consideration.

In the American Football Conference, the Seattle Seahawks decided their own destiny by defeating the New England Patriots, 24-6, to survive a four-team run at the remaining AFC postseason berth, a wild-card spot.

The ouster of the Saints paved the way to the playoffs for the Rams and San Francisco 49ers, who meet Dallas tonight (9 o'clock, TV-Channel 6) in the final game of the regular season.

If the 49ers defeat Dallas, they will be NFC West Division champions and the Rams will be the Cowboys'

(See PLAYOFFS on 4-D)

United Press International

Lansford cheers as his field goal gives the Rams a playoff spot

Pro football

REGULAR-SEASON FINALES

Atlanta 31, Buffalo 14
Baltimore 20, Houston 10
Chicago 23, Green Bay 21
Cleveland 30, Pittsburgh 10
Detroit 23, Tampa Bay 20
Kansas City 48, Denver 17
L.A. Raiders 30, San Diego 14
L.A. Rams 26, New Orleans 24
Seattle 24, New England 6

PLAYOFF QUALIFIERS

NFC division champions — Washington (14-2), Detroit (9-7) and San Francisco (9-6) or L.A. Rams (9-7).

NFC wild cards — Dallas (12-3) and San Francisco or L.A. Rams.

AFC division champions — Miami (12-4), Pittsburgh (10-6) and L.A. Raiders (12-4).

AFC wild cards — Denver (9-7) and Seattle (9-7).

PLAYOFF SCHEDULE

First round — AFC: Denver at Seattle, Saturday, 4 p.m. NFC: San Francisco or L.A. Rams at Dallas, Dec. 26, 2:30 p.m.

Conference semifinals — Dec. 31 and Jan. 1.

Conference championships — Jan. 8.

Super Bowl XVIII — Jan. 22 at Tampa, Fla., 4:30 p.m.

Detailed coverage of the NFL begins on Page 4-D.

Giant Steps

Second of five excerpts from the autobiography of Kareem Abdul-Jabbar.

Learning to walk tall in Harlem

By Kareem Abdul-Jabbar and Peter Knobler

On the New York streets where I was growing up, if you didn't know how to fight you were in big trouble, and I just didn't have the instinct. I didn't have that many fights; I just lost all of them.

When I was born in 1947, my parents — Cora and Ferdinand Lewis "Al" Alcindor — were living in Harlem. Back then, Harlem was by no means paradise, but it wasn't the war zone it is today. When I was growing up, everyone around us had a job; to be on welfare was an embarrassment. My mother would take me to play in Central Park with no fear. People would leave their front doors open. Stealing was not tolerated. Anybody who got caught snatching a purse got handled by the people in the community. Some of the worst offenders would get thrown off the roof. People didn't play around.

We moved to the Dyckman Street projects in the Inwood section of Manhattan in 1950. By then, I already knew what to expect from my parents.

It was important to them to be respectable; they were definitely not going to have a thug for a son. Their primary focus, as far as I was concerned, was my education. In fact, it was almost all we talked about.

There wasn't a lot of emotion on display in the Alcindor household. My father was stern and powerful. I knew he loved me, but he didn't often go out of his way to let me hear about it. A large man — 6 feet, 3 inches tall, 200 pounds — he carried himself as if his mere bulk and the silence he maintained were a life statement.

But there was clearly a muse on the loose inside him as well. He enrolled in the Juilliard School of Music right after I was born and gradu-

(See GIANT STEPS on 7-D)

Philadelphia Daily News

Abdul-Jabbar says he was no prodigy at basketball

Tribune Company Syndicate Inc.

A young Lew Alcindor; education was a priority

Flyers and Red Wings battle to another 3-3 tie

By Angelo Cataldi
Inquirer Staff Writer

Bobby Clarke sat frozen in the Flyers' net, a look of disbelief on his face. The clock above him indicated that time had elapsed, that the Flyers had won. The red light behind him suggested otherwise.

And so, ultimately, did the scoreboard and the standings, as the Flyers watched a win dissolve into a 3-3 tie with the Detroit Red Wings last night before 16,049 disbelieving fans at the Spectrum.

The tying goal, by Detroit's Steve Yzerman, beat Flyers goalie Pelle Lindbergh and the clock by the narrowest of margins — a couple of inches and 1 haunting second — and closed out a weekend home-and-home series in which the teams produced back-to-back 3-3 ties.

"It's disappointing," said dejected and angry Flyers coach Bob McCammon. "I think we beat ourselves when we missed all of those scoring chances before that. That was just a tough game."

The game also was more than a little controversial. McCammon attacked on several fronts after the contest, and the officiating was again the primary target of his venom.

First, he wondered about the two apparent Flyers goals — especially the last one — that referee Bryan Lewis nullified. Second, he questioned the events of those final seconds. Finally, he openly criticized the lack of calls during an inconsequential 5-minute overtime.

"If the period wasn't over," he said of the tying goal, which was officially recorded at 19 minutes, 59 seconds, "why didn't we have a face-off after that? I don't understand. He [Lewis] was so excited rooting for Detroit, I guess he forgot.

"There were at least three penalties in that overtime, and he didn't call any of them. When a penalty's a penalty, they've got to call them. If they keep it up like this, they're going to hurt the game."

The final goal was an exercise in futility that exceeded even the Flyers' norm in this frustrating season. The Wings pulled their goalie, Eddie Mio, with 49 seconds remaining, and then pressed the Flyers relentlessly. On several occasions the puck bounced precariously close to the goal, but it wasn't until the final seconds were ticking off that the real danger arose.

With about three ticks left, the puck snaked into the crease, and Lindbergh dived for it. Just before he reached it, it bounded off Ron Duguay's stick and out to Yzerman, who snapped it through a knot of bodies and into the net. Long after the play, Clarke remained in the net, as the crowd grew silent.

"One second, 5 seconds, 20 seconds, it doesn't matter," reasoned Lindbergh. "I'm disappointed, of course,

(See FLYERS on 11-D)

1983

December 19, 1983
Eagles are humiliated by St. Louis 31-7

1984

RECORD: 6-9-1, 5TH IN NFC EAST
HEAD COACH: MARION CAMPBELL

Schedule
Regular Season

Wk. 1	Sep 2	L	28-27	at New York Giants
Wk. 2	Sep 9	W	19-17	vs Minnesota Vikings
Wk. 3	Sep 16	L	23-17	at Dallas Cowboys
Wk. 4	Sep 23	L	21-9	vs San Francisco 49ers
Wk. 5	Sep 30	L	20-0	at Washington Redskins
Wk. 6	Oct 7	W	27-17	at Buffalo Bills
Wk. 7	Oct 14	W	16-7	vs Indianapolis Colts
Wk. 8	Oct 21	W	24-10	vs New York Giants
Wk. 9	Oct 28	L	34-14	vs St. Louis Cardinals
Wk. 10	Nov 4	T	23-23	at Detroit Lions (OT)
Wk. 11	Nov 11	L	24-23	at Miami Dolphins
Wk. 12	Nov 18	W	16-10	vs Washington Redskins
Wk. 13	Nov 25	L	17-16	at St. Louis Cardinals
Wk. 14	Dec 2	L	26-10	vs Dallas Cowboys
Wk. 15	Dec 9	W	27-17	vs New England Patriots
Wk. 16	Dec 16	L	26-10	at Atlanta Falcons

After a 1-4 start, the Eagles posted a 5-5-1 record in their final 11 games. Philadelphia's swarming defense set a then-club record of 60 quarterback sacks and was the catalyst for the team's improved play. Wilbert Montgomery established the Eagles' career rushing record for yards (6,538) and attempts (1,465), surpassing Steve Van Buren from 1944-1951. Kicker Paul McFadden established an Eagles' season scoring record with 116 points (top among rookies), surpassing Bobby Walston's 30-year mark of 114, and was named NFC Rookie of the Year. Quarterback Ron Jaworski suffered a broken leg at St. Louis in week 13, snapping his streak of 116 consecutive starts. Mike Quick was selected to the AFC-NFC Pro Bowl for the second straight year. By the end of the season there were widespread rumors of the team's owner Leonard Tose's financial problems.

1984 Philadelphia Eagles Stats

Passing	Comp	Att	Comp %	Yds	Y/Att	TD	Int	Rating
Ron Jaworski	234	427	54.8	2754	6.45	16	14	73.5
Joe Pisarcik	96	176	54.5	1036	5.89	3	3	70.6
Dean May	1	1	100.0	33	33.00	0	0	118.8
Wilbert Montgomery	0	2	0.0	0	0.00	0	0	39.6

Rushing	Rush	Yds	Avg	TD
Wilbert Montgomery	201	789	3.9	2
Hubie Oliver	72	263	3.7	0
Michael Haddix	48	130	2.7	1
Michael Williams	33	83	2.5	0
Andre Hardy	14	41	2.9	0
Joe Pisarcik	7	19	2.7	2
Ron Jaworski	5	18	3.6	1
Mike Quick	1	-5	-5.0	0

Receiving	Rec	Yds	Avg	TD
John Spagnola	65	701	10.8	1
Mike Quick	61	1052	17.2	9
Wilbert Montgomery	60	501	8.4	0
Michael Haddix	33	231	7.0	0
Hubie Oliver	32	142	4.4	0
Tony Woodruff	30	484	16.1	3
Kenny Jackson	26	398	15.3	1
Vyto Kab	9	102	11.3	3
Michael Williams	7	47	6.7	0
Melvin Hoover	6	143	23.8	2
Andre Hardy	2	22	11.0	0
Gregg Garrity	2	22	11.0	0

Punting	Punts	Yds	Avg	Blocked
Mike Horan	92	3880	42.2	0

Interceptions	Int	Yds	Avg	TD
Ray Ellis	7	119	17.0	0
Wes Hopkins	5	107	21.4	0
Elbert Foules	4	27	6.8	0
Herman Edwards	2	0	0.0	0
Brenard Wilson	1	28	28.0	0
Reggie Wilkes	1	6	6.0	0

Kicking	PAT Made	PAT Att	PAT %	FG Made	FG Att	FG %	Pts
Paul McFadden	26	27	96	30	37	81.1	116

The Philadelphia Inquirer
Sports Extra

section **F**

♦♦ Monday, November 26, 1984

Last-minute kick sinks Eagles

Jaworski, in the grasp of David Galloway (right) and Curtis Greer (bottom), on the play in which he was injured.

His streak, and his season, ends

By FRANK DOLSON
Sports editor

ST. LOUIS — The human body was not designed to play pro football. Not on those schoolyard-hard, plastic, green carpets that cover too many big-league playing fields in this age of multipurpose stadiums. Not when high-speed collisions with 250- and 260-pounders are all in a day's work.

Somehow, Ron Jaworski had survived in this world of super-hard knocks. From the day he made his debut at quarterback for the Philadelphia Eagles — Sept. 18, 1977 — through yesterday at Busch Stadium, Jaworski never missed a starting call. For 116 straight times — the most consecutive starts ever by an NFL quarterback — he went out

(See DOLSON on 6-F)

there, in sickness and in health, in victory and in defeat. That doesn't even count the seven postseason games he played.

Sure, there have been much longer iron-man streaks in professional sports. Heck, Lou

Gehrig made it through 2,130 consecutive games for the Yankees. But Gehrig was a baseball player, not a quarterback. He had to face only 90 m.p.h. fastballs, not King Kong-sized defensive ends and blitzing linebackers.

One of the remarkable aspects of Jaworski's streak — surely one of the most noteworthy in all of professional sports — is that hardly anybody paid any attention to it. Maybe folks were too busy chanting, "We want Joe," when the Eagles' offense sputtered. More likely, they simply took it for granted that No. 7 would be out there, shrugging off the blitzes

O'Donoghue connects as Cards win, 17-16

By Jere Longman
Inquirer Staff Writer

ST. LOUIS — The Eagles saw the light at the end of the tunnel yesterday. As usual, it was a fatal vision.

It had happened with frustrating regularity over the last two seasons. Always, the Eagles are close. Seldom are they close enough.

Last season, the Eagles lost six games by a total of 15 points. This year, they have tied Detroit and lost three one-point games, the latest coming in yesterday's 17-16 heartbreaker won by St. Louis.

As Neil O'Donoghue's 44-yard field goal drilled over the crossbar with 8 seconds left, the Eagles drifted to 5-7-1. They will have to finish the season with virtually no playoff hopes and without Ron Jaworski, who broke the fibula in his left leg three plays into the game.

Safety Ray Ellis has called the Eagles the best "almost" team in the National Football League. However, the standings measure only wins and losses.

"We've been so close, yet so far from victory," Ellis said. "We're almost there, but that's not good enough. The only thing that counts is the final score. I'd rather be the best winning team in football than the best losing team. But so far, we've been on the short end of the stick."

The Eagles had plenty of chances to win yesterday. Again, they found a way to lose. Three mistakes nailed the coffin shut.

● Early in the second quarter, with the Eagles trailing 7-3, Joe Pisarcik, in replacement of Jaworski, launched a perfect rainbow down the left sideline to Melvin Hoover.

Safety Benny Perrin and cornerback Lionel Washington ran into a pick by Mike Quick, freeing Hoover for what should have been a 50-yard touchdown pass. Instead, the ball bounced harmlessly off Hoover's right shoulder inside the 5.

"No comment," Hoover said.

Said Pisarcik, "I got hit, so I didn't see the play, but I heard he should have caught it."

● With 4:18 left in the game and the Eagles trailing 14-13, Paul McFadden lined up for a chip shot. This one was a 26-yard field goal attempt, a glorified extra point.

McFadden would kick three field goals before the game ended — from 31, 43 and 32 yards. He would set an Eagles season record with 26 field goals. But this chip shot, this 26-yarder, he would hook to the left.

"I have no excuses," McFadden said. "I just pulled the ball. The snap was 'fine, the hold was fine, the pro-

(See EAGLES on 7-F)

Pro football

Cincinnati 35, Atlanta 14
Washington 41, Buffalo 14
Cleveland 27, Houston 10
New York Giants 28, Kansas City 27
Los Angeles Rams 34, Tampa Bay 33
Pittsburgh 52, San Diego 24
Chicago 34, Minnesota 3
L.A. Raiders 21, Indianapolis 7
San Francisco 35, New Orleans 3
Seattle 27, Denver 24
Coverage of the rest of the NFL begins on Page 4-F

Off the bench, Pisarcik almost pulls out a win

By Jere Longman
Inquirer Staff Writer

ST. LOUIS — When Ron Jaworski's left leg was placed in a cast yesterday, Joe Pisarcik was suddenly cast as the Eagles' No. 1 quarterback.

The Eagles lost the game, 17-16, but Pisarcik never lost his poise. He threw 39 passes and completed 24 for 226 yards, including a 16-yard touchdown pass to Mike Quick.

"Joe did an outstanding job," Jaworski said. "He does a good job of preparing every week. He doesn't get a chance to play that often, but he's prepared to play every time. I've got so much respect for him."

With Pisarcik at quarterback, the Eagles controlled the ball for 35 of the game's 60 minutes. In fact, they controlled everything but the final score.

Pisarcik was sacked four times, but he remained relaxed in the pocket, throwing to Tony Woodruff and John Spagnola over the middle, hitting Quick on curls and corner patterns and discreetly dumping off to the running backs.

If Melvin Hoover had not dropped a potential 50-yard touchdown pass in the first half, Pisarcik — not St. Louis kicker Neil O'Donoghue — probably would have been the hero of this game.

"It's my job to come in and play the best I can and help the team to win," Pisarcik said. "This is my 11th year. I think it's expected of me to come in

(See PISARCIK on 6-F)

Joe Pisarcik
After McFadden's missed FG

Jamaican native wins Philadelphia marathon

By Mike Bruton
Inquirer Staff Writer

Ringo Adamson attacked The Hill while those all around him respected it, and that was the key to his winning the Philadelphia Independence Marathon yesterday.

Adamson, a native of Jamaica who lives in Glassboro, N.J., separated himself from a cluster of front-runners just past the 12-mile mark on a torturous incline in Chestnut Hill and held off second-place finisher Geoff Mearns to finish first in 2 hours, 16 minutes, 39 seconds.

Mearns, who came back to challenge Adamson from the 17th through the 21st mile, faltered about 2 miles from the finish line and came in at 2:17:29. Philadelphia's Mike Patterson, the pre-race favorite, was fifth at 2:20:56.

Barbara Filutze, a 38-year-old mother of three from Erie, Pa., was the women's champion with a time of 2:42:30.

The starter's gun started 3,740 runners, roughly 10 percent of them women, on their trek from Temple University's Ambler campus to the finish line at Fifth and Chestnut Streets in downtown Philadelphia.

It was a perfect day for a marathon.

The air was still and crisp, with the temperature climbing into the 50s before the race was over. The Hill was the only adverse element along the picturesque 26-mile, 385-yard course.

Adamson, 24, conquered the mile-long slope that rises 285 feet, even as that slope was intimidating other competitors.

"Everyone gets scared of running those things," said Adamson, who finished 51st in this year's Olympic marathon under the Jamaican flag. "I'm really good at running them. I rustly break people like that."

Adamson, the assistant manager of an athletic footwear store at Deptford Mall, had a mile split of 6:08 on The Hill.

Mearns, a 23-year-old first-year law student at the University of Virginia, fell back about 30 yards, leaving him just ahead of Terry Colton of England, Patterson and Frank Melo of Newark, N.J., on the slope.

"The hill seems to divide the race very quickly," said Mearns, who finished second here in 1982 and fifth last year. "My theory is that you can't win a race like that — on a hill. You

(See MARATHON on 12-F)

Ringo Adamson signals his victory as he reaches the finish line at Fifth and Chestnut

The Philadelphia Inquirer / BRYAN GRIGSBY

Analysis

Flyers soaring at quarter pole

By Al Morganti
Inquirer Staff Writer

Again and again, you hear complaints that the National Hockey League's regular season is meaningless.

Yet when you consider that before Thanksgiving — before the season was a quarter over — coaches had been fired in Vancouver and Minnesota, it becomes clear that the regular season must mean something.

It is especially meaningful in Philadelphia, where the Flyers are trying to use an almost completely restructured team to get back in the hunt for the Stanley Cup.

Although it can be argued that the early season has little bearing on what will happen in April, the young Flyers, rookie coach Mike Keenan and new general manager Bob Clarke done measuring sticks such as the quarter pole (20 games), which they reached with a 4-4 tie in Hartford Saturday night.

With that tie, the Flyers not only extended their unbeaten streak to

(See FLYERS on 9-F)

The Flyers have some surprising statistics after 20 games. Page 4-F.

November 26, 1984
Eagles QB Ron Jaworski snaps his streak of 116 consecutive starts
when he breaks his leg in a loss to St. Louis 17-16

1985

RECORD: 7-9, 4TH IN NFC EAST
HEAD COACH: MARION CAMPBELL
& FRED BRUNEY

Schedule
Regular Season

Wk. 1	Sep 8	L	21-0	at New York Giants
Wk. 2	Sep 15	L	17-6	vs Los Angeles Rams
Wk. 3	Sep 22	W	19-6	at Washington Redskins
Wk. 4	Sep 29	L	16-10	vs New York Giants (OT)
Wk. 5	Oct 6	L	23-21	at New Orleans Saints
Wk. 6	Oct 13	W	30-7	vs St. Louis Cardinals
Wk. 7	Oct 20	W	16-14	vs Dallas Cowboys
Wk. 8	Oct 27	W	21-17	vs Buffalo Bills
Wk. 9	Nov 3	L	24-13	at San Francisco 49ers
Wk. 10	Nov 10	W	23-17	vs Atlanta Falcons (OT)
Wk. 11	Nov 17	W	24-14	at St. Louis Cardinals
Wk. 12	Nov 24	L	34-17	at Dallas Cowboys
Wk. 13	Dec 1	L	28-23	vs Minnesota Vikings
Wk. 14	Dec 8	L	17-12	vs Washington Redskins
Wk. 15	Dec 15	L	20-14	at San Diego Chargers
Wk. 16	Dec 22	W	37-35	at Minnesota Vikings

On March 12, 1985, Leonard Tose, the Eagles owner since 1969, announced an agreement to sell the team to Norman Braman and Ed Leibowitz for a reported $65 million. Braman officially became the Eagles' new owner on April 29 1985. That same day, Braman elevated Harry Gamble, general manager since February 4, to vice president-general manager overseeing day-to-day operations of the club. All-time Eagles rushing leader Wilbert Montgomery did not report to camp and was traded to Detroit for linebacker Garry Cobb in the preseason. Reggie White signed a free-agent contract and ended the season as the NFC Defensive Rookie of the Year. The Eagles would struggle out of the gate again, losing four of their first five games. The Eagles would recover by winning five of their next six games to get into playoff contention. However, a four-game losing streak would end all postseason hopes, and Coach Marion Campbell was fired on December 16. In the final game of the season interim coach Fred Bruney led the Eagles to a win over the Vikings in Minnesota as the Eagles finish with a 7-9 record. Following the season the Eagles named Buddy Ryan, who was the defensive coordinator for the Chicago Bears, as their new Coach. Mike Quick, who caught 71 passes to break his own club season record, and Wes Hopkins represent Philadelphia in the AFC-NFC Pro Bowl.

1985 Philadelphia Eagles Stats

Passing	Comp	Att	Comp %	Yds	Y/Att	TD	Int	Rating
Ron Jaworski	255	484	52.7	3450	7.13	17	20	70.2
Herman Hunter	1	2	50.0	38	19.00	1	0	135.4
Randall Cunningham	34	81	42.0	548	6.77	1	8	29.8

Rushing	Rush	Yds	Avg	TD
Earnest Jackson	282	1028	3.6	5
Michael Haddix	67	213	3.2	0
Randall Cunningham	29	205	7.1	0
Herman Hunter	27	121	4.5	1
Ron Jaworski	17	35	2.1	2
Major Everettt	4	13	3.3	0
Hubie Oliver	1	3	3.0	0

Receiving	Rec	Yds	Avg	TD
Mike Quick	73	1247	17.1	11
John Spagnola	64	772	12.1	5
Michael Haddix	43	330	7.7	0
Kenny Jackson	40	692	17.3	1
Herman Hunter	28	405	14.5	1
Ron Johnson	11	186	16.9	0
Earnest Jackson	10	126	12.6	1
Gregg Garrity	7	142	20.3	0
Dave Little	7	82	11.7	0
Major Everettt	4	25	6.3	0
Keith Baker	2	25	12.5	0
Hubie Oliver	1	4	4.0	0

Interceptions	Int	Yds	Avg	TD
Wes Hopkins	6	36	6.0	1
Ray Ellis	4	32	8.0	0
Herman Edwards	3	8	2.7	1
Evan Cooper	2	13	6.5	0
Rich Kraynak	1	26	26.0	0
Mike Reichenbach	1	10	10.0	0
Roynell Young	1	0	0.0	0
Reggie Wilkes	0	2	0.0	0

Punting	Punts	Yds	Avg	Blocked
Mike Horan	91	3777	41.5	0

Kicking	PAT Made	PAT Att	PAT %	FG Made	FG Att	FG %	Pts
Paul McFadden	29	29	100	25	30	83.3	104

The Philadelphia Inquirer
Sports Extra

section
D

• • Monday, November 11, 1985

Eagles work overtime for 23-17 win

Pelle Lindbergh with his mask, ready for action

A 'Little Swede' with a big heart and a love of life

By Al Morganti
Inquirer Staff Writer

The Stanley Cup seems like a trinket now, the Vezina Trophy nothing more than worthless metal, and sports in general so much trivia.

All that matters now is that Pelle Lindbergh, 26, is brain-dead, connected to a life-support system in a New Jersey hospital.

His beating heart might seem to be caught up in a futile effort, but for those who know Pelle Lindbergh, there can be no doubt that he would give every last push to carry on with life.

It doesn't seem possible that it's over so quickly.

It doesn't seem possible that Lindbergh won't be at practice this morning as usual, dressing in his locker with the little Swedish flag on top, calling people over to look at his latest trinket and then skating onto the ice with his teammates.

It doesn't seem possible that Pelle Lindbergh is likely to soon be only a memory. Of course, his number 31 is likely to hang from the Spectrum's rafters, and his name will remain on the Vezina Trophy that he won as the NHL's best goalie last season.

But to those who know him, Lindbergh is so much more than a goalie. He is a very special person whose love of life made his transition from playing in Sweden to playing in North America as smooth as if he'd grown up in Philadelphia.

Think back to what he means, and the montage is a strange collection of on-the-ice and off-the-ice happenings. On the hockey side, there are the great saves, so many that they run into each other, and the white fiberglass mask that became both his trademark and, literally, his game face.

Away from the rink, there is the memory of Lindbergh at the Flyers' Christmas party, holding hands and skating with his fiancee, Kerstin Pietzsch; the bizarre picture of the Little Swede wearing the floppy cowboy hat at last season's all-star game in Calgary, and the sight of him driving away from practice in his red Porsche.

His love of cars was just another extension of his love of life — a fast, fun life. He wasn't a hard liver, not in the traditional sense. In fact, he hardly drank, and he was far too worried about his health to run around at all hours.

But he did love speed, and he had expensive toys. In addition to his Porsche 930 Turbo, he had a speedboat in Sweden and a collection of miniature toy cars at his home in Marlton.

Ultimately, he found tragedy in his love of driving.

"We warned him about driving too fast," said Flyers general manager Bob Clarke. "I guess I shouldn't say that, I don't know that he drove fast. But with that car and all, we were all worried about him.

"I guess, when you're that young, and that strong, and feel that much on top of the world, I guess you feel invincible. Hey,

(See APPRECIATION on 8-D)

An appreciation

Mike Quick is halted by the Falcons' Wendell Cason after making a first-half pass reception

99-yard pass tops Falcons

By Angelo Cataldi
Inquirer Staff Writer

The Eagles played another game of Russian roulette yesterday at Veterans Stadium and dodged another bullet.

This time, it was the usually lethal left foot of Atlanta kicker Mick Luckhurst that misfired. This time, it was the normally deadly feet of Mike Quick that didn't.

The scoreboard showed a 23-17 overtime victory for the Eagles over the Falcons, but the difference between success and failure in this curious game was more accurately measured in yards than in points.

Luckhurst's potential game-winning field-goal attempt missed the left upright by no more than a couple of tantalizing yards, and safety Scott Case's bid for an interception on the final play of the game fell one straining stride short.

Case's ill-advised gamble permitted Quick to collect a blur of a pass by quarterback Ron Jaworski at about the 20-yard line and then chug 80 free, happy yards to the end zone for a 99-yard touchdown and a victory that squared the Eagles' record at 5-5.

Temporarily obscured in the explosion of cheers by the 63,694 fans after Quick's jaunt was the fact that the Eagles had given away a 17-point fourth-quarter lead — and almost their season — against one of the NFL's sorriest teams.

"We dodged another bullet," nose tackle Kenny Clarke said through a relieved smile. "That's what you've got to do. There are 16 games in a season, and every one's an adventure."

If the end truly justifies the means, then the Eagles probably will rerun the film of that final play until it unravels on the reel. This was survival football at its sweetest — and its most precarious.

There were 13 minutes, 20 seconds remaining in overtime when — on second down from his 1-foot-line — Jaworski dropped back into the end zone and delivered the ball on a timing pattern to Quick, who had slipped between cornerback Bobby Butler and Case up the seam of a zone defense.

When Quick turned to look upfield after collecting the ball, he already knew what he would see there. Nothing.

"I knew there was no stopping me unless I tripped and fell," he said. "I knew I had them."

"The safety went for it," Jaworski said. "Maybe he thought I was too old to throw it like that anymore."

And so it was that the Eagles posted the first overtime victory in their history and once again rescued their hopes of making the playoffs.

(See EAGLES on 4-D)

Earnest Jackson
Rushed for 74 yards

Eagles forced to go the distance by yet another 'patsy' opponent

By FRANK DOLSON

Sports editor

The good news for the fainthearted among Eagles rooters is that their heroes have no more "patsies" to play, no more "sure victories" on their National Football League schedule.

Two weeks ago, hosting a Buffalo team that had won only one game, the Eagles didn't start playing until they were 17 points down in the final quarter, and they barely managed to pull out a 21-17 victory.

Yesterday, against an Atlanta team that had won only one game, the Eagles stopped playing in the fourth quarter, blew a 17-point lead, and came within a few feet of having the game, and their season, slip away

from them.

There would be an incredible climax to what had all the makings of a monumental collapse, a 99-yard, Ron Jaworski-to-Mike Quick touchdown pass in the second minute of overtime. But as spectacular as that goal-

(See DOLSON on 5-D)

NFL results

Dallas	13	Washington	7
Cincinnati	27	Cleveland	10
Chicago	24	Detroit	3
Green Bay	38	Minnesota	17
Buffalo	20	Houston	0
New England	34	Indianapolis	15
New York Giants	24	Los Angeles Rams	19
Pittsburgh	30	Kansas City	28
Tampa Bay	16	St. Louis	0
Seattle	27	New Orleans	3
San Diego	40	L. A. Raiders	34
Miami	21	New York Jets	17

Detailed NFL coverage begins on Page 5-D

Determined Malone scores 35 to lift Sixers to 105-97 win over Bucks

The Sixers observing a moment of silence for goalie Pelle Lindbergh before last night's game

By Mike Bruton
Inquirer Staff Writer

The Sixers won last night, in large part because Moses Malone wanted to win.

But there were other reasons why the 76ers, a team that seemed to be bent on self-destruction Friday night in a humiliating loss to San Antonio, defeated the Milwaukee Bucks, 105-97, before a crowd of 10,090 in the Spectrum.

One of them was Milwaukee forward Terry Cummings' failure to score in double figures for the first time since he entered the league in 1982-83.

Because of Charles Barkley's defense, with help off the bench from Terry Catledge, Cummings played like a man who had wandered into the building

Cummings' six-point effort snapped a 239-game streak of double-digit scoring. He had been second in that category to the Lakers' Kareem Abdul-Jabbar, who has 624 straight games with 10 or more points.

Another reason was Julius Erving's ability to neutralize Milwaukee point forward Paul Pressey.

There was a stirring of emotion in the Sixers' locker room before the game. Obviously, they were upset about Friday's 107-95 loss to San Antonio, but they also had Flyers goalie Pelle Lindbergh on their minds.

Lindbergh had been listed as brain-dead after suffering multiple injuries in an automobile crash at 5:41 a.m. yesterday in Somerdale, N.J.

"It wasn't a good day for all of Philadelphia, including myself," said Erving, who had 20 points, 12 rebounds, 3 assists and 3 steals. "We

were very, very quiet before we went out. Our hearts go out to the Flyers because it's a genuine sports tragedy."

Against the Bucks, the Sixers were at their predatory best, protecting the lane and scoring 17 points off 18 steals.

The Sixers' defense fueled the offense, and they run the fastbreak the way coach Matt Guokas had hoped they would in every game.

It all started with Malone, who set a relentless pace from the start of the game.

The Sixers center had 25 points and 12 rebounds at halftime and finished with 35 points and 14 boards.

Malone, who used Milwaukee centers Alton Lister, Paul Mokeski and Randy Breuer like props in a personal highlight film, had 15 points in

(See SIXERS on 3-D)

November 11, 1985
Eagles win their first overtime win in team history against Atlanta 23-17.
Jaworski hits Quick with a 99-yard TD reception, tying the longest TD in NFL history.

1986

RECORD: 5-10-1, 4TH IN NFC EAST
HEAD COACH: BUDDY RYAN

Schedule
Regular Season

Wk. 1	Sep 7	L	41-14	at Washington Redskins
Wk. 2	Sep 14	L	13-10	at Chicago Bears (OT)
Wk. 3	Sep 21	L	33-7	vs Denver Broncos
Wk. 4	Sep 28	W	34-20	vs Los Angeles Rams
Wk. 5	Oct 5	W	16-0	at Atlanta Falcons
Wk. 6	Oct 12	L	35-3	at New York Giants
Wk. 7	Oct 19	L	17-14	vs Dallas Cowboys
Wk. 8	Oct 26	W	23-7	vs San Diego Chargers
Wk. 9	Nov 2	L	13-10	at St. Louis Cardinals
Wk. 10	Nov 9	L	17-14	vs New York Giants
Wk. 11	Nov 16	L	13-11	vs Detroit Lions
Wk. 12	Nov 23	L	24-20	at Seattle Seahawks
Wk. 13	Nov 30	W	33-27	at Los Angeles Raiders (OT)
Wk. 14	Dec 7	T	10-10	vs St. Louis Cardinals (OT)
Wk. 15	Dec 14	W	23-21	at Dallas Cowboys
Wk. 16	Dec 21	L	21-14	vs Washington Redskins

Buddy Ryan, defensive coordinator of the Chicago Bears' Super Bowl XX Champions, was named the seventeenth head coach in Eagles history on January 29, 1986. On July 16, Norman Braham became the sole owner of the team, purchasing the remaining 35 percent from his brother-in-law Ed Leibowitz. Harry Gamble was promoted to president-chief operating officer. Ryan made sweeping changes in the Eagles roster, keeping young players and releasing several veterans. The youthful Birds struggle to a 5-10-1 record against the toughest schedule in the league. One highlight of the season was the play of second-year quarterback Randall Cunningham, who became a double threat with his throwing arm and his scrambling abilities; Cunningham took the starting job away from Ron Jaworski. The Birds placed two players on the AFC-NFC Pro Bowl roster: wide receiver Mike Quick and defensive end Reggie White. White tied a Pro Bowl record with four sacks and was named MVP of the game.

1986 Philadelphia Eagles Stats

Passing	Comp	Att	Comp %	Yds	Y/Att	TD	Int	Rating
Randall Cunningham	111	209	53.1	1391	6.66	8	7	72.9
Ron Jaworski	128	245	52.2	1405	5.73	8	6	70.2
Keith Byars	1	2	50.0	55	27.50	1	0	135.4
Matt Cavanaugh	28	58	48.3	397	6.84	2	4	53.6

Rushing	Rush	Yds	Avg	TD
Keith Byars	177	577	3.3	1
Randall Cunningham	66	540	8.2	5
Anthony Toney	69	285	4.1	1
Michael Haddix	79	276	3.5	0
Junior Tautalatasi	51	163	3.2	0
Charles Crawford	28	88	3.1	1
Ron Jaworski	13	33	2.5	0
Matt Cavanaugh	9	26	2.9	0
Mike Waters	5	8	1.6	0
Kenny Jackson	1	6	6.0	0
John Teltschik	1	0	0.0	0

Receiving	Rec	Yds	Avg	TD
Mike Quick	60	939	15.7	9
Junior Tautalatasi	41	325	7.9	2
John Spagnola	39	397	10.2	1
Kenny Jackson	30	506	16.9	6
Michael Haddix	26	150	5.8	0
Dave Little	14	132	9.4	0
Anthony Toney	13	177	13.6	0
Gregg Garrity	12	227	18.9	0
Ron Johnson	11	207	18.8	1
Keith Byars	11	44	4.0	0
Phil Smith	6	94	15.7	0
Mike Waters	2	27	13.5	0
Byron Darby	2	16	8.0	0
Bobby Duckworth	1	7	7.0	0

Interceptions	Int	Yds	Avg	TD
Andre Waters	6	39	6.5	0
Roynell Young	6	9	1.5	0
Alonzo Johnson	3	6	2.0	0
Terry Hoage	1	18	18.0	0
Elbert Foules	1	14	14.0	0
Jody Schulz	1	11	11.0	0
Seth Joyner	1	4	4.0	0
Garry Cobb	1	3	3.0	0
Evan Cooper	0	3	0.0	20

Punting	Punts	Yds	Avg	Blocked
John Teltschik	108	4493	41.6	0
Randall Cunningham	2	54	27.0	0

Kicking	PAT Made	PAT Att	PAT %	FG Made	FG Att	FG %	Pts
Paul McFadden	26	27	96	20	31	64.5	86

1986

The Philadelphia Inquirer

Sports Extra

section D

♦ ♦ ♦ ♦ Monday, October 6, 1986

Eagles make Falcons shutout victims

The Philadelphia Inquirer / JOHN PAUL FILO

Von Hayes signs autographs for fans before the game at the Vet.

The Philadelphia Inquirer / GREG LANIER

Mike Quick hauls in a pass from Ron Jaworski over Atlanta's Scott Case in the third quarter.

TD catch by Quick sets tone

By Angelo Cataldi
Inquirer Staff Writer

ATLANTA — As Mike Quick twisted his body away from the defender and stretched his left arm to its fullest extension, only his fingertips were able to touch the fading football on its flight through the end zone.

But then an amazing thing happened yesterday at Atlanta-Fulton County Stadium. The ball stuck. It didn't bounce away, it didn't slither off and it didn't flop to the ground in a cloud of dust and distress.

This time, neither the chance for a miraculous play nor the opportunity for a magnificent victory would slip through the fingers of an Eagles team that had a score to settle with the Atlanta Falcons — and settled it with this remarkable score: 16-0.

The victory was the second in a row for the Eagles after three losses, and it was their first shutout since a 38-0 win against St. Louis on Dec. 20, 1981. Atlanta, which had the top-rated offense in the NFL before the game — but certainly not after it — lost its first contest of the season.

Yet this was a game to be measured not by statistics so much as by snippets of action that suggested a startling change in fortune — and in perspective — for an Eagles franchise that has languished through four consecutive losing seasons.

It was a contest to be remembered for linebacker Garry Cobb's four stampeding sacks, halfback Junior Tautalatasi's daring 56-yard dance through the Atlanta secondary, quarterback Ron Jaworski's precise spirals and — above all — Quick's magical catch.

The game was scoreless late in the second quarter, and the Eagles were 8 tantalizing yards from the Atlanta goal line when Jaworski uncorked an arching toss toward Quick, who had cut to the middle of the field and then hooked back toward the right sideline.

There was no conceivable way for Quick to control the ball on his fingertips, pull it into his body and then land on the ground without jarring it loose. But Quick snatched it with his left hand, tucked it into his midsection and then landed with a roll that shielded the ball from his impact with the clumpy turf.

"I knew I had a chance to get my hand on the ball," Quick said, "and once I got it there, it stuck. It just stuck. I think that was one of the best catches I've ever made."

"When Mike makes a catch like that, all I can do is shake my head," said fellow wide receiver Ron John-

(See EAGLES on 4-D)

Phils cap season by beating Expos

By Peter Pascarelli
Inquirer Staff Writer

The Final Day passed with some personal goals unrealized, but the big picture remained rosy for the Phillies.

The Phils ended the 1986 season with a yawn-filled 2-1 win in 10 innings yesterday over the Montreal Expos. That left the Phils with an 86-75 record, the first time all season they were 11 games over .500.

A crowd of 25,293 left the Phils with a season home attendance of 1,933,335.

"I think we're all very satisfied with the way things went," said manager John Felske, who earlier yesterday received a contract extension through 1988.

"At no time could anyone question the players' effort," he said, "even when we didn't play well. And I think it will be exciting to look at ways to make us better over the winter, because a lot of our people are just going to get better."

If there was any disappointment yesterday, it was the failure of Von Hayes and Mike Schmidt to meet personal goals.

Hayes fell 2 RBIs short of 100, his big chance coming in the sixth inning, when he popped up with the bases loaded.

"I wanted the 100 RBIs, no doubt about it," said Hayes, who finished his magnificent season with a .305 average, 19 homers, 98 RBIs, 107 runs scored (tied for the league lead) and 46 doubles (a league high).

"But you have to give that Expos pitcher [Bob] Sebra credit. He had four pitches, and he would throw you off-speed stuff when behind in the count.

"I feel good about the season. Before opening day, I set my goal as driving in between 80 and 100 runs, and next year I'm going to raise my sights. . . . And the biggest thing was that we finished [11] games over .500. I think that makes it a successful year and an indication that we're a good team that is going to get better."

Meanwhile, Schmidt, who did not start yesterday, popped up in his only at-bat. He fell 2 RBIs short of equaling his career high of 121, finishing the year with a .290 average and with league-leading totals in homers (37) and RBIs (119). Those are numbers that likely are good enough for him to win his third Most Valuable Player award.

"I feel I have a good shot at MVP," Schmidt said. "I just came into today with nothing left. I just couldn't grind it out anymore, so it didn't make sense to play. I'm also unhappy with the way I hit the last week or so of the season, when I wanted to put up some more numbers. . . . But the year ends with the definite feeling that this team is very close to being right up there. I don't think the Mets are any better than the Phillies right now, but over 162 games they obviously were."

A big part of the Phils' strong second half and their optimism for next year was Bruce Ruffin, who yesterday pitched nine innings without a decision in his final start, allowing one run and eight hits.

"Winning nine games in a little over half of a season is pretty satisfying," Ruffin said. "If I can come out of spring training strong . . . I think winning 20 games could be a realistic goal for me."

Ruffin was nicked for a second-

(See PHILLIES on 3-D)

Bad start, promising ending

By Peter Pascarelli
Inquirer Staff Writer

Months ago such a news conference had seemed impossible. But yesterday in a final-day affirmation of the Phillies' 1986 success, club president Bill Giles announced the following developments:

• As expected, manager John Felske has had his contract extended through the 1988 season, and all five of the Phils' coaches — Lee Elia, Jim Davenport, Del Unser, Claude Osteen and Mike Ryan — have been rehired for next season.

• While Giles acknowledged that the Phils' catching was "not what it should be," he said he believed the club must improve that position from within rather than try to deal for an established catcher.

• The Phillies would like an established starting pitcher and a left-handed reliever and will seek them through trades and possibly the free-agent market. But Giles added, "I don't anticipate making a lot of deals because at least this year I don't think we have a lot we can afford to trade."

In that vein, Giles later added, "We have four players in Schmidt, Hayes, Samuel and Wilson who we will not

(See SEASON on 3-D)

On Atlanta's sideline, Campbell couldn't hide his frustrations

By FRANK DOLSON

Sports editor

ATLANTA — He came out onto the field at the last possible minute, presumably to avoid any emotional pregame hellos, and when it was over, after his old team, the Eagles, had shocked his present team, the Falcons, 16-0, and a parade of winners had come over to shake his hand and wish him luck, Marion Campbell was the first man to dash out of the Atlanta locker room.

But it wasn't necessary to talk to him yesterday to sense how much he wanted to win this game, how badly he wanted to beat Buddy Ryan, Ron Jaworski and the rest of the guys in green.

Normally, the man who was head coach of the Philadelphia Eagles through two full seasons and 15 games of a third isn't the demonstrative type.

"Marion, as you all know, likes to do all his talking and performing on the field," said Atlanta linebacker Reggie Wilkes, another longtime wearer of the green. "He doesn't try to get involved in the pregame hype or the postgame hype. He deserves a lot of credit and a lot of respect. He's a class act, whatever adjective you want to use. He's a good man."

And yesterday, on a rare October

(See DOLSON on 4-D)

Pro football

Washington	14	New Orleans	6
Chicago	23	Minnesota	0
New England	34	Miami	7
New York Giants	13	St. Louis	6
Cleveland	27	Pittsburgh	24
Detroit	24	Houston	13
Cincinnati	34	Green Bay	28
L.A. Raiders	24	Kansas City	17
Denver	29	Dallas	14
San Francisco	35	Indianapolis	14
New York Jets	14	Buffalo	13
L.A. Rams	26	Tampa Bay	20

Roy Hinson

A 7-footer in a 6-9 body

Hinson has the right stuff to avoid disappearing in Barkley's shadow

By Mike Bruton
Inquirer Staff Writer

LANCASTER — When you play alongside Charles Barkley, anonymity can become a formidable opponent.

You might as well have the word *FORWARD* stitched across the back of your jersey.

If, perchance, fans are curious, they can look you up in the game program to discover that your first name is "Other."

Bobby Jones, now retired, had no problem with that situation. He preferred keeping a low profile.

Jones' likely replacement, a pleasant man, also is not one to grapple for recognition. But it may take more than playing opposite Barkley to keep him from being noticed.

Roy Hinson is listed as being 6 feet, 9 inches tall, but he is all arms and legs, and he looks — and plays — more like a 7-footer.

When he spreads his arms in the lane, he casts an imposing shadow on any point guard looking to get the ball inside. Getting a pass by him must be like trying to throw the ball by a windmill.

The 25-year-old Trenton native is the type of player who makes opposing shooters hesitate before pulling the trigger, wondering, "Where is Hinson?" for they know they could end up with the word *Spalding* imprinted on their foreheads.

Hinson runs well, soars fluidly, scores when called on and rebounds. He is sinewy and as strong as

(See SIXERS on 8-D)

Sails are hoisted Down Under to spar for the Auld Mug

By Al Morganti
Inquirer Staff Writer

FREMANTLE, Australia — The walls of the Auld Mug Tavern on High Street are lined with pictures of J-boats, sloops and sleek 12-meter yachts that have raced for past America's Cups, but crew members aren't allowed to arm-wrestle in the pub anymore.

They still have some lively arguments about what kind of keel is going to work best in the slop and chop of the Indian Ocean, whether the vicious wind called The Doctor will blow anybody overboard, and if New Zealand really has a shot with its fiberglass boats.

The crew members can argue all they want, but arm-wrestling is taboo.

The end of that tradition, which used to settle many an argument, was sounded with a loud *snap* during the 12-meter world championships here in February. It was during those races that a winch-grinder from New Zealand broke the arm of one of his counterparts from Australia.

Some people are wondering if the tradition would have been ended if the Aussie had broken the New Zealander's arm. But that's a moot point — this is the Australians' show.

The Aussies rule the waves. So, until they lose, it's Aussie rules.

Technically, this will be the 26th defense of the America's Cup. But down here, the Americans' 132-year hold on the Cup seems to have been erased from memory, and the competition, which began yesterday, is being billed as "Australia's First Defence."

This isn't Newport, and the Americans — especially the New York Yacht Club — are given no special treatment. All right, so maybe the Aussies are looking at the Yanks as their biggest threat, but there are no guarantees that an American boat will even reach the finals.

In all probability, one of the six American teams will match up with an Australian defender in the best-of-seven America's Cup races, which are scheduled to begin Jan. 31.

But until then, the Americans have just five entries among 13 from six countries that will attempt to earn the right to challenge for the Cup. The Australians will run a simultaneous series to choose a defender.

Within the Auld Mug Tavern, there is some disagreement about which American team could come out on top. The opinion is split between America II, which is the entry of the venerable New York Yacht Club, and Stars & Stripes '87, which has Dennis Conner, now sailing for the San Diego Yacht Club, at the helm.

Conner, who won the Auld Mug as

(See CUP on 10-D)

Index

Australia's Pat Cash defeated Brad Gilbert in four sets to give his country an insurmountable lead over the United States in the Davis Cup semifinals. Sports in brief, Page 8-D.

Penn State's offense has been more imaginative than last year's. Page 7-D.

Baseball	2-D
Eagles notes	4-D
College football	7-D
High schools	8-D
Horse racing	8-D
Sixers notes	8-D
Golf	10-D

October 6, 1986
Eagles defeat Atlanta 16-0
for their first shutout since 1981

1987

RECORD: 7-8, 4TH IN NFC EAST
HEAD COACH: BUDDY RYAN

Schedule
Regular Season

Wk. 1	Sep 13	L	34-24	at Washington Redskins
Wk. 2	Sep 20	W	27-17	vs New Orleans Saints
Wk. 4	Oct 4	L	35-3	vs Chicago Bears
Wk. 5	Oct 11	L	41-22	at Dallas Cowboys
Wk. 6	Oct 18	L	16-10	at Green Bay Packers (OT)
Wk. 7	Oct 25	W	37-20	vs Dallas Cowboys
Wk. 8	Nov 1	W	28-23	at St. Louis Cardinals
Wk. 9	Nov 8	W	31-27	vs Washington Redskins
Wk. 10	Nov 15	L	20-17	vs New York Giants
Wk. 11	Nov 22	L	31-19	vs St. Louis Cardinals
Wk. 12	Nov 29	W	34-31	at New England Patriots (OT)
Wk. 13	Dec 6	L	23-20	at New York Giants (OT)
Wk. 14	Dec 13	L	28-10	vs Miami Dolphins
Wk. 15	Dec 20	W	38-27	at New York Jets
Wk. 16	Dec 27	W	17-7	vs Buffalo Bills

In March, quarterback Ron Jaworski was put on waivers after the club decided not to guarantee his contract. The Eagles split their first two games before a NFL players' strike led to the use of replacement players. The Eagles replacement team was not even competitive, losing all three games, to put the Eagles into a 1-4 hole. Making matters worse, the Cowboys regulars who crossed the picket line rolled up to score in a 41-22 humiliation in Dallas. The Eagles would get revenge in a 37-20 win when the regulars returned at the Vet. The Eagles would go on to finish with a 7-8 record, as the regulars went 7-5. Offensively, wide receiver Mike Quick earned his fifth consecutive trip to the AFC-NFC Pro Bowl while quarterback Randall Cunningham (Pro Bowl first alternate) emerged as a rising talent. Cunningham threw 23 touchdown passes and became the first quarterback to lead his team in rushing (505 yards) since the Bears' Bobby Douglass did so in 1972. Defensive end Reggie White, who was named the NFL's defensive player of the year, led the defense. White's 21 sacks set an NFC record and fell one shy of the NFL mark.

1987 Philadelphia Eagles Stats

Passing	Comp	Att	Comp %	Yds	Y/Att	TD	Int	Rating
Randall Cunningham	223	406	54.9	2786	6.86	23	12	83.0
Scott Tinsley	48	86	55.8	637	7.41	3	4	71.7
Marty Horn	5	11	45.5	68	6.18	0	0	65.7
Guido Merkens	7	14	50.0	70	5.00	0	0	64.6
Anthony Toney	0	1	0.0	0	0.00	0	0	39.6
Cris Carter	0	1	0.0	0	0.00	0	0	39.6
Otis Grant	0	1	0.0	0	0.00	0	0	39.6

Rushing	Rush	Yds	Avg	TD
Randall Cunningham	76	505	6.6	3
Anthony Toney	127	473	3.7	5
Keith Byars	116	426	3.7	3
Michael Haddix	59	165	2.8	0
Reggie Brown	39	136	3.5	0
Jacque Robinson	24	114	4.8	0
Junior Tautalatasi	26	69	2.7	0
Alvin Ross	14	54	3.9	1
John Teltschik	3	32	10.7	0
Kenny Jackson	6	27	4.5	0
Otis Grant	1	20	20.0	0
Bobby Morse	6	14	2.3	0
Scott Tinsley	4	2	0.5	0
Topper Clemons	3	0	0.0	0
Marty Horn	1	0	0.0	0
Matt Cavanaugh	1	-2	-2.0	0
Guido Merkens	3	-8	-2.7	0

Receiving	Rec	Yds	Avg	TD
Mike Quick	46	790	17.2	11
Anthony Toney	39	341	8.7	1
John Spagnola	36	350	9.7	2
Junior Tautalatasi	25	176	7.0	0
Kenny Jackson	21	471	22.4	3
Keith Byars	21	177	8.4	1
Otis Grant	16	280	17.5	0
Gregg Garrity	12	242	20.2	2
Mike Siano	9	137	15.2	1
Eric Bailey	8	69	8.6	0
Reggie Brown	8	53	6.6	0
Jimmie Giles	7	95	13.6	1
Michael Haddix	7	58	8.3	0
Kevin Bowman	6	127	21.2	1
Cris Carter	5	84	16.8	2
Jay Repko	5	46	9.2	0
Alvin Ross	5	41	8.2	0
Jacque Robinson	2	9	4.5	0
Topper Clemons	1	13	13.0	1
Dave Little	1	8	8.0	0
Bobby Morse	1	8	8.0	0
Randall Cunningham	1	-3	-3.0	0
Reggie Singletary	1	-11	-11.0	0

Interceptions	Int	Yds	Avg	TD
Elbert Foules	4	6	1.5	0
Andre Waters	3	63	21.0	0
Seth Joyner	2	42	21.0	0
Michael Kullman	2	25	12.5	0
Jerome Brown	2	7	3.5	0
Terry Hoage	2	3	1.5	0
Evan Cooper	2	0	0.0	0
Roynell Young	1	30	30.0	0
Byron Evans	1	12	12.0	0
Cedrick Brown	1	9	9.0	0
Troy West	1	0	0.0	0

Punting	Punts	Yds	Avg	Blocked
Mark Royals	5	209	41.8	0
John Teltschik	82	3131	38.2	0
Dave Jacobs	10	369	36.9	0
Guido Merkens	2	61	30.5	0

Kicking	PAT Made	PAT Att	PAT %	FG Made	FG Att	FG %	Pts
Paul McFadden	36	36	100	16	26	61.5	84
Dave Jacobs	2	4	50	3	5	60.0	11

The Philadelphia Inquirer
Sports Extra
section C
Monday, October 5, 1987

Ersatz Eagles lay an embarrassing egg

The Philadelphia Inquirer / CLEM MURRAY

Guido Merkens fumbles after being hit by Jim Althoff for one of Chicago's 11 sacks. Merkens, who was sacked 10 times, recovered.

Replacement Bears romp to 35-3 victory

By Bill Ordine
Inquirer Staff Writer

When Eagles owner Norman Braman promised "good" and "competitive" football in the NFL's replacement games, most folks knew enough to snicker at the "good" part but conceded that there probably would be a measure of competitiveness between equally ragged and ill-prepared teams.

Yesterday, however, it was evident that there are degrees of ragged and ill-prepared. Beyond bad, there is worse. Beyond worse, there is worst. And beyond worst, there are the replacement Philadelphia Eagles.

In the slapstick farce that unfolded in the empty cavern of Veterans Stadium yesterday, the only thing missing was Guido Merkens, the backup quarterback and sometime punter, getting hit in the face by a custard pie as the inept Eagles fill-ins were mauled by the fill-in Bears, 35-3.

The last time anyone saw a bunch of guys take as many pratfalls as the Eagles did yesterday, Mack Sennett was coaching the Keystone Kops.

In a game featuring two teams that had practiced for all of 10 days, it wasn't surprising to see a punt blocked, a high snap out of shotgun formation produce a loss of 32 yards and the ball, and an improvised run out of punt formation lose 9 yards. What was surprising is that all of that happened to just one team — the Eagles.

And there was more:

• The Eagles gave up 11 sacks for 70 yards. Merkens took 10 of those sacks.

• Yellow flags were falling like — well, like Guido Merkens — as Philadelphia was penalized 11 times.

• The Eagles fumbled five times, losing the ball on two of those occasions, and averaged 2.2 yards per

(See EAGLES on 4-C)

Strike Sunday: A day for losers

By FRANK DOLSON

Sports editor

You've heard it said time and time again: Nobody wins in a strike. That may be true, but seldom have we seen as many losers as turned up yesterday at Veterans Stadium.

It wasn't just the strikebreaking team disguised as the Philadelphia Eagles who lost, and lost big, to a strikebreaking team disguised as the Chicago Bears. That alone would have been no big deal.

It wasn't just Buddy Ryan, coach of the green-and-white-shirted, red-faced squad that came out on the short end of a 35-3 score (not that surprising when you consider he spent much of the week making fun of his players), who lost, and lost big.

It wasn't just the National Football League, which decided it was more important to play these games with makeshift teams and count them in the standings than to consider the best interests of the fans and the integrity of the sport, that lost, and lost big.

Sadly, the biggest loser on this day may have been the City of Philadelphia, its image battered and beaten every bit as badly as Buddy Ryan's bogus and bewildered Birds.

Surely, the lasting image of this miserable excuse for a football game will be that televised one of a fan walking out of the Vet — and smack dab into a sucker punch thrown by one of the union types who massed outside the stadium.

It was a day on which Norman Braman, the owner of the Eagles,

(See DOLSON on 5-C)

Pro football

				Attendance
Chicago	35	EAGLES	3	4,074
Tampa Bay	31	DETROIT	27	4,919
LOS ANGELES RAIDERS	35	Kansas City	17	7,500
Indianapolis	47	BUFFALO	6	9,860
Dallas	38	NEW YORK JETS	24	12,370
Green Bay	23	MINNESOTA	16	13,911
Cleveland	20	NEW ENGLAND	10	14,830
Pittsburgh	28	ATLANTA	12	16,667
San Diego	10	CINCINNATI	9	18,074
SEATTLE	24	Miami	20	19,448
WASHINGTON	28	St. Louis	21	27,728
NEW ORLEANS	37	Los Angeles Rams	10	28,745
Houston	40	DENVER	10	38,494

Home team in CAPITALS.

Report: Union ready to end strike

From Inquirer Wire Services

Player representatives from the 28 NFL teams are scheduled to meet tonight in Chicago amid growing speculation that the NFL Players Association soon will ask striking players to return to work.

Quoting unnamed union sources, yesterday's Daily Breeze in Torrance, Calif., reported that the NFLPA would announce today or tomorrow that it was dropping its demands for free agency and would ask players to return to their teams.

The sources told the paper that the union's decision to drop free agency as an issue in the 13-day strike was prompted by the massive defection of players who crossed picket lines on Friday and the threat of entire teams crossing this week. Eighty-six players have crossed the picket lines so far.

"Teams in as many as seven cities have told the union they will come across en masse this week unless free agency is dropped and bargaining resumes," one of the sources said.

Members of the Cleveland Browns, San Francisco 49ers and Los Angeles Raiders all have mentioned the possibility of having their teams cross picket lines after this weekend's games.

NFLPA executive director Gene Upshaw said that the meeting would be an attempt to get the stalled negotiations started again.

"We have to do something to get the parties to negotiate," he said. "Gene Upshaw has never represented his view, but represented the players. If the players change their mind, it's Gene Upshaw's job to change his mind.

"The player reps will determine tomorrow what we do. The majority will rule. . . . We have to do what's good for all of us."

Doug Allen, the union's assistant director, said that the fact that a meeting was being called did not mean that the union was going to concede anything.

"There is no plan to throw in the towel, no plan to go back to work without a contract," Allen said. "It's going to take good-faith negotiations

(See STRIKE on 7-C)

Afleet tops Lost Code in Derby

By Don Clippinger
Inquirer Staff Writer

Afleet, seemingly beaten in Philadelphia Park's stretch, found another gear yesterday and roared back to defeat Lost Code by 2¼ lengths in the $300,000 Pennsylvania Derby.

Afleet, ridden by Gary Stahlbaum, had matched strides with Arlington Classic winner Lost Code almost from the start. But Afleet fell back on the Bucks County track's final turn and handed Lost Code a 2½-length lead in midstretch.

The Pennsylvania Derby appeared to be over as the two front-runners headed toward the wire. But Afleet kicked in and surged again, blasting past Lost Code with 100 yards left to run and drawing away to the wire.

Although the early fractions were relatively slow, Afleet completed the Pennsylvania Derby's 1⅛ miles in a stakes record 1 minute, 48 1/5 sec-

(See DERBY on 10-C)

Index

Baseball	2-C
Phillies notes	3-C
NFL	6-C
College football	8-C
Flyers	9-C
Sports in brief	10-C
High schools	10-C
Horse racing	10-C
Golf	12-C

The Cards' Ozzie Smith doesn't have much size, and he doesn't have *any* home runs. The question is, should that make any difference?

United Press International

The case for Ozzie as MVP

By Jayson Stark
Inquirer Staff Writer

ST. LOUIS — He stands 5-foot-11. And he weighs 160 pounds. And if you stood him up next to Andre Dawson, he would look practically like Emmanuel Lewis.

Well, Ozzie Smith knows that people who are built like the star of Webster haven't won a whole lot of MVP awards. He also knows that people who go two years without hitting a home run haven't won a whole lot of MVP awards. He also knows that people who are famous mostly for their defensive acrobatics haven't won a whole lot of MVP awards.

But there's a funny thing going on. An increasing number of people think that the most valuable player in the National League this year just might be none other than Osborne Earl Smith, diminutive and homerless and glove-oriented as he might be.

His manager, Whitey Herzog, is now branding the Wizard "a very bona fide candidate." In fact, the manager is boosting Smith's candidacy these days more than the candidacy of Jack Clark — the man who was the clear-cut MVP of the first four months but only the Amelia Earhart of the last two.

And remember, the manager made a big case for Smith as the MVP in 1982, when he was just a .248-hitting leatherworker. Herzog's premise in those days was that Ozzie Smith stopped 100 runs a year with that Gold Glove of his, and heck, that was the same as knocking in 100, right?

Now here we are five years later, and he still stops as many runs as ever. But in case you hadn't noticed, Ozzie Smith doesn't just play defense anymore.

He possesses the eighth-highest batting average (.303) in the National League. And is second

(See OZZIE SMITH on 4-C)

Tigers edge Jays, rejoice over title

By Angelo Cataldi
Inquirer Staff Writer

DETROIT — While the Detroit Tigers charged onto the field in a stampede of arm-waving hysteria late yesterday afternoon, the Toronto Blue Jays stood transfixed in their dugout, unable to remove their gaze from the celebration.

After seven memorable games in 11 tense days, the emotions finally drained from both teams in that one final tableau — whoops and high fives and hugs among the winners, tears and trauma and introspection among the losers.

Every season provides a similiar scene at the end of a long, taut pennant race, but yesterday's 1-0 victory by the Tigers offered an especially vivid illustration of what it feels like to succeed, and also to fail.

"This is the best moment, the biggest moment, of my career in baseball," said Detroit manager Sparky Anderson, whose team overcame a 3½-game deficit in the final eight days of the season to win the American League East championship. "I said all year that I was proudest of this team because they gave me everything I asked, everything they had."

"You can't undo what happened," Toronto manager Jimy Williams said

(See TIGERS on 3-C)

Phillies lose, 4-2, to end season on a dismal note

By Peter Pascarelli
Inquirer Staff Writer

PITTSBURGH — During the Phillies' disheartening finish, Lee Elia resisted the temptation to emphatically enforce his will upon an often listless ball club.

But before the Phils' sorry 1987 season ended with them tied for fourth place after yesterday's 4-2 loss to the Pittsburgh Pirates, Elia made it clear that the team's lackluster season-ending play did not go unnoticed. He also said that what the Phils will need in a big way in 1988 is something called character.

"The most important thing I'd like to see is this club develop a sense of character, a sense of team," Elia said. "I've seen it at times, but I've also seen it disappear at times too.

"We simply have to get away from the singular approach to everything that has been too prevalent around here. I don't think our club has an understanding of what you call constructive criticism. Everything is taken too personally.

"It's nice to know you're good, but

(See PHILLIES on 3-C)

October 5, 1987
Eagles replacement players are embarrassed by Chicago Bears 35-3

1987

1988

RECORD: 10-6, 1ST IN NFC EAST
HEAD COACH: BUDDY RYAN

Schedule

Regular Season

Wk. 1	Sep 4	W	41-14	at Tampa Bay Buccaneers
Wk. 2	Sep 11	L	28-24	vs Cincinnati Bengals
Wk. 3	Sep 18	L	17-10	at Washington Redskins
Wk. 4	Sep 25	L	23-21	at Minnesota Vikings
Wk. 5	Oct 2	W	32-23	vs Houston Oilers
Wk. 6	Oct 10	W	24-13	vs New York Giants
Wk. 7	Oct 16	L	19-3	at Cleveland Browns
Wk. 8	Oct 23	W	24-23	vs Dallas Cowboys
Wk. 9	Oct 30	L	27-24	vs Atlanta Falcons
Wk. 10	Nov 6	W	30-24	vs Los Angeles Rams
Wk. 11	Nov 13	W	27-26	at Pittsburgh Steelers
Wk. 12	Nov 20	W	23-17	at New York Giants (OT)
Wk. 13	Nov 27	W	31-21	vs Phoenix Cardinals
Wk. 14	Dec 4	L	20-19	vs Washington Redskins
Wk. 15	Dec 10	W	23-17	at Phoenix Cardinals
Wk. 16	Dec 18	W	23-7	at Dallas Cowboys

Post Season

Divisional Playoffs

	Dec 31	L	20-12	at Chicago Bears

Under third-year head coach Buddy Ryan; the Eagles would get off to a slow start losing 3 straight after winning their season opener. The Eagles would continue to play mediocre football until the middle of the season when they sat at 4-5. However, the Eagles would catch fire winning 6 of their final 7 games to capture the NFC East with a 10-6 record. Driving the Eagles Division Title run is QB Randall Cunningham who passes 3,808 yards and adds 624 yards with his legs. However, in the Divisional Playoffs the Eagles traveled to Chicago for an NFC Divisional Playoff game against the Bears and a place in NFL history. The game, which begins in sunny, 29-degree weather, would later be dubbed "The Fog Bowl," after a thick fog rolls off Lake Michigan late in the 2nd quarter. Due to the fog, visibility on the playing field was extremely difficult and the Bears prevail, 20-12.

1988 Philadelphia Eagles Stats

Passing	Comp	Att	Comp %	Yds	Y/Att	TD	Int	Rating
Randall Cunningham	301	560	53.8	3808	6.80	24	16	77.6
Matt Cavanaugh	7	16	43.8	101	6.31	1	1	59.6
John Teltschik	1	3	33.3	18	6.00	0	0	54.9
Keith Byars	0	2	0.0	0	0.00	0	0	39.6

Rushing	Rush	Yds	Avg	TD
Randall Cunningham	93	624	6.7	6
Keith Byars	152	517	3.4	6
Anthony Toney	139	502	3.6	4
Michael Haddix	57	185	3.2	0
Terry Hoage	1	38	38.0	1
John Teltschik	2	36	18.0	0
Junior Tautalatasi	14	28	2.0	0
Walter Abercrombie	5	14	2.8	0
Cris Carter	1	1	1.0	0

Receiving	Rec	Yds	Avg	TD
Keith Jackson	81	869	10.7	6
Keith Byars	72	705	9.8	4
Cris Carter	39	761	19.5	6
Anthony Toney	34	256	7.5	1
Mike Quick	22	508	23.1	4
Ron Johnson	19	417	21.9	2
Gregg Garrity	17	208	12.2	1
Michael Haddix	12	82	6.8	0
Jimmie Giles	6	57	9.5	1
Junior Tautalatasi	5	48	9.6	0
Mark Konecny	1	18	18.0	0
Walter Abercrombie	1	-2	-2.0	0

Interceptions	Int	Yds	Avg	TD
Terry Hoage	8	116	14.5	0
Eric Allen	5	76	15.2	0
Wes Hopkins	5	21	4.2	0
Seth Joyner	4	96	24.0	0
William Frizzell	3	19	6.3	0
Andre Waters	3	19	6.3	0
Roynell Young	2	5	2.5	0
Eric Everett	1	0	0.0	0
Jerome Brown	1	-5	-5.0	0
Todd Bell	0	24	0.0	0

Punting	Punts	Yds	Avg	Blocked
Randall Cunningham	3	167	55.7	0
John Teltschik	98	3958	40.4	0

Kicking	PAT Made	PAT Att	PAT %	FG Made	FG Att	FG %	Pts
Luis Zendajas	30	31	97	19	24	79.2	87
Dean Dorsey	9	9	100	4	7	57.1	21
Dale Dawson	3	3	100	0	1	0.0	3

The Philadelphia Inquirer

SUNDAY
January 1, 1989

SPORTS

SECTION E

Eagles mauled by their mistakes

Luis Zendejas (right) watches as the third of his four field goals sails toward the goal posts through the fog that descended on Soldier Field in the second quarter.

Bears to play for NFC title

By Bill Ordine
Inquirer Staff Writer

CHICAGO — Through a surreal fog, a Soldier Field crowd serenaded Buddy Ryan with a mocking rendition of "Auld Lang Syne" as the game clock ticked off the final seconds of the Eagles' season yesterday.

Ryan, whose defense had paced the Bears' Super Bowl drive three years ago, fell short of making a triumphant postseason return to Chicago, his Eagles stumbling, 20-12, in an NFC divisional playoff game.

It was a game destined to be remembered as the "Fog Bowl," if not by some similar appellation. An incredibly dense mist crept over the south end of the stadium late in the second quarter and engulfed the field for the rest of the afternoon.

While the Bears and Eagles both groped in the gray soup, the Eagles were in a mental fog. Penalties, dropped passes and missed defensive assignments were the chief culprits in their elimination from the playoffs.

"The only thing we felt could beat us today was ourselves, and that's what happened," middle linebacker Mike Reichenbach said.

On offense, the Eagles moved inside the Chicago 20-yard line nine times without scoring a touchdown. Two TDs were called back by penalties, and tight end Keith Jackson dropped a potential scoring pass with no one around him.

As for the defense, a blown assignment in the secondary allowed the Bears to jump ahead by 7-0 in the first period, and it was a lead that Chicago would not relinquish. The touchdown came on a 64-yard pass from quarterback Mike Tomczak to a wide-open receiver Dennis McKinnon 3 minutes, 2 seconds into the game.

"We missed all kinds of opportunities, and you have to credit the Bears' defense for that," Ryan said. "They kept us out of the end zone.

"We had a couple of touchdowns called back early on because of penalties, and it just seemed like, every time we went down there, nothing was happening for us.

"All year, it's been happening for us, but we couldn't make it happen today. So you have to credit the Bears for making the plays to keep us out of the end zone."

Through their stretch drive to the NFC East championship, the Eagles
(See EAGLES on 8-E)

Birds earned their loss, but with an assist by NFL

CHICAGO — In some 30-some years of covering sports, I thought I'd seen just about everything. Yesterday, sitting in a 50-yard-line seat at Soldier Field, I saw practically nothing.

Don't feel sorry for me, though. Think, instead, of the fans who paid to see a football game and spent the entire second half in a fog. Literally. Visiting teams dream about taking the home crowd "out of the game," but this was ridiculous.

"They ran a play on the other side, and I can't tell what's going on over there," Buddy Ryan would say when it was over. "The guy sounds like he's going for 1,000 yards, and he only makes 2. You don't know what the hell's going on."

You know the fog's pretty thick when even the Eagles' head coach admits he's in it.

By FRANK DOLSON
Sports editor

Barely 30 minutes after word spread that the game had ended, the fog lifted. As this is being written, it is possible to watch the Soldier Field ground crew pulling sections of tarpaulin over the field. Why, you wonder, didn't the NFL, in its infinite wisdom, in its quest for fair play, in its deep concern for its paying patrons, hold up the game until some visibility was restored?

Funny you should ask. Eagles owner Norman Braman and president/general manager Harry Gamble were asking the same thing, even though Ryan insisted he was perfectly content that the game went on.

"That's baseball, where you delay for rain and all that," he said. "This is football. ...

It was good of him to tell us. For the last hour or so, it was hard to tell what it was we weren't seeing.

The fog had appeared without warning, billowing in from the south with a little less than two minutes to go in the first half and Eagles trailing, 17-6. It happened so fast and looked so thick that it might have been smoke from a nearby fire. A two-alarmer, at least. But no, it was a freak of nature, a cruel twist of fate that provided a
(See DOLSON on 10-E)

When all went blank, Bears led

CHICAGO — They had won a game they hadn't really seen, against the coach who once designed their carnivorous defense. They had won the right to crow, but it was the right to advance in the Super Bowl tournament that meant more to them.

So the Bears, who have never been accused of good table manners, were subdued yesterday when celebrating their fog-shrouded triumph over the Eagles in the NFC playoffs. As near as anyone could tell, the score was 20-12.

The day before, Buddy Ryan had ordered the team bus to circle Soldier Field, horn honking in a sophomoric show of defiance. And now the blowsy, blustery Bears, never candi-

By BILL LYON

dates for Miss Manners role models, surely were primed to taunt their former coach with something like: "Yo, Buddy, honk this!"

But no such vindictiveness was forthcoming.

No window-smashing, furniture-breaking carousal this time. No, they were quite content to take their win and creep gradually away. On little cat feet. Just like, ahem, fog.

The Bears had the good fortune to be in the lead when a fog bank off Lake Michigan suddenly cloaked Soldier Field and reduced visibility to invisibility. It was like trying to watch — and play — a game through gauze. And while it is true that both teams had to play, sort of, in the same squinting haze, the team on the front end of the score suddenly had a big edge when the world went blank.

The Bears seemed to know this. And they seemed, too, to realize that if Randall Cunningham could actually have seen whom he was throwing
(See LYON on 10-E)

Anthony Toney, being halted by Chicago's Mike Singletary on a carry in the second period, suffered through an afternoon he will not remember fondly. Story on Page 11-E.

What you saw was all you got

By Ron Reid
Inquirer Staff Writer

CHICAGO — The Eagles and Bears reportedly contested an exceedingly important playoff game yesterday at Soldier Field, but as to the key plays and star performers, most fans hadn't the foggiest.

What the fans did see, in the Bears' 20-12 victory that wrote a gloomy finish to the Eagles' season, was a peasoup fog that drifted in off Lake Michigan with about two minutes left in the first half.

Eerily, within a matter of minutes, the fog quickly reduced visibility to about 10 yards and produced the most bizarre NFL contest in memory.

Through most of the second half, disgruntled fans who couldn't see what was happening on the field were kept informed by the public-address announcer, doing play-by-play over the public-
(See FOG on 10-E)

Poulin ends drought as Flyers top Sabres

By Al Morganti
Inquirer Staff Writer

BUFFALO — It wasn't so very long ago that Dave Poulin was the Flyers No. 1 offensive center, the guy who pulled the trigger for wingers Tim Kerr and Brian Propp.

But times have changed, and the

Flyers captain has been assigned to a defensive role, which is why last night's performance must have been so sweet.

Poulin emerged from his role as a checking center to score a dramatic, picture-perfect backhanded goal with less than five minutes to play at the Buffalo Auditorium, where the Flyers defeated the Sabres, 3-2.

Poulin, who had only four goals during the first half of the season, broke into the Sabres' zone as part of a three-on-two break with linemates Scott Mellanby and Derrick Smith. Mellanby fed Poulin a pass from the right-wing boards, and Poulin placed a perfect backhanded shot over the blocker of goalie Daren Puppa with 4 minutes, 44 seconds to play.

Flyers goalie Ron Hextall made a couple of big saves during a Buffalo
(See FLYERS on 5-E)

Index

While the L.A. Lakers charted their downhill course, the Houston Rockets took off for a stay — albeit a brief one — atop the Midwest Division. Bob Ford, Page 3-E.

Here's how baseball can do America's hockey fans a big favor. Al Morganti, Page 4-E.

NHL, NBA	2-E	Ben Callaway	16-E
Flyers notes	5-E	Horse racing	16-E

The Bengals' Ickey Woods takes an aerial route to the goal line.

Woods and Cincinnati roll past Seattle, 21-13

By Dave Caldwell
Inquirer Staff Writer

CINCINNATI — He is a self-styled trend-setter who wears his hair in a pony tail and is the creator of the post-touchdown dance that he immodestly named the "Ickey Shuffle."

After himself, of course.

Cincinnati Bengals tailback Ickey Woods is only a rookie, but he already has made it quite clear he wants to be known as a man who likes to zig when others zag — on the field and off. And in yesterday's other NFL playoff game, Woods almost ran out of his wardrobe to boost Cincinnati to a dramatic 21-13 victory over Seattle.

As Woods, a 231-pound rookie from Nevada-Las Vegas, rumbled for a game-high 126 yards on 29 carries, a split in the seat of his white game pants widened. But Woods, like any

trouper, never considered a costume change in mid-act.

"Hey," said Cincinnati tackle Anthony Munoz, "he was into the game, and he didn't want to change his pants. When he's running like that, you let him do whatever he wants."

Woods truly made an appropriate fashion statement, because Cincinnati (13-4) had to hang on by the seat of its pants for the victory over the rambling, gambling Seahawks (9-8), who registered two touchdowns in the fourth quarter to turn an apparent blowout into a white-knuckle finish.

"It's frustrating, the finality of it all is just a situation that's so hard to
(See BENGALS on 13-E)

Previews of today's playoff games — Vikings vs. 49ers and Oilers vs. Bills — are on Page 12-E.

January 1, 1989
Eagles lose the NFC Divisional Playoff game
to Chicago 20-12 in the infamous "Fog Bowl"

1989

RECORD: 11-5, 2ND IN NFC EAST
HEAD COACH: BUDDY RYAN

Schedule

Regular Season

Wk. 1	Sep 10	W	31-7	vs Seattle Seahawks
Wk. 2	Sep 17	W	42-37	at Washington Redskins
Wk. 3	Sep 24	L	38-28	vs San Francisco 49ers
Wk. 4	Oct 2	L	27-13	at Chicago Bears
Wk. 5	Oct 8	W	21-19	vs New York Giants
Wk. 6	Oct 15	W	17-5	at Phoenix Cardinals
Wk. 7	Oct 22	W	10-7	vs Los Angeles Raiders
Wk. 8	Oct 29	W	28-24	at Denver Broncos
Wk. 9	Nov 5	L	20-17	at San Diego Chargers
Wk. 10	Nov 12	L	10-3	vs Washington Redskins
Wk. 11	Nov 19	W	10-9	vs Minnesota Vikings
Wk. 12	Nov 23	W	27-0	at Dallas Cowboys
Wk. 13	Dec 3	W	24-17	at New York Giants
Wk. 14	Dec 10	W	20-10	vs Dallas Cowboys
Wk. 15	Dec 18	L	30-20	at New Orleans Saints
Wk. 16	Dec 24	W	31-14	vs Phoenix Cardinals

Post Season

Wild Card Playoffs

	Dec 31	L	21-7	vs Los Angeles Rams

The Eagles used an aggressive, ball-hungry defense -- which led the NFL in takeaways (56) and interceptions (30), and set a team record with 62 QB sacks -- to improve their regular season record to 11-5. However, they would have to settle for the Wild Card despite beating the first place New York Giants twice. In the first post-season game at the Vet since 1981, the Los Angeles Rams shocked the Eagles by winning 21-7 on a rainy afternoon in Philadelphia and won the NFC Wild Card game.

1989 Philadelphia Eagles Stats

Passing	Comp	Att	Comp %	Yds	Y/Att	TD	Int	Rating
Randall Cunningham	290	532	54.5	3400	6.39	21	15	75.5
Roger Ruzek	1	1	100.0	22	22.00	1	0	158.3
Matt Cavanaugh	3	5	60.0	33	6.60	1	1	79.6

Rushing	Rush	Yds	Avg	TD
Randall Cunningham	104	621	6.0	4
Anthony Toney	172	582	3.4	3
Keith Byars	133	452	3.4	5
Mark Higgs	49	184	3.8	0
Heath Sherman	40	177	4.4	2
Robert Drummond	32	127	4.0	0
Mike Reichenbach	1	30	30.0	0
John Teltschik	1	23	23.0	0
Cris Carter	2	16	8.0	0
Ron Johnson	1	3	3.0	0
Matt Cavanaugh	2	-3	-1.5	0
Carlos Carson	1	-9	-9.0	0

Receiving	Rec	Yds	Avg	TD
Keith Byars	68	721	10.6	0
Keith Jackson	63	648	10.3	3
Cris Carter	45	605	13.4	11
Ron Johnson	20	295	14.8	1
Anthony Toney	19	124	6.5	0
Robert Drummond	17	180	10.6	1
Jimmie Giles	16	225	14.1	2
Mike Quick	13	228	17.5	2
Gregg Garrity	13	209	16.1	2
Heath Sherman	8	85	10.6	0
Henry Williams	4	32	8.0	0
Mark Higgs	3	9	3.0	0
Anthony Edwards	2	74	37.0	0
Dave Little	2	8	4.0	1
Carlos Carson	1	12	12.0	0

Interceptions	Int	Yds	Avg	TD
Eric Allen	8	38	4.8	0
Eric Everett	4	64	16.0	1
William Frizzell	4	58	14.5	0
Izel Jenkins	4	58	14.5	0
Byron Evans	3	23	7.7	0
Al Harris	2	18	9.0	0
Clyde Simmons	1	60	60.0	1
Mike Golic	1	23	23.0	0
Andre Waters	1	20	20.0	0
Todd Bell	1	13	13.0	0
Seth Joyner	1	0	0.0	0

Punting	Punts	Yds	Avg	Blocked
Randall Cunningham	6	319	53.2	0
John Teltschik	57	2246	39.4	0
Rick Tuten	7	256	36.6	0
Max Runager	17	568	33.4	0

Kicking	PAT Made	PAT Att	PAT %	FG Made	FG Att	FG %	Pts
Luis Zendajas	23	23	100	9	15	60.0	50
Roger Ruzek	14	14	100	8	11	72.7	38
Steve DeLine	3	3	100	3	7	42.9	12

The Philadelphia Inquirer

MONDAY
January 1, 1990

SECTION D

SPORTS EXTRA

Playoffs arrive, Eagles depart

L.A. rides fast start to victory

By Bill Ordine
Inquirer Staff Writer

The Eagles expected to take a Great Step Forward this season, but yesterday they were stopped cold in their tracks.

For the second year in a row, Buddy Ryan's team lost its opening playoff game, and the Eagles probably played worse in yesterday's NFC wild-card game than they did in their loss to the Chicago Bears in the divisional playoffs a year ago.

"I think we need to mature as a team," linebacker Seth Joyner said. "With the way we ended up last year and the way we ended up this year, it's the same. You'd think we'd learn something, but we didn't. We played terribly in a playoff game again."

The Eagles were short on offensive weapons going into the game, and the few they did have were defused by a smothering Los Angeles Rams defense. Stung by a pair of early touchdowns, the Eagles never recovered, and they exited from the playoffs, 21-7, at soggy Veterans Stadium.

"I wanted us to take that one step forward, but today wasn't the day to do it," Ryan said, repeating his oft-stated hope for the Eagles for this season. "We didn't make it happen, but we need to do that. I don't know how many times the Rams have been to the playoffs and didn't get past the first round."

Quarterback Randall Cunningham did not complete a pass for more than 2 yards until the Eagles trailed by 14-0. He finished with 24 completions in 40 attempts for 238 yards and no touchdowns, and he threw one interception. At halftime, he had thrown for only 78 yards and run for 9. The Eagles had only three first downs and had turned the ball over twice.

The Philadelphia game plan was to run, with Cunningham calling one of a couple of predetermined plays at the line of scrimmage. But two Rams touchdowns in the first 7 minutes, 20 seconds derailed that scheme. Then, when Cunningham went looking for his short-range receivers, he found a cordon of pass defenders in tight zone coverage.

"They [prepared] for what our offense does," Cunningham said. "They took tight end Keith Jackson away early. They took our wideouts away and our short passing game, as far as our tight end and halfbacks were concerned. I have to tip my hat to their defensive coordinator [Fritz Shurmur].

"A lot of times, I'd roll around the corner, and when I do that, normally, I can get a fullback or a tight end coming across. But they did a great job."

Once Mike Quick was shelved for the season after the sixth game by knee surgery, the Eagles lacked any

(See EAGLES on 4-D)

Inside

- The Rams took a novel approach on defense.
  — Page 4-D.
- Greg Bell's big run.
  — Page 4-D.
- Highlights and lowlights.
  — Page 5-D.
- A stunned secondary.
  — Page 6-D.

Henry Ellard jumps for joy after his 39-yard TD catch in the first quarter. Eric Everett (42) was unable to prevent the TD after teammate Izel Jenkins' ill-fated leap.

By FRANK DOLSON
Sports editor

Eagles talked, Rams listened

One team talked a good game. The other team played it.

You might think that sort of pregame hype wouldn't matter in the least. Think again. Football players are kids at heart. They spike footballs. They gesture. They strut. They taunt.

And when the other side talks so much, they listen. And remember. And use it to fuel their fire.

The Eagles did a lot of talking this past week. It's their style under Buddy Ryan. Be aggressive. Intimidate the opposition.

"Once the game starts, we got to go to war and take care of business," Jerome Brown had said, "because that's the way Buddy wants us to play."

"It's their trademark, their strength. But talking about it isn't enough. You have to do it, too.

The Los Angeles Rams had heard it all. They weren't intimidated; they were motivated.

"We loved that," Jim Everett, their

(See DOLSON on 5-D)

Randall Cunningham and Keith Jackson after the defeat.

A dreary day, a dreary effort

By BILL LYON

And so, once again, the Eagles perish in pea soup.

Last season, in Chicago, young and inexperienced and still new to this bewildering thing called the NFL playoffs, they expired in impenetrable fog, far from home, on tough, alien turf.

This time, with the comforts and reassurances of home, a year older and supposedly a year wiser, allegedly better equipped to cope with playoff pressure, they came out and played in a fog, literally and figuratively.

In dark, dank gloom, pelted by a cold, relentless rain, their parka-clad followers sat in sullen silence, waiting for a reason to come to life. None came.

The Eagles' fate then fell, as it usually does, at the feet of their quarterback.

The feet, on this day, were salt and pepper. Randall Cunningham was shod schizophrenically — white low-cut cleat on his right foot, black high-top on his left, as if he couldn't make up his mind. That footwear turned out to be symbolic of the way he — and the other Eagles — performed.

Bewildered by a Rams defense that he later conceded the Eagles were

unprepared for, Cunningham sputtered through another fitful, indecisive afternoon. It should be pointed out that he was severely restricted by his own team, too. The Eagles' offense is sorely limited and offers precious few options.

The result was a 21-7 loss to the Rams, who at last escaped their surfer-boys-who-can't-win-beyond-the-beach rap. And the Eagles thus concluded, abruptly and unsatisfactorily, a season that will be perceived as a disappointment even though it was a winning one.

And Buddy Ryan, who built and promotes his reputation on defensive schematics, was outcoached in his area of expertise. The Rams' game plan, especially on defense, was obviously superior. A bitter footnote is that the Eagles lost to a team

(See LYON on 5-D)

Anderson's 50-yard FG lifts Steelers past Oilers

By Mike Bruton
Inquirer Staff Writer

HOUSTON — The stadium the Houston Oilers proudly call "The House of Pain" became a pleasure palace yesterday for the Pittsburgh Steelers.

Just 3 minutes, 26 seconds into overtime, Gary Anderson kicked a 50-yard field goal to give the Steelers a 26-23 victory over the Oilers in this AFC wild-card game.

Only moments after the kick — Anderson's longest attempt of the season — split the uprights, the Steelers erupted in celebration as the Oilers, widely expected to win this game, disappeared into the bowels of the Astrodome.

Anderson's performance, which

also included field goals of 25, 30 and 48 yards, punctuated a gritty Pittsburgh showing against the self-proclaimed bad boys of the AFC.

In fact, the play that put the Steelers in position for Anderson's final kick was of the kind that Houston coach Jerry Glanville loves to see his players make.

Pittsburgh cornerback Rod Woodson, aided by nose tackle Gerald Williams, put a savage hit on running back Lorenzo White, forcing a fumble on Houston's only offensive play in overtime.

Woodson recovered his own trophy at the Houston 46-yard line and, five plays later, Anderson kicked the ball that spoiled extraordinary performances by Oilers quarterback Warren Moon and wide receiver Ernest Givins.

"It wasn't real pretty," said Steelers quarterback Bubby Brister. "It's not San Francisco football. It's Pittsburgh Steeler football. It's knock-down, drag-out. It's blood and guts. We're playing hard, dirty football."

It was almost a replay of Houston's

(See AFC on 6-D)

Index

NBA, NHL	2-D
Sixers	2-D
Baseball	8-D
Sports in brief	8-D
Horse racing	10-D

Gary Anderson is all smiles after his winning kick in overtime.

Orange Bowl: Emotion runs deep

By Jere Longman
Inquirer Staff Writer

MIAMI — Before he died of cancer in September, Sal Aunese, Colorado's suffering, inspiring quarterback, wrote a message to his teammates.

The note was read posthumously. In part, it said: "Do not be saddened that you no longer see me in the flesh, because I assure you I will always be with you in spirit. Strive only for victory each time we play . . . go get 'em, and bring home the Orange Bowl."

A victory for the fourth-ranked

Thus inspired, the top-ranked Buffaloes roamed to a perfect 11-0 season. A victory over Notre Dame tonight (Channel 3, 8 o'clock) in the Orange Bowl would give Colorado its first national championship.

"Sal is the main ingredient for getting this team close together," said all-America guard Joe Garten. "We told him we'd bring home the Orange Bowl. We didn't tell him we'd get this far and fall flat on our face."

Irish (11-1) would give Notre Dame claim to its second consecutive national title. Coach Lou Holtz's team will have played nine bowl teams after tonight. It has lost only once in the last 26 games. However, the wire-service polls, not tonight's game, will ultimately decide Notre Dame's fate.

Holtz may have thrown some gasoline onto Colorado's emotional fire last week when remarks he made to his team at practice were picked up by a Denver television station and

(See ORANGE BOWL on 8-D)

Flyers and Canucks skate to 2-2 tie

By Joe Juliano
Inquirer Staff Writer

VANCOUVER — For its final game of the 1980s, the National Hockey League sent the Flyers to Canada's Pacific Coast for a New Year's Eve contest that was in progress while their fans toasted and welcomed the new year.

While it wasn't enough to rank on anyone's list of greatest games of the decade, the Flyers and the Canucks engaged in a crisp-checking affair that ended in a 2-2 tie before 13,778

would-be revelers at the Pacific Coliseum.

Pete Peeters, one of the NHL's best goalies during a portion of the '80s but reduced to part-time status now, played a good game in goal for the Flyers in his first action since Nov. 25. He turned aside 23 of 25 Vancouver shots but remained without a win this season.

Playing without defenseman Jay Wells, who was shaken up by a shot from Tom Laidlaw in the second period of Saturday night's 6-3 win over

Los Angeles, the Flyers held leads of 1-0 and 2-1 in this game.

Keith Acton scored with less than three minutes gone in the game, but Vancouver's Brian Bradley tied it midway through the opening period. The Flyers' Doug Sulliman made it 2-1 early in the second, but ex-Flyer Rich Sutter scored with just 1 minute, 25 seconds left in the period to tie the game at 2-2.

The Flyers kept the heat on Canucks goalie Kirk McLean late in the

(See FLYERS on 3-D)

1989

January 1, 1990
First home playoff game at the Vet since 1981, the Eagles get defeated by the LA Rams 21-7 in the NFC Wild Card game

135

90's Decade in Review

Decade Win-Loss Record:
80-79-1 (2-4 postseason record)

Home Field:
Veterans Stadium 1990-1999

Playoff Appearances:
1990, 1992, 1995 and 1996

Championships:
None

Head Coaches:
Buddy Ryan 1990 (10-6) (0-1 postseason record);
Rich Kotite 1991-94 (36-28) (1-1 postseason record);
Ray Rhodes 1995-98 (29-34-1) (1-2 postseason record); Andy Reid 1999 (5-11)

Hall of Fame Inductees:
None

Award Winners:
Randall Cunningham, MVP 1990, Offensive MVP 1990, Comeback Player of the Year 1992;
Reggie White, Defensive MVP 1991; Eric Allen, NFC Defensive MVP 1993;
Jim McMahon, Comeback Player of the Year 1991; Ray Rhodes, Coach of the Year 1995

All Pro:
Jerome Brown 1990-91; Randall Cunningham 1990 and 1992; Byron Evans 1990 and 1992;
Keith Jackson 1990; Reggie White 1990-92; Eric Allen 1991 and 1992; Seth Joyner 1991-93,
Clyde Simmons 1991-92; Vai Sikahema 1992; William Fuller 1995; Andy Harmon 1995;
William Thomas 1995

Pro Bowl Selections:
Jerome Brown 1991-92; Randall Cunningham 1990-01; Keith Jackson 1990-91;
Reggie White 1990-92; Eric Allen 1990, 1992-95; Seth Joyner 1992 and 1994;
Clyde Simmons 1992-93; Fred Barnett 1993; William Fuller 1995-97;
William Thomas 1996-97; Ricky Watters 1996-97; Irving Fryar 1997-98;

First Game of the Decade:
September 9, 1990 loss to the New York Giants 27-20

Last Game of the Decade:
December 19, 1999 win over the New England Patriots 24-9

Largest Margin of Victory:
October 2, 1994 vs. the San Francisco 49ers 40-8

Largest Margin of Defeat:
September 6, 1998 vs. the Seattle Seahawks 38-0

Eagle Firsts of the Decade:
New Uniform and Logo
In 1996, changed to Midnight Green with a fiercer screaming Eagle head
First NFL Stadium with a Courtroom and Judge,
Judge Seamus P. McCaffrey presided during games
First NFL Player to score on 90-yard receiving, rushing, and returning plays in one season –
In 1994 Herschel Walker achieved this feat.

90's Decade in Review

With Ryan's firing by Norman Braman, Ryan's former Offensive Coordinator, Rich Kotite, took the helm of the franchise. Kotite would lead the Eagles to a 10-6 record in 1991 but, due to a particularly strong NFC, missed the playoffs (the team's cause was not helped by the season-ending injury incurred by Cunningham in the season's first game). In 1992, Kotite led the Eagles back into the postseason with an 11-5 record. In the Wild Card Round, the Eagles soundly beat the New Orleans Saints by a final score of 36-20. The Eagles were eliminated by Dallas in the next round (34-10). At the end of the season, DE Reggie White would leave the team through free agency. In 1993 and 1994, Kotite's Eagles would fall apart after initially promising starts, and missed the playoffs in each season. New owner Jeffrey Lurie proceeded to fire Kotite, who was almost immediately hired to coach the New York Jets, where he was by all accounts a miserable failure.

Lurie's choice to replace Kotite was San Francisco 49ers Defensive Coordinator Ray Rhodes, who successfully lobbied 49ers star Ricky Watters to join the team as a free agent. In 1995, Rhodes's first season, the Eagles got off to a slow start by losing 3 out their first 4 games: they subsequently rebounded, finishing with a 10-6 record and a playoff spot. In the Wild Card Round, the Eagles played at home and overwhelmed the Detroit Lions 58-37, with 31 of Philadelphia's points coming in the second quarter alone. Despite this dominating performance, yet again, the Eagles were eliminated in the next round by the Dallas Cowboys (30-11). 1995 was perhaps most notable in that it signaled the end of Randall Cunningham's tenure as starting quarterback. Irritated by erratic behavior on and off the field, Rhodes benched Cunningham in favor of the quotidian but manageable Rodney Peete.

In 1996, the Eagles got off to a good start, winning three of their first four games. However, a week-5 Monday night game at Veterans Stadium against the hated Cowboys would witness a season-ending knee injury to Peete and the loss of the team's momentum, and the transition to an offense led by Ty Detmer and Watters. While Watters would have a wonderful season, running for 1,411 yards, the season followed an all-too-familiar pattern: 10-6 record, and early elimination (14-0 to the 49ers) in the playoffs. In 1997 and 1998, Rhodes deteriorated under the stress of the job, and the team spiraled to the bottom of the standings. Left with little choice after a 3-13 campaign, fan revolt and sagging team morale, Lurie fired Rhodes.

TRIVIA QUESTION

Q11 WHICH OF THE FOLLOWING EAGLES DOES NOT HAVE HIS JERSEY NUMBER RETIRED BY THE TEAM?

(a) Jerome Brown   (b) Harold Carmichael
(c) Tom Brookshier   (d) Al Wistert

answer on page 254

TRIVIA QUESTION

Q12 WHO HOLDS THE EAGLES ALL TIME RECORD FOR MOST PUNTS DOWNED INSIDE THE 20?

(a) Sean Landeta   (b) John Teltschik
(c) Max Runager   (d) Jeff Feagles

answer on page 254

1990

RECORD: 10-6, 2ND IN NFC EAST
HEAD COACH: BUDDY RYAN

Schedule

Regular Season

Wk. 1	Sep 9	L	27-20	at New York Giants
Wk. 2	Sep 16	L	23-21	vs Phoenix Cardinals
Wk. 3	Sep 23	W	27-21	at Los Angeles Rams
Wk. 4	Sep 30	L	24-23	vs Indianapolis Colts
Wk. 6	Oct 15	W	32-24	vs Minnesota Vikings
Wk. 7	Oct 21	L	13-7	at Washington Redskins
Wk. 8	Oct 28	W	21-20	at Dallas Cowboys
Wk. 9	Nov 4	W	48-20	vs New England Patriots
Wk. 10	Nov 12	W	28-14	vs Washington Redskins
Wk. 11	Nov 18	W	24-23	at Atlanta Falcons
Wk. 12	Nov 25	W	31-13	vs New York Giants
Wk. 13	Dec 2	L	30-23	at Buffalo Bills
Wk. 14	Dec 9	L	23-20	at Miami Dolphins (OT)
Wk. 15	Oct 16	W	31-0	vs Green Bay Packers
Wk. 16	Dec 23	W	17-3	vs Dallas Cowboys
Wk. 17	Dec 29	W	23-21	at Phoenix Cardinals

Post Season

| Wild Card Playoffs | | | | |
| Jan 5 | L | 20-6 | vs Washington Redskins |

In February, Buddy Ryan hired Rich Kotite as offensive coordinator to improve the Eagles' sluggish attack. At season's end, the offense led the NFL in rushing (2,556) and time of possession (33:19) and the NFC in scoring (396) and touchdown passes (34). On the other side of the ball, the defense led the NFL in stopping the run (1, 169), thereby making the Birds the first team to lead the league in both rushing categories since Chicago did so in 1985. A 10-6 record put Philadelphia in the playoffs once again, but the Eagles suffered their third opening round defeat in as many seasons. The 20-6 Wild Card Game loss to Washington signaled an end to the five-year Ryan era. On January 8, 1991, owner Norman Braman announced that Ryan would not be offered a new contract. On the same day, he elevated Kotite to the head coaching position, noting that it was time for the Eagles "to reach the next plateau." Under Kotite, quarterback Randall Cunningham flourished with an NFC-leading 30 touchdown passes, 942 rushing yards, and a selection to the Pro Bowl, while rookie wide receivers Calvin Williams and Fred Barnett combined to make 17 touchdown receptions. Tight end Keith Jackson, defensive end Reggie White, and defensive tackle Jerome Brown also earned Pro Bowl berths, but running back Keith Byars, who tied a team record with 81 receptions and also threw four touchdown passes, was overlooked.

1990 Philadelphia Eagles Stats

Passing	Comp	Att	Comp %	Yds	Y/Att	TD	Int	Rating
Randall Cunningham	271	465	58.3	3466	7.45	30	13	91.6
Keith Byars	4	4	100.0	53	13.25	1	0	158.3
Jim McMahon	6	9	66.7	63	7.00	0	0	86.8
Jeff Feagles	0	1	0.0	0	0.00	0	0	39.6

Rushing	Rush	Yds	Avg	TD
Randall Cunningham	118	942	8.0	5
Heath Sherman	164	685	4.2	1
Anthony Toney	132	452	3.4	1
Thomas Sanders	56	208	3.7	1
Keith Byars	37	141	3.8	0
Roger Vick	16	58	3.6	1
Robert Drummond	8	33	4.1	1
Calvin Williams	2	20	10.0	0
Fred Barnett	2	13	6.5	0
Jeff Feagles	2	3	1.5	0
Jim McMahon	3	1	0.3	0

Interceptions	Int	Yds	Avg	TD
Wes Hopkins	5	45	9.0	0
William Frizzell	3	91	30.3	1
Eric Allen	3	37	12.3	1
Ben Smith	3	1	0.3	0
Byron Evans	1	64	64.0	1
Reggie White	1	33	33.0	0
Mike Golic	1	12	12.0	0
Seth Joyner	1	9	9.0	0
Terry Hoage	1	0	0.0	0

Receiving	Rec	Yds	Avg	TD
Keith Byars	81	819	10.1	3
Keith Jackson	50	670	13.4	6
Calvin Williams	37	602	16.3	9
Fred Barnett	36	721	20.0	8
Heath Sherman	23	167	7.3	3
Mickey Shuler	18	190	10.6	0
Anthony Toney	17	133	7.8	3
Mike Quick	9	135	15.0	1
Robert Drummond	5	39	7.8	0
Thomas Sanders	2	20	10.0	0
Kenny Jackson	1	43	43.0	0
Marvin Hargrove	1	34	34.0	1
Harper Le Bel	1	9	9.0	0

Punting	Punts	Yds	Avg	Blocked
Jeff Feagles	72	3026	42.0	2

Kicking	PAT Made	PAT Att	PAT %	FG Made	FG Att	FG %	Pts
Roger Ruzek	45	48	94	21	29	72.4	108

Lease a Loser
City's Dream Deal Isn't: **Page 3**

Tails & Heads
Why Style Hangs On: **Page 37**

MONDAY
DECEMBER 17, 1990

PHILADELPHIA DAILY
NEWS
THE PEOPLE PAPER

LATE SPORTS
35¢
50 CENTS OUTSIDE METROPOLITAN PHILADELPHIA
FOR HOME DELIVERY PHONE 665-1234

Playoff Power

1990

GEORGE REYNOLDS/DAILY NEWS

Eagles Randall Cunningham (left) and Anthony Toney rejoice during a 31-0 win that clinched a wild-card spot; seven pages in **Sports**

December 17, 1990
First home shutout since 1981,
Eagles 31-0 over Green Bay and clinch Wild Card spot

1991

RECORD: 10-6, 3RD IN NFC EAST
HEAD COACH: RICH KOTITE

Schedule
Regular Season

Wk. 1	Sep 1	W	20-3	at Green Bay Packers
Wk. 2	Sep 8	L	26-10	vs Phoenix Cardinals
Wk. 3	Sep 15	W	24-0	at Dallas Cowboys
Wk. 4	Sep 22	W	23-14	vs Pittsburgh Steelers
Wk. 5	Sep 30	L	23-0	at Washington Redskins
Wk. 6	Oct 6	L	14-13	at Tampa Bay Buccaneers
Wk. 7	Oct 13	L	13-6	vs New Orleans Saints
Wk. 9	Oct 27	L	23-7	vs San Francisco 49ers
Wk. 10	Nov 4	W	30-7	vs New York Giants
Wk. 11	Nov 10	W	32-30	at Cleveland Browns
Wk. 12	Nov 17	W	17-10	vs Cincinnati Bengals
Wk. 13	Nov 24	W	34-14	at Phoenix Cardinals
Wk. 14	Dec 2	W	13-6	at Houston Oilers
Wk. 15	Dec 8	W	19-14	at New York Giants
Wk. 16	Dec 15	L	25-13	vs Dallas Cowboys
Wk. 17	Dec 22	W	24-22	vs Washington Redskins

On January 8th, team owner Norman Braman opted not to renew the contract of Buddy Ryan, the Eagles' head coach since 1986. On the same day, Braman promoted then-offensive coordinator Rich Kotite, making him the 18th head coach in club history. They opened with a 3-1 mark, their best start since 1981, despite having lost QB Randall Cunningham for the year due to a knee injury suffered at Green Bay on opening day. After coming on to lead the Eagles to their solid start, backup QB Jim McMahon was also injured in game 5. With McMahon sidelined, the Birds suffered through a four game skid. By midseason, Philadelphia had used five quarterbacks in eight games and seen its record sink to 3-5. The Eagles regrouped, however, and surged into contention for a playoff spot with a six-game winning streak (the club's longest since the start of '81) that upped their record to 9-5. But a loss at home to Dallas in game 15 ended Philadelphia's playoff hopes. They ended the season with a record of 10-6, and joined the 49ers as the only NFL clubs to post 10-or-more wins in each of the last four seasons. The defense finished the season ranked #1 in the NFL in terms of fewest yards allowed overall, vs. the run, and vs. the pass. As such, the Birds became only the fifth club in NFL history and the first since 1975 to accomplish this rare triple.

1991 Philadelphia Eagles Stats

Passing	Comp	Att	Comp %	Yds	Y/Att	TD	Int	Rating
Jim McMahon	187	311	60.1	2239	7.20	12	11	80.3
Jeff Kemp	57	114	50.0	546	4.79	5	5	60.1
Randall Cunningham	1	4	25.0	19	4.75	0	0	46.9
Brad Goebel	30	56	53.6	267	4.77	0	6	27.0
Pat Ryan	10	26	38.5	98	3.77	0	4	10.3
Keith Byars	0	2	0.0	0	0.00	0	1	0.0

Rushing	Rush	Yds	Avg	TD
James Joseph	135	440	3.3	3
Keith Byars	94	383	4.1	1
Heath Sherman	106	279	2.6	0
Thomas Sanders	54	122	2.3	1
Jeff Kemp	16	73	4.6	0
Jim McMahon	22	55	2.5	1
Robert Drummond	12	27	2.3	2
Brad Goebel	1	2	2.0	0
Fred Barnett	1	0	0.0	0
Jeff Feagles	3	-1	-0.3	0
Pat Ryan	1	-2	-2.0	0

Receiving	Rec	Yds	Avg	TD
Fred Barnett	62	948	15.3	4
Keith Byars	62	564	9.1	3
Keith Jackson	48	569	11.9	5
Calvin Williams	33	326	9.9	3
Roy Green	29	364	12.6	0
Heath Sherman	14	59	4.2	0
James Joseph	10	64	6.4	0
Thomas Sanders	8	62	7.8	0
Mickey Shuler	6	91	15.2	0
Maurice Johnson	6	70	11.7	2
Kenny Jackson	4	29	7.3	0
Rod Harris	2	28	14.0	0
Jim McMahon	1	-5	-5.0	0

Interceptions	Int	Yds	Avg	TD
Wes Hopkins	5	26	5.2	0
Eric Allen	5	20	4.0	0
Seth Joyner	3	41	13.7	0
Rich Miano	3	30	10.0	0
Otis Smith	2	74	37.0	1
Byron Evans	2	46	23.0	0
Ben Smith	2	6	3.0	0
John Booty	1	24	24.0	0
Mike Golic	1	13	13.0	0
Andre Waters	1	0	0.0	0
Reggie White	1	0	0.0	0

Punting	Punts	Yds	Avg	Blocked
Jeff Feagles	87	3640	41.8	1

Kicking	PAT Made	PAT Att	PAT %	FG Made	FG Att	FG %	Pts
Roger Ruzek	27	29	93	28	33	84.8	111

PHILADELPHIA DAILY NEWS

Sports

FOR LATE SPORTS, SCORES: PAGE 99

Grand day for Bream, Braves
See page 82

SACKS MANIACS

BIRDS DROP AIKMAN 11 TIMES IN 24-0 WIN OVER DALLAS

Jerome Brown is congratulated by Seth Joyner (left) and Reggie White after fourth-quarter sack

MICHAEL MERCANTI / DAILY NEWS

SEE PAGE 98

NFL WEEK 3

Detroit 17	Pittsburgh 20	Chicago 20	Washington 34	Green Bay 15	Minnesota 17
Miami 13	New England 6	NY. Giants 17	Phoenix 0	Tampa Bay 13	SanFrancisco 14
Cleveland 14	Denver 16	Atlanta 13	Buffalo 23	LA Raiders 16	New Orleans 24
Cincinnati 13	Seattle 10	San Diego 10	NY Jets 20	Indianapolis 0	LA Rams 7

1991

September 16, 1991
Eagles manhandle the Cowboys 24-0,
had a team-record 11 sacks in single game

1992

RECORD: 11-5, 2ND IN NFC EAST
HEAD COACH: RICH KOTITE

Schedule

Regular Season

Wk. 1	Sep 6	W	15-13	vs New Orleans Saints
Wk. 2	Sep 13	W	31-14	at Phoenix Cardinals
Wk. 3	Sep 20	W	30-0	vs Denver Broncos
Wk. 5	Oct 5	W	31-7	vs Dallas Cowboys
Wk. 6	Oct 11	L	24-17	at Kansas City Chiefs
Wk. 7	Oct 18	L	16-12	at Washington Redskins
Wk. 8	Oct 25	W	7-3	vs Phoenix Cardinals
Wk. 9	Nov 1	L	20-10	at Dallas Cowboys
Wk. 10	Nov 8	W	31-10	vs Los Angeles Raiders
Wk. 11	Nov 15	L	27-24	at Green Bay Packers
				(at Milwaukee, WI)
Wk. 12	Nov 22	W	47-34	at New York Giants
Wk. 13	Nov 29	L	20-14	at San Francisco 49ers
Wk. 14	Dec 6	W	28-17	vs Minnesota Vikings
Wk. 15	Dec 13	W	20-17	at Seattle Seahawks (OT)
Wk. 16	Dec 20	W	17-13	vs Washington Redskins
Wk. 17	Dec 27	W	20-10	vs New York Giants

Post Season

Wild Card Playoffs	Jan 3	W	36-20	at New Orleans Saints
Divisional Playoffs	Jan 10	L	34-10	at Dallas Cowboys

Tragedy struck at the heart of the Eagles before the season even started, when linebacker Jerome Brown was killed in an automobile accident a month before the start of training camp. The Eagles dedicated the season to Brown by wearing a patch in his honor and retired his number 99. With the return of Randall Cunningham the Eagles got off to a solid 4-0 start. After struggling through the middle of the season the Eagles closed with four straight wins to make the playoffs with a solid 11-5 record. The team returned to the playoffs after a one-year absence and earned a Wild Card victory over the Saints in New Orleans 36-20. The win over the Saints was the team's first postseason victory since 1981 and its first road playoff conquest since 1949. Unfortunately, a week later their season would end in a 34-10 loss to the Cowboys in Dallas at the Divisional Playoffs. Following the season the Eagles, who had already lost tight end Keith Jackson to free agency, lost defensive end Reggie White.

1992 Philadelphia Eagles Stats

Passing	Comp	Att	Comp %	Yds	Y/Att	TD	Int	Rating
Randall Cunningham	233	384	60.7	2775	7.23	19	11	87.3
Jim McMahon	22	43	51.2	279	6.49	1	2	60.1
Herschel Walker	0	1	0.0	0	0.00	0	0	39.6
Keith Byars	0	1	0.0	0	0.00	0	0	39.6

Rushing	Rush	Yds	Avg	TD
Herschel Walker	267	1070	4.0	8
Heath Sherman	112	583	5.2	5
Randall Cunningham	7	549	6.3	5
Keith Byars	41	176	4.3	1
Jim McMahon	6	23	3.8	0
Vai Sikahema	2	2	1.0	0
Fred Barnett	1	-15	-15.0	0

Receiving	Rec	Yds	Avg	TD
Fred Barnett	67	1083	16.2	6
Keith Byars	56	502	9.0	2
Calvin Williams	42	598	14.2	7
Herschel Walker	38	278	7.3	2
Heath Sherman	18	219	12.2	1
Vai Sikahema	13	142	10.9	0
Roy Green	8	105	13.1	0
Pat Beach	8	75	9.4	2
Floyd Dixon	3	36	12.0	0
Maurice Johnson	2	16	8.0	0

Interceptions	Int	Yds	Avg	TD
Seth Joyner	4	88	22.0	2
Byron Evans	4	76	19.0	0
Eric Allen	4	49	12.3	0
John Booty	3	22	7.3	0
Wes Hopkins	3	6	2.0	0
William Thomas	2	4	2.0	0
Rich Miano	1	39	39.0	0
Andre Waters	1	23	23.0	0
Mark McMillian	1	0	0.0	0
Otis Smith	1	0	0.0	0

Punting	Punts	Yds	Avg	Blocked
Jeff Feagles	82	3459	42.2	0

Kicking	PAT Made	PAT Att	PAT %	FG Made	FG Att	FG %	Pts
Roger Ruzek	40	44	91	16	25	64.0	88

MONDAY   PHILADELPHIA DAILY NEWS   SEPTEMBER 21, 1992

Sports

Morandini makes history with solo tripleplay, but Phils lose again anyway
Page 102

NFL WEEK 3

Eagles 30
Denver 0

Washington 13
Detroit 10

Dallas 31
Phoenix 20

Pittsburgh 23
San Diego 6

Miami 26
LA Rams 10

Cleveland 28
Raiders 16

Minnesota 26
Tampa Bay 20

New Orleans 10
Atlanta 7

San Francisco 31
NY Jets 14

Houston 23
Kansas City 20 (ot)

Buffalo 38
Indianapolis 0

Seattle 10
New England 6

Green Bay 24
Cincinnati 23

NOT YOUR DAY, ELWAY

Birds crush Broncos to go to 3-0: Page 118

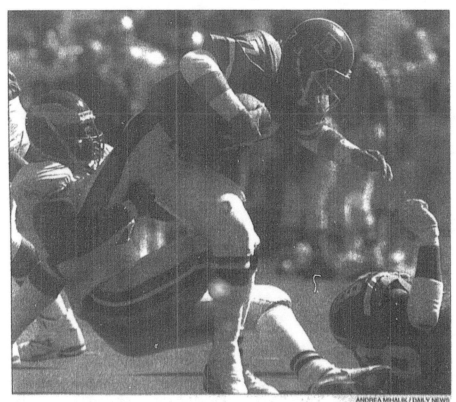

ANDREA MIHALIK / DAILY NEWS

Clyde Simmons drops John Elway in third quarter, one of the Eagles' four sacks

1992

September 21, 1992
Eagles soar over Denver 30-0
Calvin Williams and Fred Barnett gain 100 yards each, first time since 1983

1993

RECORD: 8-8, 3RD IN NFC EAST
HEAD COACH: RICH KOTITE

Schedule
Regular Season

Wk. 1	Sep 5	W	23-17	vs Phoenix Cardinals
Wk. 2	Sep 12	W	20-17	at Green Bay Packers
Wk. 3	Sep 19	W	34-31	vs Washington Redskins
Wk. 5	Oct 3	W	35-30	at New York Jets
Wk. 6	Oct 10	L	17-6	vs Chicago Bears
Wk. 7	Oct 17	L	21-10	at New York Giants
Wk. 9	Oct 31	L	23-10	vs Dallas Cowboys
Wk. 10	Nov 7	L	16-3	at Phoenix Cardinals
Wk. 11	Nov 14	L	19-14	vs Miami Dolphins
Wk. 12	Nov 21	L	7-3	vs New York Giants
Wk. 13	Nov 28	W	17-14	at Washington Redskins
Wk. 14	Dec 6	L	23-17	at Dallas Cowboys
Wk. 15	Dec 12	L	10-7	vs Buffalo Bills
Wk. 16	Dec 19	W	20-10	at Indianapolis Colts
Wk. 17	Dec 26	W	37-26	vs New Orleans Saints
Wk. 18	Jan 3	W	37-34	at San Francisco 49ers (OT)

After a flying start in which the Birds jumped out to a 4-0 record on the strength of three consecutive dramatic come-from-behind wins, season-ending injuries to quarterback Randall Cunningham, Pro Bowl wide receiver Fred Barnett and others were followed by a six-game losing streak. Despite suffering their worst skid since 1983, the resilient Eagles bounced back behind the fine play of backup QB Bubbly Brisker to win four of their final six contests---a stretch that kept them in the playoff hunt until the final week of the season. The Eagles' injury-riddled, roller-coaster ride of the 1993 campaign produced an 8-8 record.

1993 Philadelphia Eagles Stats

Passing	Comp	Att	Comp %	Yds	Y/Att	TD	Int	Rating
Randall Cunningham	76	110	69.1	850	7.73	5	5	88.1
Bubby Brister	181	309	58.6	1905	6.17	14	5	84.9
Ken O'Brien	71	137	51.8	708	5.17	4	3	67.4

Rushing	Rush	Yds	Avg	TD
Herschel Walker	174	746	4.3	1
Heath Sherman	115	406	3.5	2
Vaughn Hebron	84	297	3.5	3
James Joseph	39	140	3.6	0
Randall Cunningham	18	110	6.1	1
Bubby Brister	20	39	2.0	7
Ken O'Brien	5	17	3.4	0
Jeff Feagles	2	6	3.0	0

Receiving	Rec	Yds	Avg	TD
Herschel Walker	75	610	8.1	3
Calvin Williams	60	725	12.1	10
Mark Bavaro	43	481	11.2	6
Victor Bailey	41	545	13.3	1
James Joseph	29	291	10.0	1
Fred Barnett	17	170	10.0	0
Mike Young	14	186	13.3	2
James Lofton	13	167	12.8	0
Heath Sherman	12	78	6.5	0
Vaughn Hebron	11	82	7.5	0
Maurice Johnson	10	81	8.1	0
Jeff Sydner	2	42	21.0	0
Reggie Lawrence	1	5	5.0	0

Interceptions	Int	Yds	Avg	TD
Eric Allen	6	201	33.5	4
Rich Miano	4	26	6.5	0
William Thomas	2	39	19.5	0
Mark McMillian	2	25	12.5	0
Britt Hager	1	19	19.0	0
Byron Evans	1	8	8.0	0
Seth Joyner	1	6	6.0	0
Wes Hopkins	1	0	0.0	0
Clyde Simmons	1	0	0.0	0
Otis Smith	1	0	0.0	0

Punting	Punts	Yds	Avg	Blocked
Jeff Feagles	83	3323	40.0	0

Kicking	PAT Made	PAT Att	PAT %	FG Made	FG Att	FG %	Pts
Matt Bahr	18	19	95	8	13	61.5	42
Roger Ruzek	13	16	81	8	10	80.0	37

MONDAY   PHILADELPHIA DAILY NEWS   SEPTEMBER 13, 1993

Sports

Pete Sampras makes U.S. Open his 2nd Slam of year
Page 88

MAKING AMENS

Struggling Ruzek kicks game-winner as Eagles stun Packers, spoil White's impressive performance
Pages 99-94

Eagles tackle Antone Davis gets in the face of former teammate Reggie White.

GEORGE REYNOLDS / DAILY NEWS

1 9 9 3

PHILLIES LOSE; LEAD DOWN TO 5
PAGES 93-91

MAGIC NUMBER
15

	W	L	Pct.	GB
Phillies	87	56	.608	
Montreal	82	61	.573	5

GRANNY HAMNER DEAD AT 66
PAGE 90

September 13, 1993
Reggie White's first game back as a Packer,
but Eagles win 20-17

1994

RECORD: 7-9, 4TH IN NFC EAST
HEAD COACH: RICH KOTITE

Schedule
Regular Season

Wk. 1	Sep 4	L	28-23	at New York Giants
Wk. 2	Sep 12	W	30-22	vs Chicago Bears
Wk. 3	Sep 18	W	13-7	vs Green Bay Packers
Wk. 5	Oct 2	W	40-8	at San Francisco 49ers
Wk. 6	Oct 9	W	21-17	vs Washington Redskins
Wk. 7	Oct 16	L	24-13	at Dallas Cowboys
Wk. 8	Oct 24	W	21-6	vs Houston Oilers
Wk. 9	Oct 30	W	31-29	at Washington Redskins
Wk. 10	Nov 6	W	17-7	vs Arizona Cardinals
Wk. 11	Nov 13	L	26-7	vs Cleveland Browns
Wk. 12	Nov 20	L	12-6	at Arizona Cardinals
Wk. 13	Nov 27	L	28-21	at Atlanta Falcons
Wk. 14	Dec 4	L	31-19	vs Dallas Cowboys
Wk. 15	Dec 11	L	14-3	at Pittsburgh Steelers
Wk. 16	Dec 18	L	16-13	vs New York Giants
Wk. 17	Dec 24	L	33-30	at Cincinnati Bengals

A new chapter in Philadelphia Eagle history began on April 6th as Norman Braman, the Birds' owner since 1985, reached an agreement in principle to sell the franchise to Boston native and Hollywood-based movie producer Jeffrey Lurie. The Eagles would lose their season opener but would win 7 of their next 8 to sit right in thick of the playoff hunt with a 7-2 record. However the team would suddenly start to struggle losing their final 7 games to finish with a disappointing 7-9 record. Two days after the season finale, Rich Kotite's 4-year reign as head coach of the Birds ended when he was relieved of his duties. Despite the dismal ending, several Eagles provided memorable performances throughout the year. RB Herschel Walker etched his name into the NFL record books, as he became the first player in the 75-year history of the league to record a 90-plus yard run, reception, and kickoff return in a single season. Rookie RB Charlie Garner became only the 7th back in NFL history to eclipse the 100-yard rushing mark in his first two contests.

1994 Philadelphia Eagles Stats

Passing	Comp	Att	Comp %	Yds	Y/Att	TD	Int	Rating
Randall Cunningham	265	490	54.1	3229	6.59	16	13	74.4
Bubby Brister	51	76	67.1	507	6.67	2	1	89.1

Rushing	Rush	Yds	Avg	TD
Herschel Walker	113	528	4.7	5
Charlie Garner	109	399	3.7	3
Vaughn Hebron	82	325	4.0	2
Randall Cunningham	65	288	4.4	3
James Joseph	60	203	3.4	1
Bubby Brister	1	7	7.0	0
Calvin Williams	1	7	7.0	0

Receiving	Rec	Yds	Avg	TD
Fred Barnett	78	1127	14.4	5
Calvin Williams	58	813	14.0	3
Herschel Walker	50	500	10.0	2
James Joseph	43	344	8.0	2
Maurice Johnson	21	204	9.7	2
Victor Bailey	20	311	15.6	1
Vaughn Hebron	18	137	7.6	0
Mark Bavaro	17	215	12.6	3
Charlie Garner	8	74	9.3	0
David Alexander	2	1	0.5	0
Jeff Sydner	1	10	10.0	0

Punting	Punts	Yds	Avg	Blocked
Randall Cunningham	1	80	80.0	0
Bryan Barker	66	2696	40.8	0
Mitch Berger	25	951	38.0	0

Interceptions	Int	Yds	Avg	TD
Greg Jackson	6	86	14.3	1
Michael Zordich	4	39	9.8	1
Eric Allen	3	61	20.3	0
Bill Romanowski	2	8	4.0	0
Mark McMillian	2	2	1.0	0

Kicking	PAT Made	PAT Att	PAT %	FG Made	FG Att	FG %	Pts
Eddie Murray	33	33	100	21	25	84.0	96

William Thomas, Byron Evans, Britt Hager, and Andy Harmon all had one interception.

MONDAY · THE PHILADELPHIA DAILY NEWS · **OCTOBER 10, 1994**

Sports

Thomas, Cardinals meet, but nothing is imminent
Page 100

BACK *to* EARTH

Birds follow giddy romp over 49ers with close win vs. Redskins, 21-17

Pages 115-107

Cowboys humble Buddy, await Eagles Page 106

ALEJANDRO A. ALVAREZ/ DAILY NEWS
Randall Cunningham flips past Andre Collins on 20-yard TD run.

1994

October 10, 1994
Charlie Garner is the Eagles first rookie to gain over 100-yards in back-to-back games as Eagles defeated Washington 21-17

1995

RECORD: 10-6, 2ND IN NFC EAST
HEAD COACH: RAY RHODES

Schedule

Regular Season

Wk. 1	Sep 3	L	21-6	vs Tampa Bay Buccaneers
Wk. 2	Sep 10	W	31-19	at Arizona Cardinals
Wk. 3	Sep 17	L	27-21	vs San Diego Chargers
Wk. 4	Sep 24	L	48-17	at Oakland Raiders
Wk. 5	Oct 1	W	15-10	at New Orleans Saints
Wk. 6	Oct 8	W	37-34	vs Washington Redskins (OT)
Wk. 7	Oct 15	W	17-14	at New York Giants
Wk. 9	Oct 29	W	20-9	vs St. Louis Rams
Wk. 10	Nov 6	L	34-12	at Dallas Cowboys
Wk. 11	Nov 12	W	31-13	vs Denver Broncos
Wk. 12	Nov 19	W	28-19	vs New York Giants
Wk. 13	Nov 26	W	14-7	at Washington Redskins
Wk. 14	Dec 3	L	26-14	at Seattle Seahawks
Wk. 15	Dec 10	W	20-17	vs Dallas Cowboys
Wk. 16	Dec 17	W	21-20	vs Arizona Cardinals
Wk. 17	Dec 24	L	20-14	at Chicago Bears

Post Season

Wild Card Playoffs				
	Dec 30	W	58-37	vs Detroit Lions
Divisional Playoffs				
	Jan 7	L	30-11	at Dallas Cowboys

Under new coach Ray Rhodes the Eagles play sluggish football, losing three of their first four games, prompting Rhodes to bench quarterback Randall Cunningham. Under Cunningham's replacement Rodney Peete, the Birds rode the legs of running backs Ricky Watters and Charlie Garner to win nine of their final 12 games. Philadelphia's defense also chipped in with 48 sacks (second best in the league). The result was a 10-6 record and a spot in the playoffs as the NFC's top Wild Card team. In the Wild Card Game at the Vet the Eagles quickly soared in front to a 51-7 lead, and coasted the rest the way to a 58-37 slaughtering of the Detroit Lions at the Vet. However, a week later it was the Eagles who were slaughtered 30-11 by the Cowboys in Dallas. At season's end, Watters, defensive end William Fuller (an NFC-high 13 sacks), and linebacker William Thomas (whose seven interceptions were the most by an NFL linebacker since 1983) represented the Eagles in the Pro Bowl. Defensive tackle Andy Harmon and a pair of rookies, cornerback Bobby Taylor and punter Tom Hutton, also received numerous honors. Eleven months and a playoff victory later, first year head coach Ray Rhodes received numerous NFL Coach of the Year honors.

1995 Philadelphia Eagles Stats

Passing	Comp	Att	Comp %	Yds	Y/Att	TD	Int	Rating
Rodney Peete	215	375	57.3	2326	6.20	8	14	67.3
Randall Cunningham	69	121	57.0	605	5.00	3	5	61.5

Rushing	Rush	Yds	Avg	TD
Ricky Watters	337	1273	3.8	11
Charlie Garner	108	588	5.4	6
Rodney Peete	33	147	4.5	1
Randall Cunningham	21	98	4.7	0
Kevin Turner	2	9	4.5	0
Derrick Witherspoon	2	7	3.5	0
Fred McCrary	3	1	0.3	1
Tom Hutton	1	0	0.0	0
James Saxon	1	0	0.0	0
Calvin Williams	1	-2	-2.0	0

Receiving	Rec	Yds	Avg	TD
Calvin Williams	63	768	12.2	2
Ricky Watters	62	434	7.0	1
Fred Barnett	48	585	12.2	5
Rob Carpenter	29	318	11.0	0
Ed West	20	190	9.5	1
Kelvin Martin	17	206	12.1	0
Charlie Garner	10	61	6.1	0
Fred McCrary	9	60	6.7	0
Art Monk	6	114	19.0	0
Jimmie Johnson	6	37	6.2	0
Reggie Johnson	5	68	13.6	2
Chris T. Jones	5	61	12.2	0
Kevin Turner	4	29	7.3	0

Interceptions	Int	Yds	Avg	TD
William Thomas	7	104	14.9	1
Mark McMillian	3	27	9.0	0
Bobby Taylor	2	52	26.0	0
Bill Romanowski	2	5	2.5	0
Kurt Gouveia	1	20	20.0	0
Greg Jackson	1	18	18.0	0
Michael Zordich	1	10	10.0	0
Derrick Frazier	1	3	3.0	0
Barry Wilburn	1	0	0.0	0

Punting	Punts	Yds	Avg	Blocked
Tom Hutton	85	3682	43.3	1

Kicking	PAT Made	PAT Att	PAT %	FG Made	FG Att	FG %	Pts
Gary Anderson	33	32	103	30	22	136.4	123

Coping with comparisons
Penn State's Wally Richardson follows a very tough act. **C12.**

The Philadelphia Inquirer
Sunday
Sports

Section C

Calendar C3
College Basketball C10
College Football C2
Horse Racing C10
High Schools C12
NBA C4
NFL C6
NHL C2
Outdoors C14
Sports in Brief C3

Sunday, December 31, 1995   Philadelphia Online:

Eagles win in a big, big way

Eagles show remarkable resiliency

How can you not hand over your heart to this team of liquor-store clerks and truck drivers and other refugees from the real world who splattered the best offense in the NFL yesterday?

Really now, if you had heard only the score before kickoff, 58-37, you wouldn't have assumed that Detroit was the one with the 58?

Ray Rhodes has a way of rousing his team, but even he couldn't believe he'd end up with a laugher.

Bill Lyon

This had the look of a Super Bowl. Detroit generously played the part of the AFC team.

So the Eagles learned exactly how much the home field is worth in the playoffs.

And this is what happens to roofed teams that are forced to come outdoors and play in December and beyond.

The Eagles obliterated the Lions in yesterday's NFC wild-card playoff game at the Vet, exposing them as just another domed fraud. There were a lot of reasons for the machine-gunning, but none more compelling than this: The Eagles were much the tougher team mentally. Harder and hardier and heartier.

The Lions didn't even get a real taste of the Northeast in winter, but they shriveled up and died a hothouse plant's death anyway. The first turnover and they were looking for the exits. Since 1990, when the Lions have played teams in

See HEART on C8

The Eagles' Charlie Garner straight-arms Detroit cornerback Ryan McNeil in a bid to get outside. Garner piled up 78 yards on 12 carries.

Crush Lions in Round 1 of playoffs

By Frank Fitzpatrick
INQUIRER STAFF WRITER

Veterans Stadium shook like the Market Street El in full throttle. The Eagles' lead resembled a Sixers first-period deficit. And Rodney Peete, his index finger jabbing the sky in jubilant vindication, nearly outran his 18th and final first-half pass to the Lions' end zone.

Lions 37
Eagles 58

Peete's remarkable 43-yard touchdown heave to Rob Carpenter, on the last play of a nearly perfect hometown half, left the Lions stunned and still. It sent the Eagles dancing to the locker room with a 38-7 lead. And it typified Philadelphia's wondrous fortune on an afternoon that would fill NFL record books and embarrass Lomas Brown for eternity.

With a revived Peete throwing for 270 yards and three touchdowns, with a realigned defense intercepting six passes, and with 66,099 fans howling in green-tinged joy, the Eagles discombobulated Detroit, 58-37, yesterday in a first-round NFC playoff game.

"All week, all we heard about was how great Detroit was, how potent their offense was," coach Ray Rhodes said. "I think everybody overlooked this football team."

The lopsided victory, featuring the most points by two teams in NFL postseason history and the second-most ever for the Eagles, emphatically ended the Lions' seven-game winning streak and their fine season.

"We never thought that just because we had been playing good football, the Eagles were going to roll over and die," said Lions coach Wayne Fontes, his job security in jeopardy again. "They beat us in every way possible."

The win was the Eagles' first at home in the postseason since Jan. 11, 1981, when they defeated Dallas

See EAGLES on C8

Detroit's Brown readily eats words

He'd predicted the wild-card game would be over quickly. He didn't know how right — and how wrong — he would be.

By Phil Sheridan
INQUIRER STAFF WRITER

Here it is, the recipe for Words a la Lomas:

Saute lightly, adding a pinch of humility, and serve with a smile.

"Yes, I'm eating it today," said Lomas Brown, the veteran offensive tackle who surprised friends and teammates last week by guaranteeing a Detroit Lions victory over the Eagles.

Last week, Brown told reporters he expected the NFC wild-card playoff to be over early. He couldn't have known how right and how wrong he would be: It was the Eagles who took a 38-7 lead by halftime.

"They were the better team today," Brown said. "I have no problem admitting that. What I said was out of pure confidence. It was a re-

flection of how I felt about the guys in this locker room, about the type of team I thought we had.

"I have to take my hat off to Coach [Ray] Rhodes and to the Philadelphia Eagles. They beat us, handily beat us. The way we played, we could have played against a high school team today and not beaten them. You can't be the team to turn the ball over seven times and expect to win a playoff game."

When the record-breaking 58-37 loss was over, Brown spoke on the field with several Eagles, including Rhodes. After a brief talk with reporters at midfield, Brown jogged toward the tunnel to the Lions' locker room. Dozens of Eagles fans were waiting in the stands above the tunnel, chanting "Lomas ... Lomas" and bowing toward the men who sprayed kerosene on the Eagles' competitive fire.

"I told Coach Rhodes I would give him a call Tuesday," Brown said. "I would rather keep our conversation between him and me. Me and Coach Rhodes go way back. When he was in San Francisco, he coached some Pro Bowl squads. And I've met him a

See LIONS on C7

The Eagles' William Thomas (right) and Kurt Gouveia celebrate after Thomas scored in the fourth quarter on a 30-yard interception return.

Barnett and Garner serve special treats

The receiver dished up a surprise package with his best performance of the season. The running back provided the initial spice.

By Ron Reid
INQUIRER STAFF WRITER

Starting their playoff season yesterday with an amazing 58-37 victory over Detroit, the Eagles confronted their fans like a banquet table — offering too many good things to savor, many of them unexpected.

Chief among the latter was the play of Fred Barnett, the Eagles' six-year veteran wide receiver who could hardly have chosen a better time to turn in his finest, most surprising performance of the year.

The familiar treat was Charlie Garner, the explosive running back who scored the game's first touchdown on a scintillating 15-yard run. He racked up 78 yards on 12 carries, as the game's leading ground-gainer, and set up a field goal with a 30-yard run.

"We do have some guys who can

NFL Playoffs
Wild-card round.

■ Eagles 58, Detroit 37
■ Buffalo 37, Miami 22

■ Atlanta at Green Bay, 12:30 p.m. Ch. 29.
■ Indianapolis at San Diego, 4 p.m. Ch. 10.

help ignite our football team," said Eagles coach Ray Rhodes. "Charlie Garner is definitely one of them."

Garner didn't hang around to discuss his contributions with the media.

Arkansas Fred, as he used to be known, caught eight passes for 109 yards and a touchdown in what was a throwback to his earlier seasons with the team, when he routinely turned in the brilliant catch to scorch cornerbacks throughout the NFL.

Barnett's TD reception came in

See BARNETT on C7

Inside Sports

Villanova rallies after trailing Delaware. **C10.**

Dolphin loss Shula finale?
■ The Bills ousted the Dolphins from the playoffs, 38-22, yesterday and the humiliating defeat may wind up ending Don Shula's long tenure in Miami. **C7.**

Osborne's halo is slipping
■ A year ago, Nebraska head coach Tom Osborne was hailed as the nice guy with the model football program who finally won up a national title. Now, his program and image are targeted. **C2.**

Barber new Hershey coach
■ Bill Barber was named head coach of the AHL Hershey Bears. Meanwhile, the Flyers go for their second win in a row today, against Vancouver. **C2.**

College Basketball

Villanova 71, Delaware 58	Missouri 95, Hawaii 89
SMU 79, Penn 67	Cincinnati 103, McNeese St. 89
Oklahoma St. 49, Temple 41	Texas 74, North Carolina 72
UCLA 82, San Francisco 56	Clemson 67, Campbell 43
Georgetown 123, St. Leo 56	Virginia 76, Liberty 48
Drexel 88, Montana St. 82	Georgia 85, Jacksonville 59
Connecticut 102, Hartford 63	Louisville 98, Towson St. 72
Illinois 85, No. Carolina St. 76	**Coverage:** C10-11.

December 31, 1995
Eagles set postseason scoring record with a huge win over the Lions 58-37 in the NFC Wild Card game

149

1996

RECORD: 10-6, 2ND IN NFC EAST
HEAD COACH: RAY RHODES

Schedule

Regular Season

Wk. 1	Sep 1	W	17-14	at Washington Redskins
Wk. 2	Sep 9	L	39-13	at Green Bay Packers
Wk. 3	Sep 15	W	24-17	vs Detroit Lions
Wk. 4	Sep 22	W	33-18	at Atlanta Falcons
Wk. 5	Sep 30	L	23-19	vs Dallas Cowboys
Wk. 7	Oct 13	W	19-10	at New York Giants
Wk. 8	Oct 20	W	35-28	vs Miami Dolphins
Wk. 9	Oct 27	W	20-9	vs Carolina Panthers
Wk. 10	Nov 3	W	31-21	at Dallas Cowboys
Wk. 11	Nov 10	L	24-17	vs Buffalo Bills
Wk. 12	Nov 17	L	26-21	vs Washington Redskins
Wk. 13	Nov 24	L	36-30	at Arizona Cardinals
Wk. 14	Dec 1	W	24-0	vs New York Giants
Wk. 15	Dec 5	L	37-10	at Indianapolis Colts
Wk. 16	Dec 14	W	21-20	at New York Jets
Wk. 17	Dec 22	W	29-19	vs Arizona Cardinals

Post Season

Wild Card Playoffs				
	Dec 29	L	14-0	at San Francisco 49ers

The Eagles got off to a quick start, winning three of their first four games, before a Monday Night showdown with the Dallas Cowboys at the Vet. The Eagles lost the game 23-19 and lost quarterback Rodney Peete for the season due to a freak knee injury. Since the Eagles released Randall Cunningham prior to the season, they were forced to turn to Ty Detmer. Detmer played well, leading the Eagles to a four-game winning streak, as running back Ricky Watters stepped up and supplied the offense with a career best 1,411-yard season. The Eagles went on to finish with a 10-6 record and earned a Wild Card spot. However their season would be ended quickly as their offense got stuck in the mud in a 14-0 loss to the 49ers in San Francisco. The 1996 season marked the second consecutive year in which the Eagles compiled a 10-6 regular season record and earned a Wild Card playoff berth. As such, Ray Rhodes became the first coach to lead the Eagles into the playoffs in each of his first two seasons at the helm.

1996 Philadelphia Eagles Stats

Passing	Comp	Att	Comp %	Yds	Y/Att	TD	Int	Rating
Ty Detmer	238	401	59.4	2911	7.26	15	13	80.8
Rodney Peete	80	134	59.7	992	7.40	3	5	74.6
Mark Rypien	10	13	76.9	76	5.85	1	0	116.2

Rushing	Rush	Yds	Avg	TD
Ricky Watters	353	1411	4.0	13
Charlie Garner	66	346	5.2	1
Ty Detmer	31	59	1.9	1
Kevin Turner	18	39	2.2	0
Rodney Peete	21	31	1.5	1
Irving Fryar	1	-4	-4.0	0

Receiving	Rec	Yds	Avg	TD
Irving Fryar	88	1195	13.6	11
Chris T. Jones	70	859	12.3	5
Ricky Watters	51	444	8.7	0
Kevin Turner	43	409	9.5	1
Mark Seay	19	260	13.7	0
Jason Dunn	15	332	22.1	2
Charlie Garner	14	92	6.6	0
Freddie Solomon	8	125	15.6	0
Ed West	8	91	11.4	0
Jimmie Johnson	7	127	18.1	0
Mark Ingram	2	33	16.5	0
Calvin Williams	2	8	4.0	0
Guy McIntyre	1	4	4.0	0

Interceptions	Int	Yds	Avg	TD
Michael Zordich	4	54	13.5	0
Troy Vincent	3	144	48.0	1
William Thomas	3	47	15.7	0
Brian Dawkins	3	41	13.7	0
Bobby Taylor	3	-1	-0.3	0
James Willis	1	14	14.0	0
James Fuller	1	4	4.0	0
Ray Farmer	1	0	0.0	0

Punting	Punts	Yds	Avg	Blocked
Tom Hutton	73	3107	42.6	1

Kicking	PAT Made	PAT Att	PAT %	FG Made	FG Att	FG %	Pts
Gary Anderson	40	40	100	25	29	86.2	115

MONDAY   PHILADELPHIA DAILY NEWS   DECEMBER 23, 1996

Sports

Flyers scored upon, but tie hawks: *Page 68*
500 for Hull: *Page 69*

RETURN TICKET

Eagles squash Cards, enter playoffs vs. 49ers in homecoming for Rhodes and Watters

Pages 83-78

GEORGE REYNOLDS / DAILY NEWS

Eagles defensive end Mike Mamula sacks Arizona quarterback Kent Graham on second play of game, forcing fumble that he picked up and returned for a 4-yard touchdown.

YONG KIM / DAILY NEWS

1996

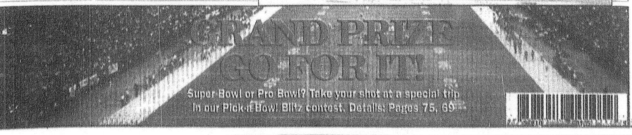

GRAND PRIZE GO FOR IT!

Super Bowl or Pro Bowl? Take your shot at a special trip in our Pick-a-Bowl Blitz contest. Details: Pages 75, 69

December 23, 1996
Gary Anderson boots five field goals to defeat the Cardinals 29-19

1997

RECORD: 6-9-1, 3RD IN NFC EAST
HEAD COACH: RAY RHODES

Schedule
Regular Season

Wk. 1	Aug 31	L	31-17	at New York Giants
Wk. 2	Sep 7	W	10-9	vs Green Bay Packers
Wk. 3	Sep 15	L	21-20	at Dallas Cowboys
Wk. 5	Sep 28	L	28-19	at Minnesota Vikings
Wk. 6	Oct 5	W	24-10	vs Washington Redskins
Wk. 7	Oct 12	L	38-21	at Jacksonville Jaguars
Wk. 8	Oct 19	W	13-10	vs Arizona Cardinals (OT)
Wk. 9	Oct 26	W	13-12	vs Dallas Cowboys
Wk. 10	Nov 2	L	31-21	at Arizona Cardinals
Wk. 11	Nov 10	L	24-12	vs San Francisco 49ers
Wk. 12	Nov 16	T	10-10	at Baltimore Ravens (OT)
Wk. 13	Nov 23	W	23-20	vs Pittsburgh Steelers
Wk. 14	Nov 30	W	44-42	vs Cincinnati Bengals
Wk. 15	Dec 7	L	31-21	vs New York Giants
Wk. 16	Dec 14	L	20-17	at Atlanta Falcons
Wk. 17	Dec 21	L	35-32	at Washington Redskins

With a record of 1-1 the Eagles were poised to beat the Cowboys in a Monday Night showdown in Dallas as they set up for field goal slightly longer then a PAT in the final seconds. However, the snap was mishandled and the Eagles lost 21-20 in one of the most embarrassing moments in team history. The Eagles recovered, and sat at 4-4 through the first 8 games. However, quarterback struggles began to catch up with Eagles, as Rodney Peete, Ty Detmer, and Bobby Hoying all struggled. The Eagles dropped their final three games and finished with a disappointing 6-9-1 record.

1997 Philadelphia Eagles Stats

Passing	Comp	Att	Comp %	Yds	Y/Att	TD	Int	Rating
Bobby Hoying	128	225	56.9	1573	6.99	11	6	83.8
Rodney Peete	68	118	57.6	869	7.36	4	4	78.0
Ty Detmer	134	244	54.9	1567	6.42	7	6	73.9

Rushing	Rush	Yds	Avg	TD
Ricky Watters	285	1110	3.9	7
Charlie Garner	116	547	4.7	3
Kevin Turner	18	96	5.3	0
Bobby Hoying	16	78	4.9	0
Ty Detmer	14	46	3.3	1
Rodney Peete	8	37	4.6	0
Duce Staley	7	29	4.1	0
Tom Hutton	1	0	0.0	0

Receiving	Rec	Yds	Avg	TD
Irving Fryar	86	1316	15.3	6
Kevin Turner	48	443	9.2	3
Ricky Watters	48	440	9.2	0
Michael Timpson	42	484	11.5	2
Freddie Solomon	29	455	15.7	3
Charlie Garner	24	225	9.4	0
Jimmie Johnson	14	177	12.6	1
Mark Seay	13	187	14.4	1
Chad Lewis	12	94	7.8	4
Jason Dunn	7	93	13.3	2
Chris T. Jones	5	73	14.6	0
Duce Staley	2	22	11.0	0

Interceptions	Int	Yds	Avg	TD
Brian Dawkins	3	76	25.3	1
Troy Vincent	3	14	4.7	0
Charles Dimry	2	25	12.5	0
William Thomas	2	11	5.5	0
Rhett Hall	1	39	39.0	0
Michael Zordich	1	21	21.0	0
Matt Stevens	1	0	0.0	0
James Willis	1	0	0.0	0

Punting	Punts	Yds	Avg	Blocked
Tom Hutton	87	3660	42.1	1

Kicking	PAT Made	PAT Att	PAT %	FG Made	FG Att	FG %	Pts
Chris Boniol	33	33	100	22	31	71.0	99

PHILADELPHIA DAILY NEWS
THE PEOPLE PAPER

MONDAY, DECEMBER 1, 1997   60¢ LATE SPORTS

'HOME ALONE 3'
Win tickets: Page 43
Keepsake photo:
Pull out Page 40

ALIVE & KICKING

Eagles still in the playoff chase – and the fans are loving it
Sports and Page 3

HOYING 7

Quarterback Bobby
Hoying leaves the field
after yesterday's 44-42
victory over the Bengals

GEORGE REYNOLDS / DAILY NEWS

12 DAYS OF CHRISTMAS   WIN A SUPER BOWL TRIP   Page 64

1997

December 1, 1997
Eagles QB Bobby Hoying throws for four touchdowns as the
Eagles edge the Bengals 44-42

1998

RECORD: 3-13, 5TH IN NFC EAST
HEAD COACH: RAY RHODES

Schedule
Regular Season

Wk. 1	Sep 6	L	38-0	vs Seattle Seahawks
Wk. 2	Sep 13	L	17-12	at Atlanta Falcons
Wk. 3	Sep 20	L	17-3	at Arizona Cardinals
Wk. 4	Sep 27	L	24-21	vs Kansas City Chiefs
Wk. 5	Oct 4	L	41-16	at Denver Broncos
Wk. 6	Oct 11	W	17-12	vs Washington Redskins
Wk. 7	Oct 18	L	13-10	at San Diego Chargers
Wk. 9	Nov 2	L	34-0	vs Dallas Cowboys
Wk. 10	Nov 8	W	10-9	vs Detroit Lions
Wk. 11	Nov 15	L	28-3	at Washington Redskins
Wk. 12	Nov 22	L	20-0	at New York Giants
Wk. 13	Nov 29	L	24-16	at Green Bay Packers
Wk. 14	Dec 3	W	17-14	vs St. Louis Rams
Wk. 15	Dec 13	L	20-17	vs Arizona Cardinals (OT)
Wk. 16	Dec 20	L	13-9	at Dallas Cowboys
Wk. 17	Dec 27	L	20-10	vs New York Giants

With the loss of Ricky Watters to free agency, Deuce Staley stepped in at runningback and supplied a solid season with 1,065 rushing yards. However, since all three Eagles quarterbacks struggled, the team went into a season long nose-dive that saw them finish with a woeful 3-13 record. Nobody demonstrated these struggles more then Bobby Hoying, who was sacked 35 times, and intercepted nine times, all without throwing a single touchdown pass. Following the season the Eagles made a change in direction that started by replacing head coach Ray Rhodes with Andy Reid.

1998 Philadelphia Eagles Stats

Passing	Comp	Att	Comp %	Yds	Y/Att	TD	Int	Rating
Koy Detmer	97	181	53.6	1011	5.59	5	5	67.7
Rodney Peete	71	129	55.0	758	5.88	2	4	64.7
Bobby Hoying	114	224	50.9	961	4.29	0	9	45.6

Rushing	Rush	Yds	Avg	TD
Duce Staley	258	1065	4.1	5
Charlie Garner	96	381	4.0	4
Kevin Turner	20	94	4.7	0
Bobby Hoying	22	84	3.8	0
Corey Walker	12	55	4.6	0
Irving Fryar	3	46	15.3	0
Rodney Peete	5	30	6.0	1
Koy Detmer	7	20	2.9	0
Dietrich Jells	2	9	4.5	0
Karl Hankton	1	-4	-4.0	0
Jason Dunn	1	-5	-5.0	0

Receiving	Rec	Yds	Avg	TD
Duce Staley	57	432	7.6	1
Irving Fryar	48	556	11.6	2
Jeff Graham	47	600	12.8	2
Kevin Turner	34	232	6.8	0
Freddie Solomon	21	193	9.2	1
Charlie Garner	19	110	5.8	0
Russell Copeland	18	221	12.3	0
Jason Dunn	18	132	7.3	0
Chris Fontenot	8	90	11.3	0
Kaseem Sinceno	3	42	14.0	1
Dietrich Jells	2	53	26.5	0
Corey Walker	2	35	17.5	0
Jimmie Johnson	2	14	7.0	0
Andrew Jordan	2	9	4.5	0
Bubba Miller	1	11	11.0	0

Punting	Punts	Yds	Avg	Blocked
Tom Hutton	104	4339	41.7	0

Interceptions	Int	Yds	Avg	TD
Brian Dawkins	2	39	19.5	0
Troy Vincent	2	29	14.5	0
Michael Zordich	2	18	9.0	0
Mike Caldwell	1	33	33.0	0
William Thomas	1	21	21.0	0
Tim McTyer	1	18	18.0	0

Kicking	PAT Made	PAT Att	PAT %	FG Made	FG Att	FG %	Pts
Chris Boniol	15	17	88	14	21	66.7	57

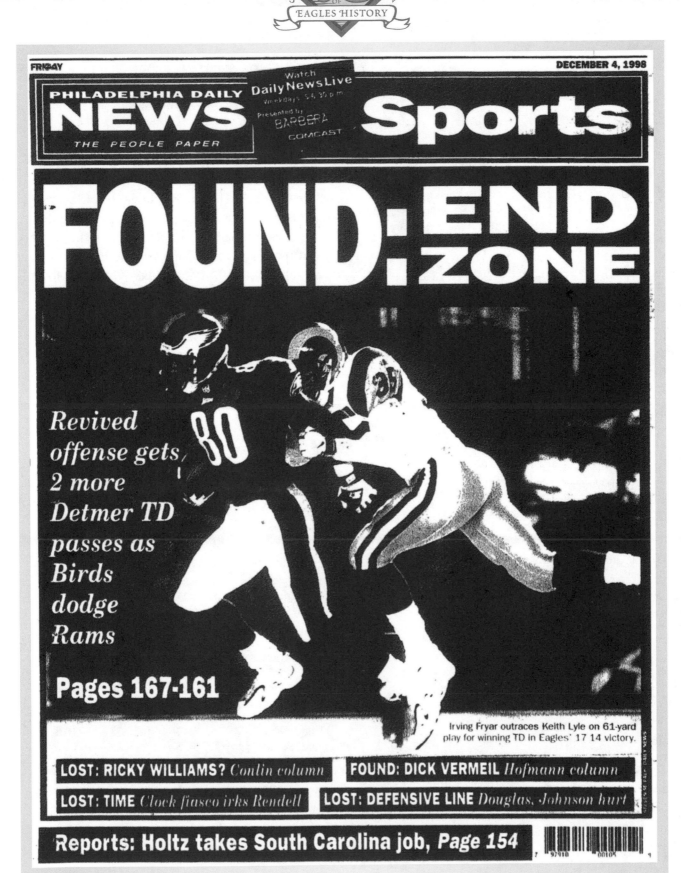

FRIDAY   DECEMBER 4, 1998

PHILADELPHIA DAILY NEWS
THE PEOPLE PAPER

Watch
Daily News Live
Weekdays 5 & 6:30 p.m.
Presented by
BARBERA
COMCAST

Sports

FOUND: END ZONE

Revived offense gets 2 more Detmer TD passes as Birds dodge Rams

Pages 167-161

Irving Fryar outraces Keith Lyle on 61-yard play for winning TD in Eagles' 17-14 victory.

| **LOST: RICKY WILLIAMS?** *Conlin column* | **FOUND: DICK VERMEIL** *Hofmann column* |
| **LOST: TIME** *Clock fiasco irks Rendell* | **LOST: DEFENSIVE LINE** *Douglas, Johnson hurt* |

Reports: Holtz takes South Carolina job, Page 154

December 4, 1998
Eagles barely win this game 17-14 over the Rams

1999

RECORD: 5-11, 5TH IN NFC EAST
HEAD COACH: ANDY REID

Schedule
Regular Season

Wk. 1	Sep 12	L	25-24	vs Arizona Cardinals
Wk. 2	Sep 19	L	19-5	vs Tampa Bay Buccaneers
Wk. 3	Sep 27	L	26-0	at Buffalo Bills
Wk. 4	Oct 3	L	16-15	at New York Giants
Wk. 5	Oct 10	W	13-10	vs Dallas Cowboys
Wk. 6	Oct 17	W	20-16	at Chicago Bears
Wk. 7	Oct 24	L	16-13	at Miami Dolphins
Wk. 8	Oct 31	L	23-17	vs New York Giants (OT)
Wk. 9	Nov 7	L	33-7	at Carolina Panthers
Wk. 10	Nov 14	W	35-28	vs Washington Redskins
Wk. 11	Nov 21	L	44-17	vs Indianapolis Colts
Wk. 12	Nov 28	L	20-17	at Washington Redskins (OT)
Wk. 13	Dec 5	L	21-17	at Arizona Cardinals
Wk. 14	Dec 12	L	20-10	at Dallas Cowboys
Wk. 15	Dec 19	W	24-9	vs New England Patriots
Wk. 17	Jan 2	W	38-31	vs St. Louis Rams

To improve their quarterback situation the Eagles drafted Donovan McNabb with the second overall pick in the draft. However, McNabb started the season on the bench as the Eagles struggled, losing their first four games. McNabb got his chance in the second half of the season and shined as the Eagles finished on a strong note, winning their last two games to finish with a 5-11 record.

1999 Philadelphia Eagles Stats

Passing	Comp	Att	Comp %	Yds	Y/Att	TD	Int	Rating
Doug Pederson	119	227	52.4	1276	5.62	7	9	62.9
Donovan McNabb	106	216	49.1	948	4.39	8	7	60.1
Koy Detmer	10	29	34.5	181	6.24	3	2	62.6
Torrance Small	0	2	0.0	0	0.00	0	0	39.6

Rushing	Rush	Yds	Avg	TD
Duce Staley	325	1273	3.9	4
Donovan McNabb	47	313	6.7	0
Eric Bieniemy	12	75	6.3	1
Doug Pederson	20	33	1.7	0
James Bostic	5	19	3.8	0
Edwin Watson	4	17	4.3	0
Kevin Turner	6	15	2.5	0
Cecil Martin	3	3	1.0	0
Koy Detmer	2	-2	-1.0	0

Receiving	Rec	Yds	Avg	TD
Torrance Small	49	655	13.4	4
Duce Staley	41	294	7.2	2
Charles Johnson	34	414	12.2	1
Luther Broughton	26	295	11.3	4
Na Brown	18	188	10.4	1
Jed Weaver	11	91	8.3	0
Cecil Martin	11	22	2.0	0
Dietrich Jells	10	180	18.0	2
Kevin Turner	9	46	5.1	0
Dameane Douglas	8	79	9.9	1
Chad Lewis	7	76	10.9	3
James Bostic	5	8	1.6	0
Eric Bieniemy	2	28	14.0	0
Brian Finneran	2	21	10.5	0
Troy Smith	1	14	14.0	0
Donovan McNabb	1	-6	-6.0	0

Interceptions	Int	Yds	Avg	TD
Troy Vincent	7	91	13.0	0
Al Harris	4	151	37.8	1
Brian Dawkins	4	127	31.8	1
Bobby Taylor	4	59	14.8	1
Jeremiah Trotter	2	30	15.0	0
Mike Mamula	1	41	41.0	1
James Darling	1	33	33.0	0
Rashard Cook	1	29	29.0	0
Damon Moore	1	28	28.0	0
Brandon Whiting	1	22	22.0	1
Mike Caldwell	1	12	12.0	0
Tim Hauck	1	2	2.0	0

Punting	Punts	Yds	Avg	Blocked
Sean Landeta	107	4524	42.3	1

Kicking	PAT Made	PAT Att	PAT %	FG Made	FG Att	FG %	Pts
Norm Johnson	25	25	100	18	25	72.0	79
David Akers	2	2	100	3	6	50.0	11

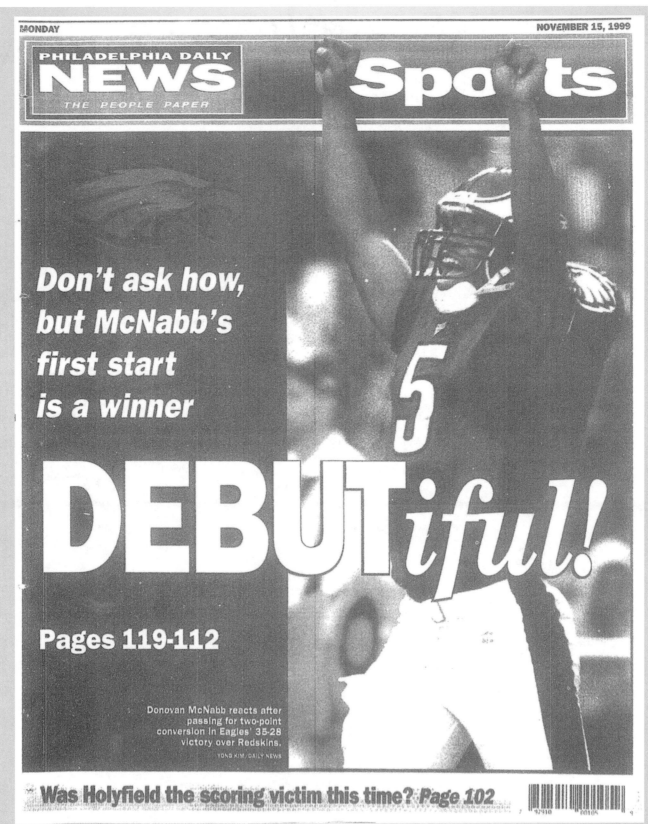

MONDAY NOVEMBER 15, 1999

PHILADELPHIA DAILY
NEWS
THE PEOPLE PAPER

Sports

Don't ask how,
but McNabb's
first start
is a winner

DEBUTiful!

Pages 119-112

Donovan McNabb reacts after
passing for two-point
conversion in Eagles' 35-28
victory over Redskins.
YONG KIM/DAILY NEWS

Was Holyfield the scoring victim this time? Page 102

1999

November 15, 1999
Rookie QB Donovan McNabb makes his first start for the Eagles as
the Eagles defeat the Redskins 35-28

2000's Decade in Review

Decade Win-Loss Record:
75-37* (8-6* postseason record)
Home Field:
Veterans Stadium 2000-02; Lincoln Financial Field 2002-Present
Playoff Appearances:
2000, 2001, 2002, 2003, 2004 and 2006
Championships:
Divisional Champions: 2001, 2002, 2003, 2004 and 2006
NFL/NFC Championship Games: 2001, 2002, 2003, and 2004
Super Bowl Appearance: XXXIV (2004)
Head Coaches:
Andy Reid 2000-Present* (75-37*) (8-6* postseason record)
Hall of Fame Inductees:
None
Award Winners:
Donovan McNabb, NFC MVP 2000 and 2004;
Andy Reid, NFL Coach of the Year 2000 and 2002
All Pro:
Hugh Douglas 200 and 2002; Jeremiah Trotter 2000; David Akers 2001-02, 2004;
Brian Dawkins 2001-04, 2006; Corey Simon 2001; Jermane Mayberry 2002;
Bobby Taylor 2002; Tra Thomas 2002; Troy Vincent 2002-03; Michael Lewis 2004;
Terrell Owens 2004; Ike Reese 2004, Lito Sheppard 2004; Tra Thomas 2004; Shawn Andrews 2006
Pro Bowl Selections:
Hugh Douglas 2001-03; Chad Lewis 2001-03; Donovan McNabb 2001-05;
Jeremiah Trotter 2001-02, 2005-06; Troy Vincent 2000-04; David Akers 2002-03, 2005;
Brian Dawkins 2000, 2002-03, 2005-07; William Thomas 2002-03, 2005;
Jermane Mayberry 2003; Jon Runyan 2003; Bobby Taylor 2003; Corey Simon 2004;
Terrell Owens 2005; Ike Reese 2005; Lito Sheppard 2005, 2007; Michael Lewis 2005;
Brian Westbrook 2005, Mike Bartrum 2006; Shawn Andrews 2007,
First Game of the Decade:
September 3, 2000 whipping of the Dallas Cowboys 41-14
Last Game of the Decade:
December 2009, not played yet
Largest Margin of Victory:
September 18, 2005 vs. San Francisco 49ers, 42-3
Largest Margin of Defeat:
December 5, 2005 vs. Seattle Seahawks, 42-0

Eagle Firsts of the Decade:
First Game at Lincoln Financial Field – September 8, 2003,
lost to Tampa Bay Buccaneers 17-0
First Win at the Linc
October 5, 2002 vs. Washington Redskins 27-25
First Playoff Game at the Linc
January 11, 2004, win over the Green Bay Packers 20-17
First Game Cancelled
August 13, 2001 vs. Baltimore Ravens in a preseason game due to
poor field conditions at Veterans Stadium
First NFL Player to intercept a pass, recover a fumble, record a sack, and catch a touchdown pass all in one game – September 29,
2002, was achieved by Brian Dawkins against the Houston Texans
First Super Bowl appearance of the decade
February 6, 2005, loss to New England Patriots 24-21

* record starting the 2007 season

2000's Decade in Review

In 2000, Andy Reid, the NFL's coach of the year, led the Eagles to the greatest turnaround in franchise history, finishing 2nd in the NFC East at 11-5. The season started with a perfectly executed onsides kick by David Akers to kickoff the season opener at Dallas. RB Duce Staley gained 201 rushing yards, the second most in club history, helped the Eagles open the 2000 NFL season with a resounding 41-14 victory. The Eagles won 10 of their next 13 contests and earned the top Wild Card spot in the NFC. In the playoffs, the Eagles overwhelmed Tampa Bay, 21-3, before losing to the eventual NFC Champion NY Giants in the Divisional Playoffs.

In 2001, we saw adversity hit this club early and often. The first preseason game was cancelled due to problems with the Veterans Stadium Nexturf. Starting C Bubba Miller was lost to a season ending foot injury. And they dropped their season opener in overtime to the Rams before true adversity devastated the entire world on September 11th when terrorist attacks struck the World Trade Center and the Pentagon. As a result, a week's worth of NFL games were postponed. The Eagles captured their first NFC Eastern Division Championship since 1988 and their first appointment in the NFC title game since 1980. In the playoffs, the Eagles defeated the Bucs again, 31-9, and in the Divisional playoffs, Donovan McNabb made his homecoming to Chicago a sweet one, winning 33-19 at Soldier Field.

The 2002 season was the 31st and final season at Veterans Stadium, the Eagles set a team record for points scored (415) and sent a league-high 10 players to the Pro Bowl. However, they fell in the NFC Championship game for the second consecutive season. Andy Reid, the consensus coach of the year, proved the Eagles were not a one-man show, winning five of six games without Donovan McNabb (broken ankle). McNabb returned for the playoffs and directed a win in the Divisional playoff after 3rd QB A.J. Feeley started the final five games, winning his first four.

Lincoln Financial Field officially became the Eagles new nest in 2003 with a season opening Monday night contest vs. Tampa Bay. In a season marred with injuries, controversy, and a slow start, the Eagles captured their third consecutive NFC East division title and third straight trip to the NFC title game, a loss to Carolina. After a 2-3 start, the Eagles rattled off nine straight wins, tying a team record previously set in 1960. That win streak was propelled by an improbable win at NYG on October 19. Trailing the Giants 10-7 with 1:34 remaining, no timeouts and a sputtering offense, Westbrook fielded a bouncing punt and raced 84 yards for the dramatic, game-winning score. The Eagles employed a unique running back trio (Westbrook, Buckhalter, and Staley), dubbed the "three-headed monster," that racked up 1,618 rushing yards, 2,465 total yards from scrimmage, and 29 total TDs. Despite giving up the ball 8 times during their 0-2 start, the team established a club record for fewest turnovers in a season with 22. They also turned in a franchise-record 6 games without a give-away.

2004, was one of the most eventful off-seasons in team history helped propel the Eagles to their first NFC Championship and subsequent Super Bowl appearance in 24 years. Although they lost a hard-fought battle to the Patriots, 24-21, in Jacksonville, the Eagles milestones were plentiful as they captured their 4th consecutive NFC East division title and won a franchise record 13 regular season games, while Andy Reid became the all-time winningest coach in franchise history surpassing Greasy Neale. The season started on the first day of the free agent signing period as they inked DE Jevon Kearse and later acquired WR Terrell Owens in a trade. Owens ended up with 77 catches for 1,200 yards and 14 scores. The Eagles stormed out to a 7-0 record and after a win at NYG on November 28, clinched the NFC East title with 5 games remaining. They went on to clinch home field advantage in the NFC after compiling a 13-1 record. In the playoffs, the Eagles topped Minnesota in the Divisional playoff round and Atlanta in the NFC Championship game

2005, the team was hit hard by injuries and a plethora of off-the field distractions, the Eagles finished with a 6-10 record and out of the playoffs for the first time since 1999. Drama appeared in the form of WR Terrell Owens, when the team suspended him for four games for conduct detrimental to the team and ended up not playing in the final nine games of the season. Despite the injury-riddled season, McNabb became the first quarterback in team history to top the 300-yard passing mark in three consecutive games and earned NFC Offensive player of the month honors in September. He also set the franchise record with 35 completions vs. San Diego. Reggie White's #92 was officially retired in an emotional halftime ceremony of a Monday night contest vs. Seattle on December 5. The ceremony included Reggie's wife, Sara, and their two children, as well as more than 20 of his former teammates and coaches.

The 2006 Eagles showed great character and toughness in claiming their fifth NFC East Division Championship in six years, as they reeled off five consecutive wins at the end of the regular season to finish 10-6. The hot start was capped off by an emotional 38-24 victory at home vs. Dallas on October 8th, in which Pro Bowl cornerback Lito Sheppard made two crucial interceptions, the second of which he returned 102 yards for a touchdown in the waning seconds. However, the team then lost five of their next six contests and quarterback Donovan McNabb for the remainder of the season to a torn ACL, which he suffered in the second quarter of a November 19th loss to Tennessee. 36-year-old Jeff Garcia was handed the reins of the quarterback position, and after a devastating 45-21 loss at Indianapolis, Garcia rallied the Eagles to five straight wins and a division title. Philadelphia had been crowned NFC East Champions once again.

2000

RECORD: 11-5, 2ND IN NFC EAST
HEAD COACH: ANDY REID

Schedule

Regular Season

Wk. 1	Sep 3	W	41-14	at Dallas Cowboys
Wk. 2	Sep 10	L	33-18	vs New York Giants
Wk. 3	Sep 17	L	6-3	at Green Bay Packers
Wk. 4	Sep 24	W	21-7	at New Orleans Saints
Wk. 5	Oct 1	W	38-10	vs Atlanta Falcons
Wk. 6	Oct 8	L	17-14	vs Washington Redskins
Wk. 7	Oct 15	W	33-14	at Arizona Cardinals
Wk. 8	Oct 22	W	13-9	vs Chicago Bears
Wk. 9	Oct 29	L	24-7	at New York Giants
Wk. 10	Nov 5	W	16-13	vs Dallas Cowboys (OT)
Wk. 11	Nov 12	W	26-23	at Pittsburgh Steelers (OT)
Wk. 12	Nov 19	W	34-9	vs Arizona Cardinals
Wk. 13	Nov 26	W	23-20	at Washington Redskins
Wk. 14	Dec 3	L	15-13	vs Tennessee Titans
Wk. 15	Dec 10	W	35-24	at Cleveland Browns
Wk. 17	Dec 24	W	16-7	vs Cincinnati Bengals

Post Season

Wild Card Playoffs				
	Dec 31	W	21-3	vs Tampa Bay Buccaneers
Divisional Playoffs				
	Jan 7	L	20-10	at New York Giants

In his first season as starter Donovan McNabb established himself as a rising star by passing for 3,365 yards and rushing for an additional 629 yards. Behind McNabb the Eagles played solid football all season, sometimes winning games in heart-stopping fashion while compiling an 11-5 record. However, two costly losses to the New York Giants cost the Eagles the division title. Settling for the Wild Card, the Eagles hosted the Tampa Bay Buccaneers in the Vet in the first round of the playoffs. In his first playoff game Donovan McNabb simply took over as the Eagles dominated the Bucs all day on the way to a 21-3 win. However, a week later the Eagles would be stymied by the Giants again, 20-10 in the Meadowlands.

2000 Philadelphia Eagles Stats

Passing	Comp	Att	Comp %	Yds	Y/Att	TD	Int	Rating
Donovan McNabb	330	569	58.0	3365	5.91	21	13	77.8
Brian Mitchell	1	4	25.0	21	5.25	0	0	49.0
Koy Detmer	0	1	0.0	0	0.00	0	1	0.0
Torrance Small	0	1	0.0	0	0.00	0	1	0.0

Rushing	Rush	Yds	Avg	TD
Donovan McNabb	86	629	7.3	6
Duce Staley	79	344	4.4	1
Darnell Autry	112	334	3.0	3
Stanley Pritchett	58	225	3.9	1
Brian Mitchell	25	187	7.5	2
Cecil Martin	13	77	5.9	0
Chris Warren	15	42	2.8	0
Charles Johnson	5	18	3.6	0
Koy Detmer	1	8	8.0	0
David Akers	1	2	2.0	0
Amp Lee	1	2	2.0	0
Torrance Small	1	1	1.0	0

Receiving	Rec	Yds	Avg	TD
Chad Lewis	69	735	10.7	3
Charles Johnson	56	642	11.5	7
Torrance Small	40	569	14.2	3
Cecil Martin	31	219	7.1	0
Duce Staley	25	201	8.0	0
Stanley Pritchett	25	193	7.7	0
Darnell Autry	24	275	11.5	1
Brian Mitchell	13	89	6.8	1
Luther Broughton	12	104	8.7	0
Todd Pinkston	10	181	18.1	0
Jeff Thomason	10	46	4.6	5
Na Brown	9	80	8.9	1
Donovan McNabb	2	5	2.5	0
Amp Lee	1	20	20.0	0
Dameane Douglas	1	9	9.0	0
Bubba Miller	1	9	9.0	0
Alex Van Dyke	1	8	8.0	0
Chris Warren	1	1	1.0	0

Interceptions	Int	Yds	Avg	TD
Troy Vincent	5	34	6.8	0
Brian Dawkins	4	62	15.5	0
Bobby Taylor	3	64	21.3	0
Damon Moore	2	24	12.0	0
Carlos Emmons	2	8	4.0	0
Jeremiah Trotter	1	27	27.0	1
Mike Caldwell	1	26	26.0	1
Hugh Douglas	1	9	9.0	0
Al Harris	0	1	0.0	0

Punting	Punts	Yds	Avg	Blocked
Sean Landeta	86	3635	42.3	0

Kicking	PAT Made	PAT Att	PAT %	FG Made	FG Att	FG %	Pts
David Akers	34	36	94	29	33	87.9	121

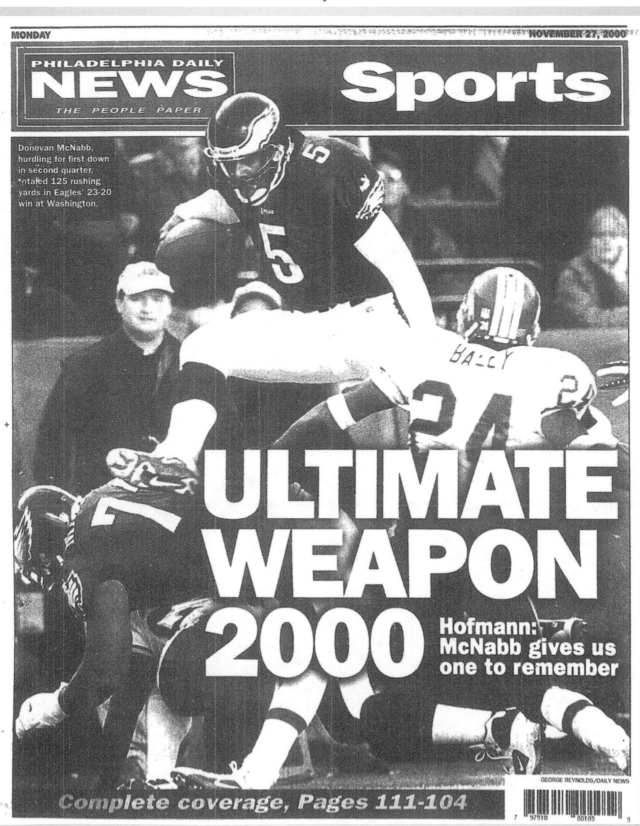

November 27, 2000
McNabb rushes for 125 yards, the most by an NFL QB since 1972,
as the Eagles win off the foot of Akers 23-20 over Redskins

2001

RECORD: 11-5, 1ST IN NFC EAST
HEAD COACH: ANDY REID

Schedule

Regular Season

Wk. 1	Sep 9	L	20-17	vs St. Louis Rams (OT)
Wk. 2	Sep 23	W	27-3	at Seattle Seahawks
Wk. 3	Sep 30	W	40-18	vs Dallas Cowboys
Wk. 4	Oct 7	L	21-20	vs Arizona Cardinals
Wk. 6	Oct 22	W	10-9	at New York Giants
Wk. 7	Oct 28	L	20-10	vs Oakland Raiders
Wk. 8	Nov 4	W	21-7	vs Arizona Cardinals
Wk. 9	Nov 11	W	48-17	vs Minnesota Vikings
Wk. 10	Nov 18	W	36-3	at Dallas Cowboys
Wk. 11	Nov 25	L	13-3	vs Washington Redskins
Wk. 12	Nov 29	W	23-10	at Kansas City Chiefs
Wk. 13	Dec 9	W	24-14	vs San Diego Chargers
Wk. 14	Dec 16	W	20-6	at Washington Redskins
Wk. 15	Dec 22	L	13-3	at San Francisco 49ers
Wk. 16	Dec 30	W	24-21	vs New York Giants
Wk. 17	Jan 6	W	17-13	at Tampa Bay Buccaneers

Post Season

Wild Card Playoffs				
	Jan 12	W	31-9	vs Tampa Bay Buccaneers
Divisional Playoffs				
	Jan 19	W	33-19	at Chicago Bears
Conference Championship				
	Jan 27	L	29-24	at St. Louis Rams

The Eagles captured their first NFC Eastern Division Championship since 1988 and their first appointment in the NFC title game since 1980. Adversity hit this club early and often. The first preseason game was cancelled due to problems with the Veterans Stadium Nexturf. Starting C Bubba Miller was lost to a season ending foot injury. And they dropped their season opener in overtime to the Rams before true adversity devastated the entire world on September 11th when terrorist attacks struck the World Trade Center and the Pentagon. As a result, a week's worth of NFL games were postponed. The Eagles were 2-2 before beating the Giants, 10-9, on Monday Night Football for the first time since 1996 (a span of nine games). The Eagles won 8 of their last 10 games, including a dramatic 24-21 win over the Giants on December 30 to clinch the NFC East title. In the playoffs, the Eagles defeated the Bucs again, 31-9, and in the Divisional playoffs, Donovan McNabb made his homecoming to Chicago a sweet one, winning 33-19 at Soldier Field.

2001 Philadelphia Eagles Stats

Passing	Comp	Att	Comp %	Yds	Y/Att	TD	Int	Rating
Donovan McNabb	285	493	57.8	3233	6.56	25	12	84.3
A. J. Feeley	10	14	71.4	143	10.21	2	1	114.0
Freddie Mitchell	0	1	0.0	0	0.00	0	0	39.6
Koy Detmer	5	14	35.7	51	3.64	0	1	17.3

Rushing	Rush	Yds	Avg	TD
Duce Staley	166	604	3.6	2
Correll Buckhalter	129	586	4.5	2
Donovan McNabb	82	482	5.9	2
James Thrash	6	57	9.5	0
Cecil Martin	9	27	3.0	0
Brian Mitchell	7	9	1.3	0
Koy Detmer	8	6	0.8	0
Rod Smart	2	6	3.0	0
Todd Pinkston	1	5	5.0	0
Freddie Mitchell	2	-4	-2.0	0

Receiving	Rec	Yds	Avg	TD
James Thrash	63	833	13.2	8
Duce Staley	63	626	9.9	2
Todd Pinkston	42	586	14.0	4
Chad Lewis	41	422	10.3	6
Cecil Martin	24	124	5.2	2
Freddie Mitchell	21	283	13.5	1
Correll Buckhalter	13	130	10.0	0
Na Brown	7	95	13.6	0
Brian Mitchell	6	122	20.3	0
Dameane Douglas	5	77	15.4	2
Tony Stewart	5	52	10.4	1
Jeff Thomason	5	33	6.6	0
Gari Scott	2	26	13.0	0
Jamie Reader	2	14	7.0	0
Mike Bartrum	1	4	4.0	1

Interceptions	Int	Yds	Avg	TD
Troy Vincent	3	0	0.0	0
Jeremiah Trotter	2	64	32.0	1
Al Harris	2	22	11.0	0
Brian Dawkins	2	15	7.5	0
Damon Moore	2	2	1.0	0
William Hampton	1	33	33.0	1
Rashard Cook	1	11	11.0	0
Bobby Taylor	1	5	5.0	0\

Punting	Punts	Yds	Avg	Blocked
Sean Landeta	97	4221	43.5	0

Kicking	PAT Made	PAT Att	PAT %	FG Made	FG Att	FG %	Pts
David Akers	37	38	97	26	31	83.9	115

EAGLES EXTRA

The NFC Championship • Rams 29, Eagles 24

End of the Run

Marshall Faulk finds himself in the middle of a pileup as he loses his helmet (top). Despite the efforts of Jeremiah Trotter (54), Faulk found his way to the end zone and put the Rams in front by 22-17.

JERRY LODRIGUSS / Inquirer Staff Photographer

Birds come up short in the NFC title game

In embers of defeat, a future that glows

ST. LOUIS — This is a loss that has the feel of a beginning more than an ending.

Just a hiccup in time. A pause before better things to come.

No defeat goes down easily, but the Eagles can wash this one down with a minimum of regret because it looks like a foreshadowing of bright tomorrows.

The NFC championship game isn't a one-time-only lottery ticket. What the Birds are building has the look of stability and permanency.

The Birds are young and on the come and improving in strobe-light bursts.

They fought the good fight yesterday, were noble losers, and acquitted themselves admirably in daunting, hostile cir-

cumstances. They were neither awed nor intimidated here at the Thunder Dome, an eardrum-shattering arena.

They forged a lead, then were on the brink of being blown out, and then they scuffled and hacked their way back to within a touchdown of a stunning upset. They lost to the best team in the NFL, but not before scaring the horns off the Rams and their clear-the-runways game.

So the Eagles will take a time-out now. In six months, they will re-huddle.

And then they will be favored to win their division, favored to advance to the NFC championship game, and, if they are doing this progression thing correctly, on
See **NFC** on E15

Bill Lyon

"A couple plays, and it could have been a changed game," says Donovan McNabb, being sacked by the Rams' Leonard Little. **E4.**

MICHAEL S. WIRTZ / Inquirer Staff Photographer

By Phil Sheridan
INQUIRER STAFF WRITER

ST. LOUIS — The dream did not die easily.

"We have got to believe," safety Brian Dawkins screamed to his teammates on the sideline as the fourth quarter and the season ticked away. "We have got to believe!"

The Eagles believed, but believing wasn't enough against the St. Louis Rams. Make that the Super Bowl-bound St. Louis Rams, who took the Eagles' best punch and held on for a 29-24 victory in a thrilling NFC title game yesterday.

The Rams will play the New England Patriots in Super Bowl XXXVI on Sunday in New Orleans. They have been installed as two-touchdown favorites to win their second NFL championship in three seasons.

For the Eagles, it was the end of a season and just maybe the beginning of an era. Their first conference championship game in 21 years may be the first of several for a young, talented group of players.

"We lost an opportunity," coach Andy Reid said. "At the same time, this was a step forward. You can look at it optimistically or pessimistically. I see it

very positively from where I'm sitting.

"It's a very empty feeling when you get this far and you don't get to the Super Bowl. And then, if you get to the Super Bowl, it's an empty feeling if you don't win it."

"This is one Super Bowl we didn't win, and we could have," Eagles owner Jeffrey Lurie said. "You want to win it every year, and it's disappointing. But I know we can now. No question about it. We were one drive, one play away, from being in the Super Bowl."

They were closer than that. They were the distance between Ndukwe Kalu's hands from winning.

So close.

The defensive end wasn't sure how he missed blocking a fourth-quarter punt by the Rams' John Baker. He broke free, beating his blocker, and hurled his body forward, arms
See **EAGLES** on E12

Super Bowl XXXVI
■ New England vs. St. Louis,
Sunday in New Orleans,
6:18 p.m., Ch. 29.

■ Patriots stop Steelers, 24-17, for AFC title. **E2.**   ■ Rams abandoned frills, turned to Faulk. **E3.**   ■ McNabb longingly watched Rams rejoice. **E4.**   ■ Birds backed off on the blitz package. **E5.**

*January 28, 2002
Eagles just couldn't pull this win off,
lose 29-24 to St. Louis*

2002

RECORD: 12-4, 1ST IN NFC EAST
HEAD COACH: ANDY REID

Schedule

Regular Season

Wk. 1	Sep 8	L	27-24	at Tennessee Titans
Wk. 2	Sep 16	W	37-7	at Washington Redskins
Wk. 3	Sep 22	W	44-13	vs Dallas Cowboys
Wk. 4	Sep 29	W	35-17	vs Houston Texans
Wk. 5	Oct 6	L	28-25	at Jacksonville Jaguars
Wk. 7	Oct 20	W	20-10	vs Tampa Bay Buccaneers
Wk. 8	Oct 28	W	17-3	vs New York Giants
Wk. 9	Nov 3	W	19-13	at Chicago Bears
Wk. 10	Nov 10	L	35-13	vs Indianapolis Colts
Wk. 11	Nov 17	W	38-14	vs Arizona Cardinals
Wk. 12	Nov 24	W	38-17	at San Francisco 49ers
Wk. 13	Dec 1	W	10-3	vs St. Louis Rams
Wk. 14	Dec 8	W	27-20	at Seattle Seahawks
Wk. 15	Dec 15	W	34-21	vs Washington Redskins
Wk. 16	Dec 21	W	27-3	at Dallas Cowboys
Wk. 17	Dec 28	L	10-7	at New York Giants (OT)

Post Season

Divisional Playoffs

Jan 11	W	20-6	vs Atlanta Falcons

Conference Championship

Jan 19	L	27-10	vs Tampa Bay Buccaneers

In the 31st and final season at Veterans Stadium, the Eagles set a team record for points scored (415) and sent a league-high 10 players to the Pro Bowl. However, they fell in the NFC Championship game for the second consecutive season. Andy Reid, the consensus coach of the year, proved the Eagles were not a one-man show, winning five of six games without Donovan McNabb (broken ankle). McNabb returned for the playoffs and directed a win in the Divisional playoff after 3rd QB A.J. Feeley started the final five games, winning his first four. Although the Eagles lost their season finale to the Giants, they were still able to clinch home field after the Jets trounced the Packers in the same stadium one day later.

2002 Philadelphia Eagles Stats

Passing	Comp	Att	Comp %	Yds	Y/Att	TD	Int	Rating
Donovan McNabb	211	361	58.4	2289	6.34	17	6	86.0
A. J. Feeley	86	154	55.8	1011	6.56	6	5	75.4
Brian Mitchell	1	1	100.0	57	57.00	1	0	158.3
Brian Westbrook	1	1	100.0	25	25.00	1	0	158.3
Koy Detmer	19	28	67.9	224	8.00	2	0	115.8
Dorsey Levens	0	2	0.0	0	0.00	0	0	39.6
Freddie Mitchell	0	1	0.0	0	0.00	0	0	39.6

Rushing	Rush	Yds	Avg	TD
Duce Staley	269	1029	3.8	5
Donovan McNabb	63	460	7.3	6
Dorsey Levens	75	411	5.5	1
Brian Westbrook	46	193	4.2	0
James Thrash	18	126	7.0	2
David Akers	1	10	10.0	0
A. J. Feeley	12	6	0.5	0
Koy Detmer	2	4	2.0	1
Sean Landeta	1	0	0.0	0
Cecil Martin	1	-4	-4.0	0
Todd Pinkston	1	-15	-15.0	0

Receiving	Rec	Yds	Avg	TD
Todd Pinkston	60	798	13.3	7
James Thrash	52	635	12.2	6
Duce Staley	51	541	10.6	3
Antonio Freeman	46	600	13.0	4
Chad Lewis	42	398	9.5	3
Dorsey Levens	19	124	6.5	1
Cecil Martin	15	126	8.4	0
Freddie Mitchell	12	105	8.8	0
Jeff Thomason	10	128	12.8	2
Brian Westbrook	9	86	9.6	0
Brian Dawkins	1	57	57.0	1
Mike Bartrum	1	8	8.0	0

Punting	Punts	Yds	Avg	Blocked
Sean Landeta	52	2229	42.9	0
Lee Johnson	14	523	37.4	0
Jason Baker	13	445	34.2	0

Interceptions	Int	Yds	Avg	TD
Bobby Taylor	5	43	8.6	1
Shawn Barber	2	81	40.5	1
Sheldon Brown	2	41	20.5	0
Brian Dawkins	2	27	13.5	0
Troy Vincent	2	1	0.5	0
Al Harris	1	0	0.0	0
Michael Lewis	1	0	0.0	0

Kicking	PAT Made	PAT Att	PAT %	FG Made	FG Att	FG %	Pts
David Akers	43	43	100	30	34	88.2	133

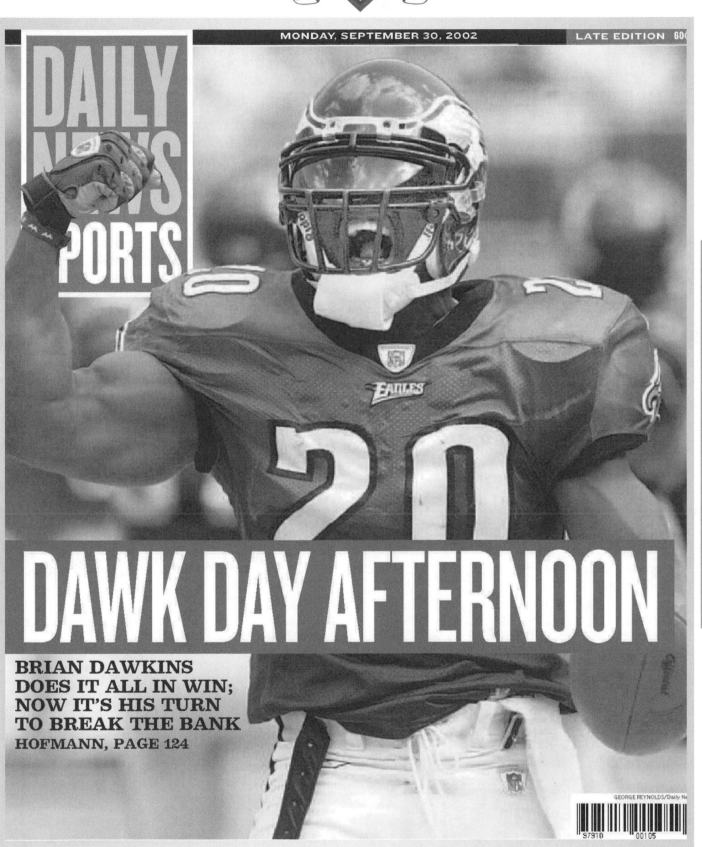

MONDAY, SEPTEMBER 30, 2002 · LATE EDITION · 60¢

DAILY NEWS SPORTS

2002

DAWK DAY AFTERNOON

**BRIAN DAWKINS
DOES IT ALL IN WIN;
NOW IT'S HIS TURN
TO BREAK THE BANK**
HOFMANN, PAGE 124

GEORGE REYNOLDS/Daily News

September 30, 2002
*Eagles defeat first time opponent Houston Texans 35-17, Safety Brain Dawkins makes his mark as the first player
in the NFL to record a sack, have an interception, recovery a fumble, and score a touchdown in a single game*

2003
RECORD: 12-4, 1ST IN NFC EAST
HEAD COACH: ANDY REID

Schedule
Regular Season

Wk. 1	Sep 8	L	17-0	vs Tampa Bay Buccaneers
Wk. 2	Sep 14	L	31-10	vs New England Patriots
Wk. 4	Sep 28	W	23-13	at Buffalo Bills
Wk. 5	Oct 5	W	27-25	vs Washington Redskins
Wk. 6	Oct 12	L	23-21	at Dallas Cowboys
Wk. 7	Oct 19	W	14-10	at New York Jets
Wk. 8	Oct 26	W	24-17	vs New York Jets
Wk. 9	Nov 2	W	23-16	at Atlanta Falcons
Wk. 10	Nov 10	W	17-14	at Green Bay Packers
Wk. 11	Nov 16	W	28-10	vs New York Giants
Wk. 12	Nov 23	W	33-20	vs New Orleans Saints
Wk. 13	Nov 30	W	25-16	at Carolina Panthers
Wk. 14	Dec 7	W	36-10	vs Dallas Cowboys
Wk. 15	Dec 15	W	34-27	at Miami Dolphins
Wk. 16	Dec 21	L	31-28	vs San Francisco 49ers (OT)
Wk. 17	Dec 27	W	31-7	at Washington Redskins

Post Season

Divisional Playoffs				
Jan 11	W	20-17	vs Green Bay Packers (OT)
Conference Championship				
Jan 18	L	14-3	vs Carolina Panthers

Lincoln Financial Field officially became the Eagles new nest with a season opening Monday Night contest vs. Tampa Bay. But the Eagles not only lost their first two contests, they were left without the services of Pro Bowl defensive backs Brian Dawkins and Bobby Taylor for a large chunk of the regular season (foot injuries). After a 2-3 start, the Eagles rattled off nine straight wins, tying a team record previously set in 1960. That win streak was propelled by an improbable win at NYG on October 19. Trailing the Giants 10-7 with 1:34 remaining, no timeouts and a sputtering offense, Westbrook fielded a bouncing punt and raced 84 yards for the dramatic, game-winning score. During that win streak, the Eagles toughed out a crucial win at Green Bay with a last-minute, game-winning drive directed by Donovan McNabb and ended up earning home-field advantage in the playoffs for the 2nd straight season. The Eagles captured their third consecutive NFC East division title and third straight trip to the NFC title game. However McNabb suffering from a rib injury sustained against Green bay wasn't able to finish the Championship game and was sidelined in the 4th quarter as the Eagles loss to Carolina 14-3.

2003 Philadelphia Eagles Stats

Passing	Comp	Att	Comp %	Yds	Y/Att	TD	Int	Rating
Donovan McNabb	275	478	57.5	3216	6.73	16	11	79.6
Freddie Mitchell	1	1	100.0	25	25.00	1	0	158.3
Koy Detmer	3	5	60.0	32	6.40	0	0	78.8

Rushing	Rush	Yds	Avg	TD
Brian Westbrook	117	613	5.2	7
Correll Buckhalter	126	542	4.3	8
Duce Staley	96	463	4.8	5
Donovan McNabb	71	355	5.0	3
James Thrash	5	52	10.4	0
Jon Ritchie	1	1	1.0	0
Todd Pinkston	1	-11	-11.0	0

Receiving	Rec	Yds	Avg	TD
James Thrash	49	558	11.4	1
Brian Westbrook	37	332	9.0	4
Todd Pinkston	36	575	16.0	2
Duce Staley	36	382	10.6	2
Freddie Mitchell	35	498	14.2	2
L. J. Smith	27	321	11.9	1
Chad Lewis	23	293	12.7	1
Jon Ritchie	17	86	5.1	3
Correll Buckhalter	10	133	13.3	1
Greg Lewis	6	95	15.8	0
Reno Mahe	1	5	5.0	0
Billy McMullen	1	2	2.0	0
Donovan McNabb	1	-7	-7.0	0

Interceptions	Int	Yds	Avg	TD
Michael Lewis	3	31	10.3	0
Troy Vincent	3	28	9.3	0
Lito Sheppard	1	34	34.0	0
Nate Wayne	1	33	33.0	0
Ndukwe Kalu	1	15	15.0	1
Sheldon Brown	1	10	10.0	0
Roderick Hood	1	5	5.0	0
Bobby Taylor	1	2	2.0	0
Brian Dawkins	1	0	0.0	0

Punting	Punts	Yds	Avg	Blocked
Dirk Johnson	79	3207	40.6	1

Kicking	PAT Made	PAT Att	PAT %	FG Made	FG Att	FG %	Pts
David Akers	42	42	100	24	29	82.8	114

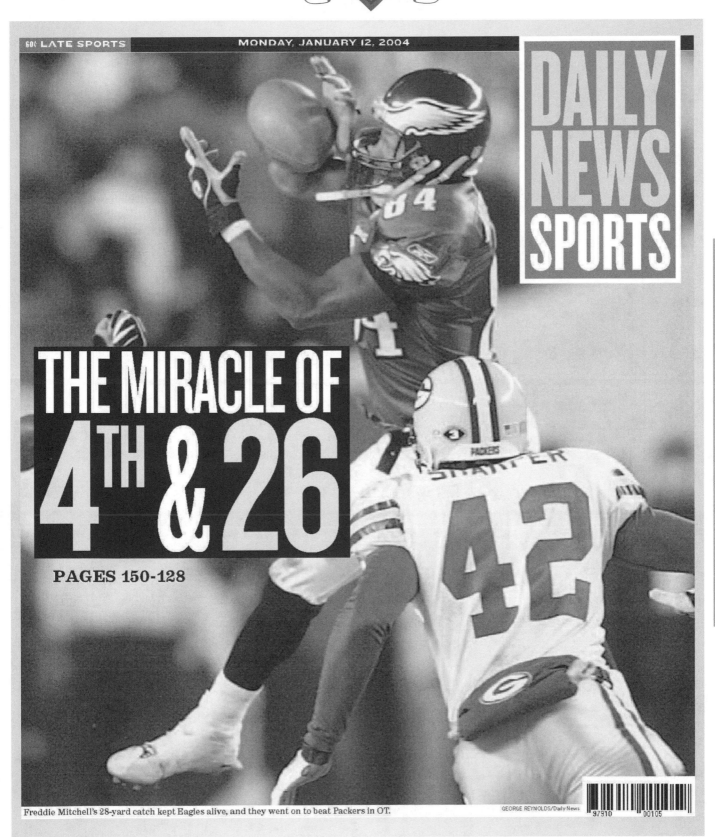

60¢ LATE SPORTS · MONDAY, JANUARY 12, 2004

DAILY NEWS SPORTS

THE MIRACLE OF 4TH & 26

PAGES 150-128

2003

Freddie Mitchell's 28-yard catch kept Eagles alive, and they went on to beat Packers in OT.

GEORGE REYNOLDS/Daily News

January 12, 2004
Eagles defeated the Packers 20-17 in an overtime
thriller including a gusty 4th and 26 yards play

2004

RECORD: 13-3, 1ST IN NFC EAST
HEAD COACH: ANDY REID

Schedule
Regular Season

Wk. 1	Sep 12	W	31-17	vs New York Giants
Wk. 2	Sep 20	W	27-16	vs Minnesota Vikings
Wk. 3	Sep 26	W	30-13	at Detroit Lions
Wk. 4	Oct 3	W	19-9	at Chicago Bears
Wk. 6	Oct 17	W	30-8	vs Carolina Panthers
Wk. 7	Oct 24	W	34-31	at Cleveland Browns (OT)
Wk. 8	Oct 31	W	15-10	vs Baltimore Ravens
Wk. 9	Nov 7	L	27-3	at Pittsburgh Steelers
Wk. 10	Nov 15	W	49-21	at Dallas Cowboys
Wk. 11	Nov 21	W	28-6	vs Washington Redskins
Wk. 12	Nov 28	W	27-6	at New York Giants
Wk. 13	Dec 5	W	47-17	vs Green Bay Packers
Wk. 14	Dec 12	W	17-14	at Washington Redskins
Wk. 15	Dec 19	W	12-7	vs Dallas Cowboys
Wk. 16	Dec 27	L	20-7	at St. Louis Rams
Wk. 17	Jan 2	L	38-10	vs Cincinnati Bengals

Post Season

Divisional Playoffs				
Jan 16	W	27-14		vs Minnesota Vikings
Conference Championship				
Jan 23	W	27-10		vs Atlanta Falcons
Superbowl				
Feb 6	L	24-21		vs New England Patriots (at Jacksonville)

One of the most eventful off-seasons in team history, the Eagles signed Jevon Kearse and Terrell Owens both helped the Eagles to their first NFC Championship and subsequent Super Bowl appearance in 24 years. The Eagles captured their 4th consecutive NFC East division title and won a franchise record 13 regular season games, while Andy Reid became the all-time winningest coach in franchise history surpassing Greasy Neale. QB Donovan McNabb became the first player in NFL history to finish a season with 30+ TD passes and fewer than 10 INTs and his 24 consecutive completions over a span of two games set an NFL record previously held by Joe Montana (22) in 1987. Eagles kicker David Akers set an NFL record with 17 FGs of 40-yards or more. The Eagles stormed out to a 7-0 record and after a win at NYG on November 28, clinched the NFC East title with 5 games remaining. They went on to clinch home field advantage in the NFC after compiling a 13-1record. In the playoffs, the Eagles topped Minnesota 27-14 in the Divisional playoff and defeated Atlanta 27-10 in the NFC Championship game. In Super Bowl XXXIV, the Eagles lost a hard-fought battle to the Patriots, 24-21, played in Jacksonville, Florida.

2004 Philadelphia Eagles Stats

Passing	Comp	Att	Comp %	Yds	Y/Att	TD	Int	Rating
Donovan McNabb	300	469	64.0	3875	8.26	31	8	104.7
Jeff Blake	18	37	48.6	126	3.41	1	1	54.6
Koy Detmer	18	40	45.0	207	5.18	0	2	40.3
Mike Bartrum	0	1	0.0	0	0.00	0	0	39.6

Rushing	Rush	Yds	Avg	TD
Brian Westbrook	177	812	4.6	3
Dorsey Levens	94	410	4.4	4
Donovan McNabb	41	220	5.4	3
Reno Mahe	23	91	4.0	0
Eric McCoo	9	54	6.0	0
Thomas Tapeh	12	42	3.5	0
Greg Lewis	4	16	4.0	0
Jeff Blake	3	6	2.0	0
Terrell Owens	3	-5	-1.7	0
Koy Detmer	10	-7	-0.7	0

Receiving	Rec	Yds	Avg	TD
Terrell Owens	77	1200	15.6	14
Brian Westbrook	73	703	9.6	6
Todd Pinkston	36	676	18.8	1
L. J. Smith	34	377	11.1	5
Chad Lewis	29	267	9.2	3
Freddie Mitchell	22	377	17.1	2
Greg Lewis	17	183	10.8	0
Reno Mahe	14	123	8.8	0
Dorsey Levens	9	92	10.2	0
Josh Parry	9	75	8.3	0
Mike Bartrum	5	45	9.0	1
Jon Ritchie	4	36	9.0	0
Billy McMullen	3	24	8.0	0
Eric McCoo	2	15	7.5	0
Thomas Tapeh	2	15	7.5	0

Interceptions	Int	Yds	Avg	TD
Lito Sheppard	5	172	34.4	2
Brian Dawkins	4	40	10.0	0
Sheldon Brown	2	33	16.5	0
Ike Reese	2	22	11.0	0
Roderick Hood	1	20	20.0	0
Dhani Jones	1	0	0.0	0
Michael Lewis	1	0	0.0	0
Quintin Mikell	1	0	0.0	0

Punting	Punts	Yds	Avg	Blocked
Dirk Johnson	72	3032	42.1	0
David Akers	1	36	36.0	0

Kicking	PAT Made	PAT Att	PAT %	FG Made	FG Att	FG %	Pts
David Akers	41	42	98	27	32	84.4	122

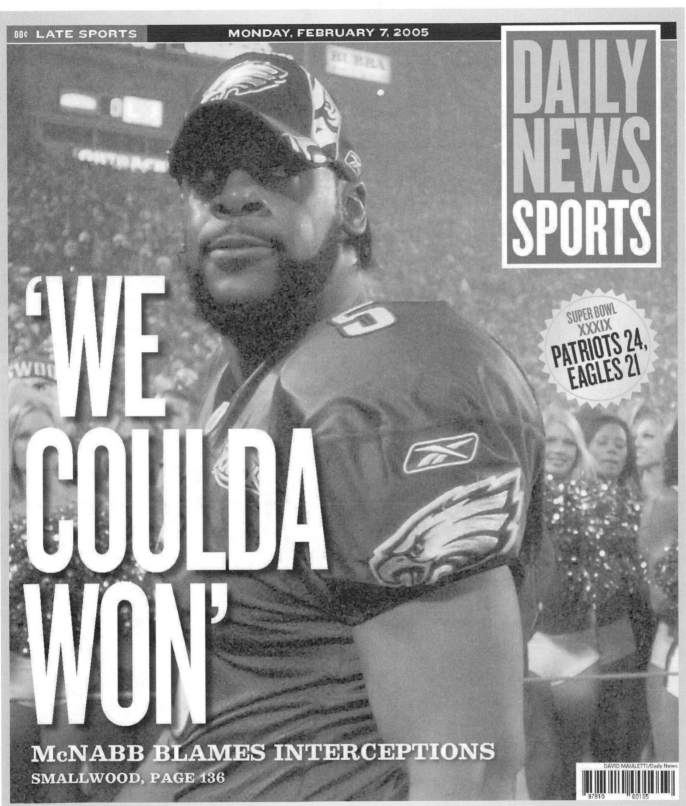

80¢ LATE SPORTS — MONDAY, FEBRUARY 7, 2005

DAILY NEWS SPORTS

SUPER BOWL XXXIX
PATRIOTS 24, EAGLES 21

2004

'WE COULDA WON'

McNABB BLAMES INTERCEPTIONS

SMALLWOOD, PAGE 136

DAVID MAIALETTI/Daily News

February 7, 2005
First Super Bowl appearance for the Eagles since 1981, however they lose
to the New England Patriots 24-21

2005

RECORD: 6-10, 4TH IN NFC EAST
HEAD COACH: ANDY REID

Schedule

Regular Season

Wk. 1	Sep 12	L	14-10	at Atlanta Falcons
Wk. 2	Sep 18	W	42-3	vs San Francisco 49ers
Wk. 3	Sep 25	W	23-20	vs Oakland Raiders
Wk. 4	Oct 2	W	37-31	at Kansas City Chiefs
Wk. 5	Oct 9	L	33-10	at Dallas Cowboys
Wk. 7	Oct 23	W	20-17	vs San Diego Chargers
Wk. 8	Oct 30	L	49-21	at Denver Broncos
Wk. 9	Nov 6	L	17-10	at Washington Redskins
Wk. 10	Nov 14	L	21-20	vs Dallas Cowboys
Wk. 11	Nov 20	L	27-17	at New York Giants
Wk. 12	Nov 27	W	19-14	vs Green Bay Packers
Wk. 13	Dec 5	L	42-0	vs Seattle Seahawks
Wk. 14	Dec 11	L	26-23	vs New York Giants (OT)
Wk. 15	Dec 18	W	17-16	at St. Louis Rams
Wk. 16	Dec 24	L	27-21	at Arizona Cardinals
Wk. 17	Jan 1	L	31-20	vs Washington Redskins

Coming off their loss in Super Bowl XXXIX, the Eagles looked like they would return to the "Bowl." However the 2005 season was a difficult one for Head Coach Andy Reid, as he was unprepared to deal with wide receiver Terrell Owens's flamboyant persona, which led Reid to permanently deactivate him midway through the season. A couple of weeks later, quarterback Donovan McNabb suffered a season ending injury, leaving the Eagles without the services of both of their star players. The team was stymied by various player injuries throughout the season. The Eagles starting the 2005 season with a loss to the Atlanta Falcons on Monday Night Football, then they won the next three games and the season looked promising. They split the next two games and then the Eagles lost eight of their last ten games and finished 6-10. This was the first time since 1999, when Andy Reid took over the team that the Eagles didn't make the playoffs. One key moment of the Eagles season was the official retirement of Reggie White's #92 jersey in an emotional halftime ceremony on Monday Night Football (against Seattle December 5).

2005 Philadelphia Eagles Stats

Passing	Comp	Att	Comp %	Yds	Y/Att	TD	Int	Rating
Donovan McNabb	211	357	59.1	2507	7.02	16	9	85.0
Mike McMahon	94	207	45.4	1158	5.59	5	8	55.2
Koy Detmer	32	56	57.1	238	4.25	0	3	45.1

Rushing	Rush	Yds	Avg	TD
Brian Westbrook	156	617	4.0	3
Ryan Moats	55	278	5.1	3
Lamar Gordon	54	182	3.4	1
Mike McMahon	34	118	3.5	3
Reno Mahe	20	87	4.4	0
Bruce Perry	16	74	4.6	0
Donovan McNabb	25	55	2.2	1
Greg Lewis	2	13	6.5	0
Reggie Brown	1	5	5.0	0
Terrell Owens	1	2	2.0	0
Koy Detmer	1	1	1.0	0

Receiving	Rec	Yds	Avg	TD
L. J. Smith	61	682	11.2	3
Brian Westbrook	61	616	10.1	4
Greg Lewis	48	561	11.7	1
Terrell Owens	47	763	16.2	6
Reggie Brown	43	571	13.3	4
Billy McMullen	18	268	14.9	1
Josh Parry	13	89	6.8	0
Reno Mahe	12	68	5.7	0
Lamar Gordon	11	79	7.2	0
Stephen Spach	7	42	6.0	0
Darnerien McCants	5	87	17.4	0
Chad Lewis	5	64	12.8	0
Ryan Moats	4	7	1.8	0
Mike Bartrum	2	6	3.0	2

Punting	Punts	Yds	Avg	Blocked
Sean Landeta	34	1483	43.6	0
Dirk Johnson	39	1615	41.4	0
Nick Murphy	7	275	39.3	0
Reggie Hodges	19	699	36.8	0

Interceptions	Int	Yds	Avg	TD
Sheldon Brown	4	67	16.8	1
Lito Sheppard	3	72	24.0	0
Brian Dawkins	3	24	8.0	0
Roderick Hood	3	17	5.7	0
Michael Lewis	2	13	6.5	0
Jeremiah Trotter	1	2	2.0	0
Dhani Jones	1	0	0.0	0

Kicking	PAT Made	PAT Att	PAT %	FG Made	FG Att	FG %	Pts
David Akers	23	23	100	16	22	72.7	71
Todd France	5	5	100	6	7	85.7	23
Jose Cortez	3	3	100	0	0	0.0	3
Mark Simoneau	1	2	50	0	0	0.0	1

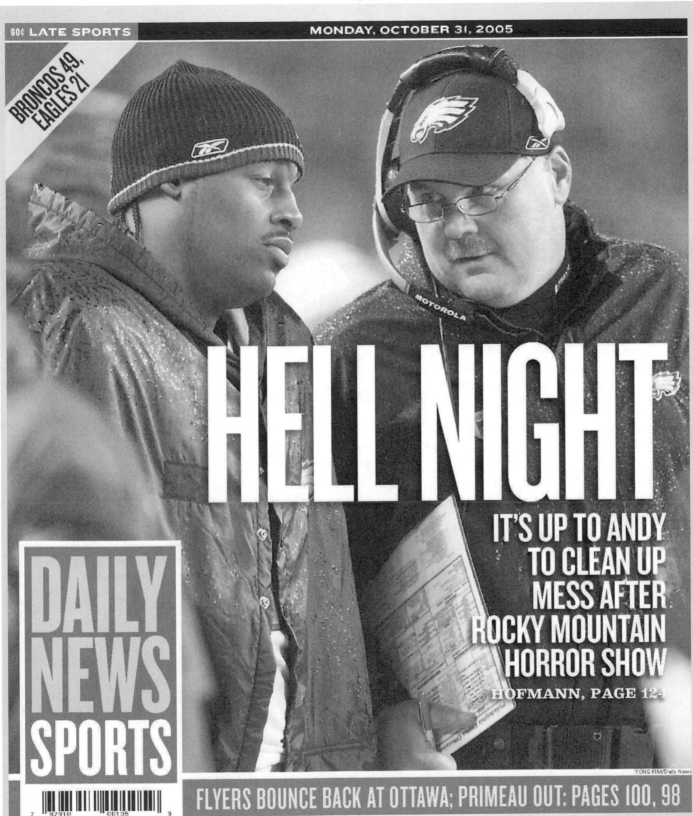

60¢ LATE SPORTS

MONDAY, OCTOBER 31, 2005

BRONCOS 49, EAGLES 21

HELL NIGHT

IT'S UP TO ANDY TO CLEAN UP MESS AFTER ROCKY MOUNTAIN HORROR SHOW

HOFMANN, PAGE 124

2005

DAILY NEWS SPORTS

FLYERS BOUNCE BACK AT OTTAWA: PRIMEAU OUT: PAGES 100, 98

YONG KIM/Daily News

October 31, 2005
Broncos run wild over Eagles 49-21

2006

RECORD: 10-6, 1ST IN NFC EAST
HEAD COACH: ANDY REID

Schedule

Regular Season

Wk. 1	Sep 10	W	24-10	at Houston Texans
Wk. 2	Sep 17	L	30-24	vs New York Giants (OT)
Wk. 3	Sep 24	W	38-17	at San Francisco 49ers
Wk. 4	Oct 1	W	31-9	vs Green Bay Packers
Wk. 5	Oct 8	W	38-24	vs Dallas Cowboys
Wk. 6	Oct 15	L	27-24	at New Orleans Saints
Wk. 7	Oct 22	L	23-21	at Tampa Bay Buccaneers
Wk. 8	Oct 29	L	13-6	vs Jacksonville Jaguars
Wk. 10	Nov 12	W	27-3	vs Washington Redskins
Wk. 11	Nov 19	L	31-13	vs Tennessee Titans
Wk. 12	Nov 26	L	45-21	at Indianapolis Colts
Wk. 13	Dec 4	W	27-24	vs Carolina Panthers
Wk. 14	Dec 10	W	21-19	at Washington Redskins
Wk. 15	Dec 17	W	36-22	at New York Giants
Wk. 16	Dec 25	W	23-7	at Dallas Cowboys
Wk. 17	Dec 31	W	24-17	vs Atlanta Falcons

Post Season

Wild Card Playoffs				
Jan 7		W	23-20	vs New York Giants
Divisional Playoffs				
Jan 13		L	27-24	at New Orleans Saints

The Eagles enjoyed a roller coaster campaign under Head Coach Andy Reid in 2006. The season appeared to be lost by October with another season-ending injury to star quarterback Donovan McNabb. The team turned a 4 and 1 start into a mid-season breakdown, which left the team 5-5. After an embarrassing defeat at the hands of the Indianapolis Colts, the Eagles were on the verge of elimination from the playoffs. Reid's game plan changed when backup quarterback Jeff Garcia rallied the 5-6 Eagles to inspiring victories over NFC rivals: the Carolina Panthers, the Washington Redskins, the New York Giants, and the hated Dallas Cowboys. The Eagles, at 10-6, won the NFC East division title, as well as winning the NFC Wild Card game against the New York Giants as David Akers kicked a 38-yard field goal. However the Eagles failed to defeat the New Orleans Saints in the NFC Divisional Round.

2006 Philadelphia Eagles Stats

Passing	Comp	Att	Comp %	Yds	Y/Att	TD	Int	Rating
Jeff Garcia	116	188	61.7	1309	6.96	10	2	95.8
Donovan McNabb	180	316	57.0	2647	8.38	18	6	95.5
A. J. Feeley	26	38	68.4	342	9.00	3	0	122.9
David Akers	1	1	100.0	11	11.00	0	0	112.5
Hank Baskett	0	1	0.0	0	0.00	0	1	0.0

Rushing	Rush	Yds	Avg	TD
Brian Westbrook	240	1217	5.1	7
Correll Buckhalter	83	345	4.2	2
Donovan McNabb	32	212	6.6	3
Jeff Garcia	25	87	3.5	0
Ryan Moats	22	69	3.1	0
Reggie Brown	3	24	8.0	1
Reno Mahe	4	18	4.5	0
Thomas Tapeh	5	9	1.8	0
A. J. Feeley	1	3	3.0	0
Dirk Johnson	1	0	0.0	0

Receiving	Rec	Yds	Avg	TD
Brian Westbrook	77	699	9.1	4
L. J. Smith	50	611	12.2	5
Reggie Brown	46	816	17.7	8
Donte' Stallworth	38	725	19.1	5
Greg Lewis	4	348	14.5	2
Correll Buckhalter	24	256	10.7	1
Hank Baskett	22	464	21.1	2
Thomas Tapeh	16	85	5.3	1
Matt Schobel	14	214	15.3	2
Jason Avant	7	68	9.7	1
Reno Mahe	5	23	4.6	0

Interceptions	Int	Yds	Avg	TD
Lito Sheppard	6	157	26.2	1
Brian Dawkins	4	38	9.5	0
Michael Lewis	2	105	52.5	1
Sheldon Brown	1	70	70.0	1
Trent Cole	1	19	19.0	1
Jeremiah Trotter	1	17	17.0	0
Omar Gaither	1	16	16.0	0
Sean Considine	1	12	12.0	0
Darwin Walker	1	6	6.0	0
LaJuan Ramsey	1	-12	-12.0	0

Punting	Punts	Yds	Avg	Blocked
Dirk Johnson	78	3326	42.6	0

Kicking	PAT Made	PAT Att	PAT %	FG Made	FG Att	FG %	Pts
David Akers	48	48	100	18	23	78.3	102

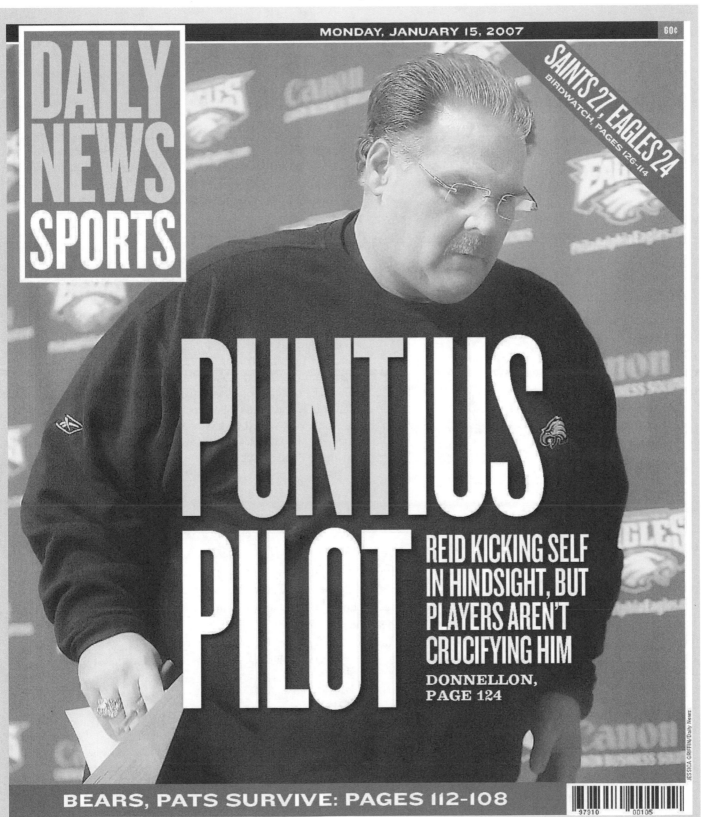

DAILY NEWS SPORTS

MONDAY, JANUARY 15, 2007   60¢

SAINTS 27, EAGLES 24
BIRDWATCH, PAGES 126-114

PUNTIUS PILOT

REID KICKING SELF IN HINDSIGHT, BUT PLAYERS AREN'T CRUCIFYING HIM

DONNELLON, PAGE 124

2006

BEARS, PATS SURVIVE: PAGES 112-108

97910 00105

JESSICA GRIFFIN/Daily News

January 14, 2007
Eagles lose Divisional Playoff game to Saints 27-24

2007 HEAD COACH: ANDY REID

Schedule
Regular Season

Wk. 1	Sep 9	L	16-13	@Green Bay
Wk. 2	Sep 17	L	20-12	Washington
Wk. 3	Sep 23			Detroit
Wk. 4	Sep 30			@N.Y. Giants
Wk. 5	BYE			BYE
Wk. 6	Oct 14			@N.Y. Jets
Wk. 7	Oct 21			Chicago
Wk. 8	Oct 28			@Minnesota
Wk. 9	Nov 4			Dallas
Wk. 10	Nov 11			@Washington
Wk. 11	Nov 18			Miami
Wk. 12	Nov 25			@New England
Wk. 13	Dec 2			Seattle
Wk. 14	Dec 9			N.Y. Giants
Wk. 15	Dec 16			@Dallas
Wk. 16	Dec 23			@New Orleans
Wk. 17	Dec 30			Buffalo

The Eagles made some gusty moves during the off-season. First they let quarterback Jeff Garcia go to the Tampa Bay Buccaneers, they signed backup A.J. Feeley to a long-term contract. Then on draft day making a trade that allowed the hated Dallas Cowboys to move into their spot in the first round, selected Houston quarterback Kevin Kolb with the 36th overall pick in the April event.

The team will open the '07 season with new starters at five different positions, including an entirely new linebacking group. The Eagles traded for Pro Bowl linebacker Takeo Spikes in March, and will plug him in on the weak side. They released strong-side linebacker Dhani Jones his long-overdue walking papers in May and have replaced him with second-year man Chris Gocong. But Gocong, a college defensive end, has never played a regular-season snap at linebacker, and still is feeling his way. In mid-August they released veteran middle linebacker Jeremiah Trotter. Trotter, a three-time Pro Bowler whose deteriorating knees had robbed him of his speed and range, will be replaced by second-year man Omar Gaither. McNabb has a new wide receiver in Kevin Curtis who appears to be a solid tradeoff for Donte Stallworth, who signed with New England.

All in all it should be a very interesting season, hopefully on the road back to the Super Bowl.

Week 1

In the first game of the '07 season against the Green Bay Packers, the Eagles could not catch a punt return. In fact, because of this problem the Eagles lost their first game 16-13. The only Green Bay touchdown came off a missed catch by Greg Lewis on his own 20-yard line, with the ball bouncing all the way into the end zone when Packers' Tracy White pounced on the ball for the score. Then near the end of the game J.R. Reed called for a fair catch and fumbled the ball away. Green Bay recovered the ball on the Eagles 31-yard line. Four plays later, Packers kicker Mason Crosby kicked a 42-yard game winning field goal. The next day the Eagles released J.R. Reed and resigned Reno Mahe.

Week 2

The Eagles home opener was a Monday Night Game lost to the Washington Redskins 20-12. The Eagles only points came off the foot of kicker David Akers, who successful kicked four field goals. The team was looked flat and baffled at times. This was the first time since the 2003 season that the Eagles have lost their first two games. Donovan McNabb reached a milestone when he became only the third quarterback in Eagles history to start 100 regular season games, as he joins Ron Jaworski and Randall Cunningham with this achievement.

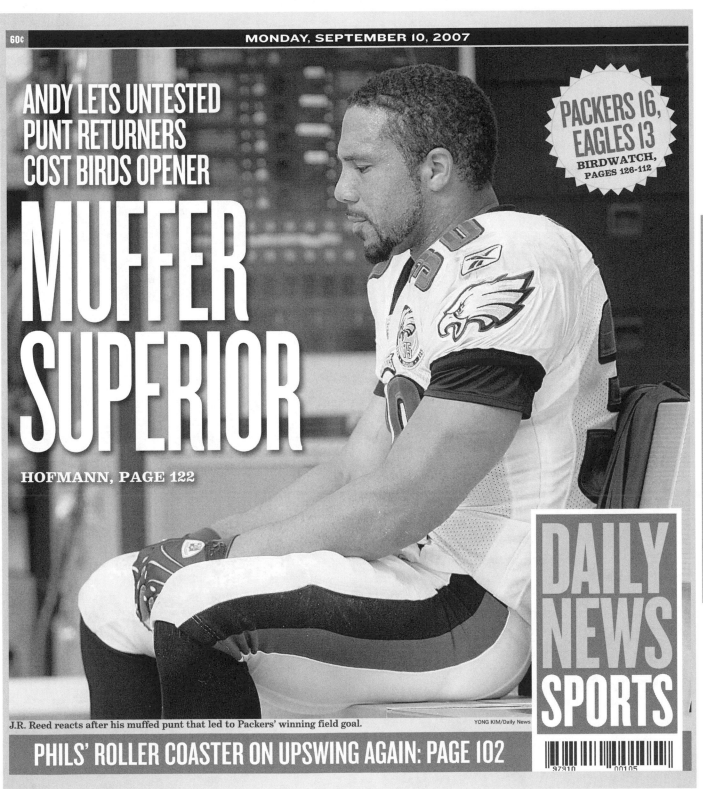

60¢

MONDAY, SEPTEMBER 10, 2007

ANDY LETS UNTESTED
PUNT RETURNERS
COST BIRDS OPENER

MUFFER SUPERIOR

HOFMANN, PAGE 122

PACKERS 16,
EAGLES 13
BIRDWATCH,
PAGES 126-112

DAILY NEWS SPORTS

J.R. Reed reacts after his muffed punt that led to Packers' winning field goal.

YONG KIM/Daily News

PHILS' ROLLER COASTER ON UPSWING AGAIN: PAGE 102

97910   00105

2007

September 10, 2007
Eagles lose season opener in Green Bay 16-13

Fondest Eagles Memories

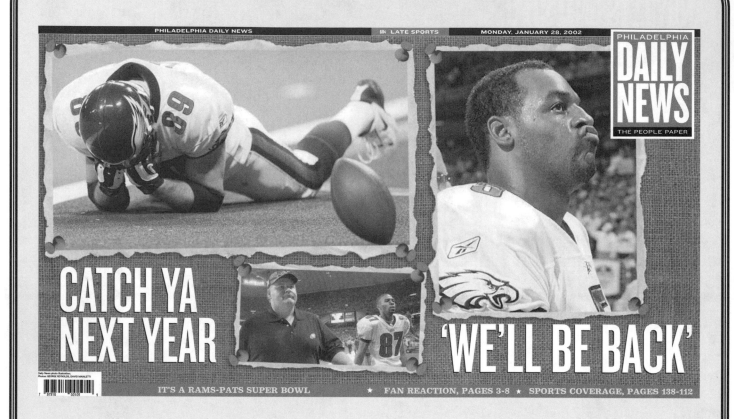

This book would not be complete without reliving some memories from the past. I was fortunate to have the opportunity to talk openly with many former and current Eagles players to hear what some of their fondest memories were while playing for the Eagles. Many spoke about the 1960 Championship game, others the play-offs, while others talked about their personal feelings becoming an Eagle. It was interesting to compare how different the players' memories were from some of the fans to whom I spoke.

Here is a collection of Eagles memories that I put together from former and current players, local sportscasters and, of course, the fans.

Fondest Eagles Memories

When I had the honor of sitting around a table with Eagle legends Tom Brookshier, Billy Ray Barnes, Theron Sapp, Pete Retzlaff, Tommy McDonald and Jimmy Gallagher. Listening to them talk about the '60s like it was yesterday. You could feel their closeness as they reminisce their stories. Recalling certain plays, what happened, what didn't happen, how they would handle things differently today. When I called some other players on the phone, I was amazed as to how cordial they were speaking with me. Never rushing, always friendly and certainly accommodating. They enjoyed talking about their past, each one had a better story to tell. As I ended my conversation almost every player I spoke with offered me another name and number for me to contact and get their memories. Some even called me back to ask if I have enough information. What a great feeling I had for a moment bonding with these legends. I have a totally different outlook now then before when I hear their names mentioned.
By: Eli Kowalski

What can I tell you, I'm proud to be the last football player to play both ends of the field. I had some big plays in my career like leveling New York Giants Frank Gifford, knocking the ball loose, and then Chuck Webber recovering the fumble and clinching the win for us. But nothing beats my tackle on Jim Taylor of the Green Bay Packers in the Championship game. We took over the lead on Ted Dean's 5-yard run, and then on the final drive of the game, Packers QB Bart Starr finds Jim Taylor over the middle of the field. Taylor shook off one tackler and was heading my way. From the corner of my eye I saw the clock ticking down.... 15,14,13 seconds. I thought to myself, "There is no way he is going by me." Then, I grabbed him and threw him down on the ground around the nine-yard line. I wouldn't let him get up. I looked up and saw the clock.... 5,4,3,2,1. I heard the gun sound off and the game was over and we won. "You can get up now, Jim," I told him, "this [expletive] game is over." I was so excited, I jumped in the air with my arms raised high. We actually won! We all started jumping around with excitement. What a feeling it was walking off the field at Franklin Field to the cheers of our fans.
By: Chuck Bednarik, Eagles Player 1949-62, and Hall of Fame Class of 1967

I remember this so vividly it was 1957, Bill Stribling got hurt in my rookie year in the ninth game and they put me out there in his place. I caught two touchdown passes, a 61-yarder and a 25-yarder. So the offensive coordinator Charlie Gauer comes up to me after the game and says, "I think we've found a spot for you." The rest is history!
By: Tommy McDonald, Eagles Player 1957-63 and Hall of Fame Class of 1998

Easy! At least, from an outstanding play perspective. Randall Cunningham on MNF- 1988, takes a shot from Carl Banks of the Giants- keeps his feet, and then throws a touchdown strike to Jimmy Giles cutting across the end zone. SWEEEEEET!
By: Michael Barkann, Sportscaster Comcast Sportsnet

To this day, Buddy Ryan will deny it, but I was one of the few reporters who knew it to be true. The so-called BOUNTY BOWL of 1989. Luis Zendejas had kicked for Ryan and the Eagles before landing with the Cowboys. He was no buddy of Ryan's. The story goes that Ryan offered a sizeable pack of cash to the first Eagle special teamer who would run the kicker down. Thus, the "Bounty Bowl". It may have been the only thing Ryan-drafted outside linebacker Jessie Small will be remembered for. Drilling Luis he did, knocked him silly.

Word got out about the bounty. Ryan and his loyal players denied it vigorously. I put in a personal call to Zendejas. Not only did he know about the bounty, he knew it was coming. Luis told me, and our channel 3 viewers that Al Roberts, the Eagles' special team coach, had called two days before the game to warn him. In fact, Zendejas had part of the conversation on tape. I heard it. I knew it to be true.

Bounty Bowl. Fog Bowl. The Body Bag game against the Redskins. Ryan's Eagles were one of a kind.
By: LT, Longtime Philadelphia Sports Anchor

Fondest Eagles Memories

About the Eagles' 1960 championship team. "They got the most out of their ability and played way over their heads, no doubt about it. I've never seen a team that had so much camaraderie. Those guys really loved each other. They fought like hell among themselves sometimes, but at the same time, they loved each other.... They weren't the best team in the league and weren't the best in their own division. But they were the best every Sunday."
By: Bill Campbell, the "Dean" of Broadcasters

One of my all-time favorite eagles moments does not seem to get nearly the attention it deserves. On 12/30/95, the Eagles played a game that will long stand out in my 32 plus years of covering this team. A 58-37 playoff win over the Detroit Lions at Veterans Stadium. The final score was a little misleading because the game was over at half-time and much more one-sided than a 21 point victory. The Vet had a festive atmosphere like rarely before on a New Year's Eve eve. The team advanced to play the Cowboys the following week in Dallas and in preparation, we spent a marvelous week at Dodgertown in Vero Beach. There was not only a feeling of optimism towards the cowboys game, but a general sense that the team under new head coach Ray Rhodes had turned a huge corner and was set for years to come. People seem to remember the loss in Dallas a lot more than the win that preceded it. Part of that is due to Randall's lost playbook and his inability to rally the team after Rodney Peete got hurt. Part of it is due to the east coast blizzard that forced us to stay in Dallas a couple of extra days amidst the gloating cowboys fans. As such, the memorable win over Detroit is mentioned very infrequently. I've long wondered how the rest of Ray's tenure would have turned out if key players from the '95 team like Barnett, McKenzie, Romanowski had remained. Still nothing can take away from a December day when the Eagles rocked Detroit in the playoffs and the Vet rocked along with them in an incredible party environment.
By: Tollie, Fox-29 TV Sportscaster and Radio Personality

In 1966, at age 11 when I started following the team. I recall listening to a home game on the radio vs. Dallas when Joe Scarpati stole the ball from Dan Reeves late in the game to protect a 24-23 lead.

Later that season my dad took me to see the Eagles beat the Browns. I vividly remember asking my dad why all those men in front of us drank from flasks and smelled from liquor. Back then his answer was "It keeps them warm". Alas, it was the last winning season until the Dick Vermeil era.
By: Mark Zeserman, Eagles fan for over forty years

The playoff win over New Orleans in the Superdome. We had lost Jerome Brown before that season so getting to the playoffs and getting the win was especially sweet. We were losing that game in the 4th quarter and scored 26 points in the last 11 minutes of the game.
By: Randall Cunningham, Eagles Player 1985-1996

As a Delaware Valley native since 1990, I've seen the good, (Andy Reid era) the bad (end of the Ray Rhodes era) and plenty in between. My favorite personal Eagle memory did not even take place on the field. Sunday January 23rd, 2005 at the Linc, NFC Championship against the Falcons. 2 hours prior to kick off I was the host of the pre game show on the Eagles Radio Network. I had also hosted the championship pregames at the Vet and the Linc the two previous years and had confidence in the Birds being victorious in both games. But this seemed different. The air of excitement and fanaticism was the same but the air of confidence was different in the "feel" around the stadium. Mother nature had interceded. The Linc was blanketed in a winter blizzard and it was bone chillingly cold that day. The dome-homed Falcons were coming into this winter wonderland with their potentially slick field handicapped running QB Michael Vick. My pregame show partner former Eagle great Bill Bergey exuded that superior confidence that was "in the air" that day. My premonition was proved out over the 3 plus hours preceding our little pregame show on the frozen tundra that was the Linc that day. Eagles 27-10 and it really wasn't as close as the score indicated and it was on to the until-that-time elusive Super Bowl. Sometimes the build-up is as good as the actual event !
By: Jody MacDonald, Sportscaster Sports Radio 950

Fondest Eagles Memories

Remember Bart Oates or Brad Benson, one of the Giants offensive linemen coming up to me and wondering who was this monster that was lining up over him by the name of Reggie White. Reggie had just joined the team and was kind of underneath the radar. It was the second or third game of the year and they had no idea who he was. There was fear in their eyes like they had seen a ghost, because Reggie had picked one of them up and thrown back into Phil Simms face. They were stuttering and asking me who was number 91 (that's the number Reggie was wearing in his first year).
By: Garry Cobb, Eagles Player 1985-87 and 610 WIP Radio Sportscaster

As we grow older and lose the people we love, I have come to the realization that what makes sports moments special is the people we share them with.

For that reason, I think the Eagles' win over the Dallas Cowboys in the 1980 NFC championship was my favorite moment. I'll never forget exchanging a "soul shake" with my dad _ who years earlier had cultivated my interest by taking me to games at Franklin Field _ in the closing seconds of the win. I remember my dad, brother and myself _ along with 60,000-plus other deliriously happy fans _ chanting "Soop-er Bowl! Soop-er Bowl!" in the final seconds. It was like we couldn't believe we were going.... and hearing it out loud somehow made the dream real.

My father died in 2002, but I think of him often whenever a big moment arrives at a game _ and how the Eagles brought so much joy to him and how they helped give the two of us a bond. When the Eagles played the Tampa Bay Bucs in the last game in the Vet's history, I went up to the same seats that my dad, brother and I sat in as season-ticket holders in the '70s and '80s. With my son at my side, I sprinkled some of my dad's ashes in the seats _ OUR seats _ and recalled how my mom would cook hot dogs before the games and put them in a warming container for us to enjoy at the game.

Stunningly, the Eagles lost to Tampa Bay that day _ by far, the most heart-breaking and unexpected defeat I have ever witnessed. But a few years later, I was there with my son when the Birds beat Atlanta in the NFC championship game and we shared hugs and kisses when the final seconds disappeared and out team was going to the Super Bowl.

I don't remember a lot of details about the game, but I DO remember the joy and connection that my son and I shared... and how precious that moment is to me. That's what makes sports such a wonderful thing. >From generation to generation, we preserve these moments and keep passing them along.
By: Sam Carchidi, Inquirer columnist and Author

The game in Texas Stadium in 1996 where the Cowboys were driving and then Troy Aikman threw an interception to James Willis and then he lateralled to Troy Vincent who ran it in for a touchdown. Better yet I was at that game and called my buddy.
By: Jason Bloom, huge Eagles fan

Holding that NFC Championship trophy over my head. We had been there so many times and hadn't gotten the job done. It was special that we had now earned a trip to the Super Bowl.
By: Brian Dawkins, Eagles Player 1996- current

The day I was drafted. I can remember visiting the Eagles and immediately I wanted to be an Eagle. It was a special time for me and my family when I was drafted.
By: William Thomas, Eagles Player 1998-current

That would have to be the game against Buffalo where Randal Cunningham loaded up from 5 deep in the end zone, and connected with Calvin Williams on the longest TD in Eagles History.
By: Socratese, a scholarly South Jersey Eagles Fan

Fondest Eagles Memories

I can make this easy. I will say when the Eagles beat Atlanta in the NFC Championship game on Jan 23, 2005. From the beginning of the game until everyone left the stadium, no one sat in their seat. From Chad Lewis' multi touchdown game and arm over arm seated dance after the last one to Brian Dawkins screaming in a hoarse voice 'Hallelujah' while holding the NFC Championship trophy. There was a group of us who got rooms in the Holiday Inn the night before and I drove us all around town trying to find a place to eat. We spent most of the night in Chickies and Pete's eating. The roads were deserted as we had a brutal snowstorm to deal with that night.

It had to be close to 0 degrees with the wind-chill during the game and it felt like 85 degrees when it ended as the adrenaline just ran through all of us in the stands. Not only was it the first NFC Championship win in 24 years, it was a whitewash. Winning 27-10. Not even that close. What made the game even more special to me was watching Josh Parry come running over to his wife and brother who were sitting in the front row of the end zone I sit in. I was standing at the rail in the end zone as Josh came over. He stood up on a wood block to give his wife a hug and then to his brother. I was right next to them as this was going on. The thing that was truly awesome was the relationship that Josh and his brother had. Josh's brother had his foot amputated a few years before and had the opportunity to play in a game on special teams 'if I am correct on that' for San Jose St. This amazing heart that Josh's brother showed gave Josh the push he needed to perform well enough to make the NFL and play well for the Eagles. I can say this as Josh told me this himself in Jacksonville when I ran into them at their hotel. The emotion shown by Josh to his family made this game even more special to me. You could just feel the energy from them all. Not to mention the energy and emotion rushing through the stadium. Nothing like it!!!!! To top it all off, hearing Brian Dawkins, 'my favorite all-time Eagle' yelling in his hoarse voice 'HALLELUJAH'!!!!!!!!!!!!!!!!!!!!!!!!!!!!!!!!!!!!!!!

By: Shaun Young

December 20, 1992 home game at Veterans Stadium vs. the Redskins. Whoever wins is in the playoffs. Eagles lead 17-13, Skins have 2nd and Goal from the Eagles' 5 with two seconds left in the game. Washington Quarterback Mark Rypien drops back and flings a pass toward wide out Gary Clark. All-pro cornerback Eric Allen breaks from his coverage to deflect the pass before it can reach its target and with that the Eagles return to the playoffs with a chance to win a Super Bowl they would dedicate to the memory of their fallen teammate Jerome Brown. The quest came up short two weeks later in Dallas, but that moment provided the hope necessary.

By: John Spitzkopf

When I made the team in my rookie year. It was 1971 and I was so elated when I went in the training room and saw my name on the list of players who had made the team.

By: Harold Carmichael, Eagles Player 1971-83 and Eagles Director Player Development

Probably the NFC Championship game win against the Atlanta Falcons because we had been there so many times without winning it.

By: Jon Runyan, Eagles Player 2000-current

That's easy. The 1960 NFL Championship game. I still remember sitting behind the end zone at Franklin Field, Section EE, watching my hero, Tommy McDonald pull in the touchdown pass from Norm Van Brocklin and tumble into the snow. Other guys remember their first date, their first car, their first prom. Me, I remember Eagles 17, Green Bay 13.

By: Ray Didinger, NFL Films Producer, Author, Radio Personality

Herman Edwards picks up a botched exchange between Joe Pisarcik and Larry Csonka and runs it in for a touchdown in the dwindling seconds to give the Eagles a 19-17 win over the New York Giants in the "Miracle of the Meadowlands."

By: Gary Discount

Fondest Eagles Memories

My sweetest moment as an Eagle occurred in the 4th and 26 game because I got a chance to redeem myself. I had missed a make able field goal in the 2nd half because of the swirling winds there in at Lincoln Financial Field. This was a playoff game and it was going to be painful if I had to go into the off-season knowing that I cost the team a playoff victory. Well it looked all was lost when Donovan connected with Freddie Mitchell on the 4th and 26. Then I went in there and made a pressurized field goal. The game went to the overtime and I got the chance to leave the stadium a winner rather leaving there as a goat. More than anybody else I appreciated that 4th and 26.
By: David Akers, Eagles Player 1999- current

A play that was called back but it was against a Hall Of Fame player. During my rookie year I beat the Redskins Darrell Green on a go route down there at RFK Stadium. The play went for 60 yards and it gave me confidence that I could play in the NFL.
By: Fred Barnett, Eagles Player 1990-95

We were backed up on the one-yard line against the Atlanta Falcons at the Vet. We had tried to run a deep seam route against them but Jaws and I weren't on the same page. We ran the same route the next play and Ron hit me in stride in the middle of their zone. I caught the ball and hit the jets. It was a wonderfully feeling because it was overtime and the split second I passed the safety, I knew it was over. There was no catching me. The play went for 99 yards and a touchdown. It's a record that will never been broken
By: Mike Quick, Eagles Player 1982-90 and Eagles Radio Broadcaster

One of my fondest Eagles memories is sitting on the floor with my dad, two uncles and cousin watching the Eagles play and listening to the chat about the plays. Growing up with the Eagles as part of the family background may be why it's such a big part of my family today. With a Navy son following the team no matter where he goes, a daughter who sits with me and cheers, and another son enjoying his career and Eagles connections in another city, it's that deep common bond of continuity that's spanning our generations.
By: Paul Parone, Founder, Tampadelphia Eagles Fan Club, Tampa FL

We playing the Tampa Buccaneers and Trent Dilfer was their starting quarterback. I was rushing outside and up field and Trent was trying to step up in the pocket. I reached out and grabbed him with one hand by the top of his jersey. He was facing the other way and my momentum was heading up field and somehow I was able to yank him up off of his feet with one hand and sling him to the ground. It made me look like I was the strongest man in the league.
By: Hugh Douglas, Eagles Player 1998-2002, 2004 and 610 WIP Sports Radio Personality

My rookie year at the Vet against the Cowboys. I was running full speed while covering a kickoff and caught Dallas kick returner Reggie Swinton as he tried to speed to through what he thought was an opening in the coverage. I nearly killed him. I also had an interception in the game. My teammates started treating me differently after that game because they realized I could help them win. That hit and interception let me know I could play on the pro level.
By: Sheldon Brown, Eagles Player 2002- current

My greatest memory of the Eagles involves Randall Cunningham and Fred Barnett. It was probably the greatest athletic play I have ever seen. Randall went back to throw against the Buffalo Bills, at about 10 yard line. He was being rushed by two Bills pass rushers. He escaped and ducked under one while on the move, he threw one about 50-60 yards on the fly into the hands of Fred Barnett. It turned out to be a 90-yard touchdown pass.
By: Adam Poppel

Fondest Eagles Memories

It was a Monday night game in 1974, the Cowboys were ahead in the game 10-0 and were on the verge of scoring again when Doug Dennison tried to go off tackle from the four yard line for a score, but I hit him chest high with everything I had and it was a thud. He coughed up the ball and Joe "The Bird" Lavender picked it up and ran 96 yards the other way for a score. We went on to win the game 13 to 10. It was the first time in years that we beat Dallas.
By: Bill Bergey, Eagles Player 1974-80

Don't know why I still remember this game but back in 1959, the Philadelphia Eagles came back from 24 points behind to win against the Chicago Cardinals. The Final score was 28-24.
By: Stanley Higbee, Go Birds!

They don't get any better than the 60's Championship win! We were such a close bunch of guys, playing a game that no one expected us to win. Van Brocklin was our leader. The whole season was interesting, as we lost the first game and then came back and stole the next nine games. After the nine game winning streak, most of the starters didn't play in the loss to the Steelers. I remember I got hurt in the Cardinals game, when I was blind-sided covering a punt. I also remember our game winning drive for the Championship, having a huge block on Packers Bill Quinlan springing Ted Dean into the end zone for our final touchdown on a five-yard swept. We were a great team, but we didn't know it at the time. It's amazing how many of us are still close, some forty-seven years later. Theron Sapp and Ed Khayat were at my wedding and I still talk to many others once a month.
By: Billy Ray Barnes, Eagles Player 1957-61

One of my favorites is about our 60's Championship team. It was an honor to be member of that squad. Every game was nerve-racking; teams scored points on us and we almost came back every game. We somehow found a way to win. How can you forget Ted Dean's 58-yard kickoff return with Billy Ray Barnes making a huge block for Ted? The mere fact that we held the Packers (who were a high scoring team that year) to only thirteen points was a great accomplishment. They had a last minute drive to beat us, but Chuck Bednarik sat on Jim Taylor as the clock was winding down, and it was over. We were the champions. It was unbelievable! Then, to top off the Championship, our Head Coach Buck Shaw left and Van Brocklin retired after that season. What a year!
By: Ed Khayat, Eagles Player 1958-61, 1964-65 and Head Coach 1971-72

One of my favorite Eagles memories would be...
All I have to say is Freddie Mitchell and the Eagles vs. Packers, 4th and 26. What a play!
By: Kim Sinclair, Love my Eagles!

First of all I was a free agent with a low percentage chance of making the team. I survived all the cuts and made the team. In the first regular season game against the Arizona Cardinals, I nearly fainted when I was standing on the sideline and Rich Kotite called my name. He told me to go into the game, and then in the huddle they called a play for me to carry the ball. They handed me the ball and I went off tackle for 33 yards. It seemed like the play took forever. When Hershel Walker was helping me up after the play, I had an out of body experience. It was like I was watching the game and I had trouble believing that I had really run for all that yardage. Later in the game, I scored a touchdown and I gave the ball to the referee because I wasn't all there. Thankfully Freddie Barnett got the ball back from the ref for me. The whole thing was like a dream but it was the game I proved I belonged in the NFL.
By: Vaughn Hebron, Eagles Player 1993-95, and Sportscaster Comcast Sportsnet

When the Eagles beat the Cowboys to go to the Super Bowl in the 80's. I cried like a baby, I was so happy.
By: Mike from S & B Sports Promotion

Fondest Eagles Memories

Well let me say this I've been a Eagles fan in and out but I must say one of the best times I've ever experience watching them had to be this. The windows were down so you could hear the entire block watching the game, it was a few years back when the Eagles were driving and then it happened... McNabb goes down and is hurt. You could hear the whole block ohhing and ahhhing, (besides other words) and it seemed all hope was gone. Now I'm a big McNabb fan so when Detmer an unknown quarterback comes into the game, well you could hear the block going "what the hell," and who is, and so on and so on.

Surprisingly he (Detmer) did well and actually got the Eagles rolling. There seemed to be an inner peace as everyone seemed to pause going WOW just maybe.... Now yes, these were the same people going "what the." It seemed like just watching a game for a few moment had everyone focusing on that instead of problems of the world and such, which kinda got me thinking at the time how incredible one sport can do this ... of course when Detmer got hurt the disbelief was back and yet again. My thing is with everything going on in the world it was nice for a few hours to have everyone on the same page and not worried about who shot who and other day-to-day problems we all face. If only all problems could be solved by watching a football game.
By: Ray, the Midas Man

It would have to be the entire 60's season. We started the season with a loss to the Cleveland Browns. Then, miraculously, we won the next nine games. What was so amazing about those nine games was that we were trailing at halftime in every game, but one, but somehow we found a way to win! Everyone knew they needed to step up and help the team. When we won the Championship against Lombardi's Green Bay Packers, it was a whole team effort. That was a great feeling and I will always remember it. I had some great years playing in Philadelphia.
By: Pete Retzlaff, Eagles Player 1956-66, and Eagles General Manager 1969-72

One of my best Eagles memories is the "4th and 26" playoff game against Green Bay. It was only the 2nd game ever where I dressed as "Andy Reid", so the people in my section at the Linc were still not sure what to make of me. Very quickly, the Eagles fell behind 14-0. Predictably, I was taking some heat.

I remember Green Bay's Coach Sherman making a gutless call to punt from his own 41 on 4th and 1. A first down would have ended the Eagles season. Instead the Packers punted into the end zone, and the Eagles had the ball at their own 20, trailing 17-14.

Obviously, the actual "4th and 26" play was a huge memory. But, the play that really sticks with me happened later that game in overtime. I announced to those seated around me that Brett Favre was really due to throw up one of his classic "trying to make too much out of nothing" interceptions. Within seconds, Favre threw up a pass that was half punt, half javelin being thrown straight into the air coming down with a dead bird (a la the old Atari "Track and Field" game). Brian Dawkins fielded it and returned it like a punt. About 10 people sitting around me starting hitting and smacking me (in a good-natured fashion) while yelling, "Andy Reid just predicted that", "the Coach guy just completely called that". I was feeling claustrophobic and euphoric at the same time.

A few plays later Akers kicked a 31-yd game winning FG in overtime and the Eagles went on to their 3rd straight NFC Championship. The rest is history (and by history, I mean, we got humiliated by the Panthers a week later).
By: Steve Odabashian, comedian/pianist and Andy Reid impersonator

When the Eagles stopped Emmitt Smith 4 times on the one-yard line and took over on downs.
By: Vinnie "the crumb," 94 WYSP Radio Personality

Fondest Eagles Memories

I was in my senior year of college in Atlanta GA and when the Eagles finally got to their first Super Bowl, I had to beg & borrow to raise the $80.00 for the ticket. One of my teammates from my college ice hockey team rode with me to Tulane University where his brother was in school. He said I could have a piece of floor to sleep on. The drive was an eye opener, going from Atlanta to New Orleans is quite an adventure for a person who spent his entire life in the north. I saw a Klu Klux Klansman in full robe on a corner in Mobile, Alabama handing out leaflets on a street corner. WOW! When I finally got to New Orleans, what a weekend it was. If you remember, the Iran hostage crisis was about to end and Reagan was about to be sworn in. The town was a buzz about that. A yellow ribbon was around the Superdome. Saturday night before the game I tried to walk down Bourbon Street, what a night. Everyone was in green or in black/silver. I was the party to end all parties. The Eagles fight song rang down from the balconies on Bourbon Street. What a build up. The game was not so good, but I would not have traded the experience for anything. I had been attending games since 1964 (age 5) and I had suffered through Joe Kuharich, Leroy Keyes, Ed Khayat, Mike McCormick, etc. This is a memory that will last me until we actually win the big one!
By: Mitch Rosenberg

Our "60s Championship team was a bunch of guys who took chances and had big dreams. Looking back, we stole many games on the way to the Championship game.
Who would ever think that the Eagles were going to defeat Lombardi's Green Bay Packers? I remember staying the night before the big game in a hotel room at 63rd and Walnut Streets, just getting mentally ready. The team was ready, but were the Green Bay Packers ready for us. The game was a usual come from behind win, when Ted Dean scored on a 5-yard run. All we had to do was hold them. On Green Bay's final drive, Bart Starr, the Packers' quarterback, went over the middle to find Jim Taylor, who did what he did all year and shook off a tackler. The only thing stopping him from scoring was Chuck Bednarik, who not only made the tackle, but wouldn't let Taylor get up to go meet his teammates at the line of scrimmage. As he was sitting on top of Taylor, the clock was winding down and we won! But, honestly, it was a complete team effort that got us the championship.
By: Tom Brookshier, Eagles Player 1953-61

So, I think it was 1961 or 62 so I was 5 or 6. My uncle Irv and my Uncle Sam had season tickets at Franklin Field. They would always take one of the nephews to a game. So I guess it was my turn. We get there. It was a December game it was freakin cold. As we are about to go in, my uncle Irv tells me to get under his trench coat, so he " sneaks" me in. I think the ticket guy knew but I thought it was the coolest thing in the world. We start walking to our seats, and we are walking and walking and walking. We were on the top row on the goal line at the open end of the Franklin Field. As we sat down I met all the regulars around them and they started their regular ritual of trading sandwiches. There was this one guy who was just silly and very funny who kept me laughing the whole game. I couldn't even begin to tell you who we were playing. The game ended and we went home. Over the years they would take me to many games, I then became a vendor first at Franklin Field and then at the VET. It was that first game and that silly guy, who I came to find out many years later, was the one and only Max Patkin.
By: Saul Braverman

We were trailing the New York Giants and hadn't really done anything that day. We preparing for a punt return and I was up at the line of scrimmage. I was responsible for faking like I was going to go for a blocked punt, then getting back downfield for and coverage guys who would try to get to Brian Westbrook. The punt was high and there was a wide receiver who was almost in Westbrook's face but he didn't signal for a fair catch, so I had to get him. I ran and hard as I could and got just a little bitty piece of his shoulder. It slowed him up enough to allow BWest to get to the sideline and the rest is history. He took it down the sideline and we won the game on that return. It turned around our season and we went on to go to the playoffs.
By: Ike Reese, Eagles Player 1998-2004

Fondest Eagles Memories

It was the first home game of the 1976 season and it was the first time I stepped onto the Vet Stadium turf for a regular season home game after sitting in the stands and watching them play for years. I had overcome some tremendous obstacles and made the team. We were hosting the New York Giants. I remember running out of the tunnel at Veterans Stadium with the crowd going crazy, then looking over my shoulder and seeing my Dad and my friends up in the stands cheering. They were so proud, I could hardly believe it. It will be a moment I will always remember because it was so special to all of us. I made a couple of big plays that day covering kickoffs and punts the on special teams. We won the game 20-7.
By: Vince Papale, Eagles Player 1976-78

I have man fond memories of attending games as for a three-year stretch I attended every game home and away. I had been to four straight championship games and a Super Bowl over the last 7 years. I have been a season ticket holder for approximately 13 years. But my fondest memory as an Eagles fan was Brian Westbrook running back the punt in New York against the Giants in the fourth quarter with a couple minutes left. See, up until that point I think the score was 13-7 Giants, and the game was boring and the New York fans were obnoxious. Everyone in the stadium, myself included, knew that the Giants had the game won, the Eagles offense was defunct and the only chance they had was a big play by Westbrook. So, obviously, kick it out of bounds. Well, everyone knows what happened and we started celebrating in our seats, as that was the turning point for the game and the season.
By: Jerry D'Addesi, proprietor Vesuvio Restaurant

I will never forget the joy I felt as we celebrated at the Vet in front of the fans in the cold, after beating the Cowboys in the 1980 NFC Championship Game. It was a dream come true. We had planned, prepared and finally beat Dallas. It was special time for Mr. Tose, Coach Vermeil and all the rest of us.
By: Ron Jaworski, Eagles Player 1977-86, and TV Sportscaster

My earliest memories as a 7 or 8 year old is listening to the Eagles on the radio during the 1948 or 49 season when they beat the Cardinals for the championship 7 to 0 in a snowstorm. I remember being with my father and grandfather listening to this game. My Favorite memories are of the 1960 season when I had season tickets for the grand price of $15 for students at Franklin Field. I remember well, the hit that my hero, Chuck Bednarik, put on Frank Gifford and will never forget the championship game against the Packers. Norm Van Brocklin was amazing, Pete Retzlaff was unstoppable and Bednarik was Bednarik. We sat in the upper deck at about the 20-yard line for all of the 8 games at home. There was no better place to watch a game. Every seat was a good one. Who would know that this was the last championship for so many years? The great fun was riding the subway and the subway surface cars to the game and stopping at the luncheonettes on Chestnut Street before the games to eat and talk football. It was a great time. Incidentally I met Chuck Bednarik many years later on a flight to Phoenix and talked football with while he was on his way to a NFL Golf outing. It was kind of a dream come true for a guy who is still a kid with certain old time sports heroes.
By: Larry Kagel

It was 1992 and we were trailing the New York Giants and there was a drizzling rain falling. I was about to receive the punt. All I remember was weaving side to side to beat the Giants defenders as I took that punt 87 yards for a touchdown. That return was and still is the Eagles record for the longest punt return. At the end of the run I put a move on long-time Giants and Eagles punter Sean Landeta and that play ended his season because he hurt his knee when I faked him out. After I scored, I started punching the goal post. I did it as a tribute to my father who watching the game and always wanted me to become a pro boxer.
By: Via Sikahema, Eagles Player 1992-93 and NBC 10 Sports Director

Fondest Eagles Memories

Buddy Ryan's last year, it was the playoff game loss to the Rams on New Years Eve. I remember it was rainy game at the Vet, we just lost and I knew they (the Eagles) would blow the team up and it would never be the same for a long time. Who knew that it was also my last year as a season ticket holder.
By: Carl Henderson, from Carl's Cards Havertown, Pa

January 11, 1981, the home Conference Championship game against the Dallas Cowboys. It was Dick Vermeil's pre-game locker room speech. He spoke about building a winning team; he thanked the coaching staff, how proud he was of everyone in this locker room. Spirits were high the weather was cold and the team was ready to defeat the Cowboys on their way to the Super Bowl. I also remember at the end of the game seeing on those policemen with dogs and horses lined up around the field. The Vet was filled with enthusiasm as the Eagles won. It truly was a special moment.
By: Jim Murray, Eagles General Manager 1969-83

The opening play of the 1961 Season. The Eagles had won the 1960 World Championship and were opening 1961 against an excellent Cleveland Browns team. I was driving down the road as Timmy Brown, one of my favorite players, took the kick-off 5 yards deep in the end zone. The great Bill Campbell was the announcer. As Timmy started to run, Bill went into a frenzy. "He's up to the 5, 20, 30, 50, fans he's going all the way! Tim ran the ball back 105 yards for a Touchdown on the opening play of the season and I almost ran my car into a pole. I later discussed this play with Timmy Brown and he told me how great it was for him.
By: Neil Poppel from Poppel.com

Nov 11, 1962, I was 9 years old and my blessed grandfather, 'Big' Nat Kleinman, took me to Franklin Field to see the Eagles play the Green Bay Packers: Horning, Taylor, Starr, Lombardi, etc. We sat on the first row of the second level (I sat on his lap) at the 50-yard line and the Packers won 49-0. I recall it also being freezing cold and wet. I was miserable. We parked miles from the stadium so we didn't have to pay for parking. I don't remember the Eagles ever coming close to a Packers player.
By: Brian "Shifty" Schiff, producer Comcast Sportsnet

One of my fondest Eagles memories would be
A game that actually occurred at the Meadowlands versus the Giants in 2003. A friend of mine had invited me to go with him to the Eagles / Giants game in the Meadowlands on a very cold winter day. Needless to say we were sitting amongst a group of rabid Giants fans in our Eagles green. The game was not going in the Eagles favor and we were hearing it loudly from the Giants fans all around us. All seemed hopeless with less than 2:00 minutes left in the game, when Brian Westbrook ran back a punt 80 some odd yards to win the game. Upon completing our high fives we quickly left the Meadowlands.
By: Neil Tobin

I grew up in Philadelphia went to school at West Philly High. I always dreamed about playing for my hometown football team. It all started in 1940, as a 15 year old kid when I was able to attend the Eagles training camp at West Chester and be a water boy, catch punts during practice and run errands for the players. Then in 1947, my dreams came true when I became a member of the Philadelphia Eagles. In 1948, our QB Tommy Thompson got injured during the Redskins game. We were going to play the powerhouse Chicago Bears in the next game. I started that game and we defeated the Bears 12-7. It was the Eagles first win ever over the Bears.
By: Bill Mackrides, Eagles Player 1947-51

Fondest Eagles Memories

I'll confess that I never loved Veterans Stadium. I spent too many years calling it a "dump" and arguing that the fans of Philadelphia deserved better. At the same time, I came to understand what the Vet meant to all the fans who spent three decades cheering and booing and sweating and freezing in its hard plastic seats. So on March 19, 2004 – the night before the implosion of the old concrete donut – I dedicated my show on WIP to the memories – Wilbert's famous run and Randall's magic and every other awe-inspiring moment. For hours, every phone line into the show was booked solid with folks wanted to share their reminiscences.

Then it occurred to me. We needed to say goodbye in person. We needed to toast the old gray building with Cold Duck and a chorus of "Auld Lang Syne" before moving on. I asked a caller if he would join me outside the Vet when I got off the air at 11 p.m. He agreed. So did the next caller. And the next. People offered to bring champagne and cigars and cheesesteaks and whatever else seemed to make sense. A Philly cop called and said we could all park around the corner without being hassled. So when my shift ended, I headed down. I hoped to find 30 fans as mentally deficient as I was to share in the moment. Instead, I found 300. The corner of Broad and Pattison was mobbed with folks who had listened to my show and wanted to hold an impromptu Irish wake for the joint the night before it went down. They drove in from Camden and Conshohocken, South Philly and Southampton. For an hour, we toasted the Vet. We lit cigars and started a bonfire with used newspapers and old programs (the cops were terrific). We raised glasses of champagne and Scotch and homemade red to Buddy Ryan and Reggie White and Wendell Davis's knees. We toasted until there was nothing left to toast and drank until there was nothing left to drink. We sang, too. "Fly, Eagles, Fly," at least a dozen times. One knucklehead even attempted a version of Bully Dave Schultz's novelty song, "Penalty Box," just for variety. For one final time, the Vet was a magnet, drawing people of all races, educations and backgrounds. We hugged and then went home. The next day they blew the place up.

Athletes come and go. Even the biggest stars are just visitors here. Coaches get fired. Owners sell out to the next rich guy. But the fans stay forever. They're the lifers. To me, they've always been the real heroes.
By: Glen Macnow, author and 610 WIP Radio Sportscaster

I have so many, but let me tell you about one from 1953, Shibe Park. December 13th, it was the last game of the season. We were playing the dreaded Cleveland Browns. They were coming in with a perfect record winning their last eleven straight games. We all thought that they were going to "clean our clocks". The team felt they had nothing to lose. Tommy Thompson threw for 3 touchdowns and somehow the team found a way to defeat the Bears 42-27. It was an unbelievable win for the team.
By: Jim Gallagher, Eagles Public Relations Director 1949-95 and member of the Eagles Honor Roll

It was 1960, I remember going with my dad to my first championship game at Franklin Field. What I remember most is seeing the various Eagles players running on and off the field. However their was one player that stood out because he never came off the field, number 60 Chuck Bednarik, he played with the offense and also with the defense. The man never rested! When the Eagles won the game and championship, I recall the fans rushing onto the field (back then they were allowed) embracing Chuck. He was so big that no one could pick him up in celebration. But the image of Chuck raising his fist in the air to say we won it will always stay in the back of my mind.
By: Steve Sabol, President NFL Films

That's easy! My fondest Eagles memory was driving down to Jacksonville and getting pulled over for speeding just North of South Of The Border. We told the trooper that we were the Birdheadz and we were performing at the Super Bowl. He didn't believe us so he had us perform "Flyin' Wit Dabirdz" right on the shoulder of I-95. Luckily he was an Eagles fan so he let us go with just a warning and oh yeah, a signed CD.
By: Birdheadz Darulah

75 yrs

OF

EAGLES HISTORY

Fondest Eagles Memories

I had a bad two years in Washington playing for the Skins so I will always remember when I came back to the Eagles. I pulled up to the Nova Care Complex expecting to walk into the locker room with little fanfare, but I saw all of those television trucks and media people waiting for me to come in and talk. I had no idea that the city cared about me so much. It really touched me because of the way I had left. I really appreciated returning to Philly to play for the Eagles because I knew the grass wasn't greener on the other side of the street.

By: Jeremiah Trotter, Eagles Player 1998-2001 and 2004-2006

We were trailing the Giants and we hadn't been able to do much in the game. It was a high punt and I saw a Giants coverage guy getting close but I didn't want to fair catch because we needed a big play. I caught the ball and made a move to get inside that first guy who was coming from the side where we had the return set up. A slight block helped me get by him. After that, I hit the gas so I could get to the wall, which we had set up down the left sideline. I just ran as fast as I could for the end zone. I remember the play so well because it helped us win that game and turned around our season.

By: Brian Westbrook, Eagles Player 2002-current

It was the 4th quarter of the NFC Championship game and I rolled out to my right and looked for Chad Lewis to make his cut outside. I spotted him and let the ball go. I knew if he caught it we were going to the Super Bowl. When he came down with the ball and the referees' signaled touchdown, I knew we had finally gotten over the hump and secured a place in the Super Bowl. Unfortunately, Chad hurt his foot on the play and wasn't able to play in the Super. But, it was something I will never forget because we had been to the NFC Championship game three other times and come up short. This was our time because we had all worked so hard to get there.

By: Donovan McNabb, Eagles Player 1999- current

When I was a young child my parents could not afford to take me to an Eagles game. I would listen to games on the radio and get so excited when they won. Then again I also was heart broken when they kept losing so many games over the years. As a teenager my friend took me to by first Eagles game with his father at the Vet. It was a blistering cold day (go figure); we got to the parking lot hours before the game and started to throw a football around trying to keep warm. I was amazed on how many people were outside tailgating, drinking and having a great time in the cold (some without jackets). People all around us were cheering, singing, watching pre-game shows on these old looking TV's others were blasting their radios. I heard stories about tailgating but unless you see it yourself first hand and experience it, well it's not the same.

Since I never was at the Vet, I had no clue where our seats were. The higher we walked up the colder it seemed. Looking down from the 700 level it looked like little people were playing. The crowds were loud they reacted on every play. High fives then boo's, you're a bum, you can't catch --- well you get the picture. But I was enjoying myself. If this was what it takes to be an Eagles fan, well I wanted it. By the time we left the game my friend and I where high fiving each other, booing with the others, doing the wave when it came around. We were part of the crowd. The Eagles defeat the Cardinals, 19-7. I had a great time!

By: Anonymous Eagles fan

TRIVIA QUESTION

Q13 IN HIS FOOTBALL CAREER, HOW MANY DIFFERENT QUARTERBACKS DID REGGIE WHITE SACK?

(a) 68   (b) 73   (c) 79   (d) 81

answer on page 254

TRIVIA QUESTION

Q14 WHICH ONE OF THE FOLLOWING EAGLES QUARTERBACKS WON HIS FIRST FOUR STARTS IN THE NEW MILLENNIUM?

(a) KOY DETMER   (b) A.J. FEELEY
(c) DOUG PEDERSON (d) BOBBY HOYING

answer on page 254

Training Camp Locations

1933	Atlantic City, NJ
1934	Atlantic City, NJ
1935	Chestnut Hill Academy, Philadelphia
1936	Temple University, (Hillcrest Hotel, Flourtown, PA)
1937	Temple University, (Oak Lane Country Day School)
1938	West Chester State Teachers College, West Chester, PA
1939	St. Joseph's College, Philadelphia
1940	West Chester State Teachers College, West Chester, PA
1941	Two Rivers, Wisconsin
1942	Two Rivers, Wisconsin
1943	St. Joseph's College, Philadelphia, PA
1944	West Chester State Teachers College, West Chester, PA
1945	West Chester State Teachers College, West Chester, PA
1946	Saranac Lake, New York
1947	Saranac Lake, New York
1948-50	Grand Rapids, Minnesota
1951-67	Hershey, PA (1964 2 weeks at Cherry Hill Inn, NJ)
1968-72	Albright College, Reading, PA
1973-79	Widener College, Chester, PA
1980-95	West Chester University, West Chester, PA
1996-Present	Lehigh University, Bethlehem, PA

TRAINING CAMPS

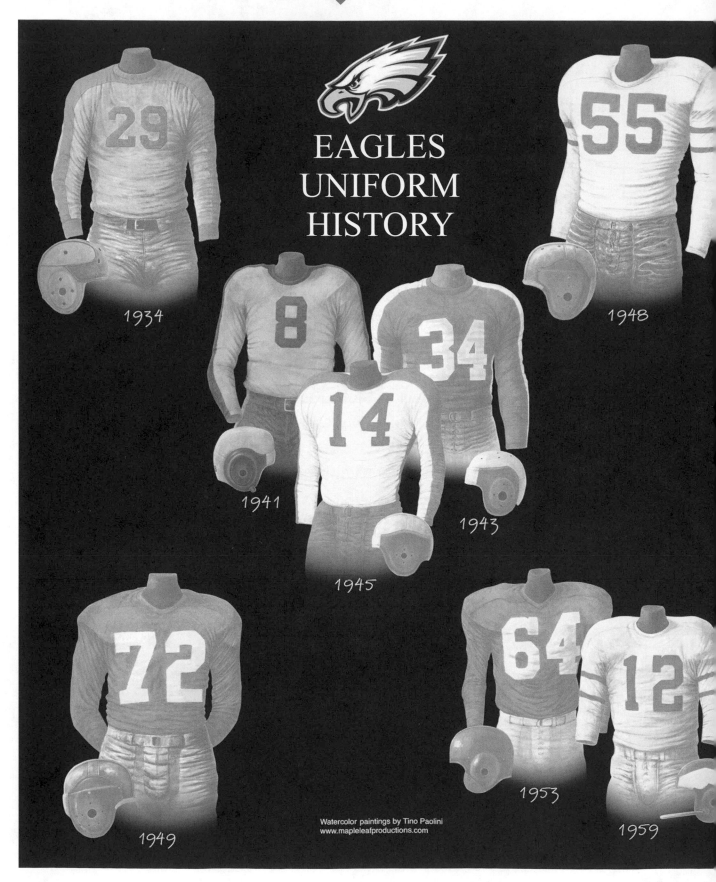

EAGLES
UNIFORM
HISTORY

1934

1941

1945

1943

1948

1949

1953

1959

Watercolor paintings by Tino Paolini
www.mapleleafproductions.com

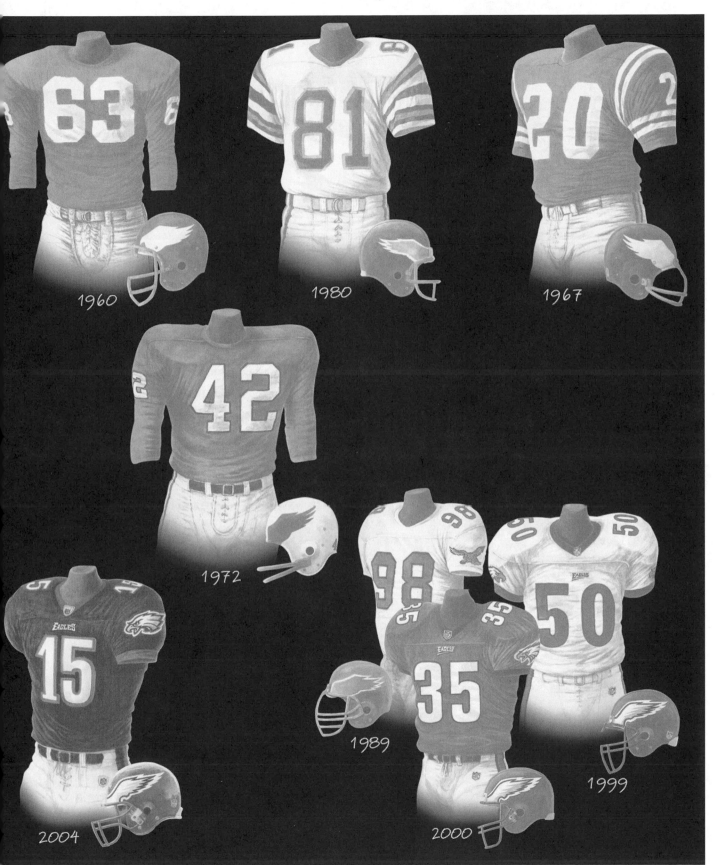

1960

1980

1967

1972

1989

1999

2004

2000

1934

1934

This yellow jersey that you see is the first jersey the team wore. Notice the blue stripes that runs from one sleeve cuff all the way up the arm, across the shoulders, and down the next arm. The numbers are small and placed high on the chest. Note also the helmet. It is very different than what we are used to seeing!

1941

This jersey isn't quite as flashy as the 1934 jersey we see on this poster. The colors have changed to black and gray, and not only on the jersey, but the helmet as well.

1945

This white jersey is a nice change from the dark colored 1941 jersey. Notice how the helmet has also changed color to match the uniform.

1941

1943

1945

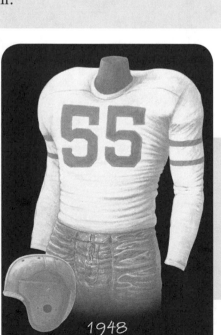

1948

1948

This white jersey has green lettering on the front, while the stripes along the shoulders and arms are removed. Note the two green horizontal stripes on the arms. The helmet has changed slightly, adding a color where there was once white.

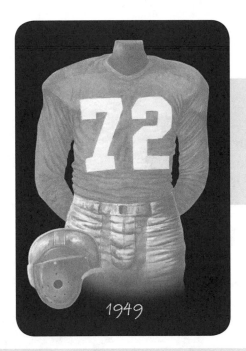

1949

1949

The team decides to stick with the basics as they remove all the stripes, and keep the same helmet as the previous season.

1953

This green jersey hasn't changed much since 1949, with exception to the numbering.
Note the helmet: it is now all green, and matches the jersey.

1959

This white jersey has adopted the green horizontal stripes on the arms once again, only this time adding white matching pants. Note the change of the helmet. They have added white eagles wings, as well as a safety bar.

1953

1959

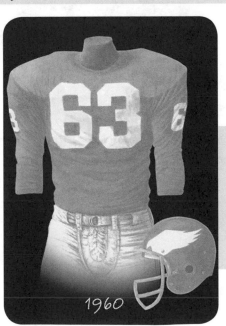

1960

1960

This green jersey has replaced the white stripes with white player numbers. Note also the change of the mask on the helmet. The logo of eagles' wings is also on the sides.

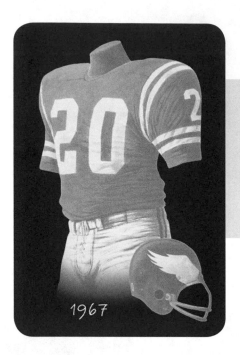

1967

This green jersey adds once again the white stripes, however changing them slightly, adding them to the arms as well as around the shoulders. The player numbers, however, are still on the arms. The helmet changes slightly, changing the mask.

1972

This jersey has abandoned the stripes, and added a black outline to the player numbers. Notice the helmet has changed the mask, and has changed to a white helmet, making the eagles wings green.

1980

This white jersey, as you can see, has added more stripes than ever, with five green stripes and two gray stripes. The player numbers have been moved to the shoulder, and if you look closely, you'll see that the collar of the jersey is also green. Note also the mask on the helmet is changed. The helmet is green, and the logo has changed, outlining the wings with white, and coloring it in with gray.

1989

This white jersey, as you can see, now has short sleeves, with no stripes. The numbers are left on the shoulder, and have been outlined with black. If you look closely, a new eagle's logo has been added to the arm of jersey. Note the mask on the helmet has changed.

2000

If you look closely at this jersey, you will note a smaller patch the NFL shield on the jersey's neckline. Most NFL uniforms added the NFL logo patch to the neck and upper left thigh of the pants beginning in 1991 - an exception being in 1994 when teams occasionally wore "throwback" uniforms celebrating the NFL's 75th anniversary.

Note the change of the mask on the helmet. This jersey is still green, although the color has changed throughout the years. The most recent change of color happened after the 1995 season. When asked about the color change, owner Jeffrey Lurie stated that "our fans want us to look less like the Jets."

2004

This Eagles black jersey was first introduced in 2003 when the Eagles played the Giants in Week 11. It is virtually opposite in color scheme to their green home jerseys and was an immediate hit with fans.

This jersey is what is referred to nowadays as a "3rd jersey". A 3rd jersey is a concept that became commonplace in baseball and hockey in the 1990's, and in the 2000's in the NFL. Most 3rd jerseys are worn occasionally at home as well as on the road, giving a team a third option as to what uniform to wear.

Eagles Retired Numbers

**Tom Brookshier, DB,
1953-61**

**Steve Van Buren, HB/S,
1944-51**

**Pete Retzlaff, RB/WR/TE,
1956-66**

**Al Wistert, OT,
1943-51**

**Chuck Bednarik, C/LB,
1949-62**

**Reggie White, DE,
1985-92**

**Jerome Brown, DT,
1986-92**

Players by the Numbers

The following players have been on the Eagles' active roster for at least one regular or postseason game during the years indicated. In addition, players who spent the entire year on the injured reserve list since 1993 and thus have accrued an NFL season are also listed below.

*=players that are on the current 2007 roster r= 1987 replacement strike players

#1
Happy Feller (K) 1971
Nick Mike-Mayer (K) 1977-78
Tony Franklin (K) 1979-83
Gary Anderson (K) 1995-9

#2
Joe Pitconis (E) 1934
Mike Michel (P/K) 1978
Mike Horan (P) 1984-85
Dean Dorsey (K) 1988
Steve DeLine (K) 1989
David Akers (K) 1999-07*

#3
Roger Kirkman (B) 1934-35
Jack Concannon (QB) 1964-66
Mark Moseley (K) 1970
Eddie Murray (K) 1994

#4
Benjy Dial (QB) 1967
Max Runager (P) 1979-83, 1989
David Jacobs (K) 1987r
Dale Dawson (K) 1988
Bryan Barker (P) 1955-98
Kevin Kolb (QB) 2007*

#5
Joe Kresky (G) 1934-35
Roman Gabriel (QB) 1973
Tom Skladany (P) 1983
Dean May (QB) 1984
Mark Royals (P) 1987r
Jeff Feagles (P) 1990-93
Donovan McNabb (QB) 1999-07*

#6
Jim MacMurdo (T) 1934-36

Gary Adams (DB) 1969
John Reaves (QB) 1972
Spike Jones (P) 1975-77
Dan Pastorini (QB) 1982-83
Matt Cavanaugh (QB) 1986-89
Bubby Brister (QB) 1993-94
Lee Johnson (P) 2002
Sav Rocca (P) 2007*

#7
Roy Zimmerman (QB) 1943-46
John Huarte (QB) 1968
Jim Ward (QB) 1971
John Reaves (QB) 1972-74
Ron Jaworski (QB) 1977-86
Roger Ruzek (K) 1989-93
Ken O'Brien (QB) 1993
Bobby Hoying (QB) 1996-98
Sean Landeta (P) 1999-02
Jason Baker (P) 2002
Jeff Garcia (QB) 2006

#8
Charles Hajek (C) 1934
Davey O'Brien (QB) 1939-40
Al Coleman (DB) 1972
Paul McFadden (K) 1984-87
Luis Zendejas (K) 1988-89
Brad Goebel (QB) 1991
Preston Jones (QB) 1993
Dirk Johnson (P) 2003-06

#9
James Zyntell (G) 1934
Sonny Jurgensen (QB) 1957-63
Jim Nettles (DB) 1965-68
Billy Walik (WR) 1970-72
Joe Pisarcik (QB) 1980-84
Don McPherson (QB) 1988-90
Jim McMahon (QB) 1990-92

Rodney Peete (QB) 1995-98
Norm Johnson (K) 1999

#10
George Kavel (B) 1934
Marv Ellstrom (B) 1934
Isadore Weinstock (B) 1935
Don Jackson (B) 1936
Maurice Harper (C) 1937-40
Tommy Thompson (QB) 1941-42
Al Sherman (B) 1943-47
Frank Tripucka (QB) 1949
Adrian Burk (QB) 1951-56
Al Dorow (QB) 1957
King Hill (QB) 1961-68
George Mira (QB) 1969
Mike Boryla (QB) 1974-76
Ove Johansson (K) 1977
John Walton (QB) 1978-79
John Teltschik (P) 1986-90
Pat Ryan (QB) 1991
Koy Detmer (QB) 1997-06

#11
Lee Woodruff (B) 1933
Joe Knapper (B) 1934
Ed Manske (E) 1936
John Ferko (G) 1937
Bernie Lee (B) 1938
Francis Murray (B) 1939-40
Lou Ghecas (B) 1941
Richard Erdlitz (B) 1942
Tommy Thompson (QB) 1945-50
John Rauch (QB) 1951
Bobby Thomanson (QB) 1952-57
Norm Van Brocklin (QB) 1958-60
Rick Arrington (QB) 1970-73
John Walton (QB) 1976-77
Jeff Christensen (QB) 1984-85
Kyle Mackey (QB) 1986
Scott Tinsley (QB) 1987r

Players by the Numbers

Casey Weldon (QB) 1992
Matt Bahr (K) 1993
Jay Fiedler (QB) 1994-95
Mark Rypien (QB) 1996
Ron Powlus (QB) 2000
Tim Hasselbeck (QB) 2002
Jeff Blake (QB) 2004
Jeremy Bloom (WR/KR) 2006

#12
John Roberts (B) 1933-34
Ed Matesic (B) 1934-35
Art Buss (T) 1936-37
Herschel Ramsey (E) 1938-40
Kent Lawrence (WR) 1969
Tom McNeill (P) 1973
Bill Troup (QB) 1975
Bob Holly (QB) 1984
Randall Cunningham (QB) 1985-95

#13
George Kenneally (E) 1933-35
Dave Smukler (B) 1936-39
Leonard Barnum (B) 1940-42
Chuck Hughes (WR) 1967-69
Rick Engles (P) 1978

#14
Swede Hanson (B) 1933-36
Rudy Gollomb (G) 1936
Elwood Dow (B) 1938-40
Bob Gambold (B) 1953
Pete Liske (QB) 1971-72
Marty Horn (QB) 1987r
Rick Tuten (P) 1969
Jeff Wilkins (K) 1994
Ty Detmer (QB) 1996-97
Doug Pederson (QB) 1999
A.J. Feeley (QB) 2001-03, 2006-07*

#15
Laf Russell (B) 1933
Dick Lackman (B) 1933
Osborne Willson (G) 1934-35
Stumy Thomason (B) 1936
William Hughes (C) 1937
Clem Woltman (T) 1938-40
Lou Tomasetti (B) 1940-41

Ted Laux (B) 1942-43
Steve Van Buren (RB) 1944-51
RETIRED

#16
Harry O'Boyle (B) 1933
Sylvester Davis (B) 1933
James Zyntell (G) 1935
John Kusko (B) 1937-38
Elmer Kolberg (B) 1940
Norm Snead (QB) 1964-70
Vern Davis (DB) 1971
Horst Muklmann (K) 1975-77
Rob Hertel (QB) 1980
Jeff Kemp (QB) 1991
Gari Scott (WR) 2000

#17
Joe Carter (E) 1935-40
James Russell (T) 1937
Ebert Van Buren (B) 1951
Fred Erike (B) 1952
Jerry Reichow (E) 1960
Ralph Guglielmi (QB) 1963
Taft Reed (B) 1967
Harold Carmichael (WR) 1971-83
Mitch Berger (P) 1994
Freddie Solomon (WR) 1995
Lonny Callicchio (K) 1997

#18
Nick Prisco (B) 1933
Porter Lainhart (B) 1933
Albert Weiner (B) 1934
Joe Pilconis (E) 1936-37
Herbert Roton (E) 1937
Rankin Britt (E) 1939
Ray Hamilton (E) 1940
Ben Hawkins (WR) 1966-73
Roman Gabriel (QB) 1974-77
Dave Archer (QB) 1991-92
Chris Bonial (K) 1997-98
Donte Stallworth (WR) 2006

#19
Roger Kirkman (B) 1933
Jim Leonard (B) 1934-37
Herman Bassman (B) 1936

Tom Burnette (B) 1938
John Ferko (G) 1938
George Somers (T) 1939-40
Harold Pegg (C) 1940
Dan Berry (B) 1967
Tom Dempsey (K) 1971-74
Guido Merkens (QB) 1987r
Tony Smith (WR) 1999
Sean Morey (WR) 2001

#20
John Lipski (C) 1933-34
Howard Bailey (T) 1935
Clyde Williams (T) 1935
Pete Stevens (C) 1936
Henry Reese (C/LB) 1937-39
Jim MacMurdo (T) 1937
Elmer Hackney (B) 1940-41
Don Stevens (B) 1952, 1954
Ed Bawel (B) 1955-56
Jim Harris (B) 1957
Frank Budd (E) 1962
Leroy Keyes (DB) 1969-72
John Outlaw (DB) 1973-78
Leroy Harris (FB) 1979-82
Andre Waters (S/LB) 1984-93
Vaughn Herbron (RB) 1994-95
Brian Dawkins (S/LB) 1996-07*

#21
James Zyntell (G) 1933
Paul Cuba (T) 1934-35
John Kusko (B) 1936
Herschel Stockton (G) 1937-38
Allison White (T) 1939
Chuck Cherundolo (C) 1940
William Boedeker (B) 1950
Al Pollard (B) 1951-53
Jim Carr (S) 1959-63
Joe Scarpati (S) 1964-69, 1971
Ray Jones (DB) 1970
Jackie Allen (DB) 1972
Wes Chesson (WR) 1973-73
Al Clark (CB) 1976
John Sciarra (DB) 1978-83
Evan Cooper (DB) 1984-87
Eric Allen (CB) 1988-94
Bobby Taylor (CB) 1995-03
Matt Ware (CB) 2004-07???
Dustin Fox (DB) 2006

Players by the Numbers

Will Peterson (DT) 2006
William James (CB) 2007*

#22

Henry Obst (G) 1933
Edward Storm (B) 1934-35
James Russell (T) 1936
Elmer Kolberg (B) 1939
Don Jones (B) 1940
Ralph Goldston (B) 1952, 1954-55
Lee Riley (DB) 1956, 1958-59
Tim Brown (RB) 1960-67
Cyril Pinder (RB) 1968-70
Larry Marshall (KR) 1974-77
Brenard Wilson (S) 1979-86
Robert Lavette (RB) 1987
Jacque Robinson (FB) 1987r
Mark Higgs (RB) 1989
Vai Sikahema (KR) 1992-93
Marvin Goodwin (S) 1994
James Saxon (FB) 1995
James Fuller (S) 1996
Duce Staley (RB) 1997-03
Eric McCoo (RB) 2004
Joselio Hanson (DB) 2006-07*

#23

Paul Cuba (T) 1933
Vince Zizak (T) 1934-37
Phil Poth (G) 1934
Harry Shaub (G) 1935
Bill Wilson (E) 1938
Zed Coston (C) 1939
Raymond George (T) 1940
William Roffler (B) 1954
Ken Keller (B) 1956-57
Carl Taseff (DB) 1961
Mike McClellan (B) 1962-63
Claude Crabb (DB) 1964-65
Willie Brown (WR) 1966
Harry Jones (RB) 1967-72
Roger Williams (DB) 1973
Clifford Brooks (DB) 1975-76
Bob Howard (CB) 1978-79
Cedrick Brown (CB) 1987
Willie Turral (RB) 1987r
Health Sherman (RB) 1989-93
Derrick Frazier (CB) 1994-95
Troy Vincent (CB) 1996-03
Ryan Moats (DB) 2005-07*

#24

Joe Carpe (T) 1933
Howard Auer (T) 1933
Dick Lackman (B) 1933-35
Joe Knapper (B) 1934
Herman Bassman (B) 1936
Joe Pilconis (E) 1937
Allen Keen (B) 1937-38
Bill Schneller (B) 1940
Dom Moselle (B) 1954
George Taliaferro (B) 1955
Don Schaefer (B) 1956
Nate Ramsey (DB) 1963-72
Artimus Parker (DB) 1974-76
Henry Monroe (CB) 1979
Zac Henderson (S) 1980
Ray Ellis (S) 1981-85
Rusell Gary (DB) 1986
Allen Reid (RB) 1987
Reggie Brown (RB) 1987r
Alan Dial (DB) 1989
Corey Barlow (CB) 1992-94
Tim McTyer (CB) 1997-98
Darnell Autry (RB) 2000
Rod Smart (RB) 2001
Blaine Bishop (S) 2002
Sheldon Brown (CB) 2002-07*

#25

Osborne Willson (G) 1933
Leonard Gudd (E) 1934
Henry Reese (C/LB) 1935-36
Emmett Kriel (G) 1939
Russ Thompson (T) 1940
Hugh McCullough (B) 1943
Toy Ledbetter (B) 1950, 1953-55
Pete Retzlaff (TE) 1956
Tommy McDonald (WR) 1957-63
Bill Mack (WR) 1964
Bob Shann (B) 1965, 1967
Larry Conjar (FB) 1968
Tommy Sullivan (RB) 1972-77
Bill Bryant (CB) 1978
Zach Dixon (RB) 1980
Dennis DeVaughn (DB) 1982-83
Anthony Toney (FB) 1986-90
Tom Gerhart (DB) 1992
Charlie Garner (RB) 1994
Greg Tremble (DB) 1995

Deral Boykin (S) 1996
Willie Clay (CB) 1997
Allen Rossum (KR) 1998-99
Je'rod Cherry (S) 2000
Monty Montgomery (CB) 2001
Dorsey Levens (RB) 2002, 2004
Dustin Fox (CB) 2006

#26

Joe Kresky (G) 1933
Dan Barnhardt (B) 1934
Javk Norby (B) 1934
Forrest McPherson (T) 1935-36
Winford Baze (B) 1937
Herschel Giddens (T) 1938
Lester McDonald (E) 1940
Dave DiFilippo (G) 1941
Clarence Peaks (FB) 1957-63
Al Nelson (DB) 1965-73
Art Malone (RB) 1975-76
John Sanders (DB) 1977-79
Michael Haddix (FB) 1983-88
Ben Smith (DB) 1990-93
Al Jackson (CB) 1994
Jerome Henderson (CB) 1995
Darnell Autry (RB) 1998
Lito Sheppard (CB) 2002-07*

#27

Milton Leathers (G) 1933
Robert Gonya (T) 1933-34
Jack Dempsey (T) 1934, 1937
Burle Robinson (E) 1935
George Rado (E) 1937-38
Milton Trost (T) 1940
Sam Bartholomew (B) 1941
Bob Davis (B) 1942
John Butler (B) 1943, 1945
Ted Laux (B) 1944
Pete Kmetovic (B) 1946
Tom Johnson (B) 1948
Clyde Scott (B) 1949-52
Neil Ferris (B) 1952
Hal Giancanelli (B) 1953-56
Billy Wells (B) 1948
Gene Johnson (B) 1959-60
Irv Cross (DB) 1961-65
Trent Johnson (WR) 1966
Po James (RB) 1972-74
Richard Blackmore (CB) 1979-82

Players by the Numbers

Topper Clemons (RB) 1987r
Siran Stacy (RB) 1992
Eric Zomalt (S) 1994-96
James Bostic (RB) 1998-99
Julian Jones (S) 2001
Quintin Mikell (DB) 2003-07*

#28

Richard Thorton (B) 1933
Myers Clark (B) 1934
Guy Turnbow (T) 1934
Max Padlow (E) 1935
Harry Kloppenberg (T) 1936
Stumpy Thomason (B) 1936
Joe Pilconis (E) 1937
Ray Keeling (T) 1938-39
Bob Jackson (B) 1960
Don Jonas (B) 1962
Paul Dudley (B) 1963
Jim Gray (B) 1967
Bill Bradley (S) 1969-76
Lou Rash (CB) 1984
Greg Harding (DB) 1987r
Don Griffen (CB) 1996
Mel Gray (KR) 1997
Clarence Love (CB) 1998
Amp Lee (RM) 2000
Correll Buckhalter (RB) 2001-2007*

#29

Ray Smith (C) 1933
Richard Fenci (E) 1933
Stephen Banas (B) 1935
Glenn Campbell (E) 1935
Stumpy Thomason (B) 1935
Herman Bassman (B) 1936
Joe Pivarnick (G) 1936
Clares Knox (T) 1937
William Hughes (C) 1938-40
John Nocera (LB) 1959-62
Israel Lang (FB) 1964-68
Harold Jackson (WR) 1969-72
Mark Burke (DB) 1976
Al Latimer (CB) 1979
Jo Jo Heath (DB) 1981
Elbert Foules (CB) 1983-87
Mark McMillian (CB) 1992-95
Adam Wlker (FB) 1996
Corey Walker (RB) 1998
Darrel Crutchfield (CB) 2001

Roderick Hood (CB) 2003-2006
Tony Hunt (RB) 2007*

#30

Art Koeninger (C) 1933
Barnes Milon (G) 1934
Harry Benson (G) 1935
Bob Masters (B) 1937-38
Don Looney (E) 1940
Mort Landsberg (B) 1941
Bosh Pritchard (B) 1942, 1946-51
John Binotto (B) 1942
Richard Erdlitz (B) 1945
Milton Smith (E) 1945
Theron Sapp (B) 1959-63
Alvin Haymond (DB) 1968
Jim Raye (DB) 1969
Joe Lavender (CB) 1973-75
Ron Lou (C) 1975
Cleveland Franklin (RB) 1977-78
Mike Hogan (FB) 1980
Don Calhoun (RB) 1982
Chris Johnson (DB) 1987r
Otis Smith (CB) 1991-94
Charlie Garner (RB) 1995-98
Brian Mitchell (KR) 2000-02
J.R. Reed (S) 2004-5, 2007*

#31

Joe Carter (E) 1933-34
Tom Graham (G) 1935
Irv Kupcinet (B) 1935
William Brian (T) 1935-36
Emmett Mortell (B) 1937-39
Jerry Ginney (G) 1940
Phil Ragazzo (T) 1940
Jim Macioszcyk (B) 1944, 1947
Dan Sandifer (DB) 1950-51
Elbert Van Buren (B) 1952-53
Ron Goodwin (E) 1963
Tom Bailey (B) 1971-74
Wilbert Montgomery (RB) 1977-84
Troy West (S) 1987r
Tyrone Jones (DB) 1989
Brian O'Neal (FB) 1994
Derrick Witherspoon (RB) 1995-97
Al Harris (CB) 1998-02
Daryon Brutley (CB) 2003
Dexter Wynn (CB) 2004-06

#32

Everitt Rowan (E) 1933
Fred Felber (E) 1933
Glenn Frey (B) 1936-37
Hugh Wolfe (B) 1940
Irving Hall (B) 1942
Charlie Gauer (E) 1943-44
Toimi Jarvi (B) 1944
John Rogalla (B) 1945
Jack Myers (B) 1948-50
Neil Worden (RB) 1954, 1957
Joe Pagliei (B) 1959
Roger Gill (B) 1964-65
Rick Duncan (P) 1968
Jack Smith (QB) 1971
Charles Ford (DB) 1974
Herb Lusk (RB) 1976-78
Earl Carr (RB) 1979
Jim Culbreath (FB) 1980
Booker Russell (FB) 1981
Michael Williams (RB) 1983-84
Michael Ulmer (QB) 1987r
Walter Abercomie (RB) 1988
James Joseph (RB) 1991-94
Ricky Watters (RB) 1995-97
Jason Bostic (RB) 1999-2000
Michael Lewis (S) 2000-06

#33

Guy Turnbow (T) 1933
Ray Spillers (T) 1937
Taldon Manton (B) 1940
Jack Banta (B) 1941, 1944-45
Bob Masters (B) 1942
Steve Sader (B) 1943
Russ Craft (B) 1946-53
Roy Barni (B) 1954-55
Willie Berzinski (B) 1956
Billy Ray Barnes (RB) 1957-61
Merrill Douglas (B) 1962
Ollie Matson (RB) 1964-66
Ron Blye (RB) 1969
Steve Preece (DB) 1970-72
Randy Jackson (RB) 1974
Po James (RB) 1975
Louie Giammona (RB) 1978-82
William Frizzell (S) 1986-90, 1992-93
Mike Waters (FB) 1986
Kevin Bouie (Rb) 1996
Tim Watson (S) 1997
Aaron Hayden (RB) 1998

Players by the Numbers

Eric Bieniemy (RB) 1999
Thomas Hamner (RB) 2000
Terrence Carroll (S) 2001
Clinton Hart (S) 2003-04

#34
Roy Lechthaler (G) 1933
Laurence Steinbach (T) 1933
Mike Sebastian (B) 1935
Jay Arnold (B) 1937-40
Lee Roy Caffey (LB) 1963
Earl Gros (FB) 1964-66
Larry Watkins (B) 1970-72
Dave Hampton (RB) 1976
James Betterson (RB) 1977-78
Hubie Oliver (FB) 1981-85
Terry Hoage (S) 1986-90
Herschel Walker (RB) 1992-94
Kevin Turner (FB) 1995-99
Jamie Reader (FB) 2001
Reno Mahe (RB) 2003-06

#35
Charles Leyendecker (T) 1933
Dick Smith (C) 1933
Forrest McPherson (T) 1937
Drew Ellis (T) 1938-40
Dick Bassi (G) 1940
Pete Pihos (E) 1947-55
Ted Dean (RB) 1960-63
Ray Poage (E) 1964-65
Adrian Young (LB) 1968-72
Mike Hogan (FB) 1976-78
Perry Harrington (RB) 1980-83
Mike Kullman (S) 1987r
Mark Konecny (RB) 1988
Kevin Bouie (RB) 1995
Deauntee Brown (CB) 1997
Anthony Marshall (S) 1998
Edwin Watson (RB) 1999
Chis Warren (RB) 2000
Bruce Perry (RB) 2005-06
Nick Graham (CB) 2007*

#36
Ed Manske (E) 1935
Carl Kane (B) 1936
Herbert Roton (E) 1937
Joe Bukant (B) 1938-40
Terry Fox (B) 19411945

John Stackpool (B) 1942
Dean Steward (B) 1943
Joe Muha (B) 1946-50
Jerry Cowhig (B) 1951
John Brewer (B) 1952-53
Dick Bielski (B) 1955-59
Tom McNeill (P) 1971-72
Norm Bulaich (RB) 1973-74
Herman Hunter (RB) 1985
Bobby Morse (RB) 1987
Robert Drummond (RB) 1989-91
Mike Zordich (S) 1994-98
Stanley Pritchett (FB) 2000
Brian Westbrook (RB) 2002-2007*

#37
Irv Kupcinet (B) 1935
Robert Rowe (B) 1935
Winford Baze (B) 1937
John Cole (B) 19381940
Bree Cuppoletti (G) 1939
Fred Gloden (B) 1941
Ernie Steele (B) 1942-48
Tom Woodeshick (RB) 1963-71
Merritt Kersey (P) 1974-75
Tommy Campbell (DB) 1976
Billy Campfield (RB) 1978-82
Taivale Tautalatasi (RB) 1986-88
Sammy Lilly (DB) 1989-90
Sean Woodson (S) 1998
Sean Considine (DB) 2005-07*

#38
Bill Fiedler (G) 1938
Jake Schuehle (B) 1939
John Huzvar (B) 1952
Rob Goode (B) 1955
Sam Baker (K) 1964-69
Tony Baker (B) 1971-72
George Amundson (RB) 1975
Bill Olds (RB) 1976
Larry Barnes (FB) 1978-79
Steve Atkins (FB) 1981
Mickey Fitzgerald (FB) 1981
Jairo Penaranda (RB) 1985
Russell Gary (DB) 1986
Rich Miano (DB) 1991-94
Dexter McNabb (FB) 1995
Charles Dimry (DB) 1997
Ceil Martin (FB) 1999-02

Thomas Tapeh (FB) 2004, 2006-07*

#39
Harry Benson (G) 1935
Bob Pylman (T) 1938-39
Foster Watkins (B) 1940
Bill Mackrides (B) 1947-51
Pete Emelianchik (E) 1967
Kermitt Alexander (DB) 1972-73
Bill Olds (RB) 1976
Bob Torrey (FB) 1980
Major everett (FB) 1983-85
Victor Bellamy (CB) 1987r
Tony Brooks (RB) 1992-93
Corey Walker (RB) 1997
Michael Reed (FB) 1998

#40
Charles Newton (B) 1939-40
Wesley McAfee (B) 1941
Sonny Karnofsky (B) 1945
Elliott Ormsbe (B) 1946
Leslie Palmer (B) 1948
Frank Reagan (B) 1949-51
Don Johnson (B) 1953-55
Tom Brookshier (CB) 1956-61
RETIRED

#41
Ted Schmidt (C) 1938-40
Foster Watkins (B) 1941
Gil Steinke (B) 1945-48
Busit Warren (B) 1945
Frank Ziegler (B) 1949-53
Jerry Norton (DB) 1954-58
Bob Freeman (DB) 1960-61
Howard Cassady (B) 1962
Harry Wilson (B) 1967-70
Richard Harvey (DB) 1970
Randy Logan (S) 1973-83
Earnest Jackson (RB) 1985-86
Keith Byars (RB) 1987-92
Alvin Ross (FB) 1987r
Fred McCrary (FB) 1995
Johnny Thomas (CB) 1996
William Hampton (CB) 2001

Players by the Numbers

#42

Carl Jorgensen (T) 1935
George Mulligan (E) 1936
Swede Hanson (B) 1936-37
Raymond George (T) 1940
Raymond Hamilton (E) 1940
Bob Hudson (B) 1954-55, 1957-58
Bob Harrison (LB) 1962-63
Aaron Martin (DB) 1966-67
Dennis Morgan (KR) 1975
Steve Wagner (S) 1980
Calvin Murray (HB) 1981-82
Keith Byars (RB) 1986
Angelo James (CB) 1987r
Eric Everett (CB) 1988-89
John Booty (DB) 1991-92
Mike Reid (S) 1993-94
David Whitmore (S) 1995
Dialleo Burks (WR) 1996
Rashard Cook (S) 1999-02

#43

Jack Hinkle (HB) 1941, 1943-47
William Jefferson (B) 1942
James Lankas (B) 1942
Jim Palmer (B) 1948-56
Robert Smith (B) 1956
Walt Kowalczyk (B) 1958-59
Ralph Heck (LB) 1963-65
Al Davis (B) 1971-72
James McAllister (RB) 1975-76
Roynell Young (CB) 1980-88
Roger Vick (RB) 1990
Erik McMillan (S) 1993
Randy Kinder (CB) 1997
Damon Moore (S) 1999-01

#44

Franklin Emmons (B) 1940
Albert Johnson (B) 1942
Ben Kish (B) 1943-49
Norm Willey (DE) 1950-51
Bob Stringer (B) 1952-53
Harry Dowda (B) 1954-55
Pete Retzlaff (TE) 1957-66
RETIRED

#45

Leo Raskowski (T) 1935

Thomas Bushby (B) 1935
Art Buss (T) 1937
Dick Riffle (B) 1938-40
Noble Doss (B) 1947-48
Joe Sutton (B) 1950-52
Tom Brookshier (CB) 1953
Rocky Ryan (E) 1956-58
Paige Cothren (B) 1959
Don Burroughs (DB) 1960-64
Ron Medved (DB) 1966-70
Pat Gibbs (DB) 1972
Marion Reeves (DB) 1974
Von Mansfield (DB) 1982
Charles Crawford (RB) 1986-87
Jeff Griffin (CB) 1987r
Thomas Sanders (RB) 1990-91
Vaughn Hebron (RB) 1993
Barry Wilburn (S) 1995-96
Matt Stevens (S) 1997-98
Tim Hauck (S) 1999-01

#46

Don Miller (B) 1954
Ted Wegert (B) 1955-56
Brad Myers (B) 1958
Glen Amerson (B) 1961
Lee Bouggess (RB) 1970-73
Herm Edwards (CB) 1977-85
Chris Gerhard (S) 1987r
Izel Jenkins (CB) 1988-92
Markus Thomas (RB) 1993
Fredric Ford (CB) 1997
Quintin Mikell (S) 2003-04
Jon Dorenbos (LS) 2006-07*

#47

Nick Basca (B) 1941
John Mallory (B) 1968
Ed Hayes (DB) 1970
Ron Bull (RB) 1971
Larry Crowe (RB) 1972
Charlie Williams (CB) 1978
Andre Hardy (RB) 1984
Greg Jackson (S) 1994-95
Charles Emanuel (S) 1997

#48

Eberle Schultz (G) 1940
Ben Scotti (CB) 1962-63

Jay Johnson (LB) 1969
Greg Oliver (RB) 1973-74
Martin Mitchell (DB) 1977
Wes Hopkins (S) 1983-93
Steve Hendrickson (LB) 1995
Andre President (TE) 1997
Jon Ritchie (FB) 2003-2004

#49

Dan DeStantis (B) 1941
Robert Thurbon (B) 1943
Mel Bleeker (B) 1944-46
Pat McHugh (B) 1947-51
Jerry Williams (B) 1953-54
Glenn Glass (B) 1964-65
Wayne Colman (LB) 1968-69
Jim Thrower (DB) 1970-72
John Tarver (RB) 1975
Eric Johnson (DB) 1977-78
Tom Caterbone (CB) 1987r
Todd Bell (LB) 1989
Luther Broughton (TE) 1997
Andrew Jordan (TE) 1998

#50

Alabama Pitts (B) 1935
Don Jackson (B) 1936
Robert Bjorklund (C) 1941
Ken Hayden (C) 1942
Alabama Wukits (C) 1943
Baptiste Manzini (C) 1944-45
Bob Kelley (C) 1955-56
Darrel Aschbacher (G) 1959
Dave Recher (C) 1966-68
Ron Porter (LB) 1969-72
Guy Morriss (C) 1974-83
Garry Cobb (LB) 1985-87
Dave Rimington (C) 1988-89
Ephesians Bartley (LB) 1992
James Willis (LB) 1995-98
Alonzo Ephraim (C) 2003
Mark Simoneau (LB) 2004
Torrance Daniels (LB) 2006
Matt McCoy (LB) 2005-07*

#51

Lyle Graham (C) 1941
Al Milling (G) 1942
Robert Wear (C) 1942
Enio Conti (G) 1944-45

Players by the Numbers

Ray Graves (C) 1946
Boyd Williams (C) 1947
Frank Szymanski (C) 1948
Chuck Weber Weber (LB) 1959-61
Jim Schrader (C) 1962-64
Dave Recher (C) 1965
Dwight Kelley (LB) 1966-72
Dick Cunningham (LB) 1973
Ron Lou (C) 1975
Reggie Wilkes (LB) 1978-85
Chuck Gorecki (LB) 1987r
Ricky Shaw (LB) 1989-90
William Thomas (LB) 1991-99
Carlos Emmons (LB) 2000-03
Takeo Spikes (LB) 2007*

#52
Ray Graves (C) 1942-43
Vic Lindskag (C) 1944-51
Wayne Robinson (LB) 1952-56
Dave Lloyd (LB) 1963-70
Kevin Reilly (LB) 1973-74
Ray Phillips (LB) 1978-81
Rich Kraynak (LB) 1983-86
Matt Battaglia (LB) 1987r
Todd Bell (LB) 1988
Jessie Small (LB) 1989-91
Louis Cooper (LB) 1993
Vaughan Johnson (LB) 1994
Sylvester Wright (LB) 1995-96
DeShawn Fogle (LB) 1997
Jon Haskins (LB) 1998
Barry Gardner (LB) 1999-02
Jason Short (LB) 2004-06
Pago Togafau (LB) 2007*

#53
Walt Masters (B) 1936
Alex Wojciechowicz (C) 1946-50
Ken Farragut (C) 1951-54
Bob Pellegrini (LB) 1956, 1958-61
John Simerson (C) 1957
Bob Butler (G) 1962
Harold Wells (LB) 1965-68
Fred Whittingham (LB) 1971
Dick Absher (LB) 1972
Dennis Franks (C) 1976-78
Jody Schulz (LB) 0983-84
Adwayne Jiles (LB) 1985-89
Fred Smalls (LB) 1987r

Maurice Henry (LB) 1990
John Roper (LB) 1993
Bill Romanowski (LB) 1994-95
N.D. Kalu (DE) 1997
Hugh Douglas (DE) 1998-02,2004
Mark Simoneau (LB) 2003
Dedrick Roper (LB) 2005-06

#54
Gerry Huth (G) 1959
Bill Lapham (C) 1960
Jim Ringo (C) 1964-67
Gene Ceppetelli (C) 1968-69
Calvin Hunt (C) 1970
Chuck Allen (LB) 1972
Tom Roussel (LB) 1973
Jim Opperman (LB) 1975
Drew Mahalic (LB) 1976-78
Zach Valentine (LB) 1982-83
Jon Kimmel (LB) 1985
Alonozo Johnson (LB) 1986-87
Kelly Kirchbaum (LB) 1987r
Britt Hager (LB) 1989-94
Kurt Gouveia (LB) 1995
Terry Crews (LB) 1996
DeShawn Fogle (LB) 1997
Jeff Herrod (LB) 1997
Jeremiah Trotter (LB) 1998-01, 2004-06
Nate Waynes (LB) 2003

#55
Frank Bausch (C) 1941
Basillio Marchi (C) 1942
Maxie Baughan (LB) 1960-65
Fred Brown (LB) 1967-68
Jerry Strum (C) 1972
Frank LeMaster (LB) 1974-83
Ray Farmer (LB) 1996-98
Quinton Carver (LB) 2001
Tyreo Harrison (LB) 2003
Dhani Jones (LB) 2004-06
Stewart Bradley (LB) 2007*

#56
Bill Hewitt (E) 1936-39
Fred Whittingham (LB) 1966
Bill Hobbs (LB) 1969-71
Bill Overmeyer (LB) 1972
Dean Halverson (LB) 1973-76
Jerry Robinson (LB) 1979-84

Byron Evans (LB) 1987-94
David Brown (LB) 1987r
Joe Kelly (LB) 1996
Darrin Smith (LB) 1997
Mike Caldwell (LB) 1998-01
Shawn Barber (LB) 2002, 2006
Derrick Burgess (DE) 2003-04

#57
Ernie Calloway (DT) 1969
James Reed (LB) 1977
Mike Osborn (LB) 1978
Mike Curcio (LB) 1981-82
Bill Cowher (LB) 1983-84
Tom Polley (LB) 1985
Scott Kowalkowski (LB) 1991-93
Marc Woodard (LB) 1994-96
James Darling (LB) 1997-00
Keith Adams (LB) 2002-04
Chris Gocong (LB/DE) 2007*

#58
Dave Cahill (LB/DT) 1966
Mel Tom (DE) 1967-70
Bob Creech (LB) 1971-72
Steve Colavito (LB) 1975
Terry Tautolo (LB) 1976-79
Anthony Griggs (LB) 1982-85
Byron Lee (LB) 1986-87
Ty Allert (LB) 1987-89
Derrick Oden (LB) 1993-95
Whit Marshall (LB) 1996
Ike Reese (LB) 1998-04
Trent Cole (DE) 2005-07*

#59
Joseph Wendlick (B) 1940
Mike Evans (C) 1968-73
Tom Ehlers (LB) 1975-77
Al Chesley (LB) 1979-82
Joel Williams (LB) 1983-85
Seth Joyner (LB) 1986-93
Carlos Bradley (LB) 1987r
Mike Mamula (DE) 1995-00
Derrick Burgess (DE) 2001-02
Tyreo Harrison (LB) 2002
Justin Ena (LB) 2003
Mike Labinjo (LB) 2004
Nick Cole (OL) 2006-07*

Players by the Numbers

#60

Bob Suffridge (G) 1941
Alvin Thacker (G) 1942
Ed Michaels (G) 1943-46
Don Weedon (G) 1947
Chuck Bednarik (C/LB) 1949-62
RETIRED

#61

Tony Cemore (G) 1941
Joseph Frank (T) 1943
Gordon Paschka (G) 1943
Duke Maronic (G) 1944-50
John Michels (G) 1953
Tom Louderback (LB) 1958-59
Howard Keys (T/C) 1960-64
Arunas Vasys (LB) 1966-68
Tony Guillory (LB) 1969
Bill Dunstan (DT) 1973-76
Mark Slater (C) 1979-83
Ben Tamburello (C/G) 1987-90
Matt Long (C) 1987r
Eric Floyd (G) 1992-93
Theo Adams (G) 1995
Steve Everitt (C) 1997-99
Giradie Mercer (DT) 2000

#62

Elwood Gerber (G) 1941-42
Mike Mandarino (G) 1944-45
Augie Lio (G) 1946
Don Talcott (T) 1947
Bill Horrell (G) 1952
Knox Ramsey (G) 1952
John Wittenborn (G) 1960-62
Jerry Mazzanti (E) 1963
Mike Dirks (G) 1968-71
Guy Morriss (C) 1973
Bill Lueck (G) 1975
Johnny Jackson (DE) 1977
Pete Perot (G) 1979-84
Nick Haden (G) 1986
Dennis McKnight (G) 1991
Brian Baldinger (G) 1992-93
Guy McIntyre (G) 1995-96
Ian Beckles (G) 1997-98
Dwight Johnson (DE) 2000
Scott Peters (OL) 2002
Max Jean-Gilles (G) 2006-07*

#63

Ralph Fritz (G) 1941
Rupert Pate (G) 1942
Bruno Banducci (G) 1944-45
Albert Baisi (G) 1947
Leo Skladany (E) 1949
Norm Willey (DE) 1952
Ken Huxhold (G) 1954-58
Tom Catlin (LB) 1959
Mike Woulfe (LB) 1962
Lynn Hoyem (G) 1964-67
Tom Luken (G) 1972-78
Ron Baker (G) 1980-88
Daryle Smith (T) 1991-92
Joe Panos (G) 1994
Raleigh McKenzie (C) 1995-96
David Diaz-Infante (G) 1999
Hank Fraley (C) 2000-04

#64

Robert McDonough (G) 1946
Mario Giannelli (G) 1948-51
George Savirsky (T) 1949
Menil Mavraides (G) 1954
Russ Carroccio (G) 1955
Abe Gibron (G) 1956-57
Bob Gaona (T) 1957
Galen Laack (G) 1958
John Simerson (C) 1958
Roy Hord (G) 1962
Ed Blaine (G) 1963-66
Dean Wink (DT) 1967-68
Randy Beisler (DE) 1968
Norm Davis (G) 1970
Joe Jones (DE) 1974-75
Ernie Janet (T) 1975
Ed George (T) 1976-78
Garry Puetz (T) 1979
Dean Miraldi (t) 1982-84
Mike Perrino (T) 1987r
Joe Rudolph (G) 1995
Sean Love (G) 1997
Stefan Rodgers (G) 2006-07*

#65

Cliff Patton (G) 1946-50
Dan Rogas (G) 1952
Jess Richardson (DT) 1953
Tom Dimmick (T) 1956
Menil Mavraides (G) 1957

Hal Bradley (G) 1958
Gerry Huth (G) 1960
Jim Beaver (G) 1962
John Mellekas (DT) 1963
Bill Stetz (G) 1967
Henry Allison (G) 1971-72
Roy Kirksey (G) 1974
Roosevelt Manning (DT) 1975
Charlie Johnson (DT) 1977-81
Mark Dennard (C) 1984-85
Bob Landsee (G/C) 1986-87
Gary Bolden (DT) 1987r
Ron Solt (G) 1988-91
Ron Hallstrom (G) 1993
Moe Elewonibi (T) 1995
Bubba Miller (C/G) 1996-01
Jamel Green (DE) 2004

#66

John Wyhonic (G) 1946-47
Baptiste Manzini (C) 1948
Ed Sharkey (T) 1954-55
Frank D'Agostino (G) 1956
Ed Meadows (E) 1958
Joe Robb (DE) 1959-60
Will Renfro (E) 1961
Bill Byrne (G) 1963
Bruce Van Dyke (G) 1973
Gordon Wright (G) 1967
Don Chuy (G) 1969
Bill Cody (LB) 1972
Roy Kirksey (G) 1973
Bill Bergey (LB) 1974-80
Ken Reeves (T) 1985-89
John Hudson (G) 1991-95
Mike Zandofsky (G) 1997
Jerry Crafts (G) 1997
Jeff Dellenbach (G/C) 1999
Bobbie Williams (G) 2000, 2003
Trey Darelik (G/T) 2004
Kimo von Oelhoffen (DT) 2007*

#67

Enio Conti (G) 1941-43
John sanders (G) 1945
John Magee (G) 1948-55
Proverb Jacobs (T) 1958
Stan Campbell (G) 1959-61
Pete Case (G) 1962-64
Erwin Will (DT) 1965

Players by the Numbers

Vern Winfield (G) 1972-73
Herb Dobbins (T) 1974
Jeff Bleamer (T) 1975-76
Lem Burnham (DE) 1977-80
Gerry Feehery (C/G) 1983-87
Steve Gabbard (T) 1989
Ryan Schau (G/T) 1999-01
Jamaal Jackson (C/G) 2005-07*

#68
Ray Romero (G) 1951
Maurice Nipp (G) 1952-53
Dick Murley (T) 1956
Bill Koman (LB) 1957-58
Bill Striegel (G) 1959
Bobby Richards (DE) 1962-65
Mark Nordquist (G) 1968-74
Blenda Gay (DE) 1975-76
Dennis Harrison (DE) 1978-84
Reggie Singletary (DT/G) 1987-90
Pete Walters (G) 1987r
Tom McHale (G/T) 1993-94
Frank Cornish (C) 1995
Morris Unutoa (C) 1996-98
Steve Sciullo (G) 2004
Pat McCoy (T) 2006-07*

#69
Dave DiFilippo (G) 1941
Joe Tyrell (G) 1952
Carl Gersbach (LB) 1970
Rich Glover (DT) 1975
Woody Peoples (G) 1978-80
Dwaine Morris (DT) 1985
Jeff Tupper (DE) 1986
Jim Angelo (G) 1987r
Bruce Collie (G) 1990-91
Burt Grossman (DE) 1994
Harry Boatswain (G/T) 19951997
George Hegamin (G/T) 1998
Jon Runyan (T) 2000-07*

#70
Joseph Frank (T) 1941
Leo Brennan (T) 1942
Al Wistert (T) 1943-51
RETIRED
Don Owens (T) 1958-60
Jim Skaggs (G) 1963-72

#71
Cecil Sturgeon (T) 1941
Frank Hrabetin (T) 1942
Eberle Schultz (G) 1943
Edmund Eiden (B) 1944
George Fritts (T) 1945
Otis Douglas (T) 1946-49
Tom Higgins (T) 1954-55
Jim Ricca (T) 1955-56
Don King (T) 1956
John Wilcox (T) 1960
Joe Lewis (T) 1962
Dick Hart (G) 1967-71
William Wynn (DE) 1973-76
Ken Clarke (DT) 1978-87
Cecil Gray (G/DT) 1990-91
Mike Chalenski (DL) 1993-95
Jermane Mayberry (G/T) 1996-04
Scott Young (G) 2005-07*

#72
Hodges West (T) 1941
Leon Cook (T) 1942
Stephen Levanities (T) 1942
Ted Doyle (T) 1943
Bob Friedman (G) 1944
Marshall Shires (T) 1945
Thomas Campion (T) 1947
Roger Harding (C) 1947
Dick Steere (T) 1951
George Mrkonic (T) 1953
Jess Richardson (DT) 1954-61
Frank Fuller (T) 1963
Flyod Peters (DT) 1964-69
Wade Key (G/T) 1970-80
Jim Fritzsche (T/G) 1983
Dave Pacella (G/C) 1984
Kevin Allen (T) 1985
David Alexander (C) 1987-94
Jeff Wenzel (T) 1987r
Joe Panos (G) 1995-97
William "Tra" Thomas (T) 1998-07*

#73
Ed Kasky (T) 1942
Rocco Canale (G) 1943-45
Henry Gude (G) 1946
Alfred Bauman (T) 1947
Fred Hartman (T) 1948
Roscoe Hansen (T) 1951

Lum Snyder (T) 1952-55
Sid Youngelman (T) 1956-88
Ed Khayat (DT) 1958-61,1964-5
Jim Norton (T) 1968
Richard Stevens (T) 1970-74
Pete Lazetich (DT) 1976-77
Steve Kenney (G) 1980-85
Paul Ryczek (C) 1987r
Ron Heller (T) 1988-92
Lester Holmes (G) 1993-96
Jerry Crafts (T/G) 1997
Steve Martin (DT) 1998
Oliver Ross (T) 1999
Jim Pyne (C/G) 2001
Shawn Andrews (G) 2004-07*

#74
Walter Barnes (G) 1948-51
Frank Wydo (T) 1957
Len Szafaryn (T) 1958
Gerry Delucca (T) 1958
Riley Gunnels (T) 1960-64
Donnie Green (T) 1977
Frank Molden (T) 1968
Steve Smith (T) 1972-74
John Niland (G) 1975-76
Leonard Mitchell (T) 1984-86
Mike Pitts (DL) 1987-92
Tim Mooney (DE) 1987r
Gerald Nichols (DT) 1993
Bernard Williams (T) 1994
Ed Jasper (DT) 1997-98
Doug Brzezinski (G) 1999-02
Winston Justice (OT) 2006-07*

#75
Bill Halverson (T) 1942
Bob Suffridge (G) 1945
George Savitsky (T) 1948-49
Walt Stickel (T) 1950-51
Frank Wydo (T) 1952-56
Tom Saidock (T) 1957
Jim McCusker (T) 1959-62
John Meyers (T) 1964-67
Tuufuli Upersa (G) 1971
Houston Antwine (DT) 1972
Dennis Wirgowski (DE) 1973
Willie Cullars (DE) 1974
Stan Walters (T) 1975-83
Jim Gilmore (T) 1986

Players by the Numbers

Scott Leggett (G) 1987r
Louis Cheek (T) 1990
Daryle Smith (T) 1990
Rob Selby (G) 1991-94
Troy Drake (T) 1995-97
John Michels (T) 1999
Juqua Thomas (DE) 2005-07*

#76

Lester McDonal (E) 1940
John Eibner (T) 1941-42
Bucko Kilroy (T) 1943-55
Len Szafaryn (T) 1957
Volney Peters (T) 1958
J.D. Smith (T) 1959-63
Bob Brown (T) 1964-68
Joe Carollo (T) 1969-70
Jerry Sisemore (T) 1973-84
Adam Schreiber (C/G) 1986-88
Broderick Thompson (T) 1993-94
Barret Brooks (T) 1995-98
John Welbourn (G/T) 1999-03
Alonzo Ephraim (C/G) 2004

#77

Phil Ragazzo (T) 1941
Bennie Kaplan (G) 1942
Tex Williams (G) 1942
Carl Fagioli (G) 1944
John Eibner (T) 1946
Jim Kekeris (T) 1947
Gus Cifelli (T) 1954
Jim Weatherall (T) 1955-57
Don Oakes (T) 1961-62
John Kapele (T) 1962
Ray Mansfield (C) 1963
Ray Rissmiller (T) 1966
Ernie Calloway (DT) 1970-72
Gerry Philbin (DE) 1973
Jerry Patton (DT) 1974
Don Ratliff (DE) 1975
Dennis Nelson (T) 1976-77
Rufus Mayes (T) 1979
Tom Jelesky (T) 1985
Michael Black (T/G) 1986
Donald Evans (DE) 1988
Antone Davis (T) 1991
Keith Millard (D/T) 1993
Howard Smothers (G) 1995
Richard Cooper (T) 1996-98

Lonnie Palelei (T/G) 1999
Artis Hicks (T) 2002-04
LaJuan Ramsey (DT) 2006-07*

#78

Mike Jarmoluk (T) 1949-55
Marion Campbell (DT) 1956-61
John Baker (DE) 1962
Dave Graham (T) 1963-69
Steve Smith (T) 1971
Wayne Mass (T) 1972
Jim Cagle (DT) 1974
Carl Hairston (DE) 1976-83
Matt Darwin (C) 1986-90
Mike Nease (C/T) 1987r
Antone Davis (T) 1991-95
Hollis Thomas (DT) 1996-04
Victor Abiamiri (DE) 2007*

#79

Vic Sears (T) 1941-43, 1945-53
Buck Lansford (T) 1955-57
Lum Snyder (T) 1958
Gene Gossage (E) 1960-62
Lane Howell (T) 1965-69
Mitch Sutton (DT) 1974-75
Manny Sistrunk (DT) 1976-79
Frank Giddens (T) 1981-82
Rusty Russell (T) 1984
Joe Conwell (T) 1986-87
Mike Schad (G) 1989-93
Mike Finn (T) 1994
Greg Jackson (DE) 1995-00
Jeremy Siechta (DT) 2002
Ian Allen (T) 2004
Todd Herremans (G/T) 2005-07*

#80

Granville Harrison (E) 1941
Kirk Hershey (E) 1941
Leonard Supulski (E) 1942
Fred Meyer (E) 1943
Bert Kuczynski (E) 1946
Neill Armstrong (E) 1947-51
Bill Stribling (E) 1955-57
Gene Mitcham (E) 1958
Ken MacAfee (E) 1959
John Tracey (DE) 1961
Ken Gregory (E) 1962

Gary Henson (E) 1963
Randy Beisler (DE) 1966-68
Don Brumm (DE) 1970-71
Clark Hoss (TE) 1972
Don Zimmerman (WR) 1973-76
Art Thomas (DE) 1977
Lither Blue (WR) 1980
Alvin Hooks (WR) 1981
Byron Williams (WR) 1983
Joe Hayes (WR) 1964
Keith Baker (WR) 1985
Bobby Duckworth (WR) 1986
Cris Carter (WR) 1987-89
Rod Harrison (WR) 1990-91
Marvin Hargrove (WR) 1990
Reggie Lawrence (WR) 1993
James Lofton (WR) 1993
Reggie Johnson (TE) 1995
Irving Fryar (WR) 1996-98
Torrance Small (WR) 1999-00
James Thrash (WR) 2001-03
Billy McMullen (WR) 2003-05
Kevin Curtis (WR)*

#81

Dick Humbert (E) 1941, 1945-49
Robert Priestly (E) 1942
Ray Reutt (E) 1943
Walt Nowak (E) 1944
John Yovicsin (E) 1944
Don McDonald (E) 1944-46
John O'Quinn (E) 1961
Ed Bawel (B) 1952
Willie Irvin (B) 1953
Eddie Bell (DB) 1955-58
Ron Goodwin (E) 1963-68
Jim Whalen (TE) 1971
Larry Estes (DE) 1972
Stan Davis (B) 1973
Oren Middlebrook (WR) 1978
Scott Fitzkee (WR) 1979-80
Ron Smith (WR) 1981-83
Kenny Jackson (WR) 1984-85
Otis Grant (WR) 1987r
Shawn Beals (WR) 1988
Henry Williams (WR) 1989
Mike Bellamy (WR) 1990
Roy Green (WR) 1991-92
Paul Richardson (WR) 1933
Robert Carpenter (WR) 1995
Mark Seay (WR) 1996-97
Jeff Graham (WR) 1998

Players by the Numbers

Charles Johnson (WR) 1999-00
Tony Stewart (TE) 2001
Billy McMullen (WR) 2003
Terrell Owens (WR) 2004-2005
Jason Avant (WR) 2006-07*

#82
Robert Krieger (E) 1941
William Combs (E) 1942
Bill Hewitt (E) 1943
Milton Smith (E) 1945
Rudy Smeja (E) 1946
Danny DiRenzo (P) 1948
Joe Restic (E) 1952
Tom Scott (DE) 1953-58
George Tarasovic (DE) 1963-65
Tim Rossovich (LB) 1968-71
Bob Picard (WR) 1973-76
Ken Payne (WR) 1978
Jerrold McRae (WR) 1979
Mike Quick (WR) 1982-90
Mickey Shuler (TE) 1991
Victor Bailey (WR) 1993-94
Chris Jones (WR) 1995-97
Karl Hankton (WR) 1998
Dameane Douglas (WR) 1999-02
L.J. Smith (TE) 2003-07*

#83
Jack Ferrante (E) 1941
Jack Smith (E) 1942
John Smith (T) 1945
Bobby Walston (E/K) 1951-62
Bill Qinlan (DE) 1963
Don Hultz (DT) 1964-73
Vince Papale (WR) 1976-78
Rodney Parker (WR) 1980-81
Tony Woodruff (WR) 1982-84
Phil Smith (WR) 1986
Jimmie Giles (TE) 1987-89
Kevin Bowman (WR) 1987r
Kenny Jackson (WR) 1990-91
Pat Beach (TE) 1992
Michael Young (WR) 1993
Ed West (TE) 1995-96
Michael Timpson (WR) 1997
Dietrich Jells (WR) 1998-99
Troy Smith (WR) 1999
Jeff Thomason (TE) 2000-02
Greg Lewis (WR) 2003-07*

#84
Larry Cabrelli (E) 1941-47
Leslie Palmer (B) 1948
Hank Burnine (E) 1956-57
Leo Sugar (DE) 1961
Mike Clark (K/E) 1963
Don Thompson (E) 1964
Jim Kelly (E) 1965-67
Richard Harris (DE) 1971-73
Keith Krepfle (TE) 1975-81
Vyto Kab (TE) 1982-85
Kenny Jackson (WR) 1986-88
Mike McCloskey (TE) 1987
Anthony Edwatds (WR) 1989-90
Floyd Dixon (Wr) 1992
Mark Bavaro (TE) 1993-94
Kelvin Martin (WR) 1995
Freddie Soloman (WR) 1996-98
Jamie Asher (TE) 1999
Luther Broughton (TE) 2000
Freddie Mitchell (WR) 2001-04
Hank Baskett (WR) 2006-07*

#85
John Shonk (E) 1941
Tony Bova (E) 1943
Bob Friedlund (E) 1944
Charlie Gauer (E) 1945
Jay MacDowell (E) 1946
Billy Hix (E) 1950
Bob Schnelker (E) 1953
Ralph Smith (E) 1962-64
Gary Ballman (TE) 1967-72
Marlin McKeever (LB) 1973
Charlrs Smith (WR) 1974-81
Mel Hoover (WR) 1982-84
Ron Johnson (WR) 1985-89
Jesse Bendross (Wr) 1987r
Mickey Shuler (TE) 1990
Jeff Sydner (WR) 1992-94
Art Monk (WR) 1995
Mark Ingram (WR) 1996
Antwuan Wyatt (WR) 1997
Chris Fontenot (TE) 1998
Na Brown (WR) 1999-01
Freedie Milons (WR) 2002
Sean Morey (WR) 2003
Jeff Thomason (TE) 2004

#86
Harold Presott (E) 1947-49
Bob McChesney (E) 1950
Bud Grant (E) 1951-52
Norm Willey (DE) 1953-57
Ed Cooke (E) 1958
Dick Stafford (E) 1962-63
Fred Hill (E) 1965-71
Charles Young (TE) 1973-76
Richard Osborne (TE) 1977-78
Ken Dunek (TE) 1980
Lewis Gilbert (TE) 1980
Steve Folsom (TE) 1981
Al Dixon (TE) 1983
Gregg Garrity (WR) 1984-89
Mike Siano (WR) 1987r
Fred Barnett (WR) 1990-95
Dialleo Burks (WR) 1996
Justin Armour (WR) 1997
Luther Broughton (TE) 1997
Russell Copeland (WR) 1998
Alex Van Dyke (WR) 1999-00
Brian Finneran (WR) 1999
Gari Scott (WR) 2000
Antonio Freeman (WR) 2002
Kori Dickerson (TE) 2003
Reggie Brown (WR) 2005-07*

#87
Jack Ferrante (E) 1944-50
Andy Nacelli (E) 1958
Art Powell (WR) 1959
Dick Lucas (E) 1960-63
Bill Cronin (E) 1965
Dave Lince (E) 1966-67
Fred Brown (LB) 1969
Kent Kramer (TE) 1971-74
Claude Humphrey (DE) 1979-81
Lawrence Sampleton (TE) 1982-84
John Goode (TE) 1985
Eric Bailey (TE) 1987r
Ron Fazio (TE) 1987r
Carlos Carson (WR) 1989
Harper LeBel (TE) 1990
Maurice Johnson (TE) 1991-94
Frank Wainwright (TE) 1995
Jason Dunn (TE) 1996-98
Jed Weaver (TE) 1999
Todd Pinkston (WR) 2000-2004
Brent Celek (TE) 2007*

Players by the Numbers

#88

John Durko (E) 1944
Herschel Ramsey (E) 1945
Jay MacDowell (E) 1947-51
John Zilly (E) 1952
Bob Hudson (B) 1953
Jerry Wilson (E) 1959-60
Gary Pettigrew (DT) 1966-74
Richard Osborne (TE) 1976
Bill Larson (TE) 1978
John Spagnola (TE) 1979-87
Keith Jackson (TE) 1988-91
Jimmie Johnson (TE) 1995-98
Kevin McKenzie (WR) 1998
Luther Broughton (TE) 1999
Mike Bartrum (TE) 2000-06

#89

Henry Piro (E) 1941
Fred Meyer (E) 1942
Tom Miller (E) 1943-44
Ben Agajanian (G) 1945
Robert Krieger (E) 1946
John Green (E) 1947-51
Bob Oristaglio (E) 1952
Don Luft (E) 1954
John Bredice (E) 1956
Mike Morgan (LB) 1964-67
Mike Ditka (E) 1968
Steve Zabel (LB) 1970-74
Wally Henry (WR) 1977-82
Glen Young (WR) 1983
Dave Little (TE) 1985-89
Jay Repko (TE) 1987r
Calvin Williams (WR) 1990-96
Dialleo Burks (WR) 1996
Chad Lewis (TE) 1997-04
Kaseem Sinceno (TE) 1998
Ron Leshinski (TE) 1999
Ed Smith (TE) 1999
Justin Swift (TE) 1999
Matt Schobel (TE) 2006-07*

#90

Aaron Brown (LB) 1985
Mike Golic (DT) 1987-92
Randall Mitchell (NT) 1987r
William Perry (DT) 1993-94
Ronnie Dixon (DT) 1995-96
Jon Harris (DE) 1997-98
Ben Williams (DT) 1999
Corey Simon (DT) 2000-04

Darren Howard (DE) 2006-07*

#91

Tim Golden (LB) 1985
Reggie White (DE) 1985
Ray Conlin (DT) 1987r
George Cumby (LB) 1987r
Scott Curtis (LB) 1988
Greg Mark (DE) 1990
Andy Harmon (DT) 1991-97
Steve Martin (DT) 1999
Uhuru Hamiter (DE) 2000-01
Sam Rayburn (DT) 2003-06

#92

Smiley Creswell (DE) 1985
Reggie White (DE) 1985-92
RETIRED

#93

Tom Strauthers (DE) 1983-86
John Dumbauld (DE) 1987-88
Ray Phillips (DE) 1987r
Dave Bailey (DE) 1990
Greg Townsend (DE) 1994
Dan Stubbs (DE) 1995
Darion Conner (DE) 1996-97
Pernell Davis (DT) 1999-00
Levon Kirkland (LB) 2002
Jevon Kearse (DE) 2004-07*

#94

Byron Darby (DE/TE) 1983-86
Dan McMillen (DE) 1987r
Steve Kaufusi (DE) 1989-90
Leonard Renfro (DT) 1993-94
Kevin Johnson (DT) 1995-96
Bill Johnson (DT) 1998-99
Kelly Gregg (DT) 1990-00
N.D. Kalu (DE) 2001-03
Montae Reagor (DT) 2007*

#95

John Bunting (LB) 1972-82
Jody Schulz (LB) 1985-87
Doug Bartlett (DT) 1988
Al Harris (LB) 1989-90
Mike Flores (DT) 1991-93
William Fuller (DE) 1994-96
Richard Dent (DE) 1997

Henry Slay (DT) 1998
Tyrone Williams (DE) 1999-00
Justin Ena (LB) 2002
Jerome McDougle (DE) 2003-07*

#96

John Sodaski (LB) 1972-73
Clyde Simmons (DE) 1986-93
Harvey Armstrong (DT) 1982-84
Marvin Ayers (DE) 1987r
Mike Flores (DT) 1994
Mark Gunn (DL) 1995-96
Keith Rucker (DT) 1996
Al Wallace (DE/LB) 1997-99
Paul Grasmanis (DT) 2000-04
Omar Gaither (LB) 2006-07*

#97

Thomas Brown (DE) 1980
Reggie Singletary (DT/G) 1986
John Klingel (DE) 1987-88
Jim Auer (DE) 1987r
Dick Chapura (DT/G) 1990
Leon Seals (DT/G) 1992
Tim Harris (DE) 1993
Rhett Hall (DT/G) 1995-98
Mark Wheeler (DT/G) 1999
Darwin Walker (DT/G) 2001-06
Brodrick Bunkley (DT) 2006-07*

#98

Mike Ditka (E) 1967
Greg Brown (DE) 1981-86
Elois Grooms (DE) 1987r
Tommy Jeter (DT) 1992-95
Michael Samson (DT) 1996
Jimmie Jones (DL) 1997
Brandon Whiting (DL) 1998-03
Mike Patterson (DT) 2005-07*

#99

Mel Tom (DE) 1971-73
Leonard Mitchell (DL) 1981-83
Joe Drake (DT) 1985
Skip Hamilton (DT) 1987r
Greg Liter (DE) 1987r
Jerome Brown (DT) 1987-91
RETIRED

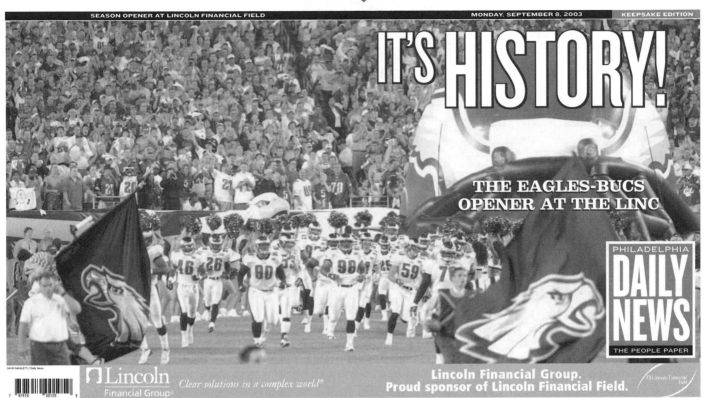

EAGLES HOME RECORDS

Home Field Records

STADIUM		RECORD	PLAYOFFS
BAKER BOWL	(1933-35)	3-11-1	0-0
TEMPLE STADIUM	(1934-35)	1-1-0	0-0
POINT STADIUM	(JOHNSTOWN, PA - 1936)	0-1-0	0-0
LAIDLEY FIELD	(CHARLESTON, WV - 1938)	1-0-0	0-0
WAR MEMORIAL STADIUM	(CHARLESTON, WV - 1942)	0-1-0	0-0
FORBES FIELD	(PITTSBURGH, PA - 1943)	2-0-0	0-0
MUNICIPAL STADIUM	(1936-39, 1941,1947, 1950, 1954)	5-14-2	0-0
SHIBE PARK/CONNIE MACK STADIUM	(1940-57)	57-35-6	1-0
FRANKLIN FIELD	(1958-70)	41-45-2	1-0
VETERANS STADIUM	(1971-2002)	144-111-2	7-4
LINCOLN FINANCIAL FIELD	(2003-PRES.**)	25-12	4-1
TOTALS		279-231-13*	13-5*

NOTE: * RECORD INCLUDES PLAYOFF RESULTS

** PRESENT RECORD AT THE START OF THE 2007 SEASON

Eagles Head Coaches

Lud Wray
Coached Eagles: 1933-35
Record: 9-21-1

Bert Bell
Coached Eagles: 1936-1940
Record: 10-44-2
1963 Hall of Fame Inductee

Earle (Greasy) Neale
Coached Eagles: 1941-50
Record: 66-44-5
Post Season Record: 3-1
1948 NFL Coach of the Year
1969 Hall of Fame Inductee

Bo McMillin
Coached Eagles: 1951
Record: 2-0

Wayne Millner
Coached Eagles: 1951
Record: 2-8

Jim Trimble
Coached Eagles: 1952-55
Record: 25-20-3

Hugh Devore
Coached Eagles: 1956-57
Record: 7-16-1

Buck Shaw
Coached Eagles: 1958-60
Record: 20-16-1
Post Season Record: 1-0
1960 NFL Coach of the Year

Nick Skorich
Coached Eagles: 1961-63
Record: 15-24-3

Joe Kuharich
Coached Eagles: 1964-68
Record: 28-41-1

Jerry Williams
Coached Eagles: 1969-71
Record: 7-22-2

Ed Khayat
Coached Eagles: 1971-72
Record: 8-15-2

Mike McCormack
Coached Eagles: 1973-75
Record: 1-25-1

Dick Vermeil
Coached Eagles: 1976-82
Record: 57-51-0
Post Season Record: 3-4
1979 NFL Coach of the Year;
1978, 1979 NFC Coach of the Year

Marion Campbell
Coached Eagles: 1983-85
Record: 17-29-1

Fred Bruney
Coached Eagles: 1985
Record: 1-0

Buddy Ryan
Coached Eagles: 1986-90
Record: 43-38-1
Post Season Record: 0-3

Rich Kotite
Coached Eagles: 1991-94
Record: 37-29
Post Season Record: 1-1

Ray Rhodes
Coached Eagles: 1995-98
Record: 30-36-1
Post Season Record: 1-2
1995 NFL Coach of the Year
1995 NFC Coach of the Year

Andy Reid
Coached Eagles: 1999- Present
Record: 80-48-0*
Post Season Record: 8-6
2000,2002 NFL Coach of the Year

* At the start of the 2007 Season

Eagles Owners

1933 to 1935, Bert Bell and Lud Wray

In 1933, with three other former college teammates (including Lud Wray, first head coach), Burt Bell became co-owner of the Eagles for $2,500.

Lud Wray was a professional American football player, coach, and co-founder, with college teammate Bert Bell, of the Philadelphia Eagles of the National Football League. He was the first coach of the Boston Braves (now Washington Redskins) in 1932 and of the Eagles, 1933-1935. His coaching record with the Eagles was 9-21-1.

1935 to 1940, Bert Bell

Taking the approach of making the overall league stronger, Bell was credited with establishing the NFL draft in 1935. He served as Eagles head coach from 1936 to 1940. By 1937, the Eagles had lost $90,000 and were put up for public auction. Bell became sole owner with a winning bid of $4,500, but after continuing financial struggles, he became co-owner of the Pittsburgh Steelers with his friend Art Rooney in a bizarre transaction in which Rooney sold the Steelers to Philadelphia businessman Alexis Thompson, who then traded franchises with Bell. By 1943, a wartime manpower shortage led the Steelers and Eagles to temporarily merge into the "Pennsylvania Steagles" (officially known as "Phil-Pitt"). The following year, the Steelers merged with the Chicago Cardinals. In 1937, Bell founded the Maxwell Football Club, which awards the Maxwell Award to the top college football player and the Bert Bell Award to the top professional.

1940 to 1949, Lex Thompson

In 1940, Lex Thompson reportly purchased the franchise for $165,000. He became the first Eagles owner to win a championship. Hired head coach Greasy Neale who at the time was an assistant football coach at his alma mater Yale. Right before selling the team, the Eagles selected Chuck Bednarik as their number one draft selection. Thompson sold the team on January 15, 1949 for $250,000 to a group of investors known as the "100 Brothers."

1949 to 1962, James P. Clark

James P. Clark was a successful businessman who organized a group of 100 Philadelphia businessman to invest $3,000 each to purchase the eagles team from Lex Thompson for the sum of $250,000. That season the Eagles won their second straight NFL championship title. This was one first of two titles the Eagles would win under the "100 Brothers" ownership before selling the team to Jerry Wolman in 1963.

1963 to 1969, Jerry Wolman

Jerry Wolman bought the Eagles franchise in 1963 for a sale price of $5.5 million . He was the youngest owner in the NFL at age 36. While living in the Washington, DC area he saw that the Redskins had a marching band for their football club. So he wanted this for he Eagles. He put together a 220-member marching band called the Philadelphia Eagles Sound of Brass. Wolman hired Joe Kuharich and after his first winning season was rewarded with a 15-year new contract as the team's coach and general manager.

He was also one of the founding owners, briefly in 1967, of the Philadelphia Flyers of the National Hockey League. Over the next two years, his $100-million financial empire crumbled into bankruptcy, and he was forced to give up his interests in both teams. In 1967, he sold his Flyers interest to his co-owners, with Ed Snider assuming control. In 1969, the team was placed on the auction block where he was forced to sell the Eagles to Leonard Tose for a reported $16.1 million, then a record price for a professional sports team.

Eagles Owners

1969 to 1985, Leonard Tose

In 1969 Tose bought the Philadelphia Eagles from Jerry Wolman for $16 million, then a record for a professional sports franchise. Tose's first official act was to fire Coach Joe Kuharich. He followed this by naming former Eagles receiving great Pete Retzlaff as General Manager and Jerry Williams as coach.

In 1976 he, along with General Manager Jimmy Murray, lured Dick Vermeil from UCLA to coach the hapless Eagles, who had one winning season from 1962-75. Vermeil's 1980 team lost to Oakland in the Super Bowl. In January 1983, Tose announced that his daughter, Susan Fletcher, the Eagles' vice president and legal counsel, would eventually succeed him as primary owner of the Eagles.

In 1985 Tose was forced to sell the Eagles to Norman Braman and Ed Leibowitz, highly successful automobile dealers from Florida, for a reported $65 million to pay off his more than $25 million in gambling debts at Atlantic City casinos.

1985 to 1994, Norman Braman

Norman Braman was an American football team owner. He was the owner of the Philadelphia Eagles. Norman and his brother-in-law, Ed Leibowitz, officially became the owners of the Eagles on April 29, 1985. Norman owned 65 percent of the team while Ed owned 35 percent until July 16, 1986 Norman bought the rest of the team from Ed. Braman will be remembered as the person who hired coach Buddy Ryan. But also fired him after the Eagles lost in the first round of the playoffs for the third consecutive year. Replacing him with offensive coorrdinator Rich Kotite. During his tenure as owner of the Eagles, the team twice won eleven games in a single season and went to the playoffs four times.

Braman was a very successful automoblie dealer in Florida and as the Eagles owner brought an aggressive marketing style to the organization. He was able to raise the Eagles fan base by some 15,000 fans and increased ticket prices three times during his first five years as owner. With new TV deals and expansion teams paid large amounts of money, Braman decided it was time to get out. He sold the Eagles franchise to Jeffrey Lurie.

1994- Present, Jeffrey Lurie

Jeffrey Lurie is a former Hollywood producer turned NFL team owner. Lurie bought the Philadelphia Eagles on May 6, 1994 from then owner Norman Braman. Lurie paid $195 million for the team. The club is now estimated to be worth $1 billion, as valuated in 2006 by Forbes.

In 1999, Lurie hired Green Bay packers assistant coach Andy Reid as his new head coach. Reid drafted Donovan McNabb in the first round. Since becoming owner of the Eagles, Lurie has been named NFL "Owner of the Year by The Sporting News in 1995 and by Pro Football Insider in 2000. He is also responsible for helping push through the deal to build a new $512 million, 68,500-seat football stadium, now called Lincoln Financial Field. Lurie currently is a member of eight different NFL committees, making him one of the most active owners. suming control. In 1969, the team was placed on the auction block where he was forced to sell the Eagles to Leonard Tose for a reported $16.1 million, then a record price for a professional sports team.

Eagles in the Hall of Fame

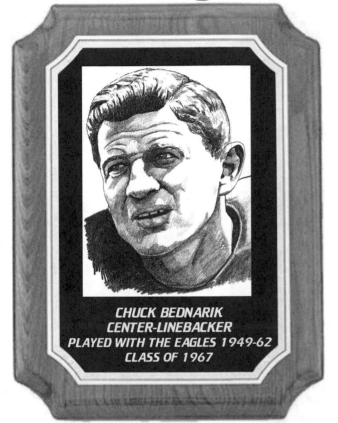

CHUCK BEDNARIK
CENTER-LINEBACKER
PLAYED WITH THE EAGLES 1949-62
CLASS OF 1967

BERT BELL
OWNER- HEAD COACH
YEARS WITH EAGLES 1933-40
CLASS OF 1963

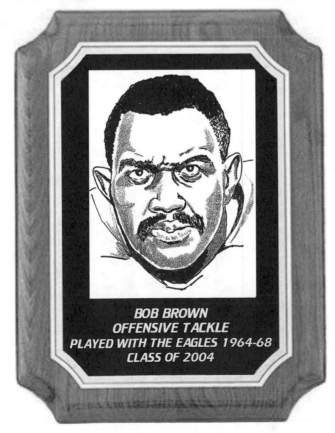

BOB BROWN
OFFENSIVE TACKLE
PLAYED WITH THE EAGLES 1964-68
CLASS OF 2004

EAGLES HALL OF FAME

Eagles in the Hall of Fame

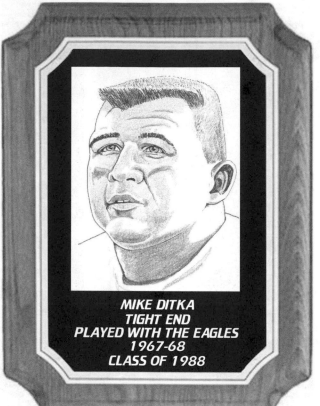

MIKE DITKA
TIGHT END
PLAYED WITH THE EAGLES
1967-68
CLASS OF 1988

SID GILLMAN
COACH
YEARS WITH EAGLES 1979-80
CLASS OF 1983

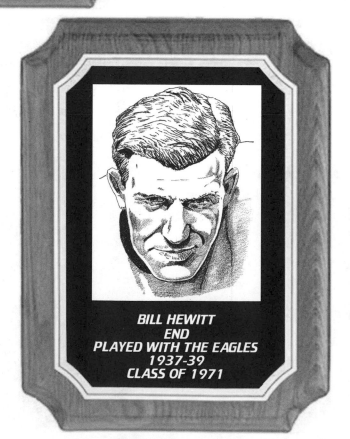

BILL HEWITT
END
PLAYED WITH THE EAGLES
1937-39
CLASS OF 1971

Eagles in the Hall of Fame

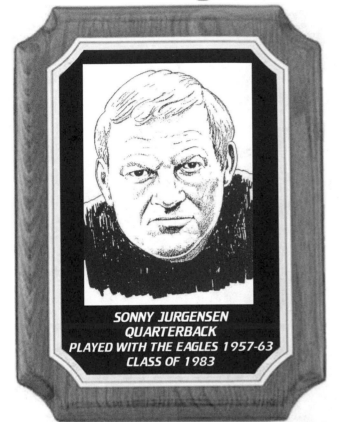

SONNY JURGENSEN
QUARTERBACK
PLAYED WITH THE EAGLES 1957-63
CLASS OF 1983

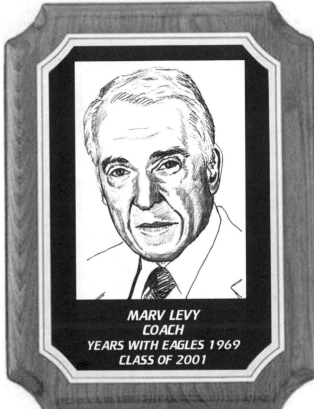

MARV LEVY
COACH
YEARS WITH EAGLES 1969
CLASS OF 2001

JAMES LOFTON
WIDE RECEIVER
PLAYED WITH THE EAGLES 1993
CLASS OF 2003

EAGLES HALL OF FAME

Eagles in the Hall of Fame

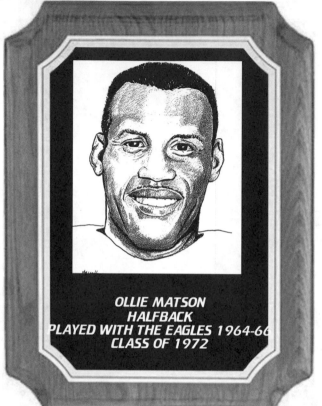

OLLIE MATSON
HALFBACK
PLAYED WITH THE EAGLES 1964-66
CLASS OF 1972

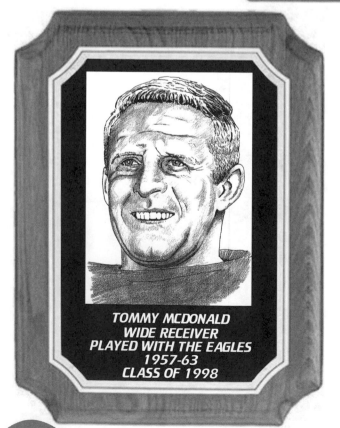

TOMMY MCDONALD
WIDE RECEIVER
PLAYED WITH THE EAGLES
1957-63
CLASS OF 1998

EARLE (GREASY) NEALE
COACH
YEARS WITH EAGLES 1941-50
CLASS OF 1969

Eagles in the Hall of Fame

PETE PIHOS
END
PLAYED WITH THE EAGLES 1947-55
CLASS OF 1970

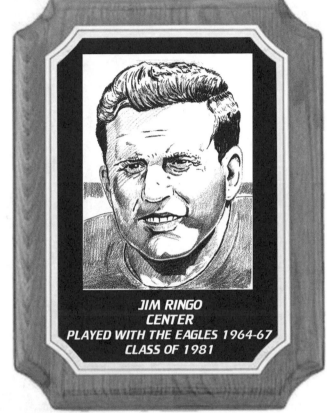

JIM RINGO
CENTER
PLAYED WITH THE EAGLES 1964-67
CLASS OF 1981

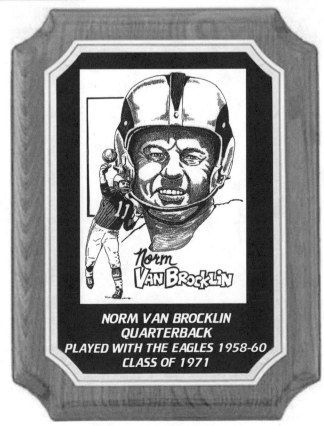

NORM VAN BROCKLIN
QUARTERBACK
PLAYED WITH THE EAGLES 1958-60
CLASS OF 1971

EAGLES HALL OF FAME

Eagles in the Hall of Fame

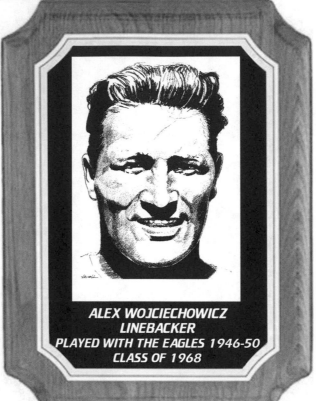

ALEX WOJCIECHOWICZ
LINEBACKER
PLAYED WITH THE EAGLES 1946-50
CLASS OF 1968

STEVE VAN BUREN
HALFBACK
PLAYED WITH THE EAGLES
1944-51
CLASS OF 1965

REGGIE WHITE
DEFENSIVE END
PLAYED WITH THE EAGLES
1985-92
CLASS OF 2006

Eagles Honor Roll

In 1987, the Eagles Honor Roll was established to honor outstanding members of the organization. Included in the inagural induction ceremony were 11 members of the Hall of Fame that played with the Eagles.

#60 Chuck Bednarik, C-LB, 1949-62, Inducted 1987

Bert Bell, founder-owner, 1933-40, Inducted 1987

#17 Harold Carmichael, WR, 1971-83, Inducted 1987

#56 Bill Hewitt, TE-DE, 1936-39 and 1943, Inducted 1987

#9 Sonny Jurgensen, QB, 1957-63, Inducted 1987

#31 Wilbert Montgomery, RB, 1977-84, Inducted 1987

"Greasy" Neale, Head Coach, 1941-50, Inducted 1987

#35 Pete Pihos, TE-DE, 1947-55, Inducted 1987

#33 Ollie Matson, RB, 1964-66, Inducted 1987

#54 Jim Ringo, C, 1964-67, Inducted 1987

#11 Norm Van Brocklin, QB, 1958-60, Inducted 1987

#15 Steve Van Buren, RB-S, 1944-51, Inducted 1987

#53 Alex Wojciechowicz, C-DT, 1946-50, Inducted 1987

#66 Bill Bergey, LB, 1974-80, Inducted 1988

#25 Tommy McDonald, WR, 1957-63, Inducted 1988

#40 Tom Brookshier, CB, 1954-61, inducted 1989

#44 Pete Retzlaff, TE, 1956-66, inducted 1989

#22 Timmy Brown, RB,1960-67, inducted 1990

#76 Jerry Sisemore, OT, 1973-84, inducted 1991

#75 Stan Walters, OT, 1975-83, Inducted 1991

#7 Ron Jaworski, QB, 1977-86, Inducted 1992

#28 Bill Bradley, S-P, 1969-76, Inducted 1993

Dick Vermeil, Head Coach, 1976-82, Inducted 1994

Jim Gallagher (American football), team executive, 1949-95, Inducted 1995

#82 Mike Quick, WR, 1982-90, Inducted 1995

#99 Jerome Brown, DT, 1987-91, Inducted 1996

Otho Davis, head trainer, 1973-95, Inducted 1999

1948 & 1949 NFL Championship Teams Inducted 2006

Monday Night Football Games

On November 23, 1970 the Eagles debuted on "Monday Night Football" on ABC versus the New York Giants in a home game played at Franklin Field which was bitter cold. The Eagles had a horrible record of 1-7-1. Eagles owner Leonard Tose threw a pregame party to celebrate the event. Impatient Howard Cosell was looking for a drink and asked that the bar be opened earlier. Well after throwing back a few vodka martinis, Howard Cosell kept on drinking trying to stay warm throughtout the broadcast. Until he finally could not finish the broadcast after halftime. The Eagles came from behind to defeat the Giants 23-20.

Other noteable games played on Monday Night was on November 12, 1990, when the Washington Redskins came into the Vet in now the infamous "Body Bag Game" in which Eagles head Coach Buddy Ryan promised a beaten so severe, that the Redskins would have to be "hauled off in body bags." Eagles won 28 –14.

On January 3, 1994 the Eagles were playing the San Francisco 49ers. The Eagles missed a game-winning field goal as the overtime period expired, which would have left the game a tie. However, a penalty against the 49ers allowed a re-kick, and the Eagles were granted one untimed down. On the second attempt, the field goal was good and the dead Eagles won 37-34 in overtime.

November 10, 1997 the Eagles on national television against the 49ers received additional attention when a fan fired off a flare gun in Veterans Stadium leading to the introduction of a courtroom which was located on the lower level of the stadium. The Eagles lost that game 24-12.

September 9, 2003, was a rematch of the previous season's NFC Champs Tampa Bay Buccaneers and it was also the first regular season game played at Lincoln Financial Field. In a much hyped rematch game the Eagles were defeated again 17-0.

November 15, 2004, The Eagles were playing the Dallas Cowboys. ABC ran a controversial "Desperate Housewives" commercial prior to the game featuring Eagle Terrell Owens and Nicolette Sheridan. Owens caught three touchdowns as the Eagles crushed the Cowboys 49-21.

"Monday Night Football" has been good to the Eagles over the years. They have a winning record of (24-21). Here are some of the sports covers from the Philadelphia Daily News.

Monday Night Football Games

November 23, 1970:
New York Giants 20, Philadelphia Eagles 23

October 2, 1972:
New York Giants 27, Philadelphia Eagles 12

September 23, 1974:
Dallas Cowboys 10, Philadelphia Eagles 13

November 3, 1975:
Los Angeles Rams 42, Philadelphia Eagles 3

MONDAY NIGHT FOOTBALL

Monday Night Football Games

People Paper / Sports

TUESDAY, SEPTEMBER 28, 1976

A Game Eagles Couldn't Win

By PHIL JASNER

Cushman: Ali Inside 12 Page 58

Hochman: Ali in the 6th Page 59

Phillies' JVs Win Page 63

Alston Calls it Quits Page 57

September 27, 1976:
Washington Redskins 20, Philadelphia Eagles 17, OT

Eagles Ride Herd

Cowboys Sag As Birds End 13-Year Jinx

PHILADELPHIA DAILY **NEWS** **SPORTS**
Tuesday, November 13, 1979

By GARY SMITH

Eagles' owner Leonard Tose (right) hugs Coach Dick Vermeil during wild locker-room scene

More on Eagles

• Win Puts Smile on Wilbert: Cushman on Page 71
• Franklin Gives Dallas Hot Foot: Smith on Page 70
• Beaten Cowboys Are Pointing Fingers: Page 66
• A Wild Day for Birds' Fans: Hochman on Page 64

November 12, 1979:
Philadelphia Eagles 31, Dallas Cowboys 21

Eagles Go Down the Tube

Falcons Win, 14-10, on National Television

By GARY SMITH

PHILADELPHIA DAILY **NEWS** **SPORTS**
Tuesday, September 11, 1979

LAWRENCE 22

Harold Carmichael lies on AstroTurf after missing a pass while Ray Easterling (32) and Rolland Lawrence celebrate

Today

• Meyers Finds NBA Tough: Cushman, Page 71
• Carmichael's Big Night: Smith, Page 70
• Brenard Wilson Worries: Greenberg, Page 69
• Falcons' Runner a Surprise: Jasner, Page 67
• Battle of the Birds: Pictures, Page 66
• Highlights, Lowlights for ABC Quinn, Page 64

Tomorrow

September 10, 1979:
Atlanta Falcons 14, Philadelphia Eagles 10

Iraq Claims It Cut Off 3 Iran Cities
Page 5

Weather
Tonight: Cool
Tomorrow: Cloudy

PHILADELPHIA DAILY **NEWS**
The People Paper

9★
20¢ **Final**

TUESDAY, SEPTEMBER 23, 1980

Look Who's No. 1

Phils in First; Eagles Win

Back Page

Eagles bury Giants during last night's nationally televised game at the Vet. Eight pages in sports on Phillies, Eagles.

September 22, 1980:
New York Giants 3, Philadelphia Eagles 35

75 yrs
1933 2007
OF
EAGLES HISTORY

Monday Night Football Games

November 30, 1981:
Philadelphia Eagles 10 , Miami Dolphins 13

October 5, 1981:
Atlanta Falcons 13, Philadelphia Eagles 16

October 10, 1988:
New York Giants 13, Philadelphia Eagles 24

October 2, 1989:
Philadelphia Eagles 13, Chicago Bears 27

Monday Night Football Games

PHILADELPHIA DAILY NEWS / TUESDAY, DECEMBER 19, 1989

Night Cap: Page 62

PM SPORTS

All-Saints Night

Randall Cunningham (12) is picture of dejection as he and teammates prepare to huddle in closing moments.

ANDREA MIHALIK/DAILY NEWS

By Tim Kawakami
Daily News Sports Writer

NEW ORLEANS — They could've been somebody. They could've been a contender. And they still might be.

But now, nobody really seems to know what they are, where they're going, and why things are never quite as simple as they appear with the Eagles.

Ever.

Now, nothing is clear.

For most of 16 weeks, these Eagles walked, talked and played like Super Bowl contenders, like a team finally ready for the big dance, like the big boys they used to be.

Then last night, in a 225-minute, nationally televised long night's journey into morning, the Eagles suddenly were thrown from their starting roles.

The Eagles are back chasing the contenders once again.

Last night, in this waterfront town, the Eagles (9-5) were unable to pull out a game they needed to maintain their front-running status in the NFC East, losing to 30-20 to the inspired — if playoff dead — New Orleans Saints (8-7).

An Eagles victory would have guaranteed them a wild-card berth,

and then a victory over the plummeting, visiting Cardinals on Sunday would have locked up the division crown for the Eagles.

But after last night's loss, the Eagles must defeat the Cardinals just to wrap up a wild-card spot. And it would take an Eagles victory plus the Raiders upsetting the New York Giants (11-4) for the Eagles to capture a division that no math last night was theirs to win.

"I wasn't satisfied with anything," coach Buddy Ryan said. "I don't believe you learn a damn thing from

losing, other than I don't like it.

"They made the turnovers, and they made the plays to win the game. That's the way the Eagles try to play."

Generally, that's the way the Eagles had been playing for most of the season. In a way that earns them mention as a true Super Bowl contender, as a team that doesn't need help from somebody else to claim a division championship.

If this is a situation that sounds rather familiar, you're not alone.

"We're in the same damn position we were in last year," linebacker Seth Joyner said in a voice that cut through the locker-room solemnity.

He was rumbling, of course, last season's final drive, when the Jets' upset of the Giants enabled the Eagles to claim the NFC East.

"I really thought we were better than this, that guys knew what we were playing for," Joyner said.

"We wouldn't that work off. Win the division, get the rest. But, for some reason, the guys didn't realize that. And now we're right back to relying on somebody to beat the Giants. Some predicament every year. It just doesn't make any sense.

See NATION Page 74

INSIDE THE EAGLES
Bill Conlin: *Page 75*
Stan Hochman: *Page 73*
Rich Hofmann: *Page 72*
TV Monday: *Page 71*
A Happy Ex-Eagle: *Page 71*
Eagles Notebook: *Page 71*
Playoff Picture: *Page 70*
Eagles Statistics: *Page 70*

Eagles' Mike Golic, alone with his thoughts on the sideline.
ANDREA MIHALIK/DAILY NEWS

It's Official: Lions Joining Big 10: Page 69

December 18, 1989:
Philadelphia Eagles 20, New Orleans Saints 30

Bullpen Battle Looms as Series Opens: Page 68

TUESDAY OCTOBER 16, 1990

PHILADELPHIA DAILY NEWS
THE PEOPLE PAPER

LATE SPORTS 35¢
50 CENTS OUTSIDE METROPOLITAN PHILADELPHIA
FOR HOME DELIVERY PHONE 665-1234

It Was Ugly, But . . .

Eagles Struggle to Pull Out a Comeback Win Against Vikings

A jubilant Buddy Ryan and Jessie Small leave the field after the Eagles rallied to defeat Minnesota, 32-24; coverage begins on Back Page
MICHAEL MERCANTI/DAILY NEWS

Neighborhood Name-Dropping: Page 6

October 15, 1990:
Minnesota Vikings 24, Philadelphia Eagles 32

Tuesday, November 13, 1990

PM SPORTS

NIGHT CAP: *Page 60*

'Skins Out Cold

By Kevin Mulligan
Daily News Sports Writer

The Eagles showed the Washington Redskins the on-ramp to I-95 South shortly after 11 p.m.

If they could have all the members of the Redskins traveling party might have dropped their equipment, gathered their lame, wounded and embarrassed, and bolted.

But they couldn't. The third quarter had just concluded and the Eagles had 15 minutes of nationally televised embarrassing to do to their 28-14 victory last night at wind-whipped Veterans Stadium.

"They acted like they didn't want to play us anymore, if you ask me," Birds defensive tackle Jerome Brown said. "It was like, after we got up 28-7, they just said, 'Beep, let's get outta here, these mugs ain't messin' around.'"

You almost couldn't blame the Redskins for wanting out.

There might not have been an offensive player in the NFL who would have traded his comfortable TV seat for a location in the same time zone as the Eagles' defense last night.

"It doesn't get much better," linebacker Seth Joyner said. "That was the old Eagle 'D' out there. All over the place."

"We gave them nowhere to go," Reggie White said. "Nowhere. It was a beautiful sight."

Lost to Beep, the Eagles rode their third consecutive victory into a second-place tie with the Redskins, at 5-4, in the NFC East.

How one-sided was it?

■ Garbage time began with the opening play of the fourth quarter and the resurrected Birds stood 28-7.

■ The Eagles reduced their fellow wild-card hunting NFC East rival to throwing a third-string running back, Brian Mitchell, in the wakes of quarterback after starter Jeff Rutledge (possible broken thumb) and reliever Stan Humphries (knee injury) were knocked out of the game.

■ The Birds allowed Washington just 144 total yards since it counted. The Skins added another 56 on a game-ending, eighth-play whimper of a scoring drive long after about 60,000 satisfied spectators had their automobiles warmed up.

■ The Eagles' defense came within a memingless play with 1:34 remaining of hosting a shutout at Washington on third-down conversions. The battered 'Skins offense finished 1-for-13 in that department.

■ The Eagles, behind Heath Sherman's franchise record-tying 25-carry, 124-yard rushing performance in his second consecutive start, outproduced Washington on the ground, 165-

See 'SKINS TAKE Page 78

INSIDE
Rich Hofmann: *Page 79*
Bill Conlin: *Page 77*
'Skins Need Ambulance: *Page 76*
Sherman Carries Load: *Page 75*
Passing Fancy Birds: *Page 74*
TV Tuesday: *Page 73*
Eagles Notebook: *Page 73*
Eagles Statistics: *Page 73*

Redskins' QB Stan Humphries is comforted by Don Warren (left) and Joe Jacoby after being stopped on fourth-and-1 in 4th quarter
GEORGE REYNOLDS/DAILY NEWS

November 12, 1990:
Washington Redskins 14, Philadelphia Eagles 28

TUESDAY, OCTOBER 1, 1991

FOR LATE SPORTS, SCORES: PAGE 79

Sports

Phillies rally to beat Chicago
See page 66

JIMMY MAC

WHEN ARE YA COMIN' BACK?

Eagles backup quarterback Pat Ryan was ineffective after replacing injured Jim McMahon in the Redskins' 23-0 victory
GEORGE REYNOLDS/DAILY NEWS

SEE PAGE 78

September 30, 1991:
Philadelphia Eagles 0, Washington Redskins 23,

Monday Night Football Games

Nash's Bullets winning somehow
See page 68

KOTITE FOR MAYOR

Birds beat Giants in a landslide, 30-7, to end four-game losing streak and ease pressure on embattled coach

SEE PAGE 78

Seth Joyner leaps into Reggie White's arms after White dropped Giants quarterback Jeff Hostetler in the first half for one of the Eagles' four sacks.

**November 4, 1991:
New York Giants 7, Philadelphia Eagles 30**

Mets will pay Bonilla $29M
See page 80

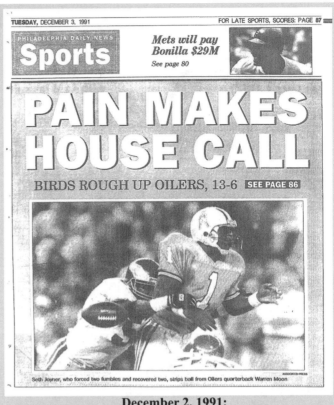

PAIN MAKES HOUSE CALL

BIRDS ROUGH UP OILERS, 13-6   SEE PAGE 86

Seth Joyner, who forced two fumbles and recovered two, strips ball from Oilers quarterback Warren Moon

**December 2, 1991:
Philadelphia Eagles 13, Houston Oilers 6**

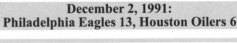

Lindros era begins; preview of Flyers, each NHL team
12-page pullout

MEN AGAINST 'BOYS

Defense, Walker star as Birds show Dallas who's boss: **Page 78**

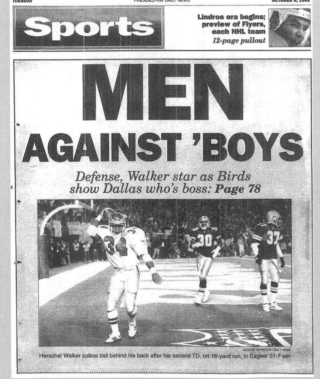

Herschel Walker spikes ball behind his back after his second TD, on 16-yard run, in Eagles' 31-7 win

**October 5, 1992:
Dallas Cowboys 7, Philadelphia Eagles 31**

Ex-Gratz star Harry Moore mourns mother's death
Page 74

CAN'T CATCH 22

Emmitt Smith carries Cowboys to 23-17 win over Birds: **Pages 79-75**

Emmitt Smith (172 yards in 23 carries) watching replay with coach Jimmy Johnson; trying to elude Seth Joyner

DAILY NEWS ALL-CITY FOOTBALL TEAM: *Page 66*

**December 6, 1993:
Philadelphia Eagles 17, Dallas Cowboys 23**

Monday Night Football Games

January 3, 1994:
San Francisco 49ers 34, Philadelphia Eagles 37, OT

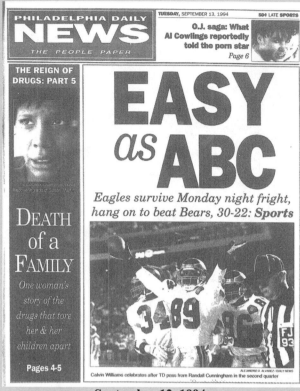

September 12, 1994:
Chicago Bears 22, Philadelphia Eagles 30

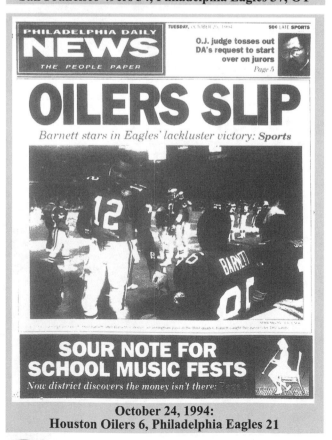

October 24, 1994:
Houston Oilers 6, Philadelphia Eagles 21

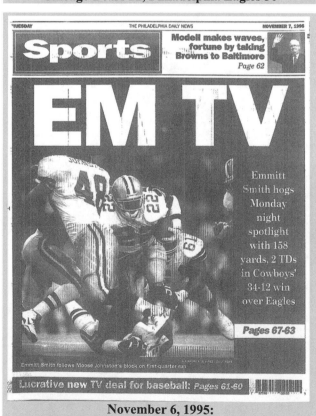

November 6, 1995:
Philadelphia Eagles 12, Dallas Cowboys 34

Monday Night Football Games

September 9, 1996:
Philadelphia Eagles 13, Green Bay Packers 39

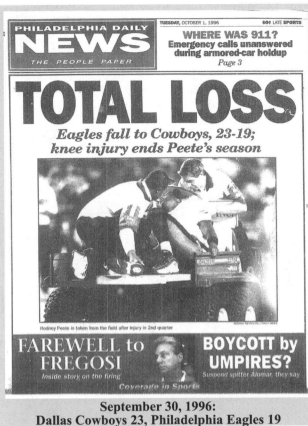

September 30, 1996:
Dallas Cowboys 23, Philadelphia Eagles 19

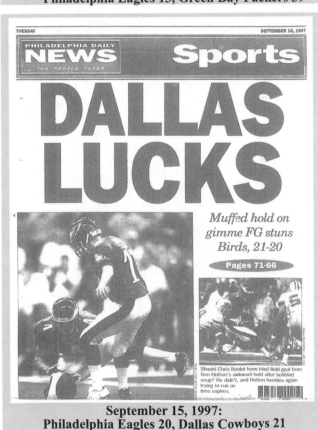

September 15, 1997:
Philadelphia Eagles 20, Dallas Cowboys 21

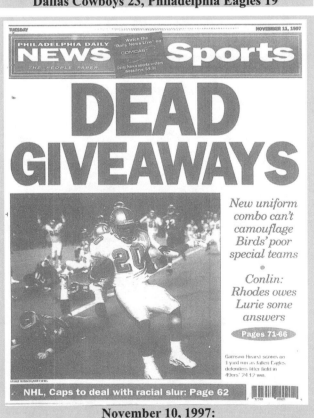

November 10, 1997:
San Francisco 49ers 24, Philadelphia Eagles 12

MONDAY NIGHT FOOTBALL

Monday Night Football Games

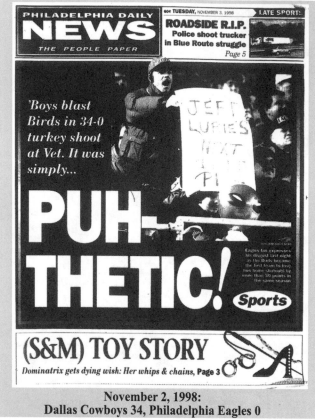

November 2, 1998:
Dallas Cowboys 34, Philadelphia Eagles 0

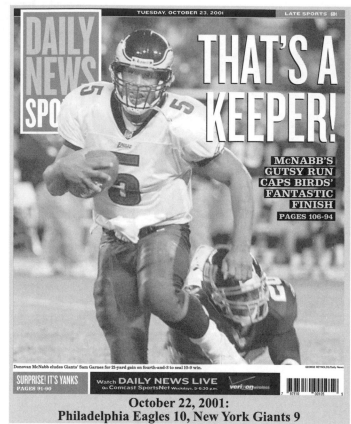

October 22, 2001:
Philadelphia Eagles 10, New York Giants 9

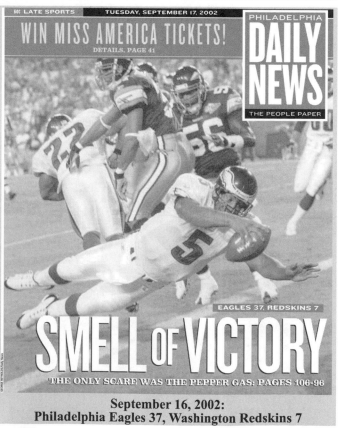

September 16, 2002:
Philadelphia Eagles 37, Washington Redskins 7

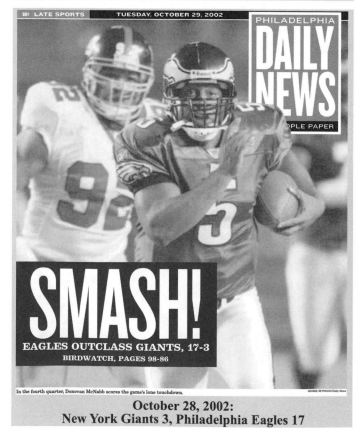

October 28, 2002:
New York Giants 3, Philadelphia Eagles 17

Monday Night Football Games

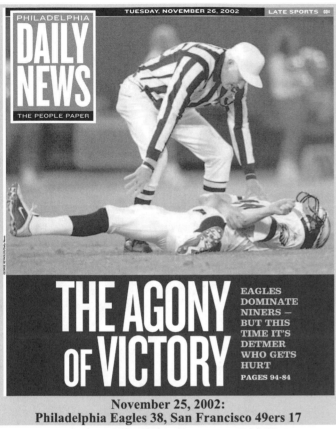

PHILADELPHIA DAILY NEWS
THE PEOPLE PAPER

TUESDAY, NOVEMBER 26, 2002 — LATE SPORTS 60¢

THE AGONY OF VICTORY

EAGLES DOMINATE NINERS — BUT THIS TIME IT'S DETMER WHO GETS HURT
PAGES 94-84

November 25, 2002:
Philadelphia Eagles 38, San Francisco 49ers 17

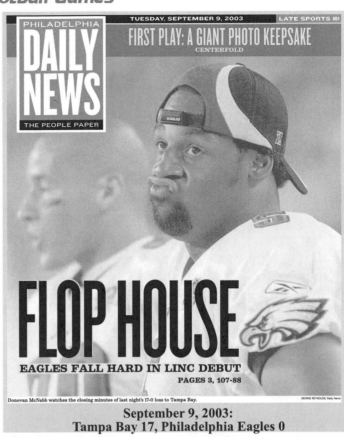

PHILADELPHIA DAILY NEWS
THE PEOPLE PAPER

TUESDAY, SEPTEMBER 9, 2003 — LATE SPORTS 60¢

FIRST PLAY: A GIANT PHOTO KEEPSAKE
CENTERFOLD

FLOP HOUSE

EAGLES FALL HARD IN LINC DEBUT
PAGES 3, 107-88

Donovan McNabb watches the closing minutes of last night's 17-0 loss to Tampa Bay.
GEORGE REYNOLDS/ Daily News

September 9, 2003:
Tampa Bay 17, Philadelphia Eagles 0

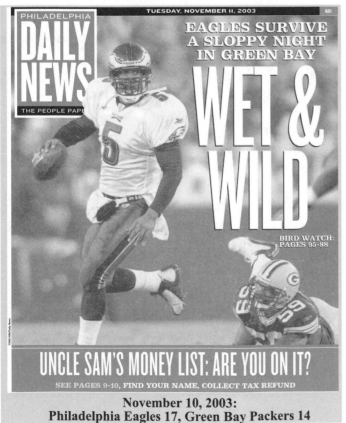

PHILADELPHIA DAILY NEWS
THE PEOPLE PAPER

TUESDAY, NOVEMBER 11, 2003 — 60¢

EAGLES SURVIVE A SLOPPY NIGHT IN GREEN BAY

WET & WILD

BIRD WATCH: PAGES 95-88

UNCLE SAM'S MONEY LIST: ARE YOU ON IT?
SEE PAGES 9-10, FIND YOUR NAME, COLLECT TAX REFUND

November 10, 2003:
Philadelphia Eagles 17, Green Bay Packers 14

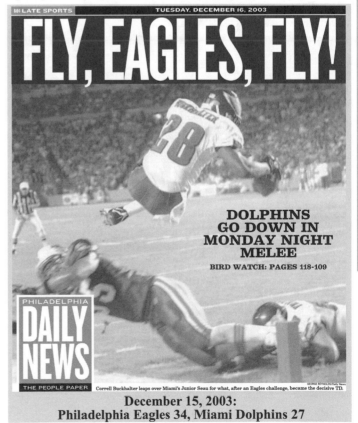

60¢ LATE SPORTS — TUESDAY, DECEMBER 16, 2003

FLY, EAGLES, FLY!

DOLPHINS GO DOWN IN MONDAY NIGHT MELEE
BIRD WATCH: PAGES 118-109

PHILADELPHIA DAILY NEWS
THE PEOPLE PAPER

Correll Buckhalter leaps over Miami's Junior Seau for what, after an Eagles challenge, became the decisive TD.
GEORGE REYNOLDS/Daily News

December 15, 2003:
Philadelphia Eagles 34, Miami Dolphins 27

MONDAY NIGHT FOOTBALL

Monday Night Football Games

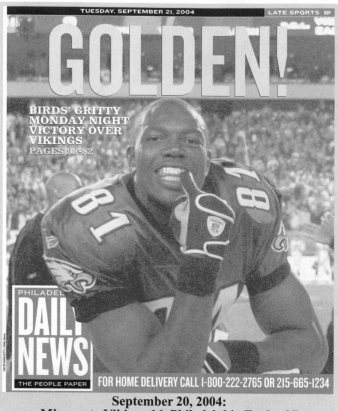

September 20, 2004:
Minnesota Vikings 16, Philadelphia Eagles 27

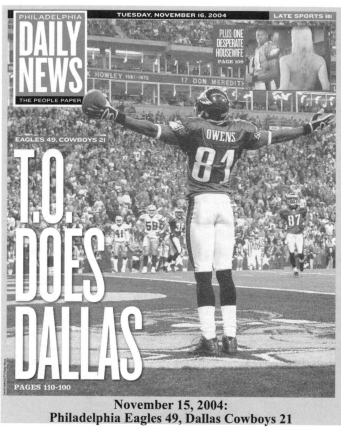

November 15, 2004:
Philadelphia Eagles 49, Dallas Cowboys 21

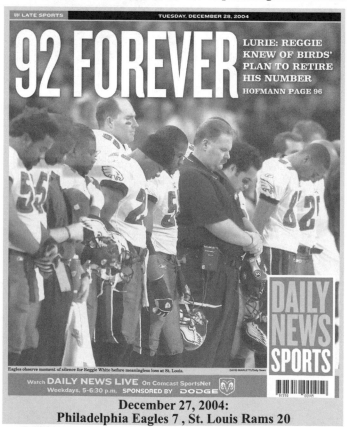

December 27, 2004:
Philadelphia Eagles 7 , St. Louis Rams 20

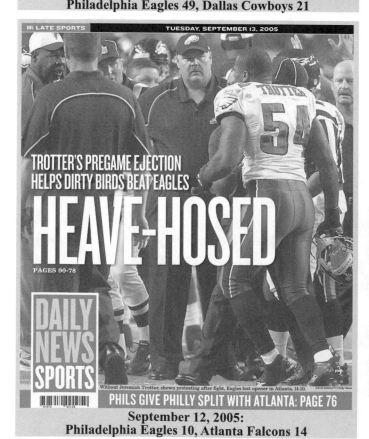

September 12, 2005:
Philadelphia Eagles 10, Atlanta Falcons 14

Monday Night Football Games

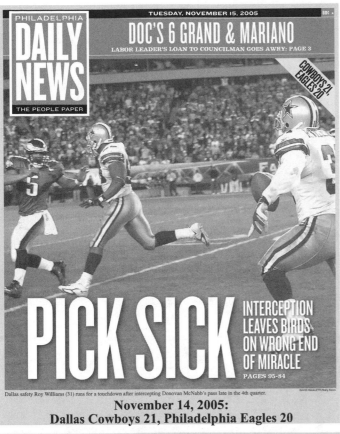

November 14, 2005:
Dallas Cowboys 21, Philadelphia Eagles 20

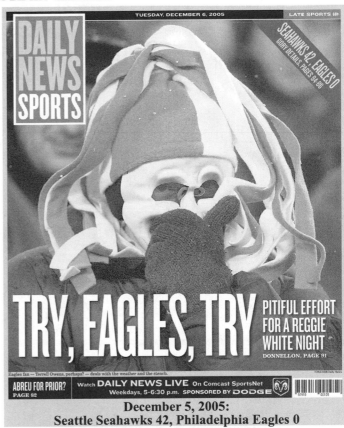

December 5, 2005:
Seattle Seahawks 42, Philadelphia Eagles 0

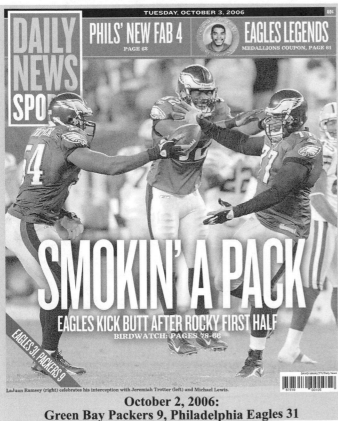

October 2, 2006:
Green Bay Packers 9, Philadelphia Eagles 31

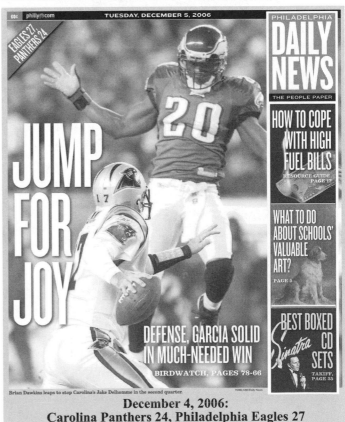

December 4, 2006:
Carolina Panthers 24, Philadelphia Eagles 27

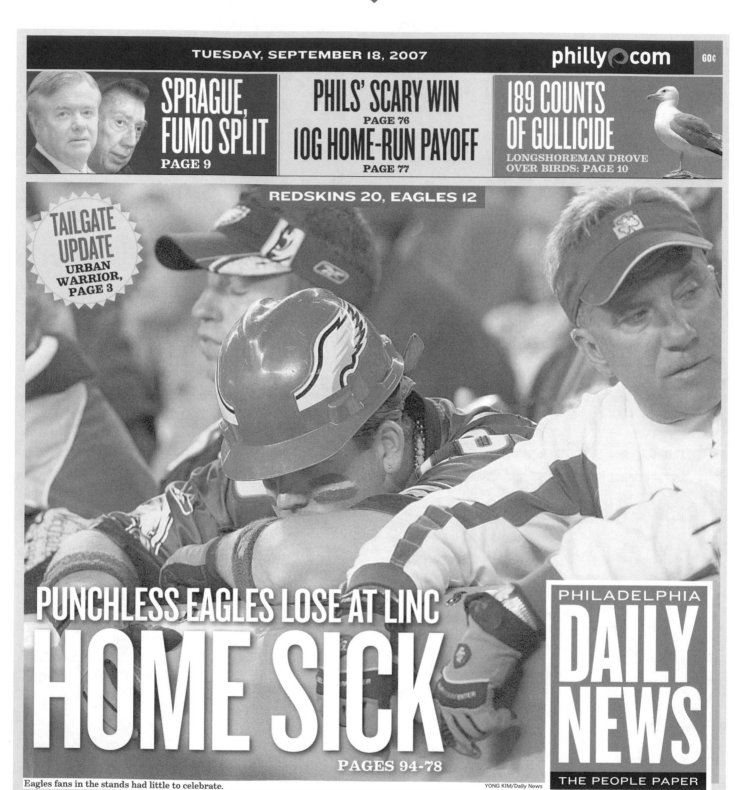

TUESDAY, SEPTEMBER 18, 2007

philly.com

60¢

SPRAGUE, FUMO SPLIT
PAGE 9

PHILS' SCARY WIN
PAGE 76
10G HOME-RUN PAYOFF
PAGE 77

189 COUNTS OF GULLICIDE
LONGSHOREMAN DROVE OVER BIRDS: PAGE 10

REDSKINS 20, EAGLES 12

TAILGATE UPDATE
URBAN WARRIOR, PAGE 3

PUNCHLESS EAGLES LOSE AT LINC

HOME SICK

PAGES 94-78

PHILADELPHIA
DAILY NEWS
THE PEOPLE PAPER

Eagles fans in the stands had little to celebrate.

YONG KIM/Daily News

September 18, 2007:
Washington Redskins 20, Philadelphia Eagles 12
Donovan McNabb's 100th regular season start

First Draft Selections per Year

1936 Jay Berwanger (HB), Chicago, 1st overall
1937 Sam Francis (FB), Nebraska, 1
1938 James McDonald (HB), Ohio State, 2
1939 Davey O'Brien (QB), Texas Christian, 4
1940 George McAfee (HB), Duke, 2
1941 Art Jones (HB), Richmond (2nd round), 11
1942 Pete Kmetovic (HB), Stanford, 3
1943 Joe Muha (FB), VMI, 2
1944 Steve Van Buren, (HB), LSU, 5
1945 John Yonaker (E), Notre Dame, 9
1946 Leo Riggs (HB), Southern California, 7
1947 Neil Armstrong (E), Oklahoma A&M, 8
1948 Clyde Scott (HB), Arkansas & Naval Acad., 8
1949 Chuck Bednarik (C), Penn (Bonus Pick), 1
 Frank Tripucka (QB), Notre Dame, 9
1950 Harry Grant (E), Minnesota, 14
1951 Ebert Van Buren (FB), LSU, 7
1952 John Bright (FB), Drake, 5
1953 Al Conway (HB), Army & Wm. Jewell
 (2nd round), 20
1954 Neil Worden (FB), Notre Dame, 9
1955 Dick Bielski (FB), Maryland, 9
1956 Bob Pellegrini (C-LB), Maryland, 4
1957 Clarence Peaks (FB), Michigan State, 7
1958 Walter Kowalczyk (FB), Michigan State, 6
1959 J.D. Smith (T), Rice (2nd round), 15
1960 Ron Burton (B), Northwestern, 9
1961 Art Baker (B), Syracuse, 14
1962 Pete Case (G), Georgia (2nd round), 27
1963 Ed Budde (T), Michigan State, 4
1964 Bob Brown (T), Nebraska, 2
1965 Ray Rissmiller (T), Georgia (2nd round), 20
1966 Randy Beisler (T), Indiana, 4
1967 Harry Jones (RB), Arkansas, 19
1968 Tim Rossovich (DE), USC, 14
1969 Leroy Keyes (RB), Purdue, 3
1970 Steve Zabel (E-LB), Oklahoma, 6
1971 Richard Harris (DE), Grambling, 5
1972 John Reaves (QB), Florida, 14

1973 Jerry Sisemore (T), Texas, 3
 Charlie Young (TE), USC, 6
1974 Mitch Sutton (DT), Kansas (3rd round), 63
1975 Bill Capraun (T), Miami (7th round), 167
1976 Mike Smith (DE), Florida (4th round), 111
1977 Skip Sharp (CB), Kansas (5th round), 119
1978 Reggie Wilkes (LB), Georgia Tech (3rd rd),66
1979 Jerry Robinson (LB), UCLA, 21
1980 Roynell Young (CB), Alcorn State, 23
1981 Leonard Mitchell (DE), Houston, 27
1982 Mike Quick (WR), North Carolina St., 20
1983 Michael Haddix (FB), Mississippi St., 8
1984 Kenny Jackson (WR), Penn State, 4
1985 Kevin Allen (T), Indiana, 9
1986 Keith Byars (RB), Ohio State, 10
1987 Jerome Brown (DT), Miami, 9
1988 Keith Jackson (TE), Oklahoma, 13
1989 Jessie Small (LB), E. Kentucky
 (2nd round), 49
1990 Ben Smith (S), Georgia, 22
1991 Antone Davis (T), Tennessee, 8
1992 Siran Stacy (RB), Alabama (2nd round), 48
1993 Lester Holmes (G), Jackson State, 19
 Leonard Renfro (DT), Colorado, 24
1994 Bernard Williams (T), Georgia, 14
1995 Mike Mamula (DE/LB), Boston College, 7
1996 Jermane Mayberry (G/T), Texas A&M ,25
1997 Jon Harris (DE), Virginia, 25
1998 Tra Thomas (T), Florida State, 11
1999 Donovan McNabb (QB), Syracuse, 2
2000 Corey Simon (DT), Florida State, 6
2001 Freddie Mitchell (WR) UCLA, 25
2002 Lito Sheppard (CB) Florida, 26
2003 Jerome McDougle (DE) Miami, 15
2004 Shawn Andrews (T/G) Arkansas, 16
2005 Mike Patterson (DT) USC, 31
2006 Brodrick Bunkley (DT) Florida State, 14
2007 Kevin Kolb (QB) Houston, (2nd round),36

ALL TIME RECORDS
- top 5 leaders -

Punt Return Leaders

(Based On Punt Return Average, min. 20 returns)

Name	Years	Yds	Avg	Lg	TDs
1. Ernie Steele	1942-48(6)	737	16.8	80	1
2. Steve Van Buren	1944-51(8)	473	13.9	NA	2
3. Pat McHugh	1947-51(5)	402	13.0	NA	1
4. Brian Westbrook	2002-06(5)	419	12.0	84t	2
5. Brian Mitchell	2000-02(3)	1369	11.7	76t	2

Most Touchdown Passes

Player	Years	TD's
1. Ron Jaworski	1977-1986	175
2. Donovan McNabb	1999-2006	152
3. Randall Cunningham	1985-1995	150
4. Norm Snead	1964-1970	111
5. Tommy Thompson	1941-1950	90

Most Points Scored

Player	Years	Pts
1. Bobby Walston	1951-62	881
2. David Akers	1999-2006	789
3. Sam Baker	1964-69	475
4. Harold Carmichael	1971-83	474
5. Steve Van Buren	1944-51	464

Most Consecutive Games Played

Player	Years	Games
1. Harold Carmichael	1972-1983	162
2. Randy Logan	1973-1983	159
3. Bobby Walston	1951-1962	148
4. Ken Clarke	1977-1987	139
5. Herman Edwards	1977-1985	135

Longest Interception Returns

Player	Game	LG
1. James Willis	*intercepted a pass 4 yds. deep in the end zone and returned it 14 yds. before lateralling to Troy Vincent, who ran 90 yds.* Nov. 3, 1996 at Cowboys - QB Troy Aikman)	104t
2. Lito Sheppard	Oct. 8, 2006 vs. Cowboys - QB Drew Bledsoe)	102t
3. Lito Sheppard	Nov. 15, 2004 at Cowboys - QB Vinny Testaverde)	101t
4. Jerry Norton	Oct. 5, 1957 vs. Giants - QB Charlie Conerly, deflected off goal post)	99t
5. Eric Allen	Oct. 3, 1993 at Jets - QB Boomer Esiason)	94t
Irv Cross	Oct. 25, 1964 at Steelers - QB Terry Nofsinger)	94t

Longest Rushing Plays

Player	Game	LG
1. Herschel Walker	Nov. 27, 1994 at Falcons	91t
2. Wilbert Montgomery	Dec. 19, 1982 vs. Oilers	90t
3. Brian Mitchell	Dec. 1, 2000 vs. Falcons	85t
4. Leroy Harris	Nov. 25, 1979 at Packers	80
5. Bosh Pritchard	Oct. 23, 1949 vs. Redskins	77t

Most Touchdowns Scored

Player	TDS
1. Harold Carmichael (WR)	79
2. Steve Van Buren (B)	77
3. Tommy McDonald (FL)	67
4. Pete Pihos (E)	63
5. Timmy Brown (B)	62

75 yrs
OF
EAGLES HISTORY

ALL TIME RECORDS
- top 5 leaders -

Longest Punts

Player	Game	LG
1. Randall Cunningham	Dec 3, 1989 at Giants	91
2. Joe Muha	Oct. 10, 1948 vs. Giants	82
3. Randall Cunningham	Oct. 16, 1994 at Cowboys	80
King Hill	Nov. 11, 1962 vs. Packers	80
5. Jeff Feagles	Sept. 15, 1991 at Cowboys	77

Most Sacks

Player	Years	Sacks
1. Reggie White	1985-92	124
2. Clyde Simmons	1986-93	76.5
3. Hugh Douglas	1998-2002, '04	54.5
4. Greg Brown	1982-86	50.5
5. Andy Harmon	1991-97	40

Leading Rushers

Player	Years	Games	Att	Yds	Avg	Lg	TDs
1. Wilbert Montgomery 1977-1984	8	100	1465	6538	4.5	90t	45
2. Steve Van Buren 1944-1951	8	83	1320	5860	4.4	70t	69
3. Duce Staley 1997-2003	7	98	1200	4807	4.0	64t	22
4. Randall Cunningham (QB) 1985-1995	11	122	677	4482	6.6	52t	32
5. Ricky Watters 1995-1997	3	48	975	3794	3.9	57	31

Most Interceptions

Player	Yards	INT's	TD's
1. Bill Bradley	536	34	1
2. Eric Allen	482	34	5
3. Herman Edwards	98	33	1
4. Brian Dawkins	489	32	2
5. Wes Hopkins	241	30	1

Most Seasons Played

Player	Years	Seasons
1. Chuck Bednarik	1949-1962	14
2. Harold Carmichael	1971-1983	13
2. Frank (Bucko) Kilroy	1943-1955	13
2. Vic Sears	1941-1953	13
5. Jerry Sisemore	1973-1984	12
Bobby Walston	1951-1962	12

Longest Field Goals

Player	Game	LG
1. Tony Franklin	Nov. 12, 1979 at Cowboys	59
2. David Akers	Sept. 14, 2003 vs. Patriots	57
3. Tom Dempsey	Dec. 12, 1971 vs. St. Louis Cardinals	54
4. David Akers	Oct. 24, 1999 at Dolphins	53
Roger Ruzek	Dec. 9, 1990 at Dolphins	53

Longest Pass Plays

Player	Game	LG
1. Ron Jaworski to Mike Quick	Nov. 10, 1985 vs. Falcons	99t*
2. Randall Cunningham to Fred Barnett	Dec. 2, 1990 at Bills	95t
3. Randall Cunningham to Herschel Walker	Sept. 4, 1994 at Giants	93
4. King Hill to Ben Hawkins	Sept. 22, 1968 vs. Giants	92t
5. Donovan McNabb to Terrell Owens	Oct. 30, 2006 at Broncos	91t
Norm Van Brocklin to Tommy McDonald	Oct. 5, 1958 vs. Giants	91t

• NFL Record

ALL TIME RECORDS
- top 5 leaders -

Most Rushing Touchdowns

Player	Years	TD's
1. Steve Van Buren	1944-51	69
2. Wilbert Montgomery	1977-84	45
3. Randall Cunningham	1985-95	32
4. Ricky Watters	1995-97	31
5. Timmy Brown	1960-67	29

Winning Percentage By A Coach

Coach	Year	Pct.
1. Andy Reid	1999-2006*	.620
2. Greasy Neale	1941-50	.596
3. Rich Kotite	1991-94	.561
4. Buck Shaw	1958-60	.554
5. Jim Trimble	1952-55	.552

*current coach

Most Yards Passing

Player	Years	Comp/Att	Total Yds
1. Ron Jaworski	1977-86	2088/3918	26,963
2. Randall Cunningham	1985-95	1874/3362	22,877
3. Donovan McNabb	1999-2006	1898/3259	22,080
4. Norm Snead	1964-70	1154/22336	15,672
5. Tommy Thompson	1941-42, 45-50	723/1396	10,240

Play By Play Radio Broadcasters

1. Merrill Reese	1977-2007*	30 years
2. Byrum Saam	1940-49, 1952-1955	14 years
3. Bill Campbell	1956-1964	9 years
4. Charlie Swift	1969-1977	9 years
5. Andy Musser	1965-1968	4 years

* current play-by-play announcer

Longest Punt Returns

Player	Game	LG
1. Vai Sikahema	Nov. 22, 1992 at Giants	87t
2. Brian Westbrook	Oct.19, 2003 at Giants	84t
3. Brian Westbrook	Dec. 21, 2003 vs. 49ers	81t
Tommy McDonald	Oct. 4, 1959 vs. Giants	81t
5. Brian Mitchell	Nov. 25, 2002 at 49ers	76t
Gregg Garrity	Nov. 30, 1986 at LA Raiders	76t

Most Receptions

Player	Years	Total Yards	Receptions
1. Harold Carmichael	1971-83	8,978	589
2. Pete Retzlaff	1956-66	7,412	452
3. Pete Pihos	1947-55	5,619	373
4. Keith Byars	1986-92	3,532	371
5. Mike Quick	1982-90	6,464	363

All-Time Eagles Roster

The following players have been on the Eagles' active roster for at least one regular or postseason game during the years indicated. In addition, players who spent the entire year on the injured reserve list since 1993 and thus have accrued an NFL season are also listed below.

*=players that are on the current 2007 roster r= 1987 replacement strike players

A

Abercrombie, Walter 1988 (RB)

Abiamiri, Victor 2007-p* (DE)

Absher, Dick 1972 (LB)

Adams, Gary 1969 (DB)

Adams, Keith 2002-05 (LB)

Adams, Theo 1995 (G)

Agajanian, Ben 1945 (G)

Akers, David 1999-p* (K)
2001-2002, 2004 All Pro Selection
2002-03, 2005 Pro Bowl

Alexander, David 1987-94 (C)
1991 Ed Block Courage Award

Alexander, Kermit 1972-73 (DB)

Allen, Chuck 1972 (LB)

Allen, Eric 1988-94 (CB)
1989, 1991, 1993 All Pro Selection
1990, 1992-95 Pro Bowl
1993 NFC Defensive MVP

Allen, Ian 2004 (T)

Allen, Jackie 1972 (DB)

Allen, Kevin 1985 (T)

Allert, Ty 1987-89 (LB)

Allison, Henry 1971-72 (G)

Amerson, Glen 1961 (B)

Amundson, George 1975 (RB)

Anderson, Gary 1995-96 (K)

Andrews, Leroy 1934 (B)

Andrews, Shawn 2004-p* (G)
2007 All-Pro
2007 Pro Bowl

Angelo, Jim 1987 (G)

Antwine, Houston 1972 (DT)

Archer, Dave 1991-92 (QB)

Armour, Justin 1997 (WR)

Armstrong, Calvin 2005- (T)

Armstrong, Harvey 1982-84 (DT)

Armstrong, Neill 1947-51 (E)

Arnold, Jay 1937-40 (B)

Arrington, Rick 1970-73 (QB)

Aschbacher, Darrel 1959 (G)

Asher, Jamie 1999 (TE)

Atkins, Steve 1981 (FB)

Auer, Howard 1933 (T)

Auer, Jim 1987r (DE)

Autry, Darnell 1998, 2000 (RB)

Avant, Jason, 2006-p* (WR)

Ayers, Marvin 1987 (DE)

B

Bahr, Matt 1993 (K)

Bailey, Dave 1990 (DE)

Bailey, Eric 1987 (TE)

Bailey, Howard 1935 (T)

Bailey, Tom 1971-74 (B)

Bailey, Victor 1993-94 (WR)

Baisi, Albert 1947 (G)

Baker, Jason 2002 (P)

Baker, John 1962 (DE)

Baker, Keith 1985 (WR)

Baker, Ron 1980-88 (G)

Baker, Sam 1964-69 (K)
1965, 1969 Pro Bowl

Baker, Tony 1971-72 (B)

Baldinger, Brian 1992-93 (G)

Ballman, Gary 1967-72 (TE)

Banas, Stephen 1935 (B)

Banducci, Bruno 1944-45 (G)
1945 All Pro Selection

Banta, Jack 1941, 1944-45 (B)

Barber, Shawn 2002, 06 (LB)
2002 Ed Block Courage Award

Barker, Bryan 1994 (P)

Barlow, Corey 1992-94 (CB)

Barnes, Billy Ray 1957-61 (RB)
1958-60 Pro Bowl

Barnes, Larry 1978-79 (FB)

Barnes, Walter 1948-51 (G)
1951 Pro Bowl

Barnett, Fred 1990-95 (WR)
1993 Pro Bowl
1994 Ed Block Courage Award

Barnhardt, Dan 1934 (B)

Barni, Roy 1954-55 (B)

All-Time Eagles Roster

Barnum, Leonard 1940-42 (B)

Barr, Stephen 1965 (WR)

Bartholomew, Sam 1941 (B)

Bartlett, Doug 1988 (DT)

Bartley, Ephesians 1992 (LB)

Bartrum, Mike 2000-06 (TE)
2006 Pro Bowl

Basca, Nick 1941 (B)

Baskett, Hank 2006-p* (WR)

Bassi, Dick 1940 (G)
1940 All Pro Selection

Bassman, Herman 1936 (B)

Battaglia, Matt 1987r (LB)

Baughan, Maxie 1960-65 (LB)
1961, 1964-65 All Pro Selection
1961-62, 1964-66 Pro Bowl

Bauman, Alfred 1947 (T)

Bausch, Frank 1940-41 (C)

Bavaro, Mark 1993-94 (TE)

Bawel, Ed 1952, 1955-56 (B)

Baze, Winford 1937 (B)

Beach, Pat 1992 (TE)

Beals, Shawn 1988 (WR)

Beaver, Jim 1962 (G)

Beckles, Ian 1997-98 (G)

Bednarik, Chuck 1949-62 (C)/LB
1950-57, 1960-61 All Pro Selection
1951-55, 1957-58, 1961 Pro Bowl
1954 Pro Bowl MVP

Beisler, Randy 1966-68 (DE)

Bell, Eddie 1955-58 (DB)

Bell, Todd 1988-89 (LB)

Bellamy, Mike 1990 (WR)

Bellamy, Victor 1987r (CB)

Bendross, Jesse 1987r (WR)

Benson, Harry 1935 (G)

Berger, Mitch 1994 (P)

Bergey, Bill 1974-80 (LB)
1974-78 All Pro Selection
1975, 1977-79 Pro Bowl

Berry, Dan 1967 (B)

Berzinski, Willie 1956 (B)

Betterson, James 1977-78 (RB)

Bielski, Dick 1955-59 (B)

Bieniemy, Eric 1999 (RB)

Binotto, John 1942 (B)

Bishop, Blaine 2002 (S)

Bjorklund, Robert 1941 (C)

Black, Michael 1986 (T/G)

Blackmore, Richard 1979-82 (CB)

Blaine, Ed 1963-66 (G)

Blake, Jeff 2004 (QB)

Bleamer, Jeff 1975-76 (T)

Bleeker, Mel 1944-46 (B)

Blue, Lither 1980 (WR)

Blye, Ron 1969 (RB)

Boatswain, Harry 1995, 1997 (G/T)

Boedeker, William 1950 (B)

Borgren, Vince 1944 (E)

Bolden, Gary 1987r (DT)

Bonial, Chris 1997-98 (K)

Booty, John 1991-92 (DB)

Boryla, Mike 1974-76 (QB)
1976 Pro Bowl

Bostic, James 1998-99 (RB)

Bostic, Jason 1999-2000 (RB)

Bouggess, Lee 1970-73 (RB)

Bouie, Kevin 1995-96 (RB)

Bova, Tony 1943 (E)

Bowman, Kevin 1987r (WR)

Boykin, Deral 1996 (S)

Bradley, Bill 1969-76 (S)
1971-73 All Pro Selection
1972-74 Pro Bowl

Bradley, Carlos 1987r (LB)

Bradley, Stewart 2007-p* (LB)

Bradley, Harold 1958 (G)

Brady, Rickey 1995 (TE)

Bredice, John 1956 (E)

Brennan, Leo 1942 (T)

Brewer, Jack 2005 (S)

Brewer, John 1952-53 (B)

Brian, William 1935-36 (T)

Bridges, Jeremy 2003 (T/G)

Brister, Bubby 1993-94 (QB)

Britt, Rankin 1939 (E)

Brodnicki, Chuck 1934 (T)

Brooks, Barret 1995-98 (T)

Brooks, Clifford 1975-76 (DB)

Brooks, Tony 1992-93 (RB)

Brookshier, Tom 1953, 1956-61 (CB)
1959-60 All Pro Selection
1960-61 Pro Bowl

Broughton, Luther 1997, 1999-2000 (TE)

Brown, Aaron 1985 (LB)

Brown, Bob 1964-68 (T)
1964-68 All Pro Selection
1966-67, 1969 Pro Bowl

Brown, Cedrick 1987 (CB)

All-Time Eagles Roster

Brown, David 1987r (LB)

Brown, Deauntee 1997 (CB)

Brown, Fred 1967-69 (LB)

Brown, Greg 1981-86 (DE)

Brown, Jerome 1987-91 (DT)
1989-91 All Pro Selection
1991-92 Pro Bowl
1992 Ed Block Courage Award

Brown, Na 1999-2001 (WR)

Brown, Reggie 2005-p* (WR)

Brown, Reggie 1987r (RB)

Brown, Sheldon 2002-p* (CB)

Brown, Thomas 1980 (DE)

Brown, Tim 1960-67 (RB)
1963, 1965-66 All Pro Selection
1963-64, 1966 Pro Bowl

Brown, Willie 1966 (WR)

Brumm, Don 1970-71 (DE)

Brutley, Daryon 2003 (CB)

Brunski, Andrew 1943 (C)

Bryant, Bill 1978 (CB)

Brzezinski, Doug 1999-2003 (G)

Buckhalter, Correll 2001-p* (RB)
2003 Ed Block Courage Award

Budd, Frank 1962 (E)

Bukant, Joe 1938-40 (B)

Bulaich, Norm 1973-74 (RB)

Bull, Ron 1971 (RB)

Bunkley, Brodrick 2006-p* (DT)

Bunting, John 1972-82 (LB)

Burgess, Derrick 2001-04 (DE)
2004 Ed Block Courage Award

Burk, Adrian 1951-56 (QB)
1955 Pro Bowl

Burke, Mark 1976 (DB)

Burks, Dialleo 1996 (WR)

Burnette, Tom 1938 (B)

Burnham, Lem 1977-80 (DE)

Burnine, Hank 1956-57 (E)

Burroughs, Don 1960-64 (DB)
1960-62 All Pro Selection

Bushby, Thomas 1935 (B)

Buss, Art 1936-37 (T)

Butler, Bob 1962 (G)

Butler, John 1943, 1945 (B)

Byars, Keith 1986-92 (RB)

Byrne, Bill 1963 (G)

Ⓒ

Cabrelli, Larry 1941-47 (E)

Caesar, Ivan 1993 (LB)

Caffey, Lee Roy 1963 (LB)

Cagle, Jim 1974 (DT)

Cahill, Dave 1966 (DT)

Caldwell, Mike 1998-2001 (LB)

Calhoun, Don 1982 (RB)

Callicchio, Lonny 1997 (K)

Calloway, Ernie 1969-72 (DT)

Campbell, Glenn 1935 (E)

Campbell, Marion 1956-61 (DT)
1960-61 Pro Bowl

Campbell, Stan 1959-61 (G)

Campbell, Tommy 1976 (DB)

Campfield, Billy 1978-82 (RB)

Campion, Thomas 1947 (T)

Canale, Rocco 1943-45 (G)

Carmichael, Harold 1971-83 (WR)
1973, 1979-80 All Pro Selection
1974, 1979-81 Pro Bowl
Carollo, Joe 1969-70 (T)

Carpe, Joe 1933 (T)

Carpenter, Robert 1995 (WR)

Carr, Earl 1979 (RB)

Carr, Jim 1959-63 (S)

Carroccio, Russ 1955 (G)

Carroll, Terrence 2001 (S)

Carson, Carlos 1989 (WR)

Carter, Cris 1987-89 (WR)

Carter, Joe 1933-40 (E)
1935-36, 1938 All Pro Selection

Case, Pete 1962-64 (G)

Cassady, Howard 1962 (B)

Castiglia, Jim 1941, 1945-46 (B)

Caterbone, Tom 1987r (CB)

Catlin, Tom 1959 (LB)

Cavanaugh, Matt 1986-89 (QB)

Caver, Quinton 2001-2002 (LB)

Celek, Brent 2007-p* (TE)

Cemore, Tony 1941 (G)

Ceppetelli, Gene 1968-69 (C)

Chalenski, Mike 1993-95 (DL)

Chapura, Dick 1990 (DT/G)

Cheek, Louis 1990 (T)

Cherry, Je'rod 2000 (S)

Cherundolo, Chuck 1940 (C)

Chesley, Al 1979-82 (LB)

Chesson, Wes 1973-74 (WR)

Christensen, Jeff 1984-85 (QB)

Chuy, Don 1969 (G)

All-Time Eagles Roster

Cifelli, Gus 1954 (T)

Clark, Al 1976 (CB)

Clark, Mike 1963 (K/E)

Clark, Algy 1934 (B)

Clark, Willie 1997 (CB)

Clarke, Adrien 2004 (G)

Clarke, Ken 1978-87 (DT)

Clayton, Don 1936 (T)

Clemons, Topper 1987r (RB)

Cobb, Garry 1985-87 (LB)

Cody, Bill 1972 (LB)

Colavito, Rocky 1975 (LB)

Cole, Nick 2006-p* (OL)

Cole, John 1938-40 (B)

Cole, Trent 2005-p* (DE)

Coleman, Al 1972-73 (DB)

Collie, Bruce 1990-91 (G)

Colman, Wayne 1968-69 (LB)

Combs, Bill 1942 (E)

Concannon, Jack 1964-66 (QB)

Conjar, Larry 1968 (FB)

Conlin, Ray 1987r (DT)

Conner, Darion 1996-97 (DE)

Considine, Sean 2005-p* (S)

Conti, Enio 1941-45 (G)

Conwell, Joe 1986-87 (T)

Cook, Leon 1942 (T)

Cook, Rashard 1999-2000 (S)

Cooke, Ed 1958 (E)

Cooper, Evan 1984-87 (DB)

Cooper, Louis 1993 (LB)

Cooper, Richard 1996-98 (T)

Copeland, Russell 1997-98 (WR)

Cornish, Frank 1995 (C)

Cortez, Joseph 2005 (K)

Coston, Zed 1939 (C)

Cothren, Paige 1959 (B)

Cowher, Bill 1983-84 (LB)

Cowhig, Jerry 1951 (B)

Crabb, Claude 1964-65 (DB)

Craft, Russ 1946-53 (B)
1952-53 Pro Bowl

Crafts, Jerry 1997-98 (T/G)

Crawford, Charles 1986-87 (RB)

Creech, Bob 1971-72 (LB)

Creswell, Smiley 1985 (DE)

Crews, Terry 1996 (LB)

Cronin, Bill 1965 (E)

Cross, Irv 1961-65, 1969 (DB)
1965-66 Pro Bowl

Crowe, Larry 1972 (RB)

Crutchfield, Darrel 2001 (CB)

Cuba, Paul 1933-35 (T)

Culbreath, Jim 1980 (FB)

Cullars, Willie 1974 (DE)

Cumby, George 1987r (LB)

Cunningham, Dick 1973 (LB)

Cunningham, Randall 1985-95 (QB)
1988, 1990, 1992 All Pro Selection
1989-91 Pro Bowl
1988 NFL MVP
1989 Pro Bowl MVP
1990 NFL MVP
1990 NFL Offensive MVP
1990 NFC Offensive MVP
1992 NFL Comeback player of the Year

Cuppoletti, Bree 1939-40 (G)

Curcio, Mike 1981-82 (LB)

Curtis, Kevin 2007-p* (WR)

Curtis, Scott 1988 (LB)

D

D'Agostino, Frank 1956 (G)

Darby, Byron 1983-86 (DE/TE)

Darelik, Trey 2004-05 (G/T)

Darling, James 1997-2000 (LB)

Darwin, Matt 1986-90 (C)

Davis, Al 1971-72 (B)

Davis, Antone 1991-95 (T)

Davis, Bob 1942 (B)

Davis, Norm 1970 (G)

Davis, Pernell 1999-2000 (DT)

Davis, Stan 1973 (B)

Davis, Sylvester 1933 (B)

Davis, Vern 1971 (DB)

Dawkins, Brian 1996-p* (S/LB)
2001-2002, 2004, 2007 All Pro Selection
2000, 2002-03, 2005-07 Pro Bowl

Dawson, Dale 1988 (K)

Dean, Ted 1960-63 (RB)
1962 Pro Bowl

DeLine, Steve 1989 (K)

Dellenbach, Jeff 1999 (G/C)

Delucca, Gerry 1959 (T)

Demas, George 1933 (G)

Dempsey, Jack 1934, 1937 (T)

Dempsey, Tom 1971-74 (K)

Dennard, Mark 1984-85 (C)

Dent, Richard 1997 (DE)

All-Time Eagles Roster

DeStantis, Dan 1941 (B)

Detmer, Koy 1997- (QB)

Detmer, Ty 1996-97 (QB)

DeVaughn, Dennis 1982-83 (DB)

Dial, Alan 1989 (DB)

Dial, Benjy 1967 (QB)

Diaz-Infante, David 1999 (G)

Dickerson, Kori 2003 (TE)

DiFilippo, Dave 1941 (G)

Dimmick, Tom 1956 (T)

Dimry, Charles 1997 (DB)

Dingle, Nate 1995 (LB)

DiRenzo, Danny 1948 (P)

Dirks, Mike 1968-71 (G)

Disend, Leo 1943 (T)

Ditka, Mike 1967-68 (E)

Dixon, Al 1983 (TE)

Dixon, Floyd 1992 (WR)

Dixon, Ronnie 1995-96 (DT)

Dixon, Zach 1980 (RB)

Dobbins, Herb 1974 (T)

Dorow, Al (QB)

Dogins, Kevin 2003 (G/C)

Dorenbos, Jon 2006-p* (LS)

Dorow, Al 1957 (B)

Dorsey, Dean 1988 (K)

Doss, Noble 1947-48 (B)

Douglas, Dameane 1999-2002 (WR)

Douglas, Hugh 1998-2002, 2004 (LB/DE)
2000, 2002 All Pro Selection
2001-03 Pro Bowl

Douglas, Merrill 1962 (B)

Douglas, Otis 1946-59 (T)

Dow, Woody 1938-40 (B)

Dowda, Harry 1954-55 (B)

Doyle, Ted 1943 (T)

Drake, Joe 1985 (DT)

Drake, Troy 1995-97 (T)

Drummond, Robert 1989-91 (RB)

Duckworth, Bobby 1986 (WR)

Dudley, Paul 1963 (B)

Dumbauld, John 1987-88 (DE)

Duncan, Rick 1968 (P)

Dunek, Ken 1980 (TE)

Dunn, Jason 1996-98 (TE)

Dunstan, Bill 1973-76 (DT)

Durko, John 1944 (E)

E

Edwards, Anthony 1989-90 (WR)

Edwards, Herm 1977-85 (CB)

Ehlers, Tom 1975-77 (LB)

Eibner, John 1941-42, 1946 (T)

Eiden, Ed 1944 (B)

Elewonibi, Moe 1995 (T)

Ellis, Drew 1938-40 (T)

Ellis, Ray 1981-85 (S)

Ellstrom, Swede 1934 (B)

Emanuel, Charles 1997 (S)

Emelianchik, Pete 1967 (E)

Emmons, Carlos 2000-03 (LB)

Emmons, Franklin 1940 (B)

Ena, Justin 2002-03, 2005 (LB)

Engles, Rick 1978 (P)

Enke, Fred 1952 (B)

Ephraim, Alonzo 2003-04 (C)

Erdlitz, Richard 1942, 1945 (B)

Estes, Larry 1972 (DE)

Evans, Byron 1987-94 (LB)
1990, 1992 All Pro Selection

Evans, Donald 1988 (DE)

Evans, Mike 1968-73 (C)

Everett, Eric 1988-89 (CB)

Everett, Major 1983-85 (FB)

Everitt, Steve 1997-99 (C)

F

Fagioli, Carl 1944 (G)

Farmer, Ray 1996-98 (LB)

Farragut, Ken 1951-54 (C)
1954 Pro Bowl

Fazio, Ron 1987r (TE)

Feagles, Jeff 1990-93 (P)

Feehery, Gerry 1983-87 (C/G)
1987 Ed Block Courage Award

Feeley, A.J. 2001-03, 2006-p* (QB)

Felber, Nip 1933 (E)

Feller, Happy 1971 (K)

Fenci, Dick 1933 (E)

Ferko, Fritz 1937-38 (G)

Ferrante, Jack 1941, 1944-50 (E)
1945, 1949 All Pro Selection

Ferrara, Frank 2003 (DE)

Ferris, Neil 1952 (B)

Fiedler, Bill 1938 (G)

All-Time Eagles Roster

Fiedler, Jay 1994-95 (QB)

Finn, Mike 1994 (T)

Finneran, Brian 1999 (WR)

Fitzgerald, Mickey 1981 (FB)

Fitzkee, Scott 1979-80 (WR)

Flanigan, Jim 2003 (DT)

Flores, Mike 1991-94 (DT)

Floyd, Eric 1992-93 (G)

Fogle, DeShawn 1997 (LB)

Folsom, Steve 1981 (TE)

Fontenot, Chris 1998 (TE)

Ford, Carl 2005- (WR)

Ford, Charles 1974 (DB)

Ford, Fredric 1997 (CB)

Foules, Elbert 1983-87 (CB)

Fox, Terry 1941, 1945 (B)

Fraham, Dick 1935 (B)

Fraley, Hank 2000-05 (C)

France, Todd 2005 (K)

Frank, Joseph 1941, 1943 (T)

Franklin, Cleveland 1977-78 (RB)

Franklin, Tony 1979-83 (K)

Franks, Dennis 1976-78 (C)

Frazier, Derrick 1993-95 (CB)

Freeman, Antonio 2002 (WR)

Freeman, Bob 1960-61 (DB)

Frey, Glenn 1936-37 (B)

Friedlund, Bob 1946 (E)

Friedman, Bob 1944 (G)

Fritts, George 1945 (T)

Fritz, Ralph 1941 (G)

Fritzsche, Jim 1983 (T/G)

Frizzell, William 1986-90, 1992-93 (S)

Fryar, Irving 1996-98 (WR)
1997-98 Pro Bowl

Fuller, Frank 1963 (T)

Fuller, James 1996 (S)

Fuller, William 1994-96 (DE)
1995 All Pro Selection
1995-97 Pro Bowl

Furio, Dominic 2004 (C)

Ⓖ

Gabbard, Steve 1989 (T)

Gabriel, Roman 1973-77 (QB)
1973 NFL Comeback Player of the Year
1974 Pro Bowl

Gaithers, Omar 2006-p* (LB)

Gambold, Bob 1953 (B)

Gaona, Bob 1957 (T)

Gardner, Barry 1999-202 (LB)

Garner, Charlie 1994-98 (RB)
1995 Ed Block Courage Award

Garrity, Gregg 1984-89 (WR)

Gary, Rusell 1986 (DB)

Gauer, Charlie 1943-45 (E)

Gay, Blenda 1975-76 (DE)

George, Ed 1976-78 (T)

George, Raymond 1949 (T)

Gerber, Woody 1941-42 (G)

Gerhard, Chris 1987r (S)

Gerhart, Tom 1992 (DB)

Gersbach, Carl 1970 (LB)

Ghecas, Lou 1941 (B)

Giammona, Louie 1978-82 (RB)

Giancanelli, Hal 1953-56 (B)

Giannelli, Mario 1948-51 (G)

Gibbs, Pat 1972 (DB)

Gibron, Abe 1956-57 (G)

Giddens, Frank 1981-82 (T)

Giddens, Wimpy 1938 (T)

Gilbert, Lewis 1980 (TE)

Giles, Jimmie 1987-89 (TE)

Gill, Roger 1964-65 (B)

Gilmore, Jim 1986 (T)

Ginney, Jerry 1940 (G)

Glass, Glenn 1964-65 (B)

Gloden, Fred 1941 (B)

Glover, Rich 1975 (DT)

Gocong, Chris 2007-p* (LB/DE)

Goebel, Brad 1991 (QB)

Golden, Tim 1985 (LB)

Goldston, Ralph 1952, 1954-55 (B)

Golic, Mike 1987-92 (DT)

Gollomb, Rudy 1936 (G)

Gonya, Robert 1933-34 (T)

Goode, John 1985 (TE)

Goode, Rob 1955 (B)

Goodwin, Marvin 1994 (S)

Goodwin, Ron 1963-68 (E)

Gordon, Lamar 2005 (RB)

Gorecki, Chuck 1987r (LB)

Gossage, Gene 1960-62 (E)

Gouveia, Kurt 1995 (LB)

All-Time Eagles Roster

Graham, Dave 1963-69 (T)

Graham, Jeff 1998 (WR)

Graham, Lyle 1941 (C)

Graham, Nick 2007-p* (CB)

Graham, Tom 1935 (G)

Grant, Bud 1951-52 (E)

Grant, Otis 1987r (WR)

Grasmanis, Paul 2000-05 (DT)

Graves, Ray 1942-43, 1946 (C)

Gray, Cecil 1990-91 (G/DT)

Gray, Jim 1967 (B)

Gray, Mel 1997 (KR)

Green, Donnie 1977 (T)

Green, Jamel 2003-04 (DE)

Green, John 1947-51 (E)
1951 Pro Bowl

Green, Roy 1991-92 (WR)

Gregg, Kelly 1999-2000 (DT)

Gregory, Ken 1962 (E)

Griffen, Don 1996 (CB)

Griffin, Jeff 1987r (CB)

Griggs, Anthony 1982-85 (LB)

Grooms, Elois 1987 (DE)

Gros, Earl 1964-66 (FB)

Grossman, Burt 1998 (DE)

Gudd, Leonard 1934 (E)

Gude, Henry 1946 (G)

Guglielmi, Ralph 1963 (QB)

Guillory, Tony 1969 (LB)

Gunn, Mark 1995-96 (DL)

Gunnels, Riley 1960-64 (T)

H

Hackney, Elmer 1940-41 (B)

Haddix, Michael 1983-88 (FB)

Haden, Nick 1986 (G)

Hager, Britt 1989-94 (LB)

Hairston, Carl 1976-83 (DE)

Hajek, Chuck 1934 (C)

Hall, Andy 2005 (QB)

Hall, Irv 1942 (B)

Hall, Rhett 1995-98 (DT/G)
1997 Ed Block Courage Award

Hallstrom, Ron 1993 (G)

Halverson, Bill 1942 (T)

Halverson, Dean 1973-76 (LB)

Hamilton, Ray 1940 (E)

Hamilton, Skip 1987 (DT)

Hamiter, Uhuru 2000-01 (DE)

Hamner, Thomas 2000 (RB)

Hampton, Dave 1976 (RB)

Hampton, William 2001 (CB)

Hankton, Karl 1998 (WR)

Hansen, Roscoe 1951 (T)

Hanson, Homer 1935 (C)

Hanson, Joselio 2006-p* (CB)

Hanson, Swede 1933-37 (B)
1933-34 All Pro Selection

Harding, Greg 1987 (DB)

Harding, Roger 1947 (C)

Hardy, Andre 1984 (RB)

Hargrove, Marvin 1990 (WR)

Harmon, Andy 1991-97 (DT)
1995 All Pro Selection

Harper, Maurice 1937-40 (C)

Harrington, Perry 1980-83 (RB)

Harris, Al 1998-2002 (CB)

Harris, Al 1989-90 (LB)

Harris, Jim 1957 (B)

Harris, Jon 1997-98 (DE)

Harris, Leroy 1979-82 (FB)

Harris, Richard 1971-73 (DE)

Harris, Rod 1990-91 (WR)

Harris, Tim 1993 (DE)

Harrison, Bob 1962-63 (LB)

Harrison, Dennis 1978-84 (DE)
1983 Pro Bowl

Harrison, Granville 1941 (E)

Harrison, Tyreo 2002-03 (LB)

Hart, Clinton 2003-04 (S)

Hart, Dick 1967-71 (G)

Hartman, Fred 1948 (T)

Harvey, Richard 1970 (DB)

Haskins, Jon 1998 (LB)

Hasselbeck, Tim 2002 (QB)

Hauck, Tim 1999-2002 (S)

Hawkins, Ben 1966-67 (WR)

Hayden, Aaron 1998 (RB)

Hayden, Ken 1942 (C)

Hayes, Ed 1970 (DB)

Hayes, Joe 1984 (WR)

Haymond, Alvin 1968 (DB)

Heath, Jo Jo 1981 (DB)

Hebron, Vaughn 1993-95 (RB)

Heck, Ralph 1963-65 (LB)

All-Time Eagles Roster

Hegamin, George 1998 (G/T)

Heller, Ron 1988-92 (T)

Henderson, Jerome 1995 (CB)

Henderson, Zac 1980 (S)

Hendrickson, Steve 1995 (LB)

Henry, Maurice 1990 (LB)

Henry, Wally 1977-82 (WR)
1980 Pro Bowl

Henson, Gary 1963 (E)

Herremans, Todd 2005-p* (T)

Herrod, Jeff 1997 (LB)

Hershey, Kirk 1941 (E)

Hertel, Rob 1980 (QB)

Hewitt, Bill 1936-39, 1943 (E)
1937-38 All Pro Selection

Hicks, Artis 2002-05 (T)

Higgins, Tom 1954-55 (T)

Higgs, Mark 1989 (RB)

Hill, Fred 1965-71 (E)

Hill, King 1961-68 (QB)

Hinkle, Jack 1941-47 (HB)
1943 All Pro Selection

Hix, Billy 1950 (E)

Hoage, Terry 1986-90 (S)

Hobbs, Bill 1969-71 (LB)

Hodges, Reggie 2005 (P)

Hogan, Mike 1976-78, 1980 (FB)

Holcomb, William 1937 (T)

Holly, Bob 1984 (QB)

Holmes, Lester 1993-96 (G)

Hood, Roderick 2003- (CB)

Hooks, Alvin 1981 (WR)

Hoover, Mel 1982-84 (WR)

Hopkins, Wes 1983-93 (S)
1984-85 All Pro Selection
1986 Pro Bowl
1988 Ed Block Courage Award

Horan, Mike 1984-85 (P)

Hord, Roy 1962 (G)

Horn, Marty 1897r (QB)

Horrell, Bill 1952 (G)

Hoss, Clark 1972 (TE)

Howard, Bob 1978-79 (CB)

Howard, Darren 2006-p* (DE)

Howell, Lane 1965-69 (T)

Hoyem, Lynn 1964-67 (G)

Hoying, Bobby 1996-98 (QB)

Hrabetin, Frank 1942 (T)

Huarte, John 1968 (QB)

Hudson, Bob 1953-55, 1957-58 (B)

Hudson, John 1991-95 (G)

Hughes, Chuck 1967-69 (WR)

Hughes, William 1937-40 (C)

Hultz, Don 1964-73 (DT)

Humbert, Dick 1941, 1945-49 (E)
1941 All Pro Selection

Humphrey, Claude 1978-81 (DE)

Hunt, Calvin 1970 (C)

Hunt, Tony 2007-p* (RB)

Hunter, Herman 1985 (RB)

Huth, Jerry 1959-60 (G)

Hutton, Tom 1995-98 (P)

Huxhold, Ken 1954-58 (G)

Huzvar, John 1952 (B)

I

Ingram, Mark 1996 (WR)

Irvin, Willie 1953 (B)

J

Jackson, Al 1994 (CB)

Jackson, Alonzo 2005 (DE)

Jackson, Bob 1960 (B)

Jackson, Don 1936 (B)

Jackson, Earnest 1985-86 (RB)

Jackson, Greg 1994-95 (FS)

Jackson, Harold 1969-72 (WR)
1972 All Pro Selection
1970, 1973 Pro Bowl

Jackson, Jamaal 2003-p* (G/O)
2007 All-Pro

Jackson, Johnny 1977 (DE)

Jackson, Keith 1988-91 (TE)
1988-90 All Pro Selection
1989-91 Pro Bowl
1988 NFL Rookie of the Year

Jackson, Kenny 1984-88, 1990-91 (WR)

Jackson, Randy 1974 (RB)

Jackson, T.J. 1966 (DB)

Jacobs, David 1987r (K)

Jacobs, Proverb 1958 (T)

James, Angelo 1987 (CB)

James, Po 1972-75 (RB)

James, William 2007-p* (CB)

Janet, Ernie 1975 (T)

Jarmoluk, Mike 1949-55 (T)
1952 Pro Bowl

Jarvi, Toimi 1944 (B)

Jasper, Ed 1997-98 (DT)

All-Time Eagles Roster

Jaworski, Ron 1977-86 (QB)
1981 Pro Bowl; 1980 NFL MVP
1980 NFL MVP
1985 Ed Block Courage Award

Jean-Gilles, Max 2006-p* (G)

Jefferson, Greg 1995-2000 (DE)

Jefferson, William 1942 (B)

Jelesky, Tom 1985-86 (T)

Jells, Dietrich 1998-99 (WR)

Jenkins, Izel 1988-92 (CB)

Jenkins, Justin 2005- (WR)

Jeter, Tommy 1992-95 (DT)

Jiles, Dwayne 1986-89 (LB)

Johansson, Ove 1977 (K)

Johnson, Albert 1942 (B)

Johnson, Alonozo 1986-87 (LB)

Johnson, Alvin 1948 (B)

Johnson, Bill 1998-99 (DT)

Johnson, Charles 1999-2000 (WR)

Johnson, Charlie 1977-81 (DT)
1981 All Pro Selection
1980-82 Pro Bowl

Johnson, Chris 1987r (DB)

Johnson, Dirk 2003- (P)

Johnson, Don 1953-55 (B)

Johnson, Dwight 2000 (DE)

Johnson, Eric 1977-78 (DB)

Johnson, Gene 1959-60 (B)

Johnson, Jay 1969-70 (LB)

Johnson, Jimmie 1995-98 (TE)

Johnson, Kevin 1995-96 (DT)

Johnson, Lee 2002 (P)

Johnson, Maurice 1991-94 (TE)

Johnson, Norm 1999 (K)

Johnson, Reggie 1995 (TE)

Johnson, Ron 2003 (DE)

Johnson, Ron 1985-89 (WR)

Johnson, Vaughan 1994 (LB)

Jonas, Don 1962 (B)

Jones, Chris T. 1995-97 (WR)

Jones, Dhani 2004-p* (LB)

Jones, Don 1940 (B)

Jones, Harry 1967-71 (RB)

Jones, Jimmie 1997 (DL)

Jones, Joe 1974-75 (DE)

Jones, Julian 2001-2002 (S)

Jones, Preston 1993 (QB)

Jones, Ray 1970 (DB)

Jones, Spike 1975-77 (P)

Jones, Tyrone 1989 (DB)

Jordan, Andrew 1998 (TE)

Jorgensen, Carl 1935 (T)

Joseph, James 1991-94 (RB)

Joyner, Seth 1986-93 (LB)
1991-93 All Pro Selection
1992, 1994 Pro Bowl

Jurgensen, Sonny 1957-63 (QB)
1961 All Pro Selection
1962 Pro Bowl

Justice, Winston 2006-p* (T)

K

Kab, Vyto 1982-85 (TE)

Kalu, N.D. 1997, 2001-05 (DE)

Kane, Carl 1936 (B)

Kapele, John 1962 (T)

Kaplan, Bennie 1942 (G)

Karnofsky, Sonny 1945 (B)

Kasky, Ed 1942 (T)

Kaufusi, Steve 1989-90 (DE)

Kavel, George 1934 (B)

Kearse, Jevon 2004-p* (DE)

Keeling, Ray 1938-39 (T)

Keen, Rabbit 1937-38 (B)

Kekeris, Jim 1947 (T)

Keller, Ken 1956-57 (B)

Kelley, Bob 1955-56 (C)

Kelley, Dwight 1966-72 (LB)

Kelly, Jim 1965-67 (E)

Kelly, Joe 1996 (LB)

Kemp, Jeff 1991 (QB)

Kenneally, George 1933-35 (E)

Kenney, Steve 1980-85 (G)

Kersey, Merritt 1974-75 (P)

Key, Wade 1970-80 (G/T)

Keyes, Leroy 1969-72 (DB)

Keys, Howard 1960-64 (T/C)

Khayat, Ed 1958-61, 1964-65 (DT)

Kilroy, Bucko 1943-55 (T)
1948-54 All Pro Selection
1953-55 Pro Bowl

Kimmel, Jon 1985 (LB)

Kinder, Randy 1997 (CB)

King, Don 1956 (T)

Kirchbaum, Kelly 1987r (LB)

Kirkland, Levon 2002 (LB)

Kirkman, Roger 1933-35 (B)

Kirksey, Roy 1973-74 (G)

All-Time Eagles Roster

Kish, Ben 1942-49 (B)

Klingel, John 1987-88 (DE)

Kloppenberg, Harry 1936 (T)

Kmetovic, Pete 1946 (B)

Knapper, Joe 1934 (B)

Knox, Charles 1937 (T)

Koeninger, Art 1933 (C)

Kolb, Kevin 2007-p* (QB)

Kolberg, Elmer 1939-40 (B)

Koman, Bill 1957-58 (LB)

Konecny, Mark 1988 (RB)

Kowalczyk, Walt 1958-59 (B)

Kowalkowski, Scott 1991-93 (LB)

Kramer, Kent 1971-74 (TE)

Kraynak, Rich 1983-86 (LB)

Krepfle, Keith 1975-81 (TE)

Kresky, Joe 1933-35 (G)

Krieger, Robert 1941, 1946 (E)

Kriel, Emmett 1939 (G)

Kuczynski, Bert 1946 (E)

Kullman, Mike 1987r (S)

Kupcinet, Irv 1935 (B)

Kusko, John 1936-38 (B)

Ḷ

Laack, Galen 1958 (G)

Labinjo, Mike 2004-05 (LB)

Lackman, Dick 1933-35 (B)

Lainhart, Porter 1933 (B)

Landeta, Sean 1999-2002, 2005 (P)

Landsberg, Mort 1941 (B)

Landsee, Bob 1986-87 (G/C)

Lang, Israel 1964-68 (FB)

Lankas, James 1942 (B)

Lansford, Buck 1955-57 (T)
1957 Pro Bowl

Lapham, Bill 1960 (C)

Larson, Bill 1978 (TE)

Latimer, Al 1979 (CB)

Laux, Ted 1942-4 (B)

Lavender, Joe 1973-75 (CB)

Lavergne, Damian 2003 (T)

Lavette, Robert 1987 (RB)

Lawrence, Kent 1969 (WR)

Lawrence, Reggie 1993 (WR)

Lazetich, Pete 1976-77 (DT)

Leathers, Milton 1933 (G)

LeBel, Harper 1990 (TE)

Lechthaler, Roy 1933 (G)

Ledbetter, Toy 1950, 1953-55 (B)

Lee, Amp 2000 (RB)

Lee, Bernie 1938 (B)

Lee, Byron 1986-87r (LB)

Leggett, Scott 1987r (G)

LeMaster, Frank 1974-83 (LB)
1982 Pro Bowl

Leonard, Jim 1934-37 (B)

Leshinski, Ron 1999 (TE)

Levanities, Stephen 1942 (T)

Levens, Dorsey 2002, 2004 (RB)

Lewis, Chad 1997-2005 (TE)
2001-03 Pro Bowl
2005 Ed Block Courage Award

Lewis, Greg 2003-p* (WR)

Lewis, Joe 1962 (T)

Lewis, Michael 2002- (S)
2004 All Pro Selection
2005 Pro Bowl

Leyendecker, Tex 1933 (T)

Lilly, Sammy 1989-90 (DB)

Lince, Dave 1966-67 (E)

Lindskag, Vic 1944-51 (C)
1951 All-Pro

Lio, Augie 1946 (G)
1946 All Pro Selection

Lipski, John 1933-34 (C)

Liske, Pete 1971-72 (QB)

Liter, Greg 1987r (DE)

Little, Dave 1985-89 (TE)

Lloyd, Dave 1963-70 (LB)

Lofton, James 1993 (WR)
1970 Pro Bowl

Logan, Randy 1973-83 (S)
1980 All Pro Selection
1980-81 Pro Bowl

Long, Matt 1987r (C)

Looney, Don 1940 (E)
1940 All Pro Selection

Lou, Ron 1975 (C)

Louderback, Tom 1958-59 (LB)

Love, Clarence 1998 (CB)

Love, Sean 1997 (G)

Lucas, Dick 1960-63 (E)

Lueck, Bill 1975 (G)

Luft, Don 1954 (E)

Luken, Tom 1972-78 (G)

Lusk, Herb 1976-78 (RB)

All-Time Eagles Roster

M

MacAfee, Ken 1959 (E)

MacDowell, Jay 1946-51 (E)

MacMurdo, Jim 1934-37 (T)

Macioszcyk, Art 1944-47 (B)

Mack, Bill 1964 (WR)

Mackey, Kyle 1986 (QB)

Mackrides, Bill 1947-51 (B)

Magee, John 1948-55 (G)

Mahalic, Drew 1976-78 (LB)

Mahe, Reno 2003- (RB)

Mallory, John 1968 (B)

Malone, Art 1975-76 (RB)

Mamula, Mike 1995-2000 (DE)
1999 Ed Block Courage Award

Mandarino, Mike 1944-45 (G)

Manning, Roosevelt 1975 (DT)

Mansfield, Ray 1963 (C)

Mansfield, Von 1982 (DB)

Manske, Ed 1935-36 (E)
1935 All Pro Selection

Manton, Taldon 1940 (B)

Manzini, Baptiste 1944-45, 1948 (C)

Marchi, Basillio 1941-42 (C)

Mark, Greg 1990 (DE)

Maronic, Duke 1944-50 (G)

Marshall, Anthony 1998 (S)

Marshall, Keyonta 2005- (DT)

Marshall, Larry 1974-77 (KR)

Marshall, Whit 1996 (LB)

Martin, Aaron 1966-67 (DB)

Martin, Ceil 1999-2002 (FB)
2000 Ed Block Courage Award

Martin, Kelvin 1995 (WR)

Martin, Steve 1998-99 (DT)

Mass, Wayne 1972 (T)

Masters, Bob 1937-38, 1941-43 (B)

Masters, Walt 1936 (B)

Matesic, Ed 1934-35 (B)

Matson, Ollie 1964-66 (RB)

Mavraides, Menil 1954, 1957 (G)

May, Dean 1984 (QB)

Mayberry, Jermane 1996-2004 (G/T)
2002 All Pro Selection
2003 Pro Bowl

Mayes, Rufus 1979 (T)

Maynard, Les 1933 (B)

Mazzanti, Jerry 1963 (E)

McAfee, Wesley 1941 (B)

McAllister, James 1975-76 (RB)

McCants, Damerien 2005 (WR)

McChesney, Bob 1950 (E)

McClellan, Mike 1962-63 (B)

McCloskey, Mike 1987 (TE)

McCoo, Eric 2004 (RB)

McCoy, Matt 2005-p* (LB)

McCoy, Pat 2006-p* (T)

McCrary, Fred 1995 (FB)

McCullough, Hugh 1943 (B)

McCusker, Jim 1959-62

McDonal, Don 1944-45 (E)

McDonald, Lester 1940 (E)

McDonald, Tommy 1957-63 (WR)
1959-1962 All Pro Selection
1959-63 Pro Bowl

McDonough, Robert 1942-46 (G)

McDougle, Jerome 2003-p* (DE)
2006 Ed Block Courage Award

McFadden, Paul 1984-87 (K)
1984 NFC Rookie of the Year

McHale, Tom 1993-94 (G/T)

McHugh, Pat 1947-51 (B)

McIntyre, Guy 1995-96 (G)

McKeever, Marlin 1973 (LB)

McKenzie, Kevin 1998 (WR)

McKenzie, Raleigh 1995-96 (C)

McKnight, Dennis 1991 (G)

McMahon, Jim 1990-92 (QB)
1991 NFL Comeback Player of the Year

McMahon, Mike 2005 (QB)

McMillan, Erik 1993 (S)

McMillen, Dan 1987r (DE)

McMillian, Mark 1992-95 (CB)

McMullen, Billy 2003-05 (WR)

McNabb, Dexter 1995 (FB)

McNabb, Donovan 1999-p* (QB)
2001-05 Pro Bowl
2000, 2004 NFC MVP

McNeill, Tom 1971-73 (P)

McPherson, Don 1988-90 (QB)

McPherson, Forrest 1935-37 (T)

McRae, Jerrold 1979 (WR)

McTyer, Tim 1997-98 (CB)

Meadows, Ed 1958 (E)

Medved, Ron 1966-70 (DB)

Mellekas, John 1963 (DT)

All-Time Eagles Roster

Mercer, Giradie 2000 (DT)

Merkens, Guido 1987 (QB)

Meyer, Fred 1942, 1945 (E)

Meyers, John 1964-67 (T)

Miano, Rich 1991-94 (DB)

Michaels, Ed 1943-46 (G)

Michel, Mike 1978 (P/K)

Michels, John 1999 (T)

Michels, John 1953 (G)

Middlebrook, Oren 1978 (WR)

Mike-Mayer, Nick 1977-78 (K)

Mikell, Quintin 2003-p* (S)
2007 All-Pro

Millard, Keith 1993 (D/T)

Miller, Bubba 1996-2001 (C/G)

Miller, Don 1954 (B)

Miller, Tom 1942-44 (E)

Milling, Al 1942 (G)

Milon, Barnes 1934 (G)

Milons, Freddie 2002 (WR)

Mira, George 1969 (QB)

Miraldi, Dean 1982-84 (T)

Mitcham, Gene 1958 (E)

Mitchell, Brian 2000-2002 (KR)

Mitchell, Freddie 2001-04 (WR)

Mitchell, Leonard 1981-86 (DE/T)

Mitchell, Martin 1977 (DB)

Mitchell, Randall 1987r (NT)

Moats, Ryan 2005-p* (RB)

Molden, Frank 1968 (T)

Monk, Art 1995 (WR)

Monroe, Henry 1979 (CB)

Montgomery, Wilbert 1977-84 (RB)
1978-79 All Pro Selection
1979-80 Pro Bowl

Mooney, Tim 1987 (DE)

Moore, Damon 1999-2001 (S)

Moreno, Zeke 2005 (LB)

Morey, Sean 2001, 2003 (WR)

Morgan, Dennis 1975 (KR)

Morgan, Mike 1964-67 (LB)

Morris, Dwaine 1985 (DT)

Morriss, Guy 1973-83 (C)

Morse, Bobby 1987 (RB)

Mortell, Emmett 1937-39 (B)

Moseley, Mark 1970 (K)

Moselle, Dom 1954 (B)

Mrkonic, George 1953 (T)

Muha, Joe 1946-50 (B)
1948, 1950 All Pro Selection

Muhlmann, Horst 1975-77 (K)

Mulligan, George 1936 (E)

Murley, Dick 1956 (T)

Murphy, Nick 2005 (P)

Murray, Calvin 1981-82 (HB)

Murray, Eddie 1994 (K)

Murray, Francis 1339-40 (B)

Myers, Brad 1958 (B)

Myers, Jack 1948-50 (B)

N

Nacelli, Andy 1958 (E)

Nease, Mike 1987r (C/T)

Nelson, Al 1965-73 (DB)

Nelson, Dennis 1976-77 (T)

Nettles, Jim 1965-68 (DB)

Newton, Charles 1939-40 (B)

Nichols, Gerald 1993 (DT)

Niland, John 1975-76 (G)

Nipp, Maurice 1952-53, 1956 (G)

Nocera, John 1959-62 (LB)

Norby, Jack 1934 (B)

Nordquist, Mark 1968-74 (G)

Norton, Jerry 1954-58 (DB)
1958-59 Pro Bowl

Norton, Jim 1968 (T)

Nowak, Walt 1944 (E)

O

Oakes, Don 1961-62 (T)

O'Boyle, Harry 1933 (B)

O'Brien, Davey 1939-40 (QB)
1939-40 All Pro Selection

O'Brien, Ken 1993 (QB)

Obst, Henry 1933 (G)

Oden, Derrick 1993-95 (LB)

Olds, Bill 1976 (RB)

Oliver, Greg 1973-74 (RB)

Oliver, Hubie 1981-85 (FB)

O'Neal, Brian 1994 (FB)

Opperman, Jim 1975 (LB)

O'Quinn, John 1951 (E)

Oristaglio, Bob 1952 (E)

Ormsbe, Elliott 1946 (B)

Osborn, Mike 1978 (LB)

Osborne, Richard 1976-78 (TE)

Outlaw, John 1973-78 (DB)

Overmeyer, Bill 1972 (LB)

Owens, Don 1958-60 (T)

Owens, Terrell 2004-05 (WR)
2004 All Pro Selection
2005 Pro Bowl

P

Pacella, Dave 1984 (G/C)

Padlow, Max 1935 (E)

Pagliei, Joe 1959 (B)

Palelei, Lonnie 1999 (T/G)

Palmer, Leslie 1948 (B)

Panos, Joe 1994-97 (G)

Papale, Vince 1976-78 (WR)

Parker, Artimus 1974-76 (DB)

Parker, Rodney 1980-81 (WR)

Parmer, Jim 1948-56 (B)

Parry, Josh 2002, 04-05 (FB)

Paschka, Gordon 1943 (G)

Pastorini, Dan 1982-93 (QB)

Pate, Rupert 1942 (G)

Patterson, Mike 2005-p* (DT)

Patton, Cliff 1946-50 (G)
1949 All Pro Selection

Patton, Jerry 1974 (DT)

Payne, Ken 1978 (WR)

Peaks, Clarence 1957-63 (FB)

Pederson, Doug 1999 (QB)

Peete, Rodney 1995-98 (QB)

Pegg, Harold 1940 (C)

Pellegrini, Bob 1956, 1958-61 (LB)

Penaranda, Jairo 1985 (RB)

Peoples, Woody 1978-80 (G)

Perot, Pete 1979-84 (G)

Perrino, Mike 1987r (T)

Perry, Bruce 2004- (RB)

Perry, William 1993-94 (DT)

Peters, Floyd 1964-69 (DT)
1965, 1967-68 Pro Bowl
1967 Pro Bowl MVP

Peters, Scott 2002 (OL)

Peters, Volney 1958 (T)

Pettigrew, Gary 1966-74 (DT)

Philbin, Gerry 1973 (DE)

Phillips, Ray 1978-81 (LB)

Phillips, Ray 1987r (DE/LB)

Picard, Bob 1973-76 (WR)

Pihos, Pete 1947-55 (E)
1947-50, 1952-55 All Pro Selection
1951-56 Pro Bowl

Pilconis, Joe 1934, 1936-37 (E)

Pinder, Cyril 1968-70 (B)

Pinkston, Todd 2000-04 (WR)

Piro, Henry 1941 (E)

Pisarcik, Joe 1980-84 (QB)

Pitts, Alabama 1935 (B)

Pitts, Mike 1987-92 (DL)

Pivarnick, Joe 1936 (G)

Poage, Ray 1964-65 (E)

Pollard, Al 1951-53 (B)

Polley, Tom 1985 (LB)

Porter, Ron 1969-72 (LB)

Poth, Phil 1934 (G)

Powell, Art 1959 (WR)

Powlus, Ron 2000 (QB)

Preece, Steve 1970-72 (DB)

President, Andre 1997 (TE)

Presott, Harold 1947-49 (E)

Priestly, Robert 1942 (E)

Prisco, Nick 1933 (B)

Pritchard, Bosh 1942, 1946-51 (B)

Pritchett, Stanley 2000 (FB)

Puetz, Garry 1979 (T)

Pylman, Bob 1938-39 (T)

Pyne, Jim 2001 (C/G)

Q

Qinlan, Bill 1963 (DE)

Quick, Mike 1982-90 (WR)
1983, 1985, 1987 All Pro Selection
1984-88 Pro Bowl
1989 Ed Block Courage Award

R

Rado, George 1937-38 (E)

Ragazzo, Phil 1940-41 (T)
1941 All Pro Selection

Ramsey, Herschel 1938-40, 1945 (E)

Ramsey, Knox 1952 (G)

Ramsey, LaJuan 2006-p* (DT)

Ramsey, Nate 1963-72 (DB)

Rash, Lou 1984 (CB)

Raskowski, Leo 1935 (T)

Ratliff, Don 1975 (DE)

Rauch, John 1951 (QB)

All-Time Eagles Roster

Rayburn, Sam 2003- (DT)

Raye, Jim 1969 (DB)

Reader, Jamie 2001 (FB)

Reagan, Frank 1949-51 (B)

Reagor, Montae 2007-p* (DT)

Reaves, John 1972-75 (QB)

Recher, Dave 1965-68 (C)

Reed, J.R. 2004-05, 2007* (S)

Reed, James 1977 (LB)

Reed, Michael 1998 (FB)

Reed, Taft 1967 (B)

Reese, Henry 1935-39 (C/LB)

Reese, Ike 1998-2004 (LB)
2004 All Pro Selection
2005 Pro Bowl

Reeves, Ken 1985-89 (T)

Reeves, Marion 1974 (DB)

Reichenbach, Mike 1984-89 (LB)

Reichow, Jerry 1960 (E)

Reid, Allen 1987 (RB)

Reid, Mike 1993-95 (S)

Reilly, Kevin 1973-74 (LB)

Renfro, Leonard 1993-94 (DT)

Renfro, Will 1961 (E)

Repko, Jay 1987r (TE)

Restic, Joe 1952 (E)

Retzlaff, Pete 1956-66 (TE)
1958, 1964-66 All Pro Selection
1959, 1961, 1964-66 Pro Bowl
1965 NFL MVP

Reutt, Ray 1943 (E)

Ricca, Jim 1955-56 (T)

Richards, Bobby 1962-65 (DE)

Richardson, Jess 1953-61 (DT)
1960 All Pro Selection
1960 Pro Bowl

Richardson, Paul 1993 (WR)

Richmond, Greg 2005- (LB)

Riffle, Dick 1938-40 (B)

Riley, Lee 1956, 1958-59 (DB)

Rimington, Dave 1988-89 (C)

Ringo, Jim 1964-67 (C)
1964, 1966 All Pro Selection;
1965-66, 1968 Pro Bowl

Rissmiller, Ray 1966 (T)

Ritchie, Jon 2003-04 (FB)

Robb, Joe 1959-60 (DE)

Roberts, John 1933-34 (B)

Robinson, Burle 1935 (E)

Robinson, Jacque 1987 (FB)

Robinson, Jerry 1979-84 (LB)
1980-81, 1983 All Pro Selection
1982 Pro Bowl

Robinson, Wayne 1952-56 (LB)
1955 All Pro Selection
1955-56 Pro Bowl

Rocca, Sav 2007-p* (P)

Rodgers, Stefan 2006-p* (G)

Roffler, William 1954 (B)

Rogalla, John 1945 (B)

Rogas, Dan 1952 (G)

Romanowski, Bill 1994-95 (LB)

Romero, Ray 1951 (G)

Roper, Dedrick 2005- (LB)

Roper, John 1993 (LB)

Rose, Ken 1990-94 (LB)

Ross, Alvin 1987r (FB)

Ross, Oliver 1999 (T)

Rossovich, Tim 1968-71 (LB)
1970 Pro Bowl

Rossum, Allen 1998-99 (KR/CB)

Roton, Herbert 1937 (E)

Roussel, Tom 1973 (LB)

Rowan, Everitt 1933 (E)

Rowe, Robert 1935 (B)

Royals, Mark 1987r (P)

Rucker, Keith 1996 (DT)

Rudolph, Joe 1995 (G)

Runager, Max 1979-83, 1989 (P)

Runyan, Jon 2000-p* (T)
2003 Pro Bowl

Russell, Booker 1981 (FB)

Russell, James 1936-37 (T)

Russell, Laf 1933 (B)

Russell, Rusty 1984 (T)

Ruzek, Roger 1989-93 (K)

Ryan, Pat 1991 (QB)

Ryan, Rocky 1956-58 (E)

Ryczek, Paul 1987r (C)

Rypien, Mark 1996 (QB)

S

Sader, Steve 1943 (B)

Saidock, Tom 1957 (T)

Sampleton, Lawrence 1982-84 (TE)

Samson, Michael 1996 (DT)

Sanders, John 1977-79 (DB)

Sanders, John 1943, 1945 (G)

Sanders, Thomas 1990-91 (RB)

Sandifer, Dan 1950-51 (DB)

All-Time Eagles Roster

Sapp, Theron 1959-63 (B)

Savirsky, George 1948-49 (T)

Saxon, James 1995 (FB)

Scarpati, Joe 1964-69, 1971 (S)

Schad, Mike 1989-93 (G)

Schaefer, Don 1956 (B)

Schau, Ryan 1999-2001 (G/T)

Schmidt, Ted 1938-40 (C)

Schnelker, Bob 1953 (E)

Schneller, Bill 1940 (B)

Schobel, Matt 2006-p* (TE)

Schrader, Jim 1962-64 (C)

Schreiber, Adam 1986-88 (C/G)

Schuehle, Jake 1939 (B)

Schultz, Eberle 1940, 1943 (G)
1943 All Pro Selection

Schulz, Jody 1983-87 (LB)
1986 Ed Block Courage Award

Sciarra, John 1978-83 (DB)

Sciullo, Steve 2004 (G)

Scott, Clyde 1949-52 (B)

Scott, Gari 2000-01 (WR)

Scott, Tom 1953-58 (DE)
1955-56 All Pro Selection
1958-59 Pro Bowl

Scotti, Ben 1962-63 (CB)

Seals, Leon 1992 (DT/G)

Sears, Vic 1941-53 (T)
1943, 1945, 1949-50, 1952 All Pro Selection

Seay, Mark 1996-97 (WR)

Sebastian, Mike 1935 (B)

Selby, Rob 1991-94 (G)

Shann, Bob 1965-67 (B)

Sharkey, Ed 1954-55 (T)

Shaub, Harry 1935 (G)

Shaw, Ricky 1989-90 (LB)

Sheppard, Lito 2002-p* (CB)
2004 All Pro Selection
2005, 2007 Pro Bowl

Sherman, Al 1943-47 (B)

Sherman, Health 1989-93 (RB)

Shires, Marshall 1945 (T)

Shonk, John 1941 (E)

Short, Jason 2004- (LB)

Shuler, Mickey 1990-91 (TE)

Siano, Mike 1987r (WR)

Sikahema, Vai 1992-93 (KR)
1992 All Pro Selection

Simerson, John 1957-58 (C)

Simmons, Clyde 1986-93 (DE)
1991-92 All Pro Selection
1992-93 Pro Bowl

Simon, Corey 2000-04 (DT)
2001 All Pro Selection
2004 Pro Bowl

Simoneau, Mark 2003-05 (LB)

Sinceno, Kaseem 1998-99 (TE)

Singletary, Reggie 1986-90 (DT/G)

Sisemore, Jerry 1973-84 (T)
1980, 1982 Pro Bowl

Sistrunk, Manny 1976-79 (DT)

Skaggs, Jim 1963-72 (G)

Skladany, Leo 1949 (E)

Skladany, Tom 1983 (P)

Slater, Mark 1979-83 (C)

Slay, Henry 1998 (DT)

Slechta, Jeremy 2002 (DT)

Small, Jessie 1989-91 (LB)

Small, Torrance 1999-2000 (WR)

Smalls, Fred 1987r (LB)

Smart, Rod 2001 (RB)

Smeja, Rudy 1946 (E)

Smith, Ben 1990-93 (DB)

Smith, Charles 1974-81 (WR)

Smith, Darrin 1997 (LB)

Smith, Daryle 1990-92 (T)

Smith, Ed 1999 (TE)

Smith, J.D. 1959-63 (T)
1962 Pro Bowl

Smith, Jack 1945 (T)

Smith, Jackie 1971 (DB)

Smith, John 1942 (T)

Smith, L.J. 2003-p* (TE)

Smith, Milton 1945 (E)

Smith, Otis 1991-94 (CB)

Smith, Phil 1986 (WR)

Smith, Ralph 1963-64 (E)

Smith, Ray 1933 (C)

Smith, Rich 1933 (C)

Smith, Robert 1956 (B)

Smith, Ron 1981-83 (WR)

Smith, Steve 1971-74 (T)

Smith, Tony 1999 (WR)

Smothers, Howard 1995 (G)

Smukler, Dave 1936-39 (B)

Snead, Norm 1964-70 (QB)
1966 Pro Bowl

Snyder, Lum 1952-55, 1958 (T)
1952-55 All Pro Selection
1954-55 Pro Bowl

All-Time Eagles Roster

Sodaski, John 1972-73 (LB)

Soloman, Freddie 1995-98 (WR)

Solt, Ron 1988-91 (G)
1990 Ed Block Courage Award

Somers, George 1939-40 (T)

Spach, Stephen 2005 (TE)

Spagnola, John 1979-87 (TE)
1984 Ed Block Courage Award

Spikes, Takeo 2007-p* (LB)

Spillers, Ray 1937 (T)

Stackpool, John 1942 (B)

Stacy, Siran 1992 (RB)

Stafford, Dick 1962-63 (E)

Staley, Duce 1997-2003 (RB)
2001 Ed Block Courage Award

Steele, Ernie 1942-48 (B)
1943 All Pro Selection

Steere, Dick 1951 (T)

Steinbach, Laurence 1933 (T)

Steinke, Gil 1945-48 (B)

Stetz, Bill 1967 (G)

Stevens, Don 1952, 1954 (B)

Stevens, Matt 1997-98 (S)

Stevens, Pete 1936 (C)

Stevens, Richard 1970-74 (T)

Steward, Dean 1943 (B)

Stewart, Tony 2001-02 (TE)

Stickel, Walt 1950-51 (T)

Stockton, Herschel 1937-38 (G)

Storm, Edward 1934-35 (B)

Strauthers, Tom 1983-86 (DE)

Stribling, Bill 1955-57 (E)

Strickland, Donald 2005- (CB)

Striegel, Bill 1959 (G)

Stringer, Bob 1952-53 (B)

Stubbs, Dan 1995 (DE)

Sturgeon, Cecil 1941 (T)

Strum, Jerry 1972 (C)

Suffridge, Bob 1941-45 (G)
1941 All Pro Selection

Sugar, Leo 1961 (DE)
1961 All Pro Selection

Sullivan, Tom 1972-77 (RB)

Supulski, Leonard 1942 (E)

Sutton, Joe 1950-52 (B)

Sutton, Mitch 1974-75 (DT)

Swift, Justin 1999 (TE)

Sydner, Jeff 1992-94 (WR)

Szafaryn, Len 1957-58 (T)

Szymanski, Frank 1948 (C)

T

Talcott, Dan 1947 (T)

Taliaferro, George 1955 (B)

Tamburello, Ben 1987-90 (C/G)

Tapeh, Thomas 2004-p* (FB)

Tarasovic, George 1963-65 (DE)

Tarver, John 1975 (RB)

Taseff, Carl 1961 (DB)

Tautalatasi, Taivale 1986-88 (RB)

Tautolo, Terry 1976-79 (LB)

Taylor, Bobby 1995-2003 (CB)
2002 All Pro Selection
2003 Pro Bowl
1998 Ed Block Courage Award

Teltschik, John 1986-90 (P)

Thacker, Alvin 1941 (G)

Thomas, Hollis 1996-05(DT)

Thomas, Johnny 1996 (CB)

Thomas, Juqua 2005-p* (DE)

Thomas, Markus 1993 (RB)

Thomas, William 1991-99 (LB)
1995 All Pro Selection
1996-97 Pro Bowl

Thomas, William "Tra" 1998-p* (T)
2002, 2004 All Pro Selection
2002-03, 2005 Pro Bowl

Thomason, Bobby 1952-57 (QB)
1954, 1956-57 Pro Bowl

Thomason, Stumpy 1935-36 (B)

Thomason, Jeff 2000-2002, 2004 (TE)

Thoms, Art 1977 (DE)

Thompson, Broderick 1993-94 (T)

Thompson, Don 1964 (E)

Thompson, Russ 1940 (T)

Thompson, Tommy 1941-42, 1945-50 (QB)
1942, 1948-49, All Pro Selection

Thorton, Richard 1933 (B)

Thrash, James 2001-03 (WR)

Thrower, Jim 1970-72 (DB)

Thurbon, Robert 1943 (B)

Timpson, Michael 1997 (WR)

Tinsley, Scott 1987r (QB)

Togafau, Pago 2007* (LB)

Tom, Mel 1967-73 (DE)

Tomasetti, Lou 1940-41 (B)

Toney, Anthony 1986-90 (FB)

Torrey, Bob 1980 (FB)

Townsend, Greg 1994 (DE)

All-Time Eagles Roster

Traccy, John 1961 (DE)

Tremble, Greg 1995 (DB)

Tripucka, Frank 1949 (QB)

Trost, Milton 1940 (T)

Trotter, Jeremiah 1998-2001, 2004-06 (LB)
2000 All Pro Selection
2001-02, 2005-06 Pro Bowl

Troup, Bill 1975 (QB)

Tupper, Jeff 1986 (DE)

Turnbow, Guy 1933-34 (T)

Turner, Kevin 1995-99 (FB)
1996 Ed Block Courage Award

Turral, Willie 1987r (RB)

Tuten, Rick 1989 (P)

Tyrell, Joe 1952 (G)

U

Ulmer, Michael 1987 (QB)

Unutoa, Morris 1996-98 (C)

Upersa, Tuufuli 1971 (G)

V

Valentine, Zach 1982-83 (LB)

Van Brocklin, Norm 1958-60 (QB)
1960 All Pro Selection
1959-61 Pro Bowl
1960 NFL MVP

Van Buren, Ebert 1951-53 (B)

Van Buren, Steve 1944-51 (RB)
1944-50 All Pro Selection

Van Dyke, Alex 1999-2000 (WR)

Van Dyke, Bruce 1966 (G)

Vasys, Arunas 1966-68 (LB)

Vick, Roger 1990 (RB)

Vincent, Troy 1996-2003 (CB)
2002 All Pro Selection
2000-04 Pro Bowl

von Oelhoffen, Kimo 2007* (DT)

W

Wagner, Steve 1980-81 (S)

Wainwright, Frank 1995 (TE)

Walik, Billy 1970-72 (WR)

Walker, Adam 1996 (FB)

Walker, Corey 1997-98 (RB)

Walker, Darwin 2000- (DT/G)

Walker, Herschel 1992-94 (RB)

Wallace, Al 1997-99 (DE/LB)

Walston, Bobby 1951-62 (E/K)
1951 All Pro Selection
1961-62 Pro Bowl
1951 NFL Rookie of the Year

Walters, Pete 1987r (G)

Walters, Stan 1975-83 (T)
1979 All Pro Selection
1979-80 Pro Bowl

Walton, John 1976-79 (QB)

Ward, Jim 1971-72 (QB)

Ware, Matt 2004-05 (CB)

Warren, Busit 1945 (B)

Warren, Chris 2000 (RB)

Waters, Andre 1984-93 (S/LB)
1993 Ed Block Courage Award

Waters, Mike 1986 (FB)

Watkins, Foster 1940-41 (B)

Watkins, Larry 1970-72 (B)

Watson, Edwin 1999 (RB)

Watson, Tim 1997 (S)

Watters, Ricky 1995-97 (RB)
1996-97 Pro Bowl

Waynes, Nate 2003-04 (LB)

Wear, Robert 1942 (C)

Weatherall, Jim 1955-57 (T)
1956-57 Pro Bowl

Weaver, Jed 1999 (TE)

Weber, Chuck 1959-61 (LB)

Weedon, Don 1947 (G)

Wegert, Ted 1955-56 (B)

Weiner, Albert 1934 (B)

Weinstock, Isadore 1935 (B)

Welbourn, John 1999-2003 (G/T)

Weldon, Casey 1992 (QB)

Wells, Billy 1958 (B)

Wells, Harold 1965-68 (LB)

Wendlick, Joseph 1940 (B)

Wenzel, Jeff 1987r (T)

West, Ed 1995-96 (TE)

West, Hodges 1941 (T)

West, Troy 1987 (SS)

Westbrook, Brian 2002-p* (RB)
2005 Pro Bowl

Whalen, Jim 1971 (TE)

Wheeler, Mark 1999 (DT/G)

Whire, John 1933 (B)

White, Allison 1939 (T)

White, Reggie 1985-92 (DE)
1986-92 All Pro Selection
1987-93 Pro Bowl
1987 Pro Bowl MVP
1987, 1991 NFL Defensive MVP
1987, 1991 NFC Defensive MVP

Whiting, Brandon 1998-2003 (DL)

Whitmore, David 1995 (S)

Whittingham, Fred 1966, 1971 (LB)

Wilburn, Barry 1995-96 (S)

Wilcox, John 1960 (T)

All-Time Eagles Roster

Wilkes, Reggie 1978-85 (LB)

Wilkins, Jeff 1994 (K)

Will, Erwin 1965 (DT)

Willey, Norm 1950-57 (DE)
1953-55 All Pro Selection
1955-56 Pro Bowl

Williams, Ben 1999 (DT)

Williams, Bernard 1994 (T)

Williams, Bobbie 2000-03 (G)

Williams, Boyd 1947 (C)

Williams, Byron 1983 (WR)

Williams, Calvin 1990-96 (WR)

Williams, Charlie 1978 (CB)

Williams, Clyde 1935 (T)

Williams, Henry 1989 (WR)

Williams, Jerry 1953-54 (B)

Williams, Joel 1983-85 (LB)

Williams, Michael 1983-84 (RB)

Williams, Roger 1973 (DB)

Williams, Ted 1973 (B)

Williams, Tex 1942 (G)

Williams, Tyrone 1999-2000 (DE)

Willis, James 1995-98 (LB)

Willson, Osborne 1933-35 (G)

Wilson, Bill 1938 (E)

Wilson, Bernard 1979-86 (S)

Wilson, Harry 1967-70 (B)

Wilson, Jerry 1959-60 (E)

Winfield, Vern 1972-73 (G)

Wink, Dean 1967-68 (DT)

Wirgowski, Dennis 1973 (DE)

Wistert, Al 1943-51 (T)
1944-51 All Pro Selection
1951 Pro Bowl

Witherspoon, Derrick 1995-97 (RB)

Wittenborn, John 1960-62 (G)

Wojciechowicz, Alex 1946-50 (C)

Wolfe, Hugh 1940 (B)

Woltman, Clem 1938-40 (T)

Woodard, Marc 1994-96 (LB)

Woodeshick, Tom 1963-71 (RB)
1968-69 All Pro Selection
1969 Pro Bowl

Woodruff, Lee 1933 (B)

Woodruff, Tony 1982-84 (WR)

Woodson, Sean 1998 (S)

Worden, Neil 1954, 1957 (RB)

Woulfe, Mike 1962 (LB)

Wright, Gordon 1967 (G)

Wright, Sylvester 1995-96 (LB)

Wukits, Al 1943 (C)

Wyatt, Antwuan 1997 (WR)

Wydo, Frank 1952-57 (T)
1953 All Pro Selection

Wyhonic, John 1946-47 (G)

Wynn, Dexter 2004-06 (CB)

Wynn, William 1973-76 (DE)

Y

Young, Adrian 1968-72 (LB)

Young, Charles 1973-6 (TE)
1973-75 All Pro Selection
1974-76 Pro Bowl
1973 NFC Rookie of the Year

Young, Glen 1983 (WR)

Young, Michael 1993 (WR)

Young, Roynell 1980-88 (CB)
1981 All Pro Selection
1982 Pro Bowl

Young, Scott 2005-p* (G)

Youngelman, Sid 1956-58 (T)

Yovicsin, John 1944 (E)

Z

Zabel, Steve 1970-74 (LB)

Zandofsky, Mike 1997 (G)

Zendejas, Luis 1988-89 (K)

Ziegler, Frank 1949-53 (B)

Zilly, John 1952 (E)

Zimmerman, Don 1972-76 (WR)

Zimmerman, Roy 1942-46 (B)
1943-44 All Pro Selection

Zizak, Vince 1934-37 (T)

Zomalt, Eric 1994-96 (S)

Zordich, Mike 1994-98 (S)

Zyntell, James 1933-35 (G)

Trivia Anwers

Q1 (c) 1936

Q2 (b) 18

Q3 (c) HANK REESE

Q4 (b) 1943

Q5 (b) 1958

Q6 (a) JESS RICHARDSON

Q7 (d) BOBBY WALSTON

Q8 (b) BALTIMORE COLTS

Q9 (d) PETE RETZLAFF

Q10 (d) PETE PIHOS

Q11 (b) HAROLD CARMICHAEL

Q12 (b) JOHN TELTSCHIK

Q13 (b) 73

Q14 (b) A.J. FEELEY

Philly Sports Challenge
Eagles Edition
(trivia book)

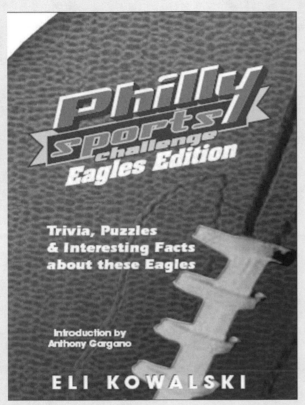

So you think you know your EAGLES football team? Well here's your chance to find out how much of an Eagle enthusiast you really are. The Philadelphia Sports Challenge Eagles Edition covers the birds' all-time great and not-so-great moments, all the numbers, the records and even the nicknames of all your favorite Eagles. Test your knowledge of the birds from their first year in the NFL to the present, with over one hundred categories on remarkable game moments, historical turning points and mind-blowing facts. The true Eagles fan will be challenged throughout the 434 pages of this book to come up with the correct answers. This 6 x 9 paperback has various black & white photos and word search puzzles scattered throughout the book for your entertainment pleasure.

It will not be easy –
but it's guaranteed to be interesting and fun!

"Philadelphia sports fans pride themselves in being passionate, opinionated and knowledgeable. Well, now they can find out just how knowledgeable they really are. The Philly sports challenge, Eagles edition, like a Wonderlic test for the 700 level. What's more, it's a lot of fun."
by Ray Didinger, NFL Films and author

"While the Philly Sports Challenge Eagles Edition looks like a trivia book, it is so much more. It is a deeply researched, compelling, FUN history of one of the NFL's oldest and greatest franchises. It will always have a place on my desk."
by Michael Barkann, Comcast SportsNet

"So finally, in this book, we have our Birds Bible to test our knowledge, study for the big test of fandom and be first team among the flock."
by Anthony Gargano, 610-WIP Radio

1-800-974-6919
available in all Philadelphia area bookstores

www.phillysportschallenge.com

Sports Page Reprints